THE STATE OF THE STATES

in Intellectual and Developmental Disabilities

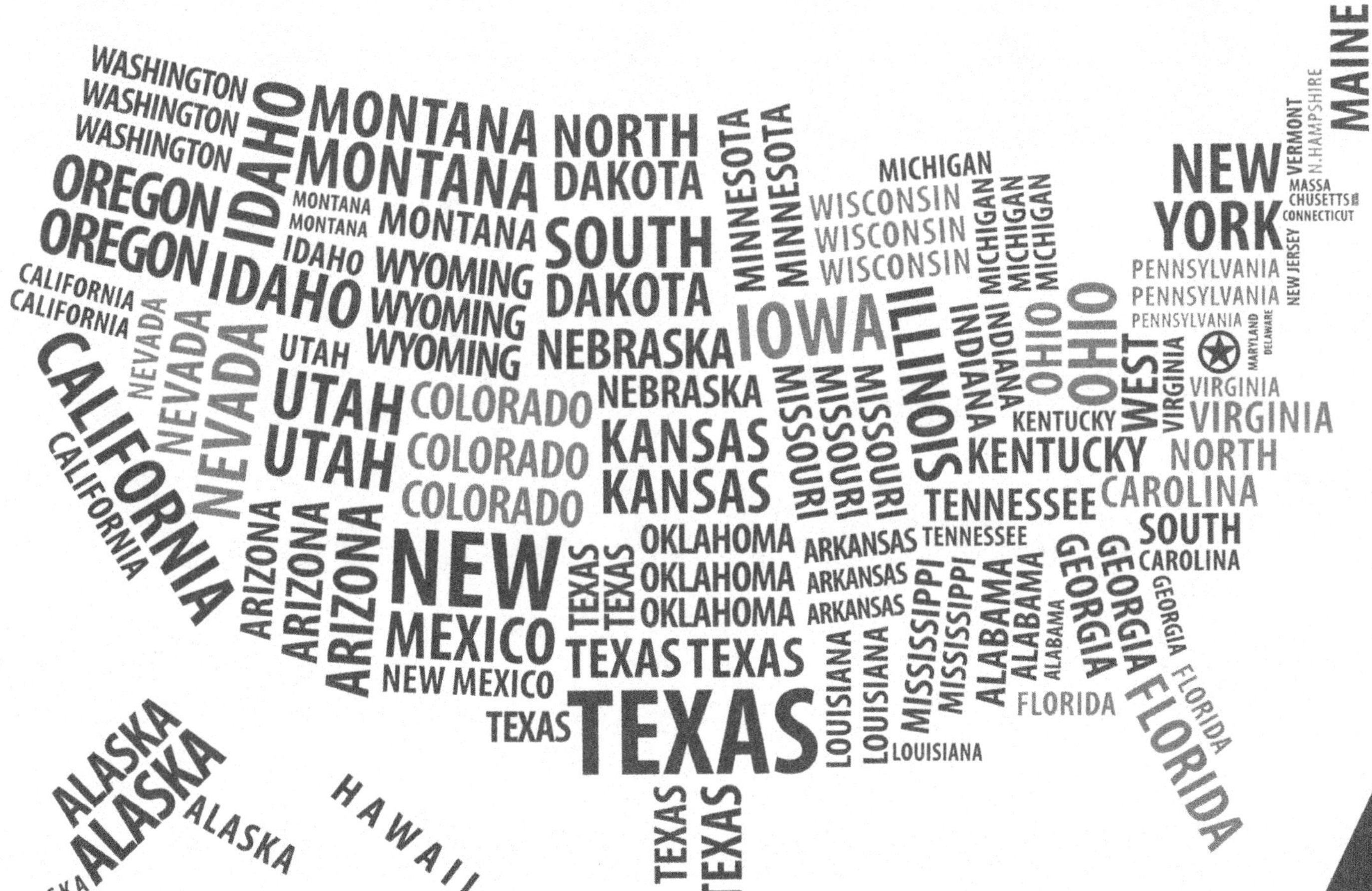

11ᵀᴴ EDITION 2017

The State of the States in Intellectual and Developmental Disabilities: 2017

*David L. Braddock, Richard E. Hemp, Emily S. Tanis,
Jiang Wu, & Laura Haffer*

Department of Psychiatry and
Coleman Institute for Cognitive Disabilities
University of Colorado

IN COLLABORATION WITH THE

Department of Disability and Human Development
University of Illinois at Chicago

11TH EDITION

American Association
on Intellectual and
Developmental Disabilities

DISTRIBUTED BY
THE AMERICAN ASSOCIATION ON INTELLECTUAL AND
DEVELOPMENTAL DISABILITIES
Washington, DC

Copyright © 2017 by David L. Braddock
All rights reserved

To order:
AAIDD Order Fulfillment
501 Third St., NW, Suite 200
Washington, DC 20001
Phone: 202-387-1968 x216
Email: books@aaidd.org
Online: http://aaidd.org/publications/bookstore-home

ISBN 978-0-9965068-7-8
Product No. 4165

**STATE OF THE STATES IN INTELLECTUAL
AND DEVELOPMENTAL DISABILITIES
WEBSITE:**

http.www.stateofthestates.org

This publication was supported in part by a cooperative agreement between the Administration on Intellectual and Developmental Disabilities, in the United States Department of Health and Human Services and University of Colorado School of Medicine's Department of Psychiatry. Grantees undertaking projects under partial government sponsorship are encouraged to express freely their findings and conclusions. Points of view or opinions do not, therefore, necessarily represent official Administration on Intellectual and Developmental Disabilities policy.

TABLE OF CONTENTS

TABLES AND FIGURES ix

ACKNOWLEDGMENTS xi

PART I. THE STATE OF THE STATES IN INTELLECTUAL
AND DEVELOPMENTAL DISABILITIES: 2017 1

I. INTRODUCTION 3
    Classification Categories 3

II. OUT-OF-HOME PLACEMENTS IN FY 2015 5

III. FEDERAL, STATE, AND LOCAL MEDICAID SPENDING: FY 2013–2015 7
    Unmatched Funds 7
    Trends in Public IDD Spending: FY 2013–2015 8
    Public and Private Spending for Institutions 11
    Community Services Spending 12

IV. FISCAL EFFORT IN THE STATES 13

V. ANNUAL COST OF CARE FOR RESIDENTS IN FIVE SETTINGS 16
    Recovering from the Great Recession 19

VI. CONCLUSION 21
    Demographic and Legal Forces 21
    Implications of Changes to Medicaid 21
    Challenges Ahead 23

VII. REFERENCES CITED 25

VIII. COLLABORATION WITH STATE INTELLECTUAL AND DEVELOPMENTAL AGENCIES
FOR DATA COLLECTION 27

PART II. PROFILES OF THE 50 STATES AND THE DISTRICT OF COLUMBIA 31
    ALABAMA 32
    ALASKA 36
    ARIZONA 40
    ARKANSAS 44
    CALIFORNIA 48
    COLORADO 52
    CONNECTICUT 56
    DELAWARE 60
    DISTRICT OF COLUMBIA 64
    FLORIDA 68
    GEORGIA 72

Table of Contents

HAWAII	76
IDAHO	80
ILLINOIS	84
INDIANA	88
IOWA	92
KANSAS	96
KENTUCKY	100
LOUISIANA	104
MAINE	108
MARYLAND	112
MASSACHUSETTS	116
MICHIGAN	120
MINNESOTA	124
MISSISSIPPI	128
MISSOURI	132
MONTANA	136
NEBRASKA	140
NEVADA	144
NEW HAMPSHIRE	148
NEW JERSEY	152
NEW MEXICO	156
NEW YORK	160
NORTH CAROLINA	164
NORTH DAKOTA	168
OHIO	172
OKLAHOMA	176
OREGON	180
PENNSYLVANIA	184
RHODE ISLAND	188
SOUTH CAROLINA	192
SOUTH DAKOTA	196
TENNESSEE	200
TEXAS	204
UTAH	208
VERMONT	212
VIRGINIA	216
WASHINGTON	220
WEST VIRGINIA	224
WISCONSIN	228
WYOMING	232
UNITED STATES	236

APPENDICES 241

    I. *The Rights of People With Cognitive Disabilities to Technology and Information Access*
(The Declaration) 243

    II. Representative Organizations Endorsing the *Declaration of the Rights of People with Cognitive Disabilities to Technology and Information Access* 244

    III. AAIDD article reprint: Braddock, D., Hoehl, J., Tanis, S., Ablowitz, E., & Haffer, L. The Rights of People With Cognitive Disabilities to Technology and Information Access. *Inclusion, 1*(2), 95–102. 252

TABLES AND FIGURES

TABLES

Table 1.	Community Services Classification Categories	4
Table 2.	U.S. Residents with IDD in Out-of-Home Settings: FY 2015	5
Table 3.	Persons with IDD in Out-of-Home Residential Settings by Size of Setting and State: FY 2015	6
Table 4:	State, County and Local Funds Potentially Available to Match Additional Federal Medicaid Funding, by State: FY 2015	9
Table 5.	Public Spending for IDD Services: FY 2013–2015	10
Table 6.	Total and Community Fiscal Effort for IDD Services in the States per $1,000 of Statewide Aggregate Personal Income	14
Table 7.	Annual Cost of Care per Resident By Setting: FY 2015	17

FIGURES

Figure 1.	Federal-State-Local Medicaid is Three-Fourths of Total IDD Spending in FY 2015	7
Figure 2.	Federal-State IDD Spending for HCBS Waiver, ICF/ID, and Related Medicaid in the U.S.: FY 1977–2015	8
Figure 3.	Thirty-Seven States Operated 133 Remaining Institutions in FY 2015	11
Figure 4.	Fiscal Effort for Intellectual and Developmental Disabilities Services in the United States: FY 1997-2015	13
Figure 5.	Individual and Family Support Cost of Support: FY 1996-2015: U.S.	18
Figure 6.	Federal Medicaid Funding for Supported Employment and Day Programs: FY1992-2015	19
Figure 7.	State and Federal IDD Spending: FY 1977–2015	20
Figure 8.	United States Estimated Number of Individuals with IDD by Age Group of Family Caregiver, FY 2015	22
Figure 9.	IDD Caregiving Families and Families Supported by State IDD Agencies: FY 1988-2015	22

ACKNOWLEDGMENTS

This is the eleventh published edition of *The State of the States in Intellectual and Developmental Disabilities*. In this new edition, we analyze financial and programmatic data across fiscal years 1977–2015. Data collected for the study were provided with the assistance of 128 intellectual and developmental disabilities (IDD) agency personnel in the 50 states and the District of Columbia. These individuals are acknowledged on pages 26–28 for their superb contributions.

Data collection for this study has always been a formidable endeavor. It is a demanding task for state officials as well. It is not an overstatement to say that we cannot thank the states enough because their participation over many years has made this longitudinal study possible. The continuing support of the National Association of State Directors of Developmental Disabilities Services, directed by Mary Lee Fay, is also central to our data collection and dissemination process. Director Fay and her predecessors Nancy Thaler and Robert M. Gettings, have been steadfast supporters of this project for four decades. We are grateful for our long-standing partnership. The Arc of the United States, led by CEO Peter Berns, and the American Association on Intellectual and Developmental Disabilities, led by CEO and Executive Director Margaret Nygren have key roles in the nationwide dissemination of this publication through their extensive national, state, and local networks.

The State of the States in Intellectual and Developmental Disabilities Project receives a significant portion of its funding as a "Project of National Significance" from the Administration on Intellectual and Developmental Disabilities (AIDD), U.S. Department of Health and Human Services. We are extremely grateful for AIDD's long-term support. We acknowledge with particular appreciation former AIDD Commissioner Aaron Bishop, Principal Deputy Administrator for ACL Sharon Lewis, and, especially, our AIDD Project Officer Katherine Cargill-Willis. We look forward to working once again with Bob Williams in his role as Deputy Commissioner, Administration on Disabilities and Director, Independent Living Administration.

Substantial non-federal resources are also contributed to support the project from the Universities of Colorado and Illinois at Chicago. Financial and administrative support for the project is provided by the University of Colorado's Anschutz School of Medicine's Department of Psychiatry, the Coleman Institute for Cognitive Disabilities, and the University of Illinois at Chicago's Department of Disability and Human Development. Jennifer Kraft provided excellent administrative support for project activities in Boulder, Colorado.

Mary Kay Rizzolo, Tamar Heller, Glenn Fujiura, Carli Friedman, Randall Owen, and Vijay Vasudevan at the University of Illinois at Chicago's Department of Disability and Human Development were key contributors to the project. Martha King at the Denver-based National Conference of State Legislatures (NCSL) contributed through a subcontract for the project's dissemination to 7,000 state legislators across the 50 states.

Prior to publication a draft of this monograph was distributed for review and comment by all 51 state IDD Agency Directors and their staffs. Their participation in this study was essential. But as is customary the listed authors bear responsibility for any errors or omissions contained herein.

DAVID BRADDOCK, Ph.D., *Coleman-Turner Chair and Professor of Psychiatry*
University of Colorado School of Medicine, and Coleman Institute Executive Director
http://stateofthestates.org

PART I
The State of the States in Intellectual and Developmental Disabilities: 2017

I. INTRODUCTION

The State of the States in Intellectual and Developmental Disabilities is a comparative nationwide longitudinal study of the financial and programmatic trends in residential and community services for people with IDD in the United States. The project spans a 39-year period across fiscal years (FY) 1977–2015. Our current study included updated IDD data for FY2014 and 2015. The State of the States in Intellectual and Developmental Disabilities provides professionals, legislators, policy analysts and advocates with reliable data to measure state and nationwide progress in the provision of services and supports for people with IDD. With our data, implementation of policies and programs can be carefully evaluated over time and systematically altered to improve outcomes. Equally important is the necessary evidence the project provides to advocates, family members, service providers, and investigators to elicit meaningful change in the programs and services that impact quality of life. To ensure appropriate information reaches key stakeholders, the study has produced over 300 publications in the past four decades and provided over 600 presentations in all 50 states, the District of Columbia and in seven foreign countries: Canada, China, Finland, Japan, Mexico, Morocco, and Sweden.

As in our previous nationwide studies of public spending for IDD services, we initiated this new study of FY 2014 and 2015 data by updating our IDD state agency contacts in all 50 states and the District of Columbia. Although state IDD agencies were our primary focus, we also collected data from state health, welfare and social services agencies across the country. These data included federal, state, and local Medicaid; federal Social Security Income (SSI), SSI state supplements; and federal Social Services Block Grants to the states established under Title XX of the Social Security Act of 1974.

Following transmittal of our individualized state survey instruments to states and the District of Columbia, we engaged in extensive communications via e-mail and telephone with 128 state program and budget officials across all the states and the District of Columbia. State responses to our survey instruments were used to construct IDD financial and programmatic profiles for each state and the District of Columbia. These graphic profiles and our data collection worksheets, provided by state agency personnel, were then forwarded to all state agency directors and their key staffs for final confirmation of FY 2014 and 2015 financial and programmatic data.

Classification Categories

The State of the States project focuses on financial outcomes of state investments in IDD services and supports. Two broad categories were employed in the classification of state revenue and spending data: *Institutional Services Funds,* which included state-operated institutions and private facilities serving 16 or more individuals; and *Community Services Funds,* supporting individuals in settings for 15 or fewer individuals. The project also collected data on day services, employment programs, and individual and family supports. Our data collection and analyses of community residential and day services also incorporated "six or fewer persons" as a defining size metric in the states.

Institutional services funds for public and private settings for 16 or more persons were sub-classified into federal, state, and local funding categories. A similar approach was used to classify community services spending. The exceptions were Medicaid HCBS Waivers, other community Medicaid funding, and SSI/ADC income maintenance benefits received by Waiver participants (Items 6b, 6c and 8 in Table 1).

We also collected data on the average annual number of individuals supported by state IDD agency funding in various sizes and types of out-of-home residential settings, full-time-equivalent participants in Medicaid Home and Community Based Services (HCBS) Waivers and in day and work programs, and non-duplicated numbers of families supported in each state and DC. Combined, the data were analyzed to generate unique financial and programmatic profiles for each state and the District of Columbia, a metric of fiscal effort, and determination of cost per participant across services and supports.

The fiscal effort calculation controls for differences in state wealth. It involves dividing the level of IDD spending in each state's fiscal year by its aggregate statewide personal income for the same year. In this study, we ranked all states in terms of funds allocated

TABLE 1
COMMUNITY SERVICES CLASSIFICATION CATEGORIES

(1) State Medicaid matching funds from State and County governments
(2) State general funds not utilized to match Medicaid funds
(3) Local government funding in 15 states: 8 states' local funds matched federal Medicaid
(4) State supplement payments for federal Supplemental Security Income (SSI) benefits
(5) Other state funds

(6) Federal Medicaid spending for community services:
    (a) Public and private Intermediate Care Facilities for Persons with Intellectual Disabilities (ICFs/ID)
    (b) Home and Community-Based Services (HCBS) Waivers
    (c) Other Federal Medicaid funding for rehabilitation services, clinic services, targeted case management, personal care services, and other State Plan Medicaid funds

Other Federal Classification Categories for Community Services Spending in the States Included:
(7) Title XX/Social Services Block Grant
(8) HCBS Waiver-related Supplemental Security Income/Adults Disabled in Childhood (SSI/ADC) funds
(9) Other Federal Funds

Source: Braddock et al., Coleman Institute and Department of Psychiatry, University of Colorado, 2017

for IDD services per $1,000 of statewide aggregate personal income in FYs 2013, 2014, and 2015 and also across FY 2013–2015 (U.S. Department of Commerce, Bureau of Economic Analysis, 2016a). Financial data collected for the study were adjusted for inflation. To do this we used the state and local sub-index of the "Gross National Product Implicit Price Deflator" (U.S. Department of Commerce, Bureau of Economic Analysis, 2016).

Reliability of the classification of IDD spending and revenue data into the various categories has been demonstrated to be high in previous studies (Braddock & Fujiura, 1991). Winer's (1971) unbiased intraclass correlation coefficients were between .88 and 1.00 in each of the state data sets. Less than perfect reliabilities for classification have typically been due to identifying expenditures overlooked in a previous edition of the study such as fringe benefits. Occasionally, we have re-classified expenditures from the institutional category to the community services category, or the reverse, as more accurate information was provided to us by state agency or federal sources.

II. OUT-OF-HOME PLACEMENTS IN FY 2015

In this update of our study, we focused on financial and programmatic trends in the states during FYs 2013–2015, a period of recovery from the *Great Recession*. During the 39-year period encompassed in our study the number of persons residing in state-operated IDD institutions declined 85% from 149,892 in FY 1977 to 21,103 in FY 2015. The number of individuals with IDD residing in settings for six or fewer persons increased exponentially from approximately 20,000 persons in FY 1977 to 559,172 persons in FY 2015. Public spending for IDD services grew 310% during FYs 1977–2015 from $15.89 billion in 1977 (constant 2015 dollars) to $65.21 billion in FY 2015.

The $65.21 billion in total IDD spending in FY 2015 supported 680,851 persons in out-of-home settings (Table 2). Settings for six persons or fewer constituted 82% of all out-of-home residents with IDD in FY 2015 (559,172 persons). Table 3 presents state-by-state data on the numbers of individuals with IDD residing in settings for six or fewer persons, 7–15 persons, and 16 or more persons. The states are ranked by the proportion of individuals in settings for six or fewer persons.

Table 2 includes the residents in Intermediate Care Facilities for Intellectual Disabilities (ICFs/ID) for three size categories: 16 or more persons; 7–15 persons; and six or fewer persons. Settings for 16 or more persons include nursing facilities[1] (Skilled and Intermediate Care Facilities) housing individuals with IDD; state institutions; and private ICFs/ID for 16 or more persons and other private facilities. Supported Living and Personal Assistance participants constituted 60% of all six-person or fewer settings, and 50% of all residential settings.

TABLE 2[1]

U.S. RESIDENTS WITH IDD IN OUT-OF-HOME SETTINGS: FY 2015		
16+ Persons	69,557	10%
Nursing Facility	27,306	39%
State Institution	21,103	30%
Private ICF/ID Institution	17,418	25%
Other Private Facility	3,730	5%
7-15 Persons	52,122	8%
Group Homes	33,186	64%
Private ICF/ID	17,671	34%
Public ICF/ID	1,265	2%
6 or Fewer Persons	559,172	82%
Supported Living/Personal Assitance	337,264	60%
Group Homes	201,228	36%
Private ICF/ID	20,412	4%
Public ICF/ID	269	0.05%
GRAND TOTAL	680,851	100%

Source: Braddock et al., Coleman Institute and Department of Psychiatry, University of Colorado, 2017

---

[1] Consult our website for more comprehensive nursing facility spending for persons with IDD, mental health needs, and physical/sensory disabilities: (http://www.stateofthestates.org).

TABLE 3
PERSONS WITH IDD IN OUT-OF-HOME RESIDENTIAL SETTINGS BY SIZE OF SETTING AND STATE: FY 2015[1]

State	1-6 Persons[2] Number	%	Rank[3]	7-15 Persons Number	%	16+ Persons[4] Number	%	Total	Rate[5]
Alabama	3,495	67%	46	651	12%	1,072	21%	5,218	107
Alaska	1,769	99%	1	16	1%	5	0%	1,790	243
Arizona	4,715	96%	5	32	1%	167	3%	4,914	72
Arkansas	4,010	60%	47	791	12%	1,881	28%	6,682	225
California	54,350	91%	18	1,561	3%	3,886	6%	59,797	153
Colorado	10,079	96%	6	128	1%	301	3%	10,508	193
Connecticut	7,429	86%	27	293	3%	913	11%	8,635	240
Delaware	1,056	85%	28	0	0%	183	15%	1,239	131
District of Columbia	1,911	99%	2	7	0%	19	1%	1,937	290
Florida	23,437	81%	32	2,118	7%	3,286	11%	28,841	143
Georgia	13,230	89%	22	0	0%	1,615	11%	14,845	146
Hawaii	749	91%	17	7	1%	68	8%	824	58
Idaho	3,841	88%	26	242	6%	299	7%	4,381	266
Illinois	12,764	48%	50	8,104	31%	5,590	21%	26,458	206
Indiana	9,186	69%	42	2,436	18%	1,700	13%	13,322	201
Iowa	5,766	68%	44	803	9%	1,890	22%	8,459	271
Kansas	2,819	89%	24	37	1%	317	10%	3,173	109
Kentucky	14,514	91%	16	215	1%	1,160	7%	15,889	359
Louisiana	4,277	56%	49	1,611	21%	1,725	23%	7,613	163
Maine	3,178	85%	29	392	11%	161	4%	3,731	281
Maryland	8,426	95%	9	0	0%	463	5%	8,889	148
Massachusetts	14,326	90%	19	775	5%	738	5%	15,839	233
Michigan	28,454	92%	14	1,378	4%	1,188	4%	31,020	313
Minnesota	20,220	93%	11	523	2%	885	4%	21,628	395
Mississippi	1,585	36%	51	710	16%	2,119	48%	4,414	147
Missouri	9,689	78%	34	1,092	9%	1,603	13%	12,384	204
Montana	1,621	72%	37	432	19%	205	9%	2,258	219
Nebraska	3,709	88%	25	9	0%	510	12%	4,228	223
Nevada	1,973	92%	15	0	0%	179	8%	2,152	75
New Hampshire	2,531	95%	10	25	1%	114	4%	2,670	201
New Jersey	8,357	71%	38	678	6%	2,729	23%	11,764	131
New Mexico	4,547	96%	7	120	3%	93	2%	4,760	228
New York	49,618	69%	43	18,024	25%	4,444	6%	72,086	364
North Carolina	24,419	89%	23	150	1%	2,863	10%	27,432	274
North Dakota	1,529	70%	41	438	20%	231	11%	2,198	292
Ohio	28,664	77%	35	2,669	7%	5,661	15%	36,994	319
Oklahoma	3,090	58%	48	625	12%	1,588	30%	5,303	136
Oregon	15,890	98%	4	195	1%	168	1%	16,253	405
Pennsylvania	16,074	77%	36	543	3%	4,153	20%	20,770	162
Rhode Island	1,885	90%	20	135	6%	66	3%	2,086	198
South Carolina	4,400	71%	40	902	14%	927	15%	6,229	128
South Dakota	1,887	68%	45	623	22%	277	10%	2,787	325
Tennessee	7,674	84%	31	667	7%	789	9%	9,130	139
Texas[6]	55,184	89%	21	552	1%	6,118	10%	61,854	226
Utah	2,420	71%	39	96	3%	906	26%	3,422	115
Vermont	1,854	99%	3	0	0%	28	1%	1,882	301
Virginia	9,059	80%	33	668	6%	1,649	14%	11,376	136
Washington	17,672	93%	12	140	1%	1,124	6%	18,936	265
West Virginia	3,758	84%	30	392	9%	303	7%	4,453	241
Wisconsin	23,836	96%	8	20	0%	1,103	4%	24,959	433
Wyoming	2,246	92%	13	97	4%	93	4%	2,436	416
United States	**559,172**	**82%**		**52,122**	**8%**	**69,557**	**10%**	**680,851**	**212**

[1] Table reports average daily residents for FY 2015; all states' sum is 100%; some settings' percentages rounded up or down.

[2] Settings for 1-6 persons included 337,264 supported living/personal assistance participants.

[3] States' ranking, highest to lowest, on percentage of total persons with IDD in out-of-home settings who reside in 1-6 person settings.

[4] 16+ settings include state-operated institutions, private ICFs/ID and non-ICFs/ID, and nursing facilities. In Alaska, New Mexico, and Vermont, 16+ settings are exclusively persons with I/DD in nursing facilities.

[5] Utilization rate, per 100,000 citizens of the general population, for all IDD out-of-home placements in the state.

[6] Texas reported out-of-home placements in the following categories: 8 or fewer, 9-13 and 14+ persons.

Source: Braddock et al., Coleman Institute and Department of Psychiatry, University of Colorado, 2017.

III. FEDERAL, STATE, AND LOCAL MEDICAID SPENDING: FY 2013-2015

Federal, state, and local Medicaid funding totaled $49.4 billion and constituted 76% of funding for IDD services and supports in the United States in FY 2015.

Established in 1981, nationwide federal-state Home and Community Based Services (HCBS) Waiver funds totaled $34.5 billion in FY 2015. The HCBS Waiver federal-state spending comprised 53% of total IDD spending and 70% of Medicaid spending ($49.4 billion) in 2015 (Figure 1).

Funding for Medicaid Intermediate Care Facilities for People with Intellectual Disabilities (ICF/ID) was $11.0 billion, 22% of Medicaid, and $3.9 billion (8%), financed State Plan Medicaid services including personal care, rehabilitative services, clinic services, and targeted case management.

Figure 2 presents the 1977–2015 trend in inflation-adjusted federal, state, and local Medicaid spending for the HCBS Waiver, all public and private ICFs/ID, and for State Plan Medicaid services. Note the rapid growth in Waiver spending, and the marked decline in ICF/ID spending during 2013–2015. We address Medicaid spending trends in more detail in the pages following.

Unmatched Funds

State and local unmatched funds totaled $7.97 billion (Table 4). Unmatched funds constituted 12% of total IDD spending (up from 11% in 2013). These funds were

Figure 1
FEDERAL, STATE, and LOCAL MEDICAID IS THREE-FOURTHS OF TOTAL IDD SPENDING IN FY 2015

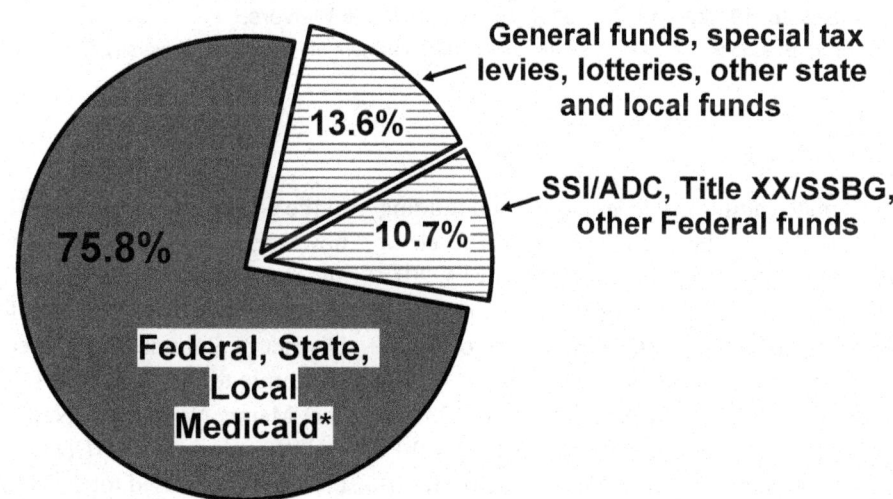

TOTAL IDD SPENDING: $65.21 BILLION

*TOTAL FEDERAL-STATE MEDICAID: $49.4 BILLION
  a) HCBS WAIVER (70%)
  b) PUBLIC & PRIVATE ICFs/ID (22%)
  c) STATE PLAN MEDICAID (8%)

Source: Braddock et al., Coleman Institute and Department of Psychiatry, University of Colorado, 2017.

Figure 2
FEDERAL AND STATE IDD SPENDING FOR HCBS WAIVER, ICF/ID, AND RELATED MEDICAID IN THE U.S.: FY 1977-2015

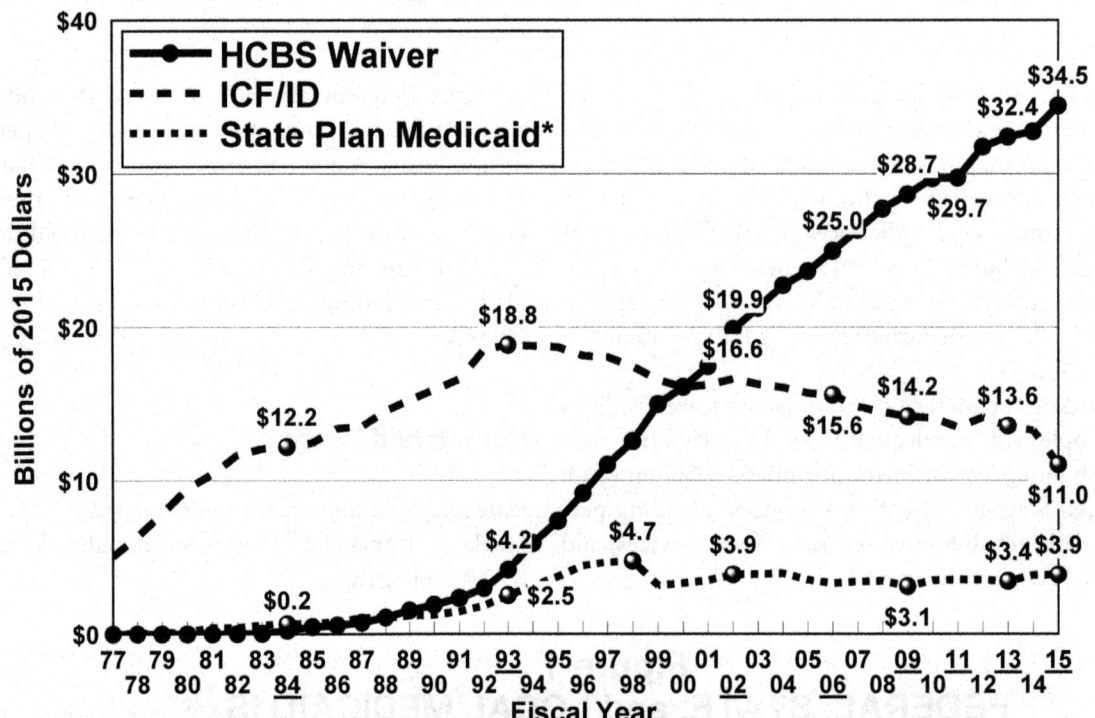

*State Plan Medicaid includes Clinic and Rehabilitative Services, Targeted Case Management, Personal Assistance, and Community Administrative Services. Waivers include Sections 1115, 1915a/b, 1915b/c, 1915c, 1915i, 1915j, and 1915k Waivers.

Source: Braddock et al., Coleman Institute and Department of Psychiatry, University of Colorado, 2017.

available to match additional federal Medicaid funding in the states. The ten states with the highest levels of potentially unmatched state/local funding in FY 2015 included New York ($2.20 billion), California ($1.17 billion), Massachusetts ($0.97 billion), Ohio ($0.82 billion), New Jersey ($0.42 billion), Georgia ($0.29 billion), North Carolina, and Pennsylvania ($0.23 billion), Virginia ($0.19 billion), and Connecticut ($0.17 billion). Note the states are ranked in unmatched funding as a percentage of total IDD spending.

Trends in Public IDD Spending: FY 2013-2015

Spending for persons with IDD and their families was strong in most states during FYs 2013-2015. This period encompassed states' recovery from the impact of the Great Recession.[2] Total IDD spending increased, however, by 3.3% in 2012; 0.7% in 2013; 0.6% in 2014; and 3.5% in 2015. During FY 2013-2015, total IDD spending increased 4.1% and forty-one states and the District of Columbia increased IDD spending in real economic terms. Nine states: Hawaii, Kansas, Louisiana, Maine, New Jersey, New York, Ohio, Oklahoma, and Wyoming *reduced IDD spending during 2013-2015*. Five states increased total IDD spending quite dramatically by 20% to 50% during the 2013-2015 period (Table 5). The states were: Kentucky (50% growth); Idaho (25%); Delaware (24%); North Carolina (21%); and North Dakota (20%).

Eighty-eight percent of FY 2015 financial resources in the U.S. was allocated for community residential

---
[2] The National Bureau of Economic Research (2017) defined the duration of the Great Recession as: December 2007-June 2009.

TABLE 4
STATE, COUNTY AND LOCAL FUNDS POTENTIALLY AVAILABLE TO MATCH ADDITIONAL FEDERAL MEDICAID FUNDING, BY STATE: FY 2015[1,2]

Rank		Total Federal, State, County & Local IDD Spending	Total Unmatched State, County & Local Funds	Unmatched % of Total Spending
38	Alabama	$404,099,733	$6,556,662	1.6%
24	Alaska	$210,140,720	$13,847,970	6.6%
35	Arizona	$987,977,823	$19,624,763	2.0%
42	Arkansas	$595,812,179	$6,441,970	1.1%
8	California	$7,153,803,689	$1,173,095,964	16.4%
15	Colorado	$624,463,901	$65,635,477	10.5%
12	Connecticut	$1,279,088,392	$166,907,872	13.0%
10	Delaware	$216,390,346	$30,231,250	14.0%
14	District of Columbia	$347,354,588	$41,056,143	11.8%
29	Florida	$1,749,178,764	$68,207,678	3.9%
2	Georgia	$994,311,241	$285,627,950	28.7%
18	Hawaii	$155,907,657	$12,609,480	8.1%
40	Idaho	$273,075,276	$4,074,260	1.5%
21	Illinois	$1,727,321,894	$127,591,674	7.4%
45	Indiana	$1,526,601,925	$2,022,830	0.1%
32	Iowa	$968,340,077	$20,254,330	2.1%
41	Kansas	$429,115,258	$4,840,509	1.1%
30	Kentucky	$1,163,381,717	$32,065,413	2.8%
36	Louisiana	$1,436,379,021	$28,296,008	2.0%
39	Maine	$448,192,411	$6,953,915	1.6%
11	Maryland	$1,105,422,862	$150,153,453	13.6%
1	Massachusetts	$2,462,225,103	$967,434,598	39.3%
31	Michigan	$1,559,298,066	$36,068,791	2.3%
33	Minnesota	$1,906,552,072	$39,585,758	2.1%
20	Mississippi	$414,270,689	$32,700,000	7.9%
16	Missouri	$1,081,031,938	$107,710,369	10.0%
6	Montana	$187,045,479	$35,847,257	19.2%
17	Nebraska	$413,053,481	$33,821,771	8.2%
7	Nevada	$185,193,710	$34,647,721	18.7%
34	New Hampshire	$298,939,164	$6,062,540	2.0%
5	New Jersey	$1,965,588,844	$422,190,287	21.5%
28	New Mexico	$404,072,903	$18,444,805	4.6%
4	New York	$10,228,587,300	$2,210,784,239	21.6%
13	North Carolina	$1,864,605,378	$227,045,183	12.2%
37	North Dakota	$340,121,606	$5,757,372	1.7%
3	Ohio	$3,370,684,768	$818,609,791	24.3%
25	Oklahoma	$509,943,199	$27,234,923	5.3%
44	Oregon	$835,232,432	$3,575,947	0.4%
23	Pennsylvania	$3,293,586,568	$225,871,620	6.9%
46	Rhode Island	$286,870,506	$333,049	0.1%
19	South Carolina	$695,021,799	$55,336,129	8.0%
22	South Dakota	$189,504,678	$13,621,836	7.2%
49	Tennessee	$977,591,522	$0	0.0%
27	Texas	$2,797,204,384	$129,009,168	4.6%
47	Utah	$313,839,473	$156,025	0.0%
49	Vermont	$196,211,764	$0	0.0%
9	Virginia	$1,355,841,260	$190,802,518	14.1%
26	Washington	$1,141,277,363	$59,478,473	5.2%
49	West Virginia	$508,912,735	$0	0.0%
48	Wisconsin	$1,493,887,168	$0	0.0%
43	Wyoming	$136,574,177	$878,632	0.6%
	United States	**$65,209,129,005**	**$7,969,104,372**	**12.2%**

[1] States ranked lowest have the highest percentage of Unmatched Funds as a percentage of total IDD Spending. Unmatched funds consisted of total IDD spending, minus federal-state Medicaid, federal SSI/ADC for HCBS Waiver participants, SSI state supplementation, and social services and other federal funds.

[2] County governments provided 20% of Ohio's unmatched state and local funds; unmatched funds in Iowa & Wisconsin also included county and other local government funding.

Source: Braddock et al., Coleman Institute and Department of Psychiatry, University of Colorado, 2017

TABLE 5
PUBLIC SPENDING FOR IDD SERVICES: FY 2013-2015[1]

STATE	FY 2015 TOTAL IDD	% CHANGE[2]	FY 2015 COMMUNITY	% CHANGE[2]	TOTAL INSTITUTION 16+	% CHANGE[2]	PUBLIC INST. 16+	% CHANGE[2]	PRIVATE INST. 16+	% CHANGE[2]
Alabama	$404.1	6.8%	$404.1	6.8%						
Alaska	$210.1	4.7%	$210.1	4.7%						
Arizona	$988.0	12.9%	$959.5	13.3%	$28.5	0.7%	$13.1	-7.6%	$15.4	9.0%
Arkansas	$595.8	9.2%	$430.3	13.5%	$165.5	-0.7%	$139.7	0.8%	$25.7	-8.2%
California	$7,153.8	8.3%	$6,599.2	9.5%	$554.6	-4.3%	$511.2	-3.8%	$43.4	-9.6%
Colorado	$624.5	13.7%	$584.5	16.6%	$39.9	-16.1%	$39.9	-16.1%		
Connecticut	$1,279.1	1.7%	$1,085.3	6.8%	$193.8	-19.9%	$188.8	-20.0%	$4.9	-15.1%
Delaware	$216.4	23.5%	$170.6	23.8%	$45.8	22.8%	$23.5	-15.7%	$22.3	136.0%
District of Columbia	$347.4	19.1%	$347.4	19.1%						
Florida	$1,749.2	12.0%	$1,422.9	8.3%	$326.3	31.4%	$118.0	0.0%	$208.3	60.0%
Georgia	$994.3	10.6%	$931.3	11.1%	$63.0	3.4%	$56.0	4.1%	$6.9	-1.9%
Hawaii	$155.9	-6.7%	$155.9	-6.7%						
Idaho	$273.1	24.7%	$248.3	30.5%	$24.8	-13.6%	$6.3	-38.9%	$18.5	0.6%
Illinois	$1,727.3	2.2%	$1,311.8	5.7%	$415.5	-7.7%	$279.6	-4.9%	$135.9	-13.0%
Indiana	$1,526.6	10.6%	$1,506.7	11.7%	$19.9	-35.5%			$19.9	-35.5%
Iowa	$968.3	6.2%	$741.9	10.9%	$226.5	-6.9%	$115.3	-6.9%	$111.2	-6.8%
Kansas	$429.1	-15.3%	$376.8	-15.6%	$52.3	-13.0%	$52.3	-13.0%		
Kentucky	$1,163.4	50.2%	$1,017.4	63.0%	$146.0	-2.9%	$115.9	-4.1%	$30.1	2.0%
Louisiana	$1,436.4	-3.0%	$1,270.8	-0.7%	$165.6	-18.1%	$104.7	-10.1%	$60.9	-29.0%
Maine	$448.2	-3.3%	$434.4	-4.3%	$13.8	48.1%			$13.8	48.1%
Maryland	$1,105.4	4.5%	$1,050.1	4.5%	$55.3	4.9%	$55.3	4.9%		
Massachusetts	$2,462.2	13.6%	$2,329.4	18.8%	$132.8	-36.1%	$132.8	-36.1%		
Michigan	$1,559.3	1.4%	$1,534.3	1.9%	$25.0	-19.6%			$25.0	-19.6%
Minnesota	$1,906.6	7.4%	$1,873.7	7.7%	$32.8	-9.5%			$32.8	3.1%
Mississippi	$414.3	6.7%	$208.2	25.1%	$206.1	-7.1%	$151.1	-8.2%	$55.0	-4.0%
Missouri	$1,081.0	2.0%	$981.9	3.4%	$99.1	-10.3%	$88.2	-11.4%	$10.9	0.1%
Montana	$187.0	6.6%	$175.2	7.8%	$11.9	-8.8%	$11.9	-8.8%		
Nebraska	$413.1	7.7%	$343.4	9.5%	$69.6	-0.3%	$49.7	-4.1%	$20.0	10.3%
Nevada	$185.2	9.6%	$170.9	9.9%	$14.3	5.4%	$10.4	4.6%	$3.9	7.7%
New Hampshire	$298.9	3.0%	$294.5	2.8%	$4.4	17.3%			$4.4	17.3%
New Jersey	$1,965.6	-4.9%	$1,413.2	10.9%	$552.4	-30.2%	$477.3	-32.4%	$75.1	-12.0%
New Mexico	$404.1	6.5%	$404.1	6.5%						
New York	$10,228.6	-6.8%	$9,659.3	-3.7%	$569.3	-40.2%	$247.4	-60.9%	$321.9	1.1%
North Carolina	$1,864.6	20.5%	$1,455.1	21.9%	$409.5	16.1%	$280.7	-0.1%	$128.8	79.2%
North Dakota	$340.1	20.3%	$306.8	22.7%	$33.3	1.6%	$26.4	-0.3%	$6.9	9.7%
Ohio	$3,370.7	-0.2%	$2,882.5	1.4%	$488.2	-8.8%	$189.9	-8.1%	$298.3	-9.2%
Oklahoma	$509.9	-4.7%	$443.6	-0.7%	$66.3	-24.8%	$30.6	-40.5%	$35.8	-2.8%
Oregon	$835.2	0.8%	$835.2	0.8%						
Pennsylvania	$3,293.6	13.7%	$2,769.8	15.1%	$523.8	7.0%	$327.6	10.3%	$196.2	2.0%
Rhode Island	$286.9	8.4%	$281.0	8.6%	$5.9	0.5%			$5.9	0.5%
South Carolina	$695.0	11.9%	$586.2	14.8%	$108.8	-1.3%	$108.8	-1.3%		
South Dakota	$189.5	6.9%	$158.5	7.7%	$31.0	3.1%	$24.2	4.6%	$6.8	-2.0%
Tennessee	$977.6	1.8%	$897.3	3.4%	$80.3	-13.9%	$66.6	-16.9%	$13.7	4.4%
Texas	$2,797.2	1.2%	$1,952.3	2.4%	$844.9	-1.3%	$830.2	-0.6%	$14.8	-28.9%
Utah	$313.8	8.5%	$241.1	9.5%	$72.7	5.4%	$37.3	6.9%	$35.4	3.9%
Vermont	$196.2	6.2%	$196.2	6.2%						
Virginia	$1,355.8	0.3%	$1,156.3	8.6%	$199.6	-30.6%	$167.2	-34.5%	$32.4	-0.3%
Washington	$1,141.3	4.8%	$955.9	5.4%	$185.4	1.8%	$184.0	4.0%	$1.3	-73.4%
West Virginia	$508.9	1.4%	$507.6	1.9%	$1.3	-62.6%			$1.3	-62.6%
Wisconsin	$1,493.9	2.5%	$1,360.5	5.2%	$133.4	-18.6%	$109.1	-13.9%	$24.4	-34.7%
Wyoming	$136.6	-10.6%	$117.3	-9.2%	$19.3	-18.4%	$19.3	-18.4%		
UNITED STATES	**$65,209.1**	**4.1%**	**$57,750.7**	**6.5%**	**$7,458.5**	**-11.3%**	**$5,390.3**	**-15.3%**	**$2,068.2**	**1.02%**

[1]Spending in $Millions. [2]Percent change in inflation-adjusted spending: FY 2013-2015. Blank cell indicates the State had no institution.

Source: Braddock et al., Coleman Institute and Department of Psychiatry, University of Colorado, 2017

services for 15 or fewer persons (611,294 individuals). This included supported living for 337,264 persons and an array of day programs and community supports such as supported employment for 109,954 workers and family support for 523,501 families. The remaining 12% of funds financed care for 69,557 individuals in the nation's public and private institutions for 16 or more persons.

Inflation-adjusted spending for community services advanced 6.5% during FY 2013–2015. This is in marked contrast to spending for public and private institutions for 16 or more persons. Institutional spending dropped 11.3% during FYs 2013–2015. This precisely matched the 11.3% institutional spending reduction during FYs 2012–2014. Most growth in IDD spending in the United States during FYs 2013–2015 was financed with the HCBS Waiver. Nationwide public spending for the HCBS Waiver surpassed spending for the ICF/ID program in FY 2000 (Figure 2).

Public and Private Spending for Institutions

Spending for public and private facilities for 16 or more persons totaled $7.5 billion and constituted 11.4% of total IDD nationwide spending in FY 2015 (Table 5). Seventy-one percent ($5.4 billion) was allocated to support 21,103 residents in the nation's remaining 133 state-operated institutions for 16 or more persons (Figure 3).

The remaining $2.1 billion, 29%, supported 21,148 persons residing in privately-operated facilities for 16 or more persons in the states.

Public institutions. The vast majority of the states, 28 to be precise, reduced spending for state-operated 16 or more person institutions during FY2013–2015 and nationwide institutional spending fell 11.3%. However, 37 states still operated institutional facilities (Figure 3); as noted, 28 of these states reduced spending. Reductions

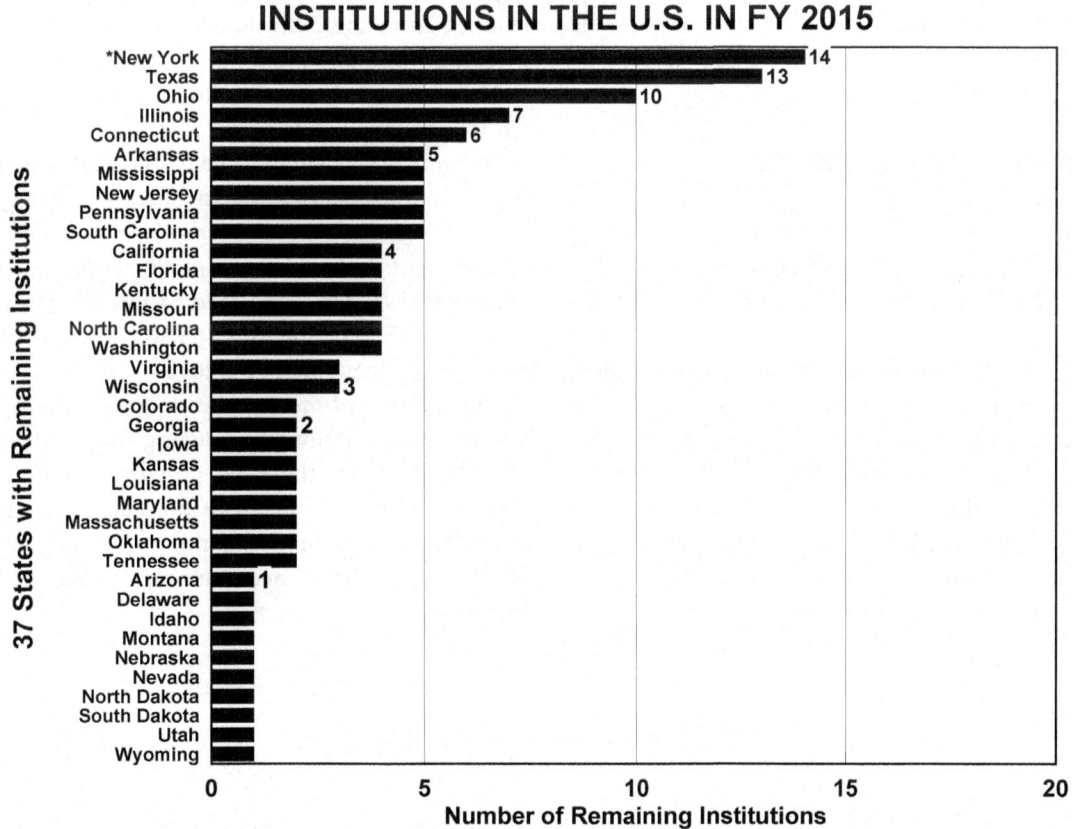

Figure 3
THIRTY-SEVEN STATES OPERATED 133 REMAINING INSTITUTIONS IN THE U.S. IN FY 2015

*New York's 14 remaining institutions included two large facilities, Brooklyn and Broome, and 12 special units where large institutions had closed.
Source: Braddock et al., Coleman Institute and Department of Psychiatry, University of Colorado, 2017.

ranged from 61% in New York and 41% in Oklahoma to −0.1% in North Carolina. Moreover, 34 of the 37 states with state-operated institutions reduced their census during FY 2013–2015. But two states, Montana and South Dakota, increased their number of residents by five and one person, respectively. Utah's institutional census was stable across FYs 2013–2015. Eight states increased state-operated institutional spending between 11% and 1%: Pennsylvania (10%); Utah, (7%); Nevada, South Dakota, and Maryland (5%); Georgia and Washington (4%); and Arkansas (1%). As indicated in Figure 3, ten states operated only one remaining state institution. New York reduced the number of remaining facilities from 24 in 2013 to 14 in 2015.

Private Institutions. Spending for private facilities for 16 or more persons increased by only 1.02% nationwide during FY 2013–2015 (Table 5). However, among the 37 states that operated private institutions in 2015, 17 states increased spending during 2013–2015. The largest increases were in Delaware (136%), North Carolina (79%), and Florida (60%). There was reduced spending in privately-operated institutional facilities in the remaining 21 states during FY 2013–2015. The largest spending reductions were in Washington State (−73%), West Virginia (−63%), Indiana (−36%), Wisconsin (−35%), and Louisiana and Texas (−29%).

Community Services Spending

Community spending in the United States grew 6.5% from $54.23 billion (inflation-adjusted) in 2013 to $57.75 billion in 2015 (*Table 5*). Kentucky's remarkable growth began in FY 2009 with a class action lawsuit (*Michelle P, et al. v. Morgan et al.*, 2001, amended 2008). The lawsuit addressed a lengthy wait list for Medicaid services despite increases in state funds. Adjusted community spending increased each year in Kentucky during 2009–2015—by 42% in 2010, 15% in 2011, 22% in 2012, 14% in 2013, 54% in 2014, and 6% in 2015. This analysis of spending growth includes spending for 7–15 person residential settings.

The Home and Community Based Services (HCBS) Waiver was the engine of community services growth in virtually all states posting strong community spending increases during 2013–2015. Kentucky increased Waiver spending by 82%. Nine other states increased community services spending during FY 2013–2015 from 15% to 63%. The nine states included Idaho (153% Waiver growth), Mississippi (55%) Massachusetts (46%), North Dakota (27%), North Carolina (26%), Delaware (25%), District of Columbia (20%), Pennsylvania (19%), and Colorado (16%).

In contrast, seven states reduced inflation-adjusted spending for community services during 2013–2015: Kansas (−18%), Maine (−15%), New York (−10%), Wyoming (−12%), Hawaii (−7%), Louisiana (−3%), and Oklahoma (−0.7%). All states reducing community spending also had slower Waiver growth during 2013–2015—ranging from −0.3% to −18%.

Using a *"six person or fewer"* metric to define community services across the states, community services spending increased 8.8%—from $50.9 billion in FY 2013 to $55.4 billion in FY 2015. This was greater than the 6.5% increase for community services including facilities for 15 person or fewer persons. This resulted from the exclusion of more expensive 7–15 person group homes and public and private ICFs/ID. Inflation-adjusted spending for 7–15 person settings fell 15% nationally during 2013–2015.

Individual and family supports is a subcomponent of community services. It includes family support, supported living/personal assistance, and supported employment. *Individual and family support* spending nationwide was $16.0 billion in FY 2015. It constituted 28% of the $57.5 billion for 15 person or fewer community services spending in FY 2015.

Individual and family support grew rapidly at an adjusted 13% nationwide during 2013–2015. This growth was twice the 6.5% growth for community services overall. However, as presented later in this report, there are millions of families that do not receive monetary support for necessary care and services (see Figure 9).

IV. FISCAL EFFORT IN THE STATES

Fiscal effort measures the states' financial capacity to fund IDD services. As an analytical tool, it measures differences in states' wealth. Fiscal effort is defined as a state's spending for IDD services from federal, state, and local sources per $1,000 aggregate state-wide personal income (U.S. Department of Commerce, 2016a).

Total nationwide IDD fiscal effort in FY2015 was $4.30 per $1,000 of statewide personal income. From FY 2010, the peak year before the major impact of the Great Recession, through FY 2015, total IDD fiscal effort in the U.S. declined 4%. Figure 4 presents the nation's community fiscal effort level ($3.81), institutional services fiscal effort ($0.49), and total fiscal effort ($4.30).

The institutional fiscal effort is much lower due to the downsizing and closing of many public institutions across the United States. Institutional facility fiscal effort fell 28% during 2010–2015. This was the most dramatic decline in institutional fiscal effort in the 39 year history of The States of the States in Intellectual and Developmental Disabilities Project. Community fiscal effort increased 1% during FY 2010–2015. Table 6 includes the states' rankings in total fiscal effort and community fiscal effort in 2015. The states' percent change in total and community fiscal effort during FY 2013–2015 is also ranked from largest to smallest.

Community services fiscal effort. Community Services fiscal effort grew only 1.8% from FY2013 to FY2015. It advanced from 1% to 58% across 36 states and the District of Columbia

Institutional fiscal effort. In contrast to community services, 16 or more public/private institutional services fiscal effort peaked over three decades ago in FY 1980 at $1.71 per $1,000 of statewide aggregate personal income. It declined to a low of $0.49 per $1,000 in FY 2015 (Figure 4).

In FY 2015 Alabama, Alaska, District of Columbia, Hawaii, New Mexico, Oregon, and Vermont had "$0.00" institutional fiscal effort because these states no longer operated public or private 16 or more person institutions. Another 21 states had institutional fiscal effort levels in FY2015 below the national average of $.50. These states were Arizona, California, Colorado, Florida, Georgia, Idaho, Indiana, Kansas, Maine, Maryland, Massachusetts, Michigan, Minnesota, Missouri, Montana, Nevada, New Hampshire, Oklahoma, Tennessee, Virginia, and West Virginia.

Figure 4
FISCAL EFFORT FOR INTELLECTUAL AND DEVELOPMENTAL DISABILITIES SERVICES IN THE UNITED STATES: FY 1977-2015

Source: Braddock et al., Coleman Institute and Department of Psychiatry, University of Colorado, 2017.

TABLE 6
TOTAL AND COMMUNITY FISCAL EFFORT FOR IDD SERVICES IN THE STATES
PER $1,000 OF STATEWIDE AGGREGATE PERSONAL INCOME

STATE	TOTAL FISCAL EFFORT				COMMUNITY FISCAL EFFORT			
	FY 2015	RANK	% CHANGE FYs 2013-15	RANK	FY 2015	RANK	% CHANGE FYs 2013-15	RANK
Alabama	$2.20	48	4%	19	$2.20	44	4%	25
Alaska	$5.12	20	1%	31	$5.12	17	1%	37
Arizona	$3.77	33	7%	11	$3.67	29	7%	15
Arkansas	$5.28	16	7%	10	$3.81	27	11%	9
California	$3.50	37	2%	28	$3.23	34	3%	30
Colorado	$2.29	47	4%	23	$2.14	45	6%	17
Connecticut	$5.25	18	0.5%	33	$4.46	19	5.6%	20
Delaware	$4.95	21	18%	2	$3.90	25	18%	6
District of Columbia	$7.15	6	9%	7	$7.15	4	9%	10
Florida	$1.99	50	5%	15	$1.62	49	2%	35
Georgia	$2.47	45	5%	16	$2.31	42	5%	22
Hawaii	$2.31	46	-11%	49	$2.31	43	-11%	49
Idaho	$4.39	27	17%	3	$3.99	23	23%	3
Illinois	$2.72	44	-1%	36	$2.06	47	2%	31
Indiana	$5.60	14	8%	9	$5.53	12	9%	11
Iowa	$6.88	9	3%	24	$5.27	14	8%	13
Kansas	$3.15	40	-16%	51	$2.77	37	-16%	51
Kentucky	$6.96	7	45%	1	$6.09	9	58%	1
Louisiana	$7.25	5	-6%	43	$6.42	8	-4%	43
Maine	$8.02	2	-6%	42	$7.77	2	-7%	47
Maryland	$3.35	38	3%	27	$3.18	36	3%	29
Massachusetts	$5.94	12	8%	8	$5.62	11	13%	7
Michigan	$3.71	35	-3%	41	$3.65	30	-3%	42
Minnesota	$6.95	8	3%	25	$6.83	6	4%	27
Mississippi	$4.02	31	6%	13	$2.02	48	24%	2
Missouri	$4.27	28	0.3%	34	$3.87	26	2%	34
Montana	$4.41	26	4%	18	$4.13	21	6%	19
Nebraska	$4.51	25	5%	17	$3.75	28	6%	16
Nevada	$1.57	51	4%	20	$1.45	51	4%	24
New Hampshire	$4.12	30	1%	32	$4.05	22	0%	38
New Jersey	$3.73	34	-8%	46	$2.68	39	7%	14
New Mexico	$5.17	19	3%	26	$5.17	16	3%	28
New York	$9.06	1	-9%	47	$8.56	1	-6%	45
North Carolina	$4.66	24	17%	4	$3.63	31	18%	5
North Dakota	$7.92	3	17%	5	$7.14	5	19%	4
Ohio	$6.77	10	-3%	40	$5.79	10	-1%	40
Oklahoma	$2.87	42	-11%	48	$2.50	41	-7%	48
Oregon	$4.88	22	-6%	45	$4.88	18	-6%	46
Pennsylvania	$5.26	17	11%	6	$4.43	20	12%	8
Rhode Island	$5.54	15	5%	14	$5.43	13	6%	21
South Carolina	$3.80	32	6%	12	$3.21	35	9%	12
South Dakota	$4.73	23	4%	21	$3.96	24	5%	23
Tennessee	$3.62	36	-2%	39	$3.32	33	-0.3%	39
Texas	$2.19	49	-6%	44	$1.53	50	-5%	44
Utah	$2.75	43	1%	29	$2.11	46	2%	32
Vermont	$6.53	11	4%	22	$6.53	7	4%	26
Virginia	$3.18	39	-2%	38	$2.71	38	6%	18
Washington	$3.13	41	-2%	37	$2.62	40	-1%	41
West Virginia	$7.57	4	1%	30	$7.55	3	1%	36
Wisconsin	$5.73	13	-0.5%	35	$5.22	15	2.1%	33
Wyoming	$4.13	29	-14%	50	$3.55	32	-13%	50
UNITED STATES	$4.30		-0.4%		$3.81		1.8%	

Source: Braddock et al., Coleman Institute and Department of Psychiatry, University of Colorado, 2017

Total statewide aggregate personal income in the U.S., adjusted for inflation, increased only 0.3% on average during the ten year period from 2005 to 2014; but it advanced 6.5% in FY 2015 and 3.4% in FY 2016. In the face of strong personal income growth in 2015, 32 states and the District of Columbia increased total IDD fiscal effort from 2013–2015 and 38 states increased community IDD fiscal effort during 2013–2015. In this analysis, community services fiscal effort included community services for 15 or fewer people and individual and family support, and it excluded spending for state and private institutions for 16 or more people.

There was substantial growth during FY 2013–2015 in total IDD fiscal effort in Kentucky, Delaware, Idaho, North Carolina, North Dakota, Pennsylvania, District of Columbia, Indiana, Arizona, and Arkansas. New York State led the nation in total fiscal effort in 2015, spending $9.06 per $1,000 of statewide personal income for IDD services. Other states with high total fiscal effort commitments in FY 2015 were Maine, North Dakota, West Virginia, Louisiana, District of Columbia, Kentucky, Minnesota, Iowa, and Ohio. At the other end of the spectrum, Nevada committed only $1.57 per $1,000 of its aggregate state wealth for total IDD services. Florida was the only other state spending less than $2.00 per $1,000 of statewide personal income for IDD services.

The most substantial growth in *community fiscal effort* between FY 2013 and FY 2015 occurred in Kentucky, Mississippi, Idaho, North Dakota, North Carolina, Delaware, Massachusetts, and Pennsylvania. These states posted community fiscal effort increases of 10% or more. New York led the nation in community fiscal effort in FY 2015. The State spent $8.56 per $1,000 of state personal income for IDD services. Other states with the most substantial financial commitments to community IDD services in FY2015 included, in rank order, Maine, West Virginia, District of Columbia, North Dakota, Minnesota, Vermont, Louisiana, Kentucky, and Ohio. Nevada committed the least effort—only $1.45 per $1,000 of the State's aggregate wealth was allocated for community IDD services in 2015. Other states spending less than $2.10 per $1,000 of state wealth for community services fiscal effort were Texas, Florida, Mississippi, and Illinois.

V. ANNUAL COST OF CARE FOR RESIDENTS IN FIVE SETTINGS

Costs varied widely in FY 2015 by state and by type of residential setting. Nationwide average annual cost per resident ranged from $27,593 in supported living to $210,110 in state-operated 16 or more person public institutions. Table 7 presents annual costs of care in five settings: a) private institutions for 16 or more persons (ICFs/ID and non-ICFs/ID); b) state-operated institutions for 16 or more persons; c) private ICFs/ID for 15 or fewer persons; d) public ICFs/ID for 15 or fewer persons; and e) supported living/personal assistance.

The number of individuals with IDD served in 16 or more person state-operated institutions has declined by an average of 5% each year for 39 consecutive years. During FY 2013–2015 the census fell from 24,695 to 21,103 persons, a 15% decline. Average annual cost of care per person in state-operated 16 or more institutions, based on the number of average daily residents during FY2015, ranged from below $200,000 in Arkansas, Arizona, Florida, Illinois, Kansas, Mississippi, South Carolina, South Dakota, and Utah to more than $300,000 in California, Connecticut, Delaware, Kentucky, Maryland, Nebraska, New York, North Dakota, Oklahoma, Pennsylvania, Tennessee, and Virginia. The national average cost per resident was $210,110.

Costs in private facilities. In FY2015, 21,148 persons with IDD resided in private facilities for 16 or more persons. The vast majority of these individuals were living in private ICF/ID facilities; 17,418 persons compared to 3,730 persons in non-ICFs/ID settings. The average annual per person cost of care across all 16 or more person private institutions was $95,758. However, costs varied from less than $50,000 in California, Connecticut, Illinois, Michigan, Missouri, Texas, Washington, and Oklahoma to more than $200,000 in Arizona, Delaware, Maine, Nevada, New Jersey, North Dakota, Rhode Island, and Virginia.

Private facilities for 16 or more people consisted of ICFs/ID in 33 states and non-ICFs/ID in nine states. California, Illinois, Iowa, New Jersey, and New York operated both types of facilities. The weighted average private facility cost shown in Table 1 is $95,758. The nationwide average private ICF/ID cost per resident was $112,873, considerably greater than the average non-ICF/ID private institutional cost of $50,195 per resident.

In FY2015, 38,083 persons were served in *private ICFs/ID for 15 or fewer persons*. The average annual cost per resident in the 35 states that offered these settings was $106,553. The cost ranged dramatically from below $50,000 in Alabama, California, Oklahoma, and Utah to more than $200,000 in Connecticut, District of Columbia, Florida, Kansas, Nebraska, Vermont, and Virginia. *Publicly operated ICFs/ID for 15 or fewer persons* served 2,204 individuals in 11 states in FY 2015. Publicly operated 15 or fewer ICF/ID annual cost ranged from $79,490 in South Carolina and $82,136 in Minnesota to over $100,000 in Arizona, Kentucky, Louisiana, Mississippi, New Mexico, New York, Rhode Island, Tennessee, and Texas. The national average cost was $165,054 (Table 7).

Costs for supported living/personal assistance settings. The last column in Table 7 presents the average annual cost per person for supported living and personal assistance. At $27,593 in 2015, supported living cost approximately 80% less than the average annual cost of all institutional ICF/ID settings.

Supported living was defined in this study as housing in which individuals choose where and with whom they live. Ownership must be by someone other than the support provider, such as the individual, his/her family, a landlord, or a housing cooperative. The individual must also have a personalized support plan that changes as her or his needs and abilities change. *Personal assistance*, in addition to the criteria defining supported living, is financed by state funds, Medicaid state plan personal care, or HCBS Waiver funds. In general, people with IDD are choosing to live in their own homes or their family's home, and the State also defines this type of support as "personal assistance" (Braddock et al., 2015). Supported living cost $30,795 per person per year in FY2015 compared to $21,653 per person for personal assistance.

Forty-eight states reported providing supported living and personal assistance services for 337,264 individuals with IDD in FY2015. Total cost was $6.75 billion.

TABLE 7
ANNUAL COST OF CARE PER RESIDENT
BY SETTING: FY 2015

STATE	INSTITUTIONS FOR 16+ PERSONS		ICFs ID FOR 15 OR FEWER PERSONS		SUPPORTED LIVING/PERSONAL ASSISTANCE
	PRIVATE	PUBLIC	PRIVATE	PUBLIC	
Alabama			$36,237		$15,756
Alaska			$157,871		$38,081
Arizona	$480,157	$140,801		$154,953	$50,245
Arkansas	$74,185	$152,213	$81,375		$48,979
California	$25,115	$502,529	$49,614		$26,645
Colorado		$269,772	$183,528		$13,711
Connecticut	$48,453	$403,496	$201,134		$12,641
Delaware	$280,743	$434,505			$46,742
District of Columbia			$273,576		$39,210
Florida	$135,975	$152,453	$224,917		$13,241
Georgia	$61,259	$216,439			$12,301
Hawaii			$104,195		$0
Idaho	$88,931	$275,080	$55,137		$18,635
Illinois	$45,607	$162,183	$59,440		$22,978
Indiana	$155,359		$119,533		$48,976
Iowa	$130,661	$292,613	$115,436		$56,908
Kansas		$165,023	$207,129		$3,793
Kentucky	$195,655	$440,524		$222,412	$15,738
Louisiana	$74,087	$222,469	$94,647	$735,007	$72,420
Maine	$246,781		$138,633		$50,802
Maryland		$453,520			$51,500
Massachusetts		$287,434			$13,244
Michigan	$45,807				$19,696
Minnesota	$82,743		$74,445	$82,136	$15,661
Mississippi	$79,020	$140,332		$122,140	$18,469
Missouri	$30,469	$212,549	$60,736		$54,574
Montana		$215,665			$15,109
Nebraska	$92,025	$427,079	$234,173		$26,627
Nevada	$215,689	$222,074	$100,025		$47,197
New Hampshire	$177,587				$7,669
New Jersey	$418,169	$280,521			$50,149
New Mexico			$107,105	$766,392	$44,098
New York	$156,203	$421,185	$170,058	$250,330	$17,998
North Carolina	$159,039	$235,093	$107,538		$18,833
North Dakota	$231,637	$321,529	$175,129		$73,783
Ohio	$97,196	$205,843	$92,422		$35,446
Oklahoma	$37,035	$462,991	$37,323		$124,931
Oregon					$15,595
Pennsylvania	$143,256	$327,749	$131,498		$23,968
Rhode Island	$280,146			$116,281	$33,144
South Carolina		$161,651		$79,490	$16,761
South Dakota	$136,146	$172,642			$5,020
Tennessee	$153,909	$465,114	$153,909	$368,682	$60,572
Texas	$40,826	$233,904	$92,675	$228,795	$18,595
Utah	$64,169	$177,863	$46,499		$13,803
Vermont			$233,725		$10,256
Virginia	$207,414	$348,559	$325,283		$25,062
Washington	$386	$209,737	$120,361		$40,991
West Virginia	$54,947		$134,796		$56,242
Wisconsin	$56,427	$281,076	$54,002		$26,292
Wyoming		$275,184			$19,095
UNITED STATES	$95,758	$210,110	$106,553	$165,054	$27,593

Source: Braddock et al., Coleman Institute and Department of Psychiatry, University of Colorado, 2017

Figure 5
COST OF INDIVIDUAL AND FAMILY SUPPORT: FY 1996-2015
UNITED STATES

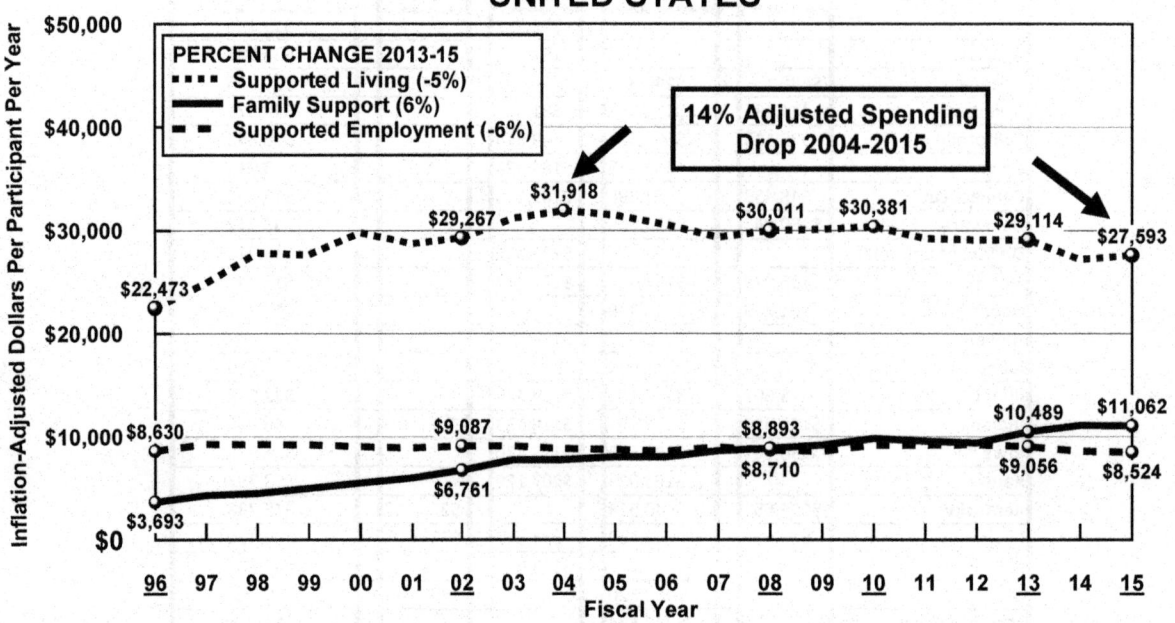

Source: Braddock et al., Coleman Institute and Department of Psychiatry, University of Colorado, 2017

Participants increased 13% from 2013–2015. In FY 2015, personal assistance services were provided to 118,124 persons in 30 states and supported living was provided to 219,140 individuals in 47 states. Twenty-five states provided both supported living and personal assistance. In FY 2015, supported living/personal assistance participants constituted 50% of all IDD residential settings in the United States.

Every state except Hawaii[3] provided supported living or personal assistance services in FY2015. Spending per participant ranged from below $15,000 per year in Colorado, Florida, Georgia, Kansas, Massachusetts, New Hampshire, South Dakota, Utah, Vermont, Mississippi, and West Virginia to over $50,000 in Arizona, Maine, Maryland, Missouri, New Jersey, North Dakota, Oklahoma, Tennessee, and West Virginia.

When supported living is combined with family support and supported employment the total spending grew from one percent of total IDD nationwide in 1986 to 25% in 2015. Spending for individual supports (supported living and supported employment) and for family support each grew an average 10% per year during 1986–2015. Individuals and families supported totaled 970,718 nationwide in 2015. Compared to the level of resources required for group homes and other community residential services and day programs, considerably fewer financial resources are provided for Individual and Family Support.

Annual inflation-adjusted costs per participant in supported living, supported employment, and family support during 1996–2015 are presented in Figure 5. During FY 2013–2015, adjusted supported employment cost per worker declined 6%. Costs per supported living/personal assistance participant fell 5% during FY 2013–2014, but increased 2% in 2015. Adjusted cost per family increased by 6% during 2013–2015. However, this increase followed a family cost reduction of 3% in 2012. Cost per family in 2015 was $11,062—4% of the annual cost per person in state-operated institutions in the U.S. ($253,832).

Inflation-adjusted cost per participant for supported living and personal assistance declined 14% during FY

---

[3]Hawaii reported that all supported living participants were adults choosing to live with their families. Participants and spending were categorized by the state as "a subset of family support."

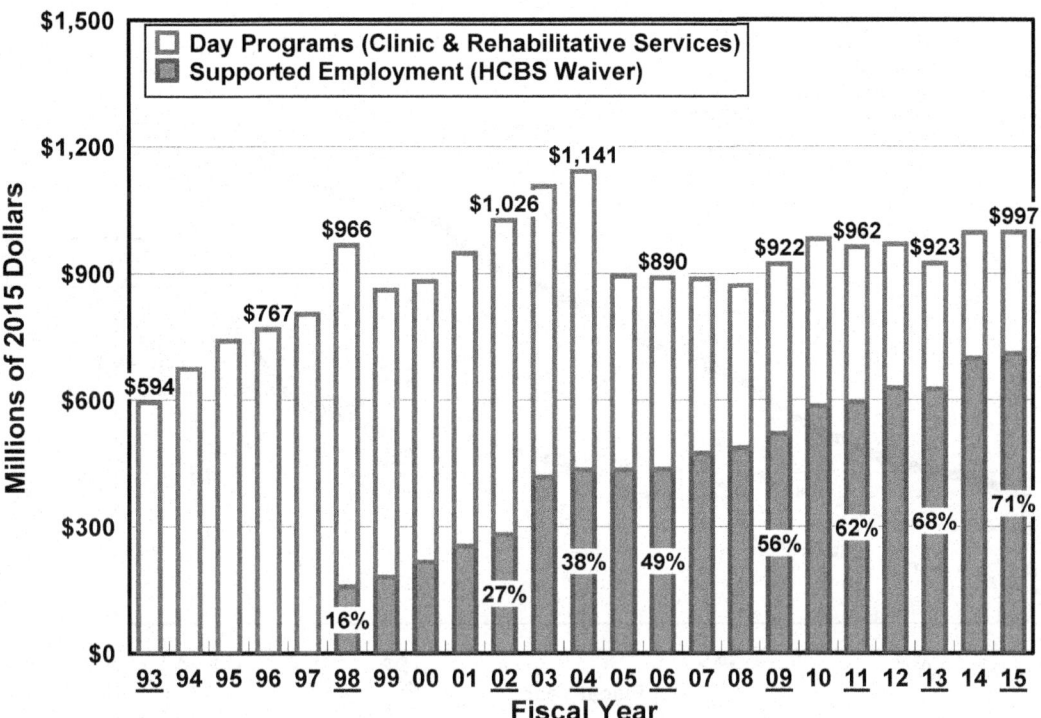

Figure 6
FEDERAL MEDICAID FUNDING FOR SUPPORTED EMPLOYMENT AND DAY PROGRAMS: FY 1992-2015

Source: Braddock et al., Coleman Institute and Department of Psychiatry, University of Colorado (2017).

2004–2015. It dropped from $31,918 to $27,593. This reduction was likely due to the experience that states have gained in providing more cost-effective systems of support for individuals with IDD.

For example, the major factor in the cost reduction during FY 2004–2015 in Medicaid spending for supported employment and clinic/rehabilitation programs in the states is due to the growing use of HCBS Waiver funding. The Federal Waiver share of total Medicaid spending for clinic/rehab programs and supported employment grew from only 16% in 1998 to 71% in FY 2015, as the clinic/rehab Medicaid share dropped from 84% in FY 1998 to only 29% in FY 2015 (Figure 6). Adjusted total Medicaid spending for clinic/rehab programs and supported employment dropped 13% during FYs 2004–2015.

Costs of care for all people with disabilities are also declining in real terms as the Waiver and other community Medicaid options continued to replace more expensive nursing facilities and other congregate settings (Hemp, Braddock, Tanis, & King, 2016).

Recovering from the Great Recession

Total spending for IDD services grew 4.1% during FY 2013–2015 (2% on an average annual basis). In contrast, IDD spending grew only 0.3% per year during 2009–2011 and it dropped 0.8% in 2011 (Figure 7). However, when state funding declined precipitously across the country during 2009–2011, the federal government utilized "enhanced" federal Medical Assistance Percentage (FMAP) rates to mitigate the effects of the *Great Recession* in the states.

Moreover, from 2010 to 2012, as state FMAP rates fell to pre-*Recession* levels, inflation-adjusted total IDD spending grew 2.5%. Federal spending dropped 9.5% and adjusted state IDD spending jumped 23%. In real economic terms, total IDD average annual spending advanced only 2% per year during 2013–2015. But this was seven times the 0.3% annual inflation-adjusted growth during 2009–2011.

In FY 2015 federal and state IDD spending had returned to the annual growth rate established before

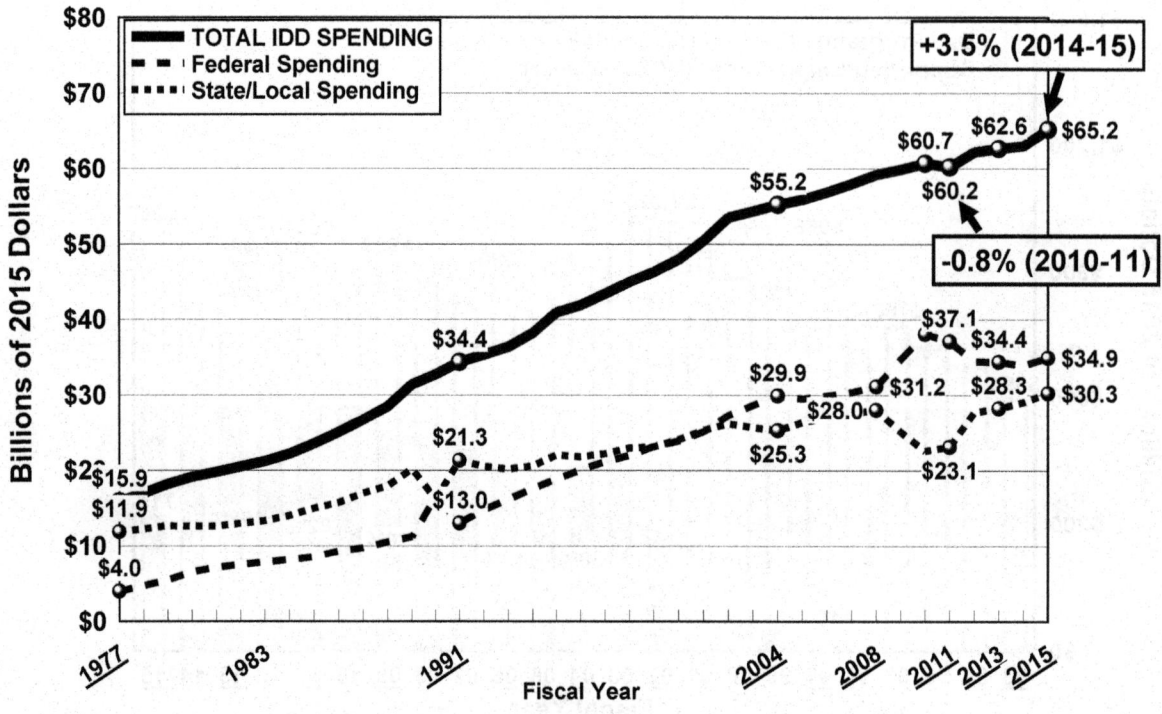

Figure 7
STATE AND FEDERAL IDD SPENDING: FY 1977-2015

Source: Braddock et al., Coleman Institute and Department of Psychiatry, University of Colorado, 2017.

the Great Recession in 2008. However, despite nationwide growth in IDD spending in FY 2015, 25 states in FY 2016, and a projected 24 states in FY 2017 reported reductions in their state general funds. This raised concerns regarding state fiscal health. In addition, state budget leaders are facing Congress and President Trump's repeal of the Affordable Care Act. Low energy prices and potential reductions in federal funding may also result in reduced tax revenues and adversely impact services in the states (Kamp, 2017).

VI. CONCLUSION

As a result of the 1999 U.S. Supreme Court's *Olmstead v. L.C.* decision and the increased utilization of the HCBS Waiver and individual and family support, states are very likely to continue to downsize and close many state-operated institutions in the future. However, in FY 2015, 37 states still continued to operate 133 state-operated institutions for people with IDD.

Total public and private inflation-adjusted spending for IDD institutions fell 50% in the last two decades. Inflation-adjusted institutional spending dropped dramatically: −5.3% in 2009–2011; −6.2% in 2011–2013; and −11.3% in 2013–2015. Consequently, institutional spending reductions and closures are likely to gain greater momentum in the future and the rapid growth of individual and family supports for people with IDD is absolutely essential.

Demographic and Legal Forces

The need for long-term services and supports for people with IDD and their families will continue to increase. Three powerful demographic and legal forces will impose pressure on the states and the U.S. Government to increase public financial commitments for out-of-home services and to support families.

The number of Americans aged 65 years and older will reach 55 million in less than three years (2020) and 98 million by 2060 (U.S. Census Bureau, 2016; Centers for Disease Control and Prevention, 2016). Moreover, as family caregivers age beyond their caregiving capabilities, supported living options must be established to support their relatives with IDD (Braddock et al., 2015). In FY2015, approximately 3.6 million of the 5.1 million people with IDD in the United States were receiving residential care and supports from family caregivers (Figure 8).

Moreover, an estimated 871,420 persons with IDD were residing with caregivers aged 60 years or more. How long can aging caregivers provide adequate supports for their adult children absent sufficient assistance from federal and state governments? Clearly, many caregiving families need substantial IDD state agency support now and in the future (Fujiura, 2012).

Note the rapid growth and a near quadrupling in families supported during 1988–2015 (Figure 9). However, the proportion of families supported dropped during 2011–2013, although this was followed by increases in 2014–2015.

A second factor promoting growing demand for IDD long-term care services and supports in the near future is the increasing lifespan for people with IDD. The mean age at death for persons with IDD in the United States was 59 years in the 1970s. It increased to 66 years in 1993 (Janicki, 1996; Janicki, Dalton, Henderson, & Davidson; 1999; Jokinen, Janicki, Keller, McCallion, and the National Task Force on Intellectual Disabilities and Dementia Practices, 2013). The mean age at death for the U.S. general population in 1993 was 70 years. In 2016, life expectancy for all Americans had increased to 78 years (Centers for Disease Control and Prevention, 2016). Janicki (1996) has maintained for over 20 years that with continued improvement in health status, many individuals with IDD, including many of those with the most significant impairments, will have a lifespan approximately equal to that of the general population.

A third growth factor is the stimulus of class-action litigation. It remains a strong force shaping the development and funding of community services and supports for people with IDD. Litigation in the 1990s led to considerable progress in the states. Lawsuits were filed (1) to force states to expand services for people on waiting lists; (2) to urge states to meet the requirements of constitutional and legislative community integration mandates such as the 1999 *Olmstead* Supreme Court decision; and (3) to provide services on behalf of individuals eligible for Medicaid but not receiving them (Priaulx, 2016).

Implications of Changes to Medicaid

The new Presidential administration and Congress are proposing "Medicaid Block Grants" or "Per Capita Caps" to the states to reduce domestic federal spending. This alteration to the federal program now providing 76% of funding for people with IDD could have a negative impact on children, adults, and families receiving IDD services and supports.

Twenty-one years ago we evaluated Congress' Block Grant proposal, termed "Medi-Grants" (Braddock

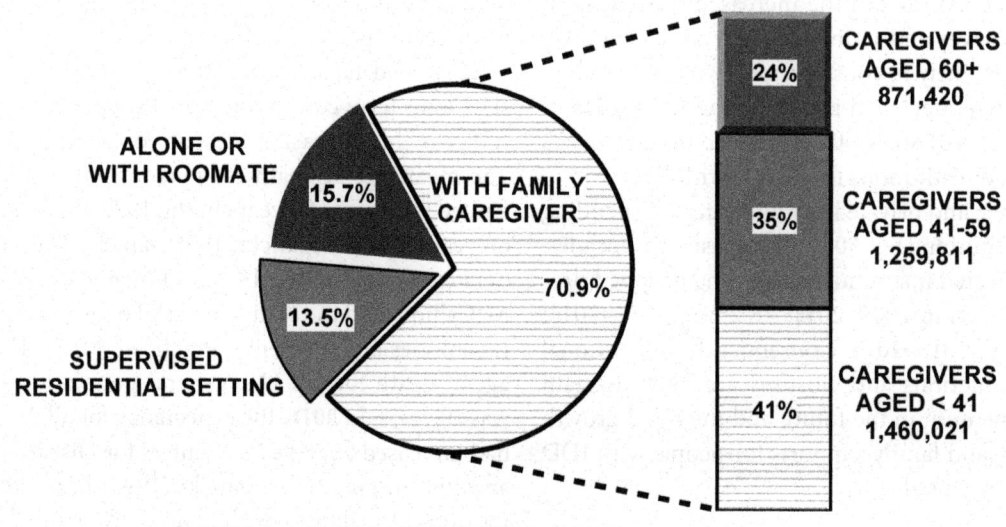

Figure 8
UNITED STATES
ESTIMATED NUMBER OF INDIVIDUALS WITH IDD BY AGE GROUP OF FAMILY CAREGIVER, FY 2015

Source: Braddock et al., Coleman Institute and Department of Psychiatry, University of Colorado, 2017, based on Fujiura (2015).

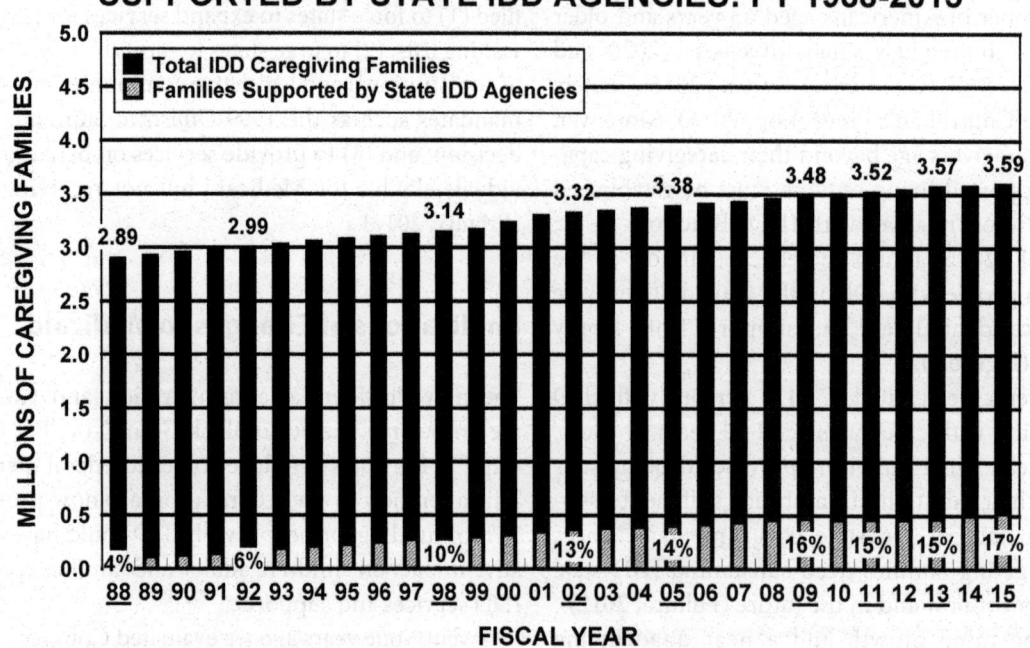

Figure 9
IDD CAREGIVING FAMILIES AND FAMILIES SUPPORTED BY STATE IDD AGENCIES: FY 1988-2015

Source: Braddock et al., Coleman Institute and Department of Psychiatry, University of Colorado, 2017.

& Hemp, 1996). This legislation was vetoed by President Clinton and not implemented. But if the "Medi-Grants" had taken effect in 2002, they would have eliminated between 24,431 (9%) and 84,342 (32%) of the recipients with IDD receiving Medicaid services and supports—depending on whether the Senate or House proposal was implemented (Braddock & Hemp, 1996, pp. 23–26).

The currently proposed Medicaid Block Grants (U.S. House of Representatives, 2016) could also force onerous financial and programmatic constraints on states, families, and people with IDD. Medicaid services and supports such as Waivers, personal care, rehabilitation services, case management, and group home ICFs/ID are "optional" and not "mandatory" services such as hospitals, nursing facilities, and physician services. Medicaid cuts could put great pressure on states to place individuals with IDD into nursing homes and other congregate care settings to maximize their "mandatory" Medicaid reimbursements.

The U.S. House of Representatives (2016) recently estimated that $913 billion is to be removed from federal Medicaid appropriations over the next 10 years (2016–2025). Total federal Medicaid spending was $368 billion in FY 2016. It would not reach that level again until 2025 (U.S. House, 2016, pp. 38–39).

To determine the potential impact of Medicaid Block Grants on recipients of IDD Medicaid services and supports during 2016–2025, we calculated the average annual inflation-adjusted percentage change in spending during FYs 2003–2015 for total federal Medicaid (3.1% per year) and for IDD federal Medicaid (1.5% per year).

Using these annual growth rates, we project that total federal Medicaid spending would advance from $328.3 billion in FY 2015 to $444.1 billion in FY 2025. We also projected that federal IDD Medicaid funds would increase from $28.0 billion in 2015 to $32.5 billion in 2025, supporting an estimated 920,000 Medicaid recipients with IDD compared to the 720,000 supported in 2015.

Total projected federal Medicaid funds, however, must be reduced 18% from $444.1 to $365 billion in order to match the federal block grant spending target in 2025. The proportionate 18% reduction for IDD spending would drop $5.9 billion to $26.6 billion in 2025. Based on the known 27% reduction during FYs 2003–2015 in inflation-adjusted IDD Medicaid cost per participant, we estimated that using the FY 2015 IDD Medicaid participant cost of $35,330 would provide a conservative cost estimate for 2025.

This IDD cost per participant, when applied to the reduced IDD Medicaid spending in 2025 ($26.6 billion), could support only 754,162 of the projected 920 thousand participants with IDD in 2025. As a result, *165,000 children and adults would lose IDD services and supports in 2025* to meet the spending reductions in the proposed Medicaid block grants (United States House of Representatives, 2016).

Challenges Ahead

To meet the needs of people with IDD, we must address at least six key challenges in the future:

(1) Enhance the near-poverty level wages and benefits of direct support staff in community services programs, to improve the quality of services they provide, and minimize staff turnover (Braddock et al., 2015; Butterworth, Smith, Winsor, Timmons, Migliore, & Domin, 2015);

(2) Develop additional Medicaid-funded, person-centered, community residential services, supported living and family support programs to reduce waiting lists in the states (Braddock et al., 2015; Larson, Hallas-Muchow, Aiken, Taylor, Pettingell, Hewitt, Sowers, & Fay, 2016);

(3) Develop and implement dramatically more health promotion and disease prevention programs in residential and community services settings nationwide (Braddock et al., 2015; Schiller, Lucas, Ward, & Peregoy, 2012);

(4) Reduce the 75%–80% unemployment rates for persons with IDD and dramatically expand supported employment programs (Butterworth, et al., 2015);

(5) Accelerate the development and utilization of assistive and cognitive technologies for people with IDD to support independent living, productivity, health, and safety, and to reduce the rapidly growing "cognitive digital divide" experienced by people with IDD in our society (Braddock, 2012; Braddock, Hoehl, Tanis, Ablowitz, & Haffer, 2013); and

(6) Support *The Rights of People with Cognitive Disabilities to Technology and Information Access*. A nationwide coalition of disability organizations and individuals asserted this right in a formal

declaration presented at the 13th Annual Coleman Institute National Conference on Cognitive Disability and Technology in 2013 (Braddock et al., 2013). Join this movement by endorsing *The Declaration* on our website: http://www.coleman institute.org/technology-and-information access.

People with IDD, and their families and advocates as well, have confronted and prevailed over many challenges encountered in recent decades. These have included addressing repressive segregation in overcrowded, under-staffed residential institutions, and until more recently, a near total lack of community and family supports throughout the country, as well as blatant discrimination in employment, housing, education and health care.

Progress has been achieved in recent decades, but the challenges we face today remind us that abuses removed call even greater attention to the more galling ones that remain.

VII. REFERENCES

Braddock, D. (2012). Foreword. In Marcia J. Scherer, *Assistive technologies and other supports for people with brain impairment* (pp. ix–x). New York City: Springer Publishing Company.

Braddock, D., & Fujiura, G.T. (1991). Politics, public policy, and the development of community mental retardation services in the US. *American Journal on Mental Retardation, 95*, 369–387.

Braddock, D., & Hemp, R. (1996). Medicaid spending reductions and developmental disabilities. *Journal of Disability Policy Studies,7*(1), 1–72. https://doi.org/10.1177/104420739600700101

Braddock, D., Hemp, R., Rizzolo, M.C., Tanis, E.S., Haffer, L., & Wu, J. (2015). *The state of the states in intellectual and developmental disabilities: Emerging from the Great Recession, 10th Edition*. Washington, DC: American Association on Intellectual and Developmental Disabilities.

Braddock, D., Hoehl, J., Tanis, S., Ablowitz, E., & Haffer, L. (2013). The rights of people with cognitive disabilities to technology and information access. *Inclusion,1*(2), 95–102. https://doi.org/10.1352/2326-6988-01.02.95

Butterworth, J., Smith, F.A., Winsor, J., Timmons, J.C., Migliore, A., & Domin, D. (2015). *StateData: The National Report on Employment Services and Outcomes: 2015*. Boston, MA: Institute for Community Inclusion.

Centers for Disease Control and Prevention (CDC). (2016, March 29). Deaths: Final data for 2014, *National Vital Statistics Reports. Vol. 65*(4). Washington, DC.

Fujiura, G. T. (2012). *Structure of Intellectual and Developmental Disabilities Households in the United States: Demographics of the Family in 2010*. Presented at AAIDD 136th Annual Meeting, Charlotte, NC, June 2012.

Hemp, R., Braddock, D., Tanis, E.S., & King, M. (2016). U.S. disability services and spending. *LegisBrief, 24*(18), National Conference of State Legislatures.

Janicki, M.P. (1996). Longevity increasing among older adults with an intellectual disability. *Aging, Health, and Society, 2*, 2.

Janicki, M. P., Dalton, A. J., Henderson, C. M., & Davidson, P. W. (1999). Mortality and morbidity among older adults with intellectual disability: Health service considerations. *Disability and Rehabilitation, 21*(5-6), 284–294. https://doi.org/10.1080/096382899297710

Janicki, M. P., Henderson, M. C., & Rubin, I. L. (2008). Neurodevelopmental conditions and aging: Report on the Atlanta Study Group Charrette on Neurodevelopmental Conditions and Aging. *Disability and Health Journal, 1*(2), 116–124. https://doi.org/10.1016/j.dhjo.2008.02.004

Jokinen, S.M., Janicki, M. P., Keller, P., McCallion, L. T., & the National Task Group on Intellectual Disabilities and Dementia Practices. (2013). *Guidelines for structuring community care and supports for people with intellectual disabilities affected by dementia*. Washington, DC: American Academy for Developmental Medicane and Dentistry.

Kamp, J. (2017, January 20). Revenue shortfalls fuel state budget woes. *The Wall Street Journal*, U.S. News, p. A6.

Larson, S. A., Hallas-Muchow, L., Aiken, F., Taylor, B., Pettingell, S., Hewitt, A., Sowers, M., & Fay, M. L. (2016). *In-home and residential long-term supports and services for persons with intellectual or developmental disabilities: Status and trends through 2013*. Minneapolis, MN: University of Minnesota, Research and Training Center on Community Living, Institute on Community Integration.

Michelle P. v. Holsinger, No. 3:02-23-JMH (E.D. Ky. Feb. 11, 2005).

National Bureau of Economic Research (NBER). (2017). *United States business cycles and contractions*. Retrieved from http://nber.org/cyclles/cyclesmain.html.

Olmstead v. L.C., 119 S. Ct. 2176 (1999).

Priaulx, E. (2016). *Docket of cases related to enforcment of the ADA Title II integration regulations*. Washington, DC: Administration on Developmental Disabilities.

Schiller, J.S., Lucas, J.W., Ward, B.W., & Peregoy, J.A. (2012). Summary health statistics for U.S. adults: National Health Interview Survey, 2010. National Center of Health Statistics. *Vital Health Stat. 10*, 252.

Testimony at The United States Congress Long Term Care Commission, 113th Cong. (2013) (Testimony of David Braddock).

United States Census Bureau. (2016). *U.S. interim projections by age, sex, race, and Hispanic origin*. Retrieved from http://www.census.gov/population/projections/

United States Department of Commerce, Bureau of Economic Analysis. (2016). *National income and product accounts, Table 1.1.4 Implicit price deflators for gross domestic product [index numbers 2009=100]*, last revised November 15, 2016.

United States Department of Commerce, Bureau of Economic Analysis. (2016a). *Quarterly personal income, by state*, last revised November 15, 2016.

United States House of Representatives. (2016, March). *A balanced budget for a stronger America*.

Winer, B. J. (1971). *Statistical principles in experimental design*. New York, NY: McGraw-Hill.

VIII. COLLABORATION WITH STATE INTELLECTUAL AND DEVELOPMENTAL DISABILITIES AGENCIES FOR DATA COLLECTION

Alabama. Andy Slate, Director, Fiscal Operations, Karen Coffey, Director, Systems Management, and Courtney Tarver, Associate Commissioner for Department of Mental Health/Division of Developmental Disabilities.

Alaska. Anastasiya S. Podunovich, Research and Analysis Unit, and Duane Mayes, Director, Senior & Disabilities Services, Department of Health & Social Services.

Arizona. Joseph Tansill, Business Administrator, Ben Kauffman, Finance Manager, and Laura Love, Ph.D., Assistant Director, Division of Developmental Disabilities, Department of Economic Security.

Arkansas. Shelley Lee, Assistant Director for Quality Assurance, Regina Davenport, Program Administrator; QA Outreach; Jerry Hodge, Waiver Policy Administrator; Stephen Sullivan, Contracts; Kim Goh Walker, DDS Fiscal Manager, and Mellissa Stone, Director, Developmental Disabilities Services, Department of Human Services.

California. John Doyle, Chief Deputy Director; Carie Powell, Chief, Federal Program Operations Section; Yasir Ali, Assistant Chief, Federal Program Operations Section, and Nancy Bargman, Director, California Department of Developmental Services.

Colorado. Sally Langston, Lazlo Frohs, Emily Blanford, Budget and Finance Director, and Barbara D. Ramsey, Director, Division for Developmental Disabilities, Department of Human Services.

Connecticut. Tim Deschenes-Desmond, Planning Specialist, Office of the Commissioner; Victoria Berman, Research Analyst, Shawn Boisclair, Director of Audit, Billing and Rate Setting, Jordan Scheff, Acting Commissioner, Department of Developmental Services.

Delaware. Lennie Warren, Program Evaluator, Marie Nonnenmacher, and Jill Rogers, Director, Division of Developmental Disabilities Services, Department of Health and Social Services.

District of Columbia. Erin Leveton and Olga Figueroa, State Office of Disability Administration, Darlene Richardson, Administrative Officer, Srinivas Bheemreddy, Chief Information Officer, Jared Morris, Deputy Director for the Department on Disability Services.

Florida. Susan Chen, Todd Gregory, Denzil Weimorts, Susan Nipper, Lisa Robertson, Tina Weber, Denise Arnold, Lorena Fulcher, David Dobbs, Tom Rice, Cheryl Smith, Tim Graves, Tom Rankin, and Barbara Palmer, Director, Agency for Persons with Disabilities.

Georgia. Esther Park, Eddie Towson, Director of Quality Assurance, and Ronald Wakefield, Director, Division of Developmental Disabilities, Department of Behavior Health and Developmental Disabilities.

Hawaii. Deb Tsutsui, Research Statistician, and Mary Brogan, DDS, Chief, Developmental Disabilities Division, Department of Health.

Idaho. Aaron Haws, Rebecca Fadness, DD Policy Program Manager, Arthur Evans, Chief, Division of Medicaid; Tom Rosenthal, Division of Finance, Department of Health and Welfare,. and Cameron Gilliland, Deputy Administrator, Division of Developmental Disabilities.

Illinois. Tom Armitage, Contracted Support Division, Reta Hoskin, Gary Kramer, Bureau Chief, Reimbursement & Support, and Greg Fenton, Director, Developmental Disabilities, Department of Human Services.

Indiana. Thomas G. Williams, Data Manager and Kylee Hope, Director, Division of Disability and Rehabilitative Services, Family and Social Services Administration.

Iowa. Kim Rose and Theresa Armstrong, Community Services and Planning, and Rick Shults, Division Administrator, Division of Mental Health and Disability Services, Department of Human Services.

Kansas. George Van Hoozer, Program Oversight Manager, and Kari Bruffett, Community Services and Programs Commission, Kansas Department for Aging and Disability Services.

Kentucky. James Kimble, Ericka Jenkins, Tabatha Burkhart-Wilson, and Claudia Johnson, Commissioner, Department for Behavioral Health and Developmental and Intellectual Disabilities, Cabinet for Health and Family Services.

Louisiana. Beth Jordan, Program Manager, Kin Hodge, Pam Sund, Julia Kenny, Laura Brackin, Ph.D., Director, and Mark Thomas, Assistant Secretary, Office for Citizens with Developmental Disabilities, Department of Health and Hospitals.

Maine. Cynthia Eurich, David Berry, Jim Martin, Director, Bridget Bagley, HCBS Waiver Program Manager, Terry Sandusky, Information Services Manager, Deb Gellatly, Resource Development Manager, Joy Swift, Senior Staff Accountant, Gary Wolcott, Director, Office of Aging and Disability Services, Department of Health and Human Services.

Maryland. Karen Mason, Peter deFries, Assistant Director, Gary Wolcott, Director, and Bernard A. Simons, Deputy Secretary, Developmental Disabilities Administration, Department of Health and Mental Hygiene.

Massachusetts. Kathy Phillips, Janet George, Assistant Commissioner for Policy Planning and Children's Services, Jeanette Maillet, Division of Policy, Planning and Children's Services, and Elin Howe, Commissioner, Department of Developmental Services.

Michigan. Kathleen Haines, Division for Quality Management and Planning, Debra Tsutsui, Managed Care Specialist, William Harrison, DCH Consultant, Judy Webb, Director, Division of Quality Management and Planning, and Lynda Zeller, Deputy Director, Behavioral Health and Developmental Disabilities Administration, Department of Community Health.

Minnesota. Melanie Fry, Lead Policy Consultant, Mahesh Gorregattu, Sarah J. Thorson, and Alex Bartolic, Director, Disability Services Division, Department of Human Services.

Mississippi. Matt Armstrong, Ashley Lacoste and Kenneth Leggett, and Renee Brett, Bureau of Intellectual and Developmental Disabilities, Department of Mental Health.

Missouri. Gary Schanzmeyer, Fiscal Manager, and Valerie Huhn, Director, Division of Developmental Disabilities, Department of Mental Health.

Montana. Jennifer Finnegan, Budget Analyst, and Novelene Martin, Bureau Chief, Developmental Disabilities Program, Department of Public Health and Human Services.

Nebraska. Lorie Harder, Scott Hartz, Kathie Lueke, Deputy Administrator of Quality Improvement, Scott Hartz, Data/Financial Analyst, Mike Kaczmarczyk, Program Analyst, DHHH Financial and Program Analysis (FAPA), and Courtney Miller, Director, Division of Developmental Disabilities, Nebraska Department of Health and Human Services.

Nevada. Jim Cribari, Program Evaluator, Rosie Melarkey, Clinical Program Planner, and Jane Gruner, Administrator, Aging and Disability Services Division, Department of Health and Human Services.

New Hampshire. Ken Lindberg, Bureau Liaison, Karen Kimball, Medicaid and Finance Administrator, and Christine Santaniello, Bureau of Developmental Services, Division of Community Based Care Services, Department of Health and Human Services.

New Jersey. Patrick Boyle, Thomas Papa, Chief of Staff, and Elizabeth Shea, Assistant Commissioner, New Jersey Division of Developmental Disabilities, Department of Human Services.

New Mexico. Mark Kolman, Christopher Futey, Cathy Stevenson, Wendy Corry, Director of Systems Improvement, Roberta Duran, Bureau Chief of the Community Programs, Developmental Disabilities Supports Division, Gene Lujan, Business Analyst, Information Technology Services Division, and Kathyleen Kunkel, Director, New Mexico Department of Health.

New York. Laura Rosenthal, Christine Muller, Becki Lifford, Christine Carey, Martha Dalton, Kim Thayer, and Kerry A. Delaney, Acting Commissioner, Office for People with Developmental Disabilities.

North Carolina. Mya Williams, Shealy Thompson, Ph.D., Lead, Quality Management, Terrie Qadura, and Dr. Jason Vogler, Acting Director, Division of Mental

Health, Developmental Disabilities, and Substance Abuse Services, Department of Health and Human Services.

North Dakota. Brianne Skachenko, Residential and Day Services Administrator, and Tina Bay, Director, Developmental Disabilities Services Division, Department of Human Services.

Ohio. Clay Weidner, Fiscal Administration, Hope McGonigle, and John Martin, Director, Department of Developmental Disabilities.

Oklahoma. Joanne Goin, Chief Fiscal Officer, and Marie Moore, Interim Director, Developmental Disabilities Services, Department of Human Services.

Oregon. Leaann Stutheit, Laura Bastien, Budget Analyst, DHS Budget Division, Vera Kraynick, Research Analyst, Office of Business Intelligence, and Lilia Teninty, Director, Developmental Disability Services, Oregon Department of Human Services.

Pennsylvania. Theresa Boucher, Budget Analyst III and Timothy O'Leary, Chief, Division of Financial Management; Suzanne Puzak and Connie Meeker, Director, Bureau of Policy and Program Support; and Nancy Thaler, Deputy Secretary, Office of Developmental Programs, Department of Public Welfare.

Rhode Island. Deborah Mazzone, Principal Rate Analyst, Linda Reilly, Amy Vincenzi, Administrator and, Kerri Zanchi, Director, Division of Developmental Disabilities, Department of Behavioral Healthcare, Developmental Disabilities, and Hospitals, Department of Human Services.

South Carolina. Emily Limoges, Nancy Rumbaugh, Trina Smalley, Lisa Weeks, South Carolina Department of Disabilities and Special Needs (DDSN) Budget Division; Tom Waring, Associate State Director, Administration and Beverly Buscemi, Ph.D., State Director.

South Dakota. Colin Hutchison, Nicholas Cotton, Office of Budget & Finance, Tammie Herrlein, Laura Ellenbecker, Darryl Millner, and Dan Lusk, Director, Division of Developmental Disabilities, Department of Human Services.

Tennessee. Melinda Lanza, Budget Director; Lance Iverson, Deputy Commissioner, Fiscal and Administrative Services; Debra K. Payne, Commissioner, Department of Intellectual and Developmental Disabilities.

Texas. Janie Eubanks, Quality Reporting, Michelle Martin, Kristi Jordan, Corliss Powell, and Chris Adams, Director, Center for Policy and Innovation, and Sonja Gaines, IDD and Behavioral Health Services, Texas Department of Health and Human Services.

Utah. Mel Castillo, Robert Downing, Tyler D. Black, Administration, and Angella Pinna, Director, Division of Services for People with Disabilities, Department of Human Services.

Vermont. June Bascom, M.A., Program Development and Policy Analyst, and Roy Gerstenberger, Director, Developmental Disabilities Services Division, Department of Disabilities, Aging and Independent Living.

Virginia. Rupinder Kaur, Cheri Stierer, Ph.D., Community Resource Manager, and Connie Cochran, Assistant Commissioner for Developmental Services, Department of Behavioral Health and Developmental Services.

Washington. Kristin Ohler, Lisa Weber and Chris Shelley, Steve Kuehn, Jennifer Usrey-Scott and Dave Cook, Management Services Division; Department of Social and Health Services, and Evelyn Perez, Assistant Secretary.

West Virginia. Cassandra Toliver, Patricia Nisbet, Deborah Reed, and Jim Cremeans, Community Supports, and Beth Morrison, Director, Division of Intellectual and Developmental Disabilities, Behavioral Health and Health Facilities, Department of Health and Human Resources.

Wisconsin. Michelle Prost, Budget and Policy Analyst, Michael Pancook, Senior Rate Analyst, Dave Varana, Bureau of Financial Management Director, and Curtis Cunningham, Division of Long-Term Care Administrator, Department of Health and Family Services.

Wyoming. Colleen Noon, Data Analyst/Epidemiologist, Aaron Wales, Accounting Analyst-Medicaid, Kevin Kulow, Business Office Manager-WLRC and Lee Grossman, Administrator, Developmental Disabilities Division, Wyoming Department of Health.

PART II
Profiles of the 50 States and the District of Columbia

ALABAMA

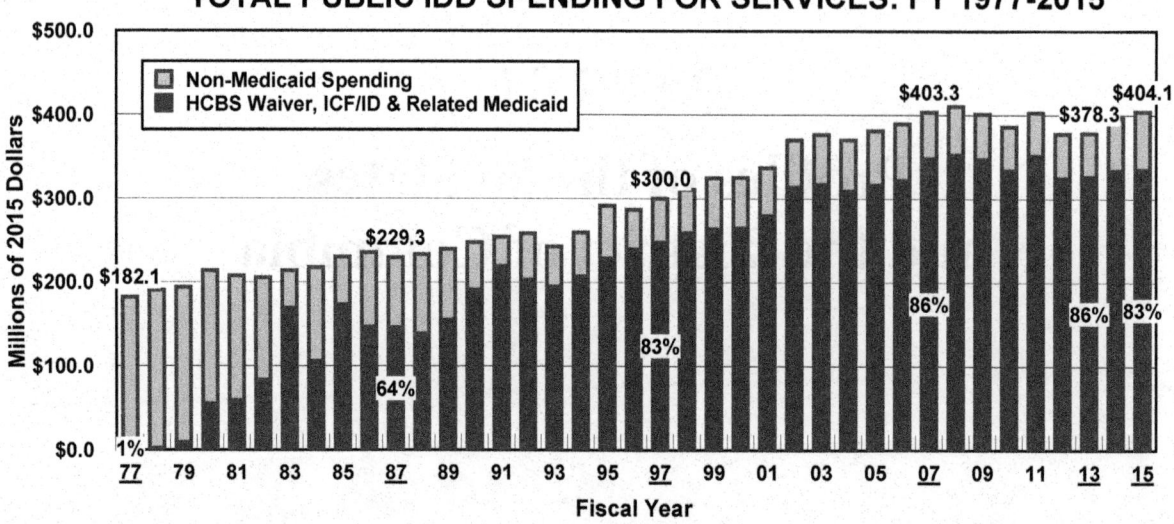

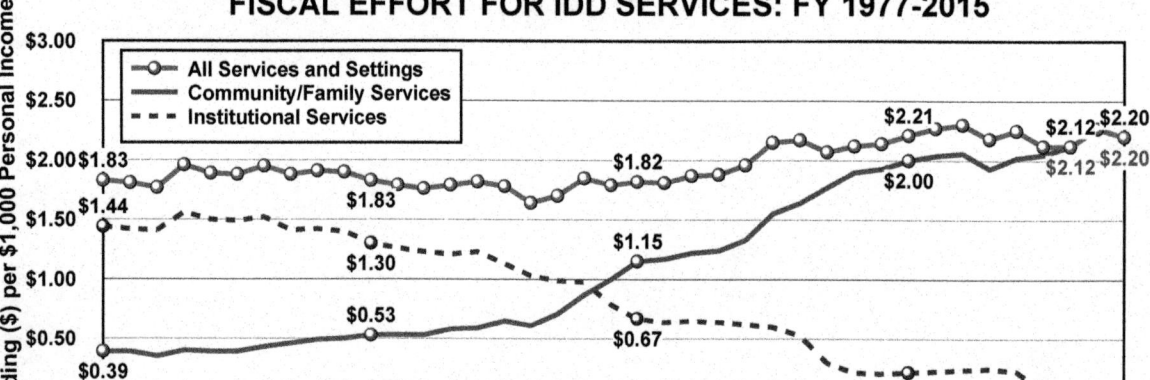

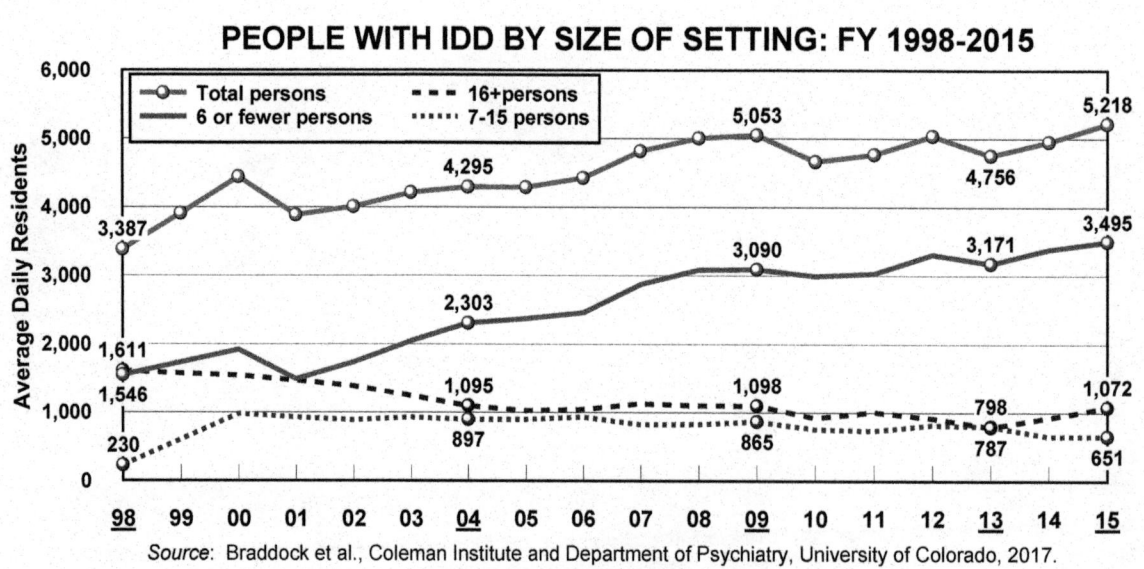

Source: Braddock et al., Coleman Institute and Department of Psychiatry, University of Colorado, 2017.
http://stateofthestates.org

ALABAMA

FEDERAL IDD MEDICAID SPENDING BY REVENUE SOURCE

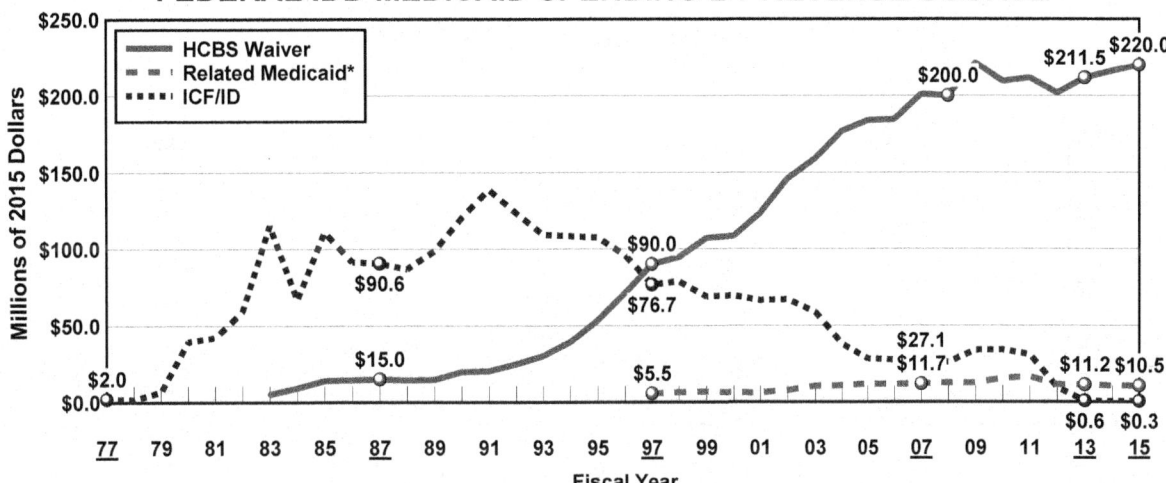

*In 2015, "Related Medicaid" was targeted case management ($6.9 million) and administration ($3.6 million).

FEDERAL-STATE-LOCAL MEDICAID AS A PERCENTAGE OF TOTAL IDD SPENDING IN FY 2015

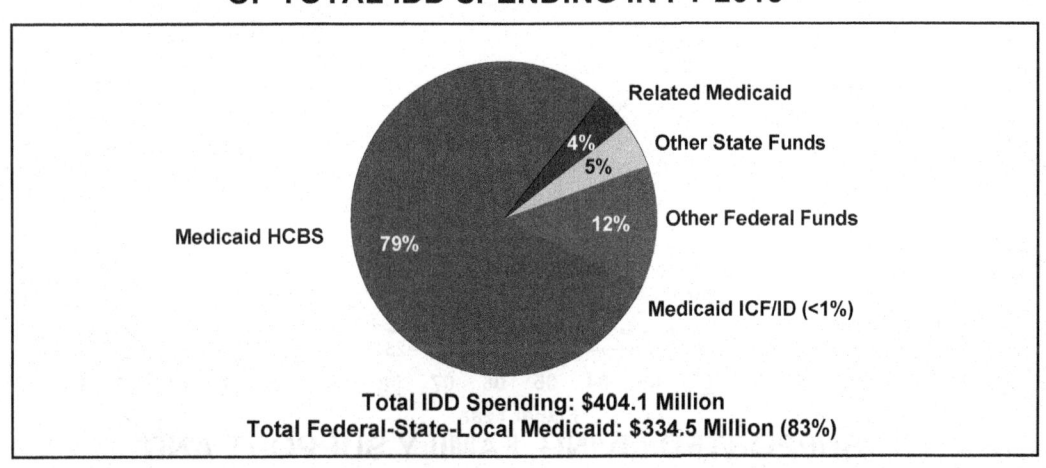

Total IDD Spending: $404.1 Million
Total Federal-State-Local Medicaid: $334.5 Million (83%)

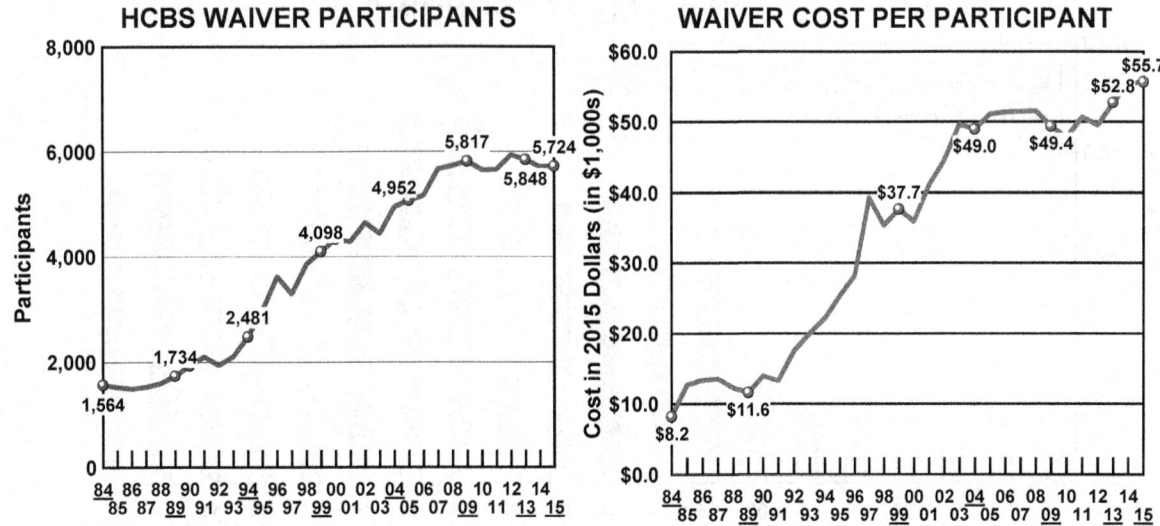

Source: Braddock et al., Coleman Institute and Department of Psychiatry, University of Colorado, 2017.
http://stateofthestates.org

ALABAMA

INDIVIDUAL AND FAMILY SUPPORT
SPENDING: FY 1996-2015

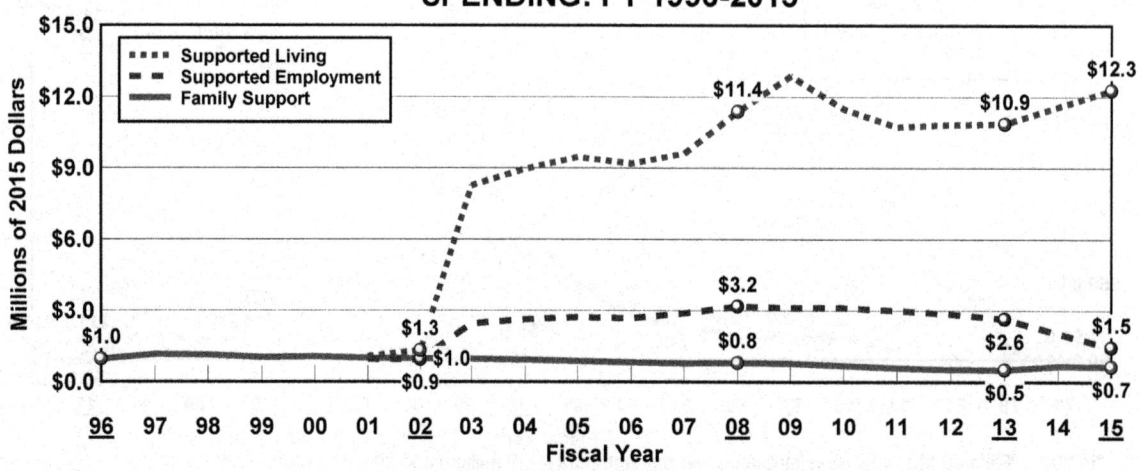

PARTICIPANTS: FY 1996-2015

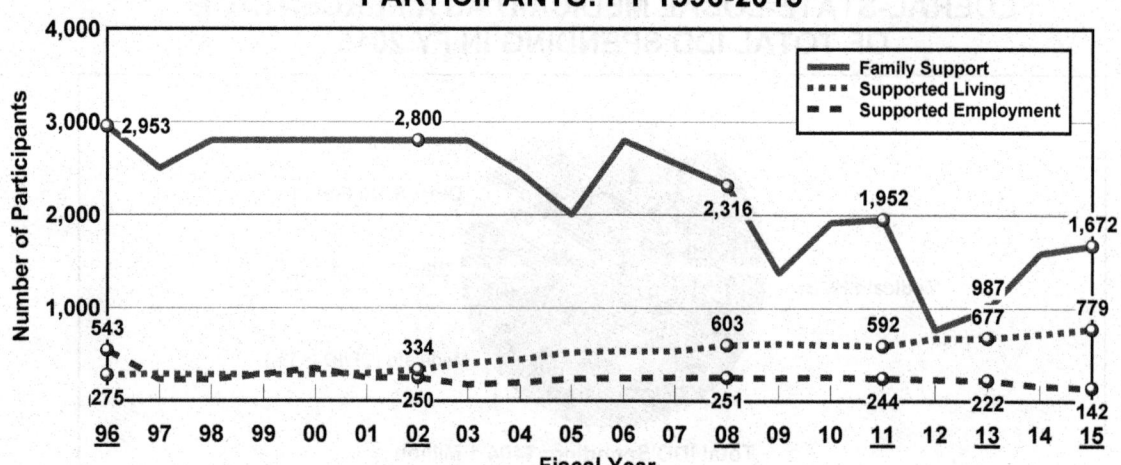

SUPPORTED LIVING, FAMILY SUPPORT AND
SUPPORTED EMPLOYMENT SPENDING: FY 1996-2015

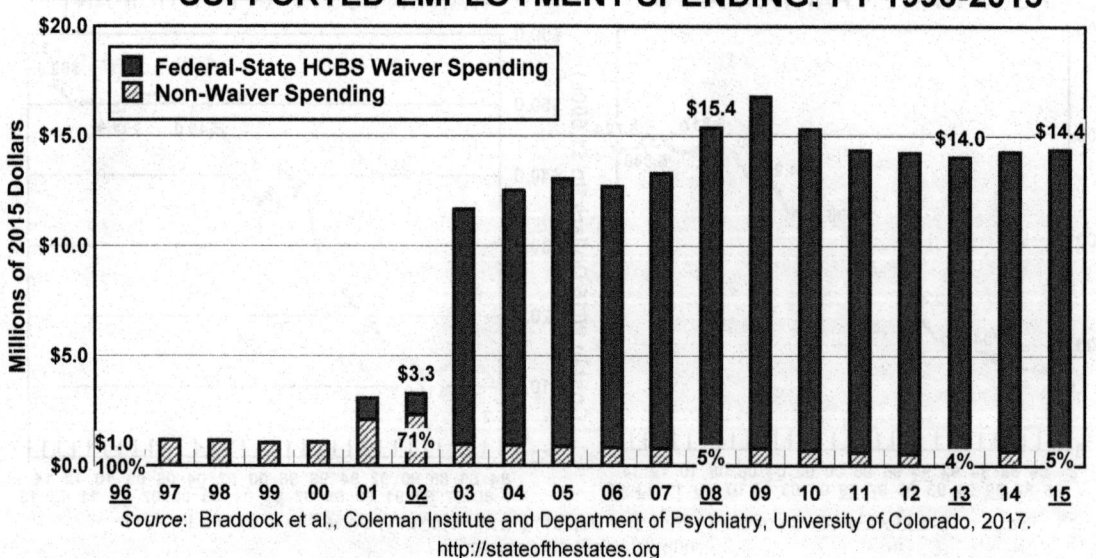

Source: Braddock et al., Coleman Institute and Department of Psychiatry, University of Colorado, 2017.
http://stateofthestates.org

ALABAMA

ANNUAL COST OF CARE BY RESIDENTIAL SETTING: FY 2015

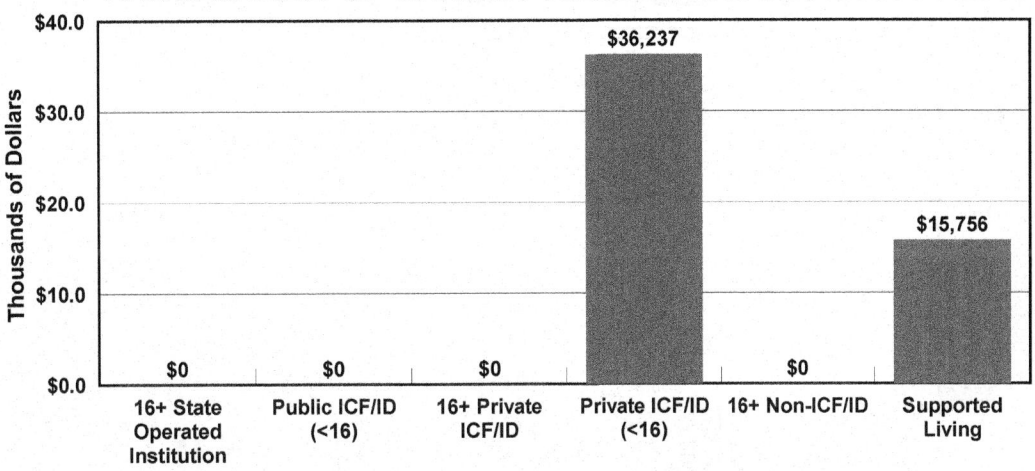

ESTIMATED NUMBER OF INDIVIDUALS WITH IDD BY AGE GROUP LIVING WITH FAMILY CAREGIVERS: FY 2015

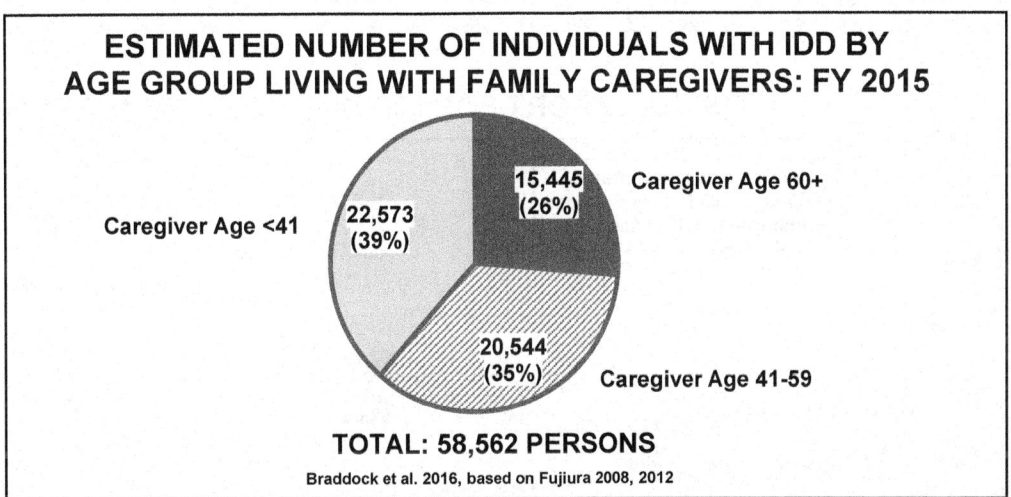

TOTAL: 58,562 PERSONS

Braddock et al. 2016, based on Fujiura 2008, 2012

ESTIMATED NUMBER OF IDD CAREGIVING FAMILIES AND FAMILIES SUPPORTED BY IDD AGENCIES: FY 1988-2015

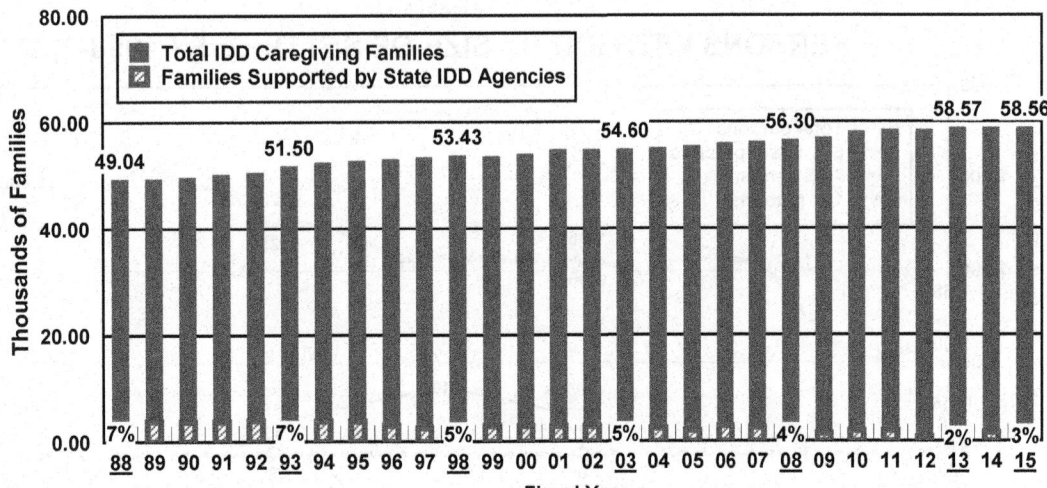

Source: Braddock et al., Coleman Institute and Department of Psychiatry, University of Colorado, 2017.
http://stateofthestates.org

ALASKA

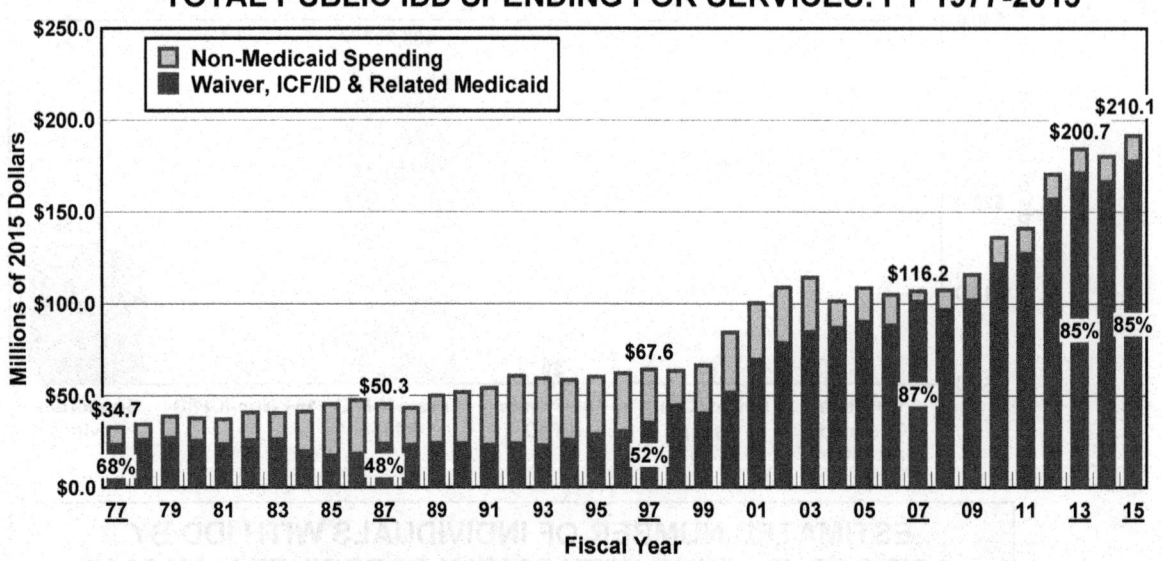

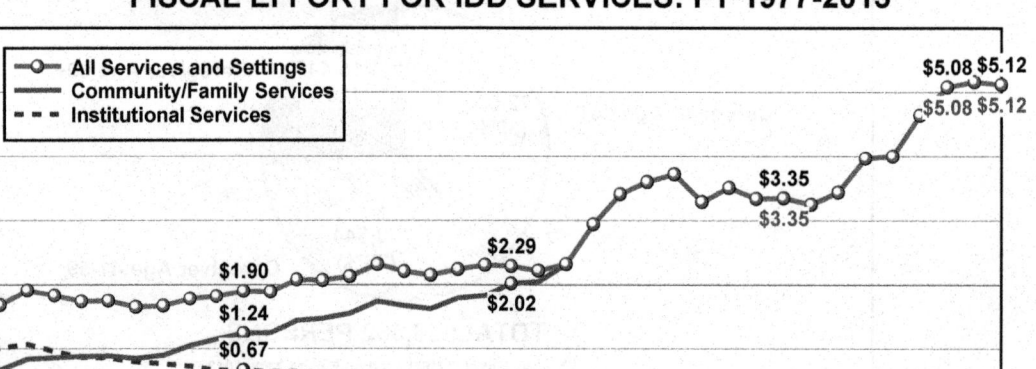

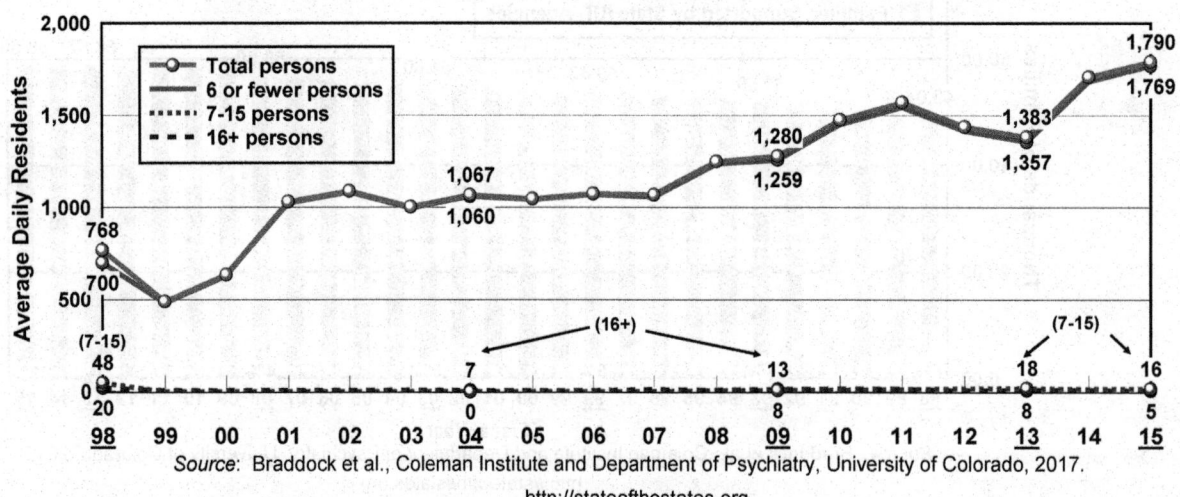

Source: Braddock et al., Coleman Institute and Department of Psychiatry, University of Colorado, 2017.
http://stateofthestates.org

ALASKA

FEDERAL IDD MEDICAID SPENDING BY REVENUE SOURCE

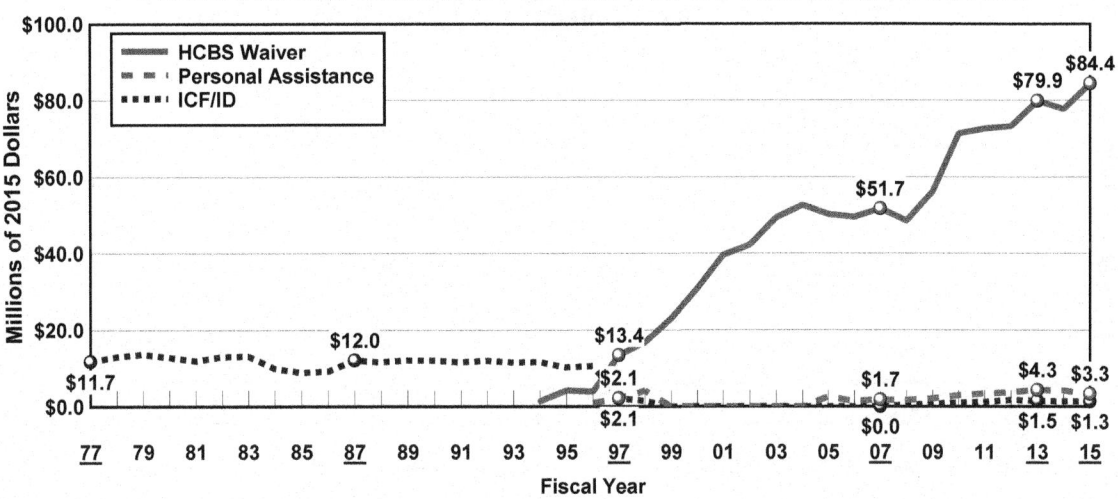

FEDERAL-STATE MEDICAID AS A PERCENTAGE OF TOTAL IDD SPENDING IN FY 2015

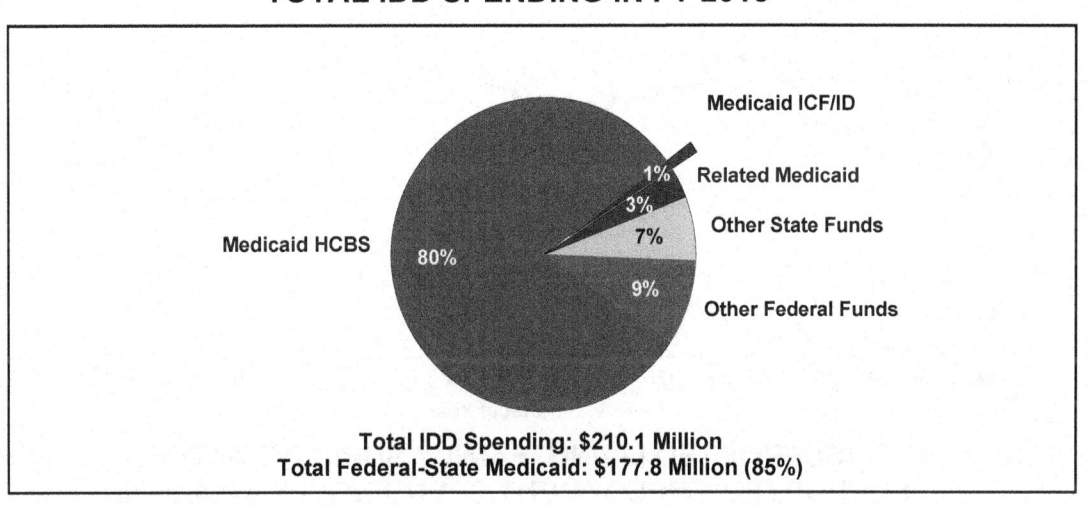

Total IDD Spending: $210.1 Million
Total Federal-State Medicaid: $177.8 Million (85%)

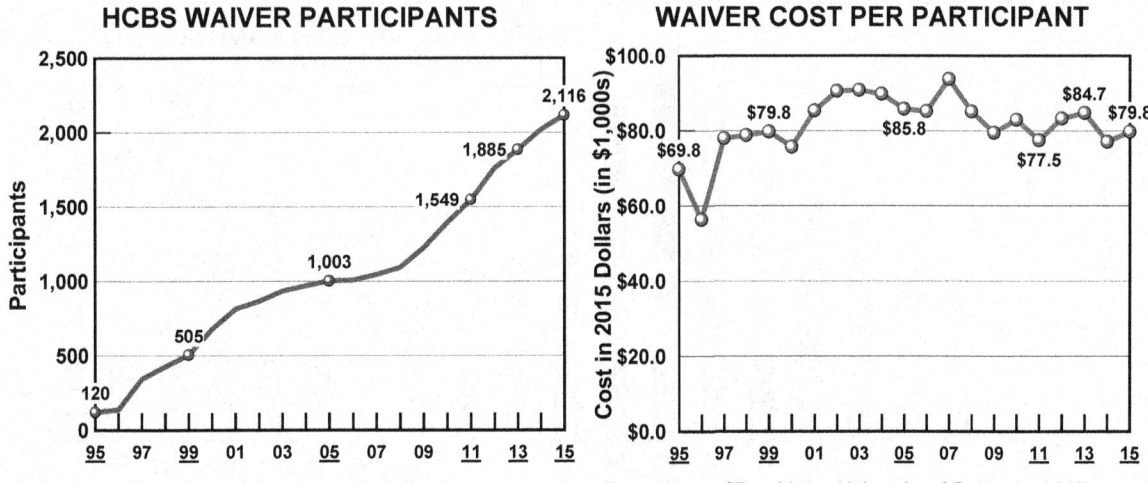

Source: Braddock et al., Coleman Institute and Department of Psychiatry, University of Colorado, 2017.

http://stateofthestates.org

ALASKA

INDIVIDUAL AND FAMILY SUPPORT
SPENDING: FY 1996-2015

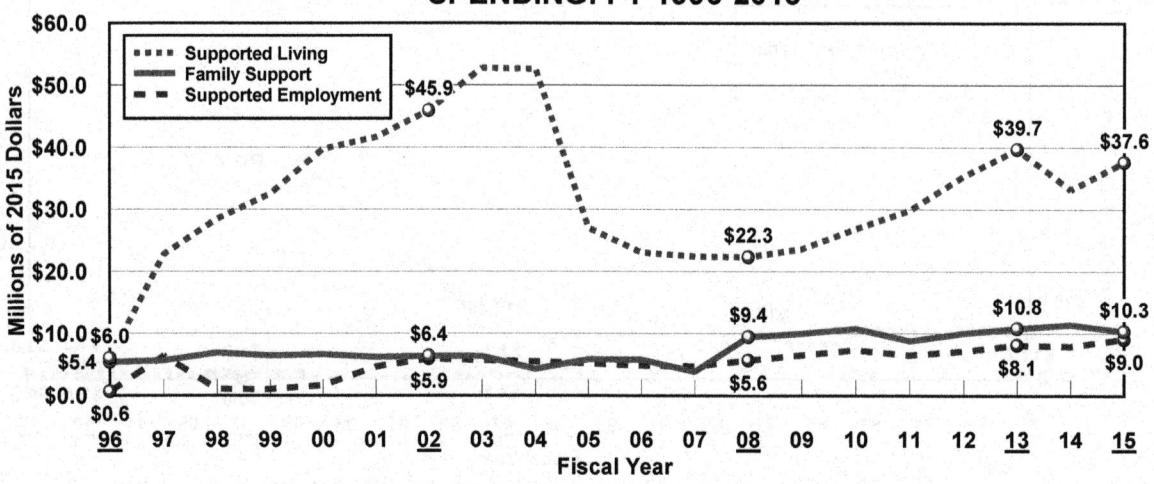

PARTICIPANTS: FY 1996-2015

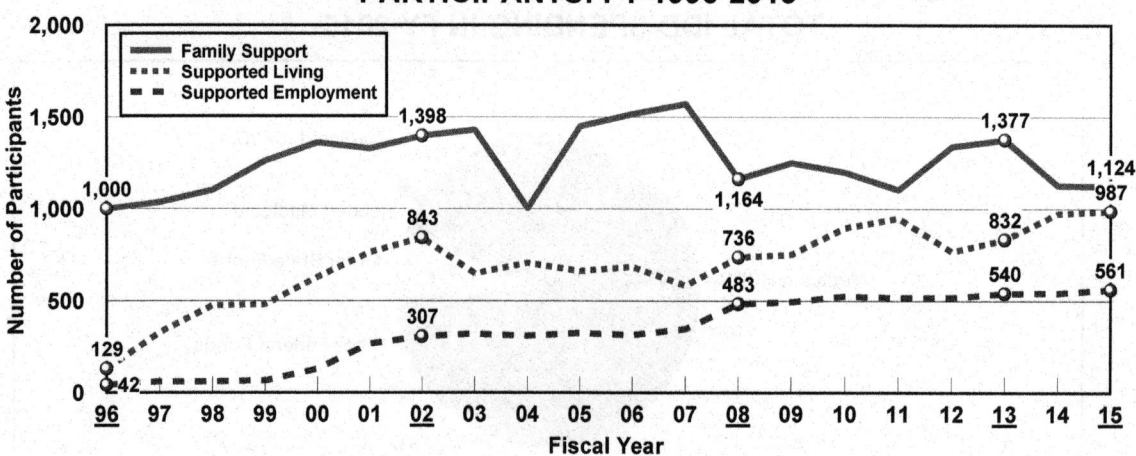

SUPPORTED LIVING, FAMILY SUPPORT AND SUPPORTED EMPLOYMENT SPENDING: FY 1996-2015

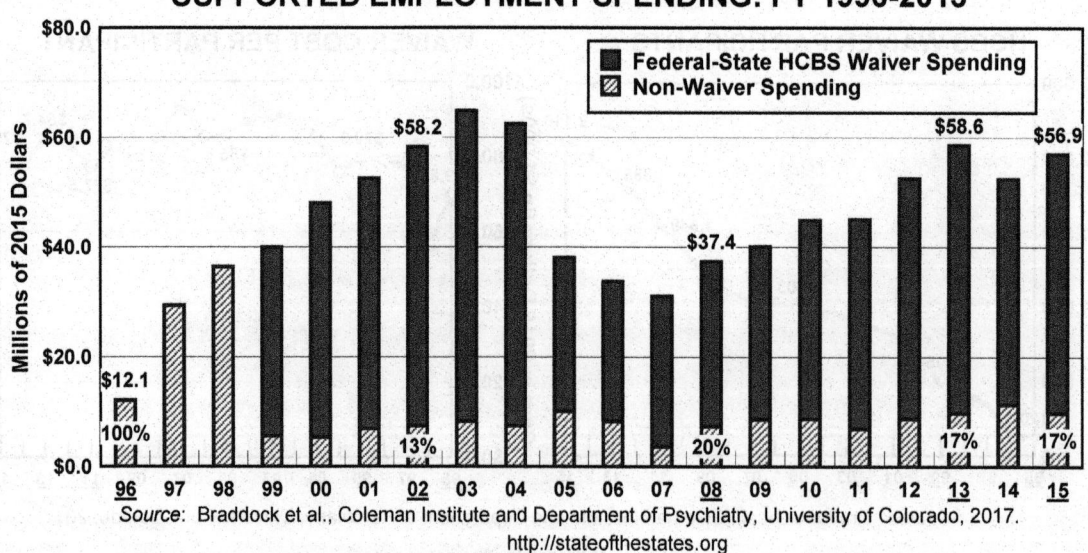

Source: Braddock et al., Coleman Institute and Department of Psychiatry, University of Colorado, 2017.
http://stateofthestates.org

ALASKA

ANNUAL COST OF CARE BY RESIDENTIAL SETTING: FY 2015

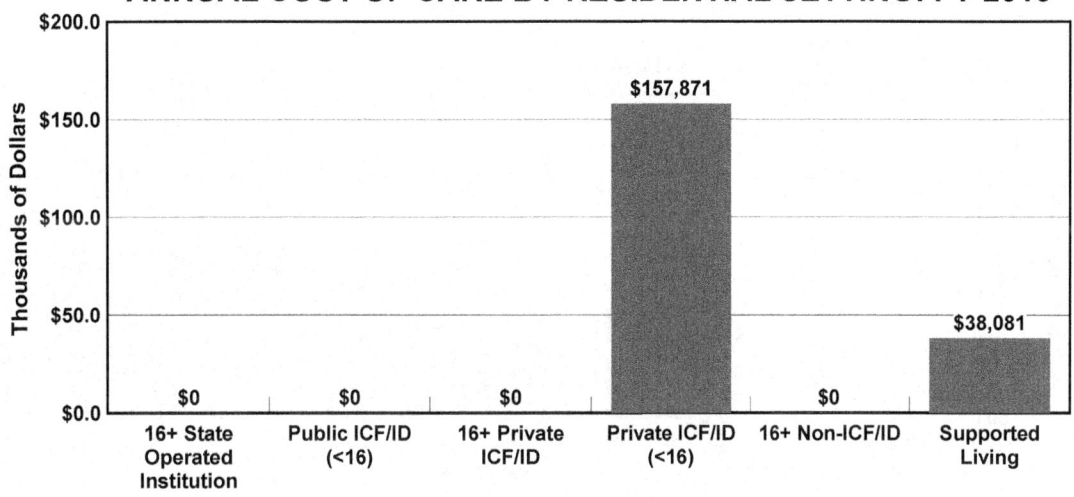

ESTIMATED NUMBER OF INDIVIDUALS WITH IDD BY AGE GROUP LIVING WITH FAMILY CAREGIVERS: FY 2015

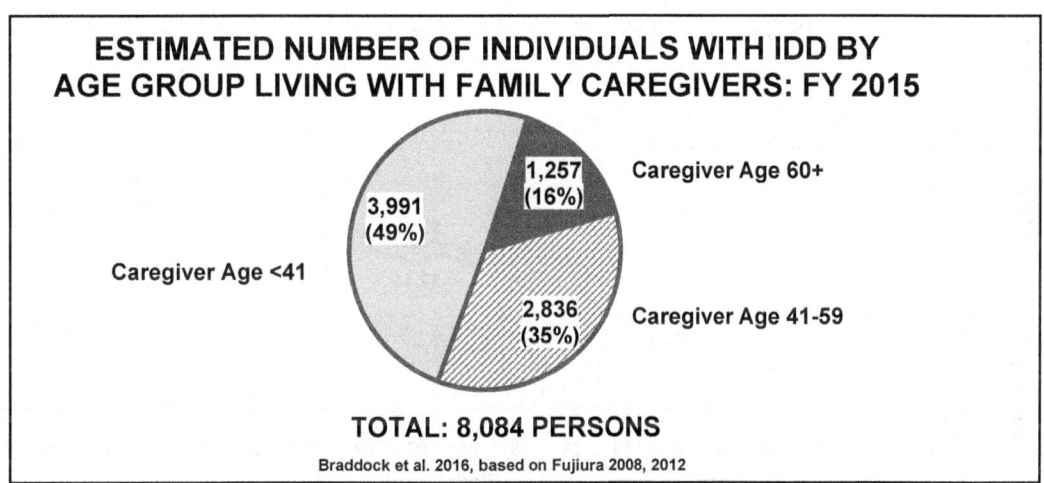

TOTAL: 8,084 PERSONS

Braddock et al. 2016, based on Fujiura 2008, 2012

ESTIMATED NUMBER OF IDD CAREGIVING FAMILIES AND FAMILIES SUPPORTED BY IDD AGENCIES: FY 1988-2015

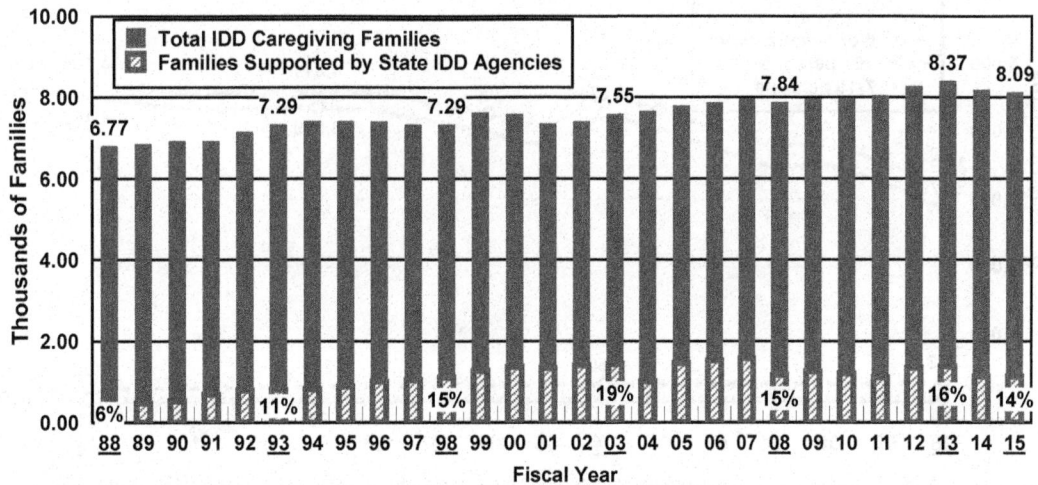

Source: Braddock et al., Coleman Institute and Department of Psychiatry, University of Colorado, 2017.
http://stateofthestates.org

ARIZONA

TOTAL PUBLIC IDD SPENDING FOR SERVICES: FY 1977-2015

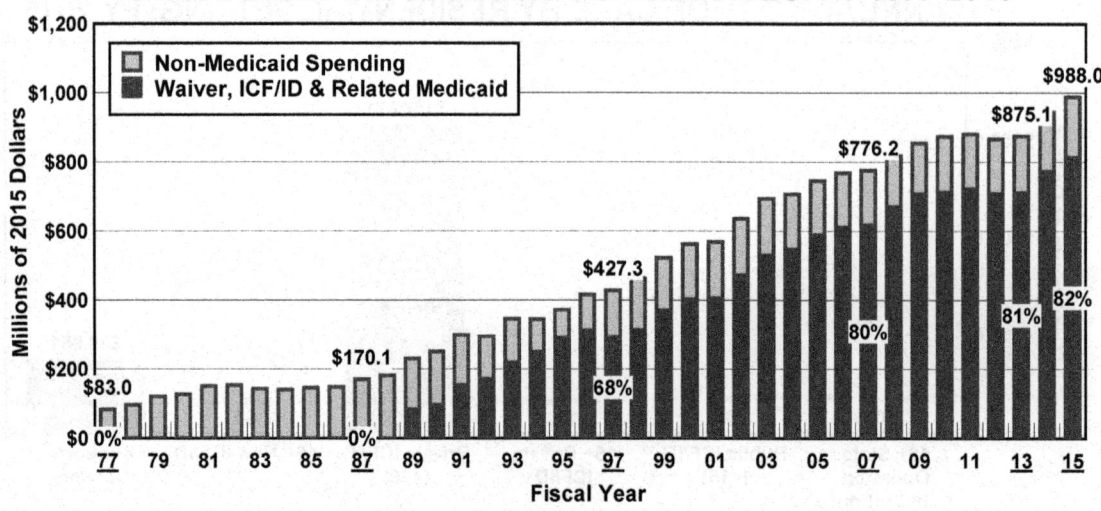

FISCAL EFFORT FOR IDD SERVICES: FY 1977-2015

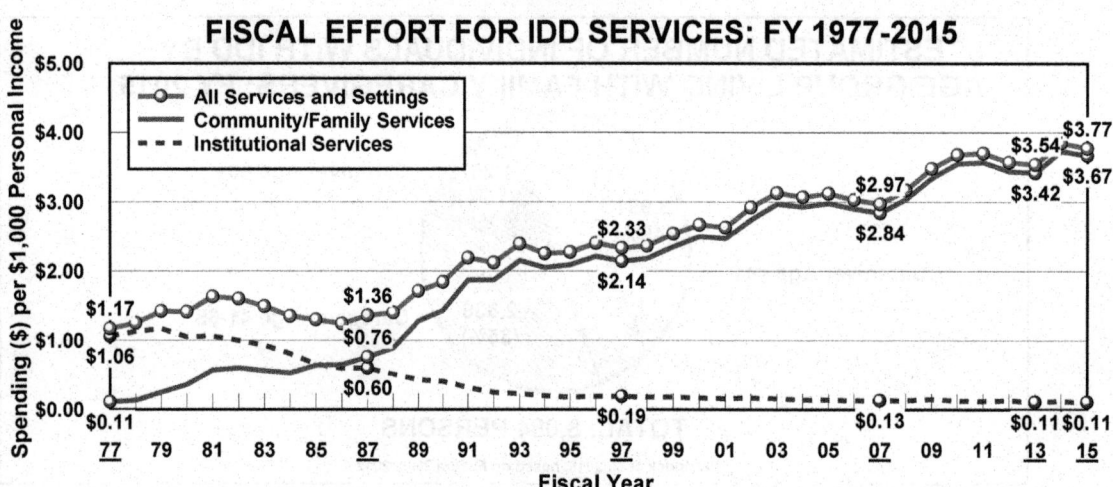

PERSONS WITH IDD BY SIZE OF SETTING: FY 1998-2015

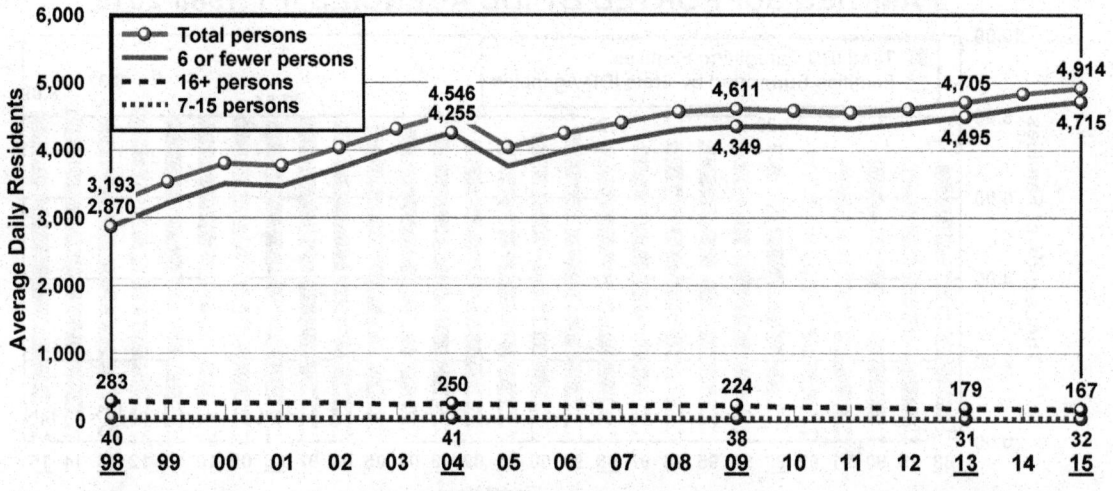

Source: Braddock et al., Coleman Institute and Department of Psychiatry, University of Colorado, 2017.
http://stateofthestates.org

Profiles of the 50 States and the District of Columbia

ARIZONA

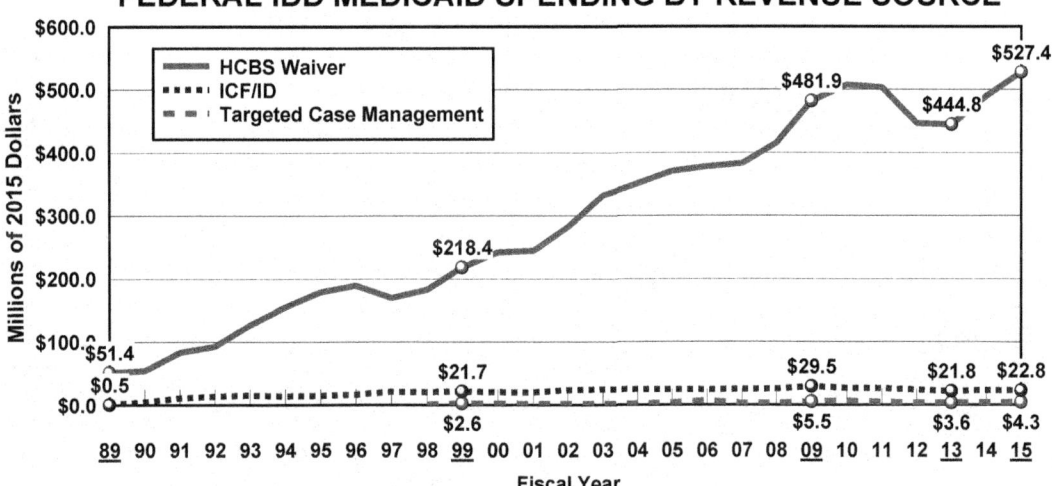

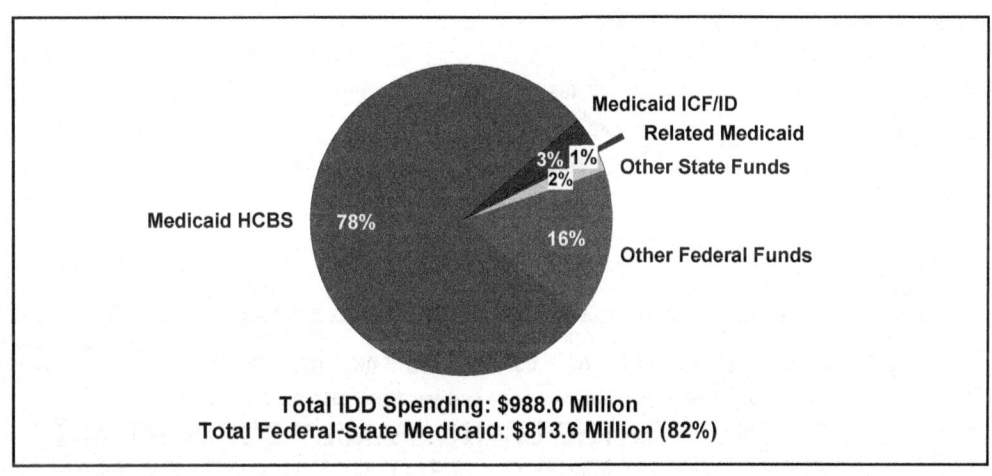

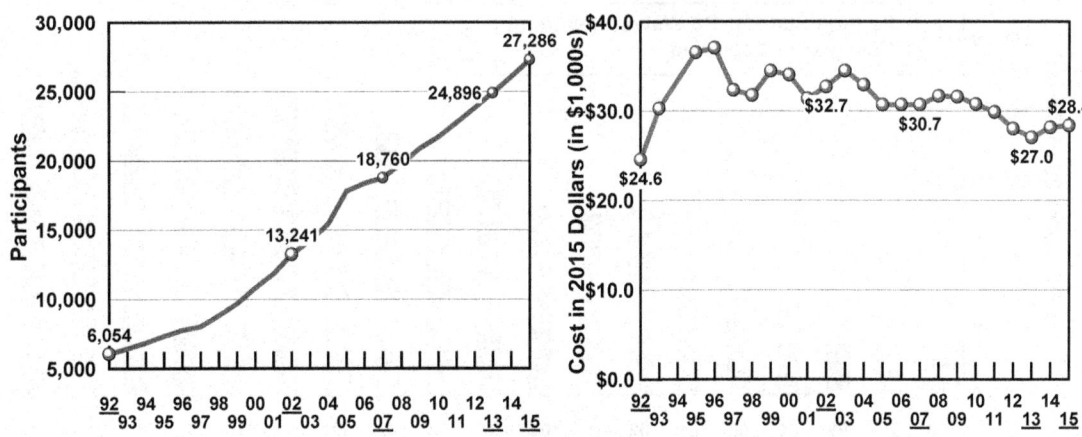

Source: Braddock et al., Coleman Institute and Department of Psychiatry, University of Colorado, 2017.
http://stateofthestates.org

ARIZONA

INDIVIDUAL AND FAMILY SUPPORT
SPENDING: FY 1996-2015

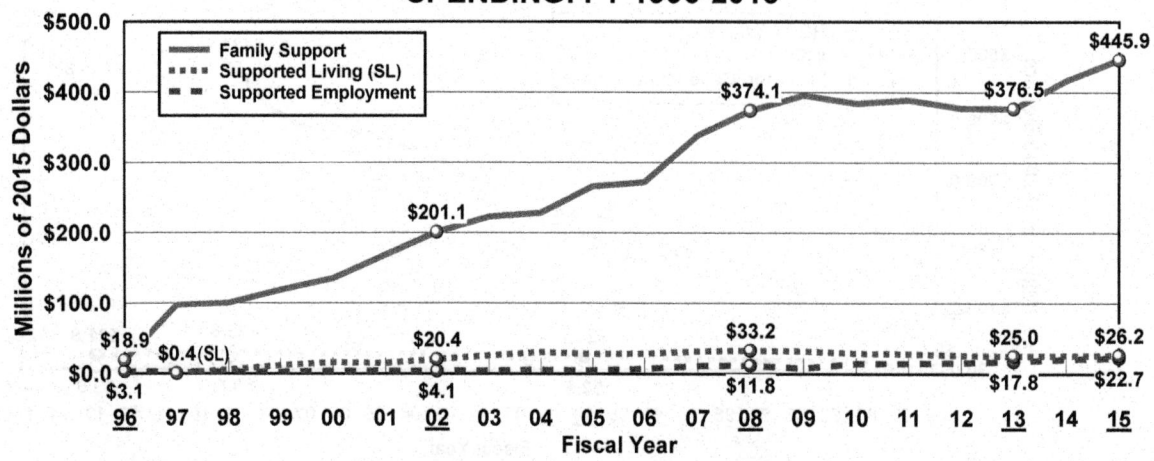

PARTICIPANTS: FY 1996-2015

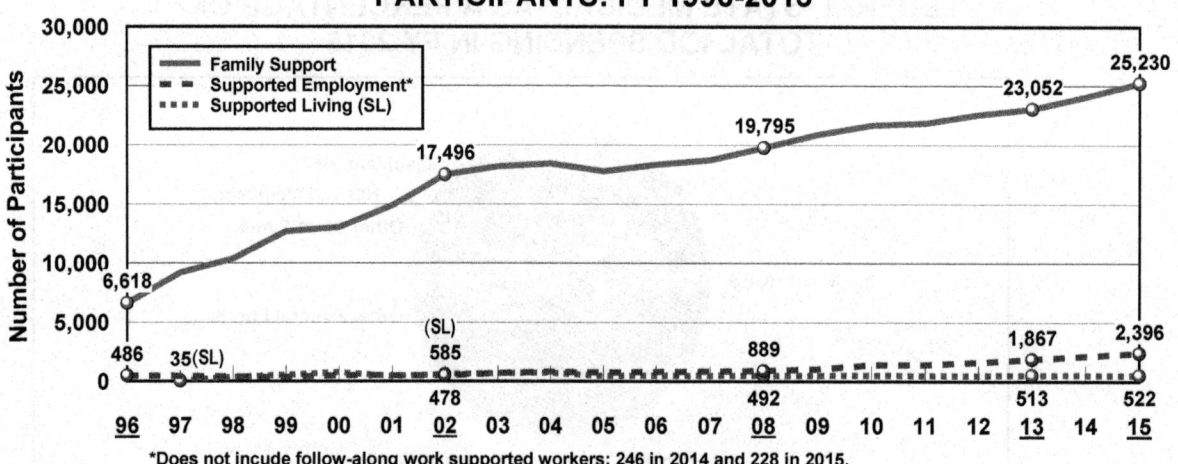

*Does not include follow-along work supported workers: 246 in 2014 and 228 in 2015.

SUPPORTED LIVING, FAMILY SUPPORT AND SUPPORTED EMPLOYMENT SPENDING: FY 1996-2015

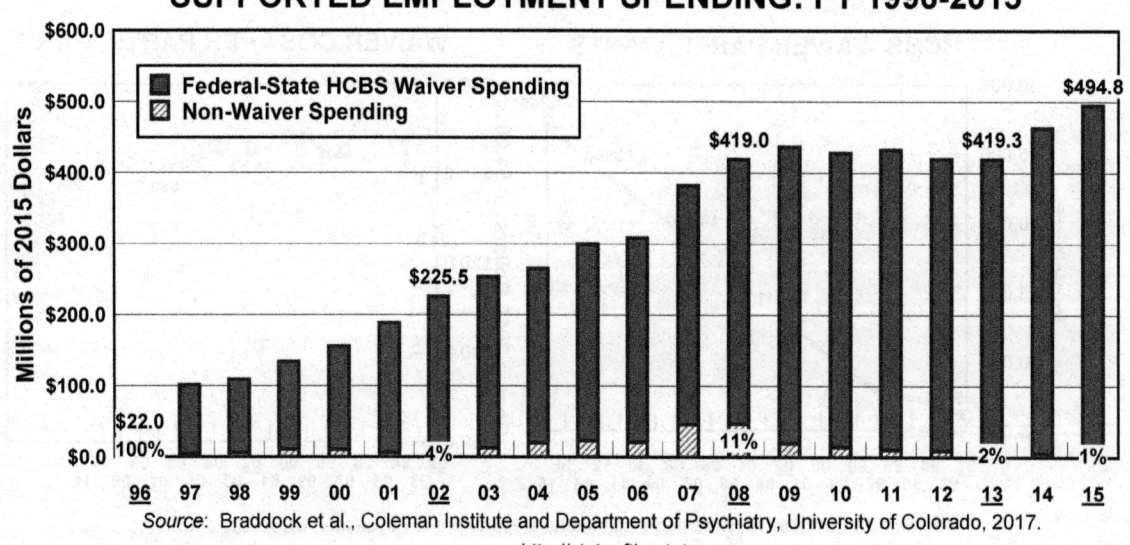

Source: Braddock et al., Coleman Institute and Department of Psychiatry, University of Colorado, 2017.
http://stateofthestates.org

ARIZONA

ANNUAL COST OF CARE BY RESIDENTIAL SETTING: FY 2015

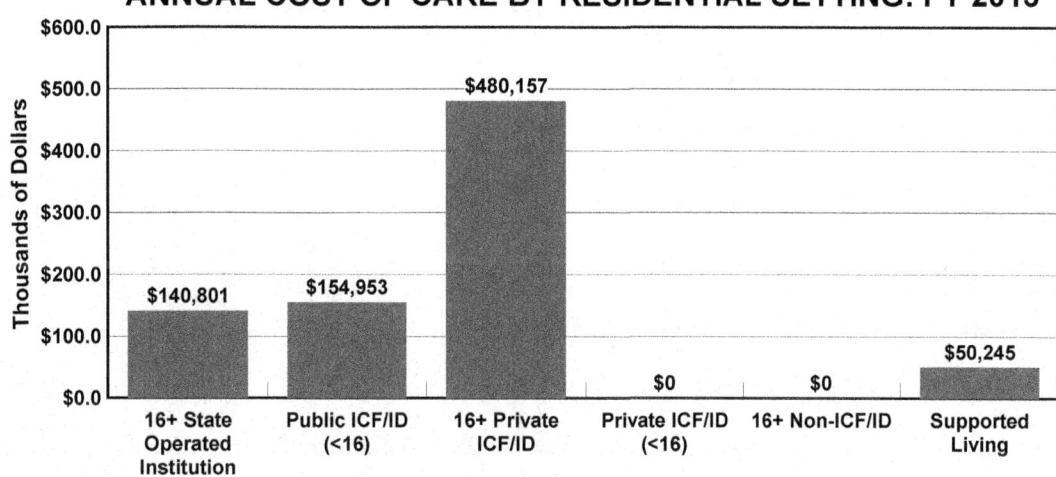

ESTIMATED NUMBER OF INDIVIDUALS WITH IDD BY AGE GROUP LIVING WITH FAMILY CAREGIVERS: FY 2015

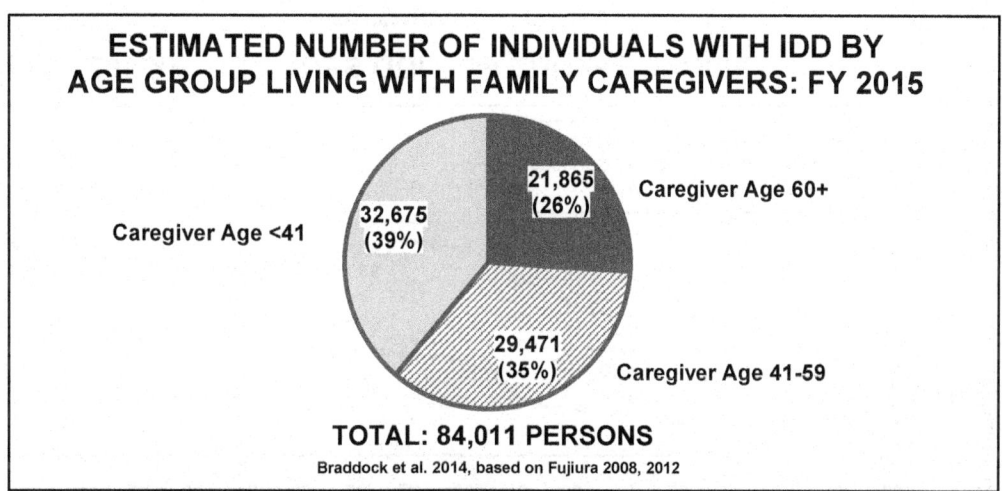

TOTAL: 84,011 PERSONS
Braddock et al. 2014, based on Fujiura 2008, 2012

ESTIMATED NUMBER OF IDD CAREGIVING FAMILIES AND FAMILIES SUPPORTED BY IDD AGENCIES: FY 1988-2015

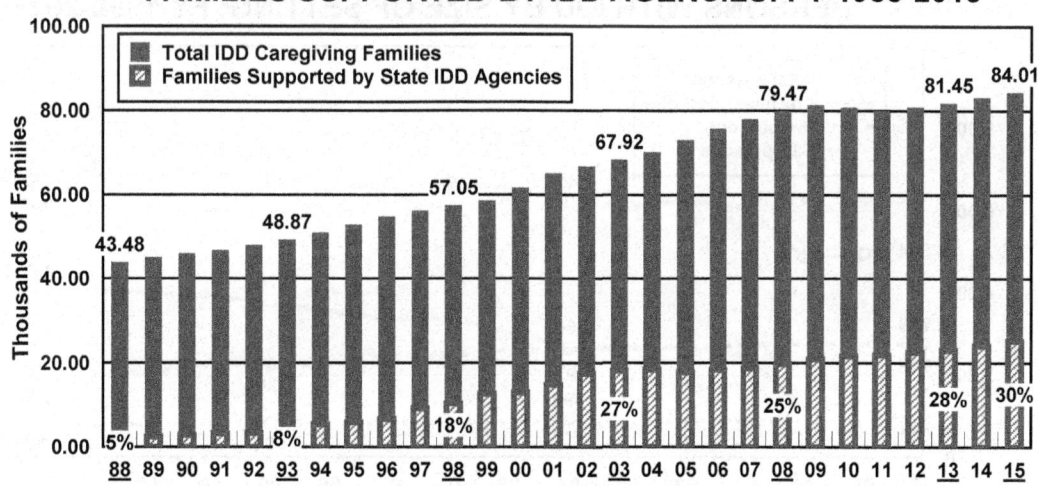

Source: Braddock et al., Coleman Institute and Department of Psychiatry, University of Colorado, 2017.
http://stateofthestates.org

ARKANSAS

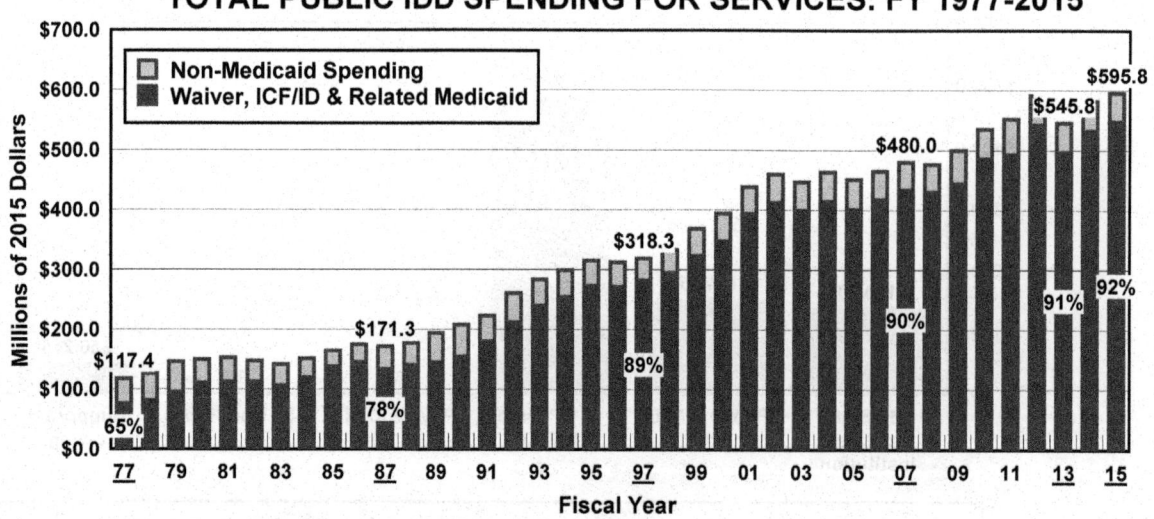

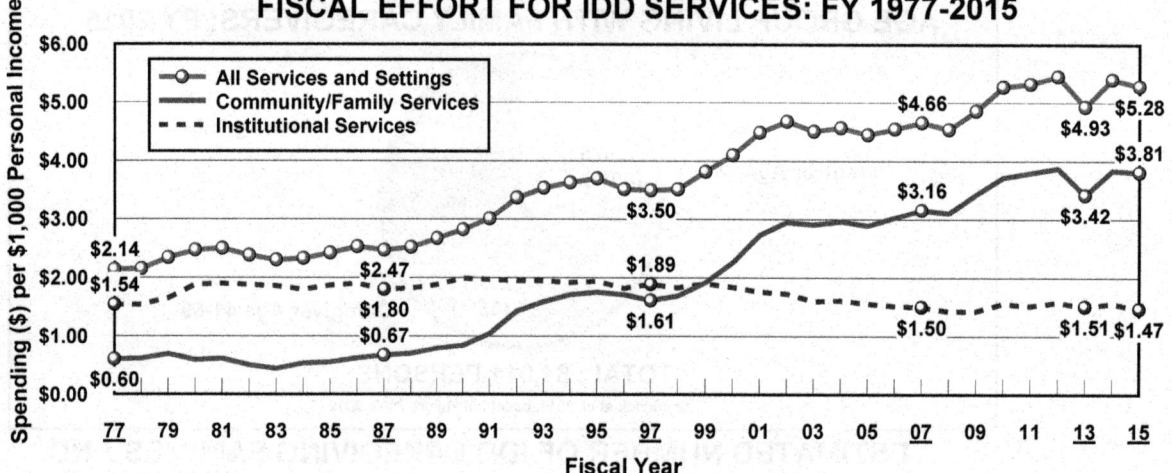

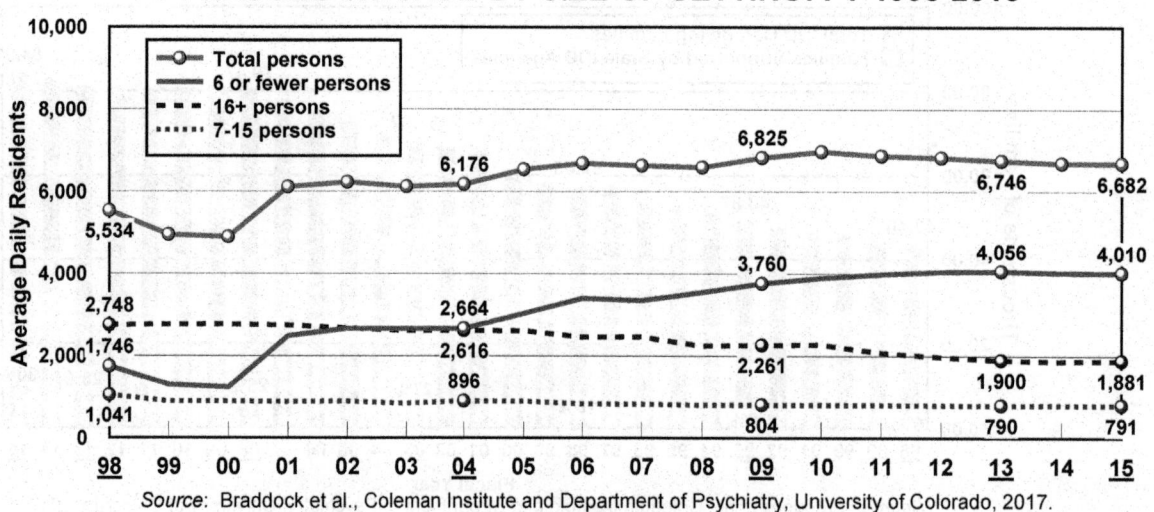

Source: Braddock et al., Coleman Institute and Department of Psychiatry, University of Colorado, 2017.
http://stateofthestates.org

ARKANSAS

FEDERAL IDD MEDICAID SPENDING BY REVENUE SOURCE

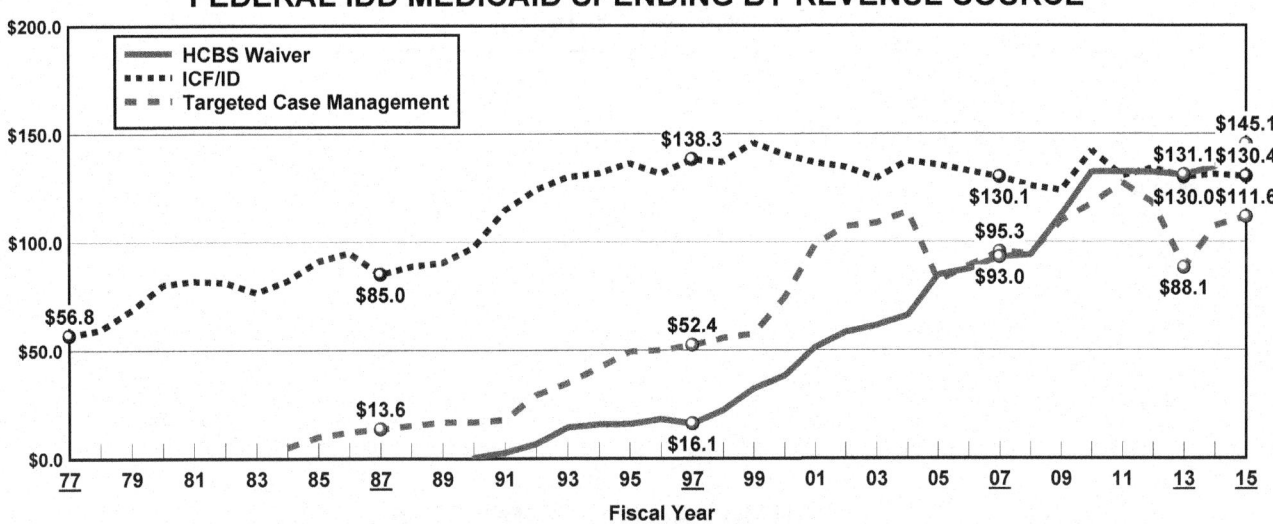

FEDERAL-STATE MEDICAID AS A PERCENTAGE OF TOTAL IDD SPENDING IN FY 2015

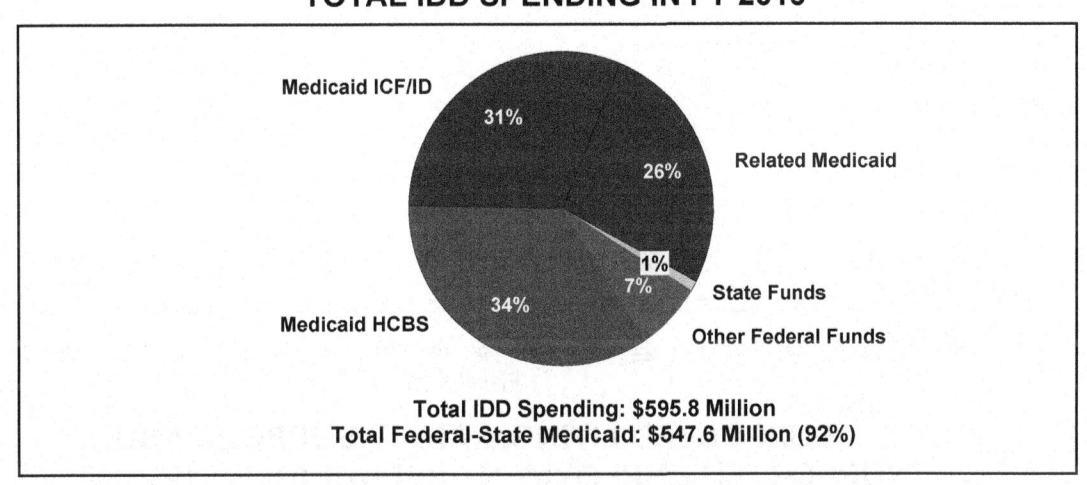

Total IDD Spending: $595.8 Million
Total Federal-State Medicaid: $547.6 Million (92%)

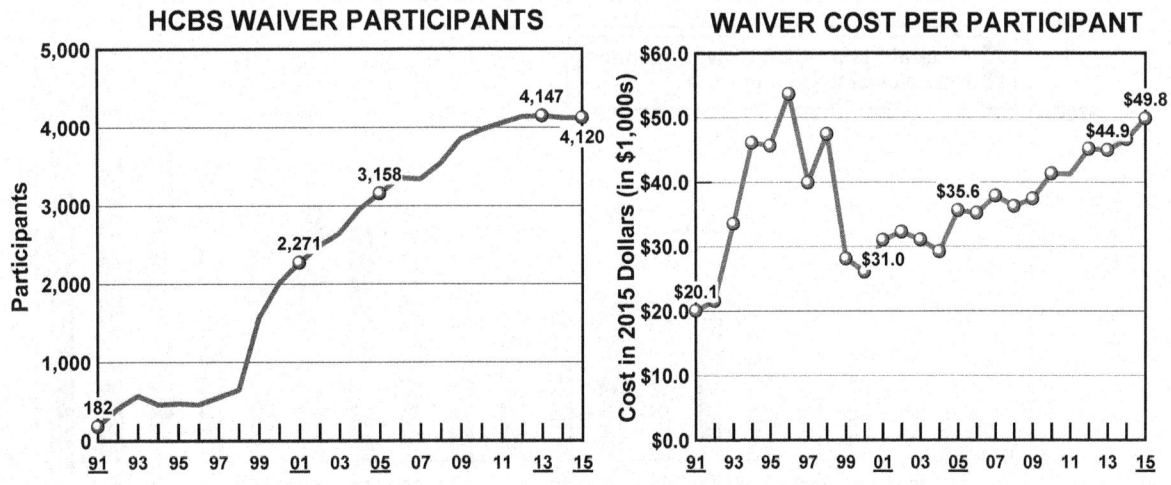

Source: Braddock et al., Coleman Institute and Department of Psychiatry, University of Colorado, 2017.
http://stateofthestates.org

ARKANSAS
INDIVIDUAL AND FAMILY SUPPORT
SPENDING: FY 1996-2015

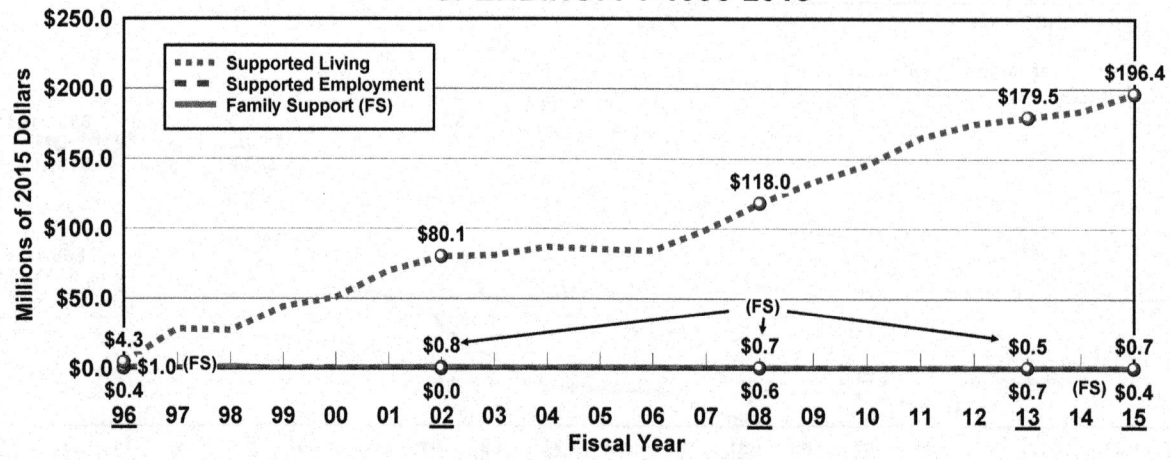

PARTICIPANTS: FY 1996-2015

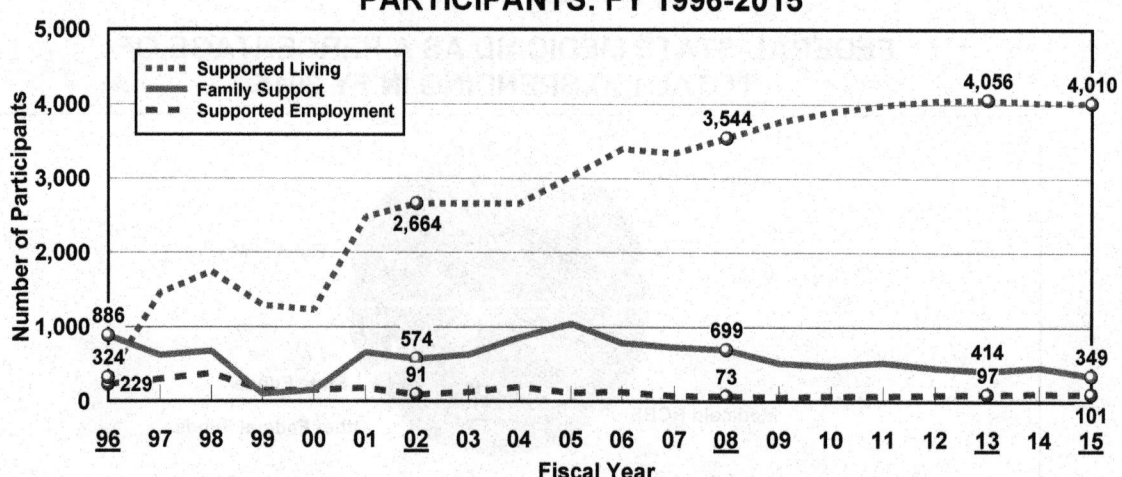

SUPPORTED LIVING, FAMILY SUPPORT AND SUPPORTED EMPLOYMENT SPENDING: FY 1996-2015

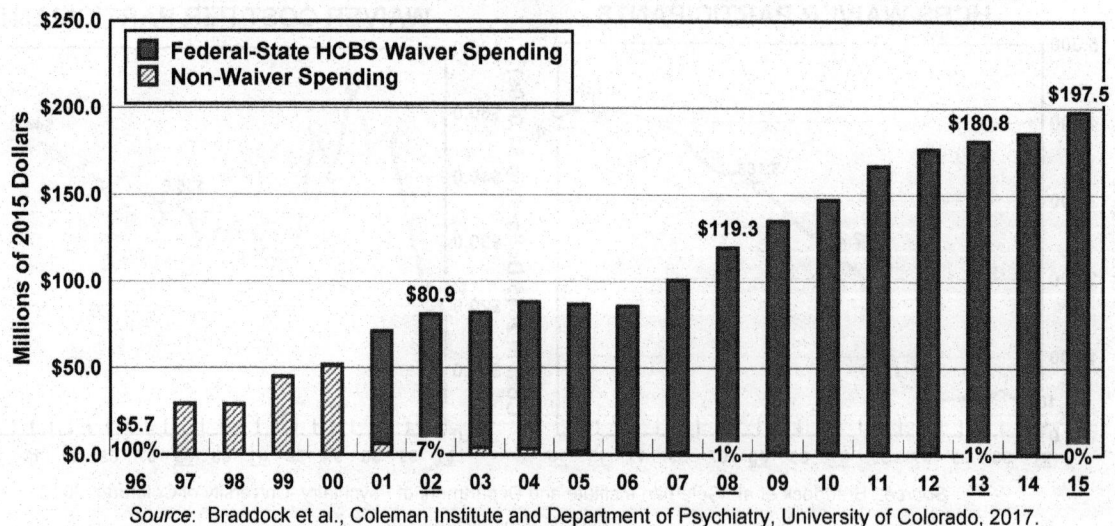

Source: Braddock et al., Coleman Institute and Department of Psychiatry, University of Colorado, 2017.
http://stateofthestates.org

ARKANSAS

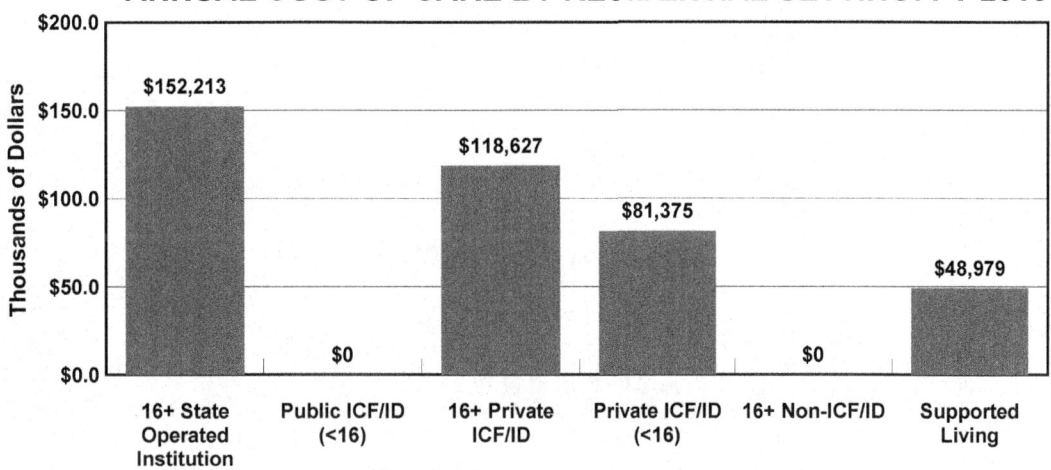

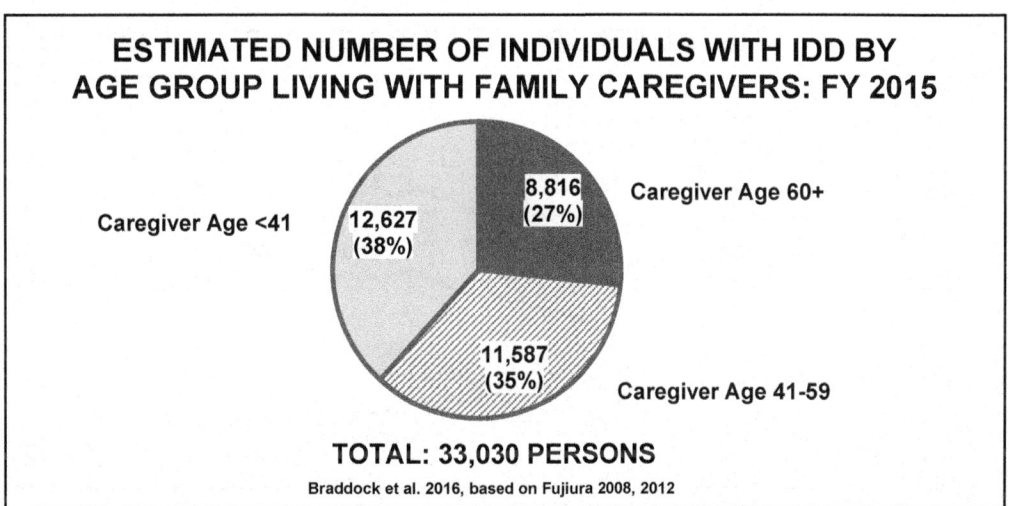

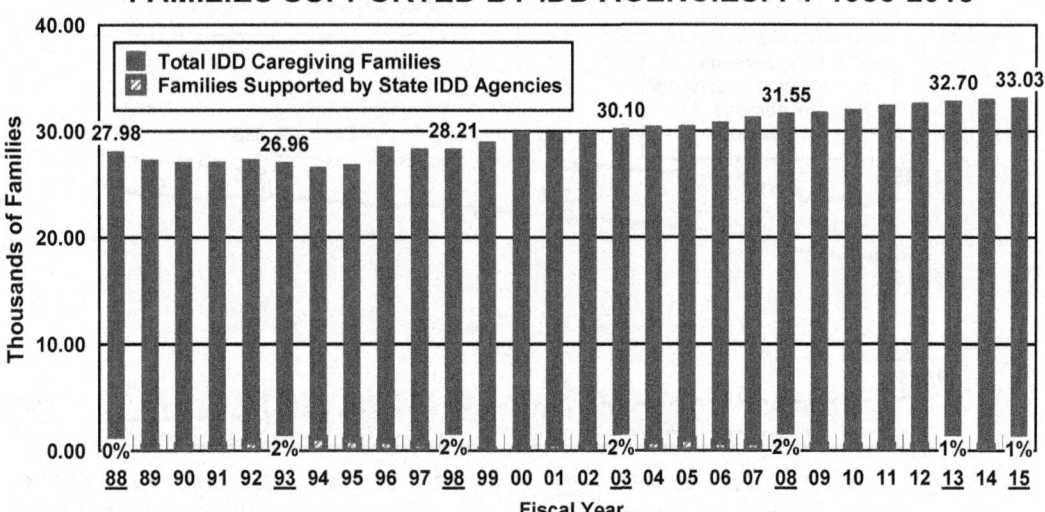

Source: Braddock et al., Coleman Institute and Department of Psychiatry, University of Colorado, 2017.
http://stateofthestates.org

CALIFORNIA

TOTAL PUBLIC IDD SPENDING FOR SERVICES: FY 1977-2015

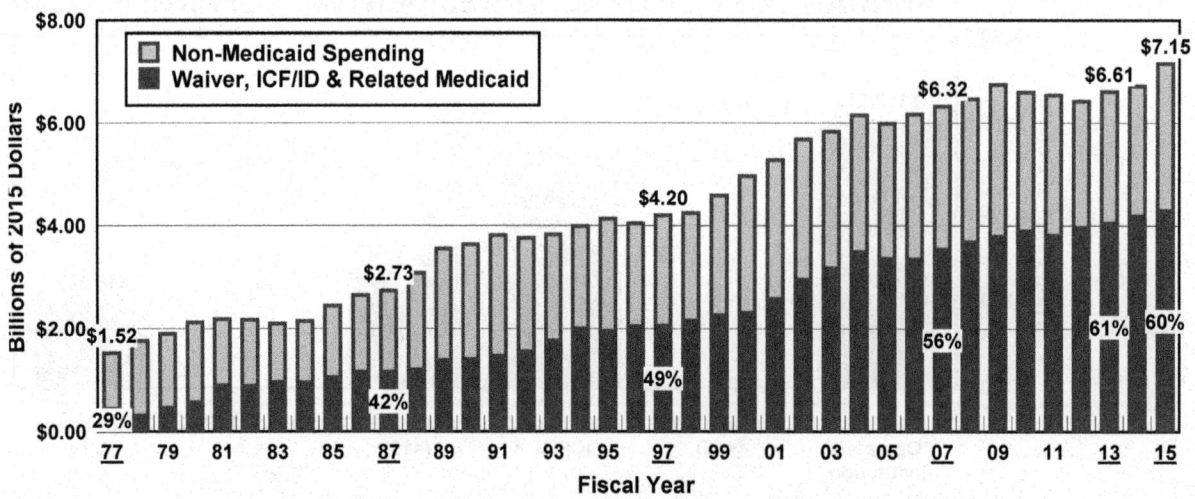

FISCAL EFFORT FOR IDD SERVICES: FY 1977-2015

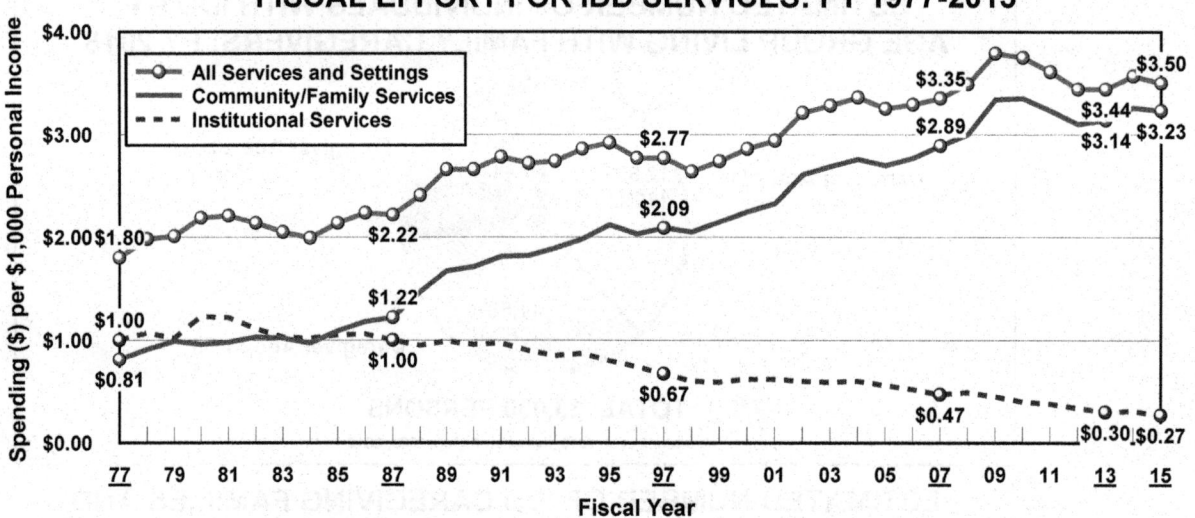

PERSONS WITH IDD BY SIZE OF SETTING: FY 1998-2015

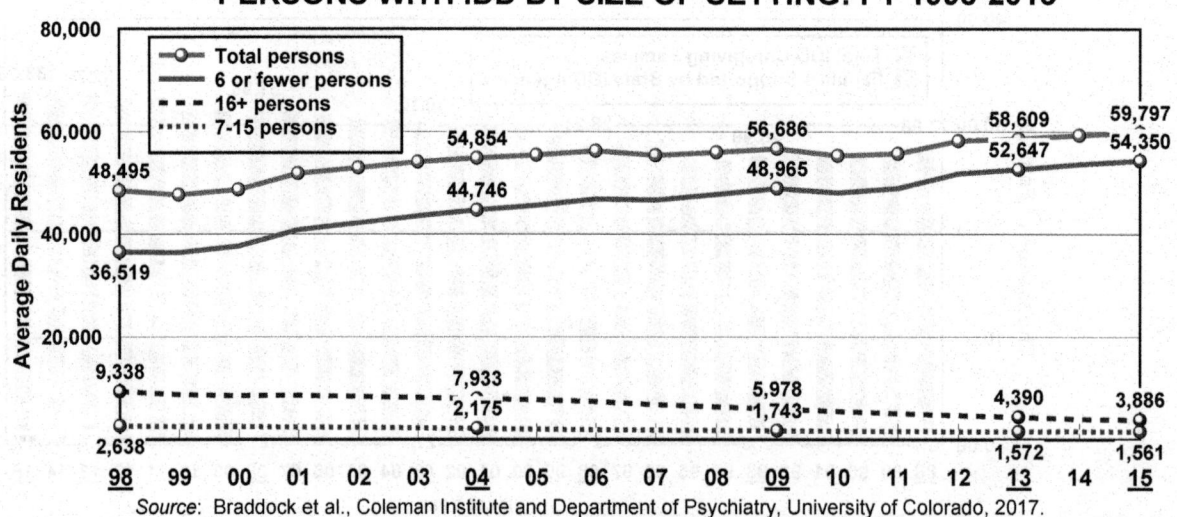

Source: Braddock et al., Coleman Institute and Department of Psychiatry, University of Colorado, 2017.

http://stateofthestates.org

CALIFORNIA

FEDERAL IDD MEDICAID SPENDING BY REVENUE SOURCE

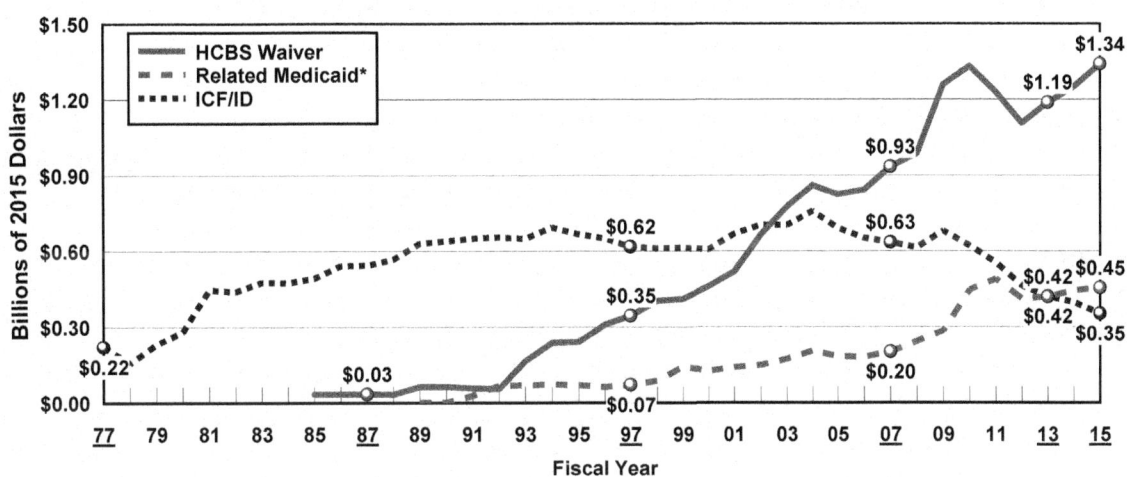

*In 2015, "Related Medicaid" was targeted case management ($165.0 million) and administration ($289.2 million).

FEDERAL-STATE MEDICAID AS A PERCENTAGE OF TOTAL IDD SPENDING IN FY 2015

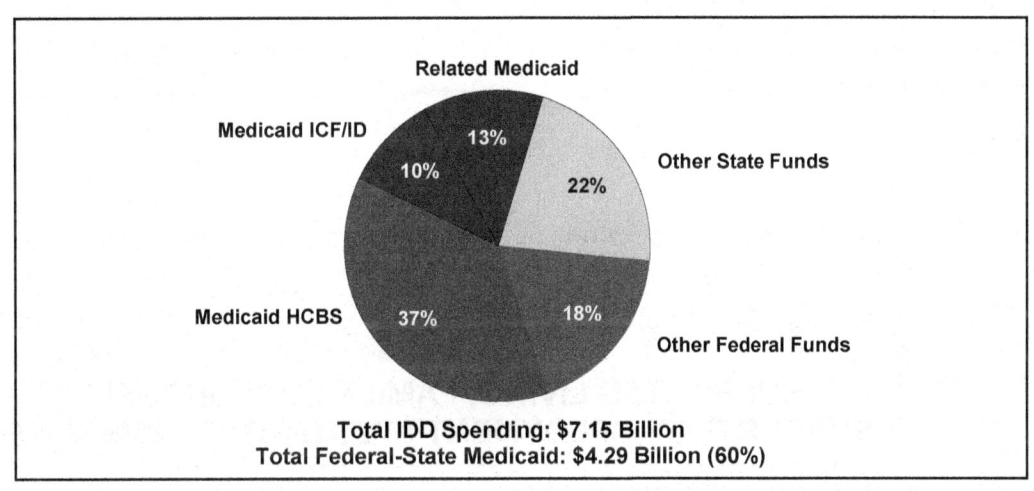

Total IDD Spending: $7.15 Billion
Total Federal-State Medicaid: $4.29 Billion (60%)

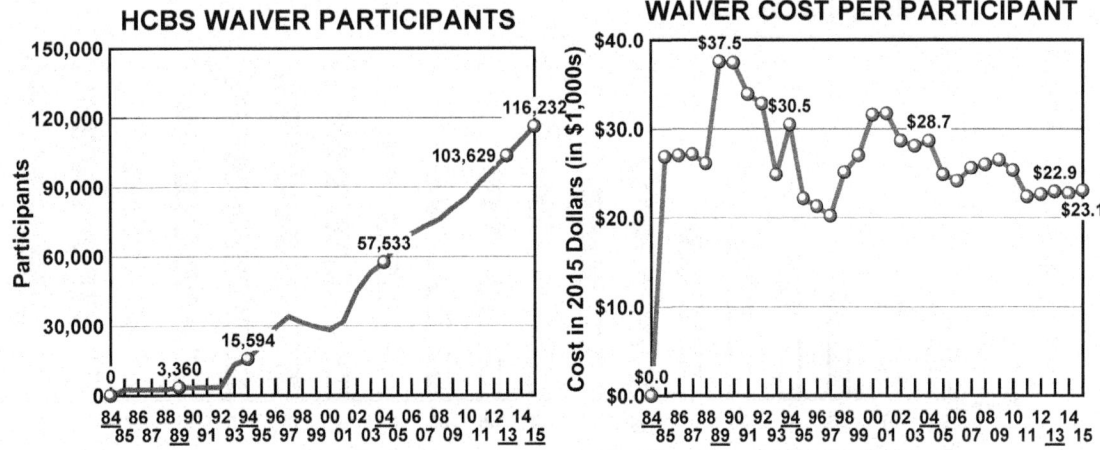

Source: Braddock et al., Coleman Institute and Department of Psychiatry, University of Colorado, 2017.
http://stateofthestates.org

CALIFORNIA
INDIVIDUAL AND FAMILY SUPPORT

SPENDING: FY 1996-2015

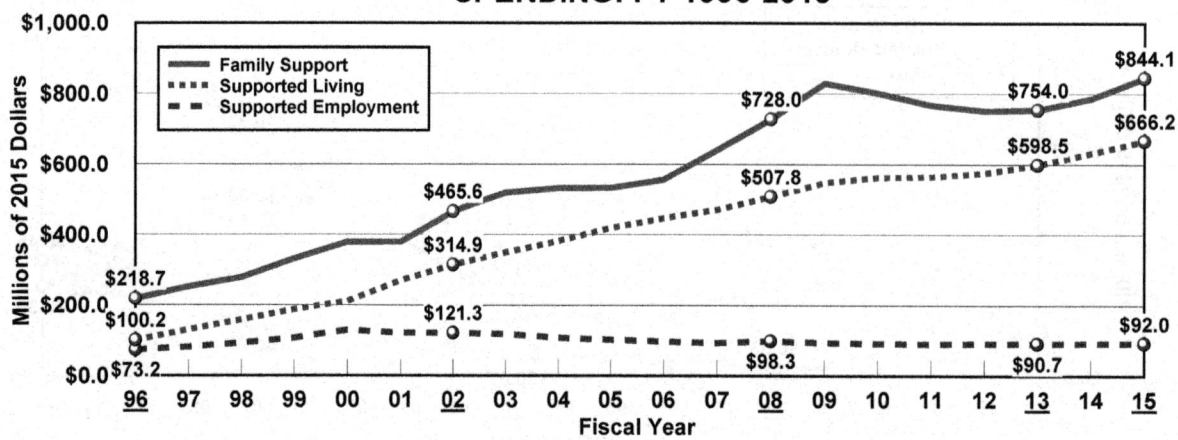

PARTICIPANTS: FY 1996-2015

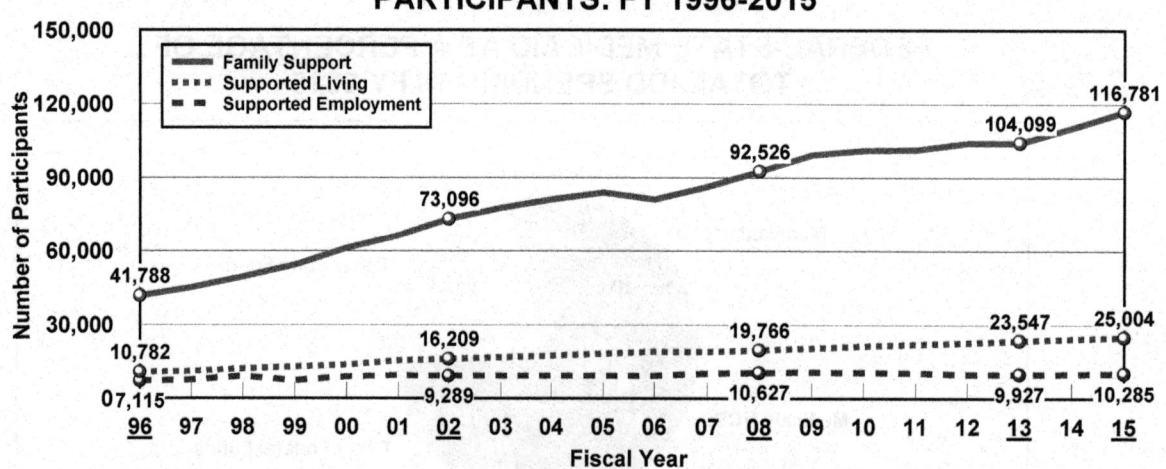

SUPPORTED LIVING, FAMILY SUPPORT AND SUPPORTED EMPLOYMENT SPENDING: FY 1996-2015

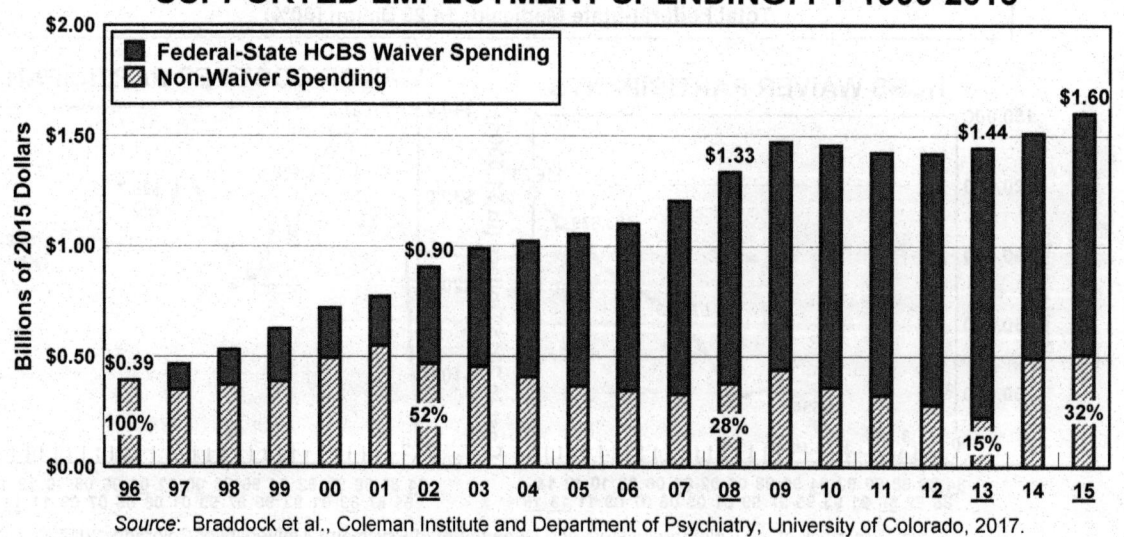

Source: Braddock et al., Coleman Institute and Department of Psychiatry, University of Colorado, 2017.
http://stateofthestates.org

CALIFORNIA

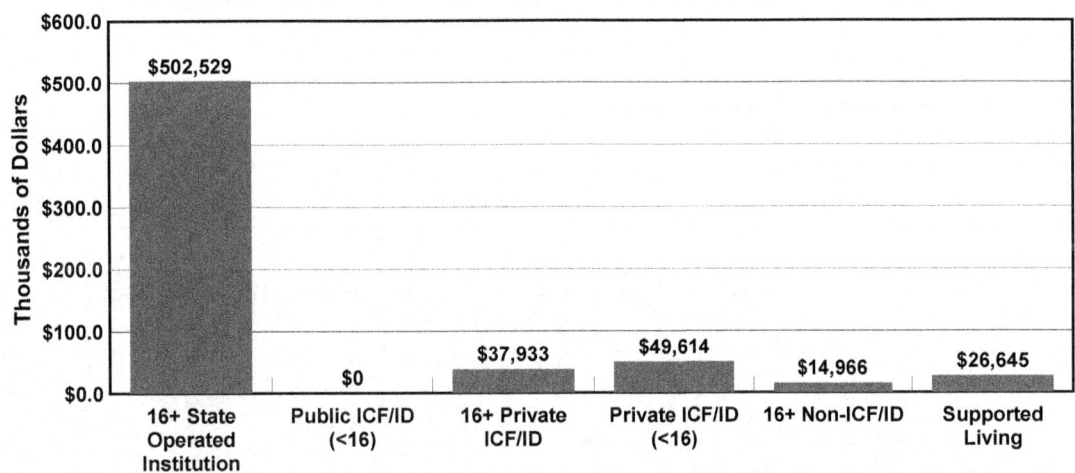

ANNUAL COST OF CARE BY RESIDENTIAL SETTING: FY 2015

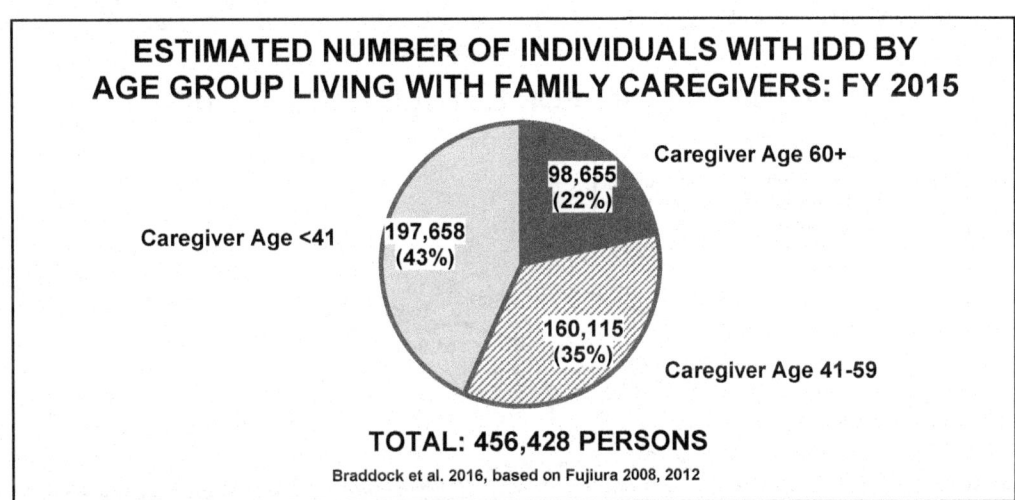

ESTIMATED NUMBER OF INDIVIDUALS WITH IDD BY AGE GROUP LIVING WITH FAMILY CAREGIVERS: FY 2015

TOTAL: 456,428 PERSONS

Braddock et al. 2016, based on Fujiura 2008, 2012

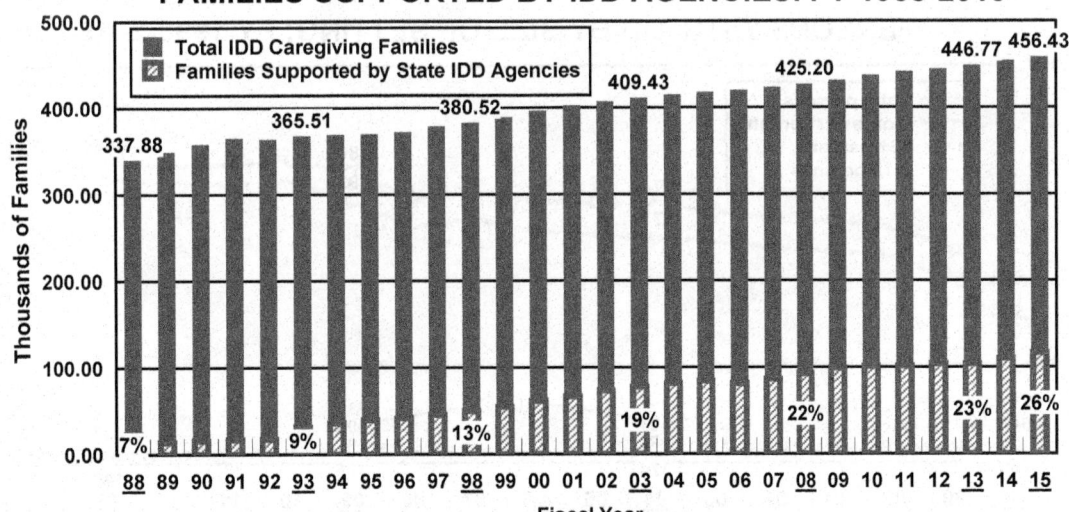

ESTIMATED NUMBER OF IDD CAREGIVING FAMILIES AND FAMILIES SUPPORTED BY IDD AGENCIES: FY 1988-2015

Source: Braddock et al., Coleman Institute and Department of Psychiatry, University of Colorado, 2017.
http://stateofthestates.org

COLORADO

TOTAL PUBLIC IDD SPENDING FOR SERVICES: FY 1977-2015

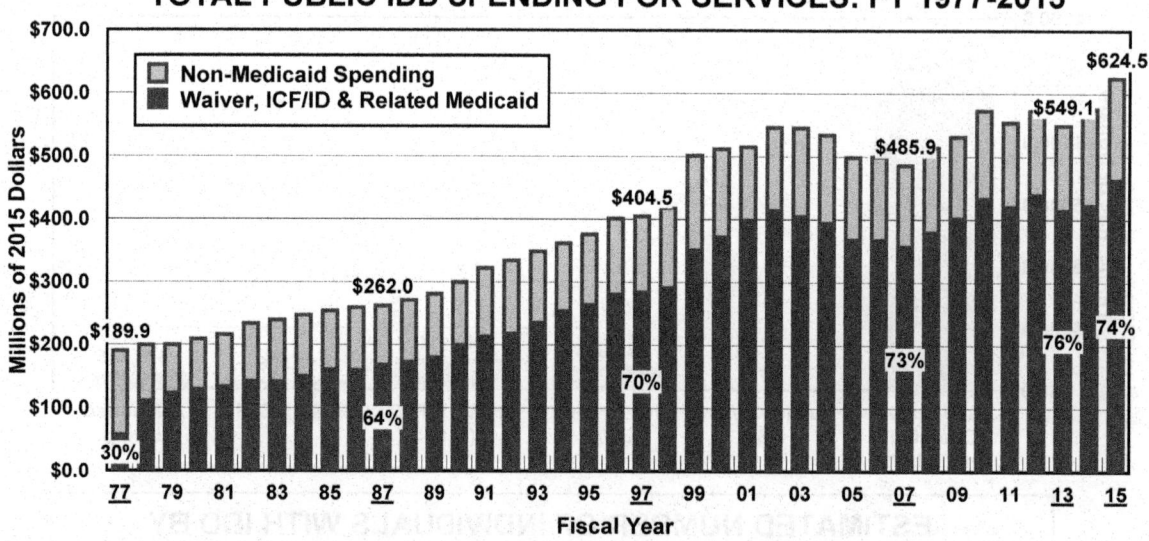

FISCAL EFFORT FOR IDD SERVICES: FY 1977-2015

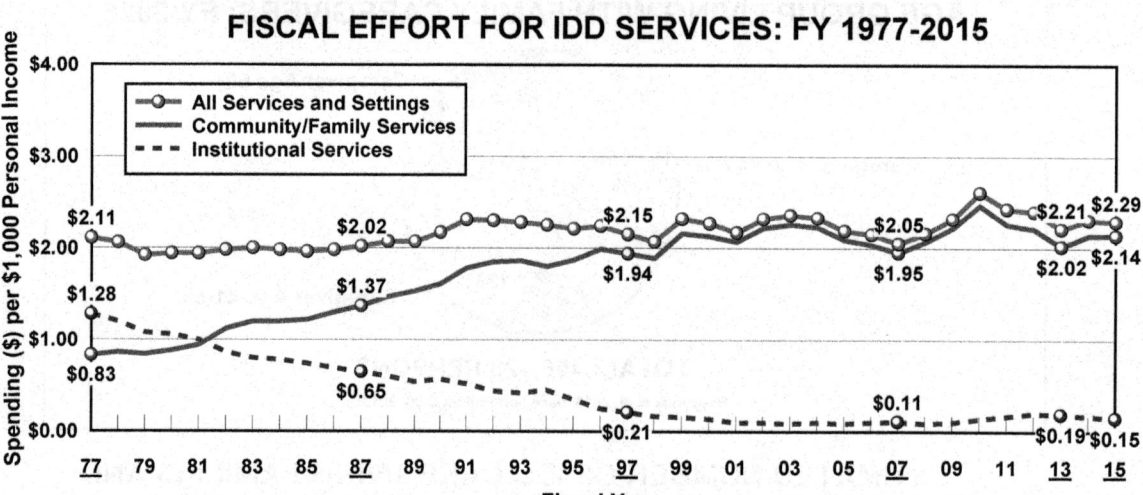

PERSONS WITH IDD BY SIZE OF SETTING: FY 1998-2015

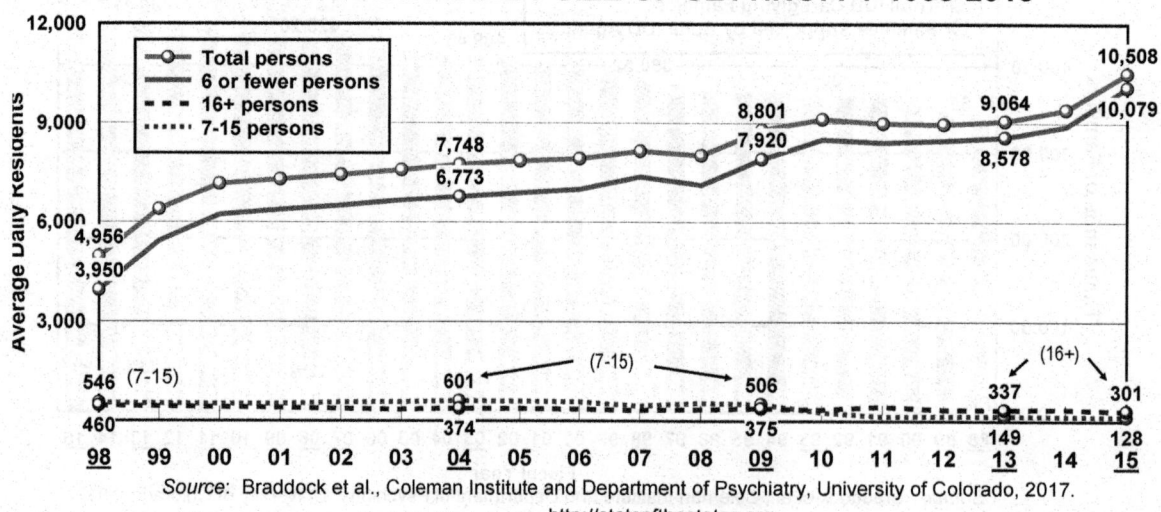

Source: Braddock et al., Coleman Institute and Department of Psychiatry, University of Colorado, 2017.
http://stateofthestates.org

COLORADO

FEDERAL IDD MEDICAID SPENDING BY REVENUE SOURCE

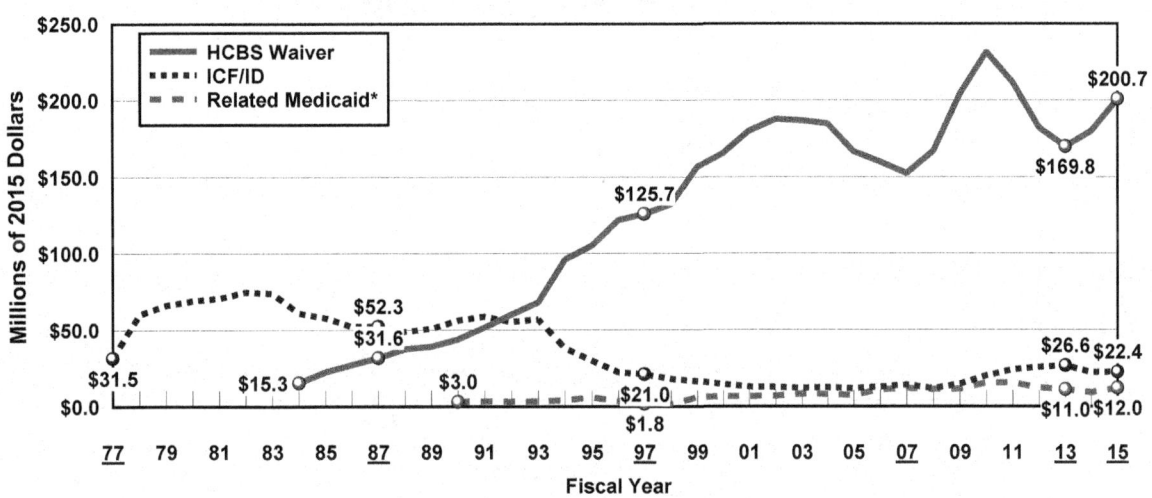

*In 2015, "Related Medicaid" was targeted case management ($10.6 million) and administration ($1.5 million).

FEDERAL-STATE MEDICAID AS A PERCENTAGE OF TOTAL IDD SPENDING IN FY 2015

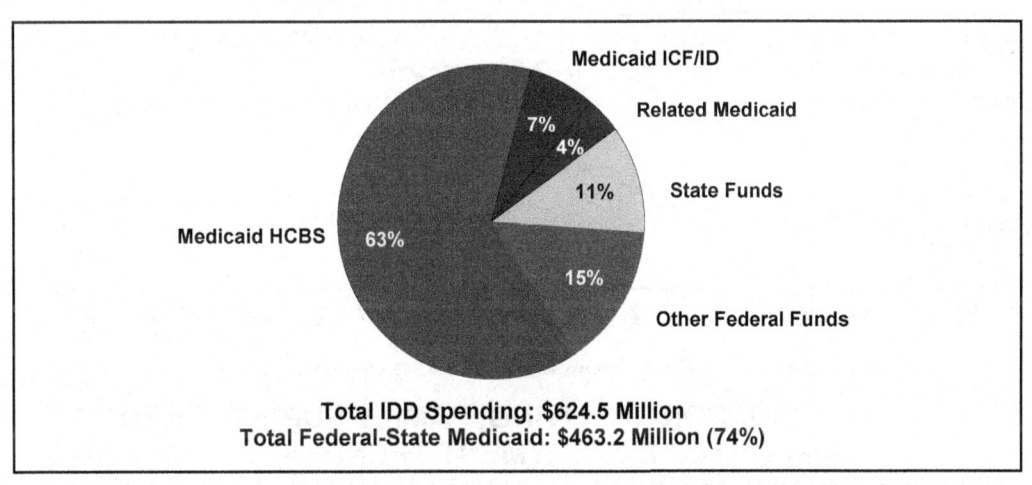

Total IDD Spending: $624.5 Million
Total Federal-State Medicaid: $463.2 Million (74%)

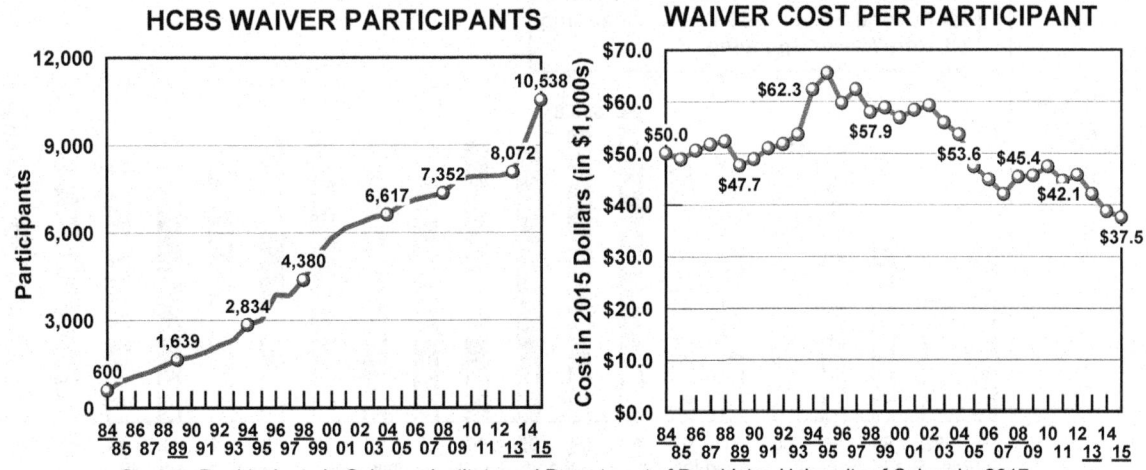

Source: Braddock et al., Coleman Institute and Department of Psychiatry, University of Colorado, 2017.
http://stateofthestates.org

COLORADO
INDIVIDUAL AND FAMILY SUPPORT
SPENDING: FY 1996-2015

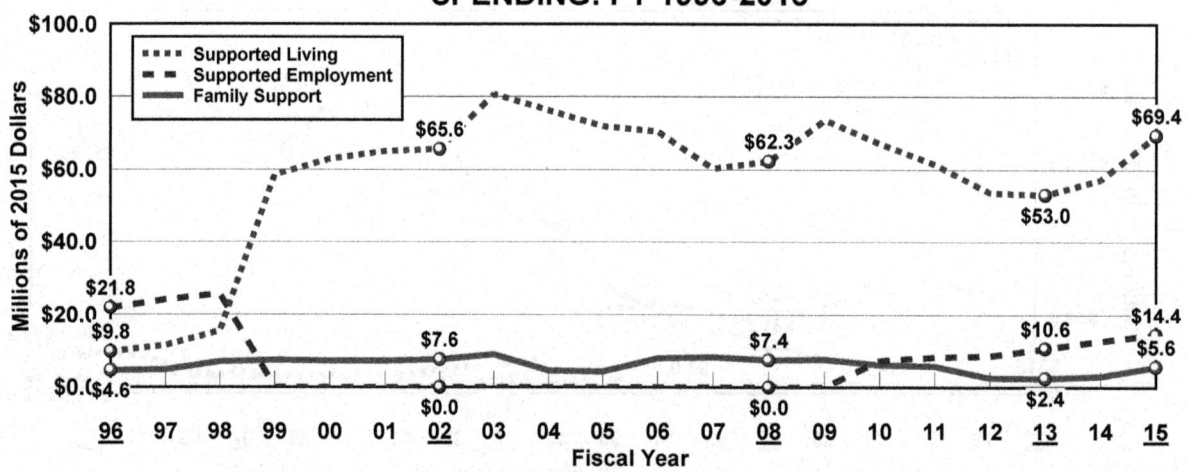

PARTICIPANTS: FY 1996-2015

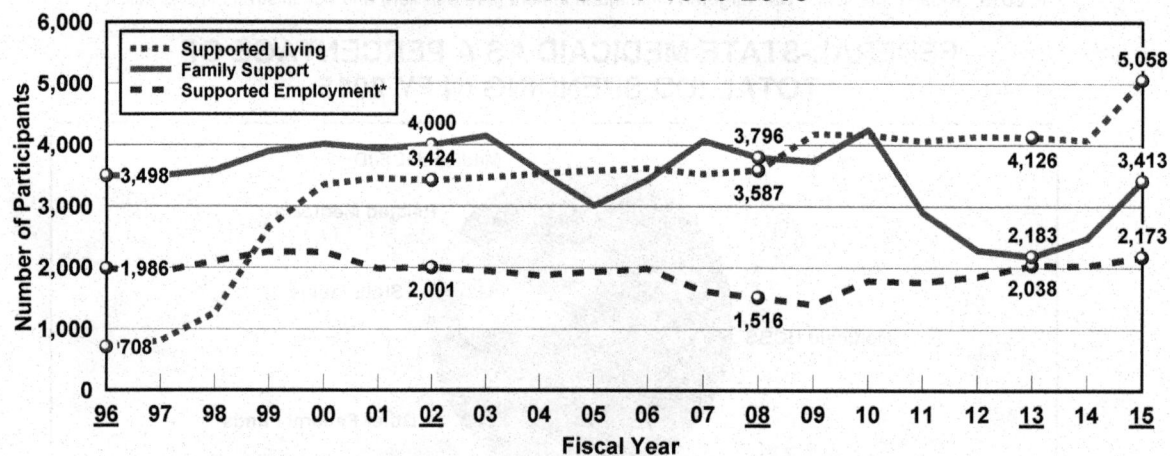

* Does not include 306 follow-long work support workers in 2014 and 346 workers in 2015.

SUPPORTED LIVING, FAMILY SUPPORT AND SUPPORTED EMPLOYMENT SPENDING: FY 1996-2015

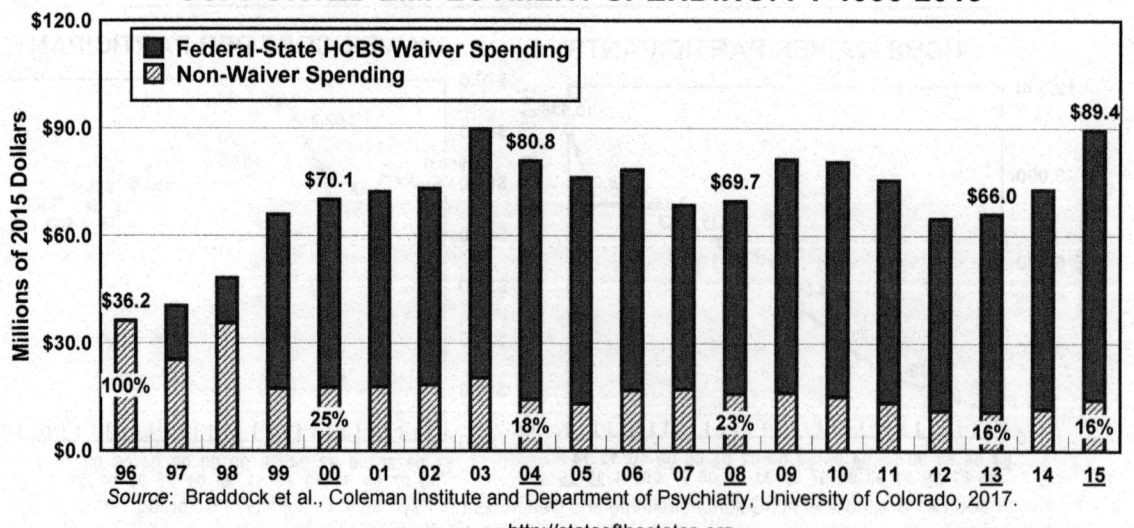

Source: Braddock et al., Coleman Institute and Department of Psychiatry, University of Colorado, 2017.

http://stateofthestates.org

COLORADO

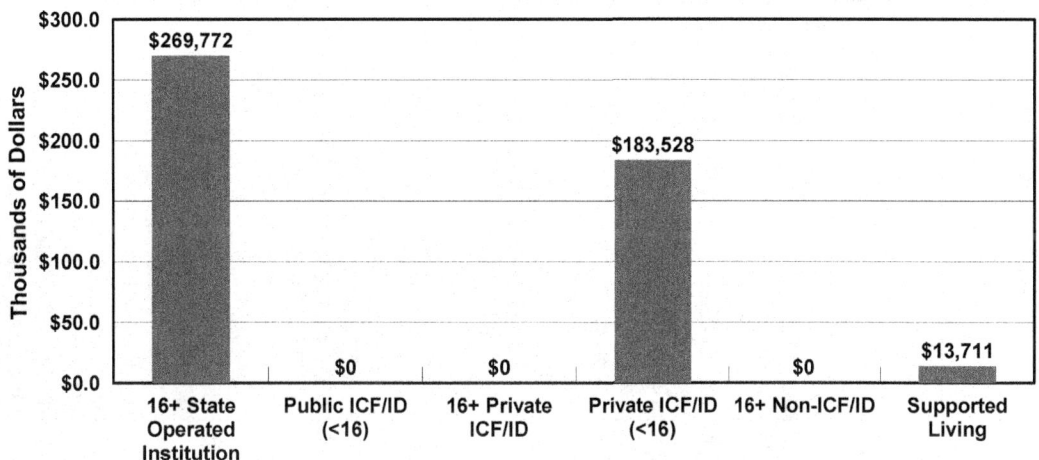

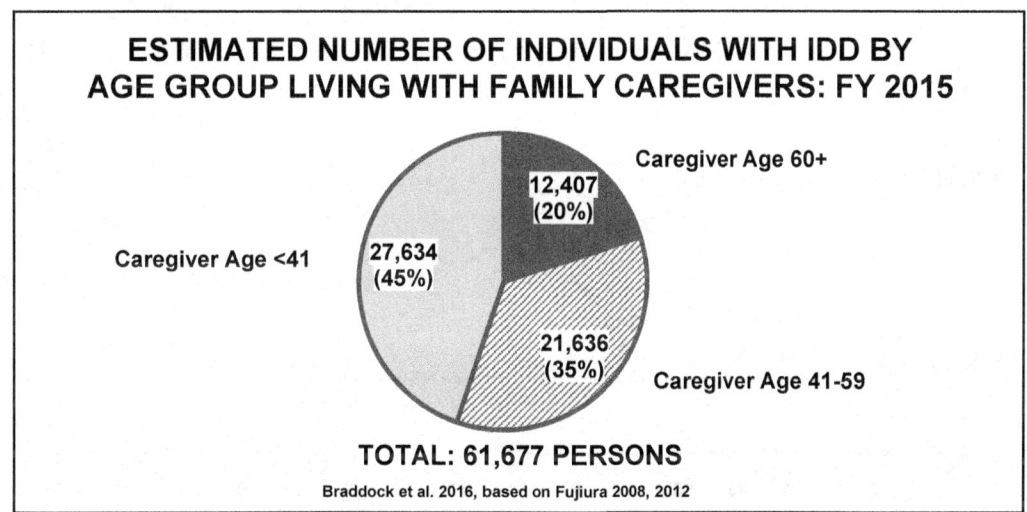

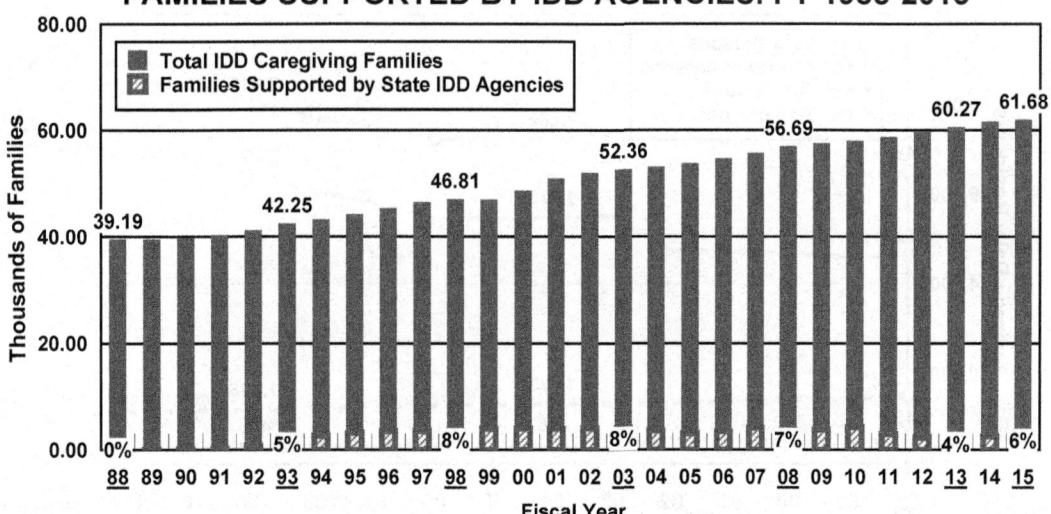

Source: Braddock et al., Coleman Institute and Department of Psychiatry, University of Colorado, 2017.
http://stateofthestates.org

CONNECTICUT

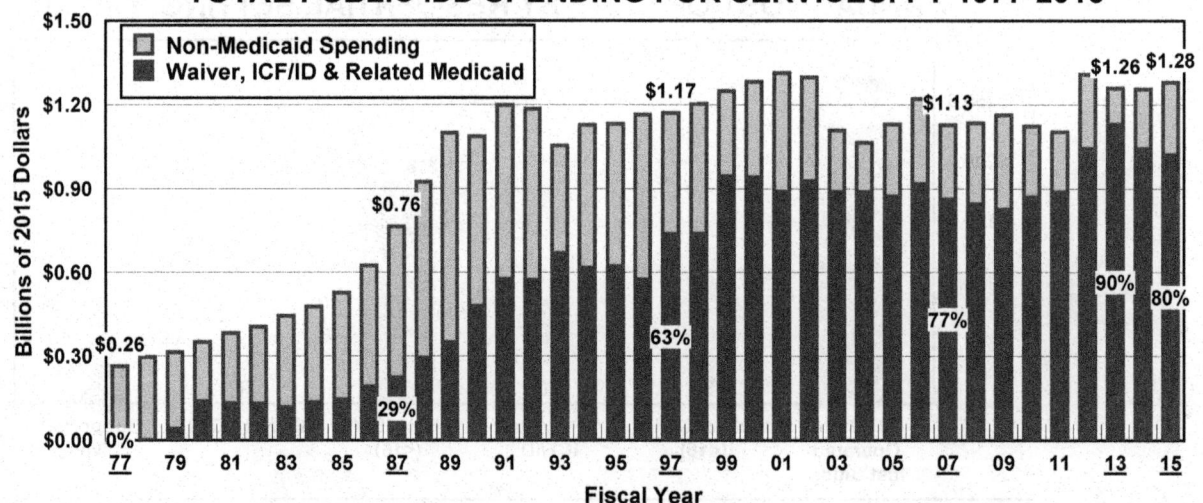

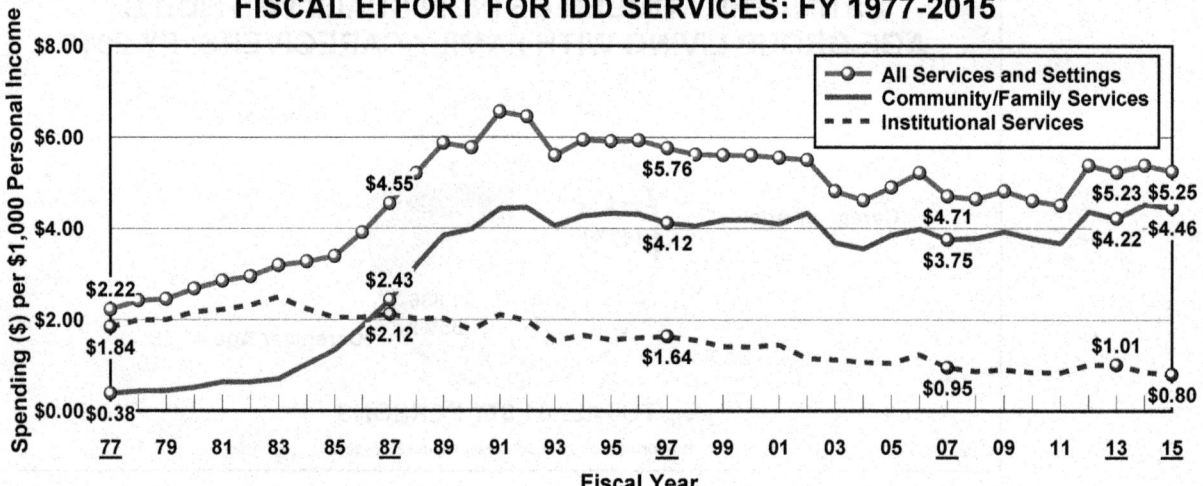

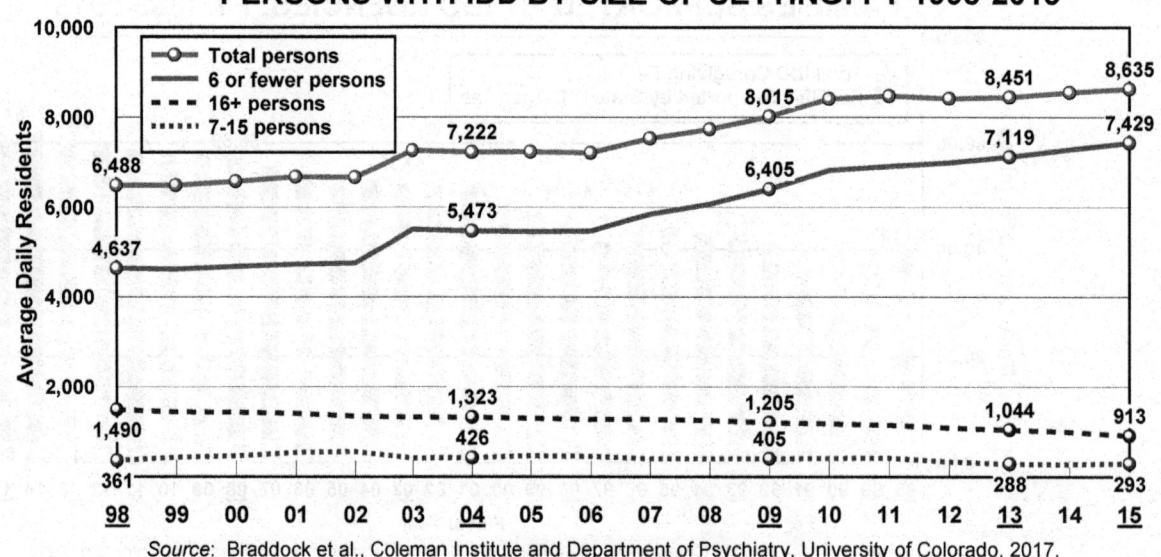

Source: Braddock et al., Coleman Institute and Department of Psychiatry, University of Colorado, 2017.
http://stateofthestates.org

CONNECTICUT

FEDERAL IDD MEDICAID SPENDING BY REVENUE SOURCE

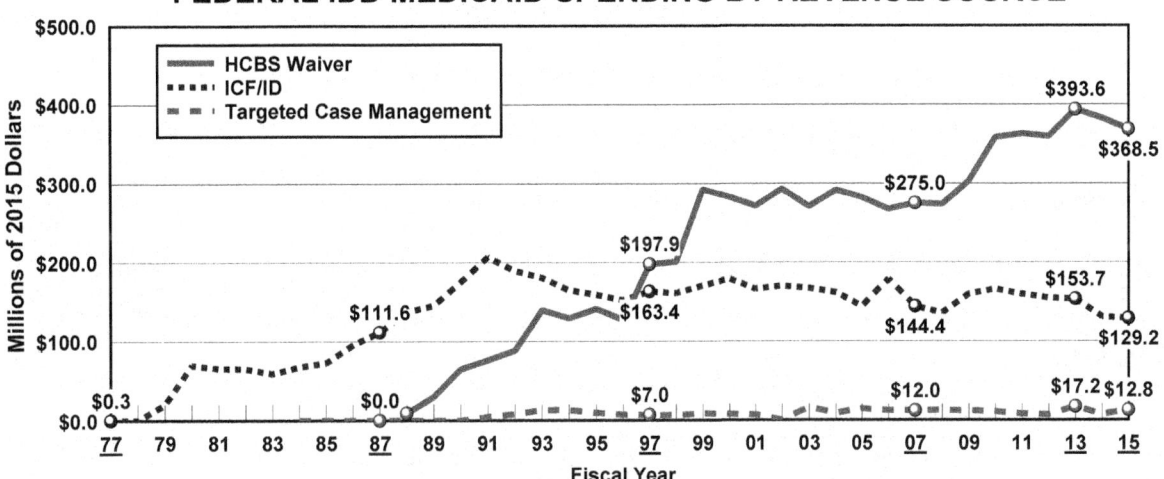

FEDERAL-STATE MEDICAID AS A PERCENTAGE OF TOTAL IDD SPENDING IN FY 2015

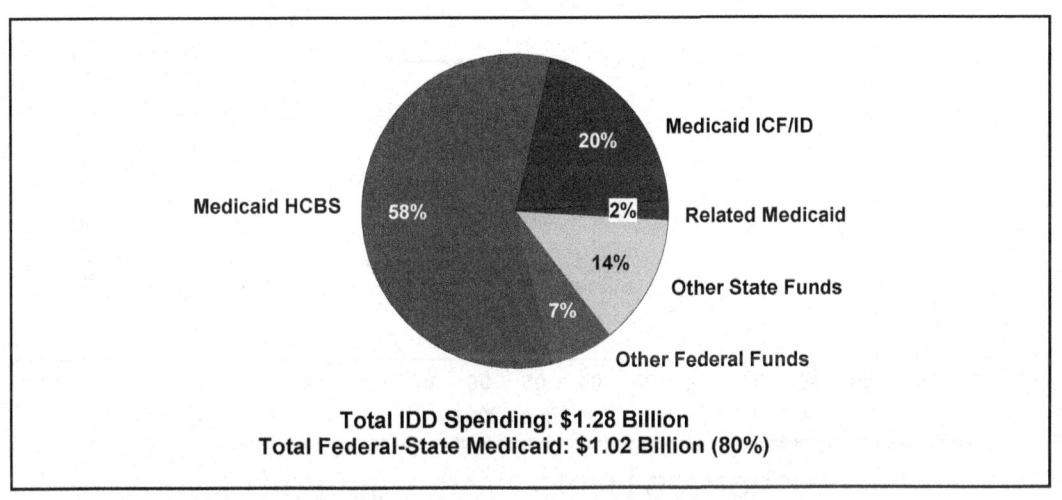

Total IDD Spending: $1.28 Billion
Total Federal-State Medicaid: $1.02 Billion (80%)

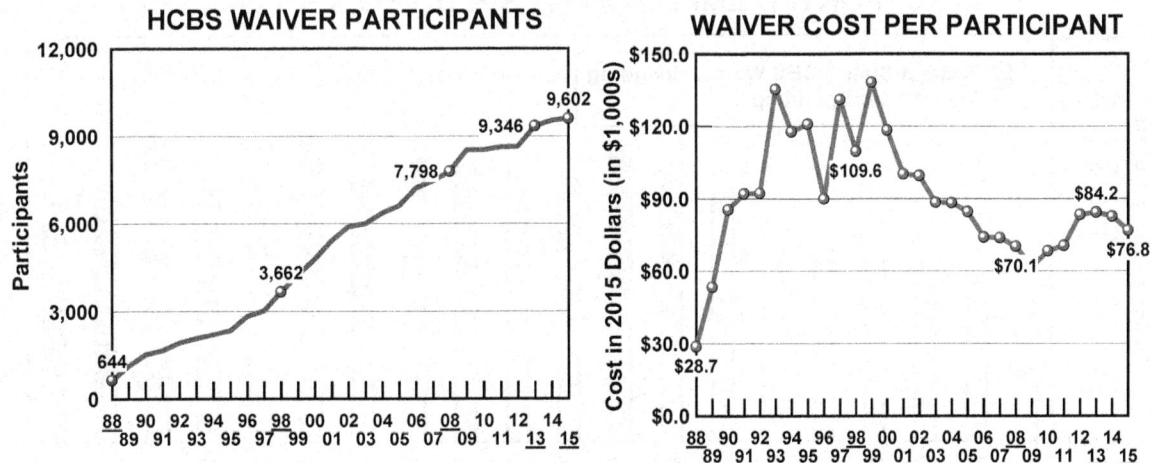

Source: Braddock et al., Coleman Institute and Department of Psychiatry, University of Colorado, 2017.
http://stateofthestates.org

CONNECTICUT
INDIVIDUAL AND FAMILY SUPPORT
SPENDING: FY 1996-2015

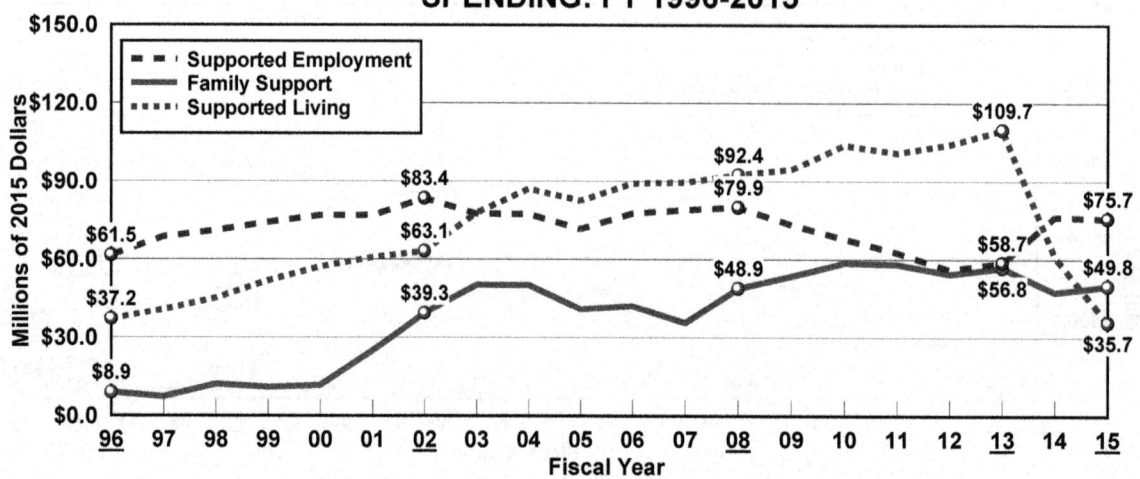

PARTICIPANTS: FY 1996-2015

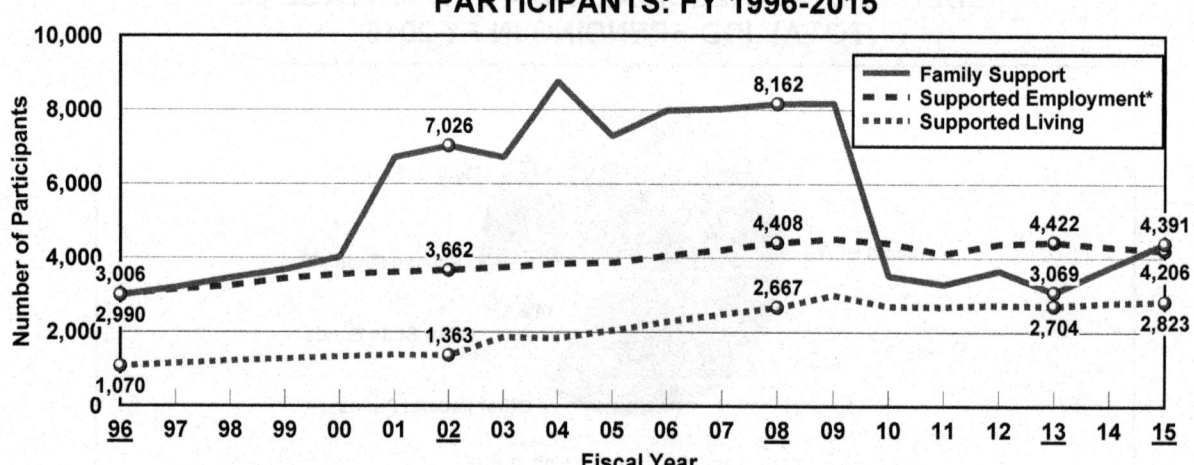

*Does not include 319 follow-along work supported workers in 2014 and 311 workers in 2015.

SUPPORTED LIVING, FAMILY SUPPORT AND SUPPORTED EMPLOYMENT SPENDING: FY 1996-2015

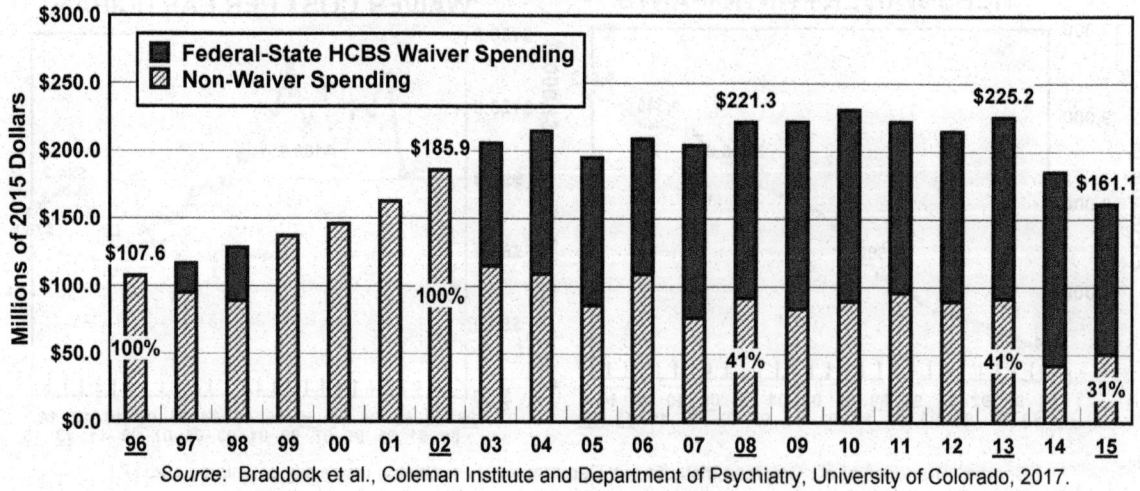

Source: Braddock et al., Coleman Institute and Department of Psychiatry, University of Colorado, 2017.

http://stateofthestates.org

CONNECTICUT

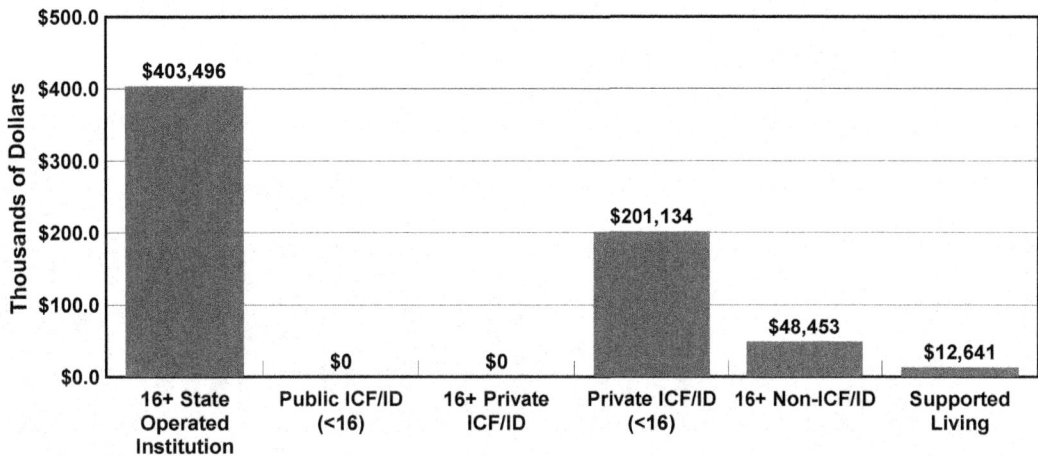

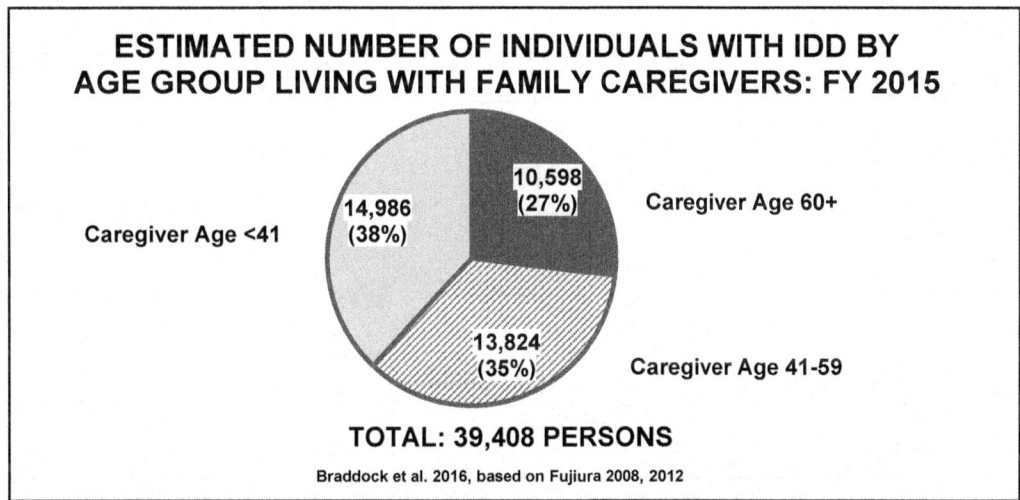

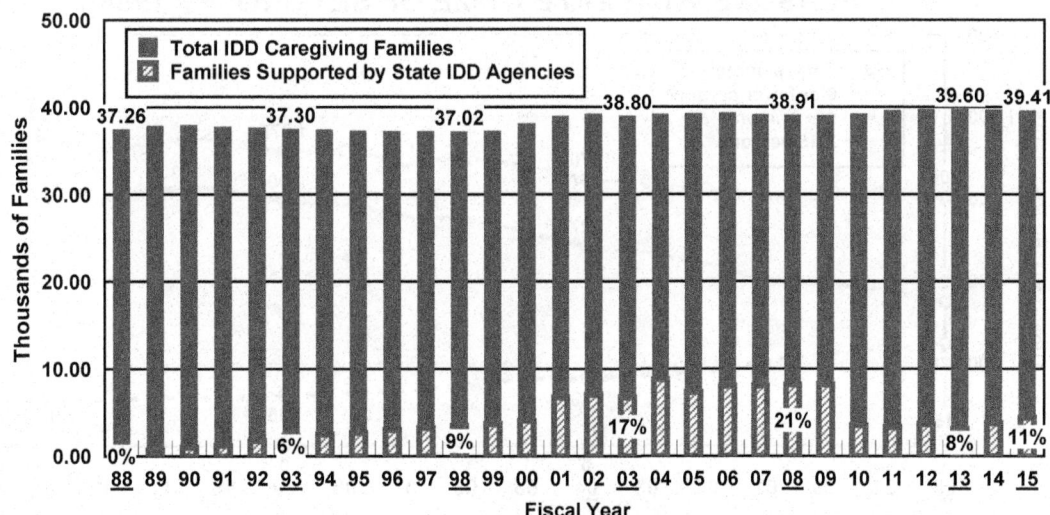

Source: Braddock et al., Coleman Institute and Department of Psychiatry, University of Colorado, 2017.
http://stateofthestates.org

DELAWARE

TOTAL PUBLIC IDD SPENDING FOR SERVICES: FY 1977-2015

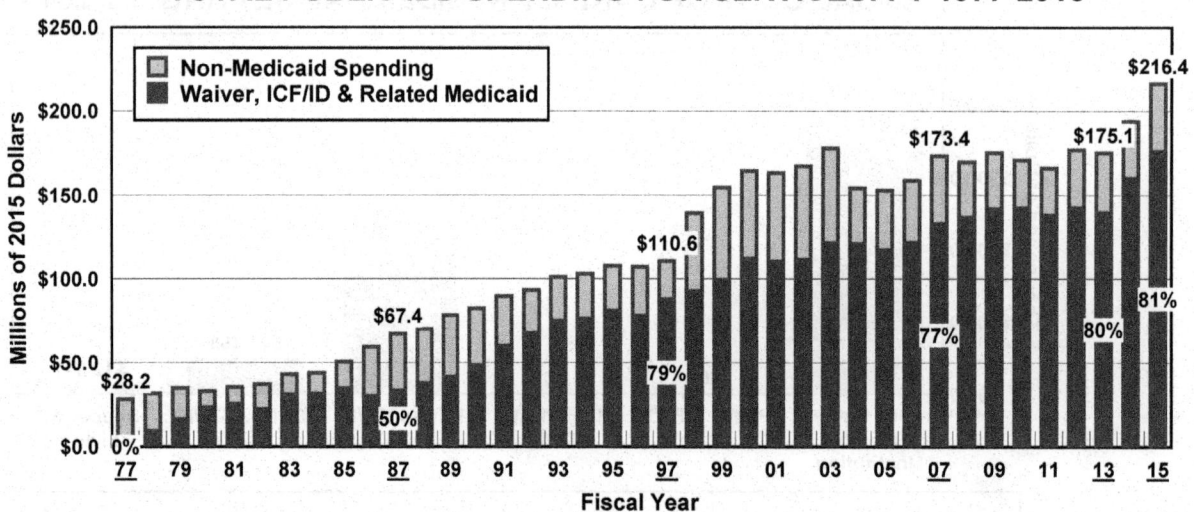

FISCAL EFFORT FOR IDD SERVICES: FY 1977-2015

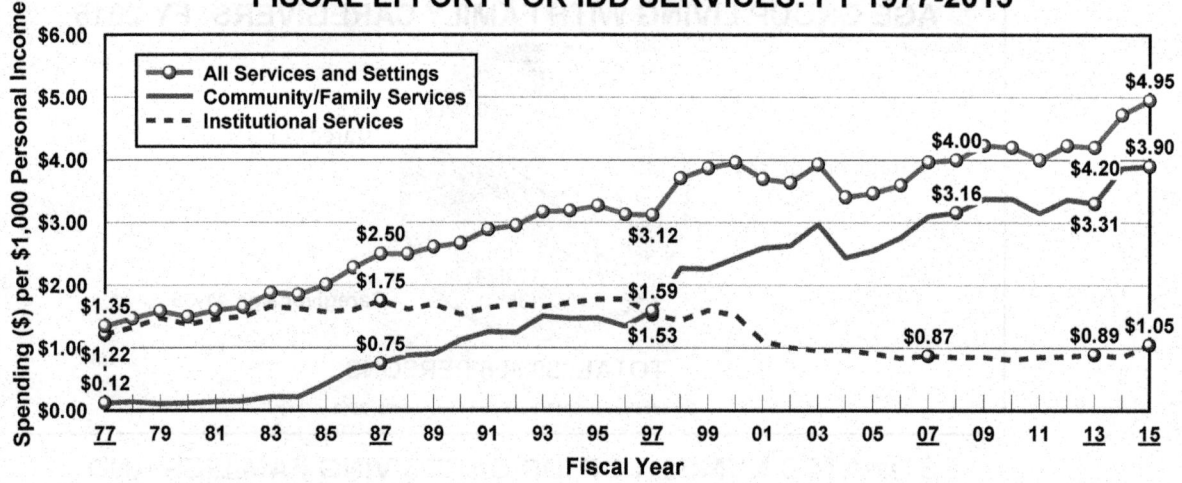

PERSONS WITH IDD BY SIZE OF SETTING: FY 1998-2015

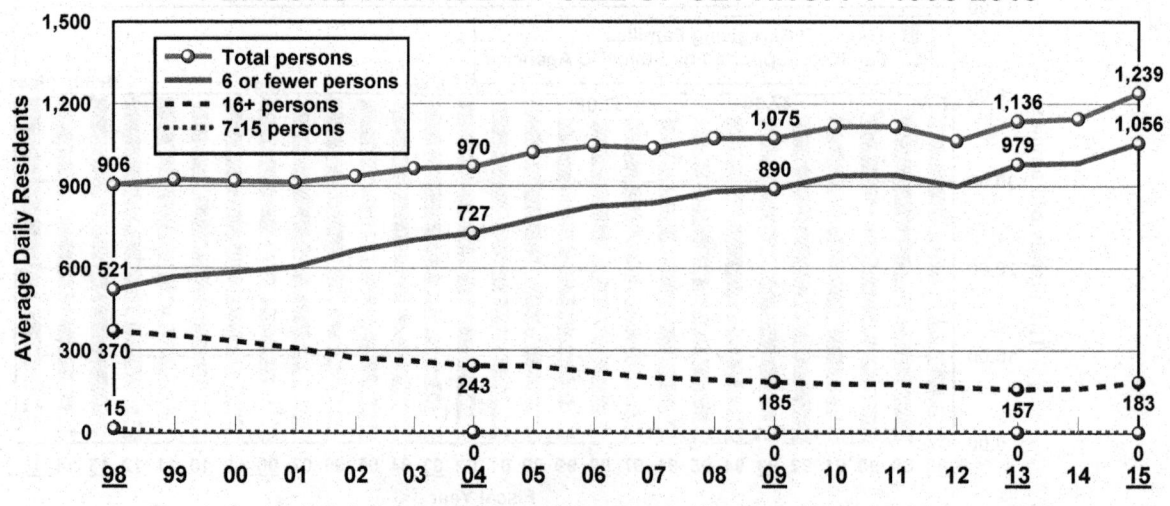

Source: Braddock et al., Coleman Institute and Department of Psychiatry, University of Colorado, 2017.
http://stateofthestates.org

DELAWARE

FEDERAL IDD MEDICAID SPENDING BY REVENUE SOURCE

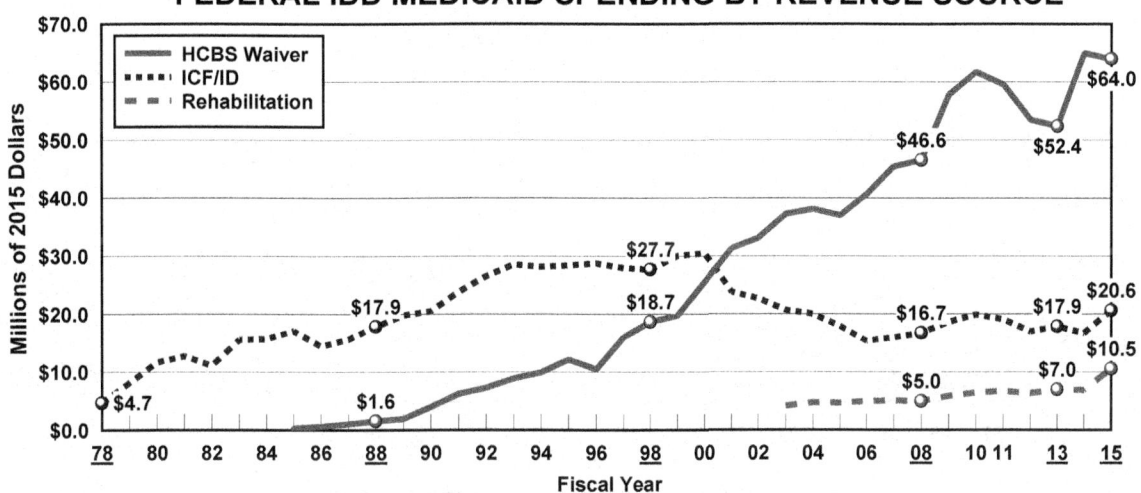

FEDERAL-STATE MEDICAID AS A PERCENTAGE OF TOTAL IDD SPENDING IN FY 2015

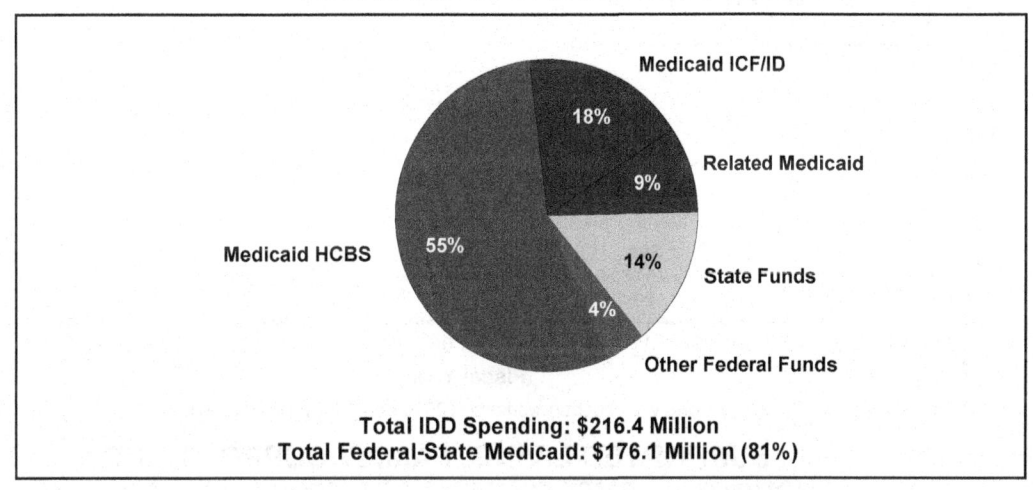

Total IDD Spending: $216.4 Million
Total Federal-State Medicaid: $176.1 Million (81%)

HCBS WAIVER PARTICIPANTS / WAIVER COST PER PARTICIPANT

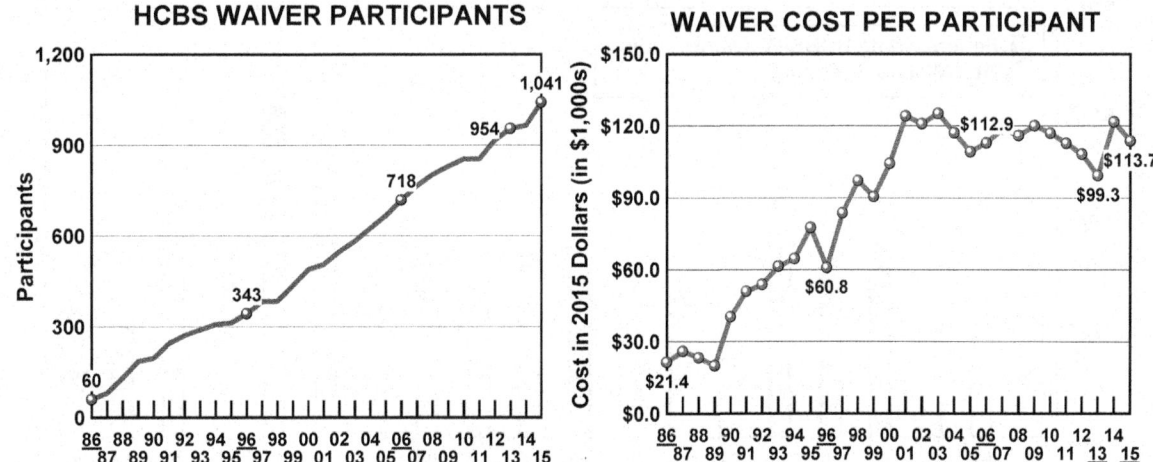

Source: Braddock et al., Coleman Institute and Department of Psychiatry, University of Colorado, 2017.
http://stateofthestates.org

DELAWARE

INDIVIDUAL AND FAMILY SUPPORT
SPENDING: FY 1996-2015

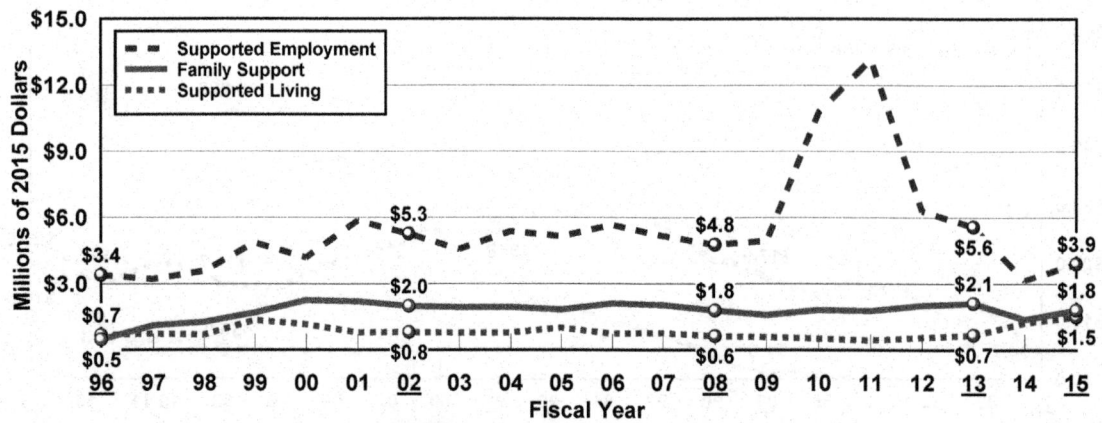

PARTICIPANTS: FY 1996-2015

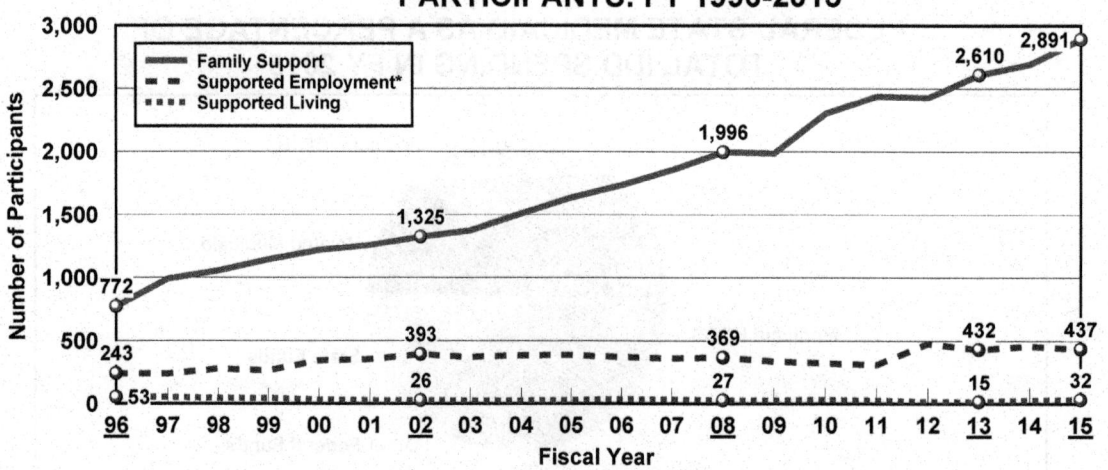

*Does not include 133 follow-along work support workers in 2014 and 560 workers in 2015.

SUPPORTED LIVING, FAMILY SUPPORT AND SUPPORTED EMPLOYMENT SPENDING: FY 1996-2015

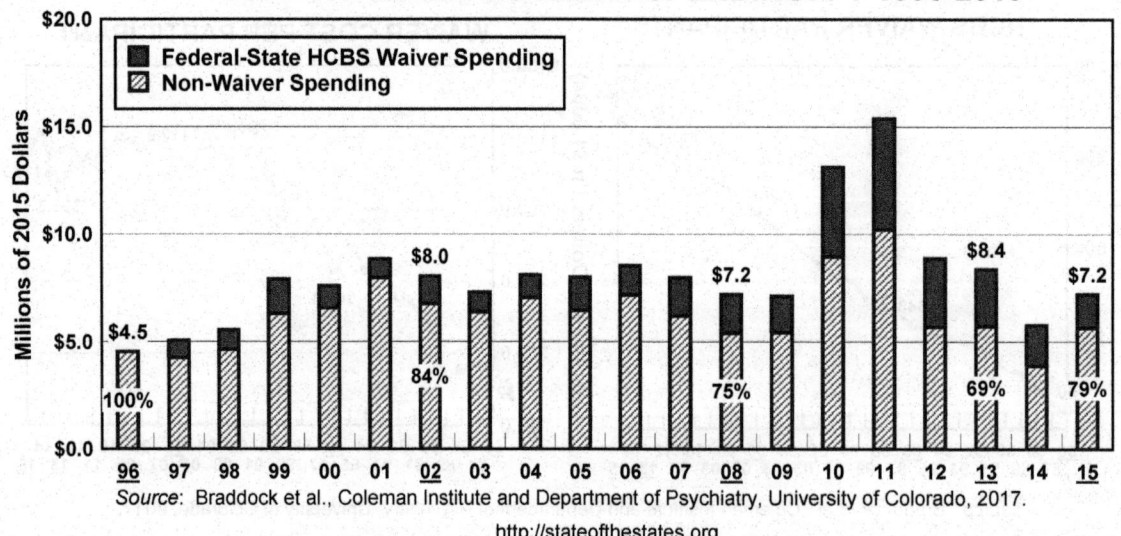

Source: Braddock et al., Coleman Institute and Department of Psychiatry, University of Colorado, 2017.
http://stateofthestates.org

DELAWARE

ANNUAL COST OF CARE BY RESIDENTIAL SETTING: FY 2015

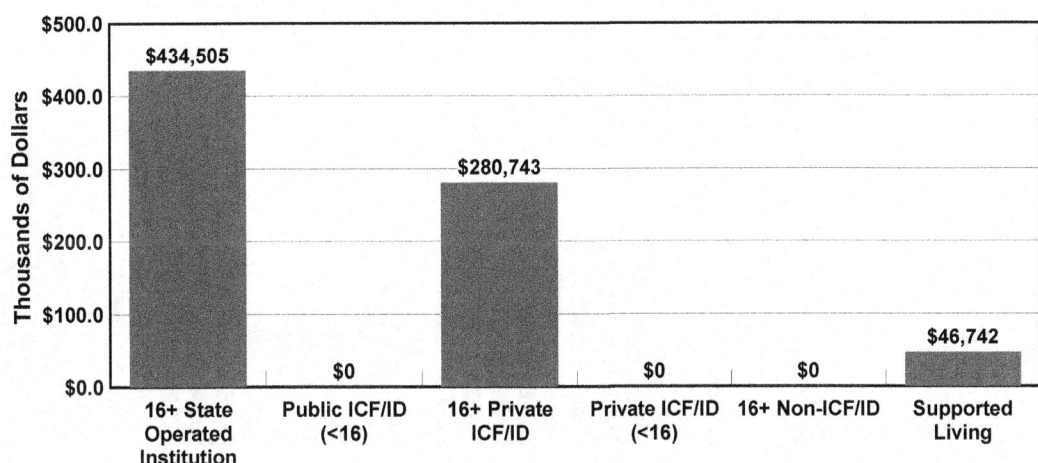

ESTIMATED NUMBER OF INDIVIDUALS WITH IDD BY AGE GROUP LIVING WITH FAMILY CAREGIVERS: FY 2015

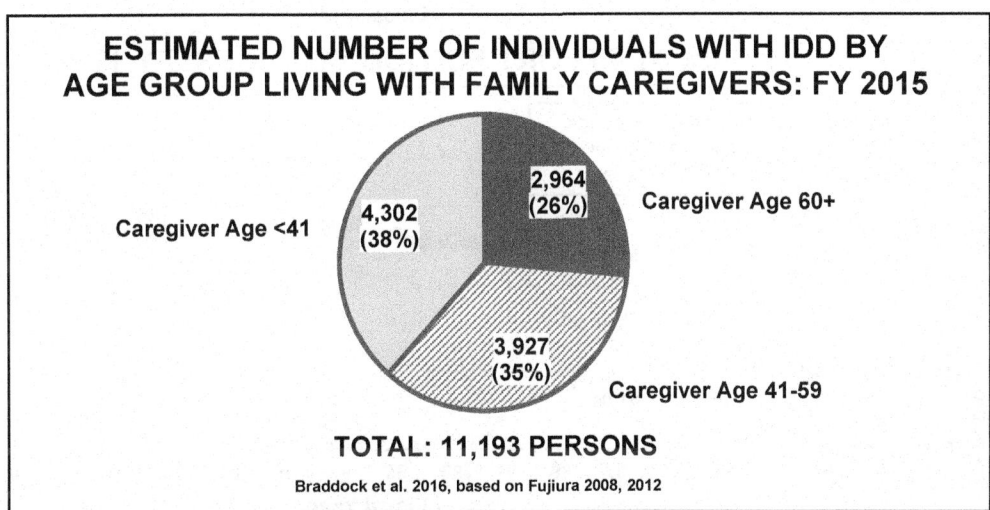

TOTAL: 11,193 PERSONS

Braddock et al. 2016, based on Fujiura 2008, 2012

ESTIMATED NUMBER OF IDD CAREGIVING FAMILIES AND FAMILIES SUPPORTED BY IDD AGENCIES: FY 1988-2015

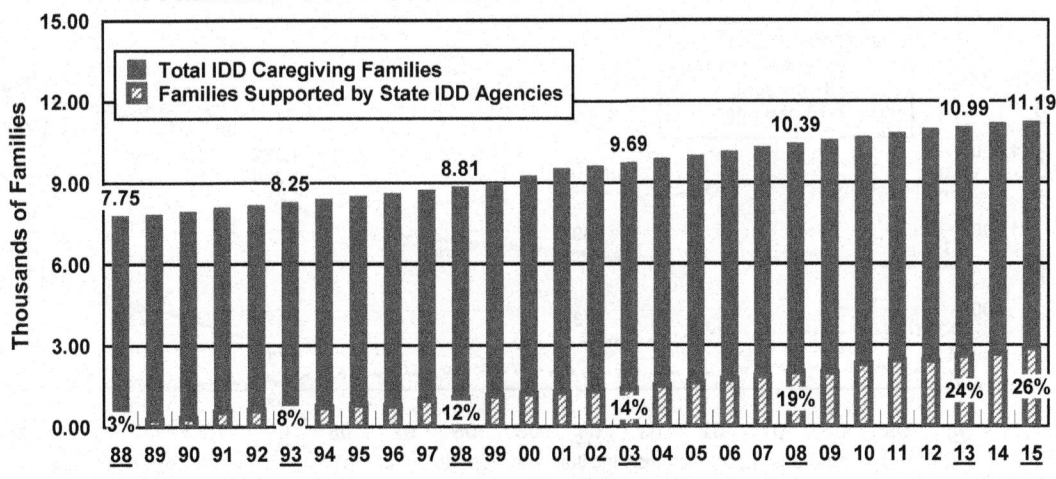

Source: Braddock et al., Coleman Institute and Department of Psychiatry, University of Colorado, 2017.

http://stateofthestates.org

DISTRICT OF COLUMBIA

TOTAL PUBLIC IDD SPENDING FOR SERVICES: FY 1977-2015

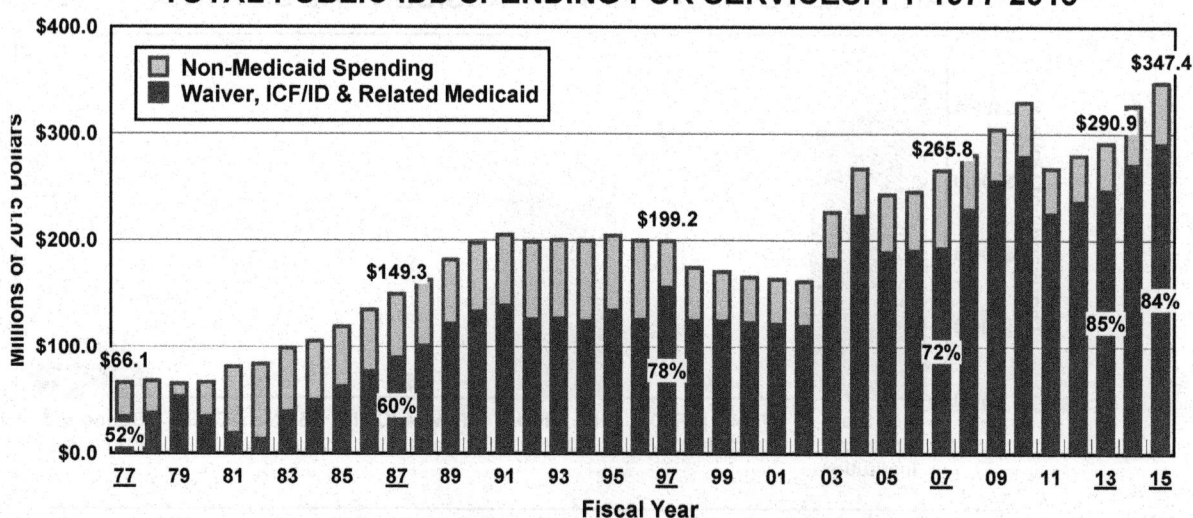

FISCAL EFFORT FOR IDD SERVICES: FY 1977-2015

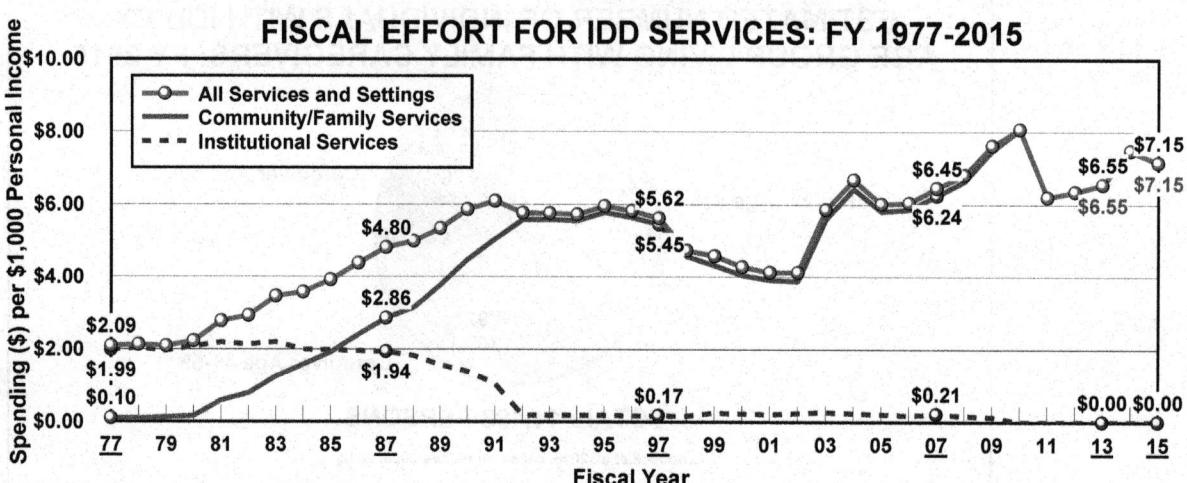

PERSONS WITH IDD BY SIZE OF SETTING: FY 1998-2015

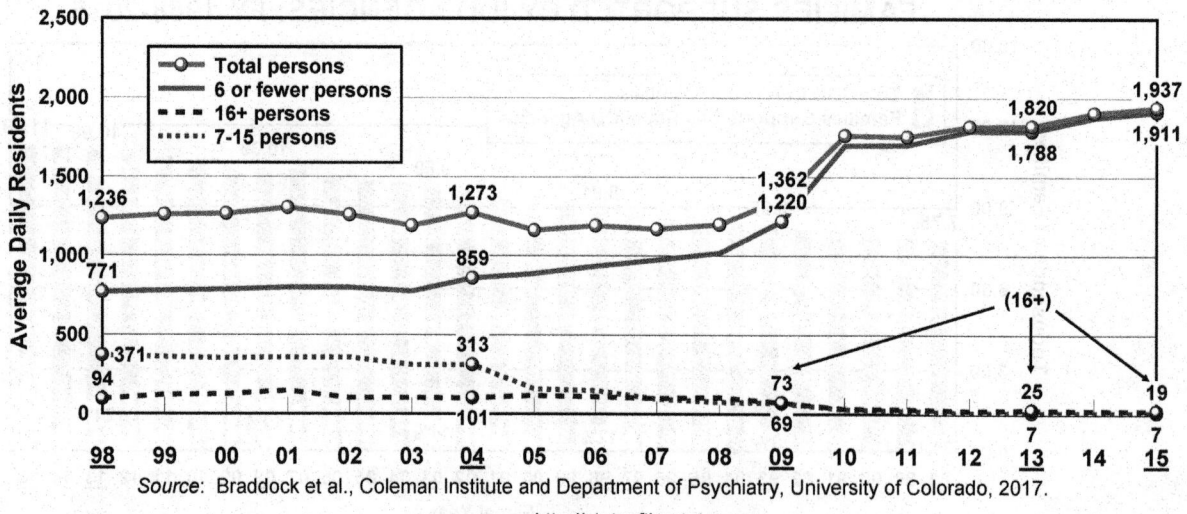

Source: Braddock et al., Coleman Institute and Department of Psychiatry, University of Colorado, 2017.
http://stateofthestates.org

DIDTRICT OF COLUMBIA

FEDERAL IDD MEDICAID SPENDING BY REVENUE SOURCE

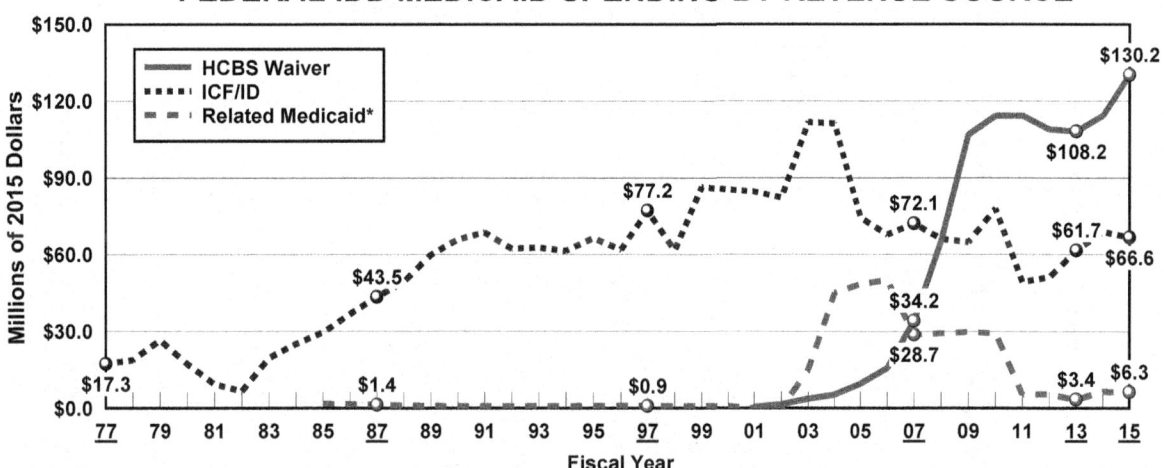

*In 2015, "Related Medicaid" was clinic rehabitiation (0.2 million) and administration ($6.1 million).

FEDERAL-STATE MEDICAID AS A PERCENTAGE OF TOTAL IDD SPENDING IN FY 2015

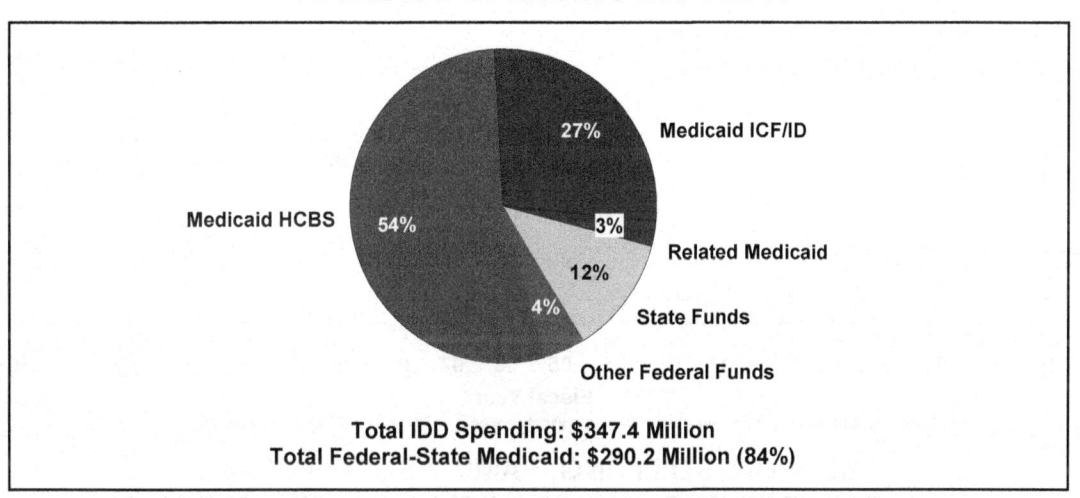

Total IDD Spending: $347.4 Million
Total Federal-State Medicaid: $290.2 Million (84%)

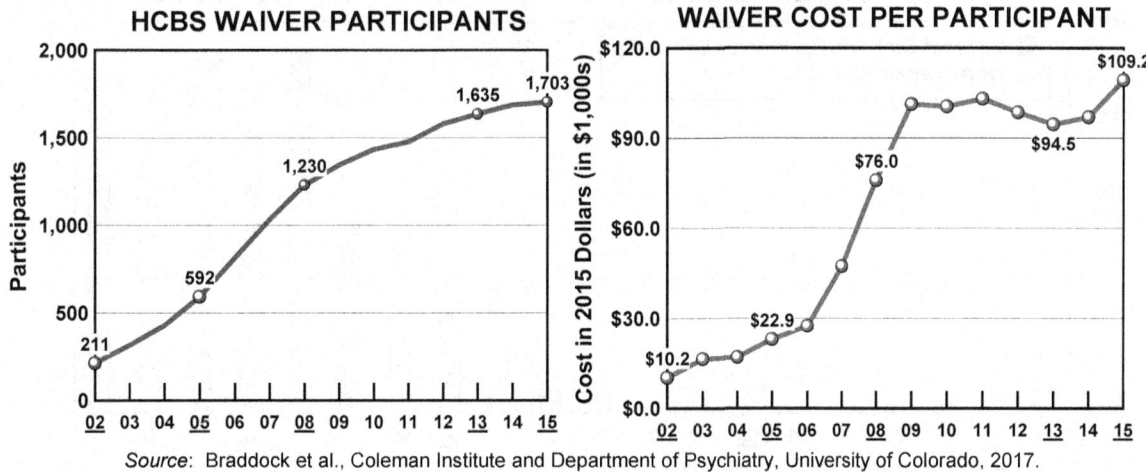

Source: Braddock et al., Coleman Institute and Department of Psychiatry, University of Colorado, 2017.
http://stateofthestates.org

DISTRICT OF COLUMBIA
INDIVIDUAL AND FAMILY SUPPORT
SPENDING: FY 1996-2015

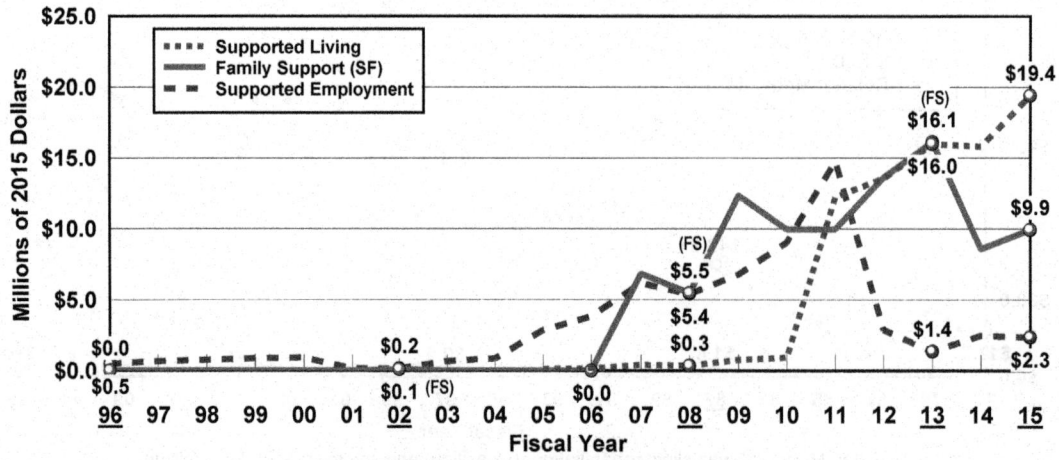

PARTICIPANTS: FY 1996-2015

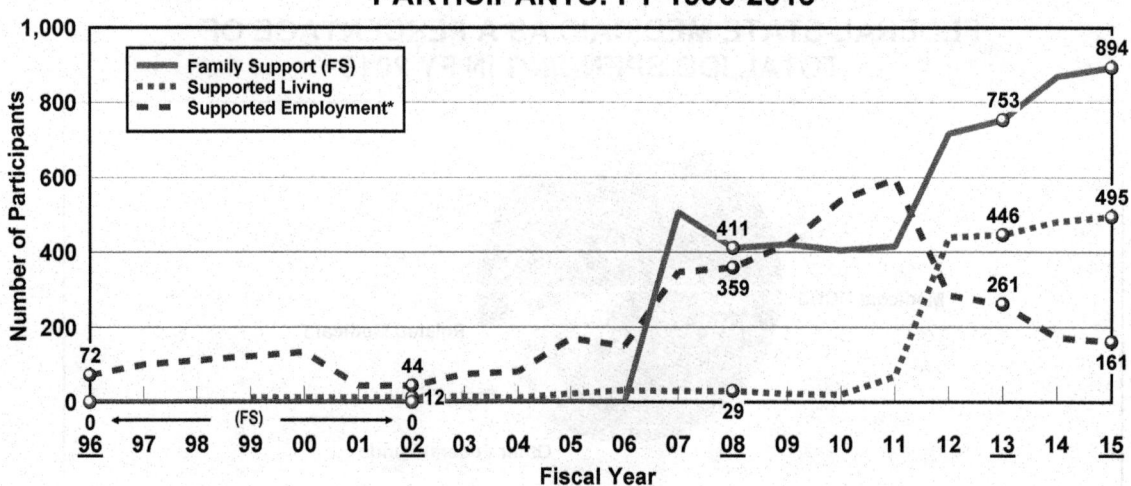

*Does not include 253 follow-along work support workers in 2014 and 269 workers in 2015.

SUPPORTED LIVING, FAMILY SUPPORT AND SUPPORTED EMPLOYMENT SPENDING: FY 1996-2015

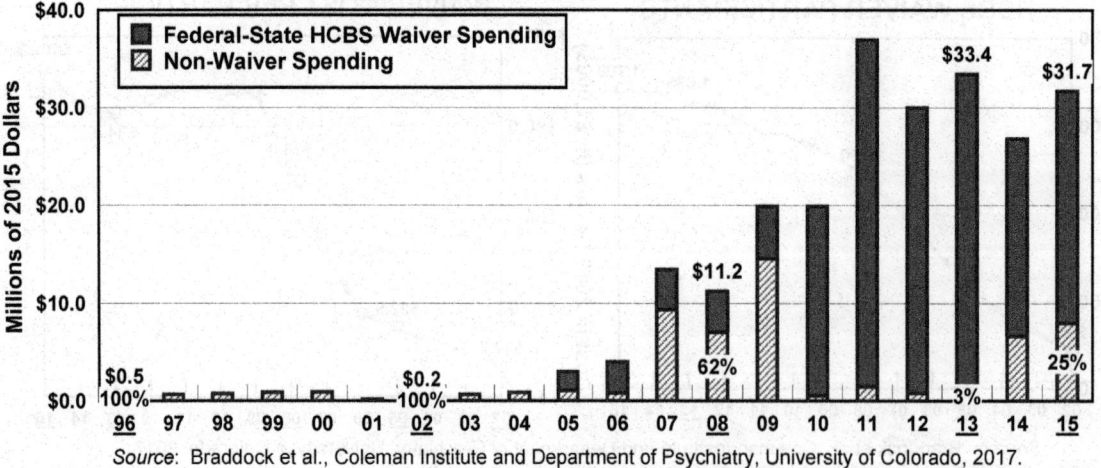

Source: Braddock et al., Coleman Institute and Department of Psychiatry, University of Colorado, 2017.

http://stateofthestates.org

DISTRICT OF COLUMBIA

ANNUAL COST OF CARE BY RESIDENTIAL SETTING: FY 2015

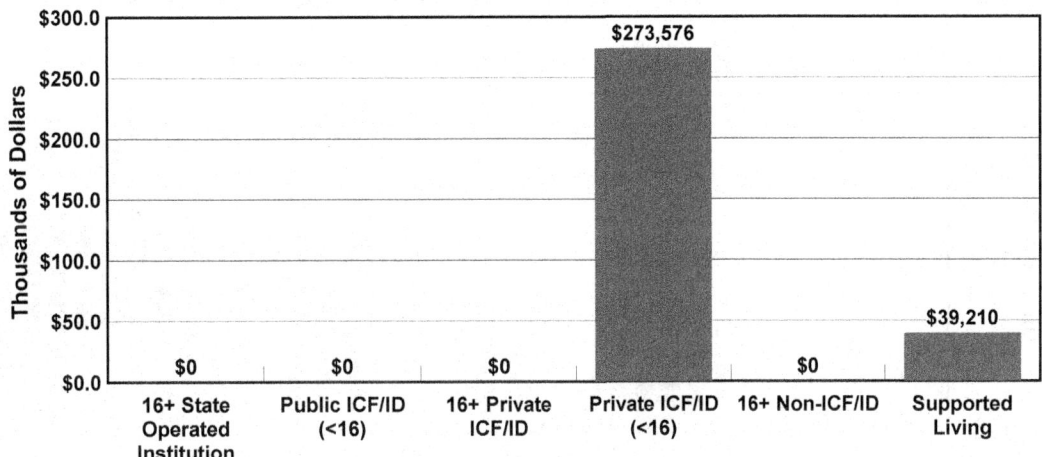

ESTIMATED NUMBER OF INDIVIDUALS WITH IDD BY AGE GROUP LIVING WITH FAMILY CAREGIVERS: FY 2015

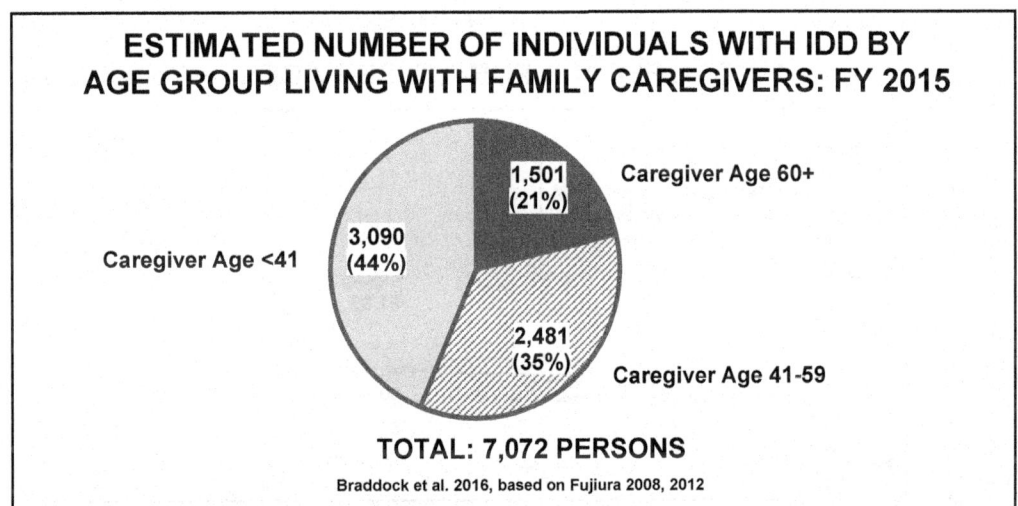

TOTAL: 7,072 PERSONS

Braddock et al. 2016, based on Fujiura 2008, 2012

ESTIMATED NUMBER OF IDD CAREGIVING FAMILIES AND FAMILIES SUPPORTED BY IDD AGENCIES: FY 1988-2015

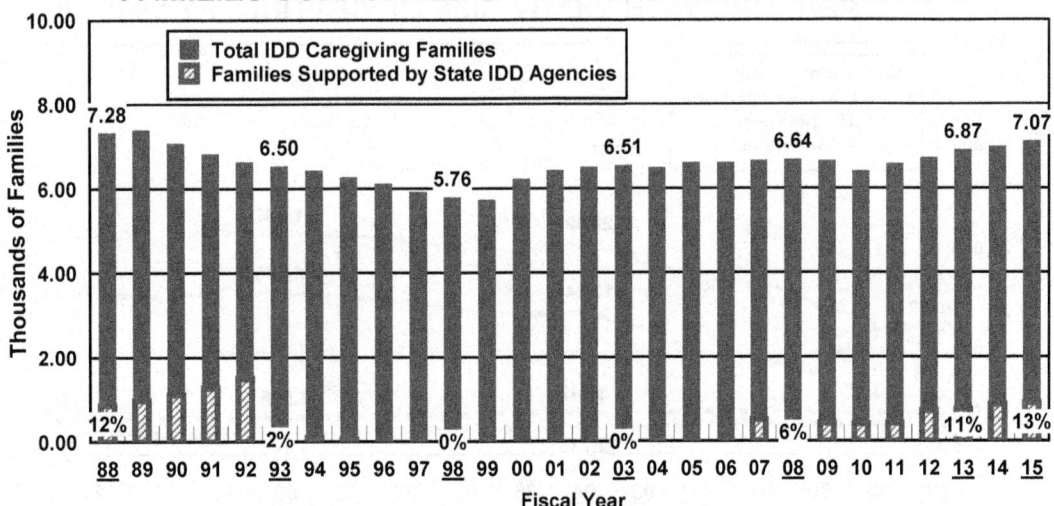

Source: Braddock et al., Coleman Institute and Department of Psychiatry, University of Colorado, 2017.
http://stateofthestates.org

FLORIDA

TOTAL PUBLIC IDD SPENDING FOR SERVICES: FY 1977-2015

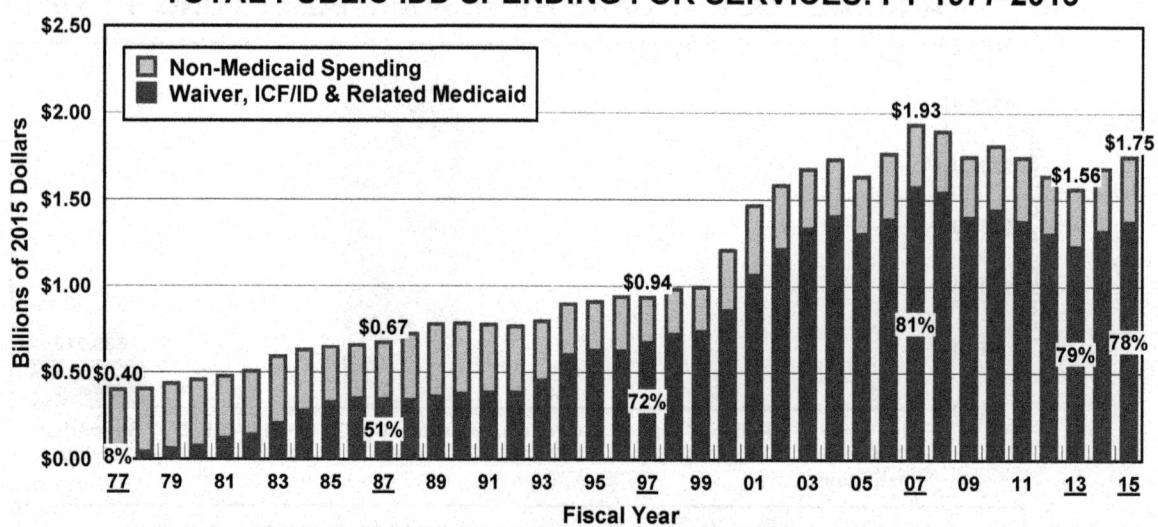

FISCAL EFFORT FOR IDD SERVICES: FY 1977-2015

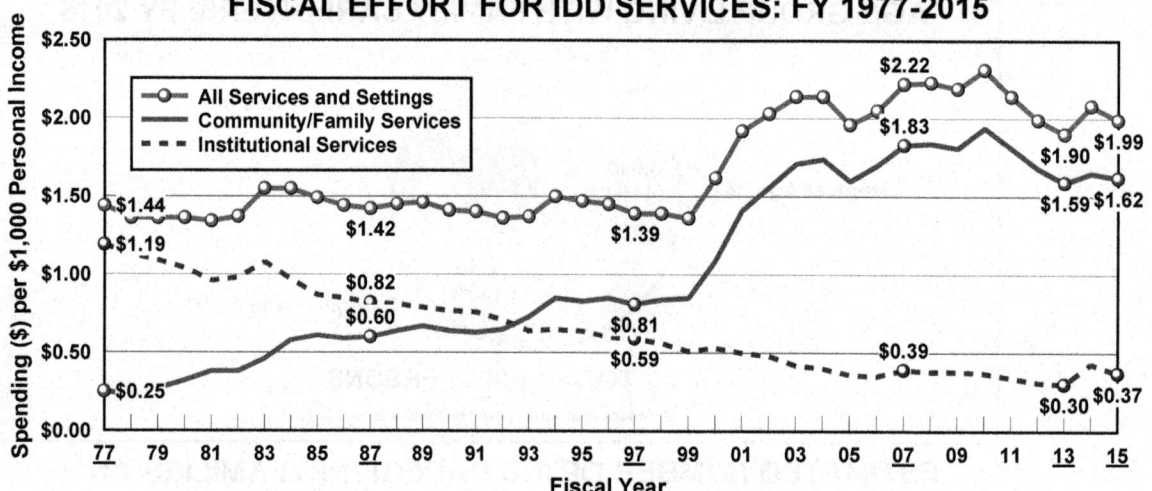

PERSONS WITH IDD BY SIZE OF SETTING: FY 1998-2015

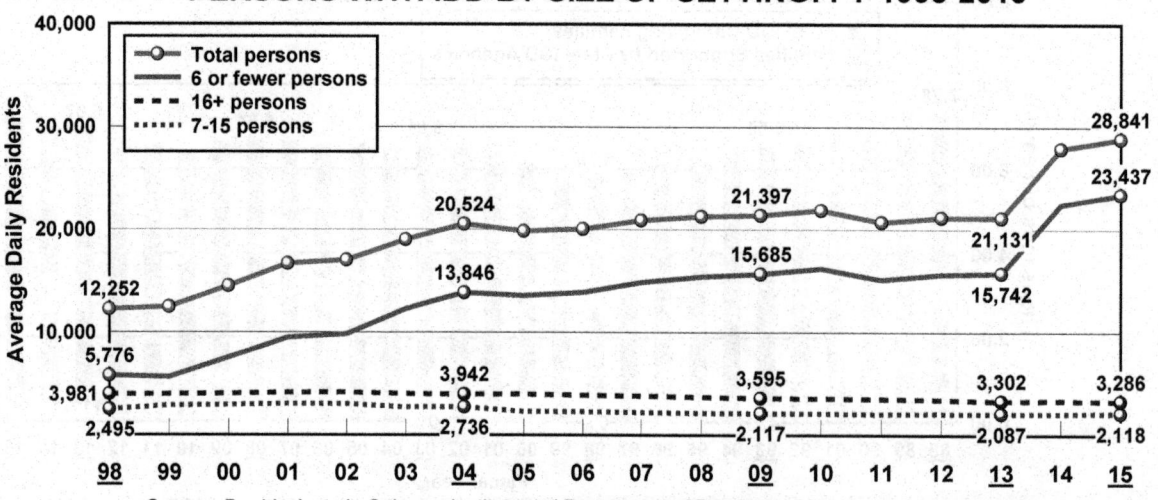

Source: Braddock et al., Coleman Institute and Department of Psychiatry, University of Colorado, 2017.
http://stateofthestates.org

FLORIDA

FEDERAL IDD MEDICAID SPENDING BY REVENUE SOURCE

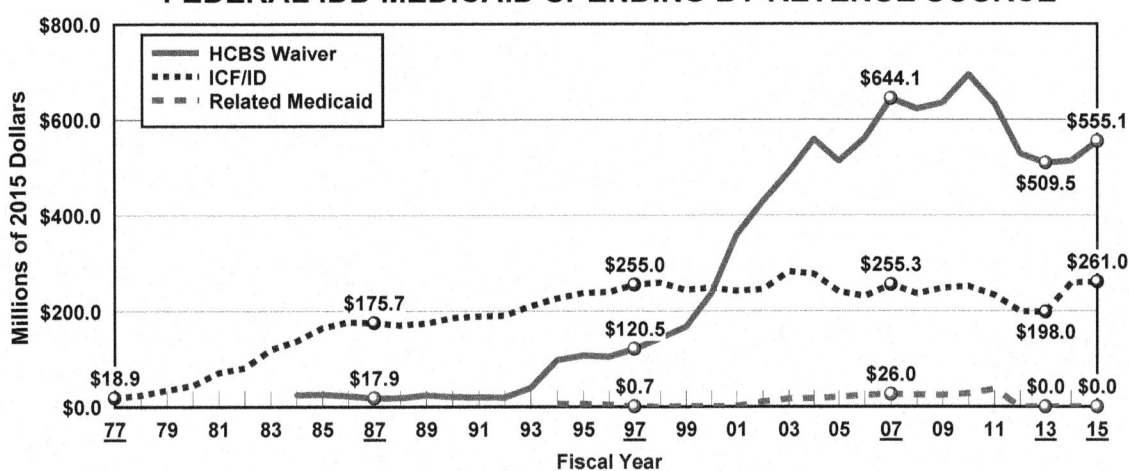

FEDERAL-STATE MEDICAID AS A PERCENTAGE OF TOTAL IDD SPENDING IN FY 2015

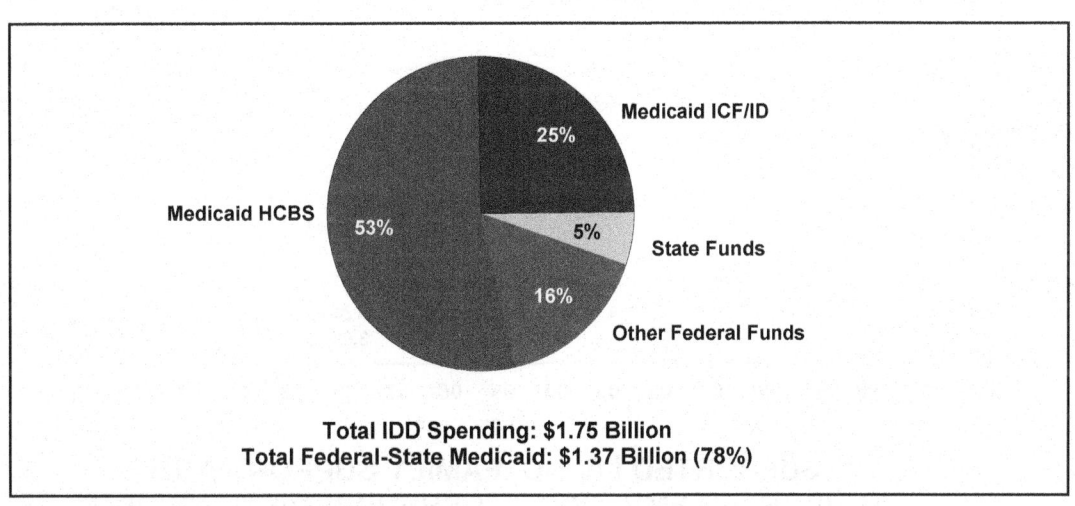

Total IDD Spending: $1.75 Billion
Total Federal-State Medicaid: $1.37 Billion (78%)

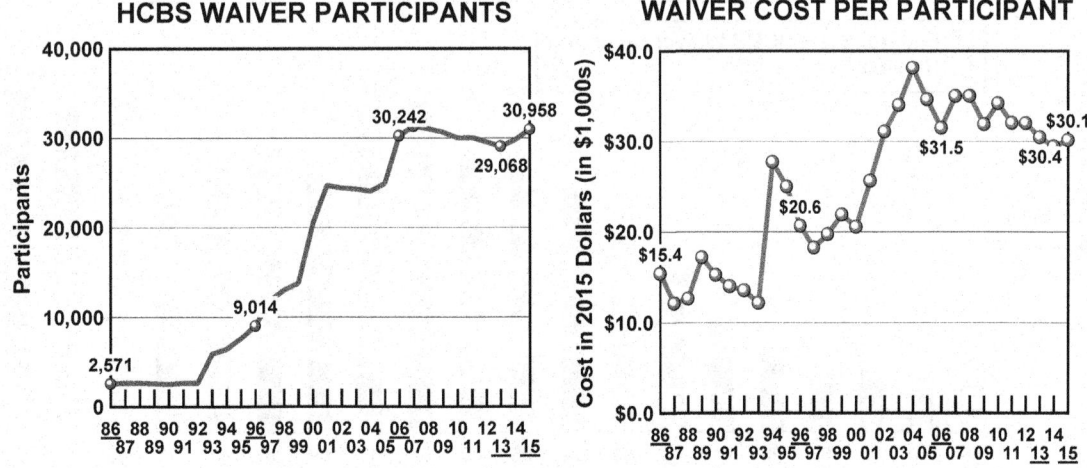

Source: Braddock et al., Coleman Institute and Department of Psychiatry, University of Colorado, 2017.
http://stateofthestates.org

FLORIDA

INDIVIDUAL AND FAMILY SUPPORT SPENDING: FY 1996-2015

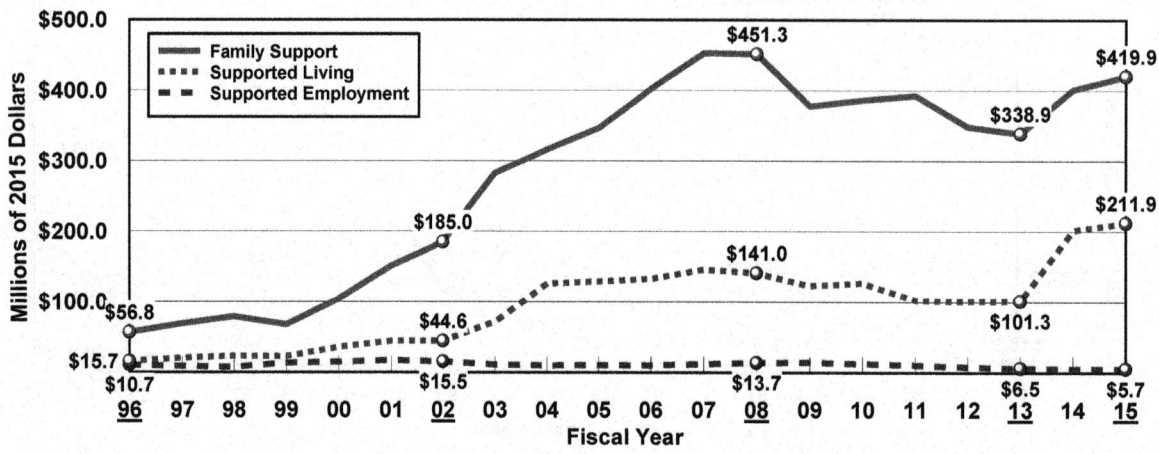

PARTICIPANTS: FY 1996-2015

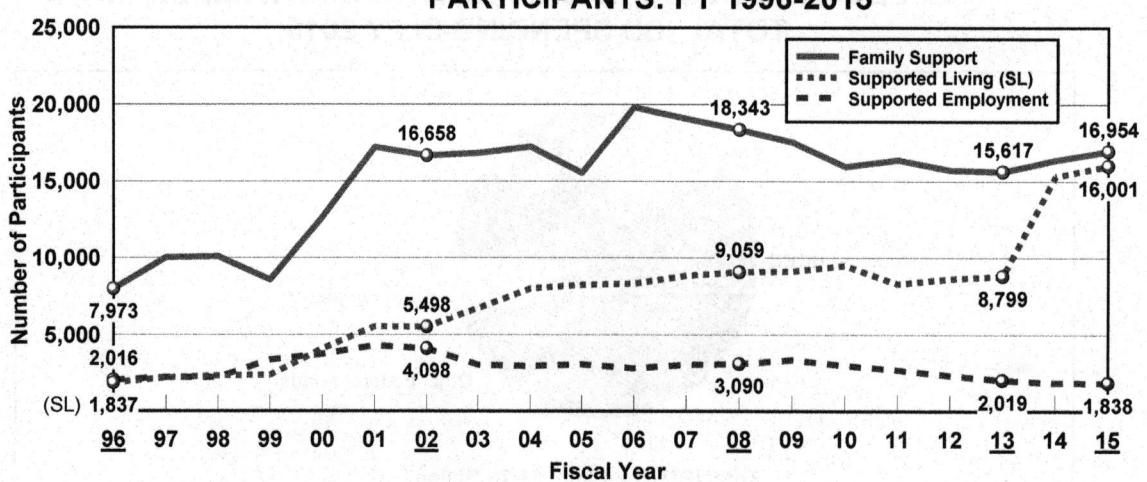

SUPPORTED LIVING, FAMILY SUPPORT AND SUPPORTED EMPLOYMENT SPENDING: FY 1996-2015

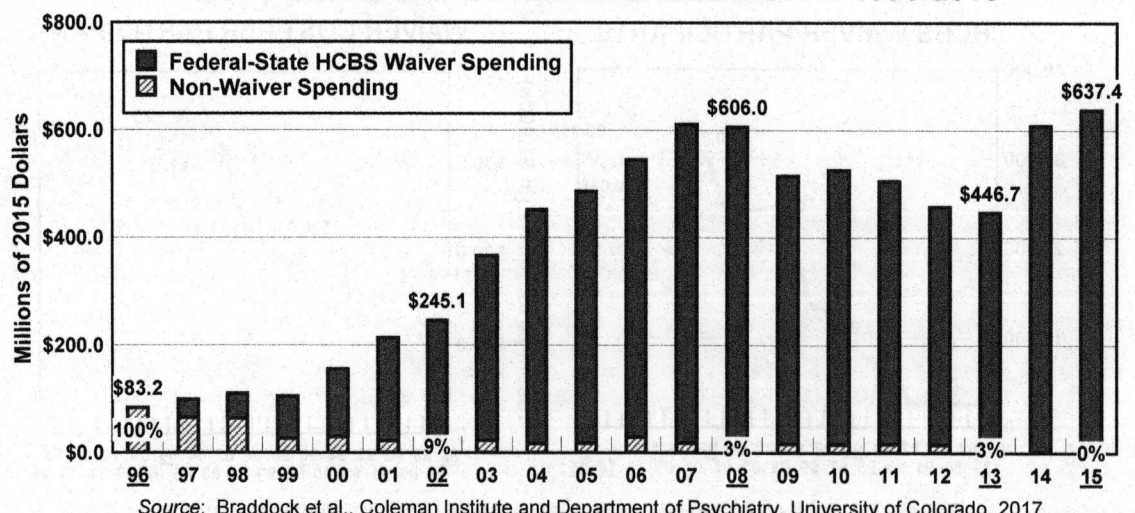

Source: Braddock et al., Coleman Institute and Department of Psychiatry, University of Colorado, 2017.
http://stateofthestates.org

FLORIDA

ANNUAL COST OF CARE BY RESIDENTIAL SETTING: FY 2015

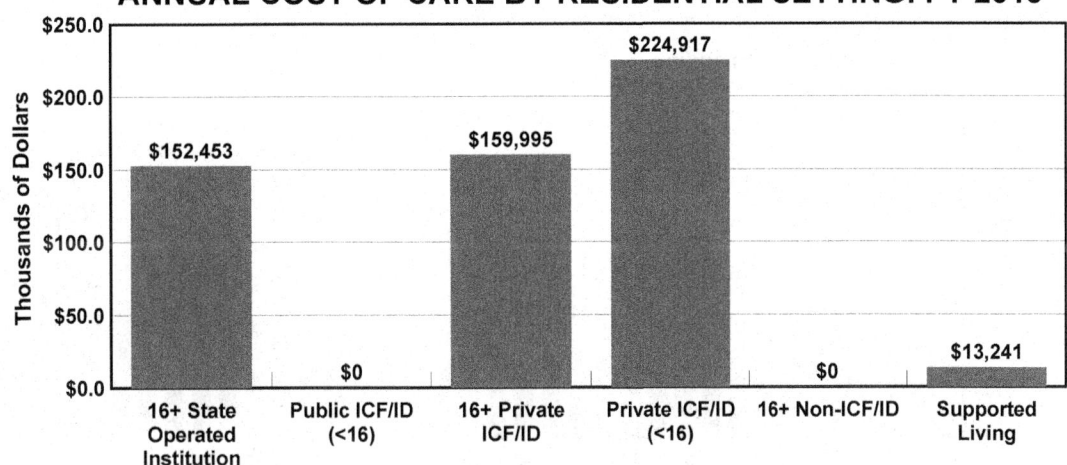

ESTIMATED NUMBER OF INDIVIDUALS WITH IDD BY AGE GROUP LIVING WITH FAMILY CAREGIVERS: FY 2015

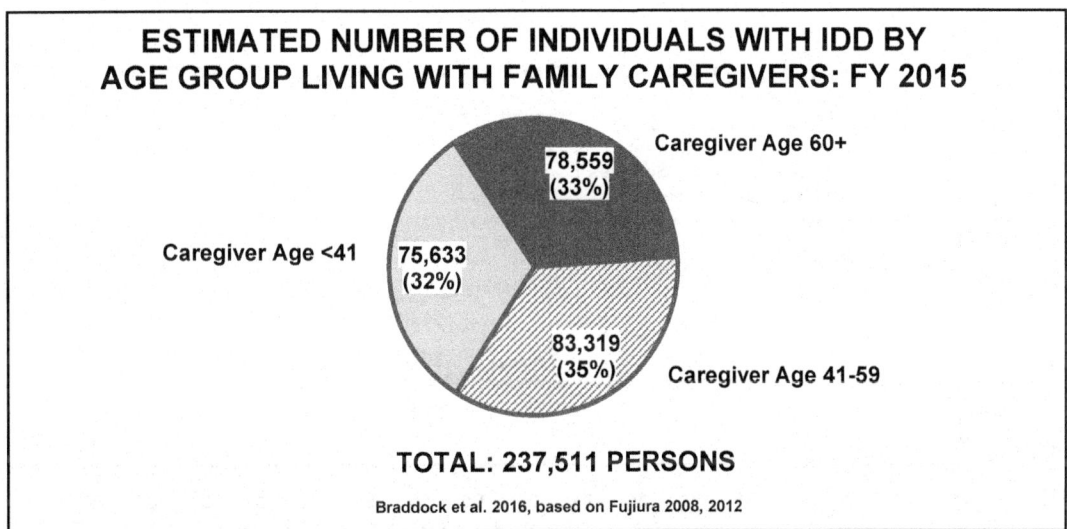

TOTAL: 237,511 PERSONS

Braddock et al. 2016, based on Fujiura 2008, 2012

ESTIMATED NUMBER OF IDD CAREGIVING FAMILIES AND FAMILIES SUPPORTED BY IDD AGENCIES: FY 1988-2015

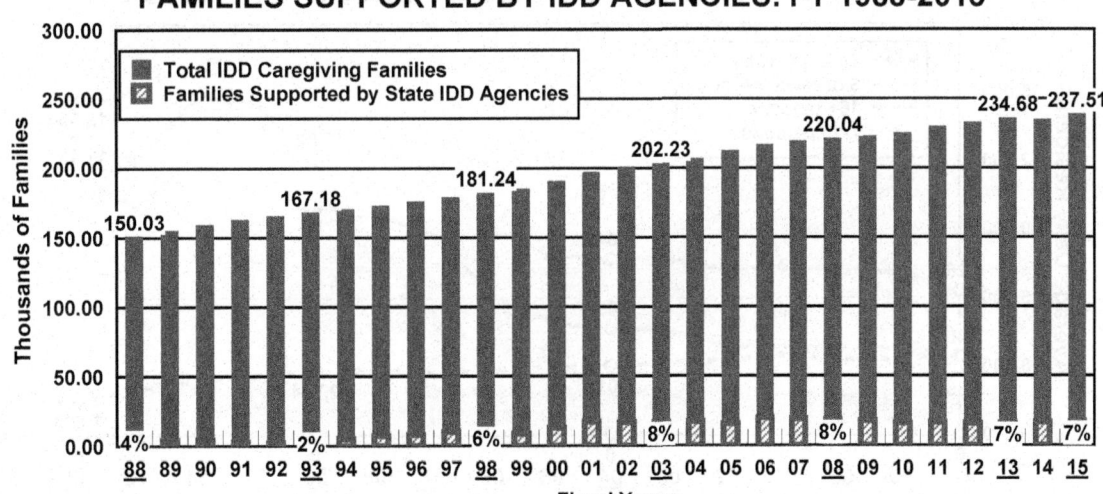

Source: Braddock et al., Coleman Institute and Department of Psychiatry, University of Colorado, 2017.

http://stateofthestates.org

GEORGIA

TOTAL PUBLIC IDD SPENDING FOR SERVICES: FY 1977-2015

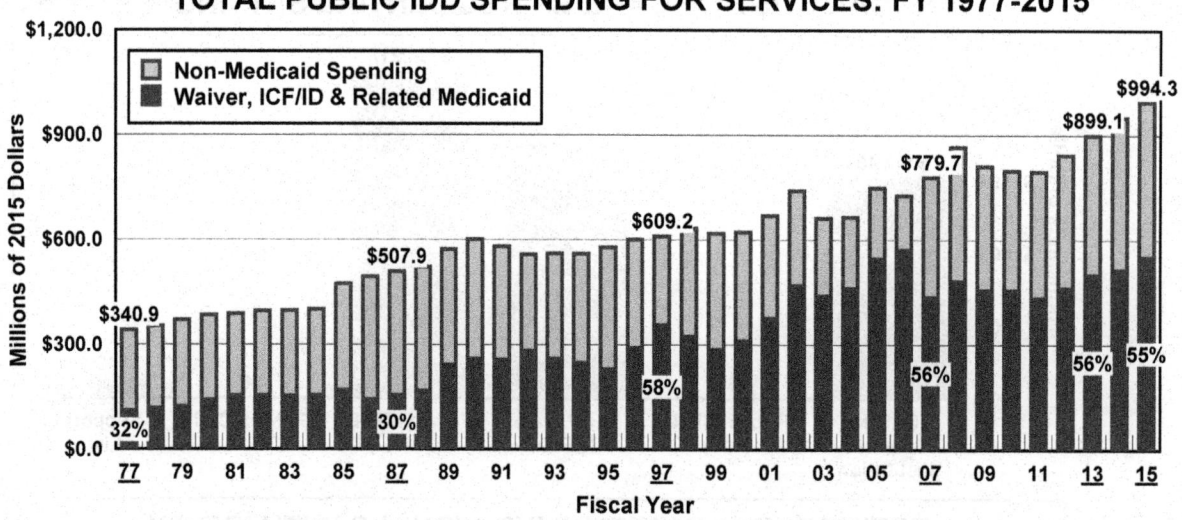

FISCAL EFFORT FOR IDD SERVICES: FY 1977-2015

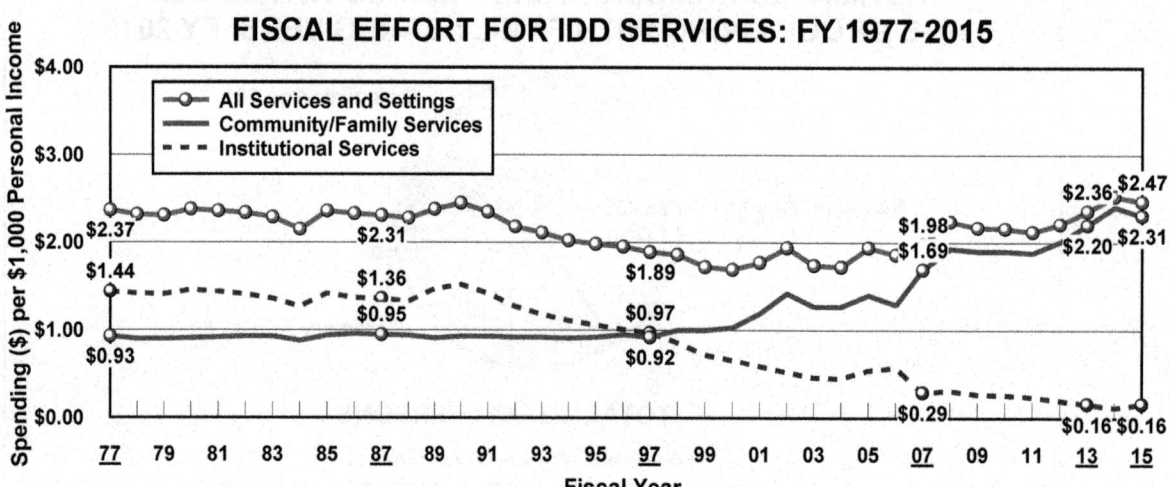

PERSONS WITH IDD BY SIZE OF SETTING: FY 1998-2015

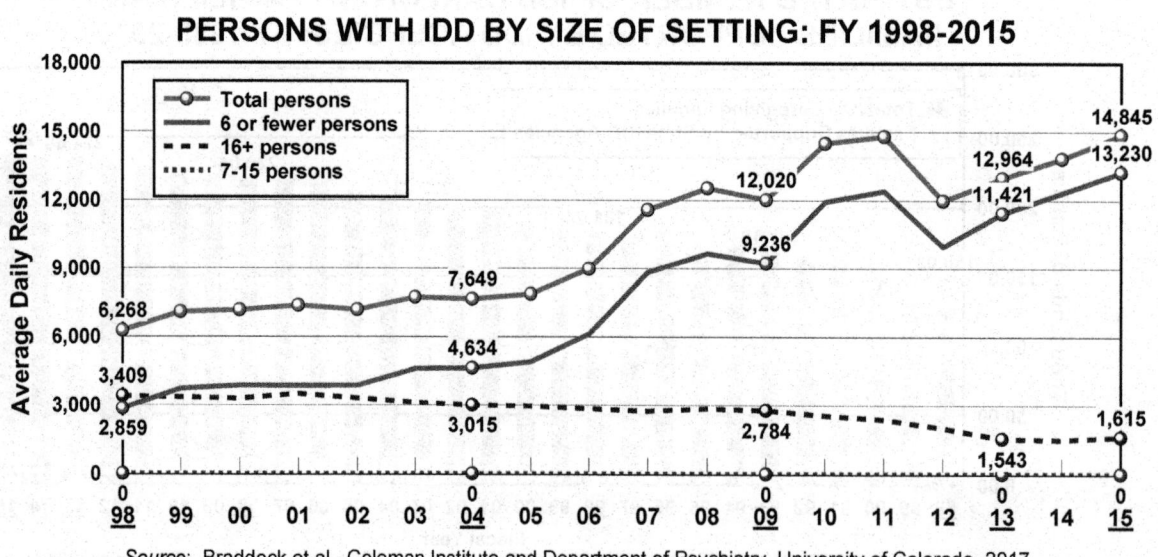

Source: Braddock et al., Coleman Institute and Department of Psychiatry, University of Colorado, 2017.
http://stateofthestates.org

GEORGIA

FEDERAL IDD MEDICAID SPENDING BY REVENUE SOURCE

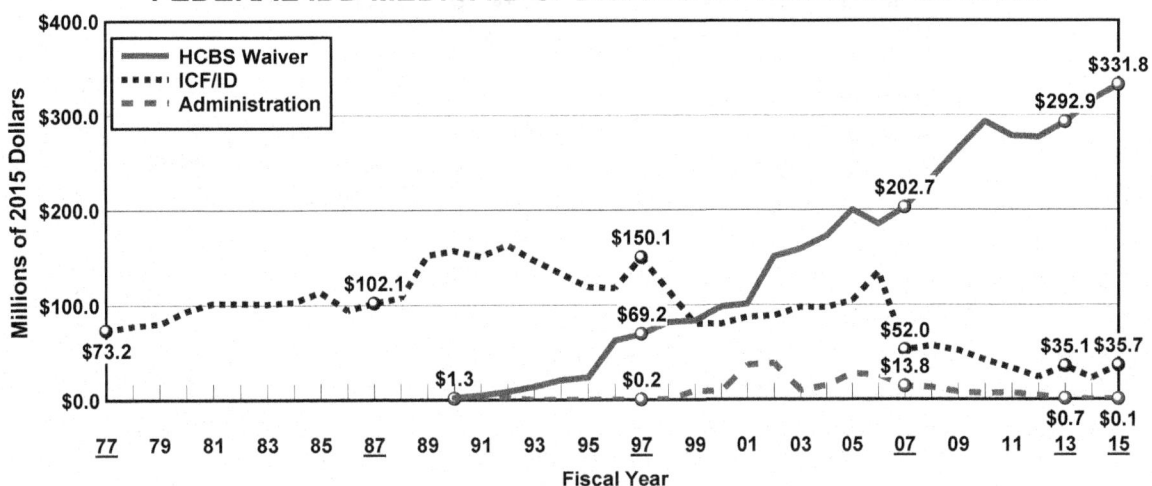

FEDERAL-STATE MEDICAID AS A PERCENTAGE OF TOTAL IDD SPENDING IN FY 2015

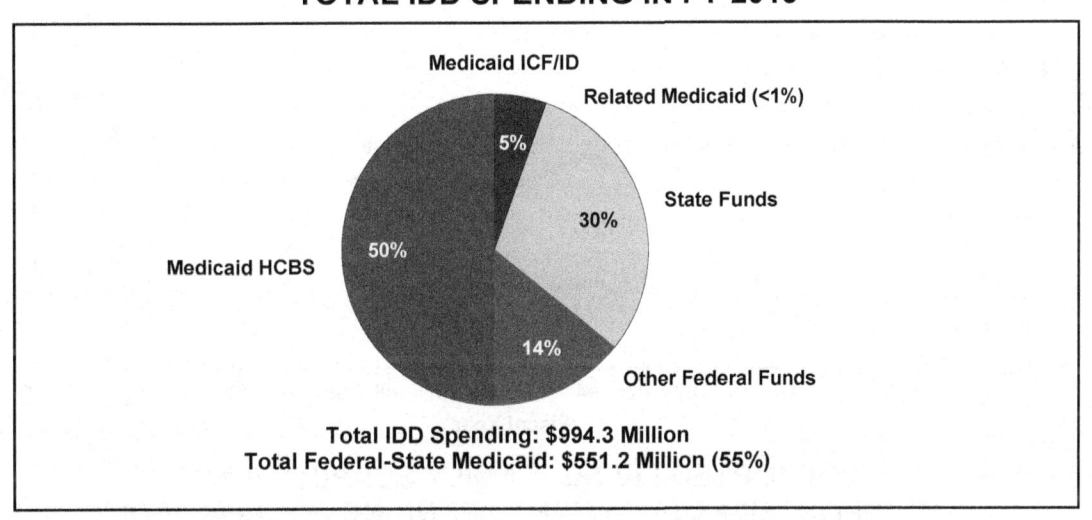

Total IDD Spending: $994.3 Million
Total Federal-State Medicaid: $551.2 Million (55%)

HCBS WAIVER PARTICIPANTS / WAIVER COST PER PARTICIPANT

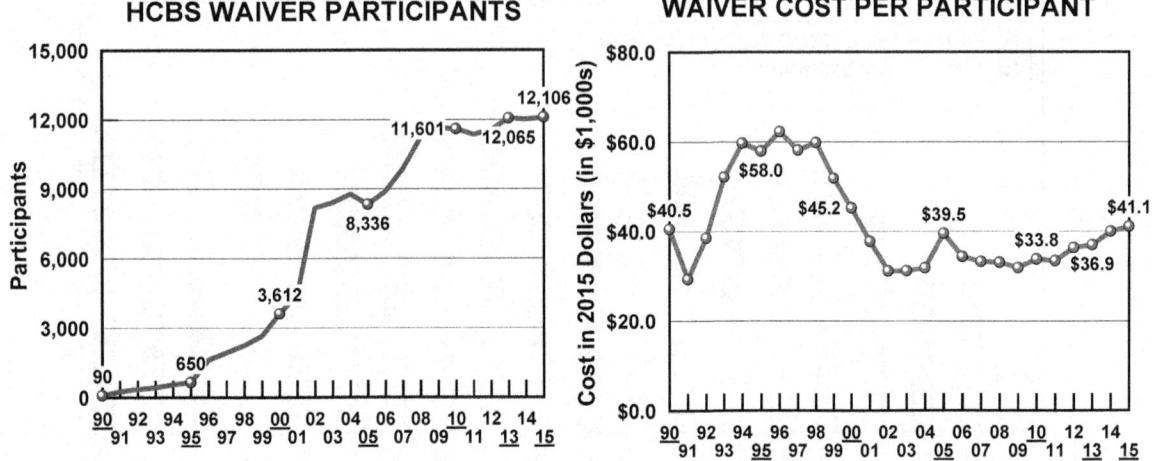

Source: Braddock et al., Coleman Institute and Department of Psychiatry, University of Colorado, 2017.
http://stateofthestates.org

GEORGIA

INDIVIDUAL AND FAMILY SUPPORT
SPENDING: FY 1996-2015

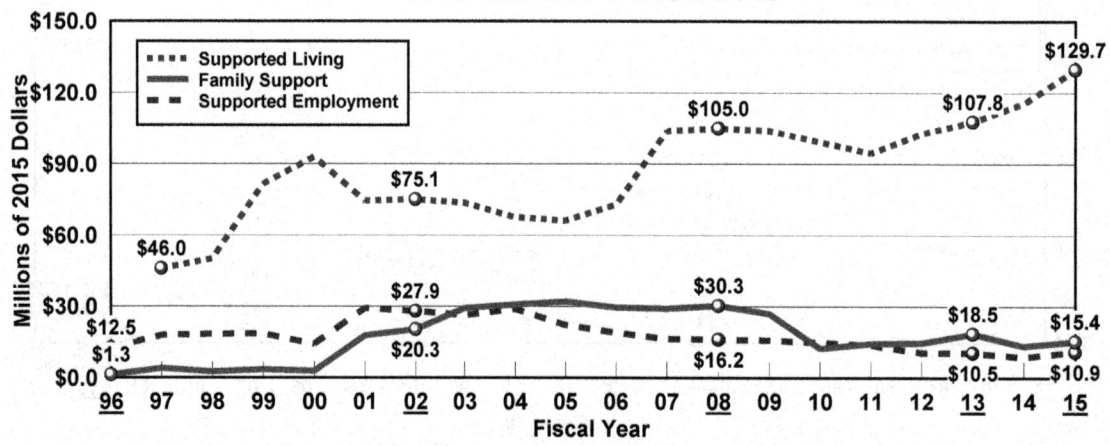

PARTICIPANTS: FY 1996-2015

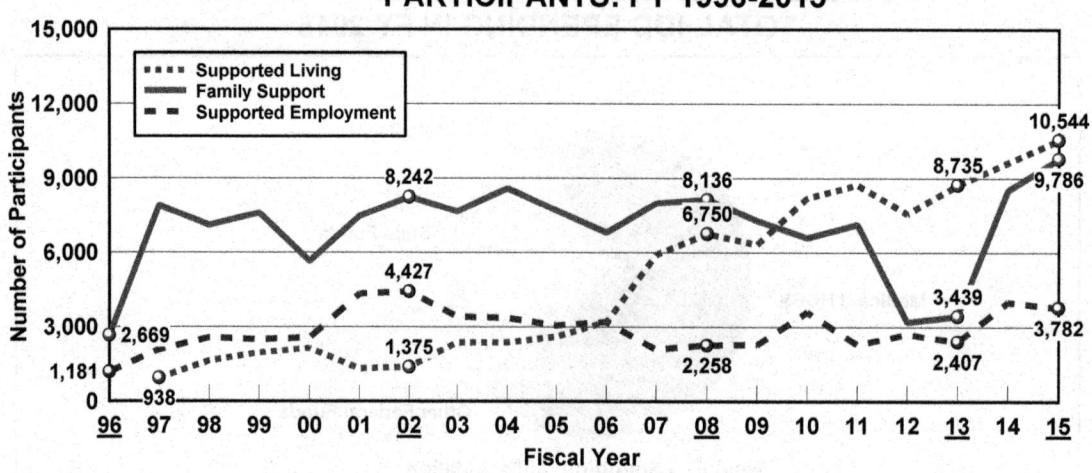

SUPPORTED LIVING, FAMILY SUPPORT AND SUPPORTED EMPLOYMENT SPENDING: FY 1996-2015

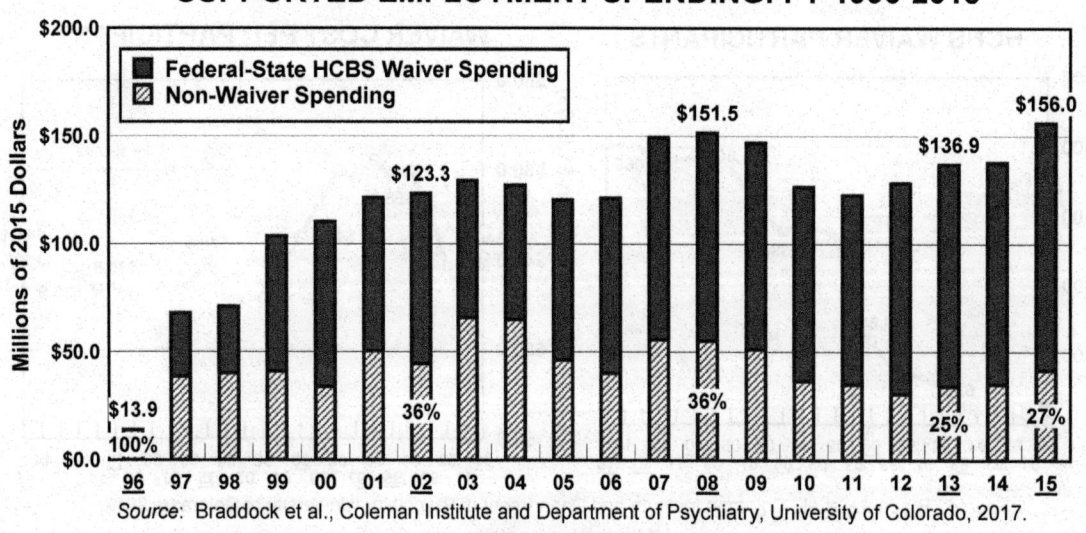

Source: Braddock et al., Coleman Institute and Department of Psychiatry, University of Colorado, 2017.
http://stateofthestates.org

GEORGIA

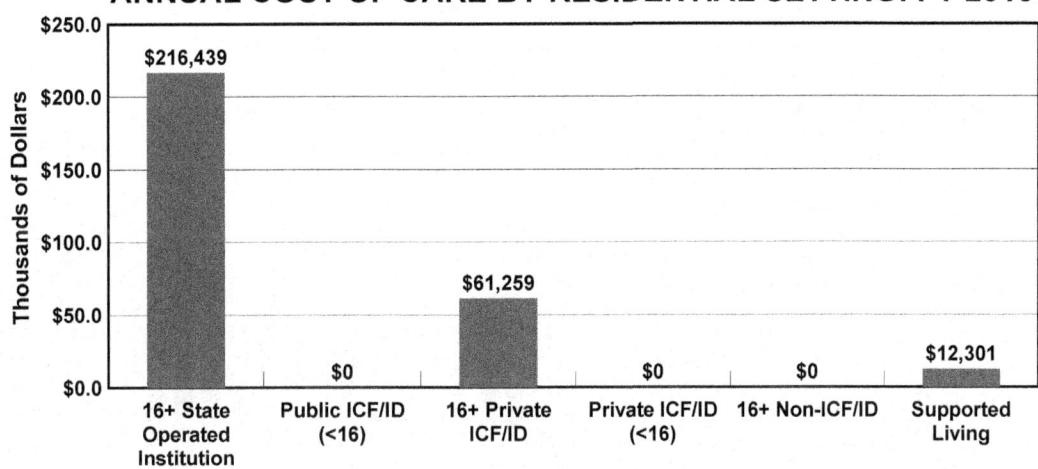

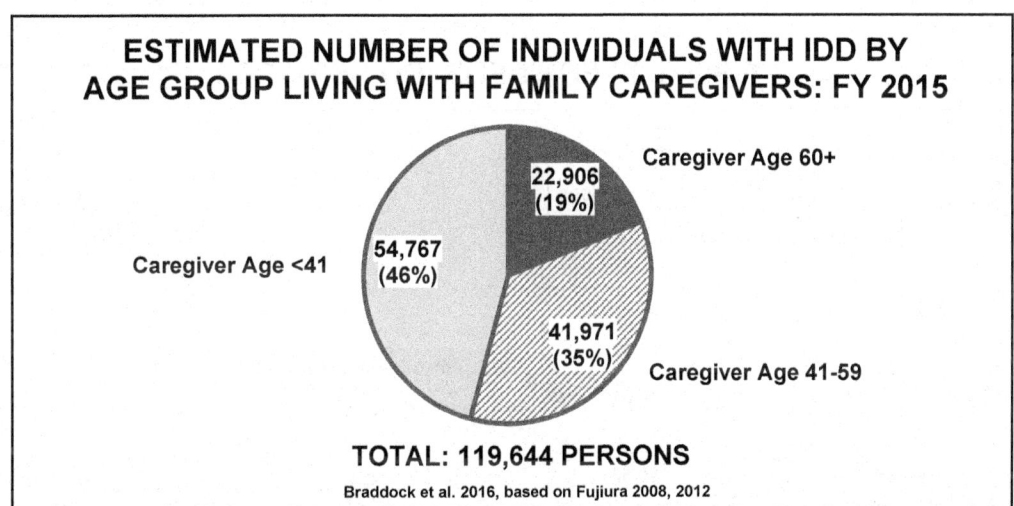

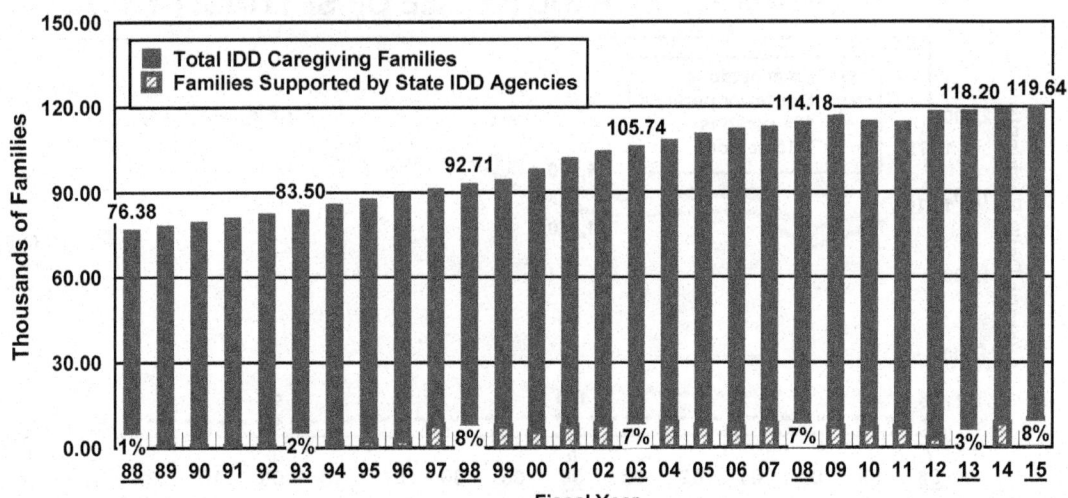

Source: Braddock et al., Coleman Institute and Department of Psychiatry, University of Colorado, 2017.

http://stateofthestates.org

HAWAII

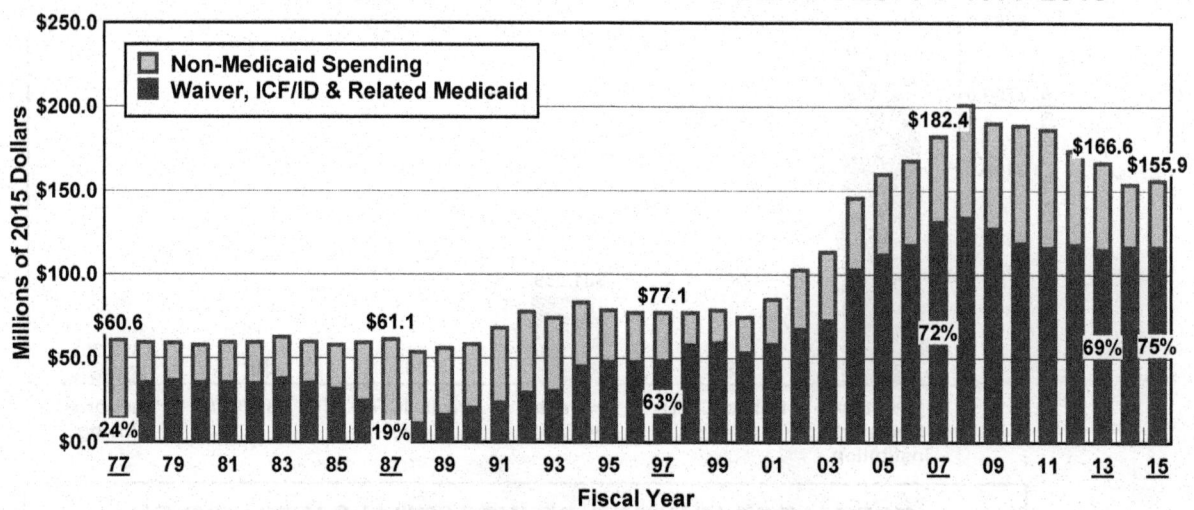

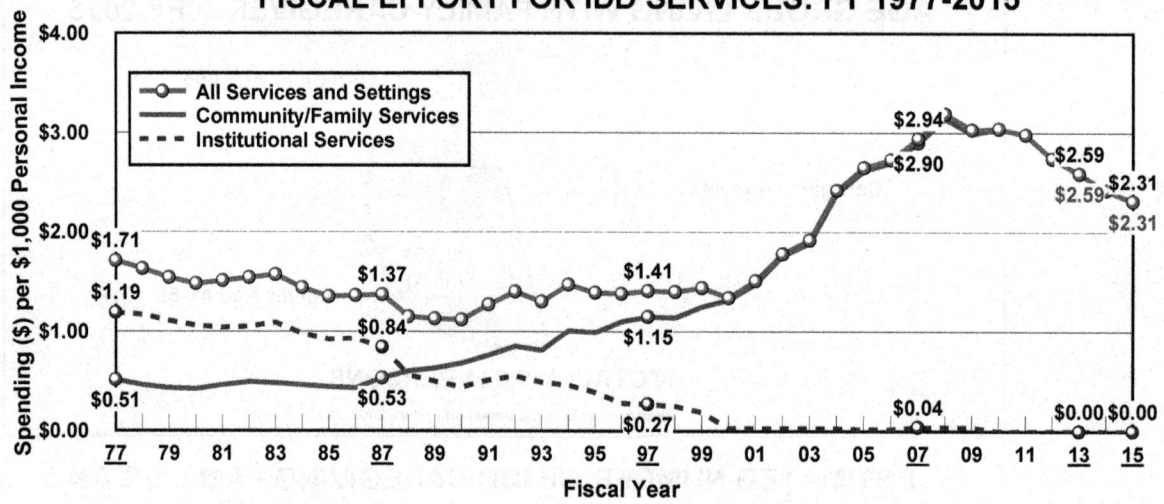

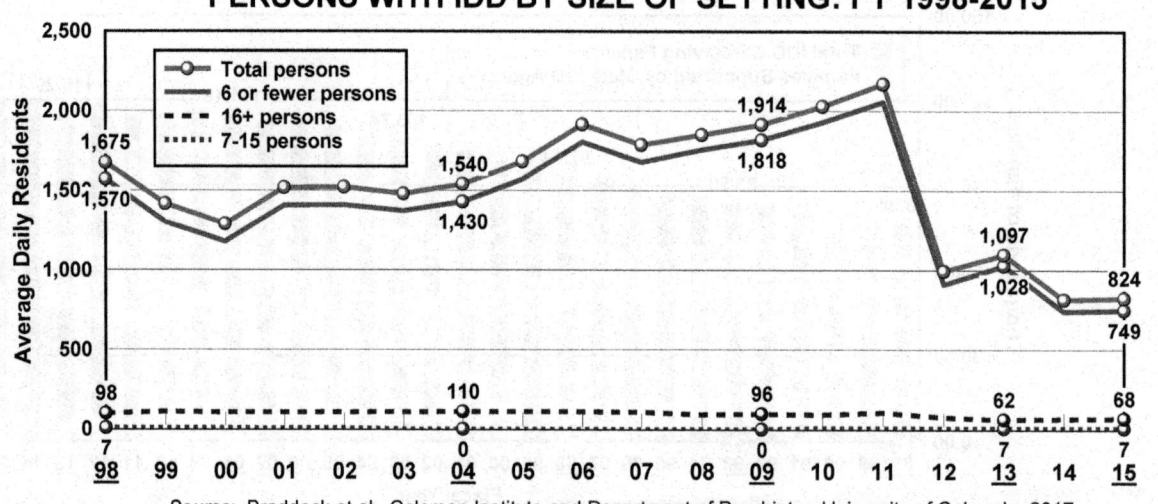

Source: Braddock et al., Coleman Institute and Department of Psychiatry, University of Colorado, 2017.
http://stateofthestates.org

HAWAII

FEDERAL IDD MEDICAID SPENDING BY REVENUE SOURCE

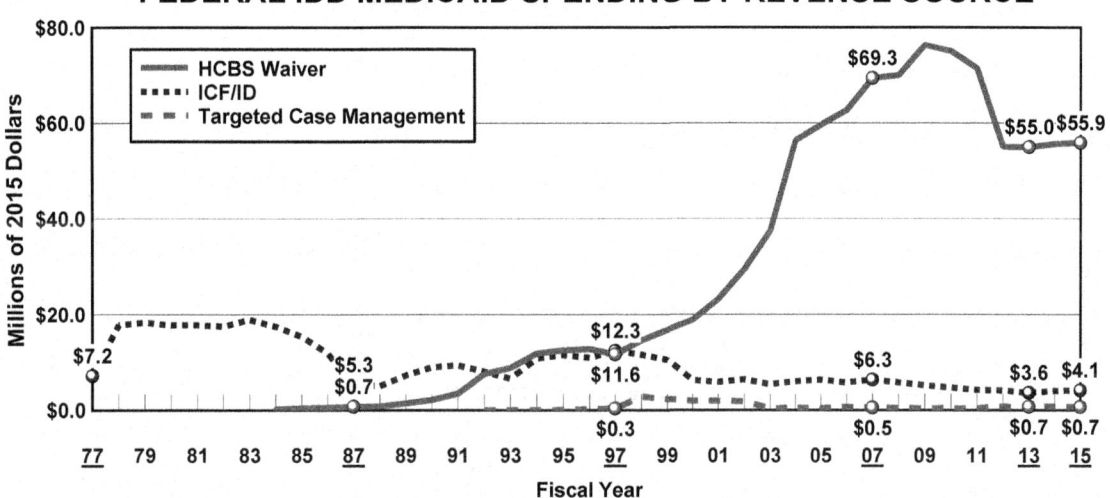

FEDERAL-STATE MEDICAID AS A PERCENTAGE OF TOTAL IDD SPENDING IN FY 2015

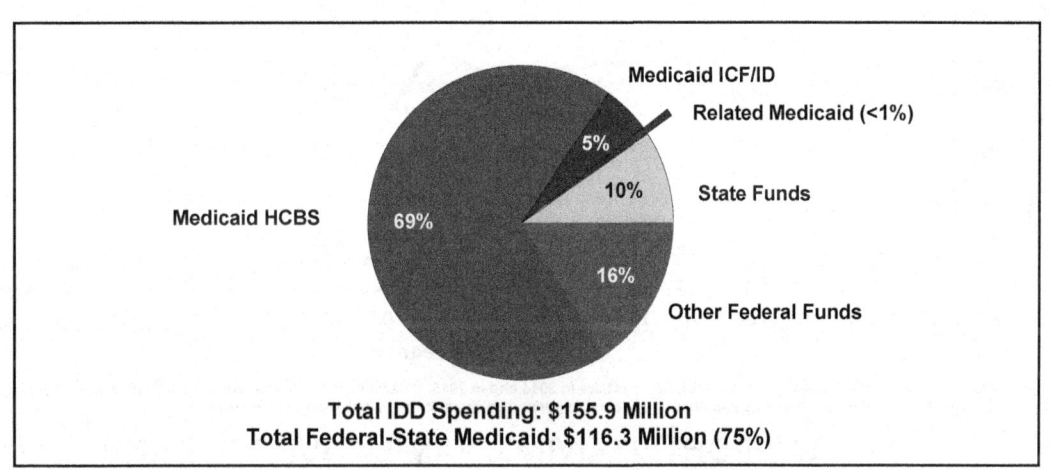

Total IDD Spending: $155.9 Million
Total Federal-State Medicaid: $116.3 Million (75%)

HCBS WAIVER PARTICIPANTS / WAIVER COST PER PARTICIPANT

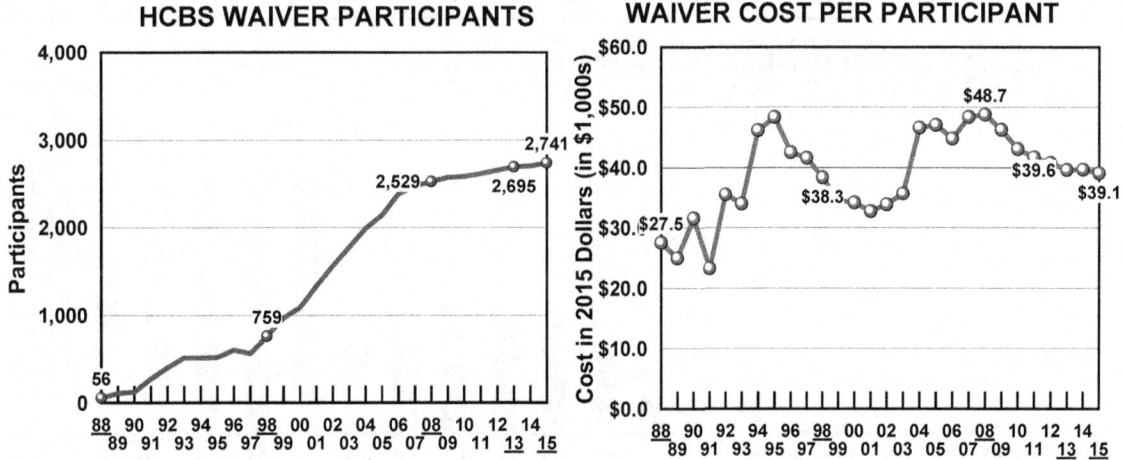

Source: Braddock et al., Coleman Institute and Department of Psychiatry, University of Colorado, 2017.

http://stateofthestates.org

HAWAII

INDIVIDUAL AND FAMILY SUPPORT SPENDING: FY 1996-2015

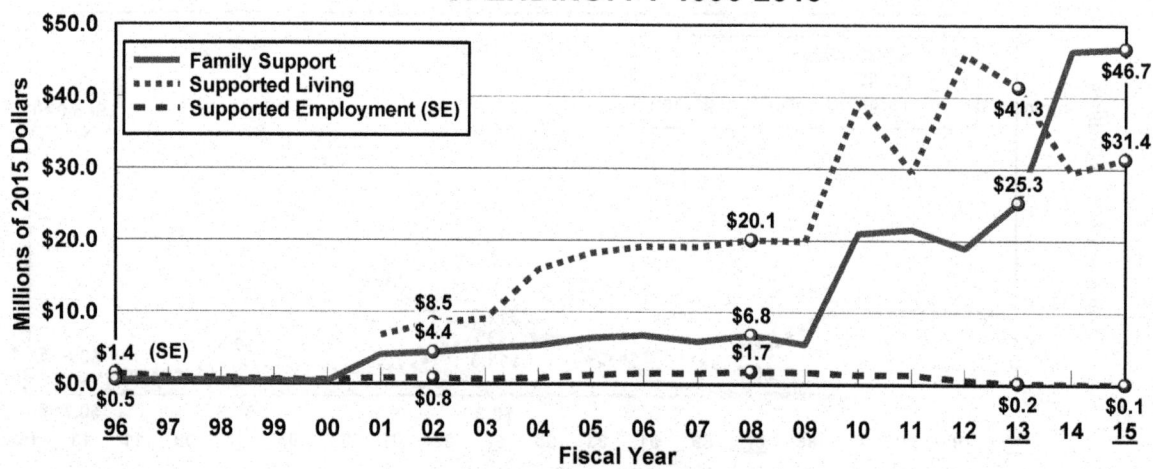

PARTICIPANTS: FY 1996-2015

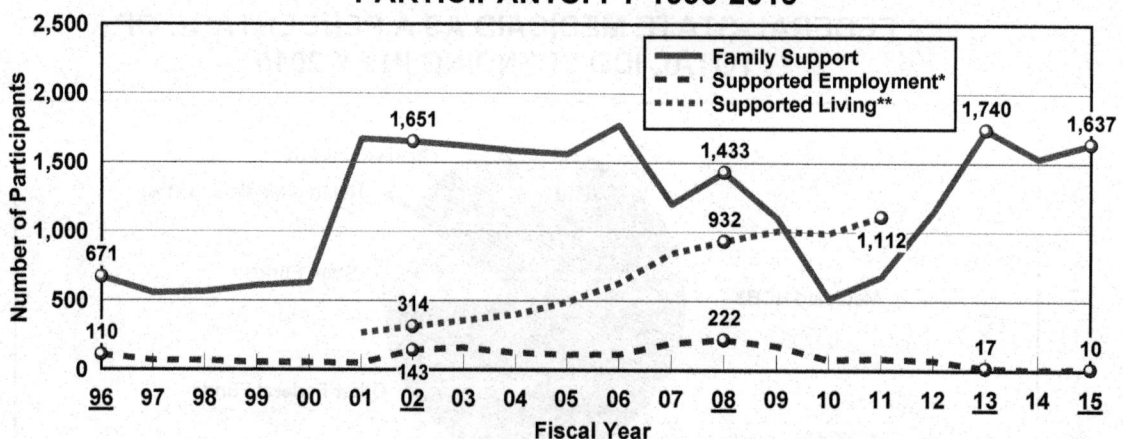

*Does not include 177 follow-along work support workers in 2014 and in 2015. **Hawaii reported that all SL participants were adults choosing to live with their families. Participants and spending were categorized by the state as "a subset of family support."

SUPPORTED LIVING, FAMILY SUPPORT AND SUPPORTED EMPLOYMENT SPENDING: FY 1996-2015

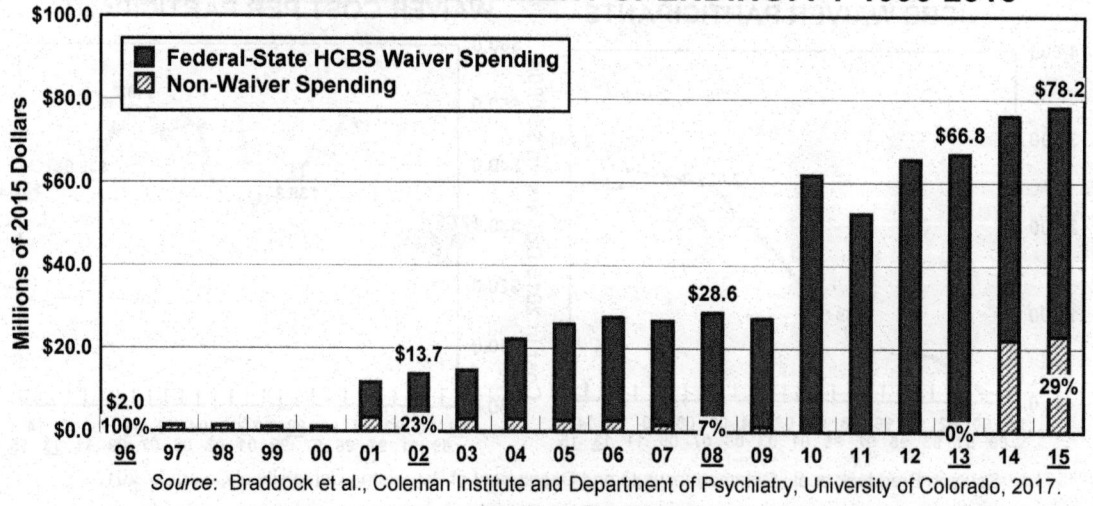

Source: Braddock et al., Coleman Institute and Department of Psychiatry, University of Colorado, 2017.
http://stateofthestates.org

HAWAII

ANNUAL COST OF CARE BY RESIDENTIAL SETTING: FY 2015

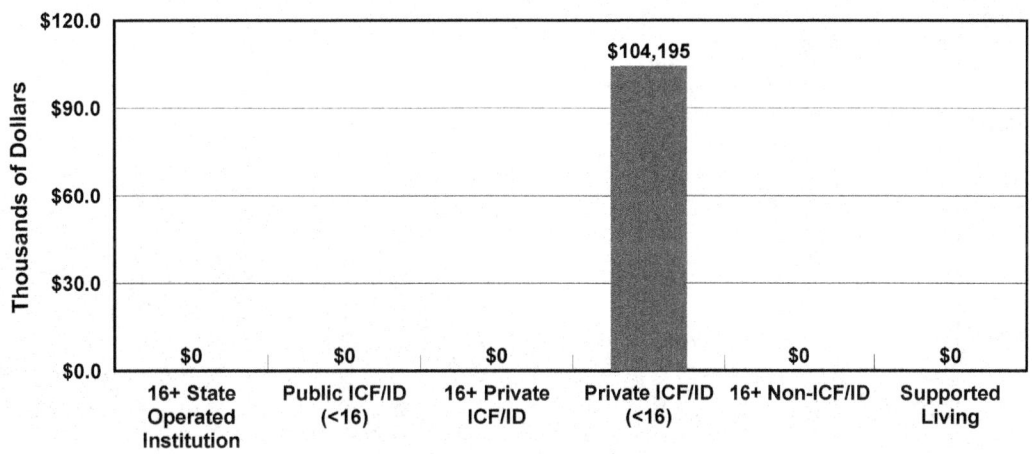

ESTIMATED NUMBER OF INDIVIDUALS WITH IDD BY AGE GROUP LIVING WITH FAMILY CAREGIVERS: FY 2015

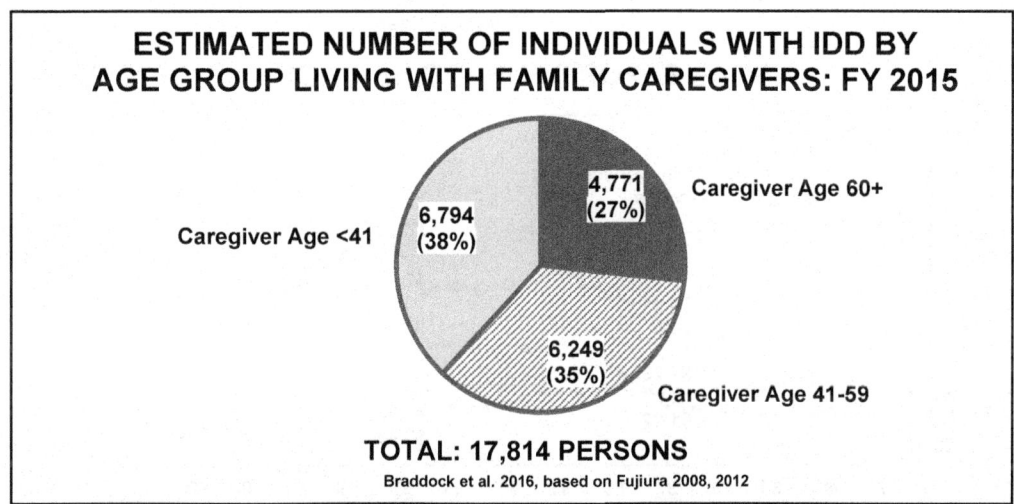

TOTAL: 17,814 PERSONS
Braddock et al. 2016, based on Fujiura 2008, 2012

ESTIMATED NUMBER OF IDD CAREGIVING FAMILIES AND FAMILIES SUPPORTED BY IDD AGENCIES: FY 1988-2015

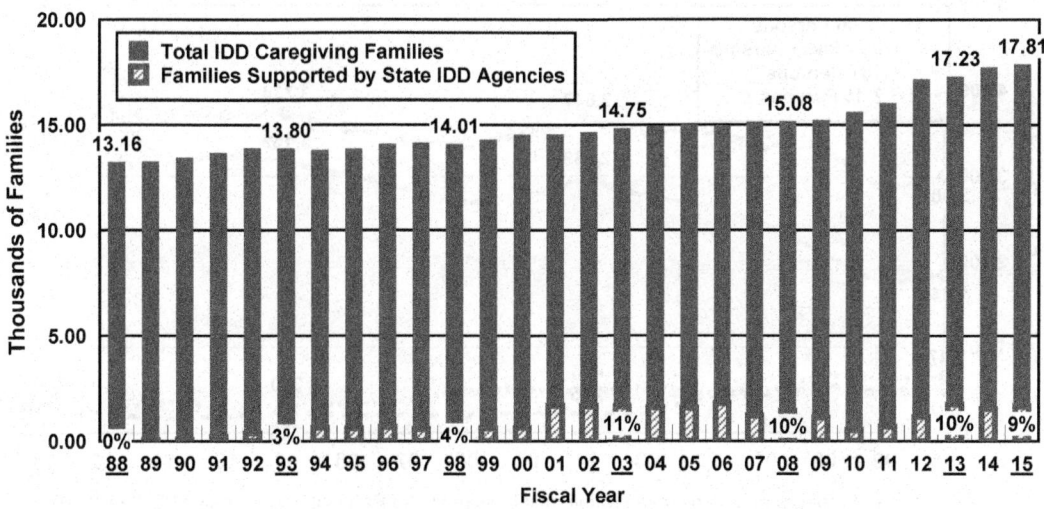

Source: Braddock et al., Coleman Institute and Department of Psychiatry, University of Colorado, 2017.
http://stateofthestates.org

IDAHO

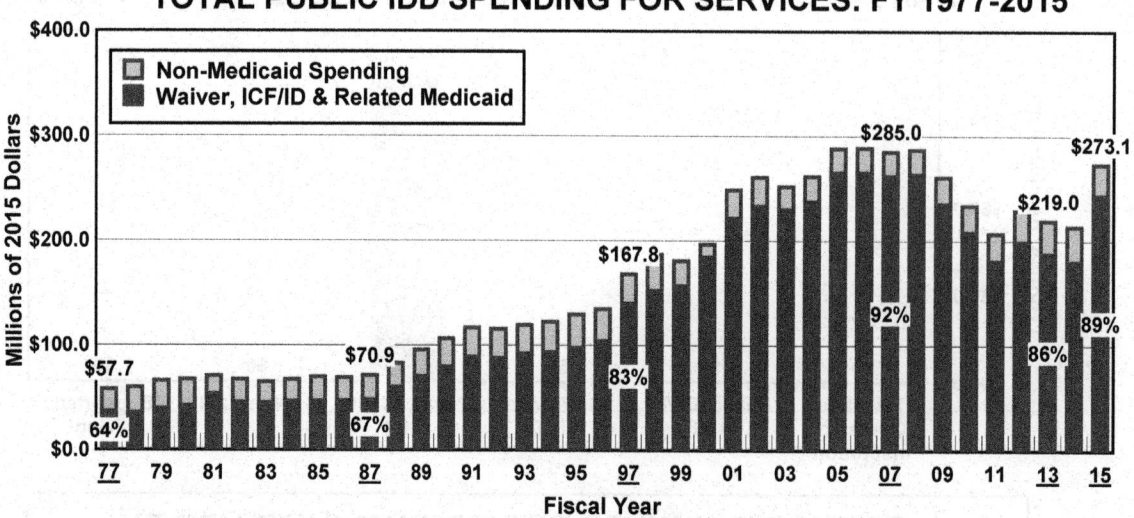

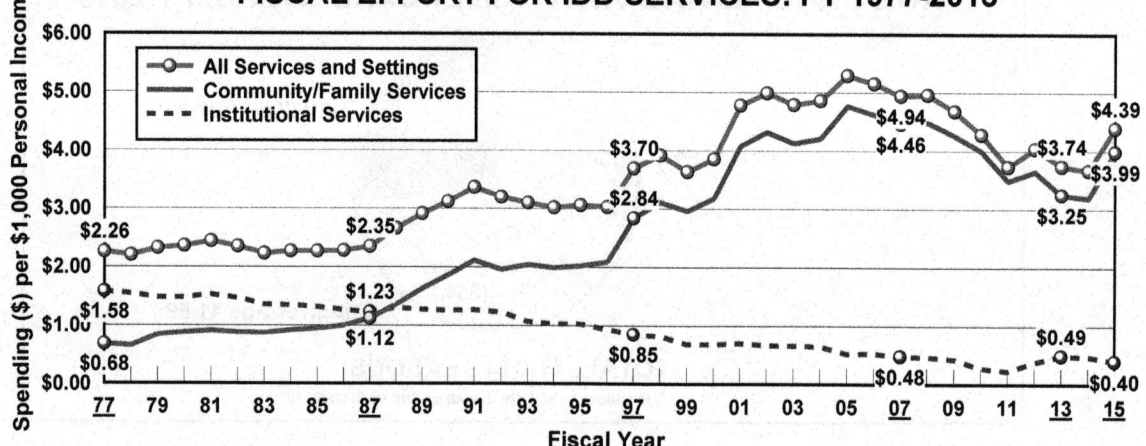

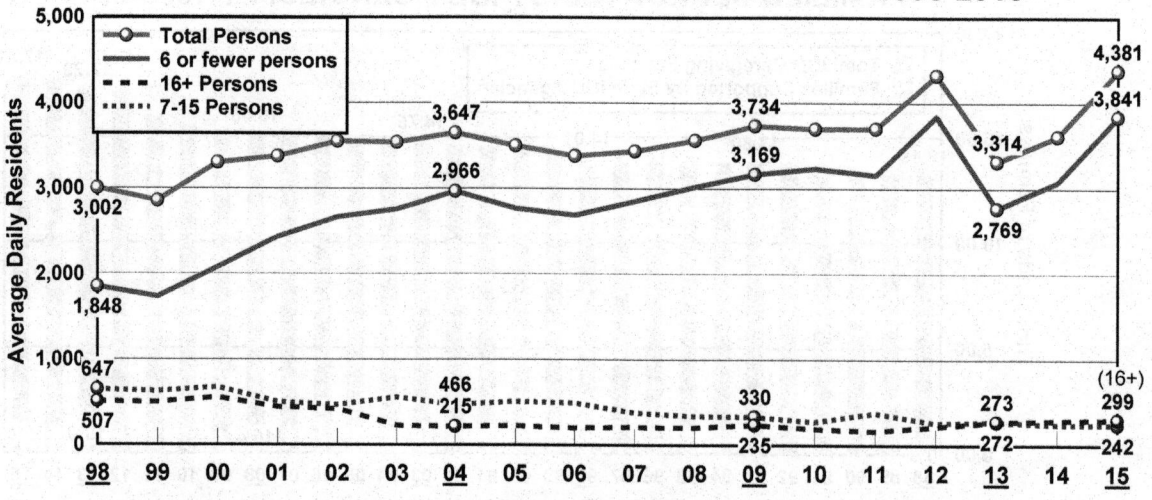

Source: Braddock et al., Coleman Institute and Department of Psychiatry, University of Colorado, 2017.
http://stateofthestates.org

IDAHO

FEDERAL IDD MEDICAID SPENDING BY REVENUE SOURCE

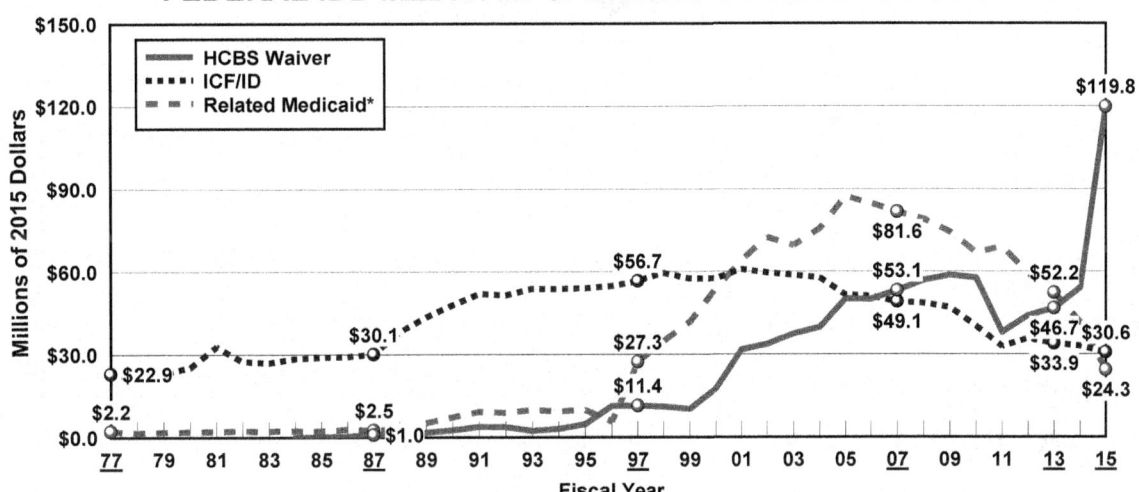

*In 2015, "Related Medicaid" was clinic rehabilitation ($16.7 million), personal assistance ($3.7 million) and targeted case management ($3.9 million).

FEDERAL-STATE MEDICAID AS A PERCENTAGE OF TOTAL IDD SPENDING IN FY 2015

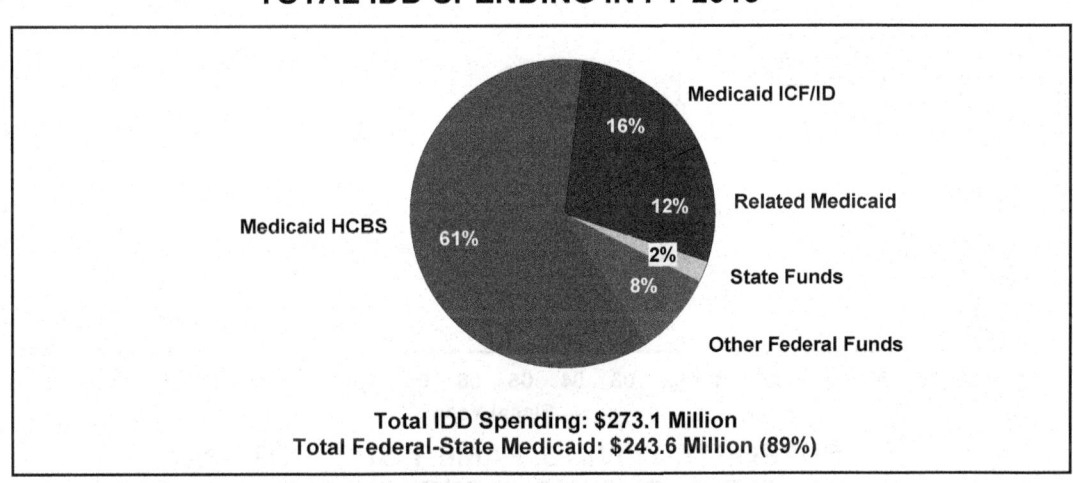

Total IDD Spending: $273.1 Million
Total Federal-State Medicaid: $243.6 Million (89%)

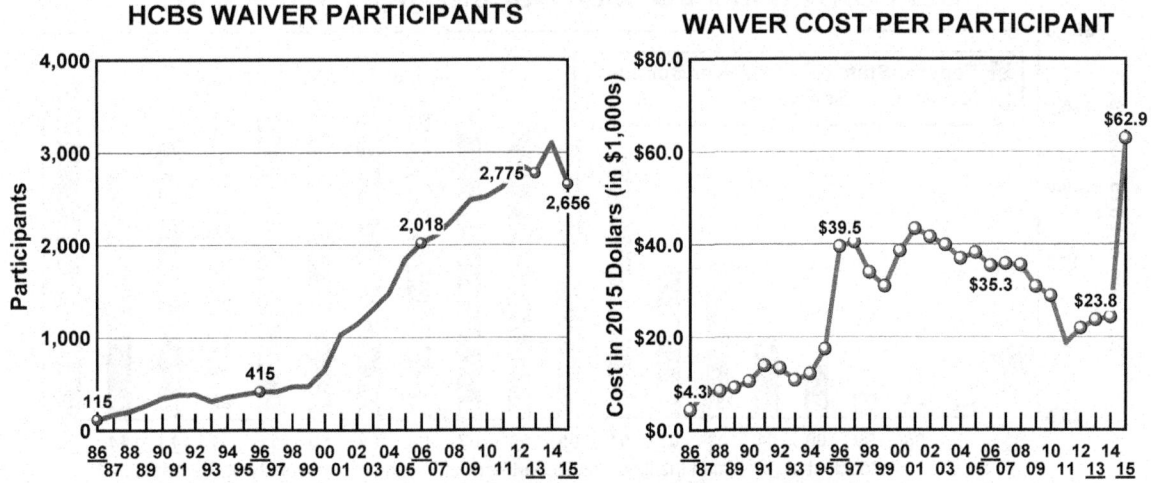

Source: Braddock et al., Coleman Institute and Department of Psychiatry, University of Colorado, 2017.
http://stateofthestates.org

IDAHO
INDIVIDUAL AND FAMILY SUPPORT
SPENDING: FY 1996-2015

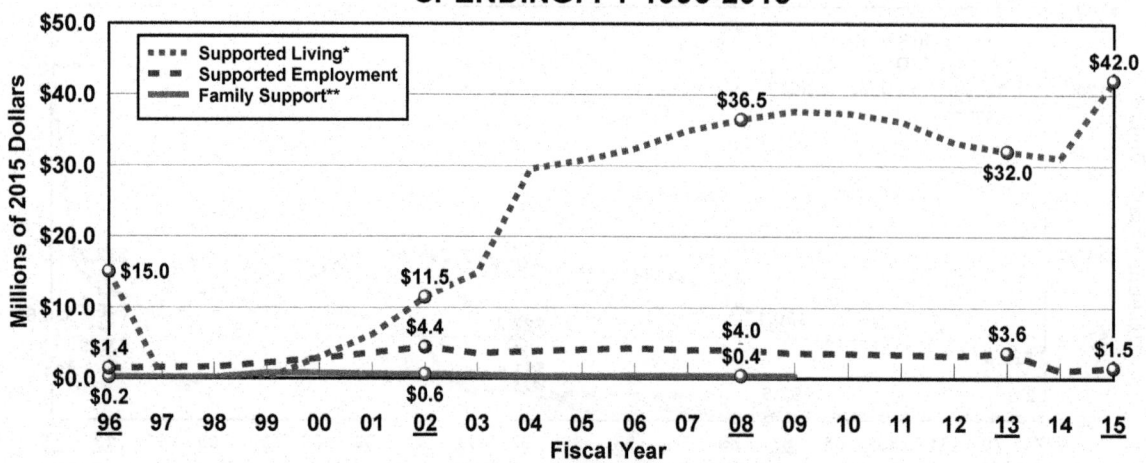

*State provided no Supported Living spending data during 1997-98. **Family support program termined in 2010.

PARTICIPANTS: FY 1996-2015

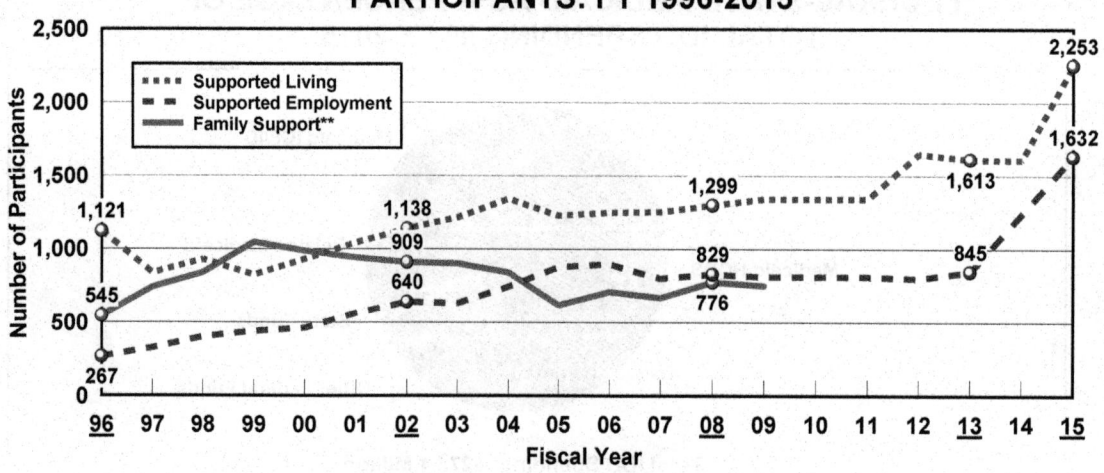

SUPPORTED LIVING, FAMILY SUPPORT AND SUPPORTED EMPLOYMENT SPENDING: FY 1996-2015

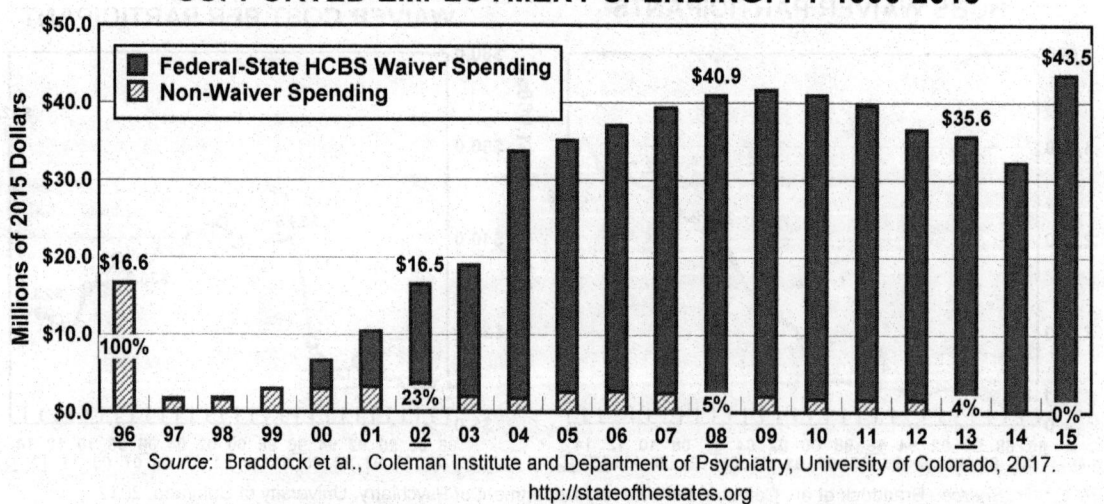

Source: Braddock et al., Coleman Institute and Department of Psychiatry, University of Colorado, 2017.
http://stateofthestates.org

IDAHO

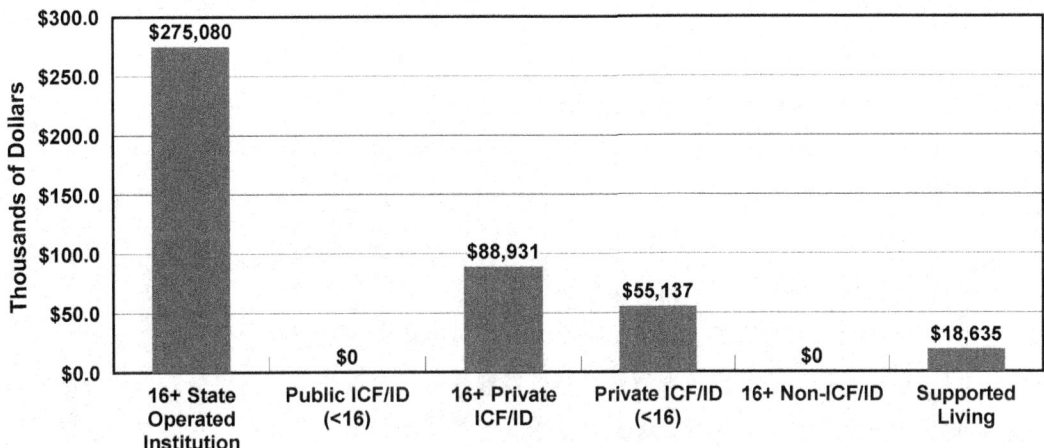
ANNUAL COST OF CARE BY RESIDENTIAL SETTING: FY 2015

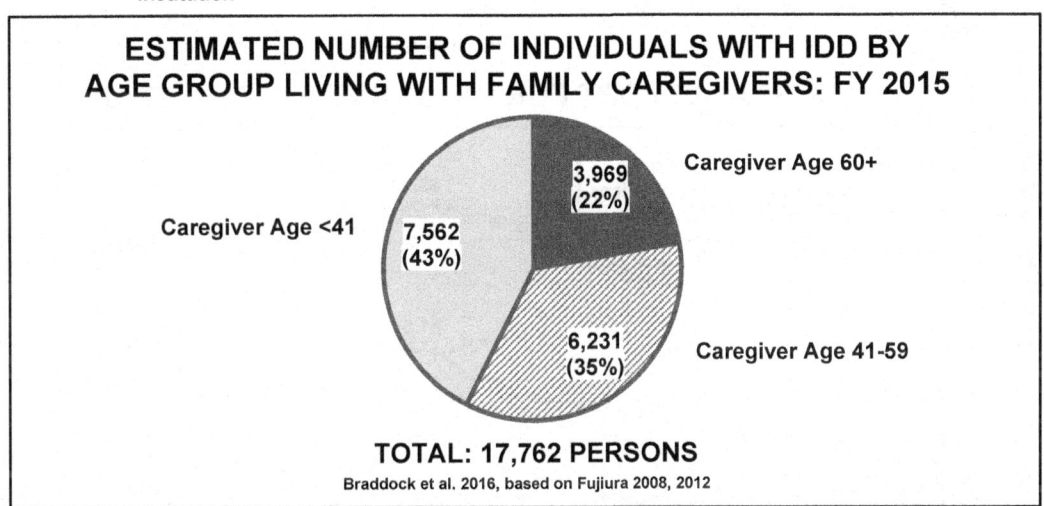
ESTIMATED NUMBER OF INDIVIDUALS WITH IDD BY AGE GROUP LIVING WITH FAMILY CAREGIVERS: FY 2015

TOTAL: 17,762 PERSONS
Braddock et al. 2016, based on Fujiura 2008, 2012

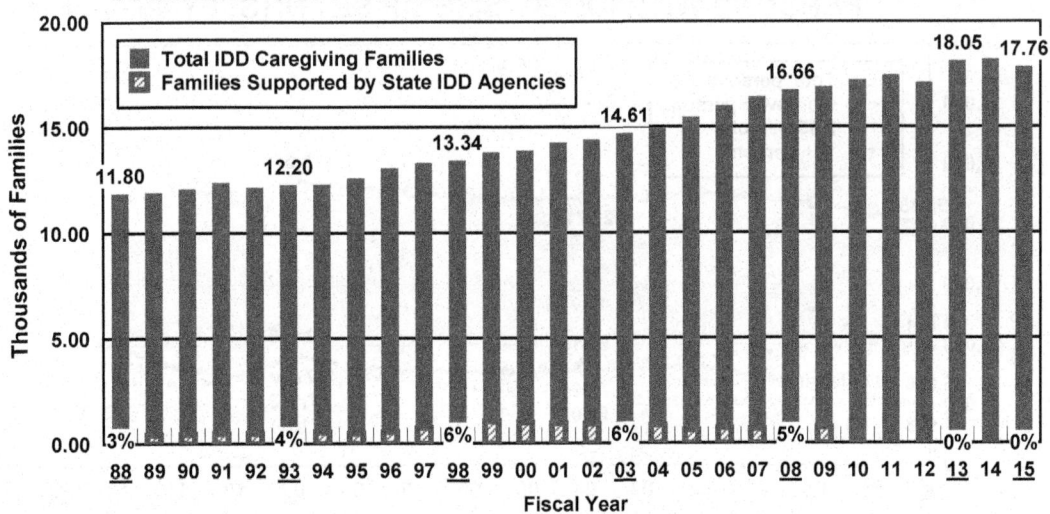
ESTIMATED NUMBER OF IDD CAREGIVING FAMILIES AND FAMILIES SUPPORTED BY IDD AGENCIES: FY 1988-2015

Source: Braddock et al., Coleman Institute and Department of Psychiatry, University of Colorado, 2017.
http://stateofthestates.org

ILLINOIS

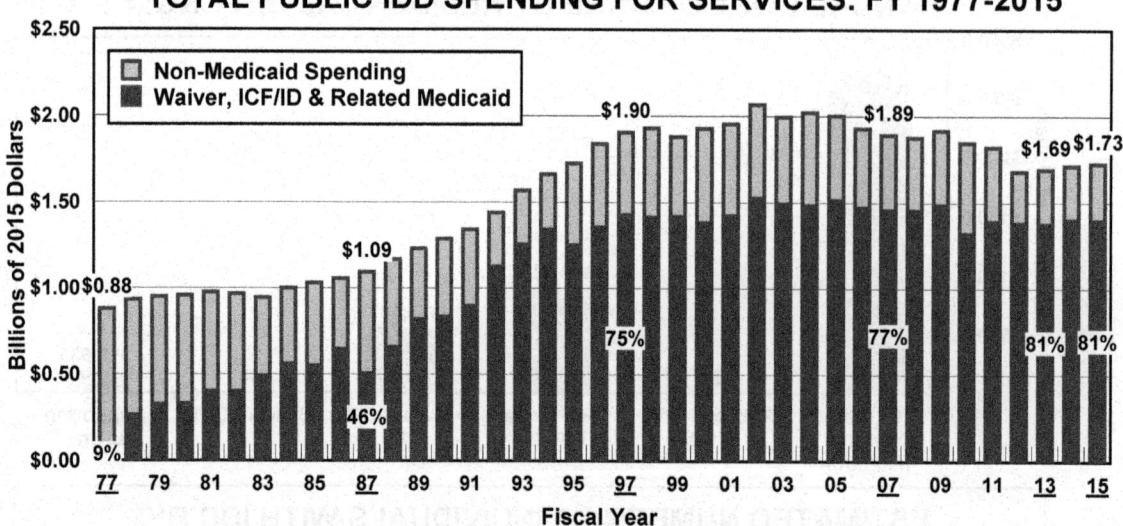

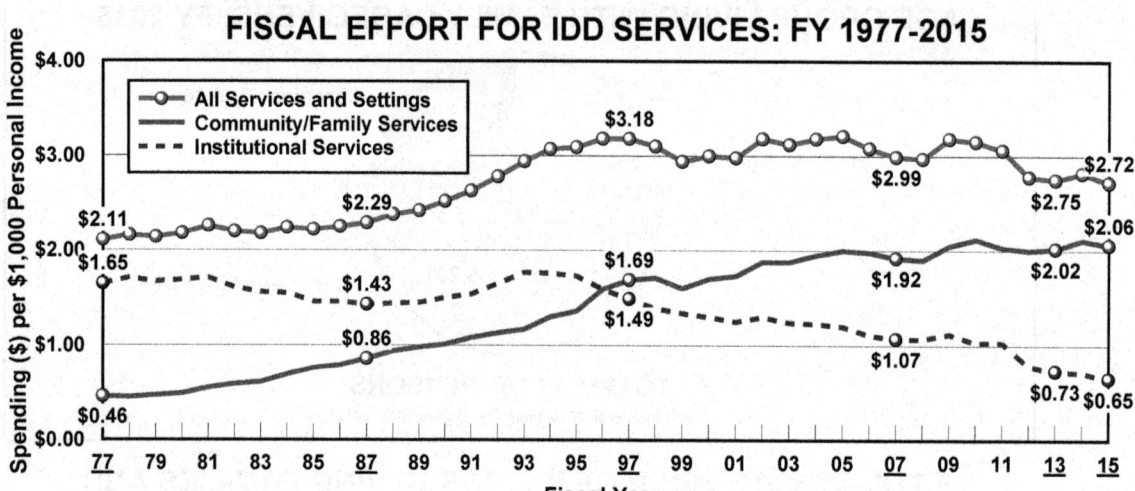

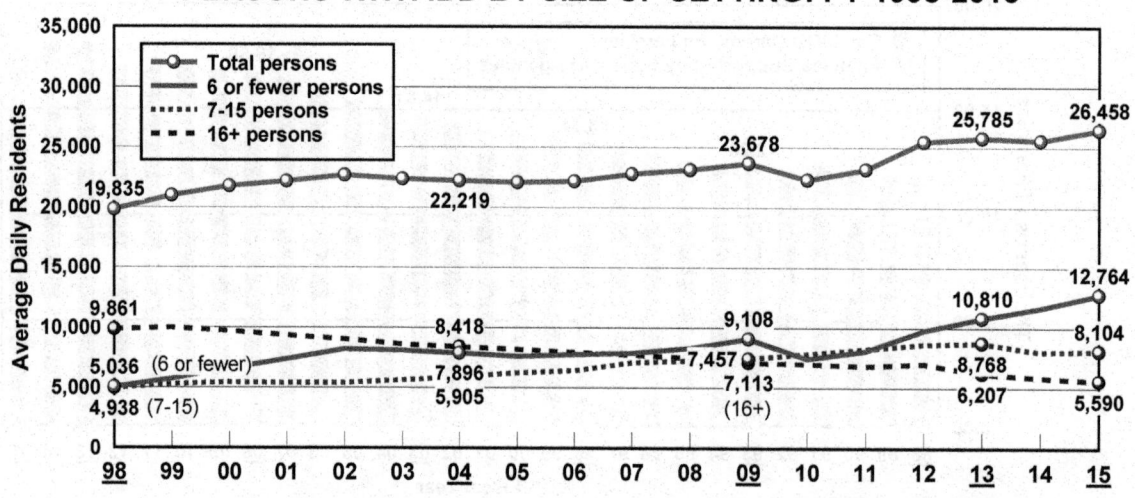

Source: Braddock et al., Coleman Institute and Department of Psychiatry, University of Colorado, 2017.
http://stateofthestates.org

ILLINOIS

FEDERAL IDD MEDICAID SPENDING BY REVENUE SOURCE

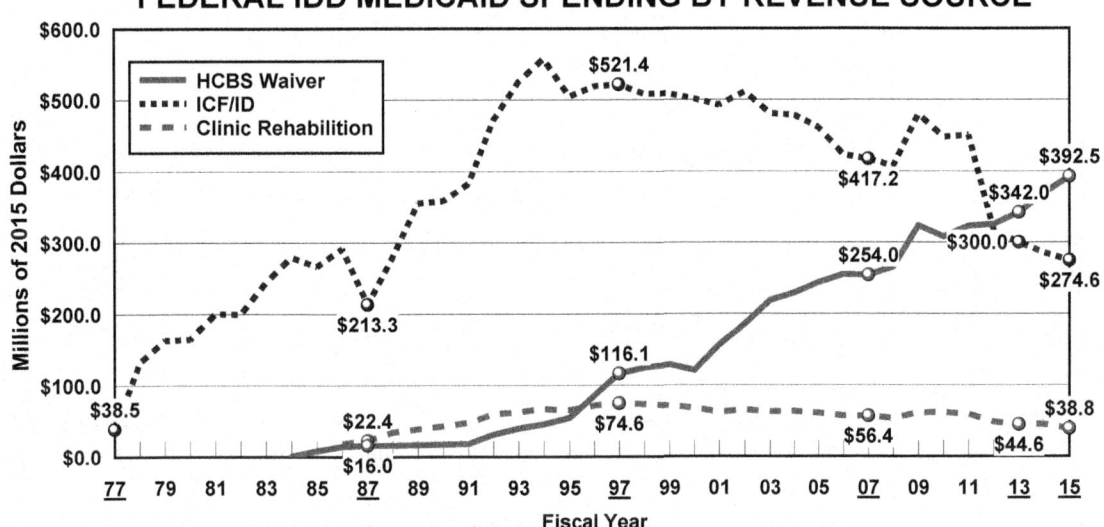

FEDERAL-STATE MEDICAID AS A PERCENTAGE OF TOTAL IDD SPENDING IN FY 2015

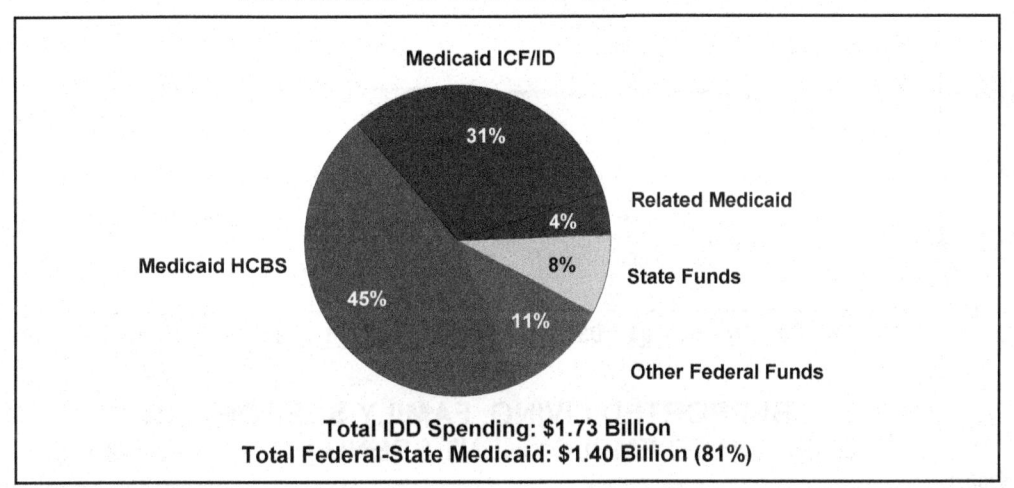

Total IDD Spending: $1.73 Billion
Total Federal-State Medicaid: $1.40 Billion (81%)

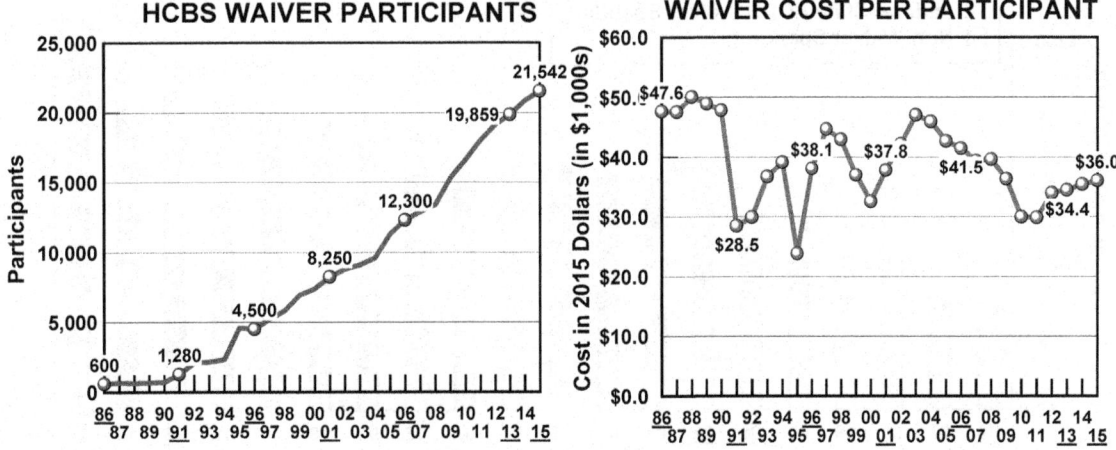

Source: Braddock et al., Coleman Institute and Department of Psychiatry, University of Colorado, 2017.
http://stateofthestates.org

ILLINOIS
INDIVIDUAL AND FAMILY SUPPORT
SPENDING: FY 1996-2015

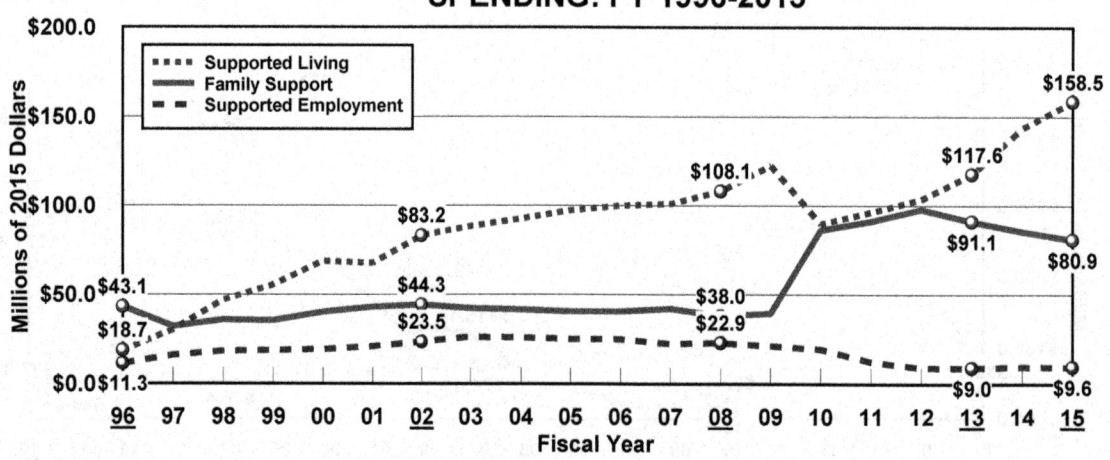

PARTICIPANTS: FY 1996-2015

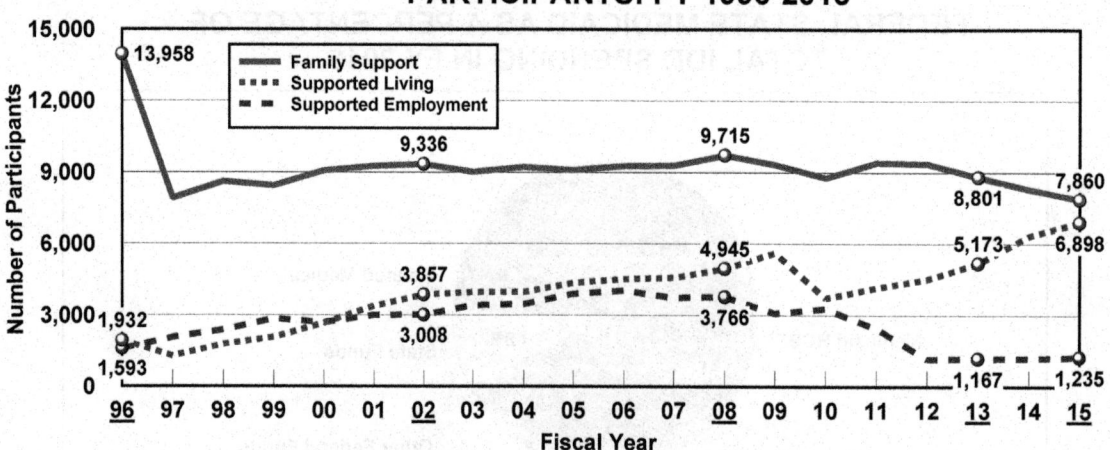

SUPPORTED LIVING, FAMILY SUPPORT AND SUPPORTED EMPLOYMENT SPENDING: FY 1996-2015

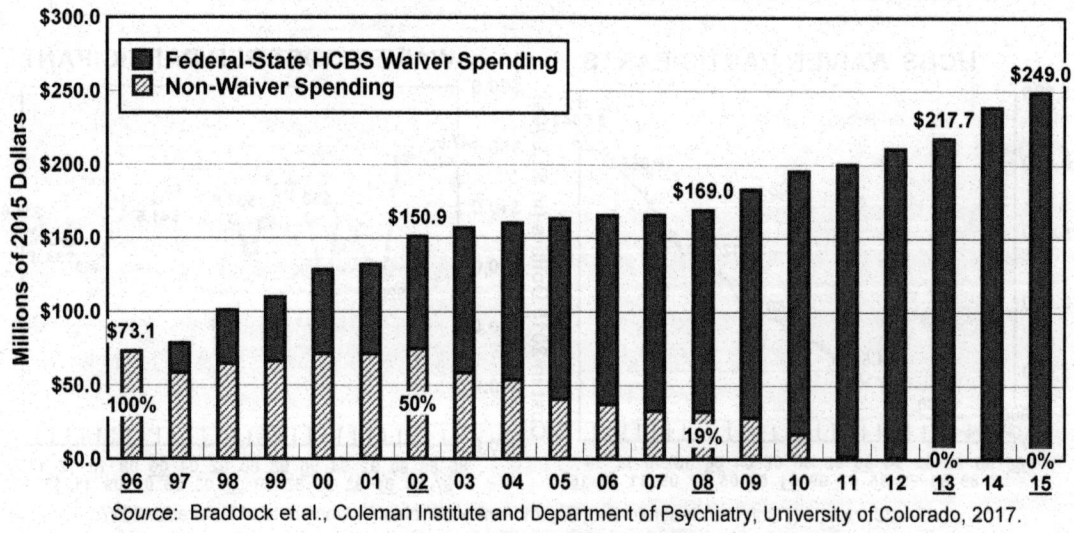

Source: Braddock et al., Coleman Institute and Department of Psychiatry, University of Colorado, 2017.

http://stateofthestates.org

ILLINOIS

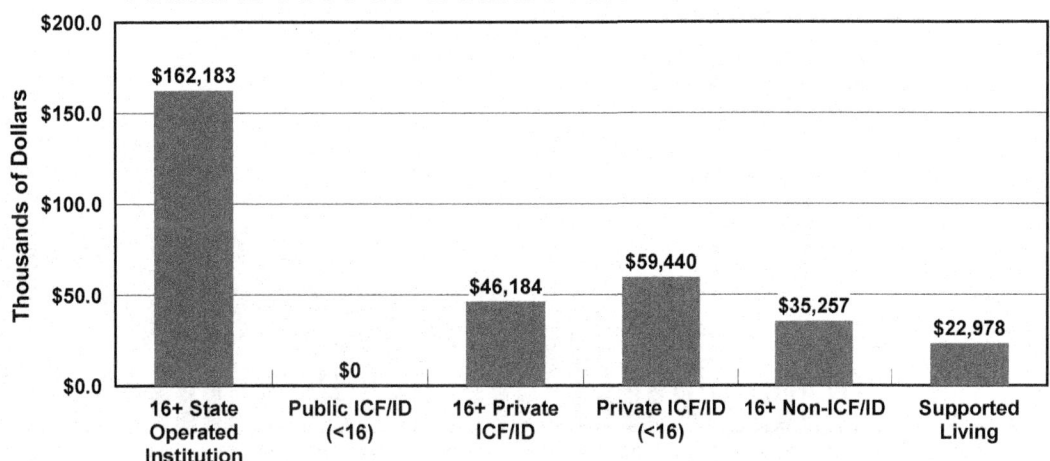

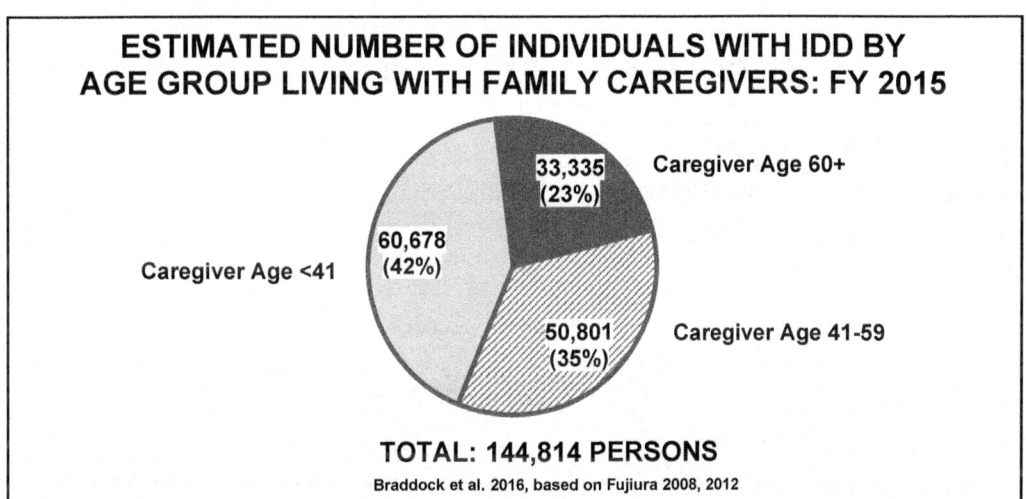

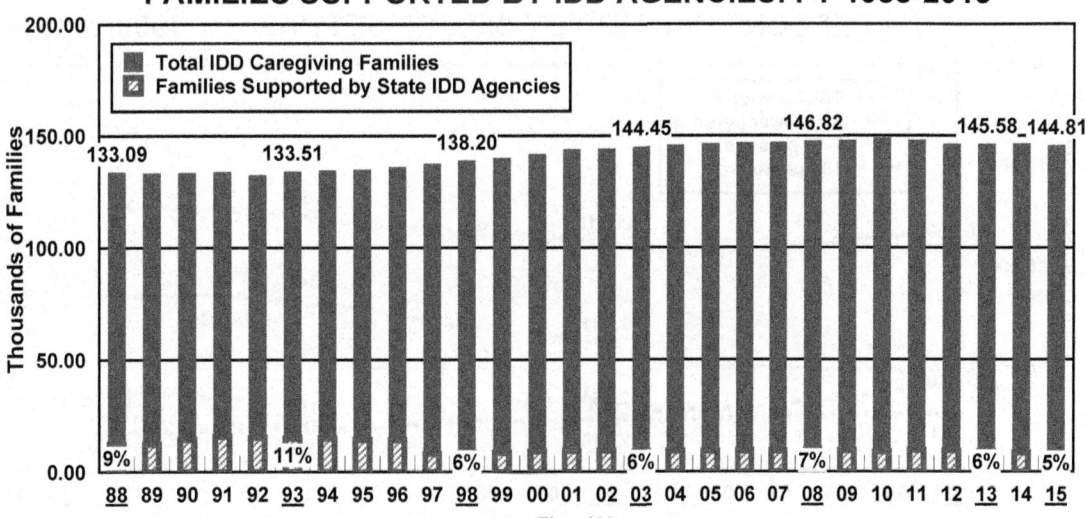

Source: Braddock et al., Coleman Institute and Department of Psychiatry, University of Colorado, 2017.
http://stateofthestates.org

INDIANA

TOTAL PUBLIC IDD SPENDING FOR SERVICES: FY 1977-2015

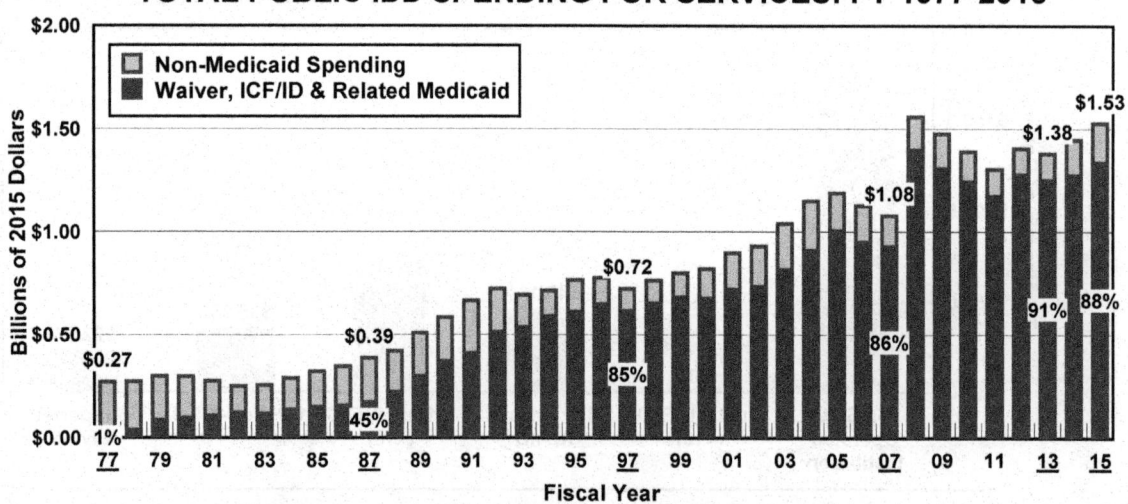

FISCAL EFFORT FOR IDD SERVICES: FY 1977-2015

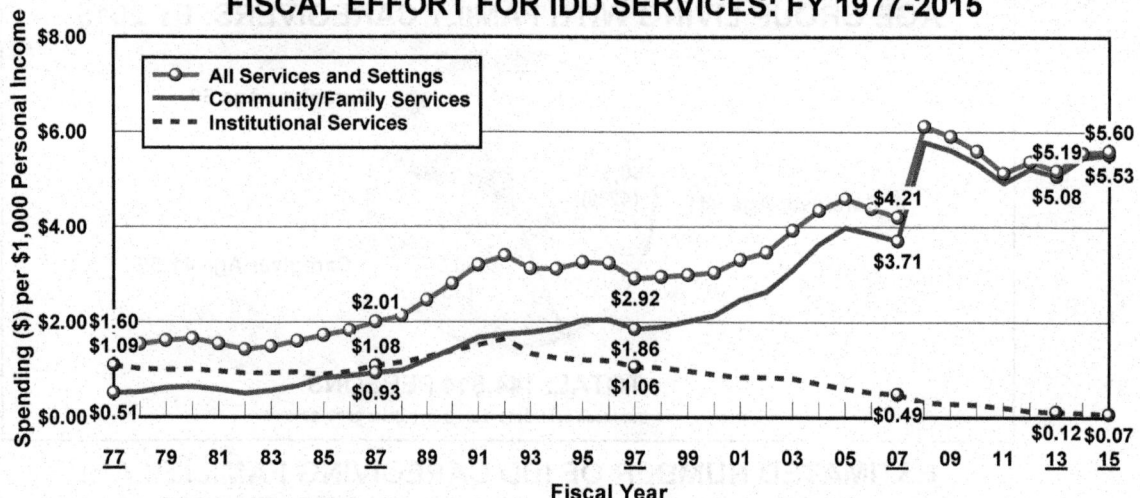

PERSONS WITH IDD BY SIZE OF SETTING: FY 1998-2015

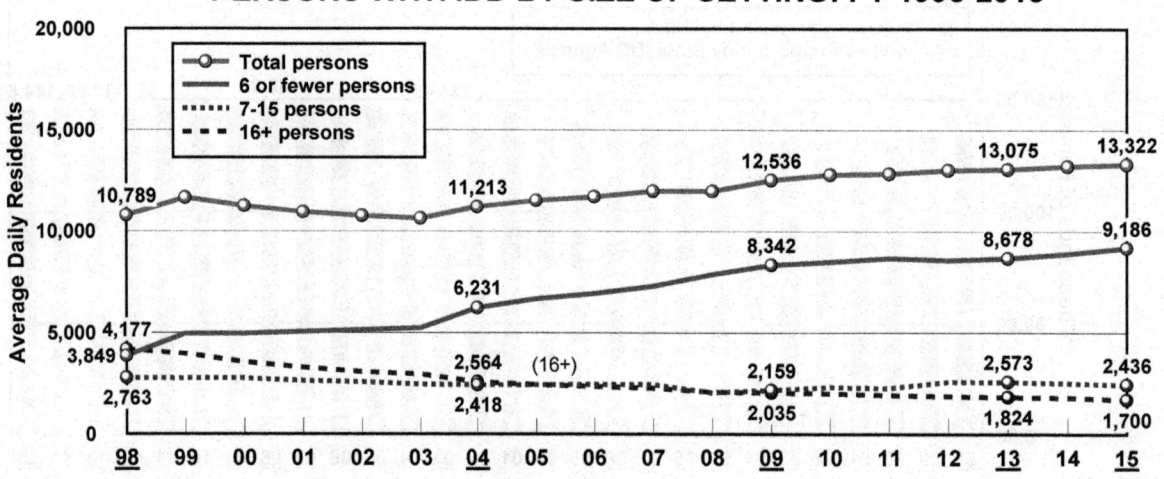

Source: Braddock et al., Coleman Institute and Department of Psychiatry, University of Colorado, 2017.
http://stateofthestates.org

INDIANA

FEDERAL IDD MEDICAID SPENDING BY REVENUE SOURCE

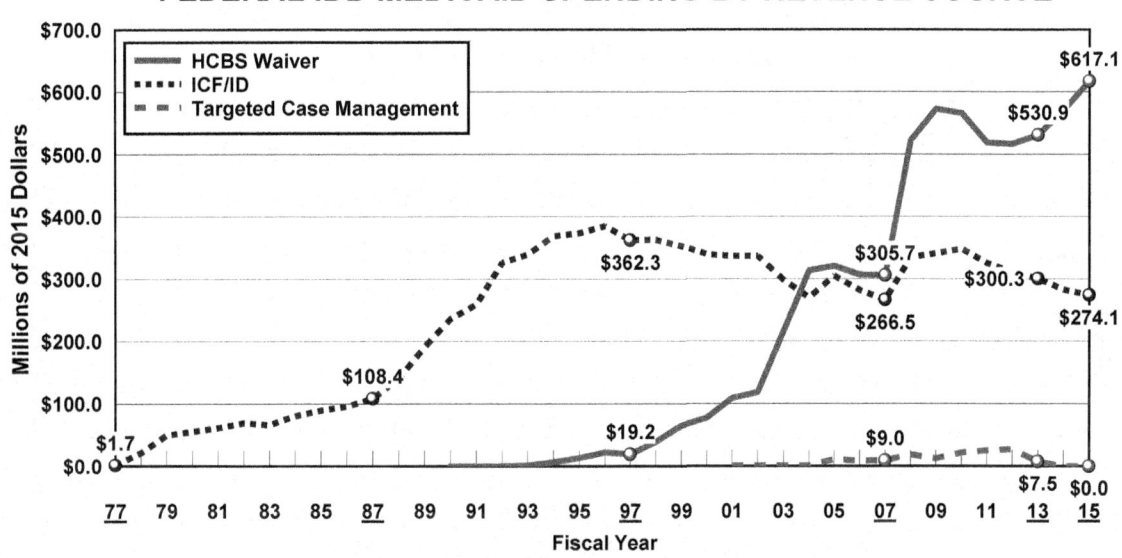

FEDERAL-STATE MEDICAID AS A PERCENTAGE OF TOTAL IDD SPENDING IN FY 2015

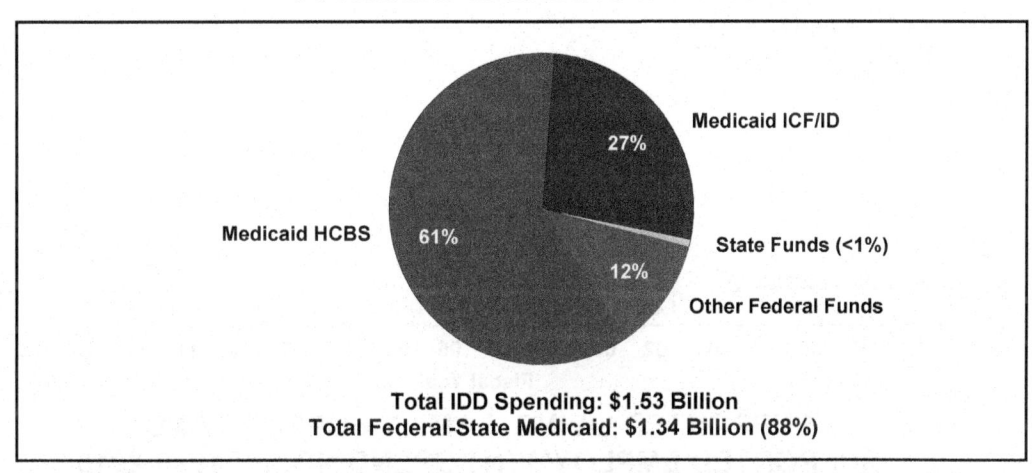

Total IDD Spending: $1.53 Billion
Total Federal-State Medicaid: $1.34 Billion (88%)

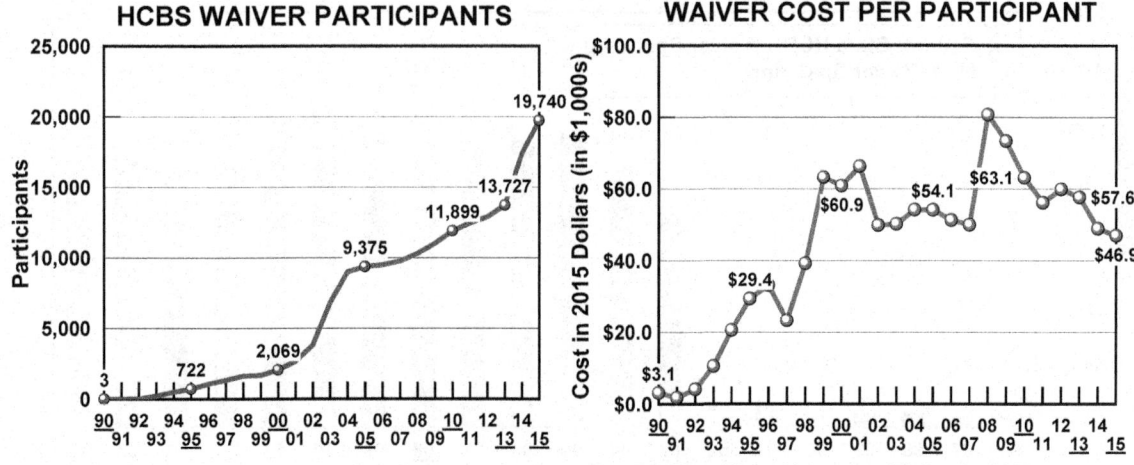

Source: Braddock et al., Coleman Institute and Department of Psychiatry, University of Colorado, 2017.
http://stateofthestates.org

INDIANA

INDIVIDUAL AND FAMILY SUPPORT SPENDING: FY 1996-2015

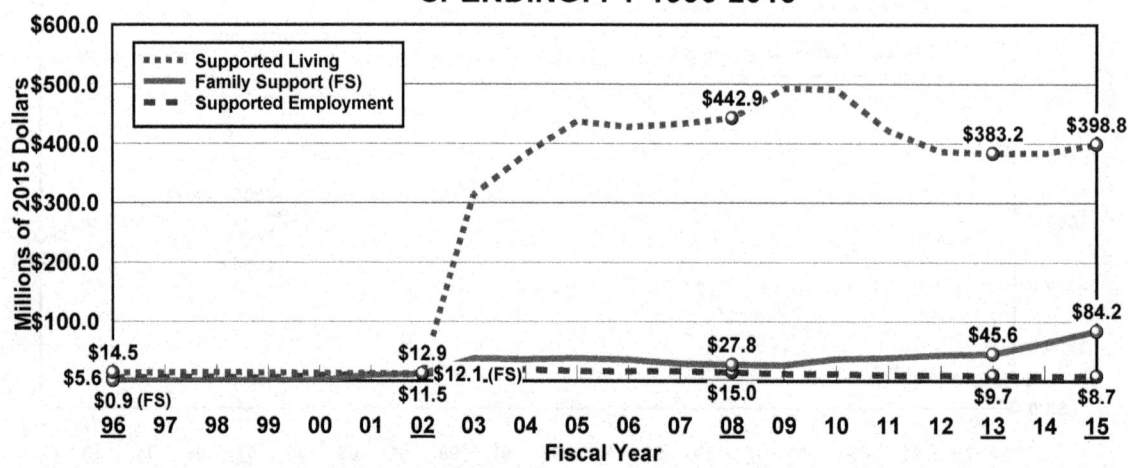

PARTICIPANTS: FY 1996-2015

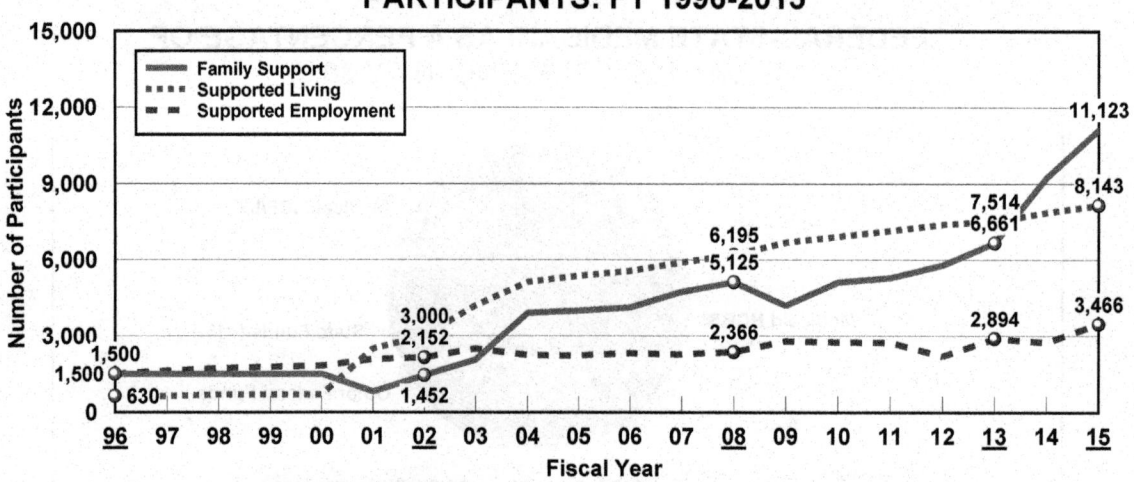

SUPPORTED LIVING, FAMILY SUPPORT AND SUPPORTED EMPLOYMENT SPENDING: FY 1996-2015

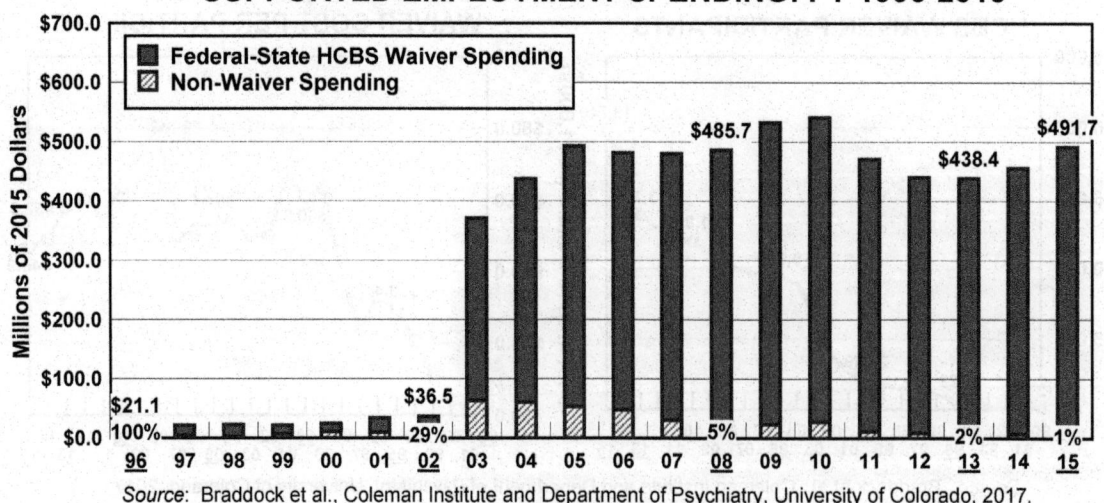

Source: Braddock et al., Coleman Institute and Department of Psychiatry, University of Colorado, 2017.
http://stateofthestates.org

INDIANA

ANNUAL COST OF CARE BY RESIDENTIAL SETTING: FY 2015

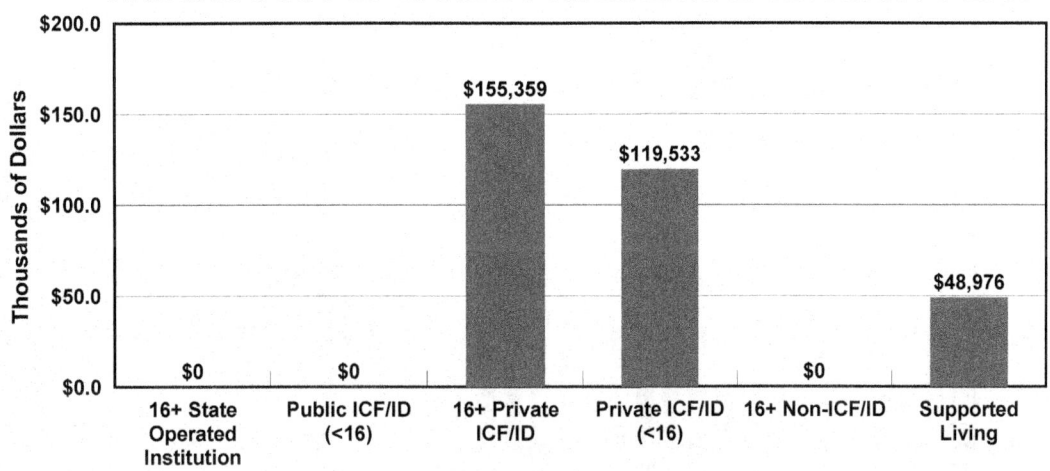

ESTIMATED NUMBER OF INDIVIDUALS WITH IDD BY AGE GROUP LIVING WITH FAMILY CAREGIVERS: FY 2015

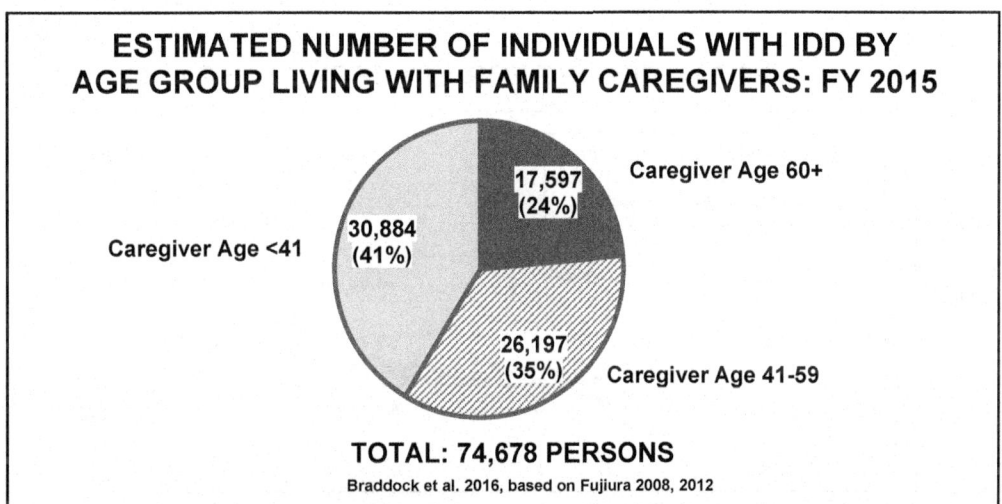

TOTAL: 74,678 PERSONS
Braddock et al. 2016, based on Fujiura 2008, 2012

ESTIMATED NUMBER OF IDD CAREGIVING FAMILIES AND FAMILIES SUPPORTED BY IDD AGENCIES: FY 1988-2015

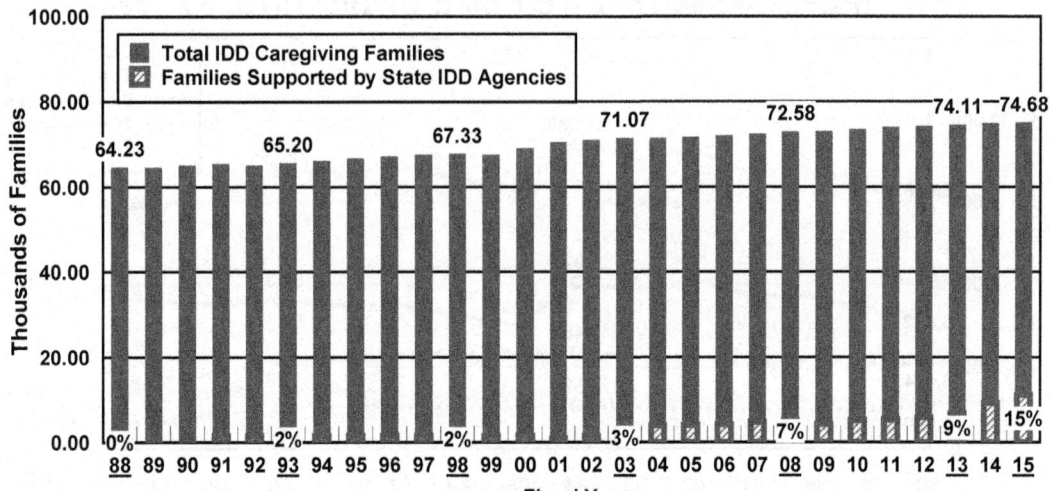

Source: Braddock et al., Coleman Institute and Department of Psychiatry, University of Colorado, 2017.
http://stateofthestates.org

IOWA

TOTAL PUBLIC IDD SPENDING FOR SERVICES: FY 1977-2015

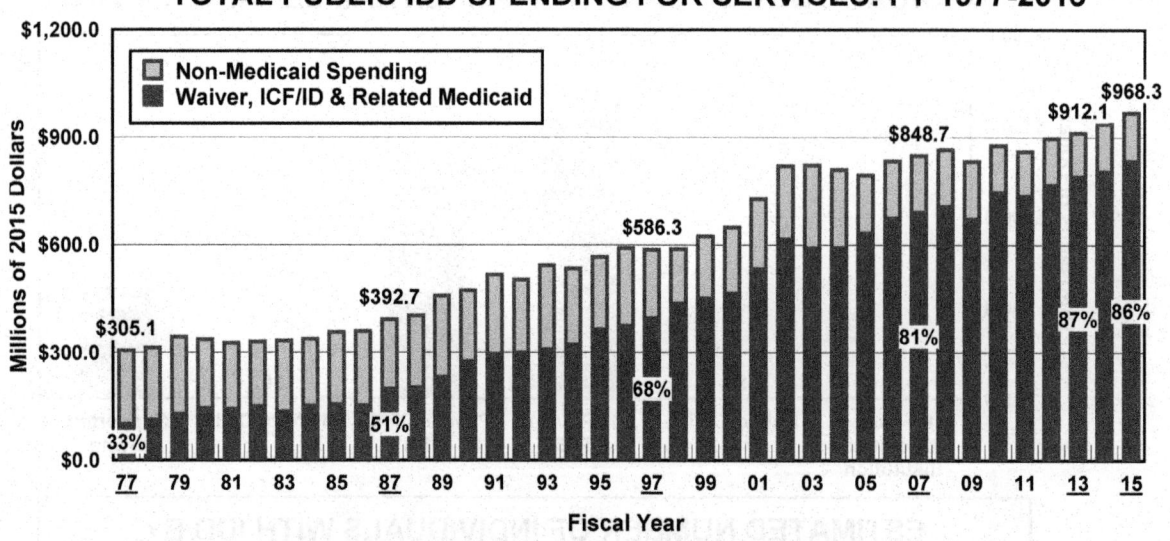

FISCAL EFFORT FOR IDD SERVICES: FY 1977-2015

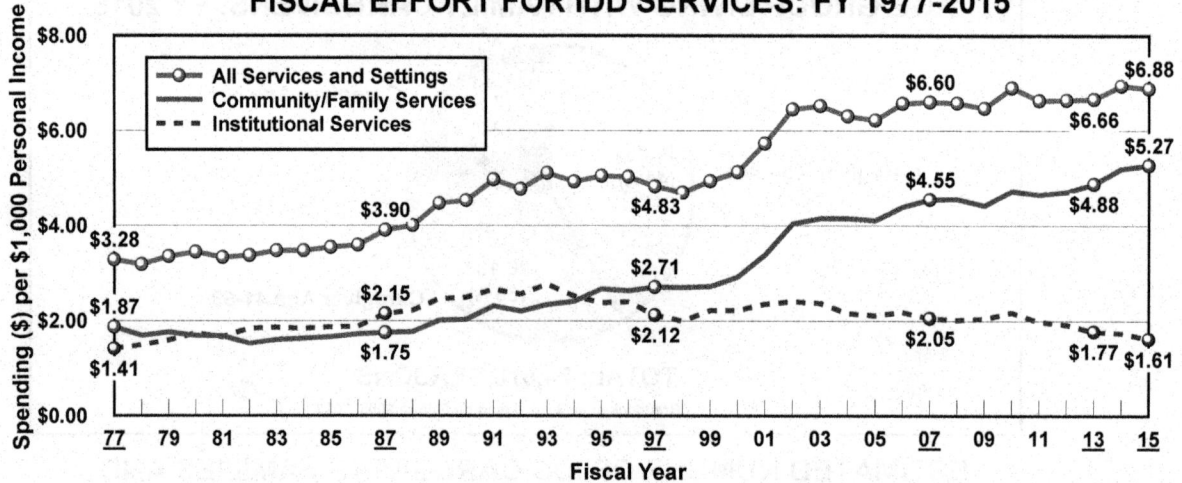

PERSONS WITH IDD BY SIZE OF SETTING: FY 1998-2015

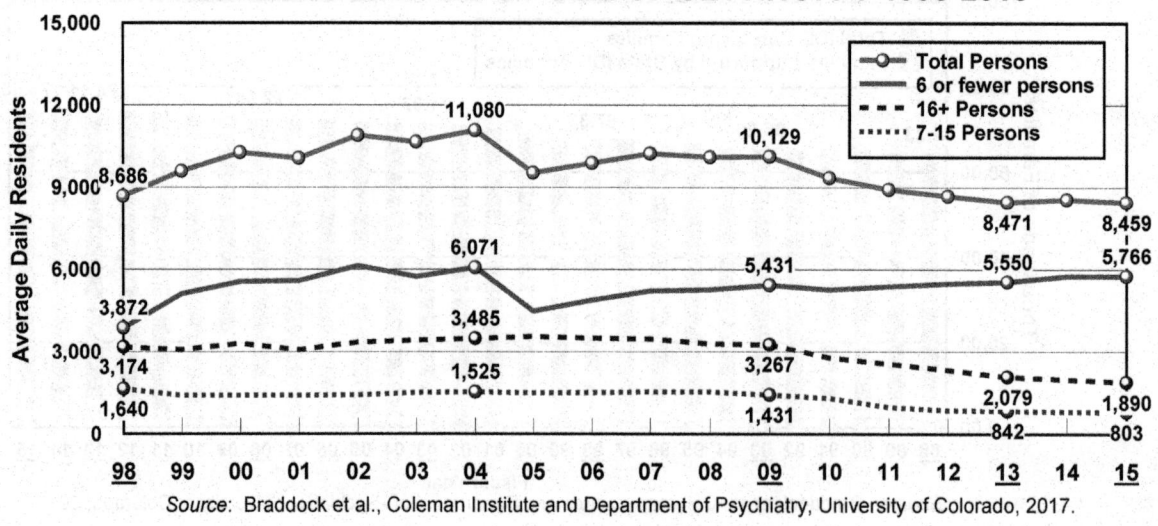

Source: Braddock et al., Coleman Institute and Department of Psychiatry, University of Colorado, 2017.
http://stateofthestates.org

IOWA

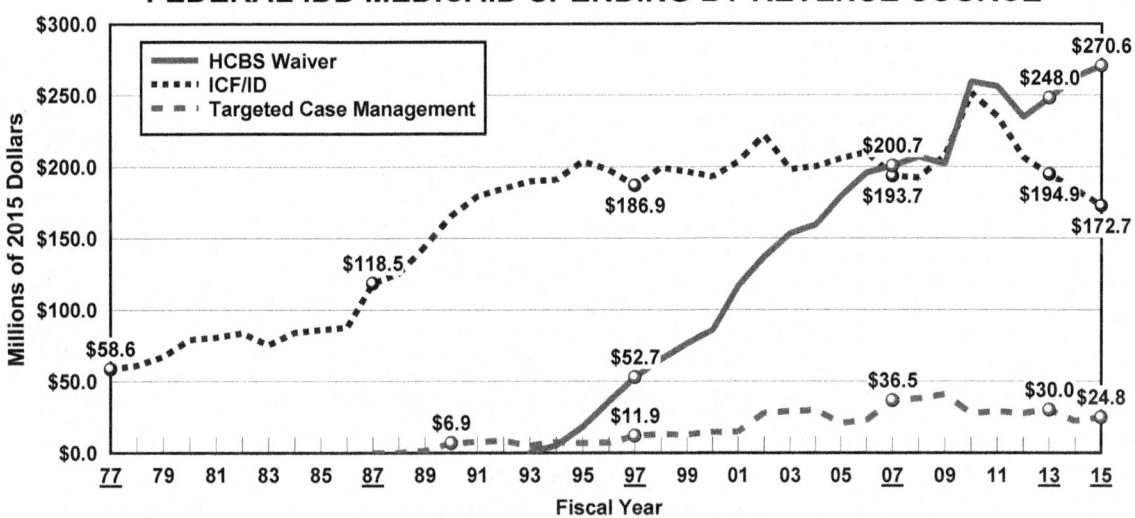

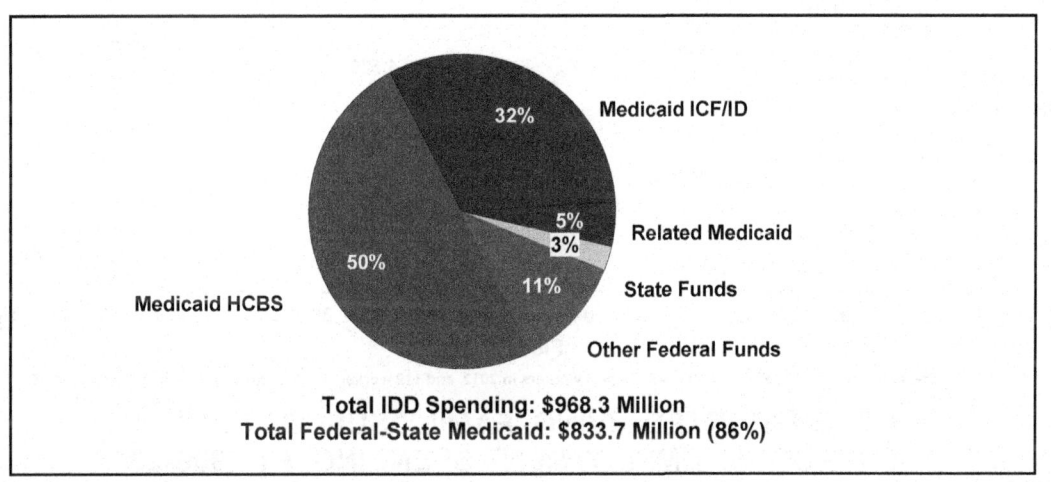

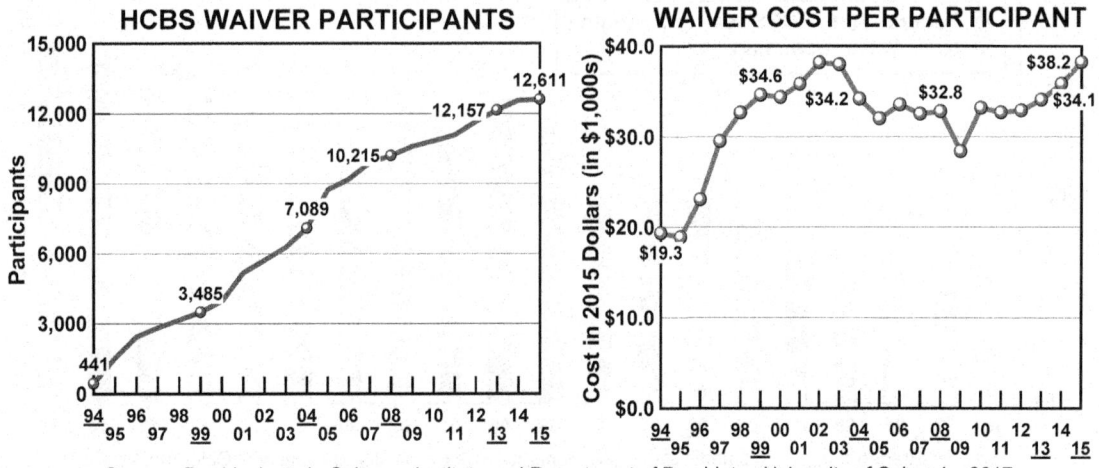

Source: Braddock et al., Coleman Institute and Department of Psychiatry, University of Colorado, 2017.
http://stateofthestates.org

IOWA

INDIVIDUAL AND FAMILY SUPPORT
SPENDING: FY 1996-2015

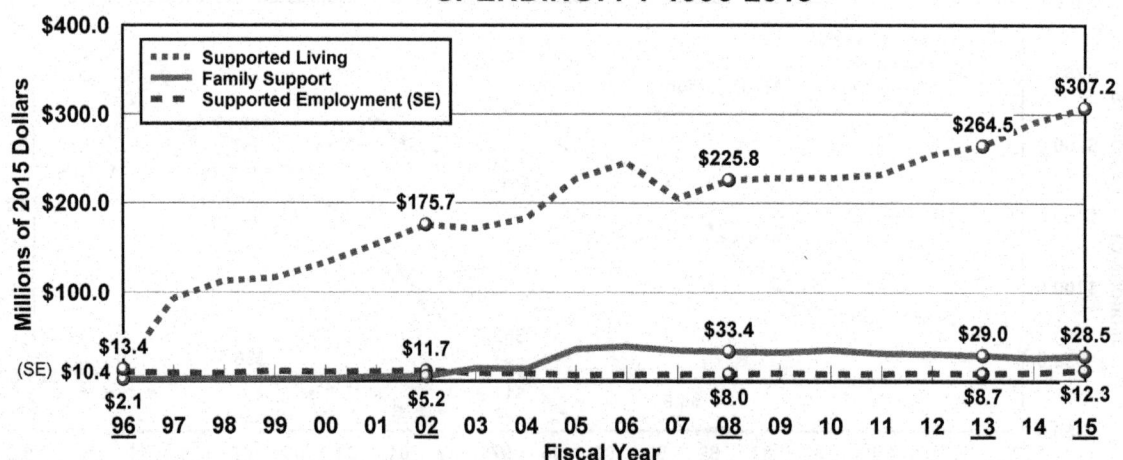

PARTICIPANTS: FY 1996-2015

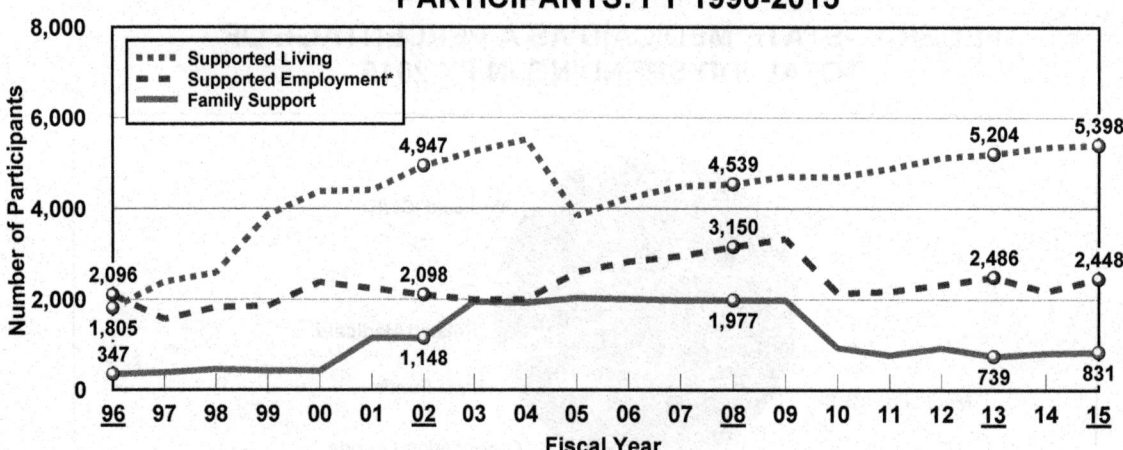

*Does not include 138 follow-along work support workers in 2012, and 112 workers in 2013, none reported in 2014 and 2015.

SUPPORTED LIVING, FAMILY SUPPORT AND SUPPORTED EMPLOYMENT SPENDING: FY 1996-2015

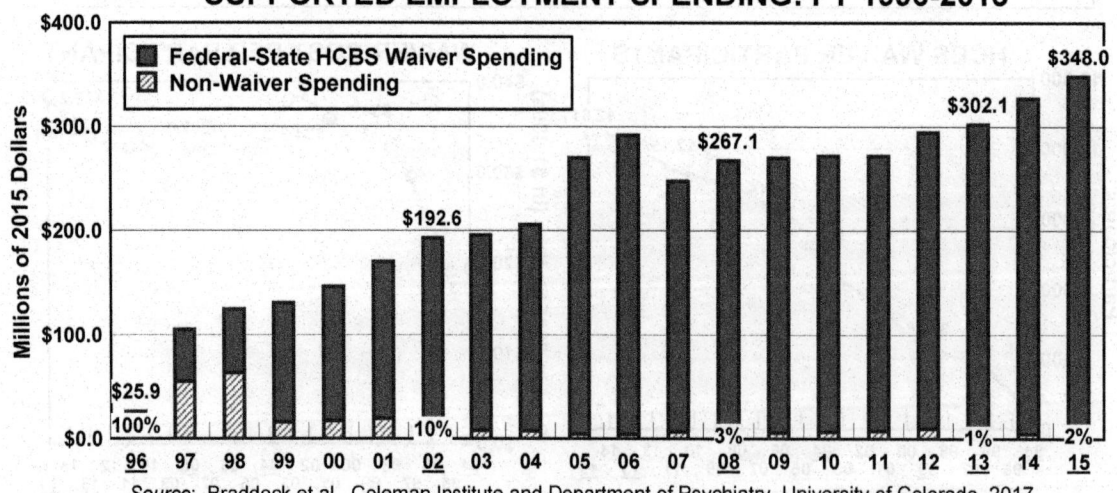

Source: Braddock et al., Coleman Institute and Department of Psychiatry, University of Colorado, 2017.
http://stateofthestates.org

IOWA

ANNUAL COST OF CARE BY RESIDENTIAL SETTING: FY 2015

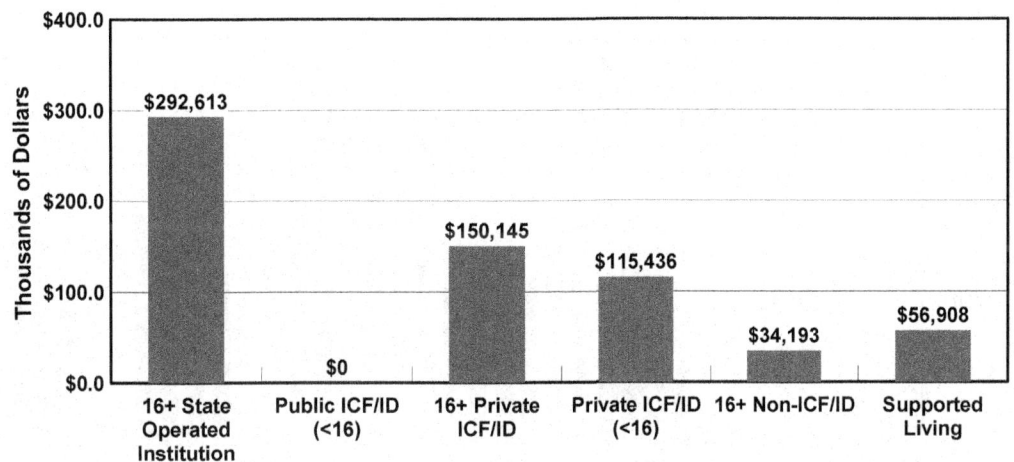

ESTIMATED NUMBER OF INDIVIDUALS WITH IDD BY AGE GROUP LIVING WITH FAMILY CAREGIVERS: FY 2015

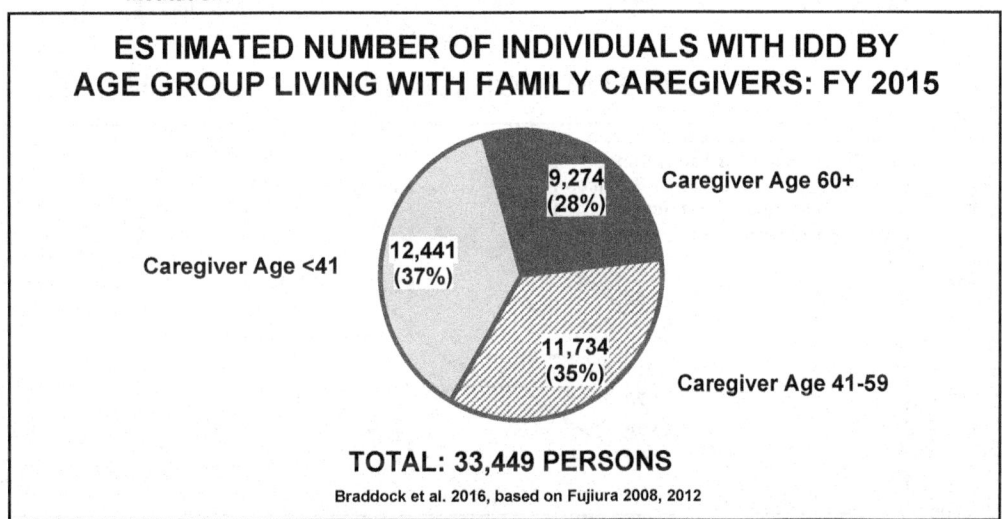

TOTAL: 33,449 PERSONS

Braddock et al. 2016, based on Fujiura 2008, 2012

ESTIMATED NUMBER OF IDD CAREGIVING FAMILIES AND FAMILIES SUPPORTED BY IDD AGENCIES: FY 1988-2015

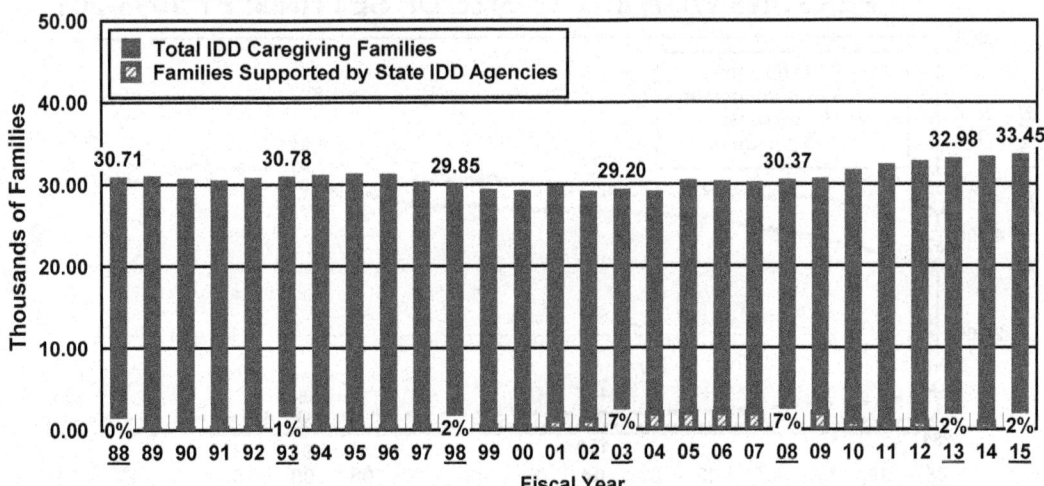

Source: Braddock et al., Coleman Institute and Department of Psychiatry, University of Colorado, 2017.
http://stateofthestates.org

KANSAS

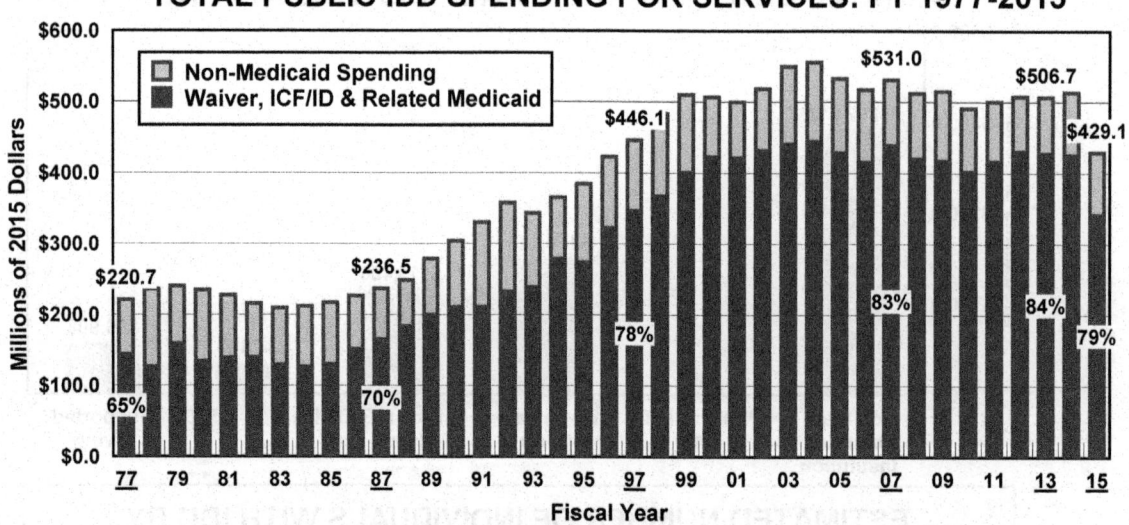

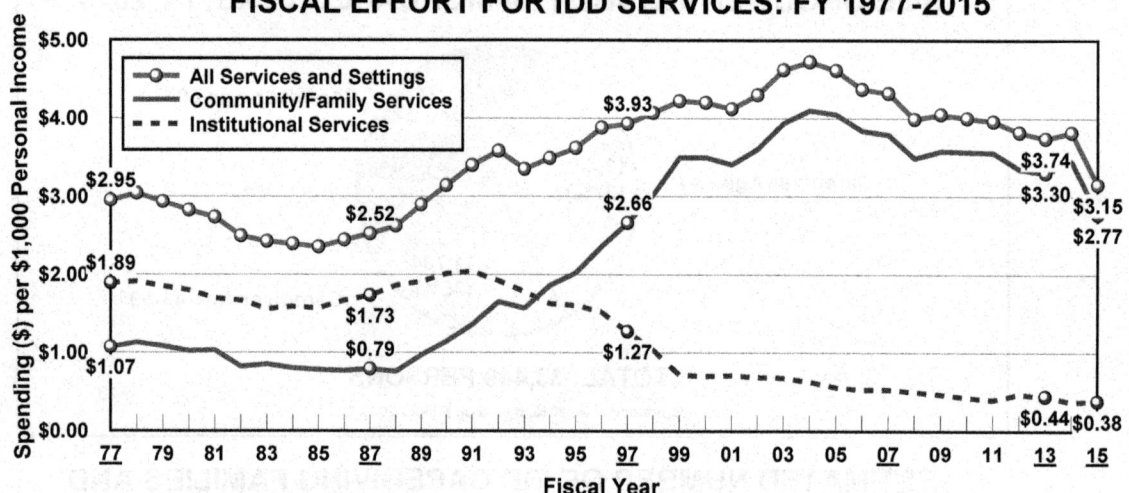

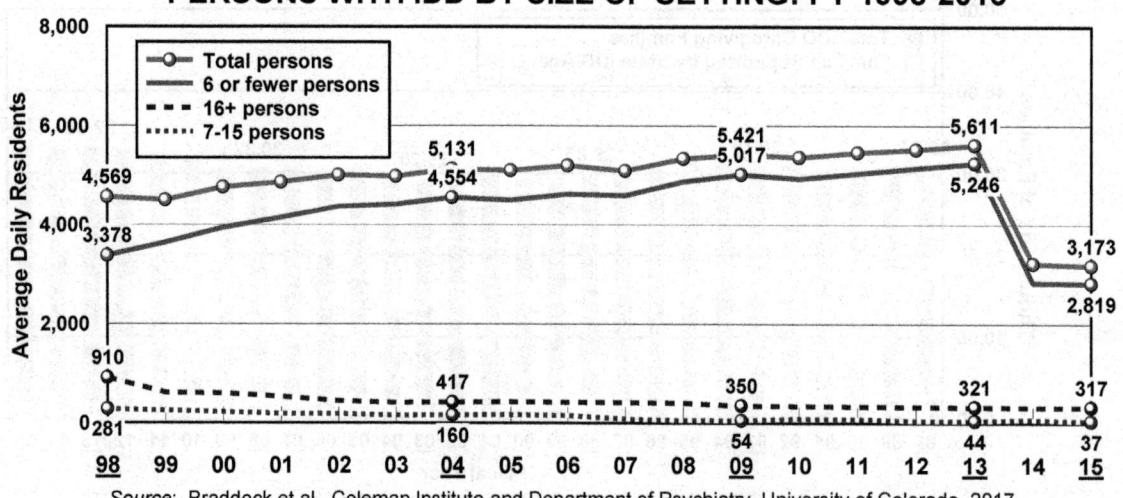

Source: Braddock et al., Coleman Institute and Department of Psychiatry, University of Colorado, 2017.
http://stateofthestates.org

KANSAS

FEDERAL IDD MEDICAID SPENDING BY REVENUE SOURCE

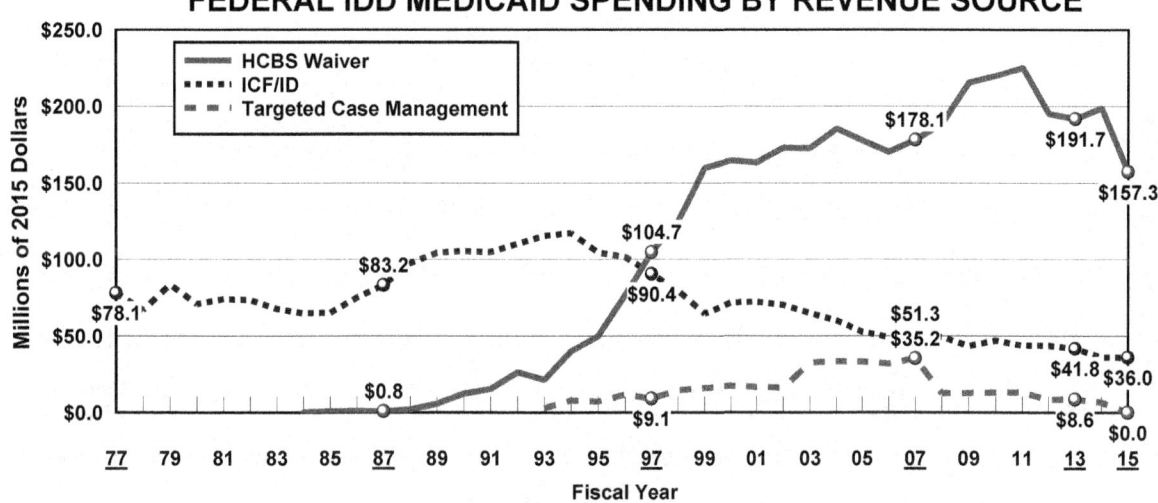

FEDERAL-STATE MEDICAID AS A PERCENTAGE OF TOTAL IDD SPENDING IN FY 2015

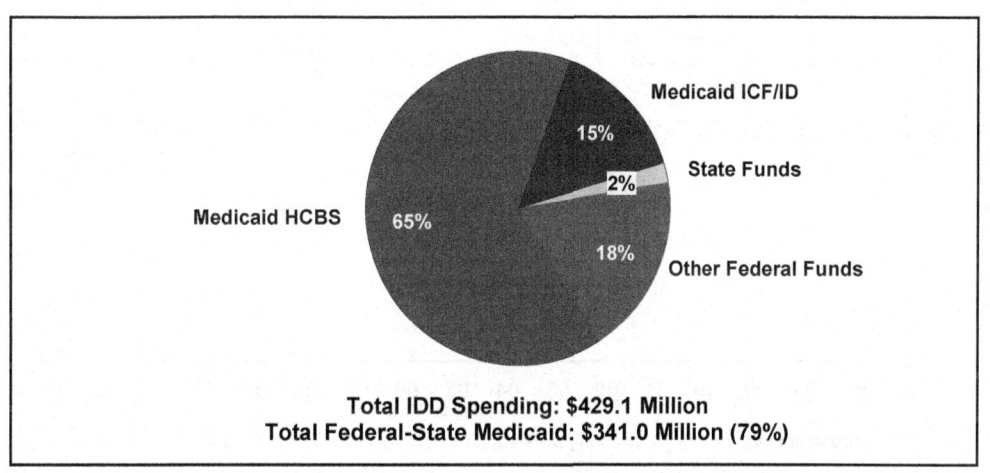

Total IDD Spending: $429.1 Million
Total Federal-State Medicaid: $341.0 Million (79%)

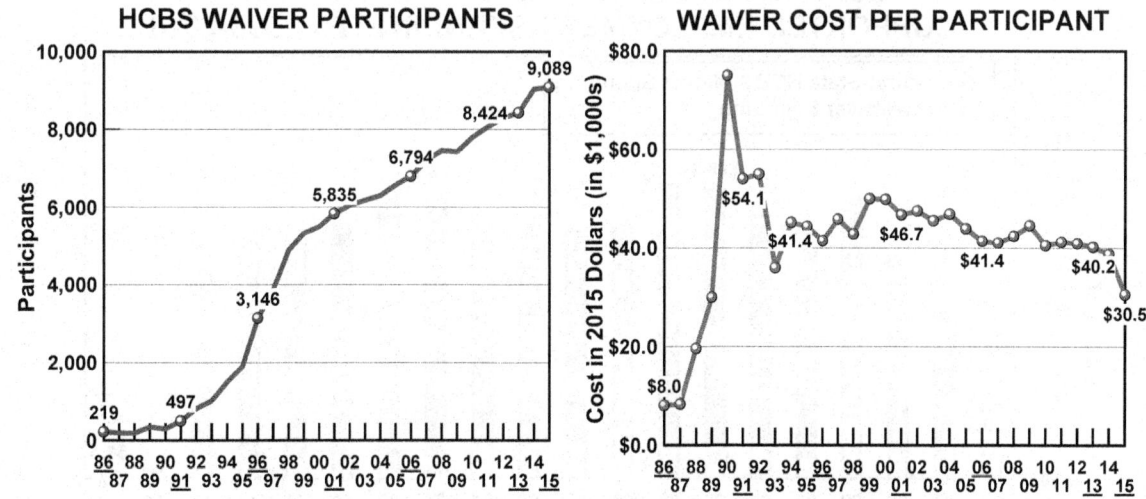

Source: Braddock et al., Coleman Institute and Department of Psychiatry, University of Colorado, 2017.
http://stateofthestates.org

KANSAS
INDIVIDUAL AND FAMILY SUPPORT
SPENDING: FY 1996-2015

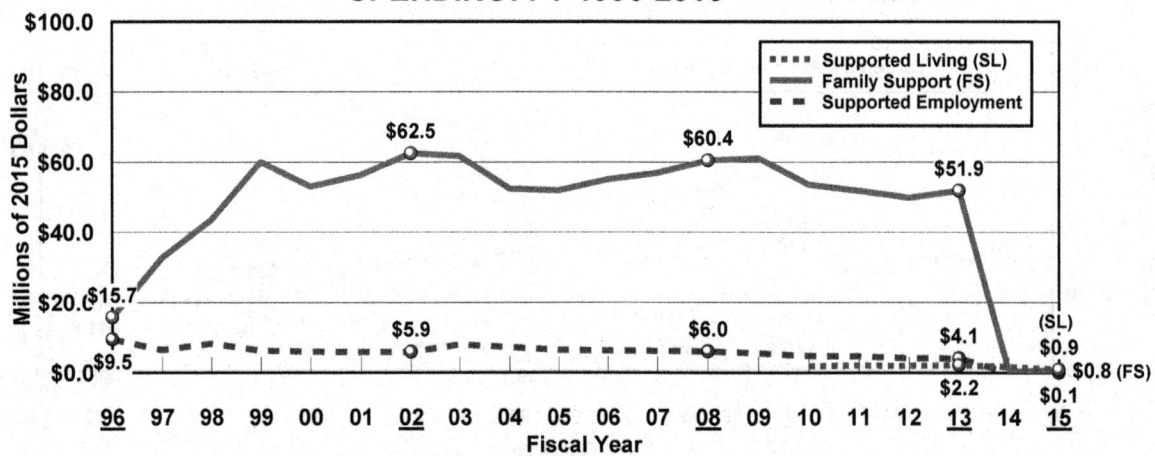

PARTICIPANTS: FY 1996-2015

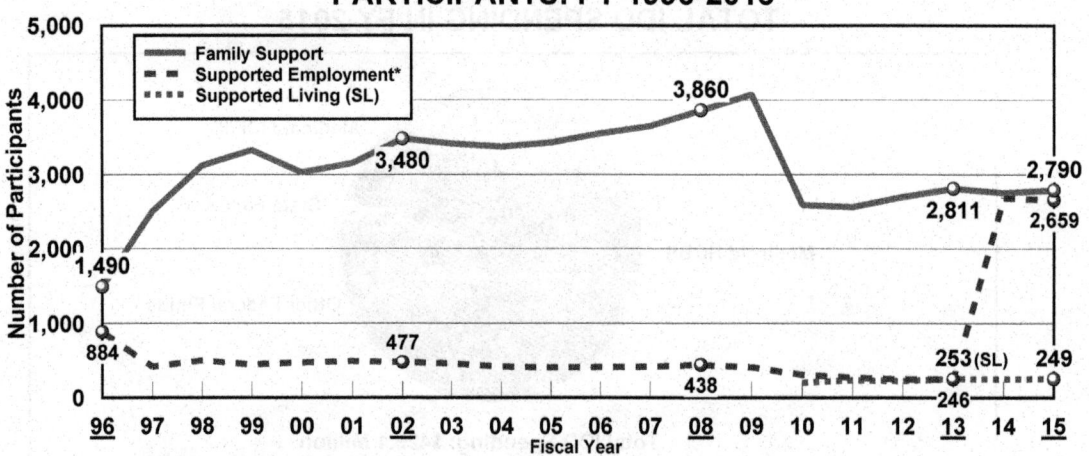

*Does not include 575 follow-along work support workers in 2014 and in 2015.

SUPPORTED LIVING, FAMILY SUPPORT AND SUPPORTED EMPLOYMENT SPENDING: FY 1996-2015

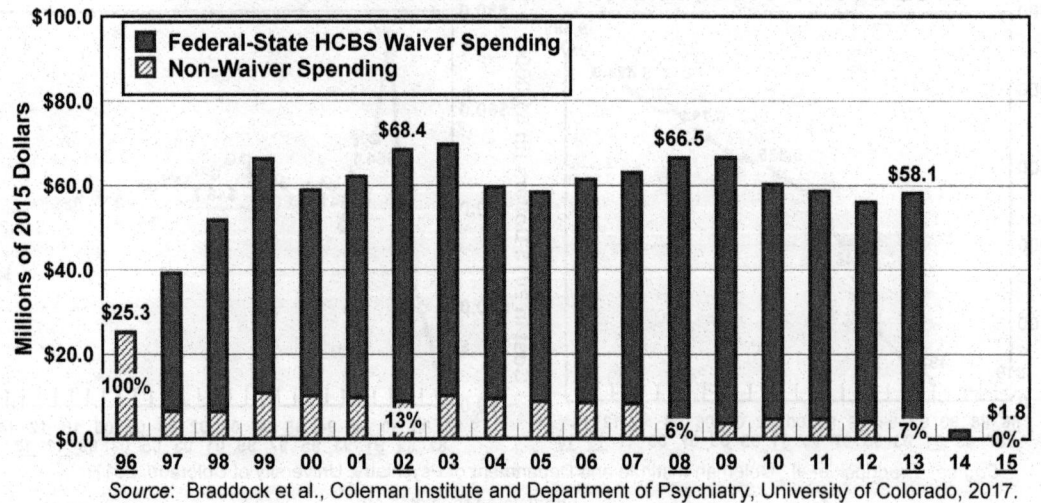

Source: Braddock et al., Coleman Institute and Department of Psychiatry, University of Colorado, 2017.
http://stateofthestates.org

KANSAS

ANNUAL COST OF CARE BY RESIDENTIAL SETTING: FY 2015

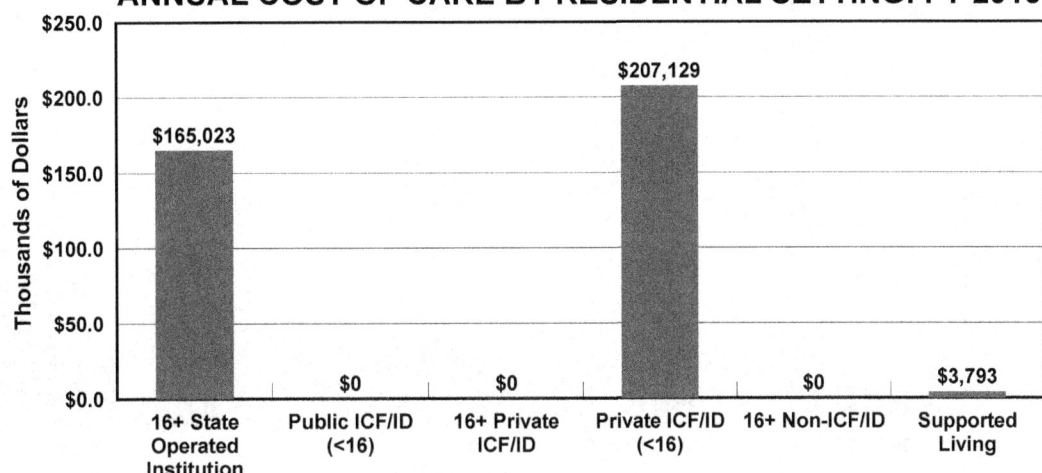

ESTIMATED NUMBER OF INDIVIDUALS WITH IDD BY AGE GROUP LIVING WITH FAMILY CAREGIVERS: FY 2015

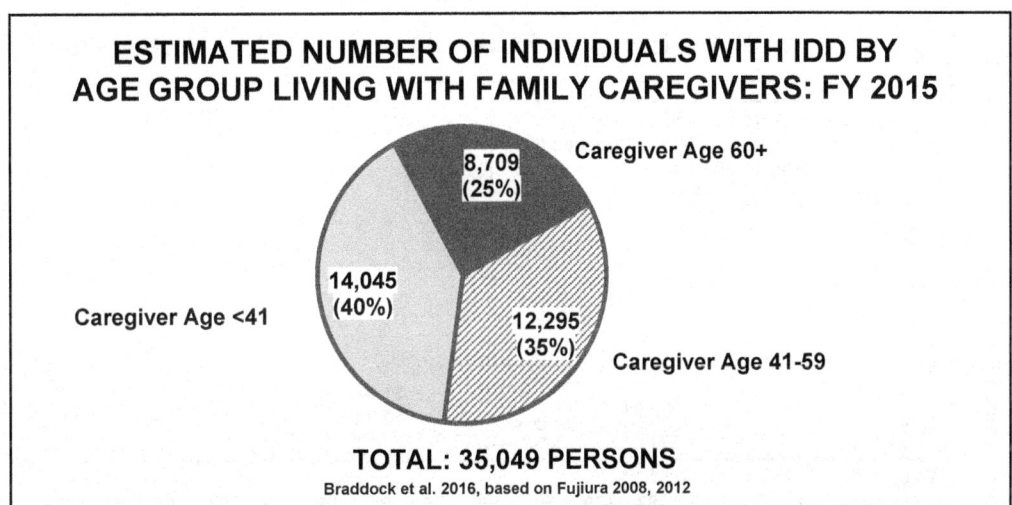

TOTAL: 35,049 PERSONS
Braddock et al. 2016, based on Fujiura 2008, 2012

ESTIMATED NUMBER OF IDD CAREGIVING FAMILIES AND FAMILIES SUPPORTED BY IDD AGENCIES: FY 1988-2015

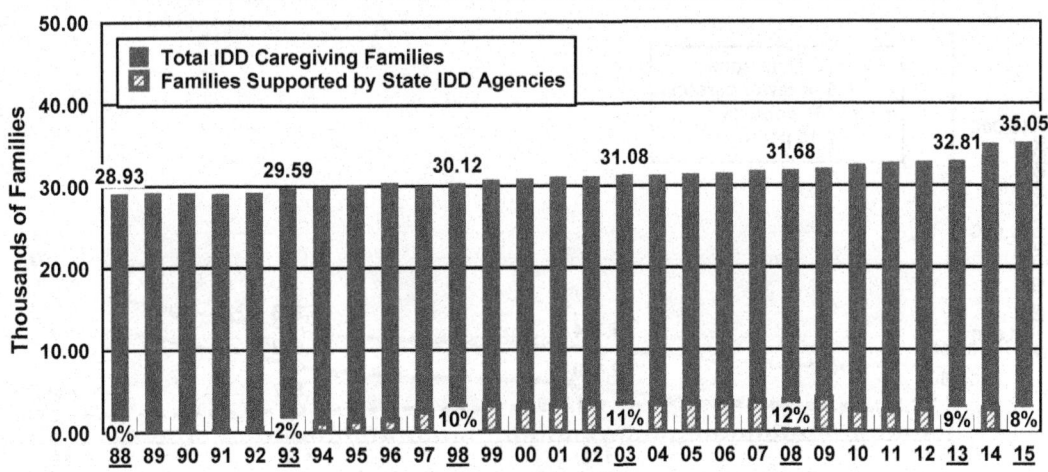

Source: Braddock et al., Coleman Institute and Department of Psychiatry, University of Colorado, 2017.
http://stateofthestates.org

KENTUCKY

TOTAL PUBLIC IDD SPENDING FOR SERVICES: FY 1977-2015

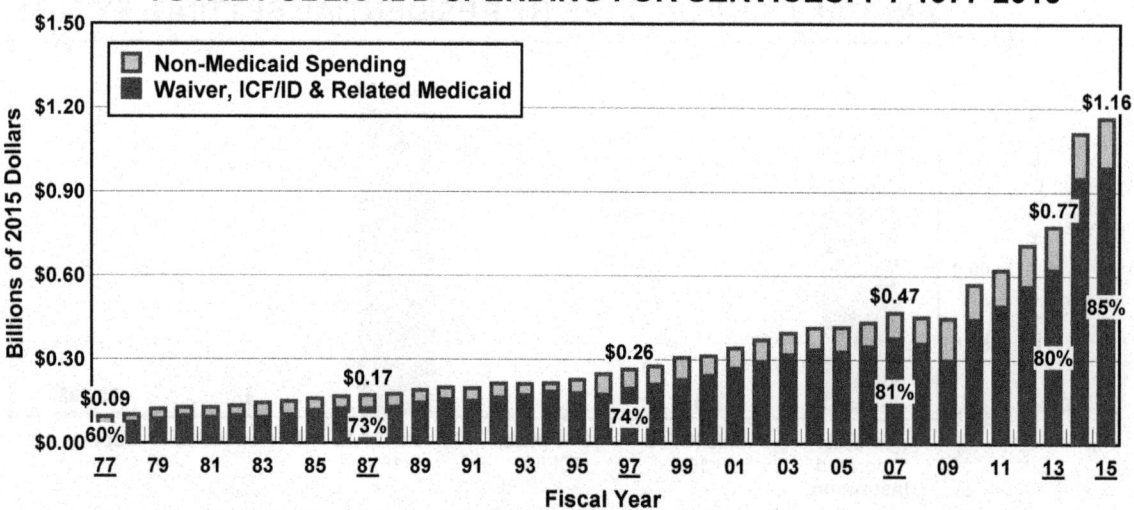

FISCAL EFFORT FOR IDD SERVICES: FY 1977-2015

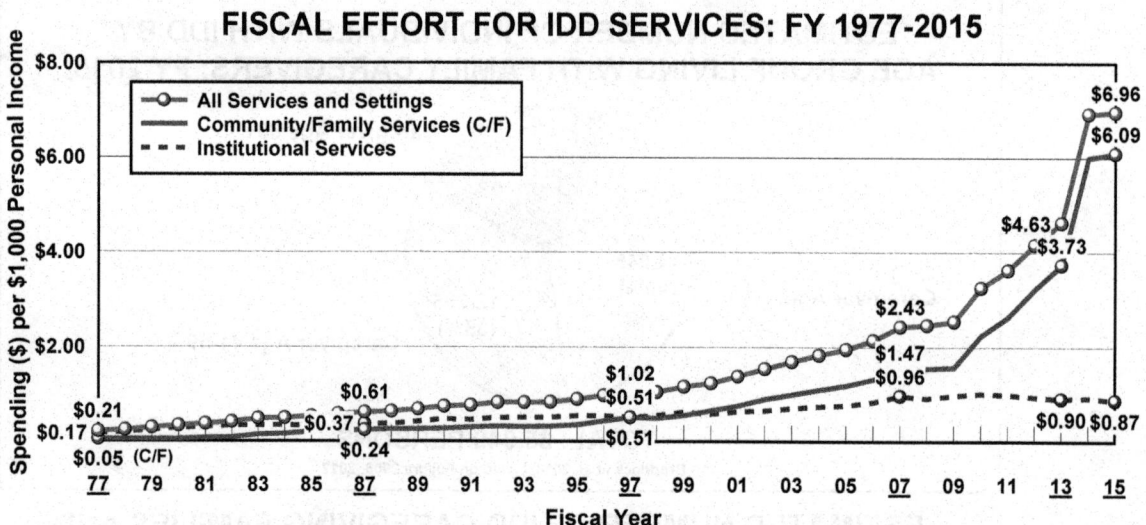

PERSONS WITH IDD BY SIZE OF SETTING: FY 1998-2015

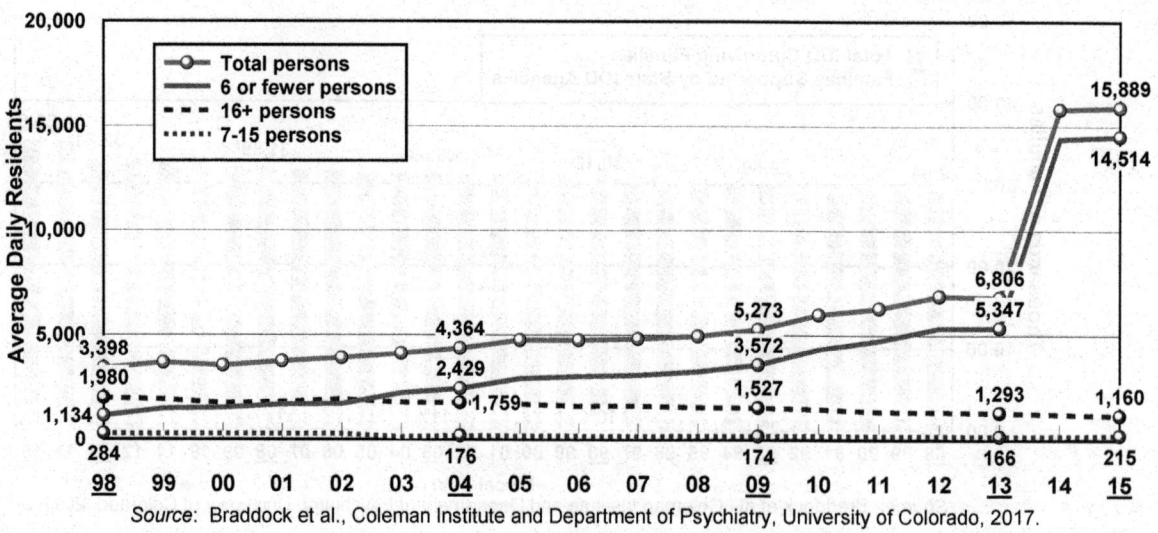

Source: Braddock et al., Coleman Institute and Department of Psychiatry, University of Colorado, 2017.
http://stateofthestates.org

KENTUCKY

FEDERAL IDD MEDICAID SPENDING BY REVENUE SOURCE

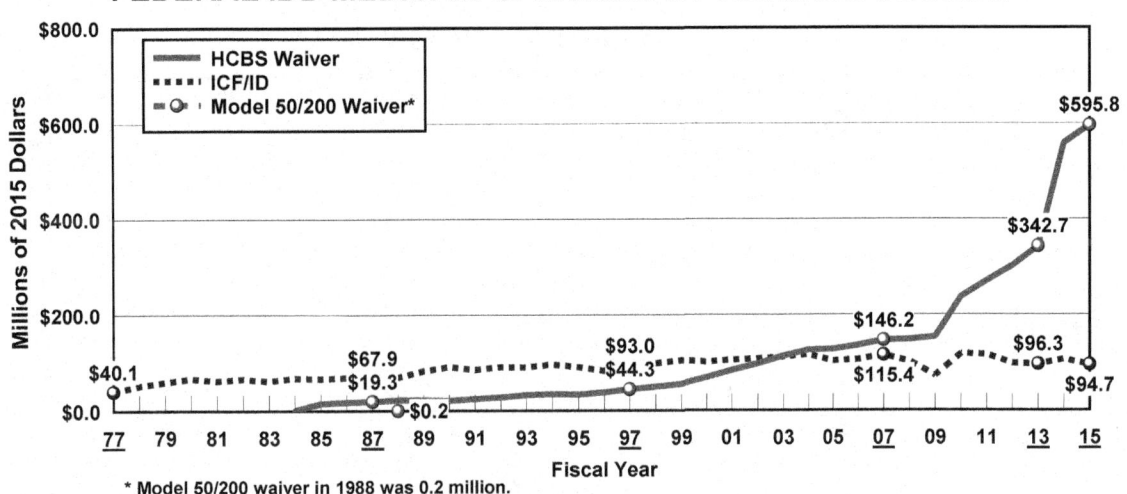

* Model 50/200 waiver in 1988 was 0.2 million.

FEDERAL-STATE MEDICAID AS A PERCENTAGE OF TOTAL IDD SPENDING IN FY 2015

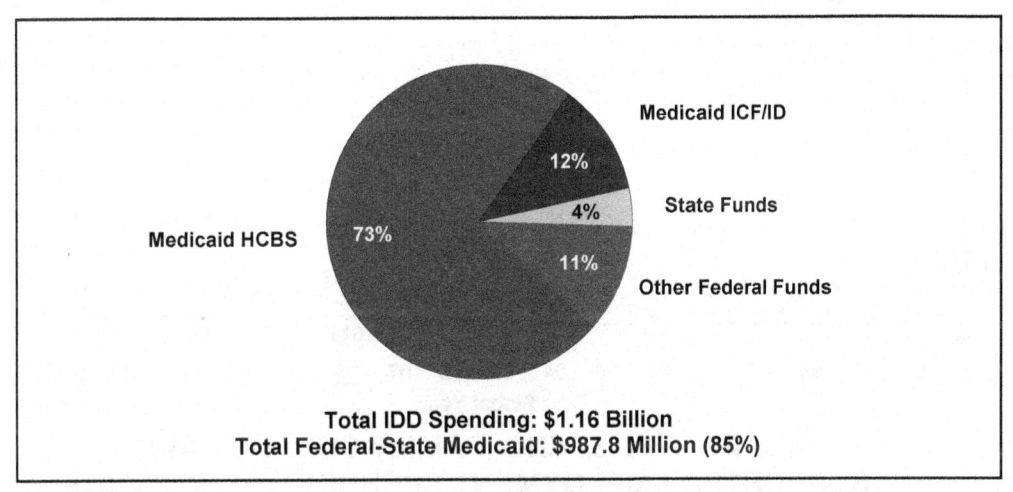

Total IDD Spending: $1.16 Billion
Total Federal-State Medicaid: $987.8 Million (85%)

HCBS WAIVER PARTICIPANTS / WAIVER COST PER PARTICIPANT

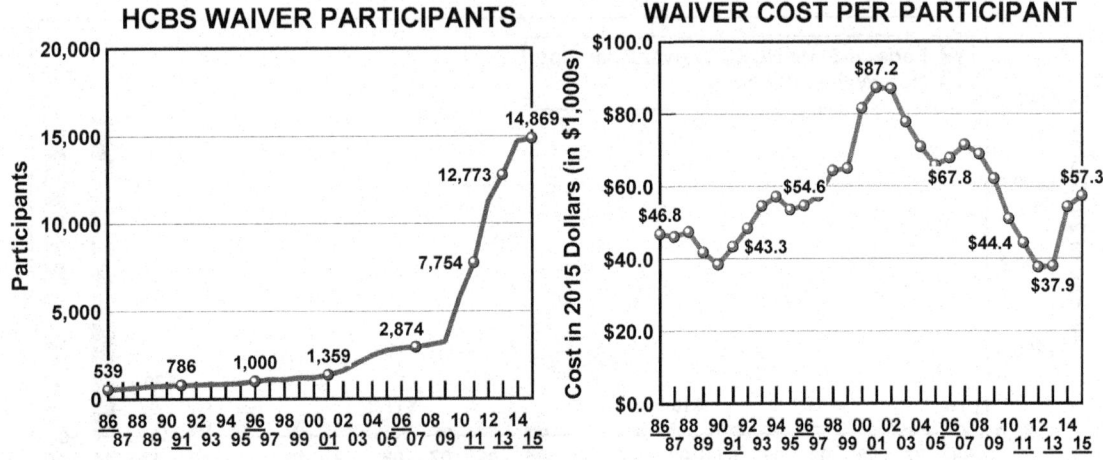

Source: Braddock et al., Coleman Institute and Department of Psychiatry, University of Colorado, 2017.
http://stateofthestates.org

KENTUCKY

INDIVIDUAL AND FAMILY SUPPORT
SPENDING: FY 1996-2015

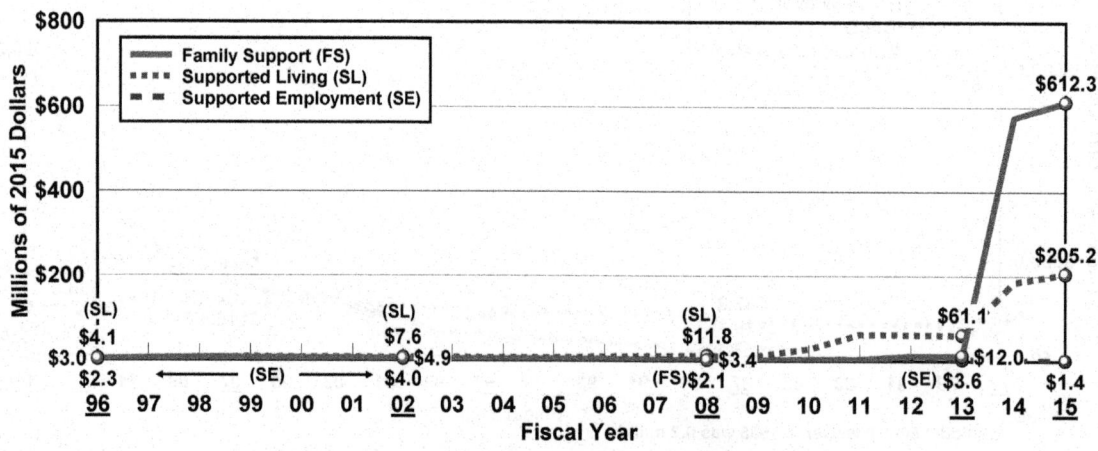

PARTICIPANTS: FY 1996-2015

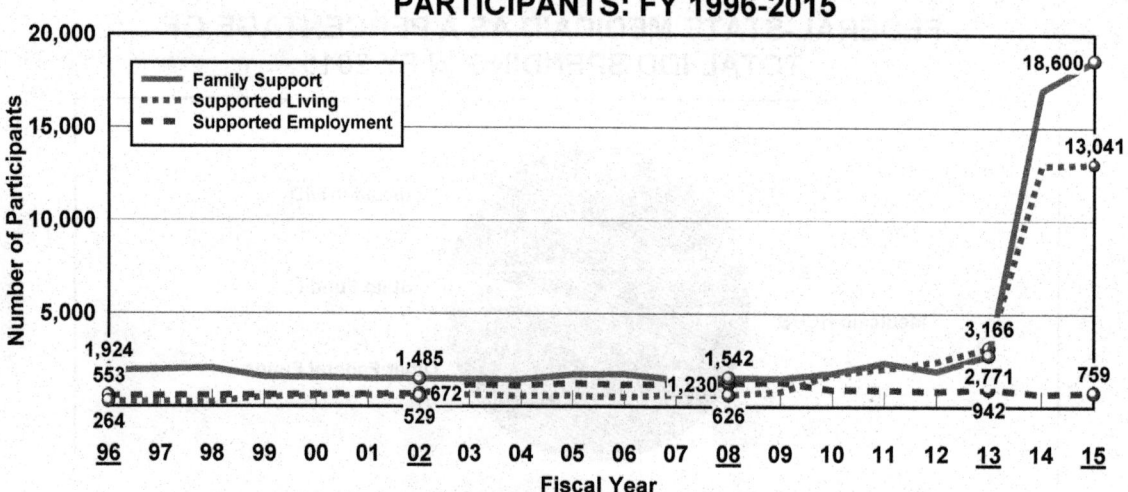

SUPPORTED LIVING, FAMILY SUPPORT AND SUPPORTED EMPLOYMENT SPENDING: FY 1996-2015

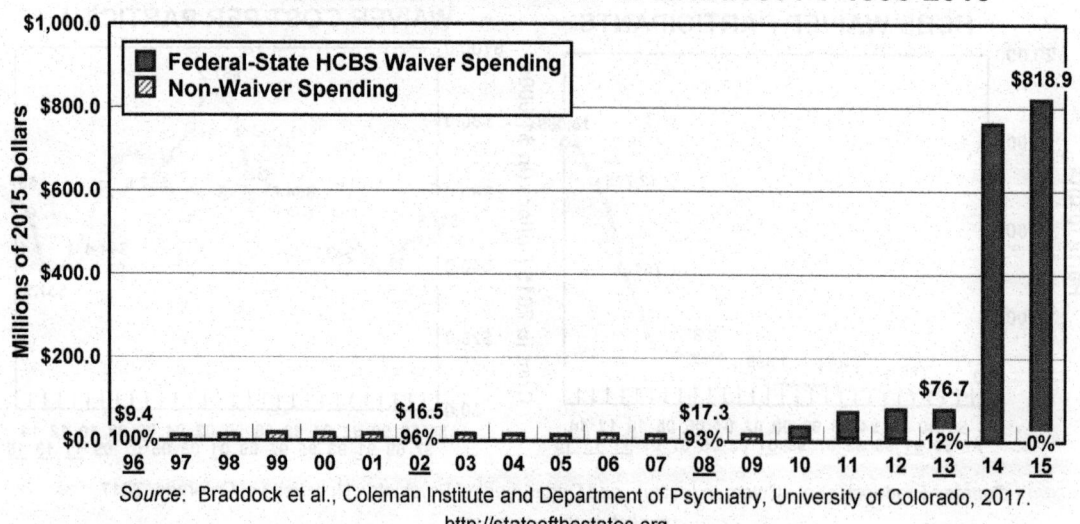

Source: Braddock et al., Coleman Institute and Department of Psychiatry, University of Colorado, 2017.
http://stateofthestates.org

KENTUCKY

ANNUAL COST OF CARE BY RESIDENTIAL SETTING: FY 2015

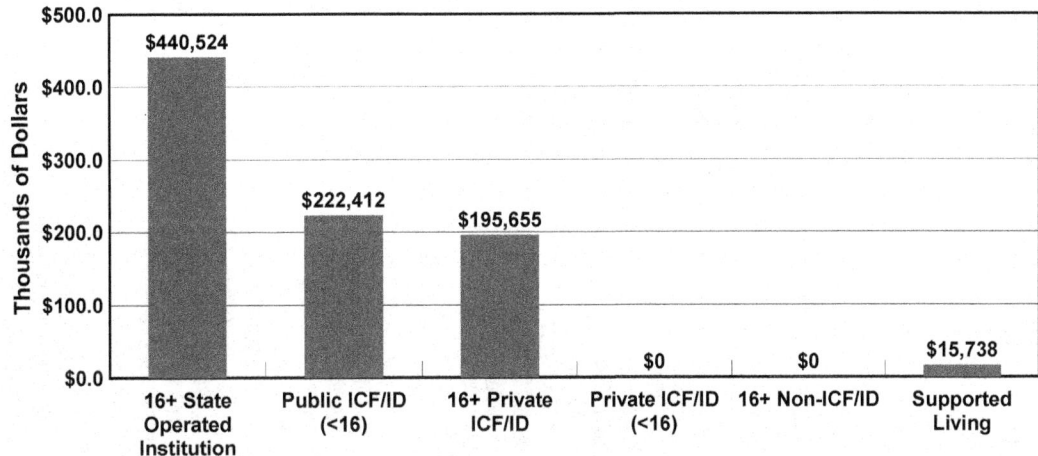

ESTIMATED NUMBER OF INDIVIDUALS WITH IDD BY AGE GROUP LIVING WITH FAMILY CAREGIVERS: FY 2015

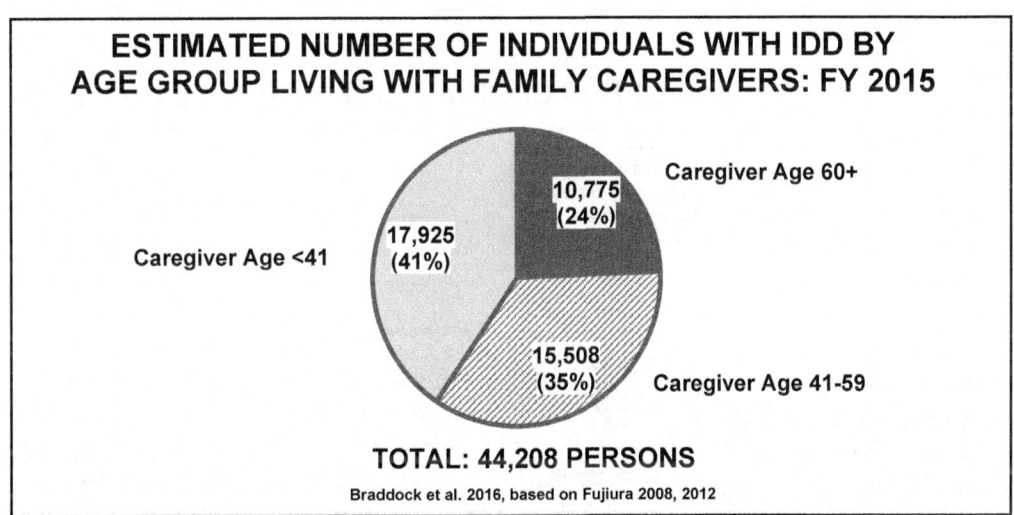

TOTAL: 44,208 PERSONS

Braddock et al. 2016, based on Fujiura 2008, 2012

ESTIMATED NUMBER OF IDD CAREGIVING FAMILIES AND FAMILIES SUPPORTED BY IDD AGENCIES: FY 1988-2015

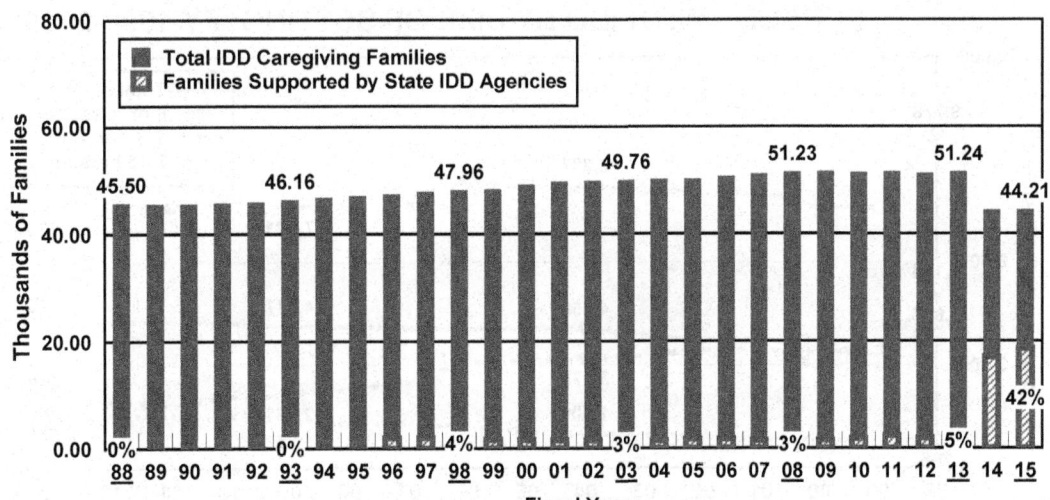

Source: Braddock et al., Coleman Institute and Department of Psychiatry, University of Colorado, 2017.
http://stateofthestates.org

LOUISIANA

TOTAL PUBLIC IDD SPENDING FOR SERVICES: FY 1977-2015

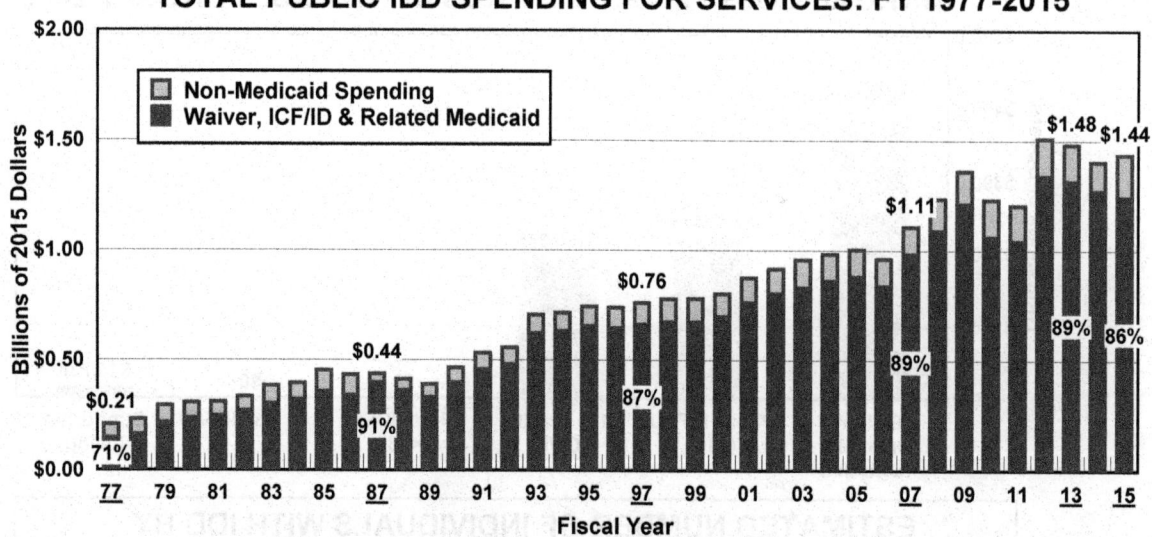

FISCAL EFFORT FOR IDD SERVICES: FY 1977-2015

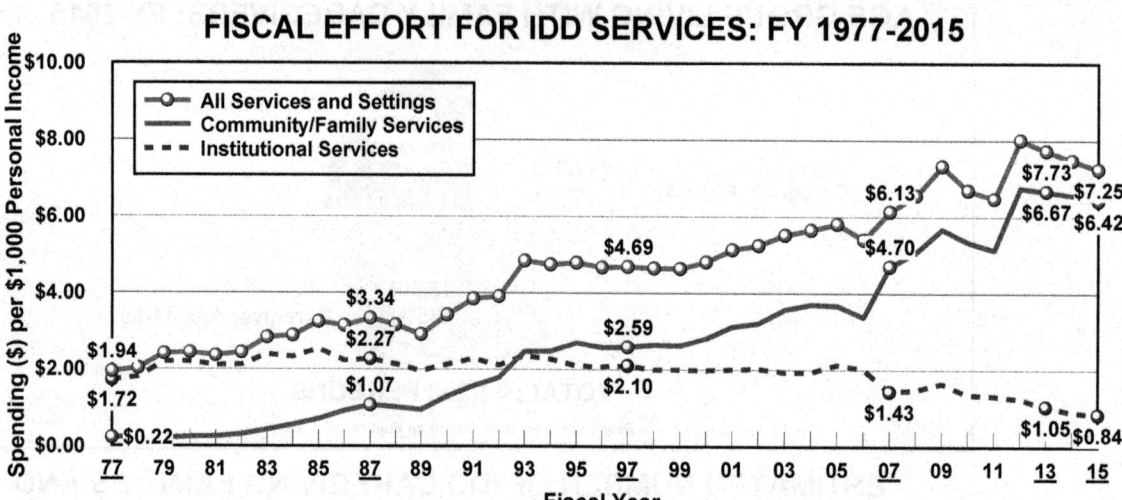

PERSONS WITH IDD BY SIZE OF SETTING: FY 1998-2015

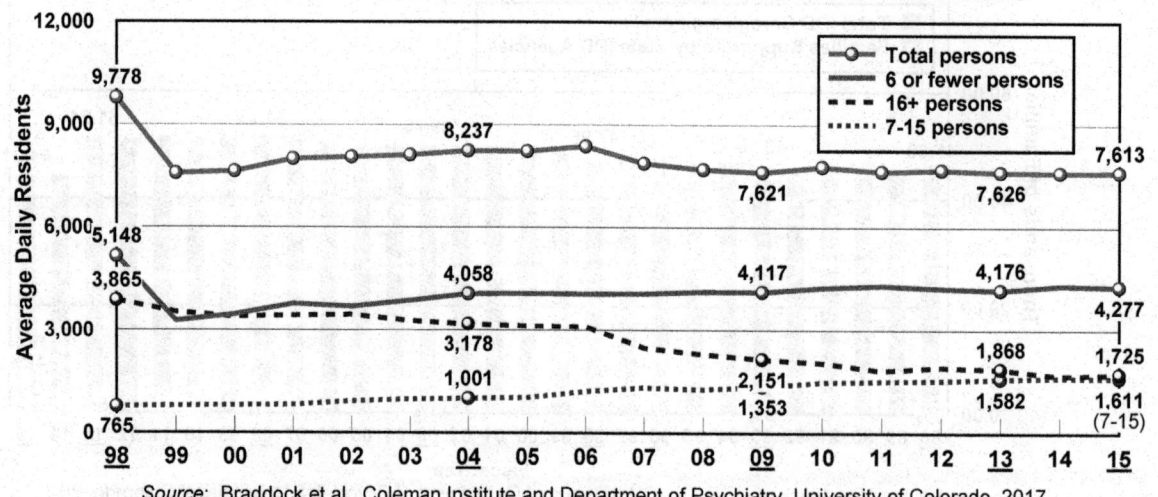

Source: Braddock et al., Coleman Institute and Department of Psychiatry, University of Colorado, 2017.
http://stateofthestates.org

LOUISIANA

FEDERAL IDD MEDICAID SPENDING BY REVENUE SOURCE

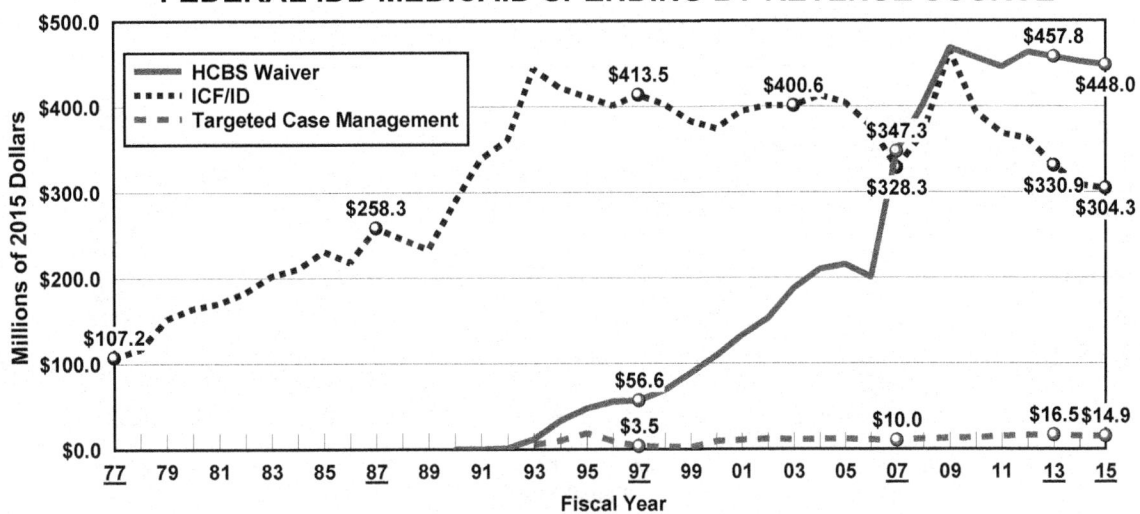

FEDERAL-STATE MEDICAID AS A PERCENTAGE OF TOTAL IDD SPENDING IN FY 2015

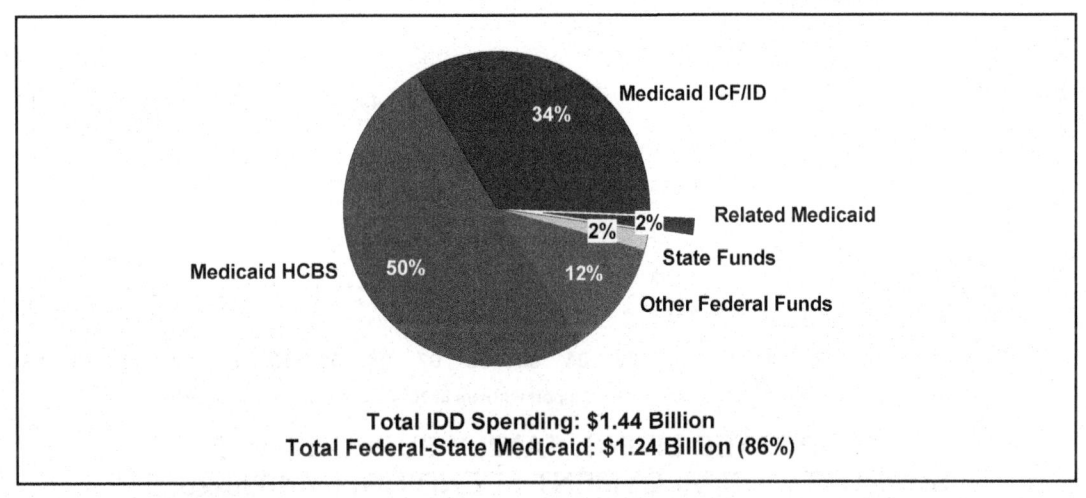

Total IDD Spending: $1.44 Billion
Total Federal-State Medicaid: $1.24 Billion (86%)

HCBS WAIVER PARTICIPANTS / WAIVER COST PER PARTICIPANT

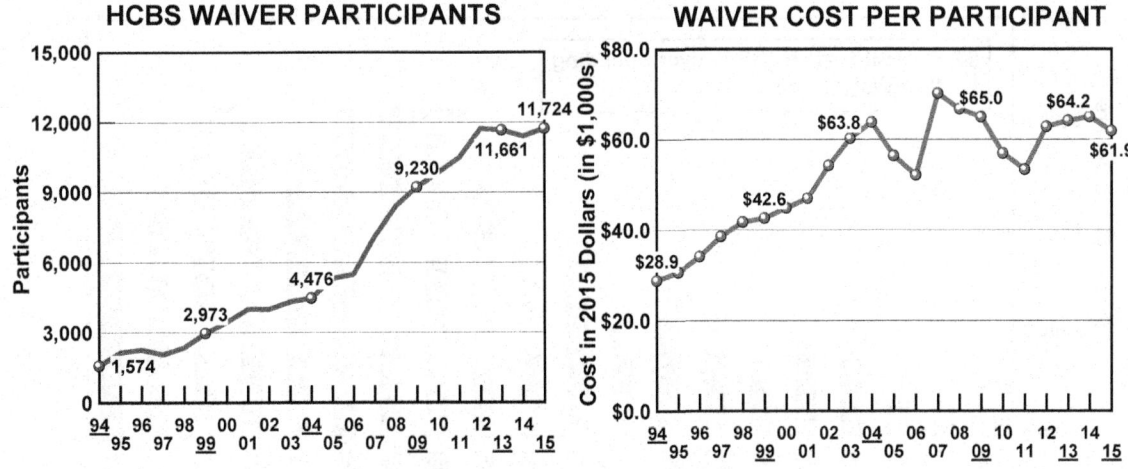

Source: Braddock et al., Coleman Institute and Department of Psychiatry, University of Colorado, 2017.
http://stateofthestates.org

LOUISIANA
INDIVIDUAL AND FAMILY SUPPORT
SPENDING: FY 1996-2015

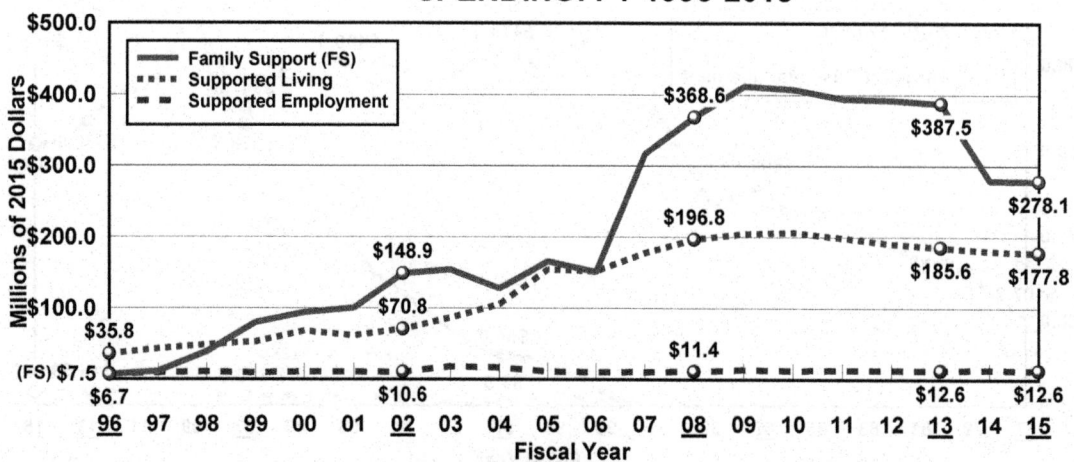

PARTICIPANTS: FY 1996-2015

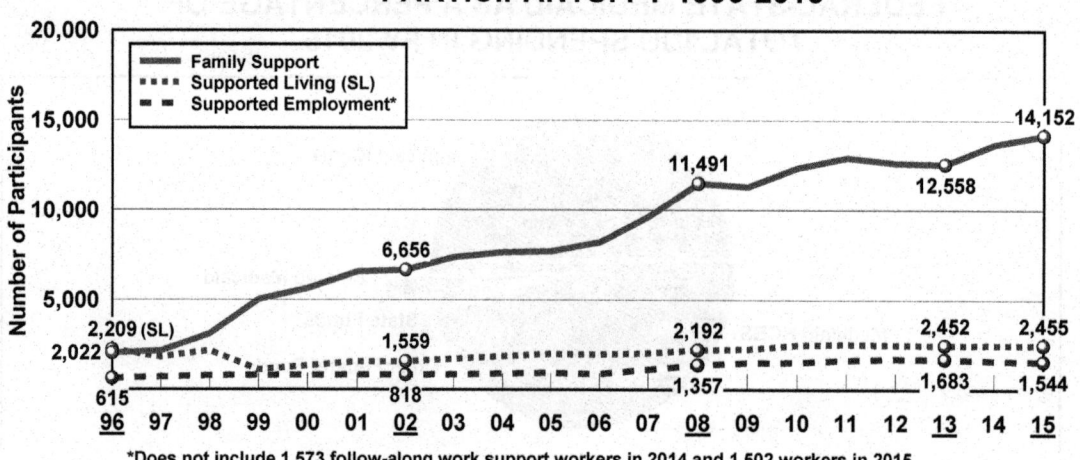

*Does not include 1,573 follow-along work support workers in 2014 and 1,502 workers in 2015.

SUPPORTED LIVING, FAMILY SUPPORT AND SUPPORTED EMPLOYMENT SPENDING: FY 1996-2015

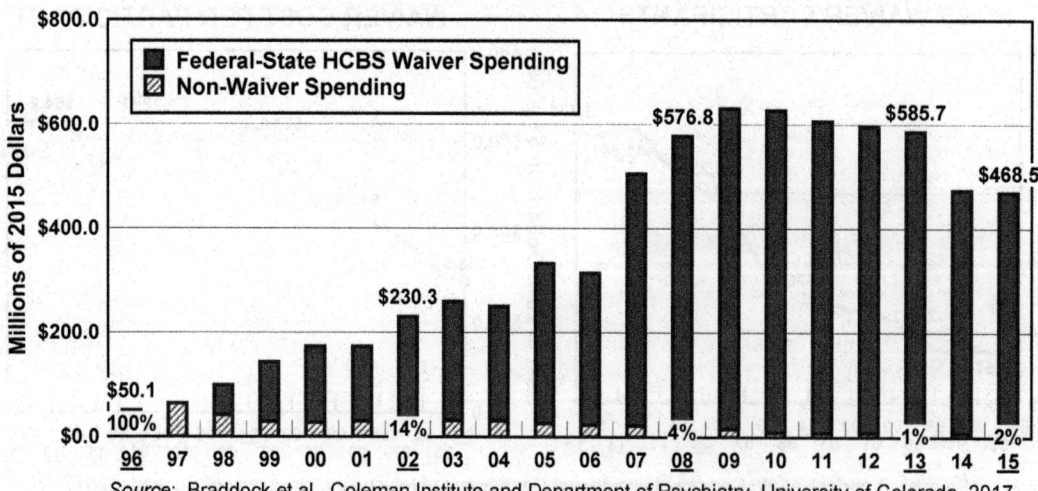

Source: Braddock et al., Coleman Institute and Department of Psychiatry, University of Colorado, 2017.
http://stateofthestates.org

LOUISIANA

ANNUAL COST OF CARE BY RESIDENTIAL SETTING: FY 2015

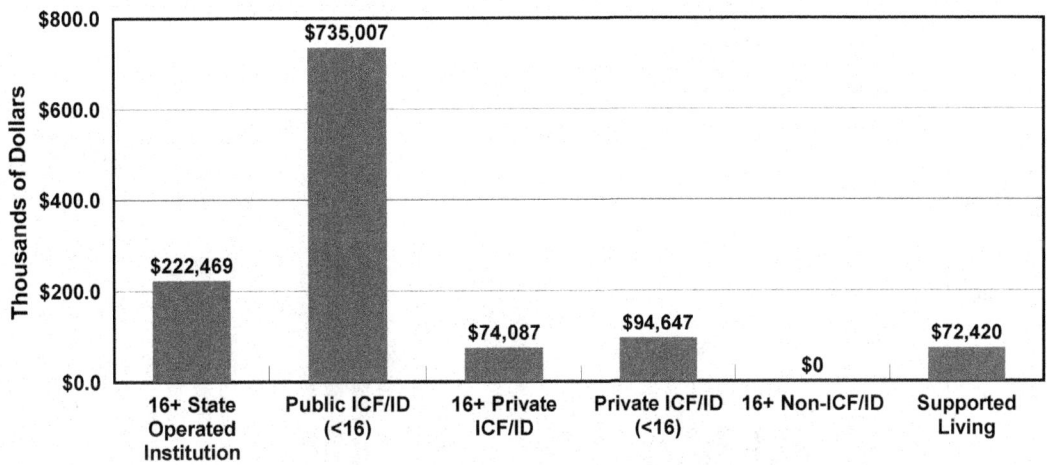

ESTIMATED NUMBER OF INDIVIDUALS WITH IDD BY AGE GROUP LIVING WITH FAMILY CAREGIVERS: FY 2015

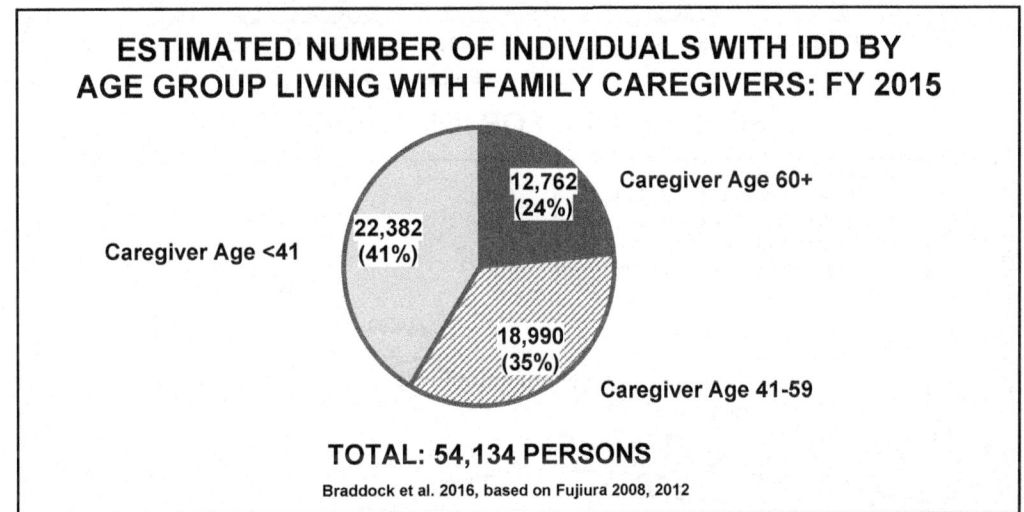

TOTAL: 54,134 PERSONS

Braddock et al. 2016, based on Fujiura 2008, 2012

ESTIMATED NUMBER OF IDD CAREGIVING FAMILIES AND FAMILIES SUPPORTED BY IDD AGENCIES: FY 1988-2015

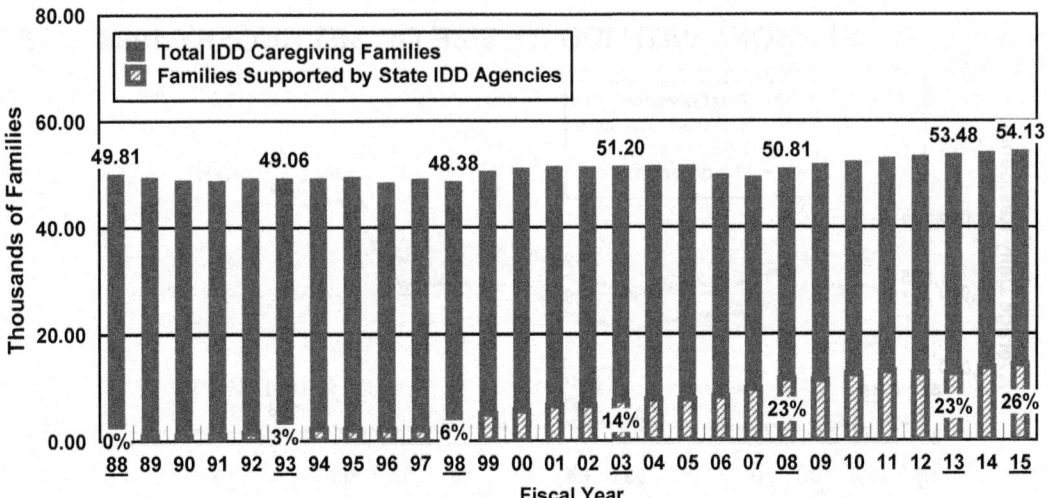

Source: Braddock et al., Coleman Institute and Department of Psychiatry, University of Colorado, 2017.
http://stateofthestates.org

MAINE

TOTAL PUBLIC IDD SPENDING FOR SERVICES: FY 1977-2015

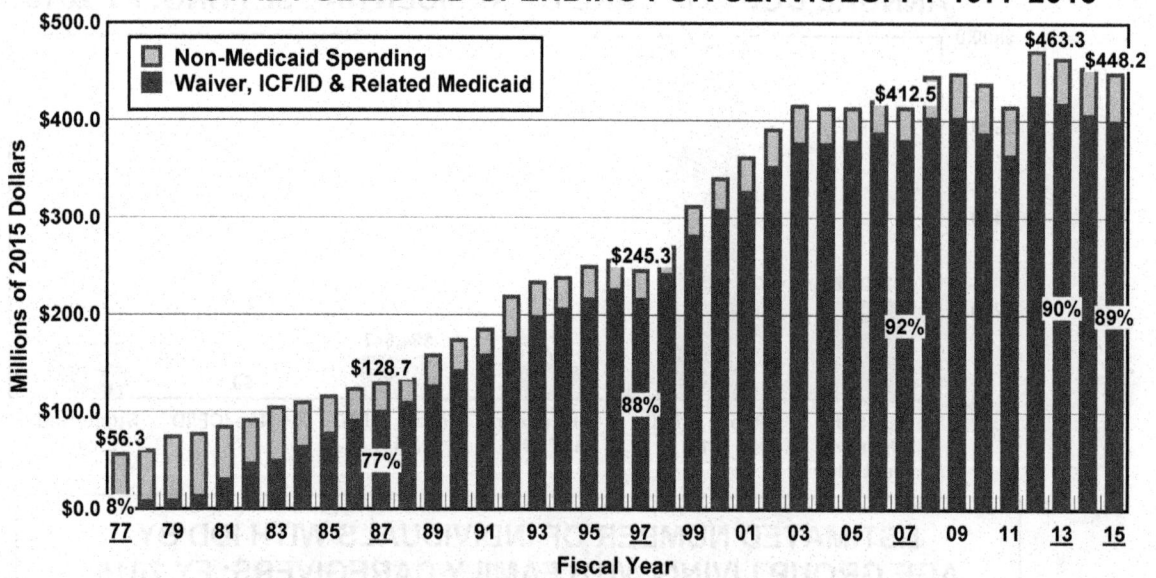

FISCAL EFFORT FOR IDD SERVICES: FY 1977-2015

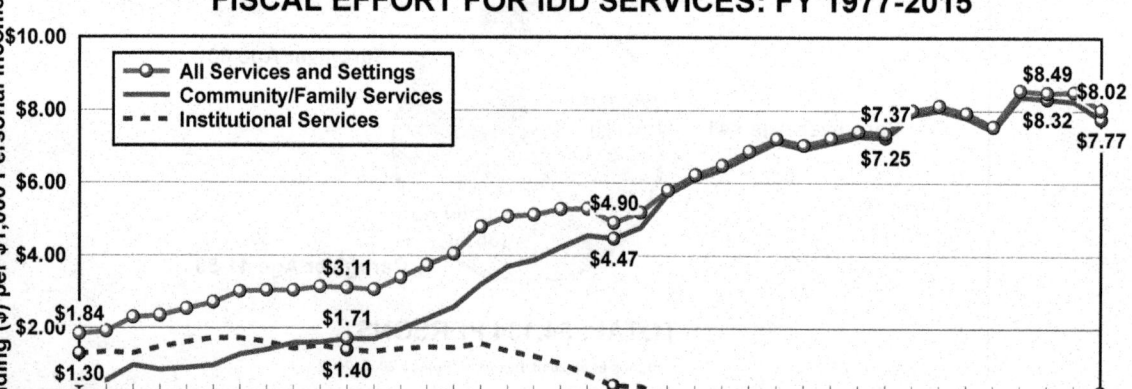

PERSONS WITH IDD BY SIZE OF SETTING: FY 1998-2015

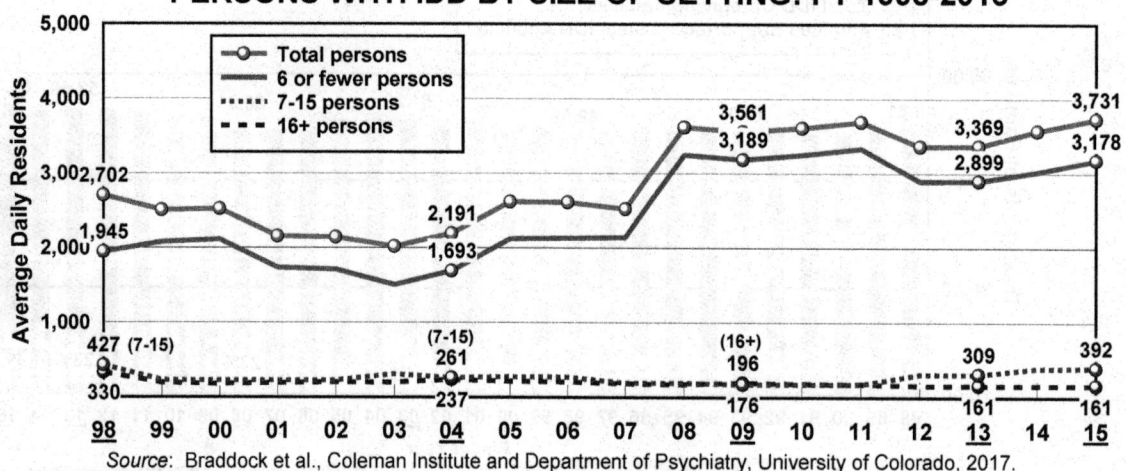

Source: Braddock et al., Coleman Institute and Department of Psychiatry, University of Colorado, 2017.
http://stateofthestates.org

MAINE

FEDERAL IDD MEDICAID SPENDING BY REVENUE SOURCE

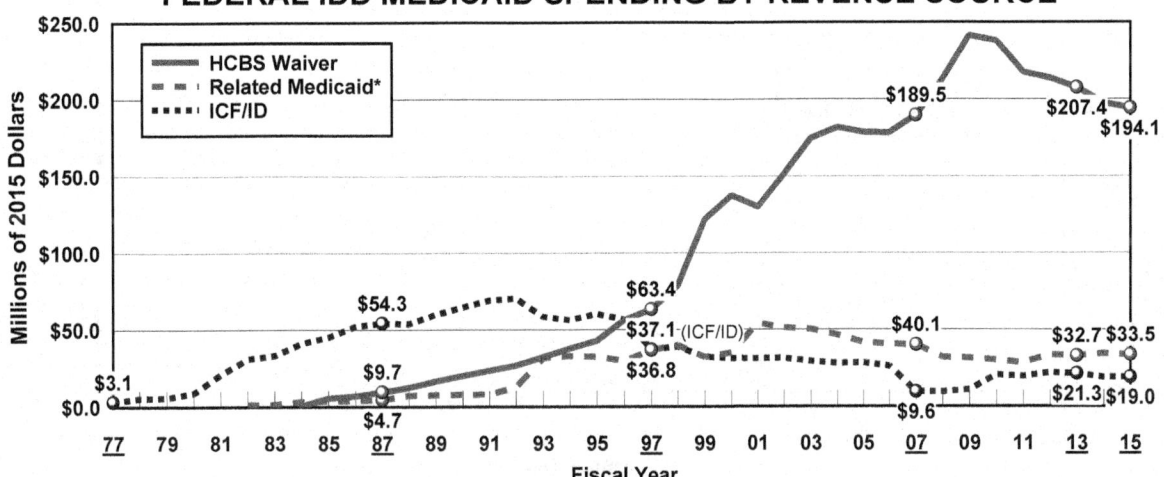

*In 2015, "Related Medicaid" was targeted case management ($10.0 million), clinic rehab ($9.90 million), personal assistant ($1.35 million) and administration ($12.21 million).

FEDERAL-STATE MEDICAID AS A PERCENTAGE OF TOTAL IDD SPENDING IN FY 2015

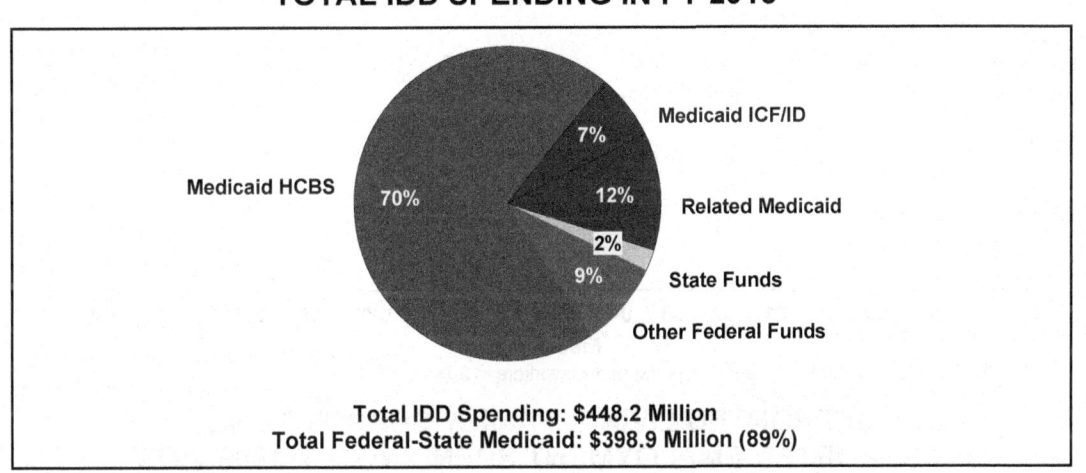

Total IDD Spending: $448.2 Million
Total Federal-State Medicaid: $398.9 Million (89%)

HCBS WAIVER PARTICIPANTS / WAIVER COST PER PARTICIPANT

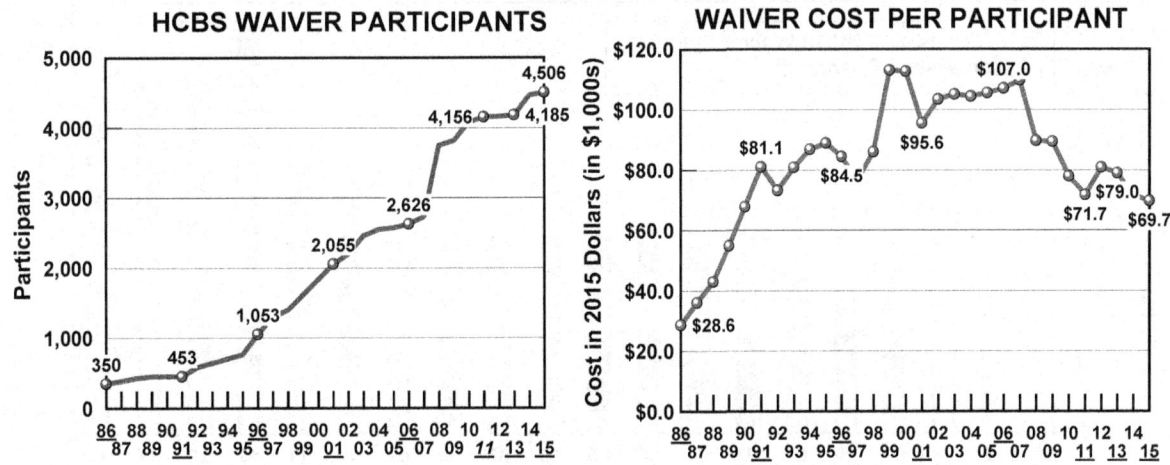

Source: Braddock et al., Coleman Institute and Department of Psychiatry, University of Colorado, 2017.

http://stateofthestates.org

MAINE

INDIVIDUAL AND FAMILY SUPPORT
SPENDING: FY 1996-2015

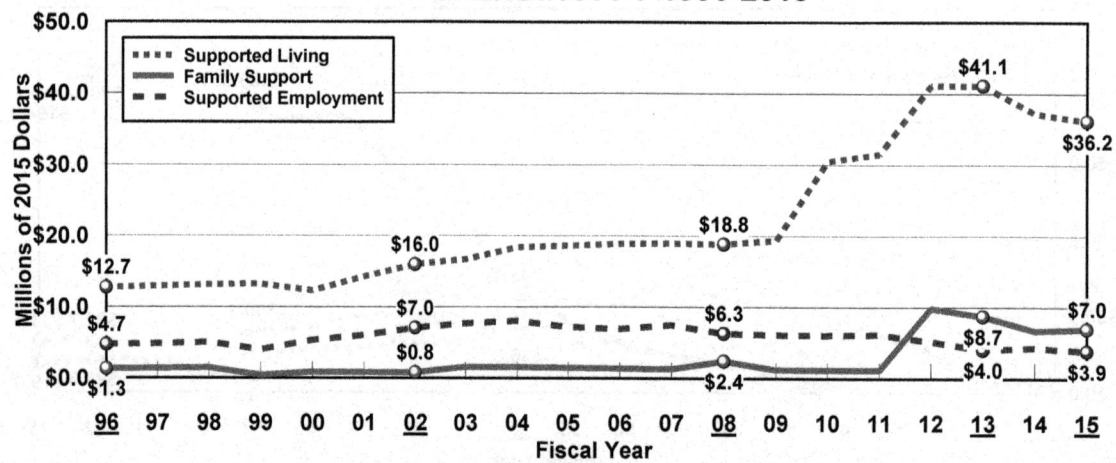

PARTICIPANTS: FY 1996-2015

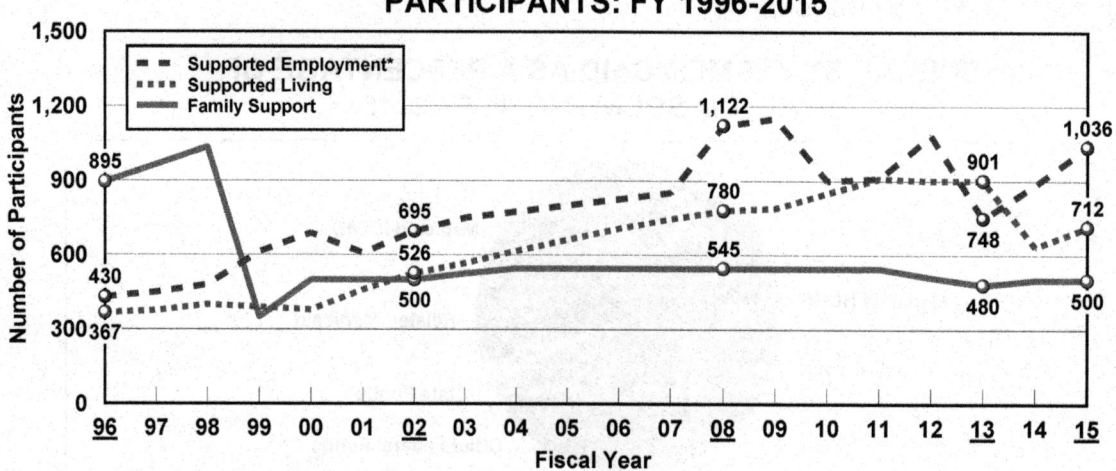

*Does not include 150 follow-along work supported workers in 2014 and 2015.

SUPPORTED LIVING, FAMILY SUPPORT AND SUPPORTED EMPLOYMENT SPENDING: FY 1996-2015

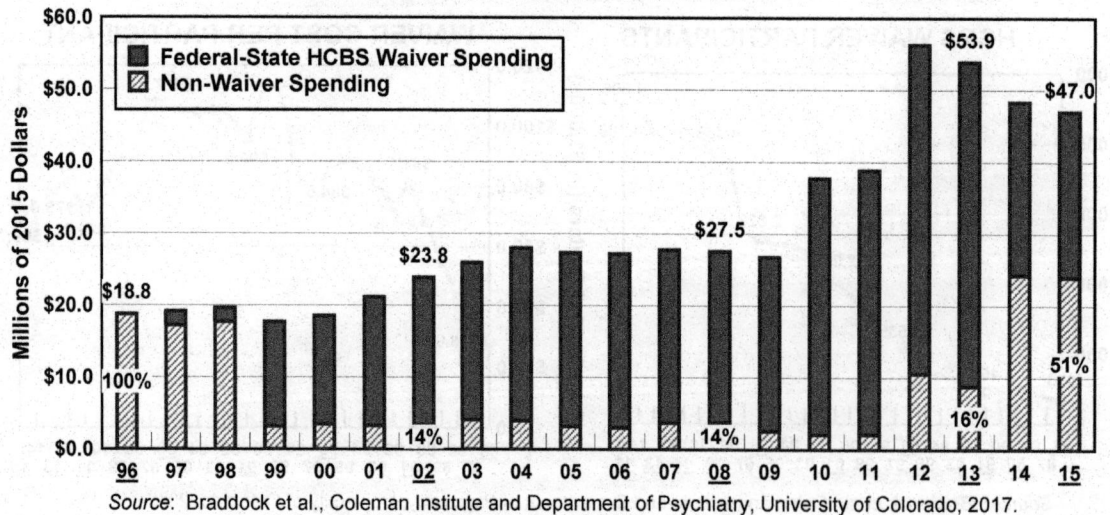

Source: Braddock et al., Coleman Institute and Department of Psychiatry, University of Colorado, 2017.
http://stateofthestates.org

MAINE

ANNUAL COST OF CARE BY RESIDENTIAL SETTING: FY 2015

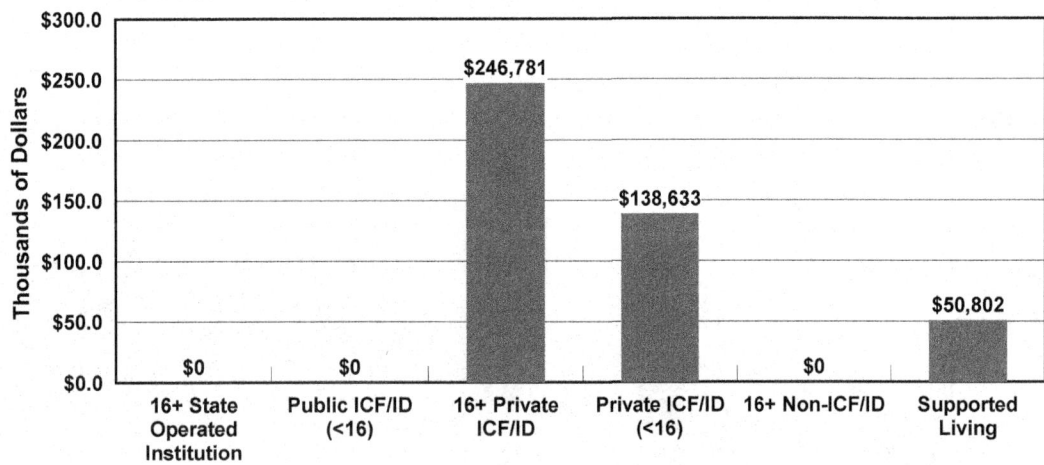

ESTIMATED NUMBER OF INDIVIDUALS WITH IDD BY AGE GROUP LIVING WITH FAMILY CAREGIVERS: FY 2015

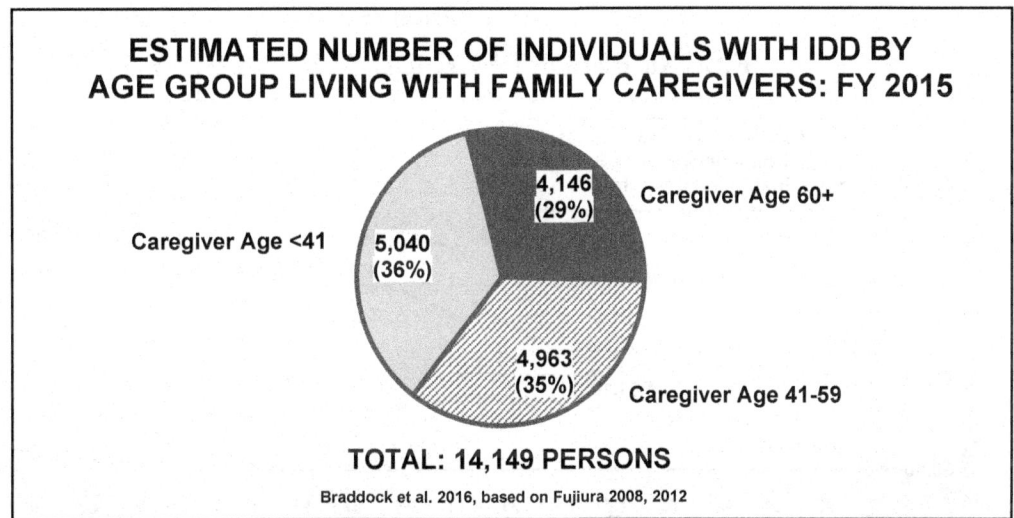

TOTAL: 14,149 PERSONS

Braddock et al. 2016, based on Fujiura 2008, 2012

ESTIMATED NUMBER OF IDD CAREGIVING FAMILIES AND FAMILIES SUPPORTED BY IDD AGENCIES: FY 1988-2015

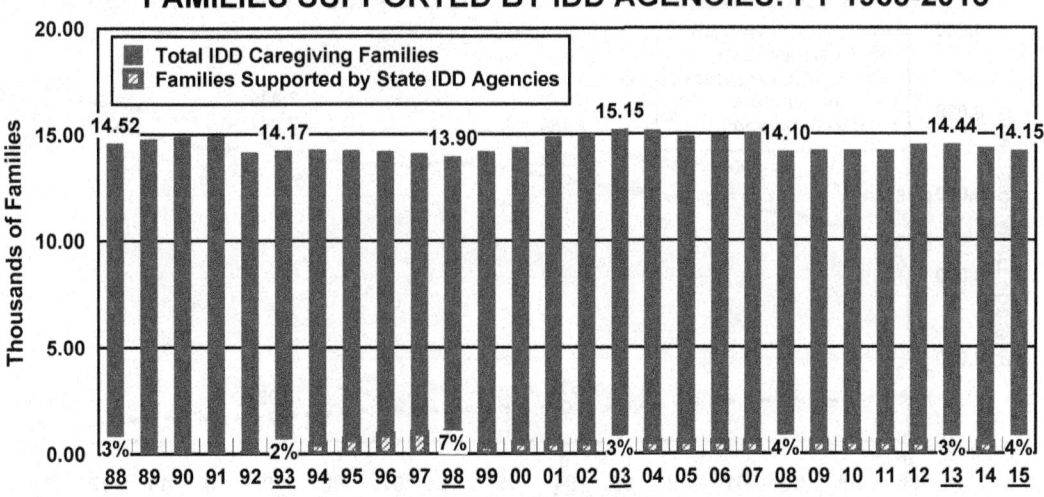

Source: Braddock et al., Coleman Institute and Department of Psychiatry, University of Colorado, 2017.
http://stateofthestates.org

MARYLAND

TOTAL PUBLIC IDD SPENDING FOR SERVICES: FY 1977-2015

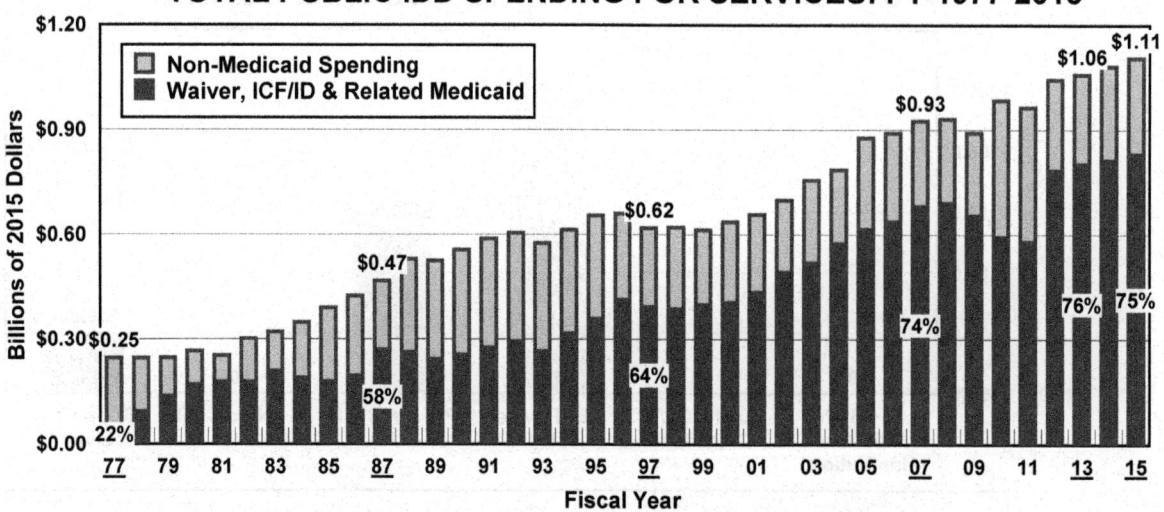

FISCAL EFFORT FOR IDD SERVICES: FY 1977-2015

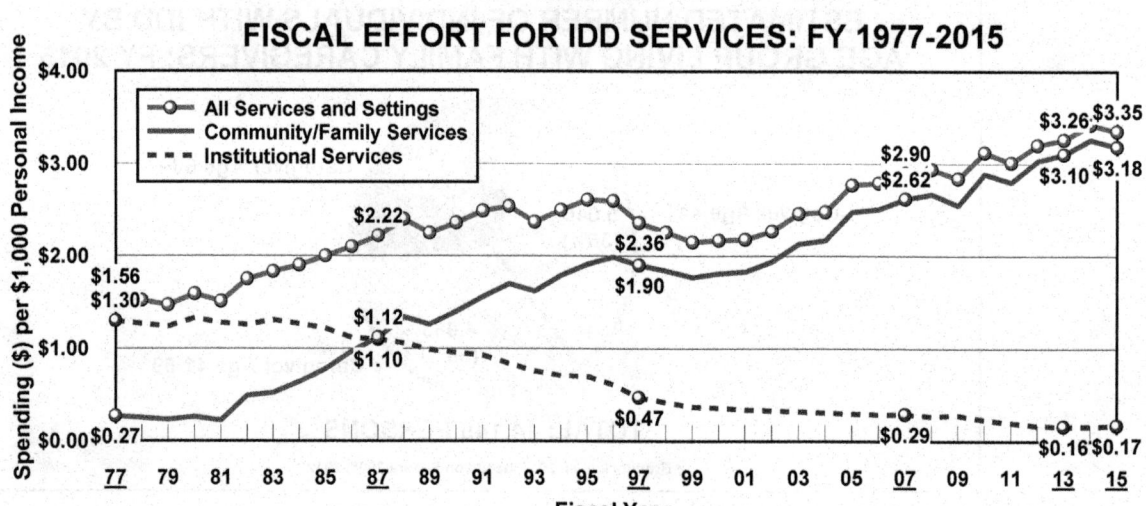

PERSONS WITH IDD BY SIZE OF SETTING: FY 1998-2015

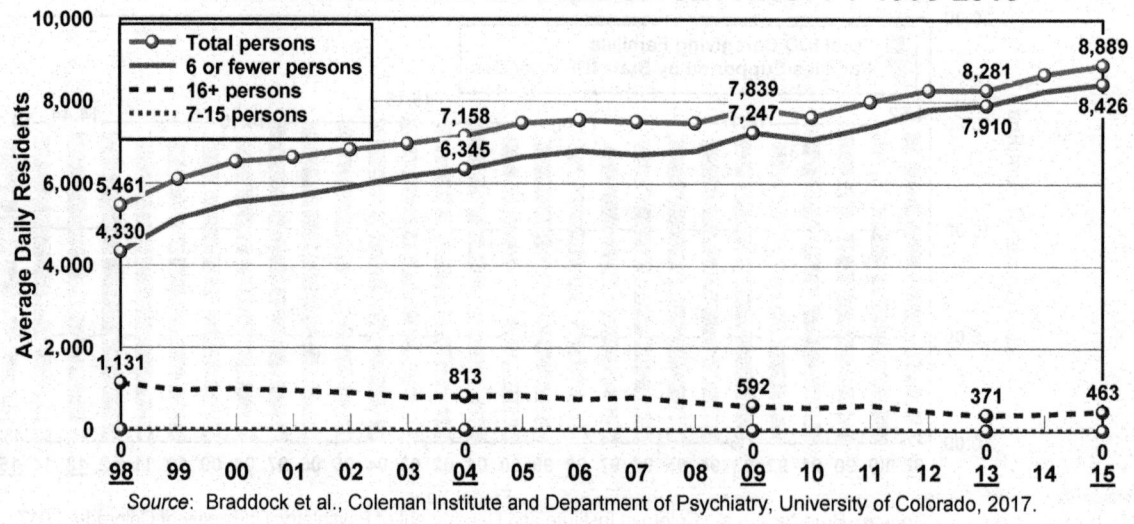

Source: Braddock et al., Coleman Institute and Department of Psychiatry, University of Colorado, 2017.

http://stateofthestates.org

MARYLAND

FEDERAL IDD MEDICAID SPENDING BY REVENUE SOURCE

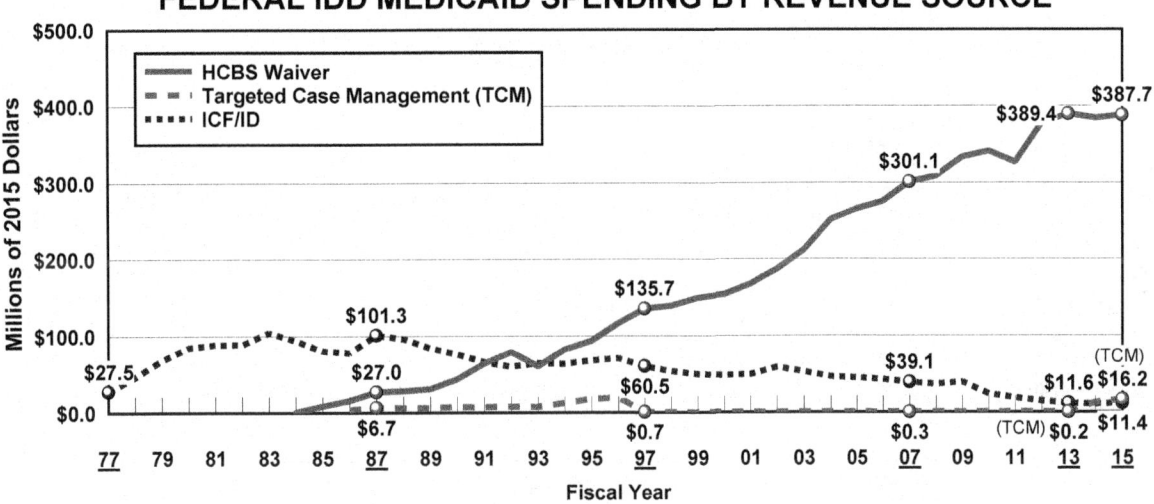

FEDERAL-STATE MEDICAID AS A PERCENTAGE OF TOTAL IDD SPENDING IN FY 2015

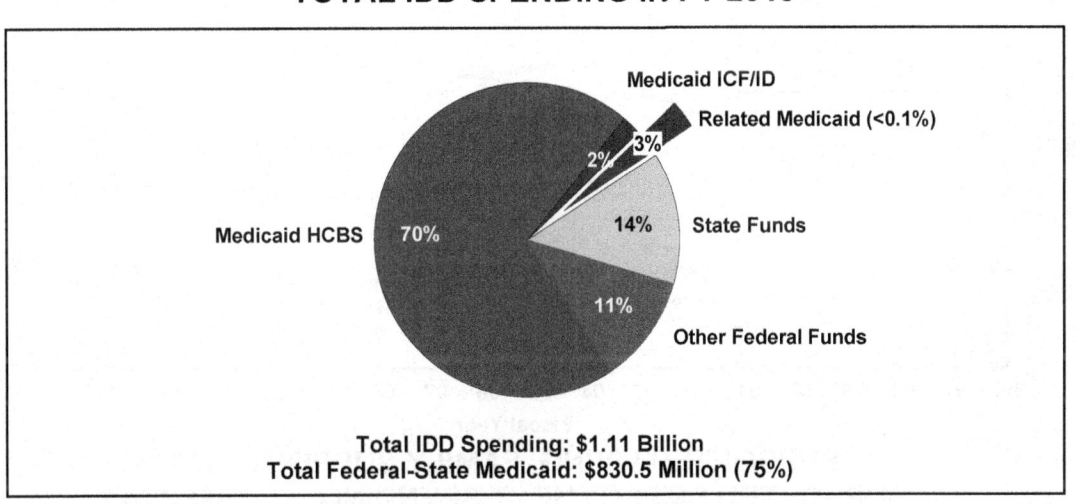

Total IDD Spending: $1.11 Billion
Total Federal-State Medicaid: $830.5 Million (75%)

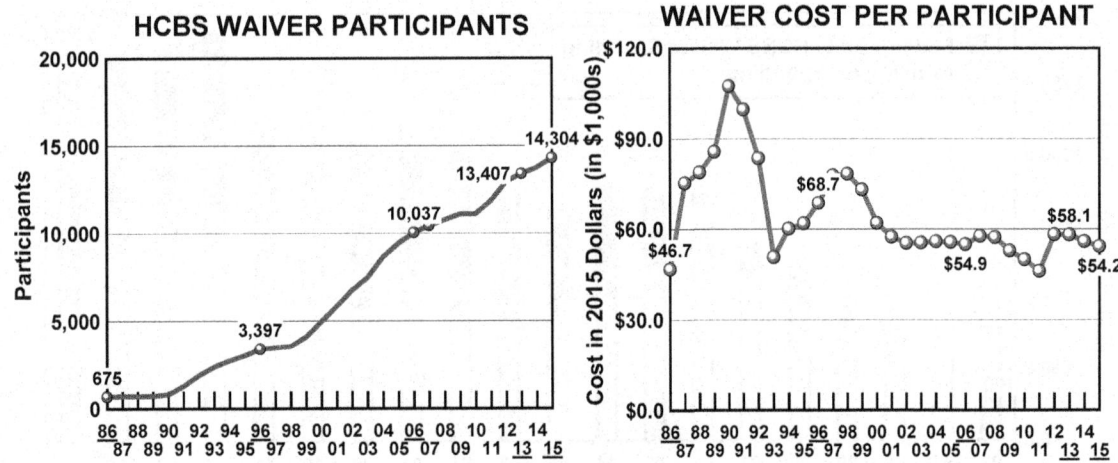

Source: Braddock et al., Coleman Institute and Department of Psychiatry, University of Colorado, 2017.
http://stateofthestates.org

MARYLAND
INDIVIDUAL AND FAMILY SUPPORT

SPENDING: FY 1996-2015

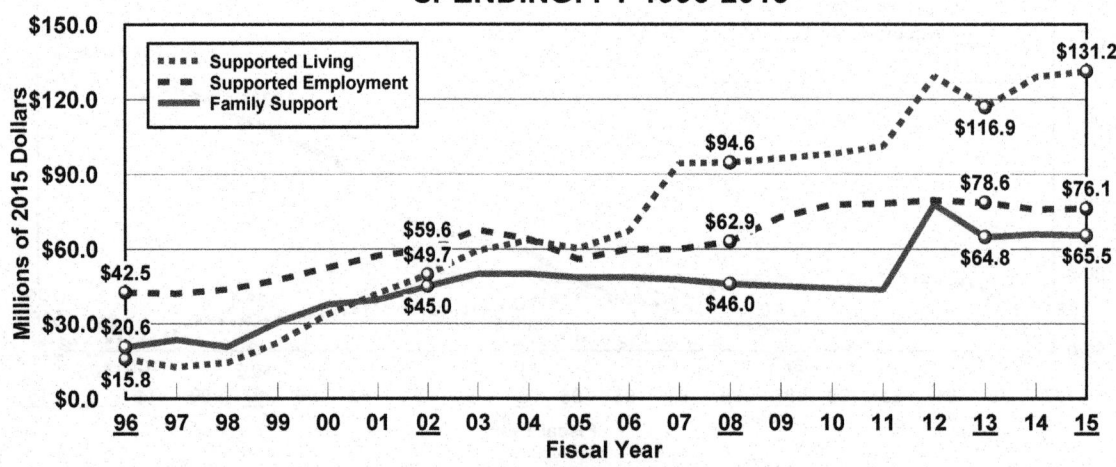

PARTICIPANTS: FY 1996-2015

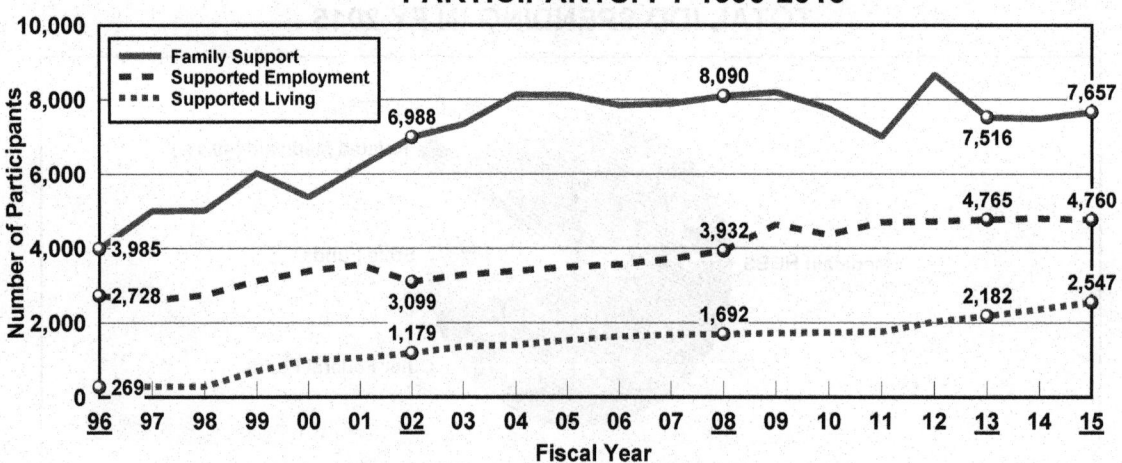

SUPPORTED LIVING, FAMILY SUPPORT AND SUPPORTED EMPLOYMENT SPENDING: FY 1996-2015

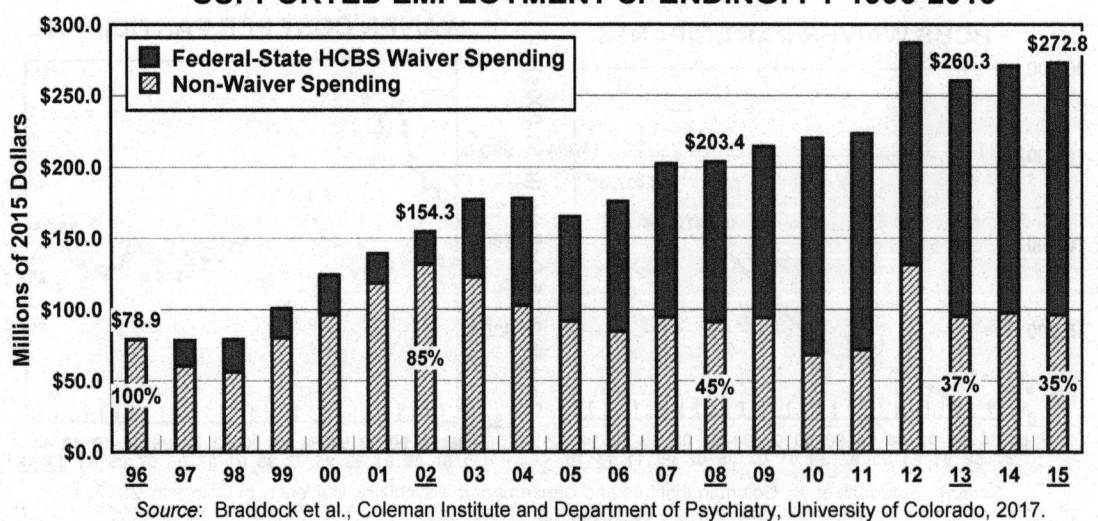

Source: Braddock et al., Coleman Institute and Department of Psychiatry, University of Colorado, 2017.
http://stateofthestates.org

MARYLAND

ANNUAL COST OF CARE BY RESIDENTIAL SETTING: FY 2015

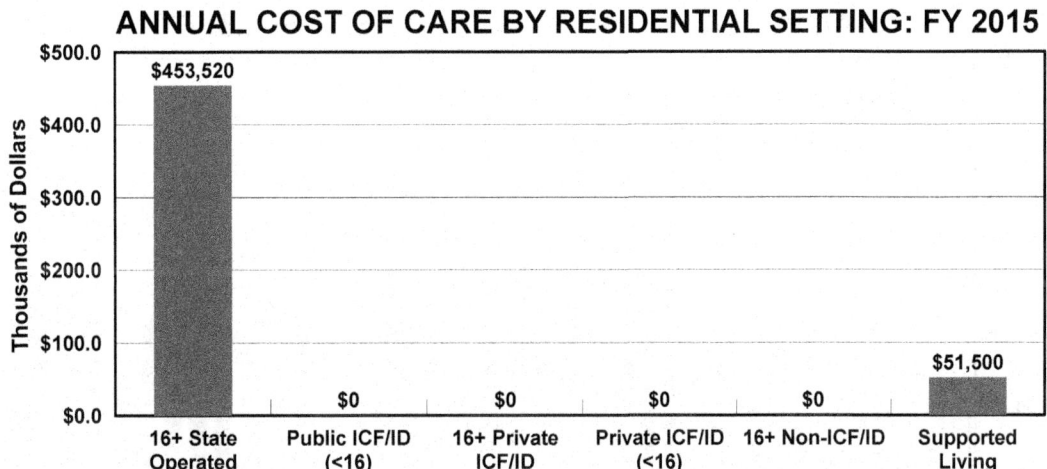

ESTIMATED NUMBER OF INDIVIDUALS WITH IDD BY AGE GROUP LIVING WITH FAMILY CAREGIVERS: FY 2015

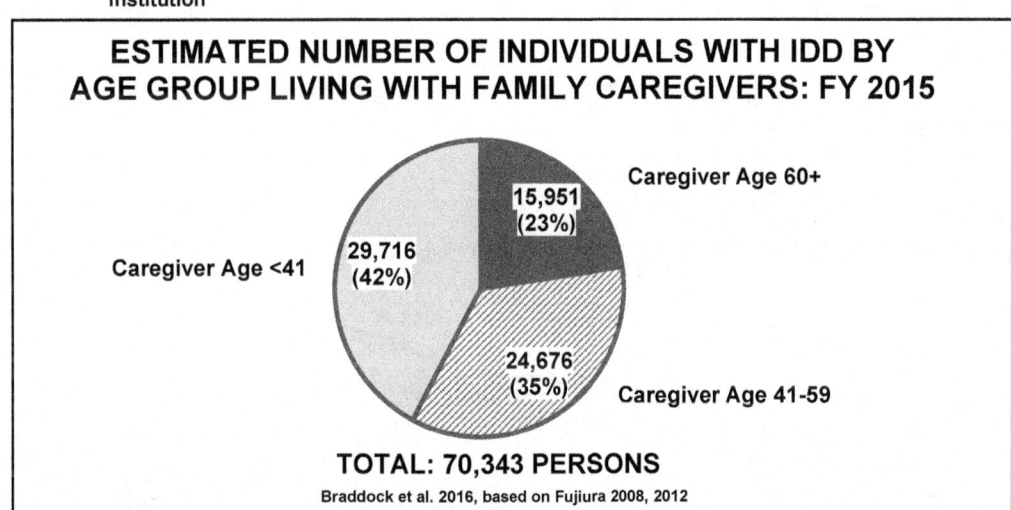

TOTAL: 70,343 PERSONS

Braddock et al. 2016, based on Fujiura 2008, 2012

ESTIMATED NUMBER OF IDD CAREGIVING FAMILIES AND FAMILIES SUPPORTED BY IDD AGENCIES: FY 1988-2015

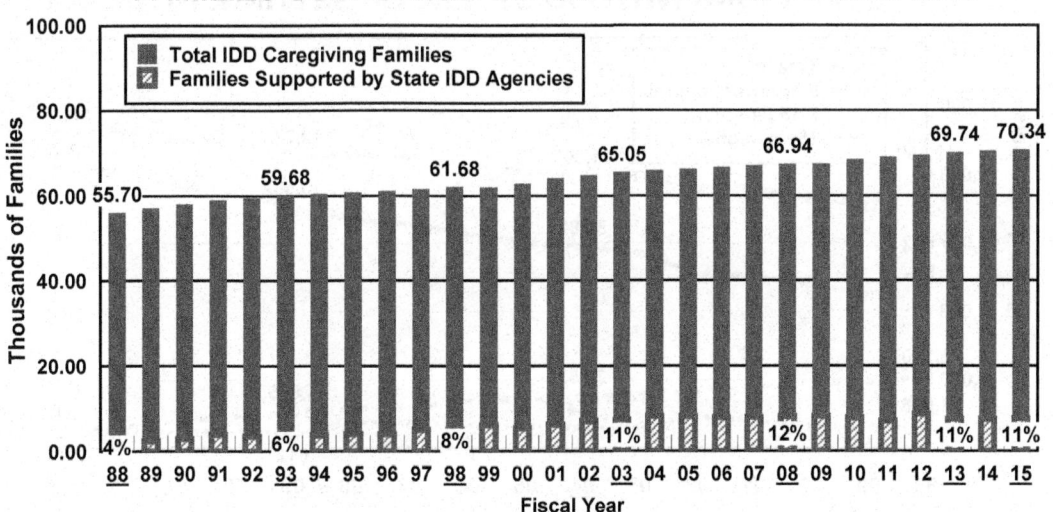

Source: Braddock et al., Coleman Institute and Department of Psychiatry, University of Colorado, 2017.
http://stateofthestates.org

MASSACHUSETTS

TOTAL PUBLIC IDD SPENDING FOR SERVICES: FY 1977-2015

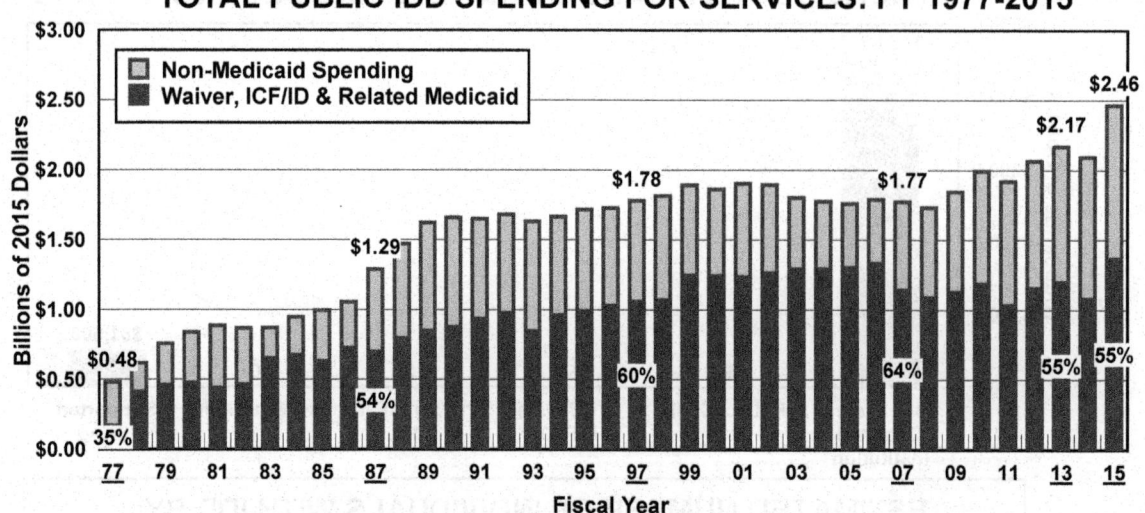

FISCAL EFFORT FOR IDD SERVICES: FY 1977-2015

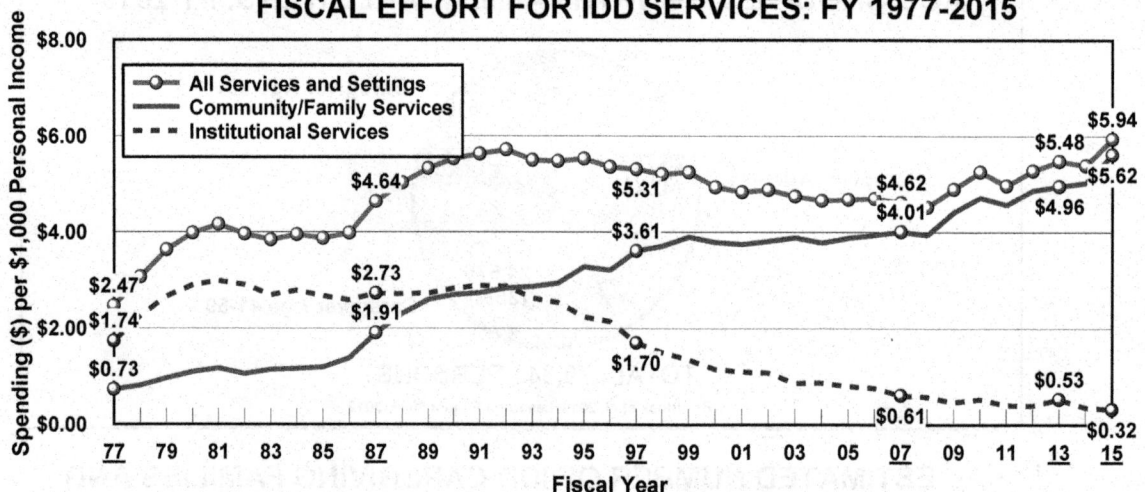

PERSONS WITH IDD BY SIZE OF SETTING: FY 1998-2015

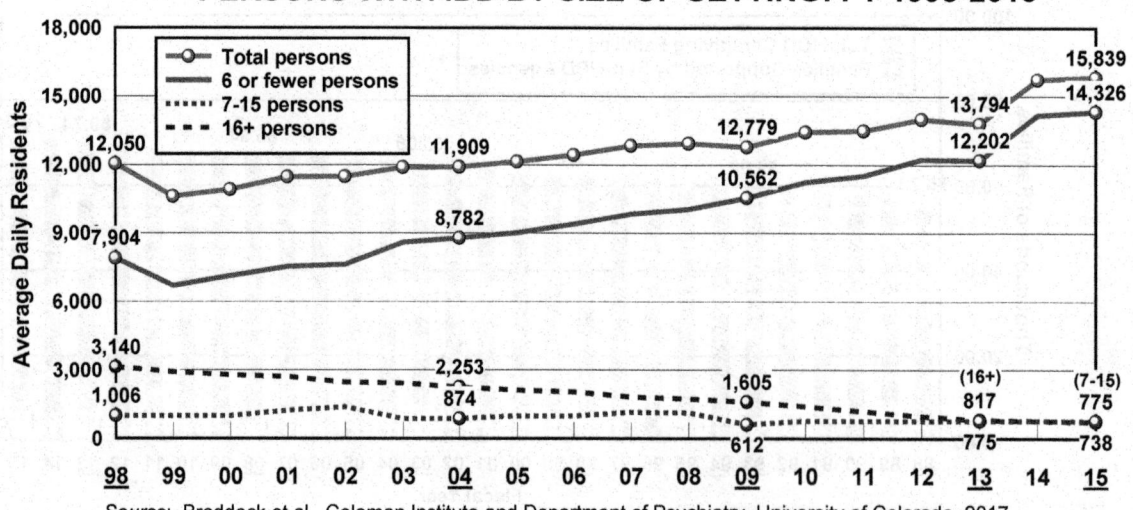

Source: Braddock et al., Coleman Institute and Department of Psychiatry, University of Colorado, 2017.
http://stateofthestates.org

MASSACHUSETTS

FEDERAL IDD MEDICAID SPENDING BY REVENUE SOURCE

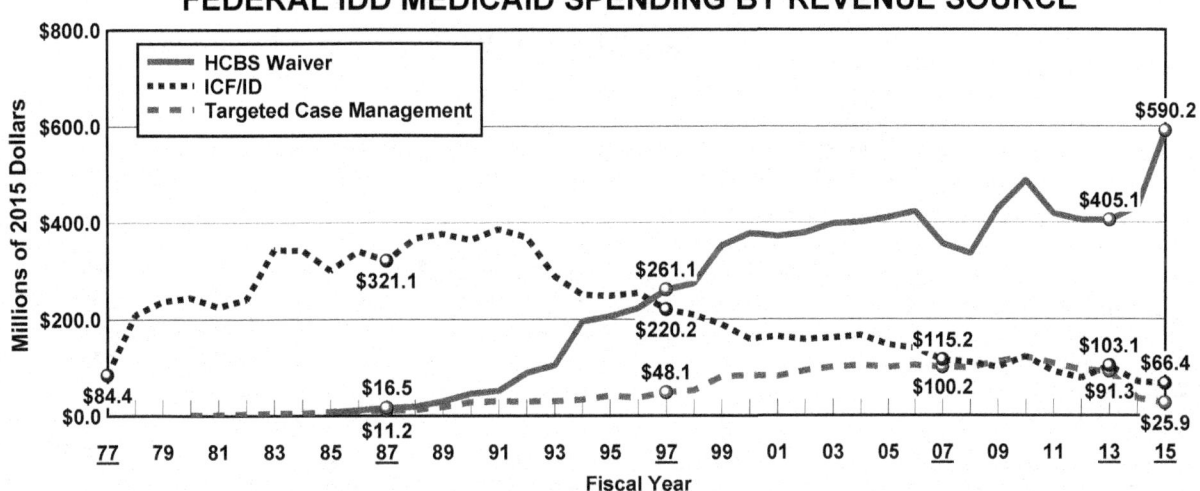

FEDERAL-STATE MEDICAID AS A PERCENTAGE OF TOTAL IDD SPENDING IN FY 2015

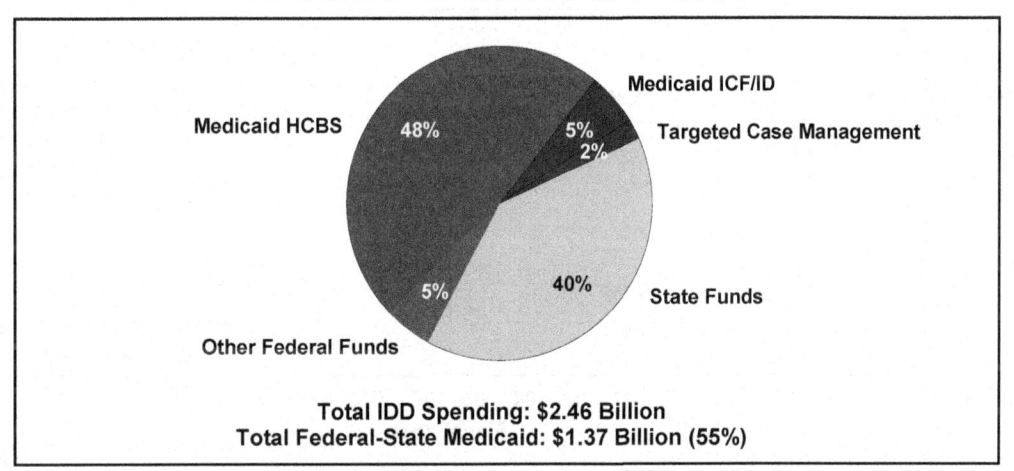

Total IDD Spending: $2.46 Billion
Total Federal-State Medicaid: $1.37 Billion (55%)

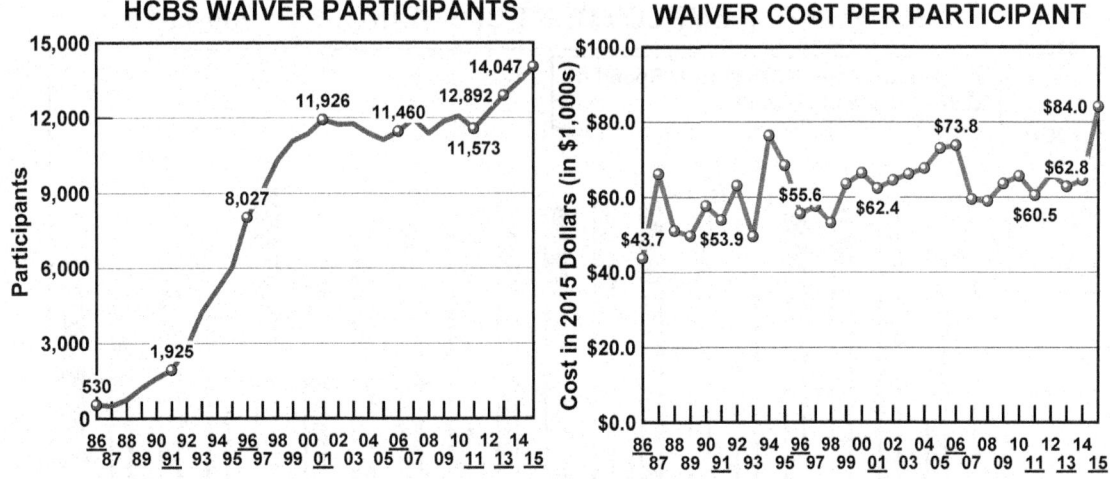

Source: Braddock et al., Coleman Institute and Department of Psychiatry, University of Colorado, 2017.
http://stateofthestates.org

MASSACHUSETTS
INDIVIDUAL AND FAMILY SUPPORT
SPENDING: FY 1996-2015

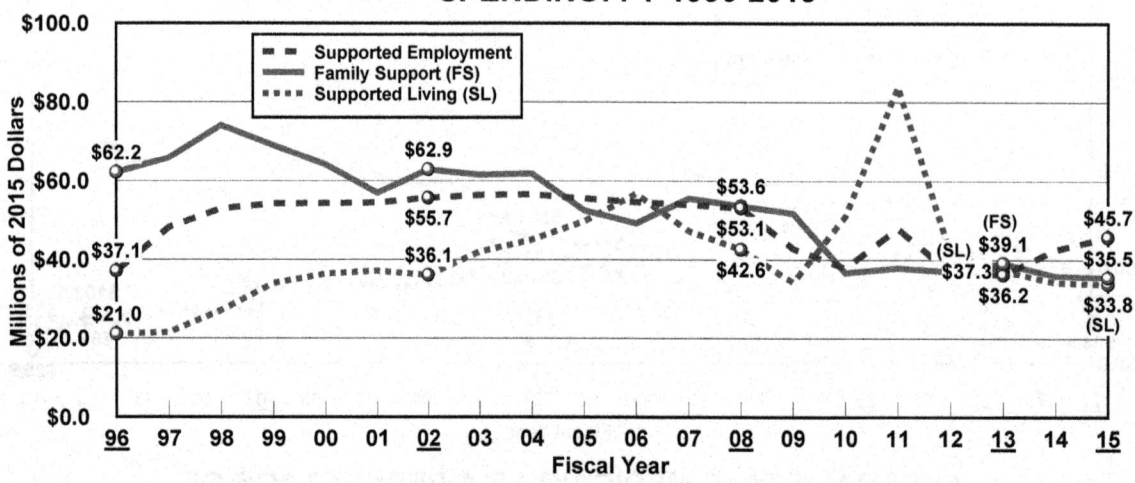

PARTICIPANTS: FY 1996-2015

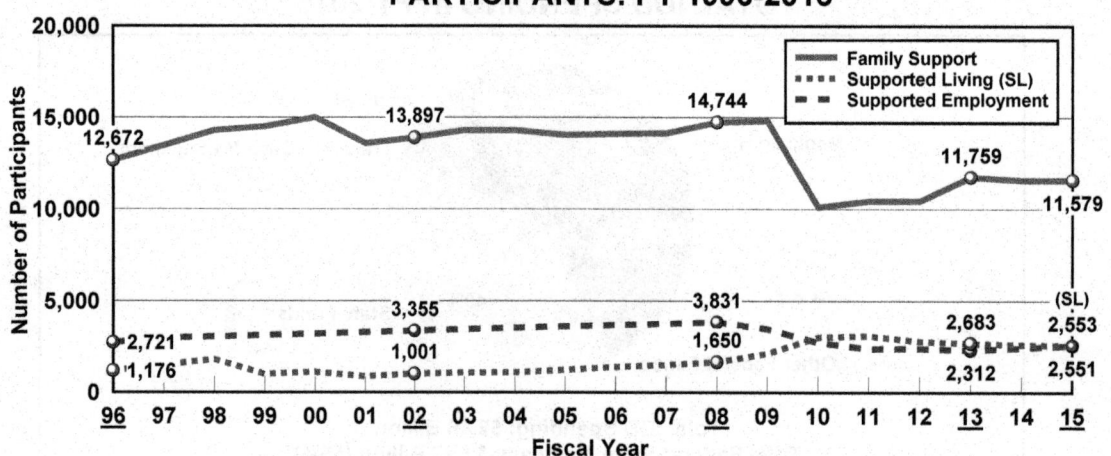

SUPPORTED LIVING, FAMILY SUPPORT AND SUPPORTED EMPLOYMENT SPENDING: FY 1996-2015

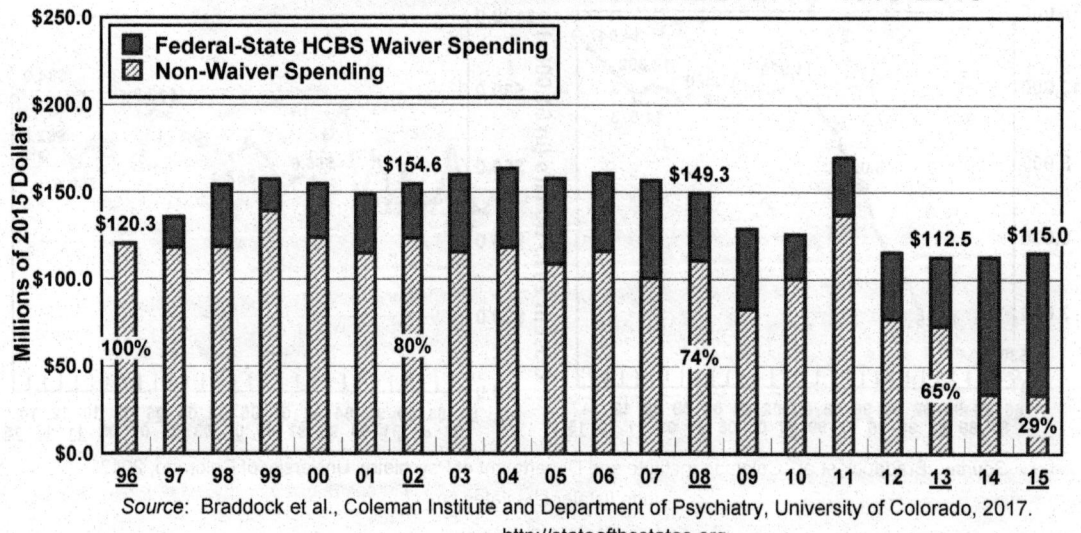

Source: Braddock et al., Coleman Institute and Department of Psychiatry, University of Colorado, 2017.
http://stateofthestates.org

MASSACHUSETTS

ANNUAL COST OF CARE BY RESIDENTIAL SETTING: FY 2015

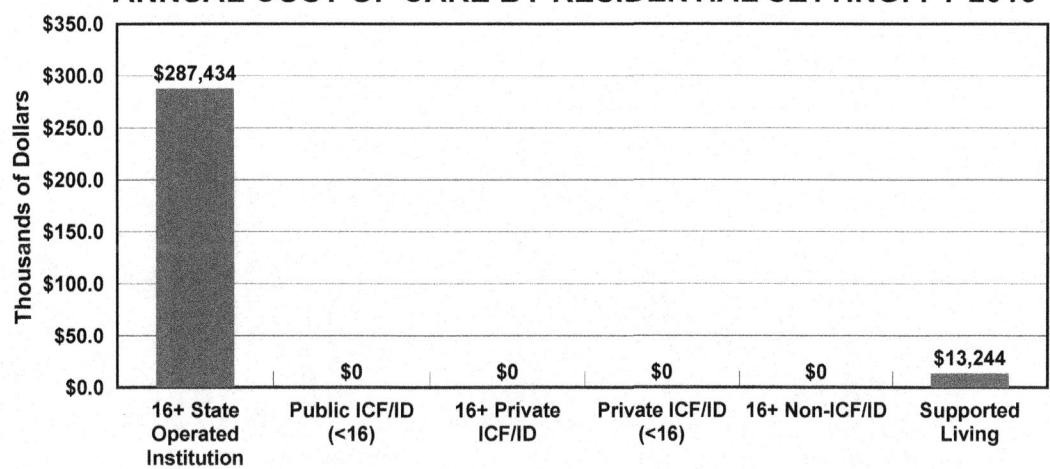

ESTIMATED NUMBER OF INDIVIDUALS WITH IDD BY AGE GROUP LIVING WITH FAMILY CAREGIVERS: FY 2015

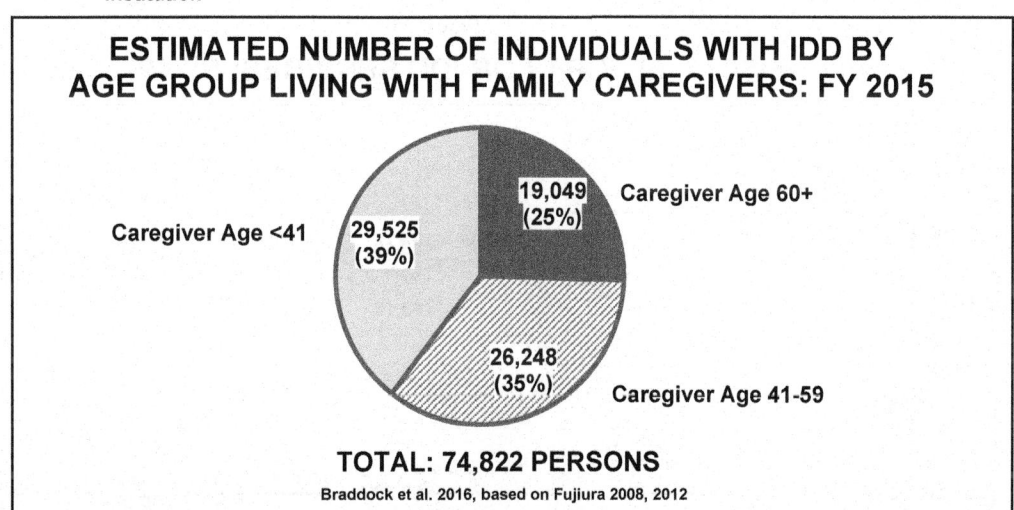

TOTAL: 74,822 PERSONS
Braddock et al. 2016, based on Fujiura 2008, 2012

ESTIMATED NUMBER OF IDD CAREGIVING FAMILIES AND FAMILIES SUPPORTED BY IDD AGENCIES: FY 1988-2015

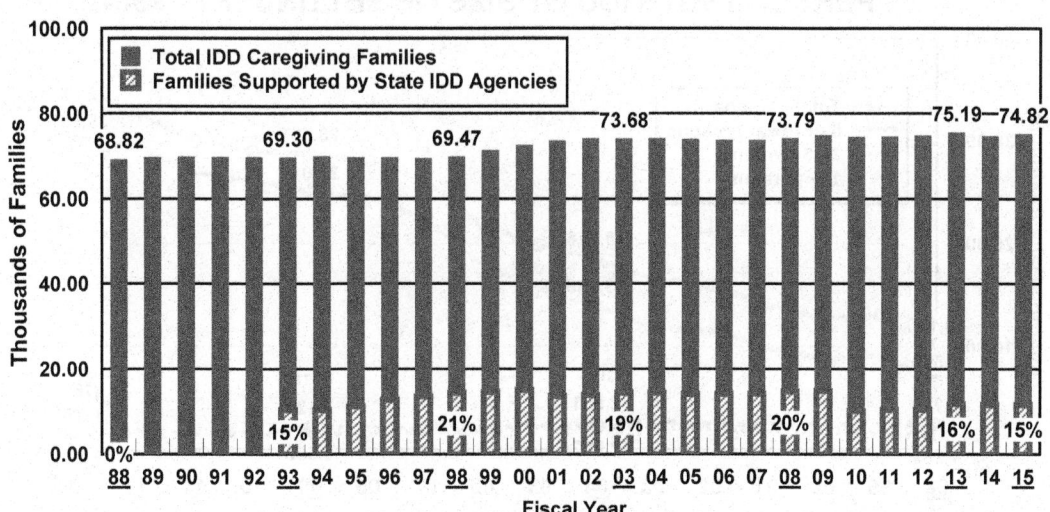

Source: Braddock et al., Coleman Institute and Department of Psychiatry, University of Colorado, 2017.
http://stateofthestates.org

MICHIGAN

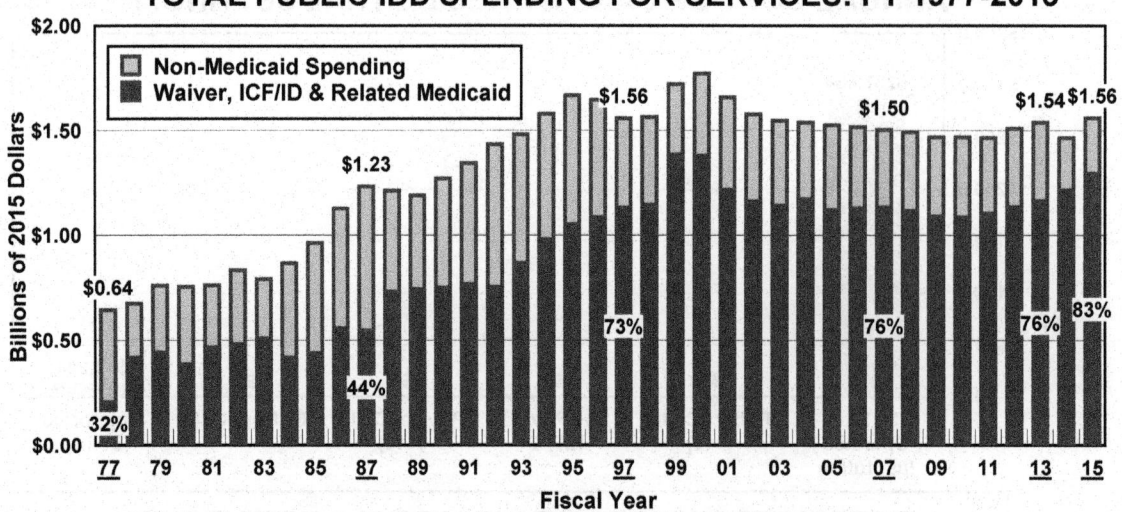

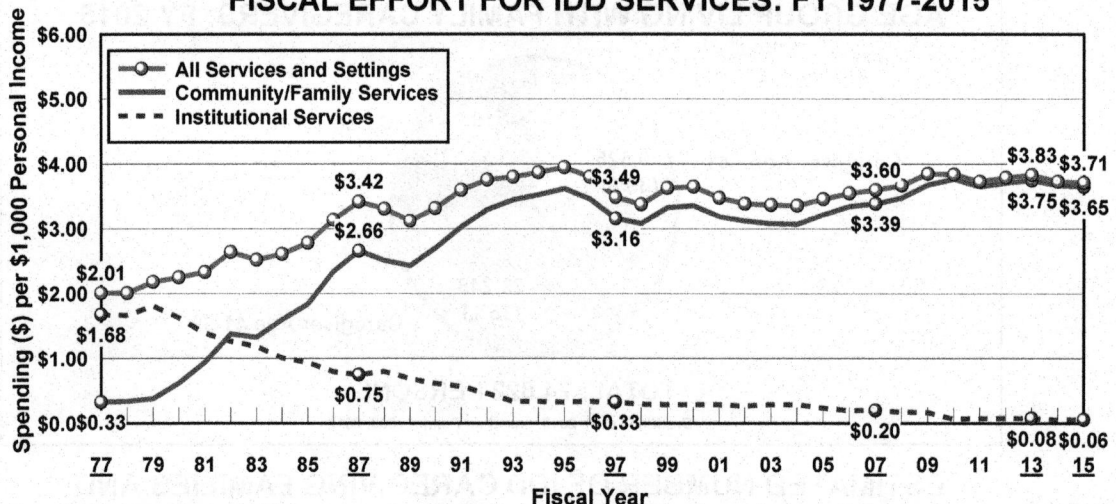

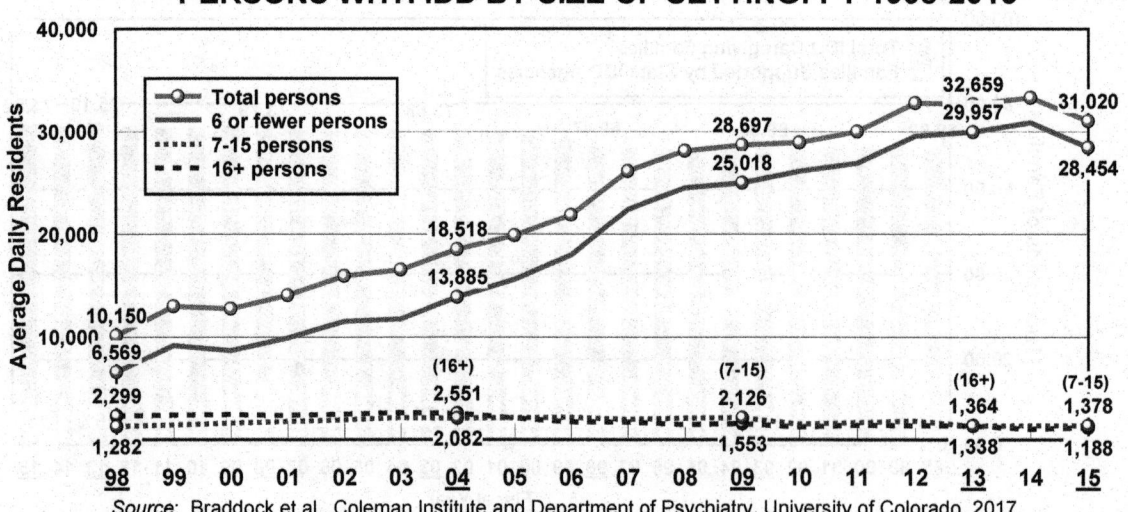

Source: Braddock et al., Coleman Institute and Department of Psychiatry, University of Colorado, 2017.
http://stateofthestates.org

MICHIGAN

FEDERAL IDD MEDICAID SPENDING BY REVENUE SOURCE

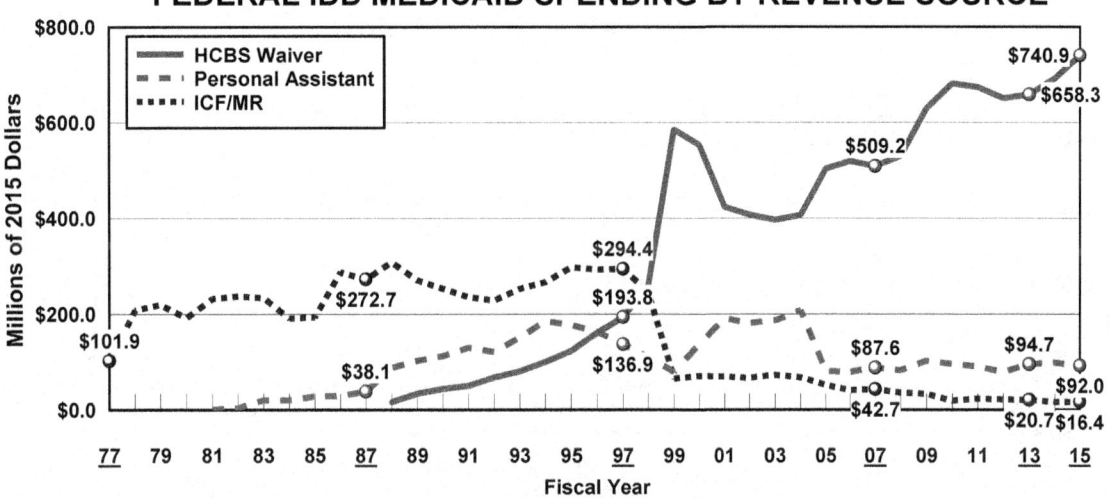

FEDERAL-STATE MEDICAID AS A PERCENTAGE OF TOTAL IDD SPENDING IN FY 2015

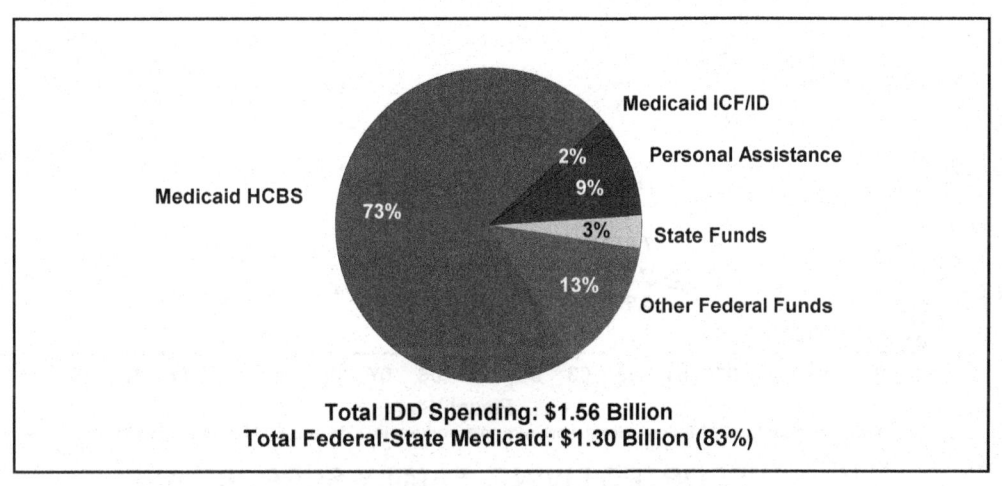

Total IDD Spending: $1.56 Billion
Total Federal-State Medicaid: $1.30 Billion (83%)

HCBS WAIVER PARTICIPANTS / WAIVER COST PER PARTICIPANT

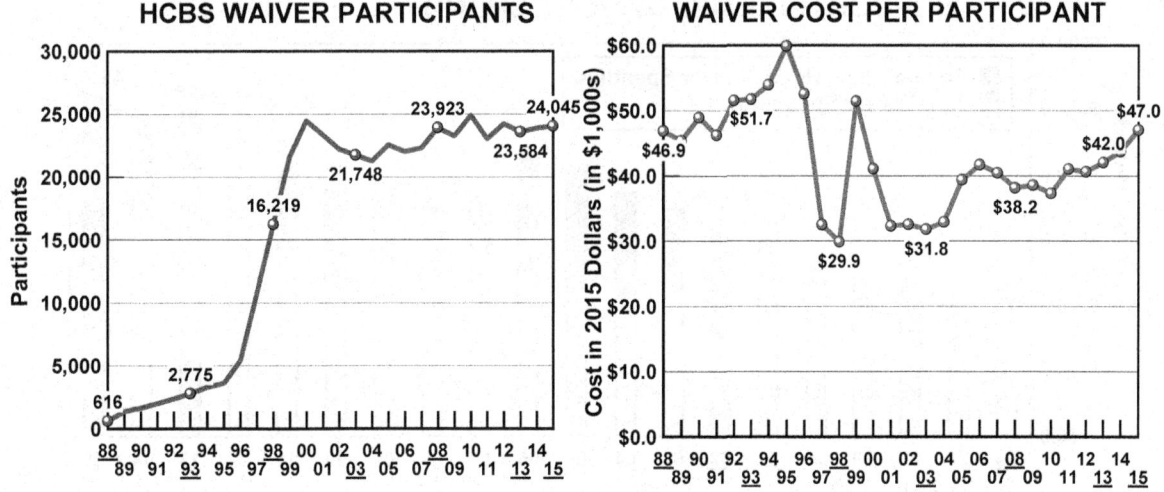

Source: Braddock et al., Coleman Institute and Department of Psychiatry, University of Colorado, 2017.
http://stateofthestates.org

MICHIGAN
INDIVIDUAL AND FAMILY SUPPORT
SPENDING: FY 1996-2015

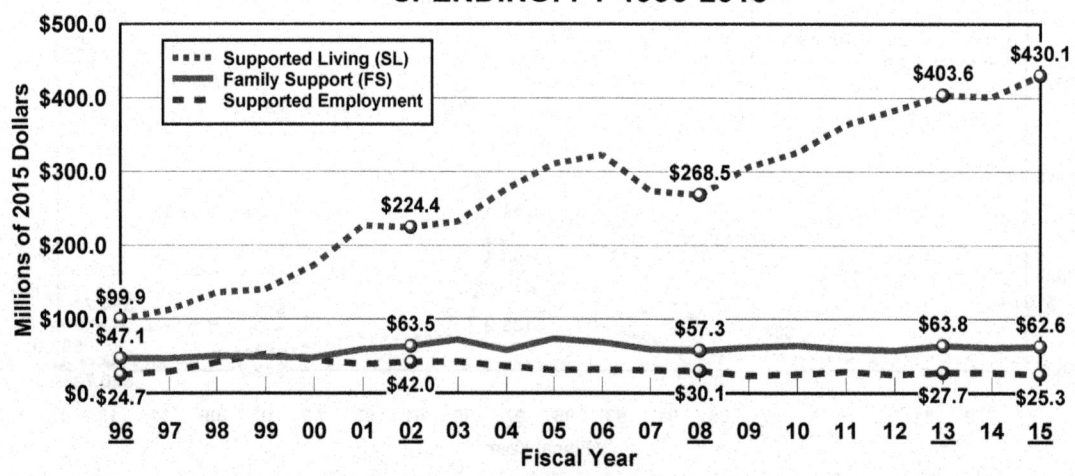

PARTICIPANTS: FY 1996-2015

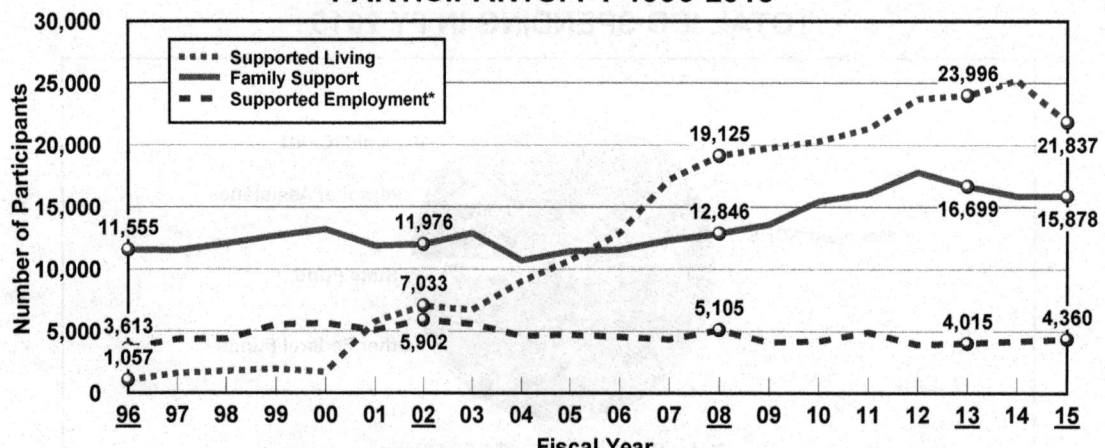

*Does not include 2,757 follow-along work support workers in 2014 and 2,391 workers in 2015.

SUPPORTED LIVING, FAMILY SUPPORT AND SUPPORTED EMPLOYMENT SPENDING: FY 1996-2015

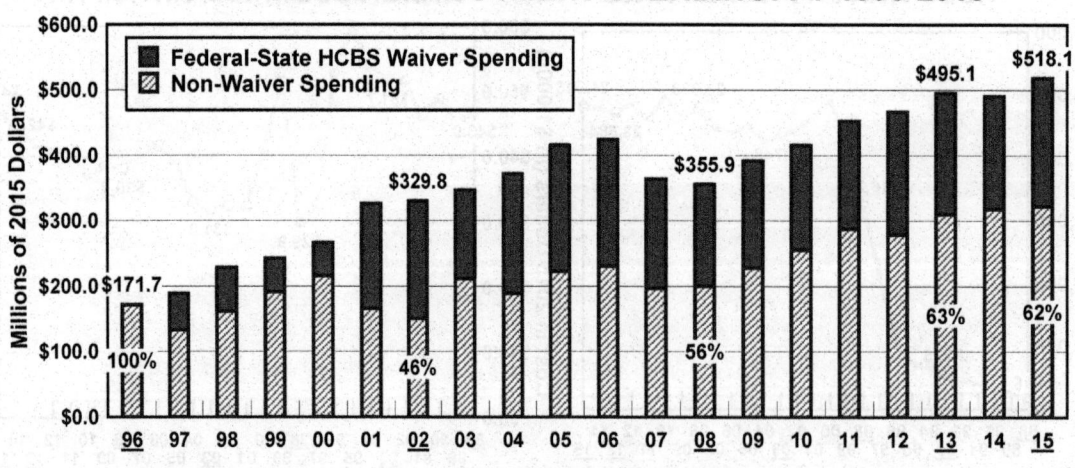

Source: Braddock et al., Coleman Institute and Department of Psychiatry, University of Colorado, 2017.
http://stateofthestates.org

MICHIGAN

ANNUAL COST OF CARE BY RESIDENTIAL SETTING: FY 2015

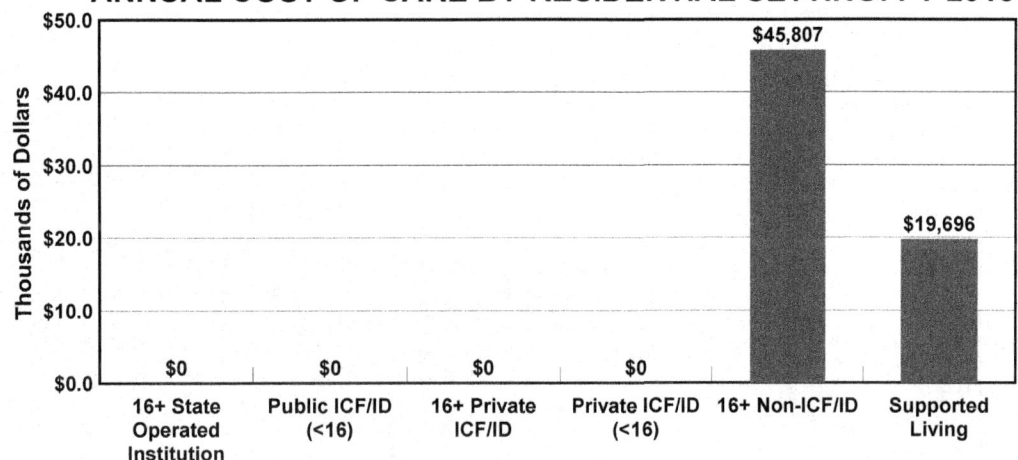

ESTIMATED NUMBER OF INDIVIDUALS WITH IDD BY AGE GROUP LIVING WITH FAMILY CAREGIVERS: FY 2015

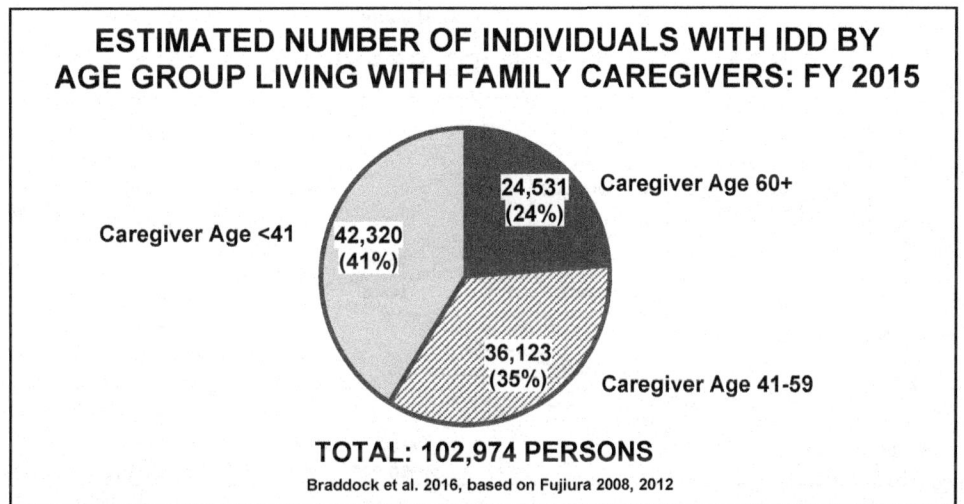

TOTAL: 102,974 PERSONS
Braddock et al. 2016, based on Fujiura 2008, 2012

ESTIMATED NUMBER OF IDD CAREGIVING FAMILIES AND FAMILIES SUPPORTED BY IDD AGENCIES: FY 1988-2015

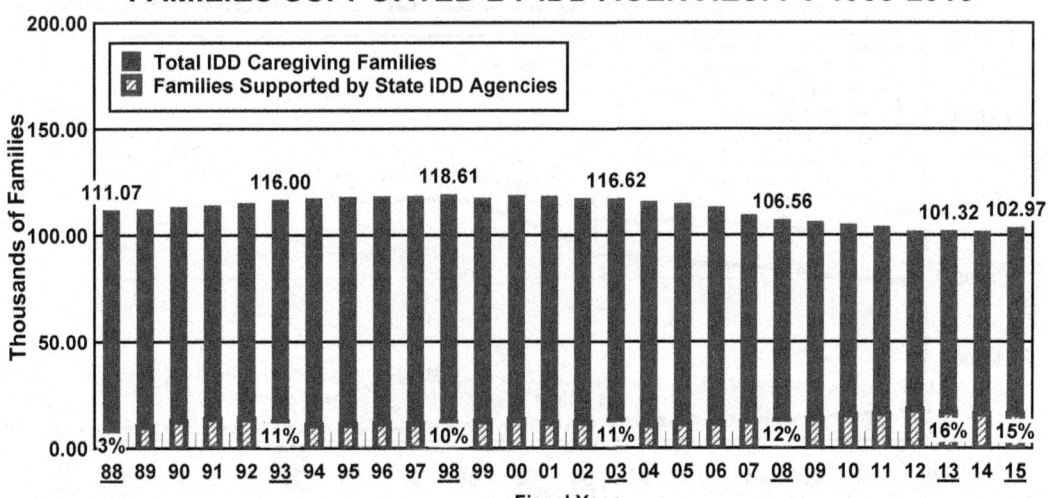

Source: Braddock et al., Coleman Institute and Department of Psychiatry, University of Colorado, 2017.
http://stateofthestates.org

MINNESOTA

TOTAL PUBLIC IDD SPENDING FOR SERVICES: FY 1977-2015

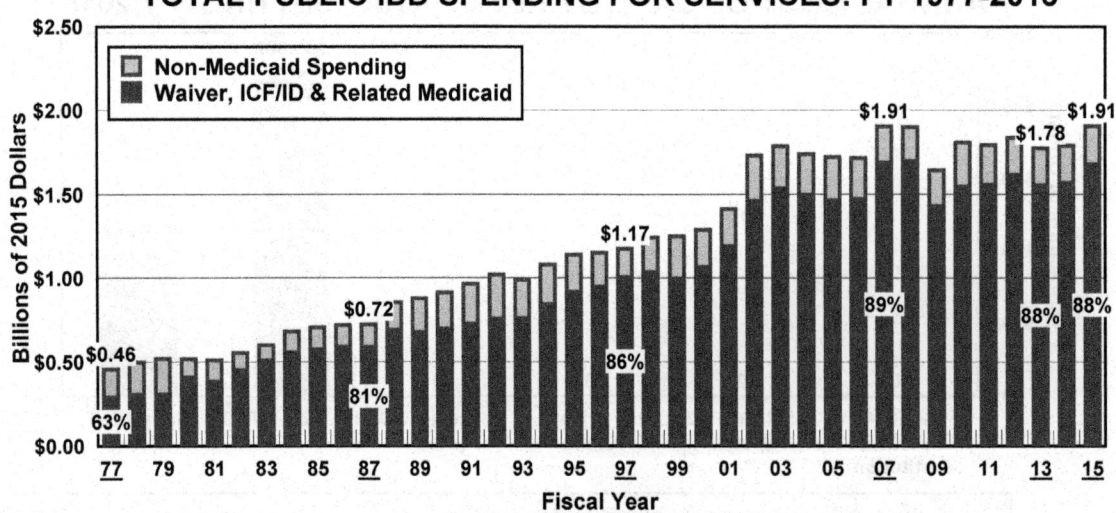

FISCAL EFFORT FOR IDD SERVICES: FY 1977-2015

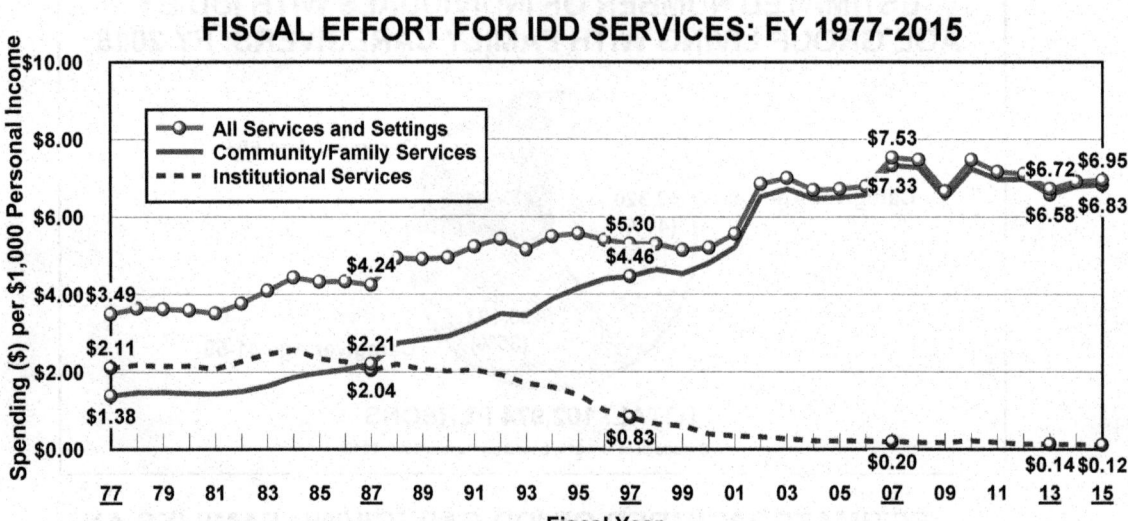

PERSONS WITH IDD BY SIZE OF SETTING: FY 1998-2015

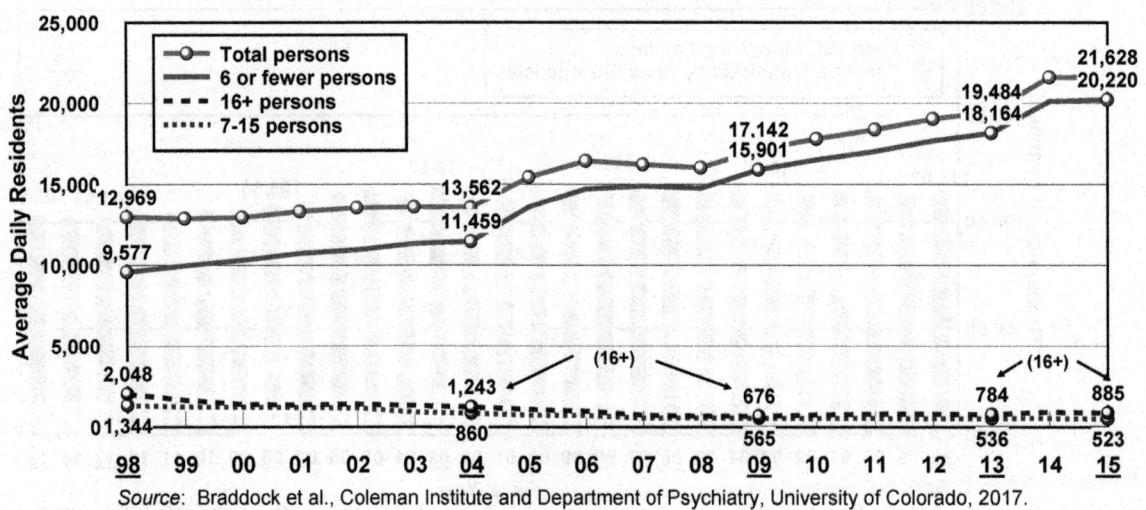

Source: Braddock et al., Coleman Institute and Department of Psychiatry, University of Colorado, 2017.
http://stateofthestates.org

MINNESOTA

FEDERAL IDD MEDICAID SPENDING BY REVENUE SOURCE

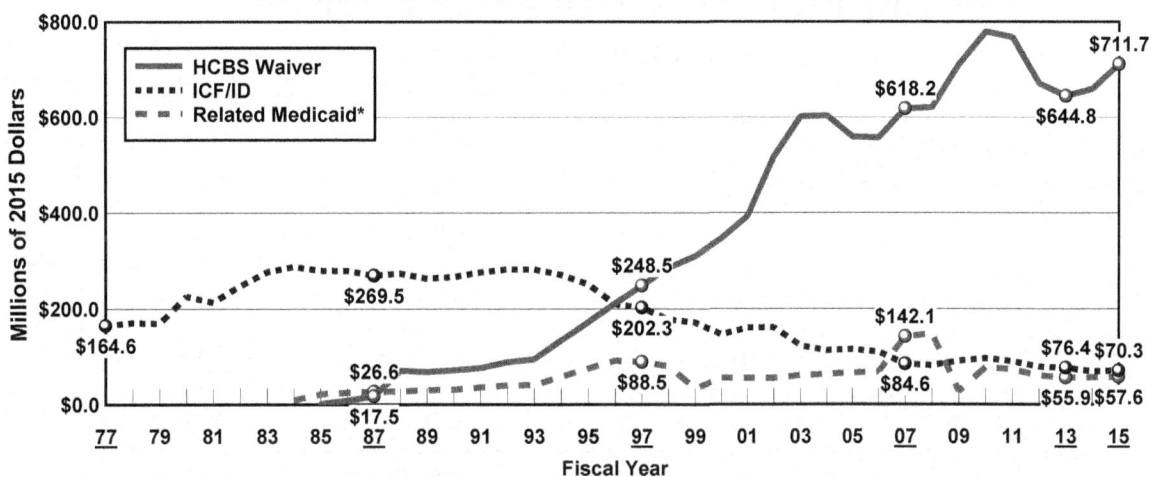

*In 2015, "Related Medicaid" was personal assistance ($29.2 million), targeted case management ($10.8 million) and administration ($17.6 million).

FEDERAL-STATE MEDICAID AS A PERCENTAGE OF TOTAL IDD SPENDING IN FY 2015

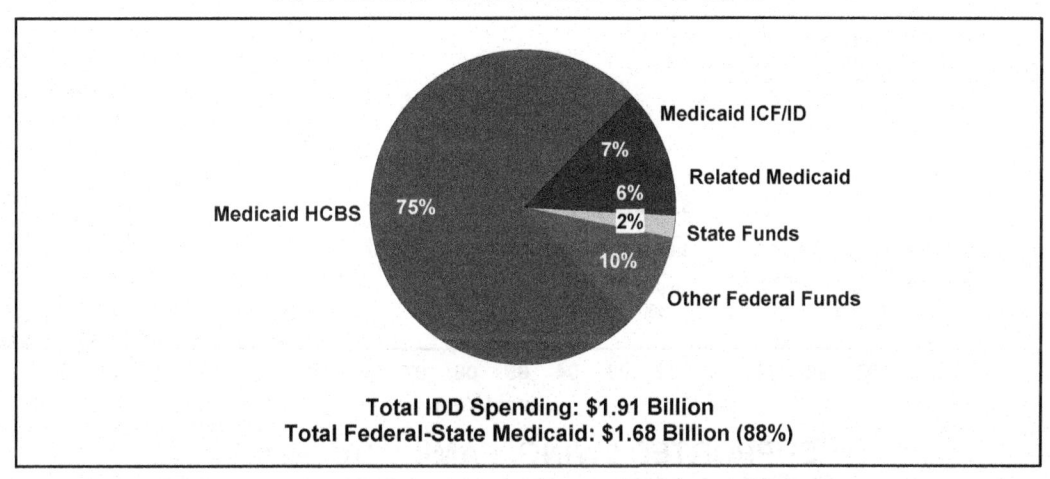

Total IDD Spending: $1.91 Billion
Total Federal-State Medicaid: $1.68 Billion (88%)

HCBS WAIVER PARTICIPANTS / WAIVER COST PER PARTICIPANT

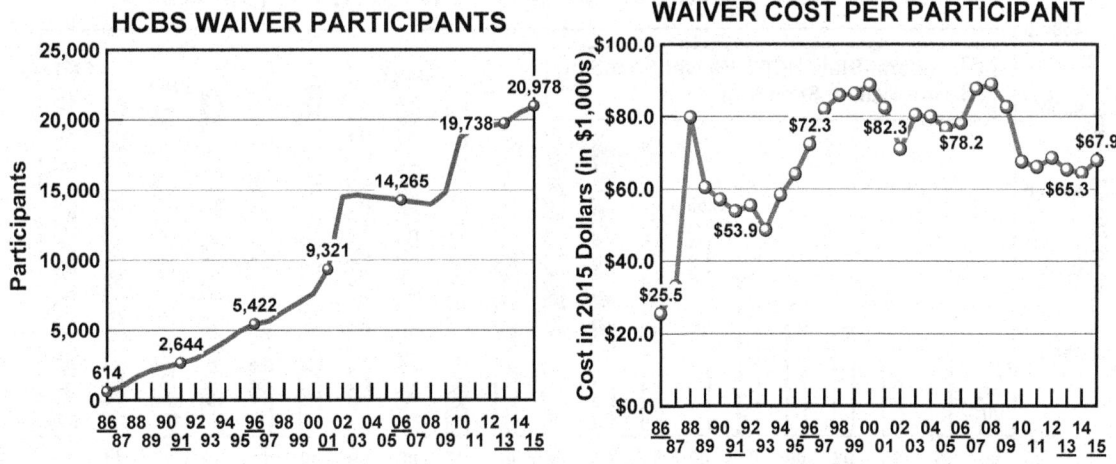

Source: Braddock et al., Coleman Institute and Department of Psychiatry, University of Colorado, 2017.
http://stateofthestates.org

MINNESOTA
INDIVIDUAL AND FAMILY SUPPORT
SPENDING: FY 1996-2015

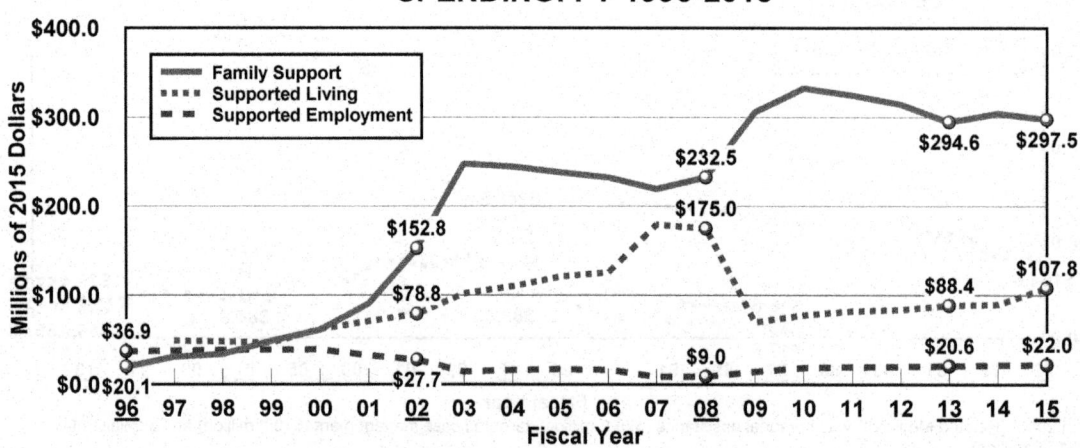

PARTICIPANTS: FY 1996-2015

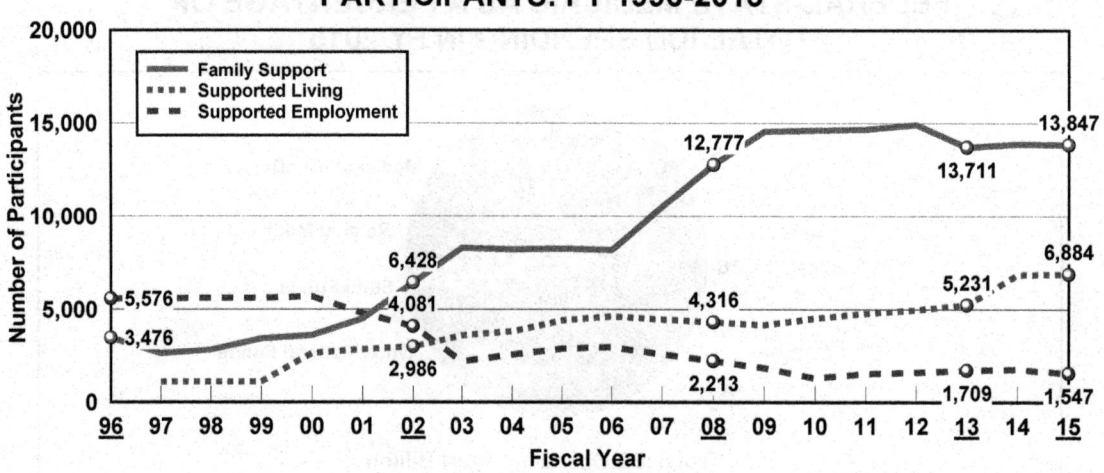

SUPPORTED LIVING, FAMILY SUPPORT AND SUPPORTED EMPLOYMENT SPENDING: FY 1996-2015

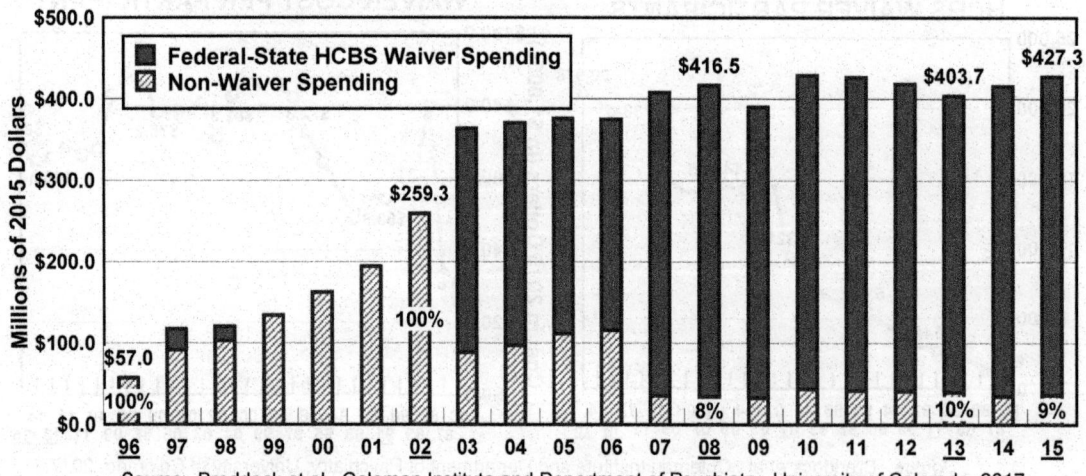

Source: Braddock et al., Coleman Institute and Department of Psychiatry, University of Colorado, 2017.
http://stateofthestates.org

MINNESOTA

ANNUAL COST OF CARE BY RESIDENTIAL SETTING: FY 2015

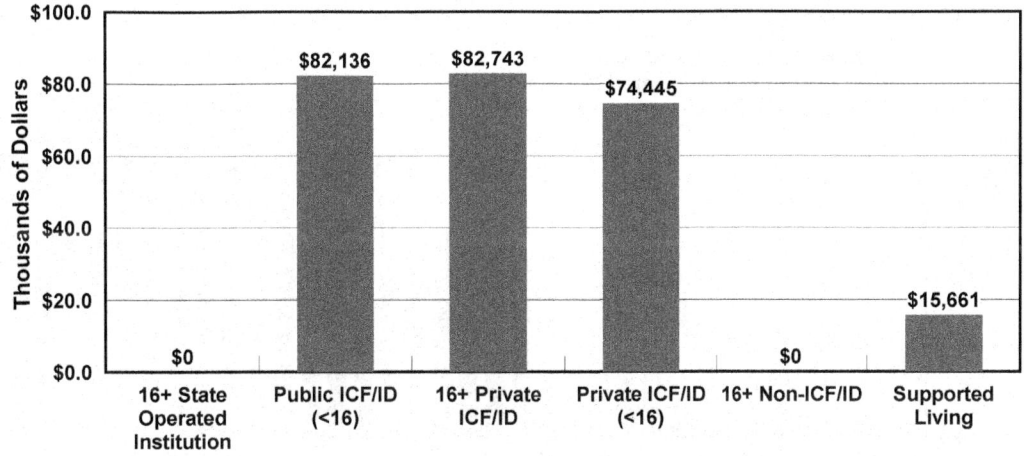

ESTIMATED NUMBER OF INDIVIDUALS WITH IDD BY AGE GROUP LIVING WITH FAMILY CAREGIVERS: FY 2015

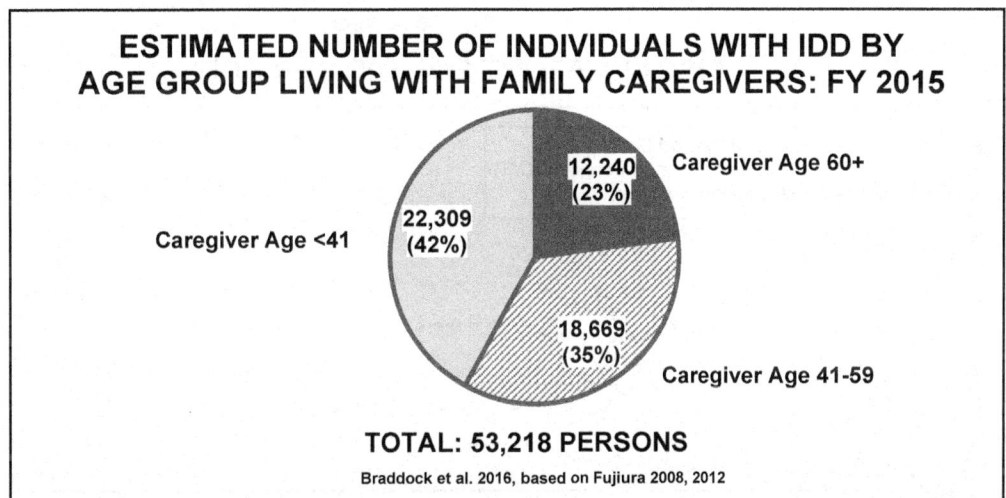

TOTAL: 53,218 PERSONS

Braddock et al. 2016, based on Fujiura 2008, 2012

ESTIMATED NUMBER OF IDD CAREGIVING FAMILIES AND FAMILIES SUPPORTED BY IDD AGENCIES: FY 1988-2015

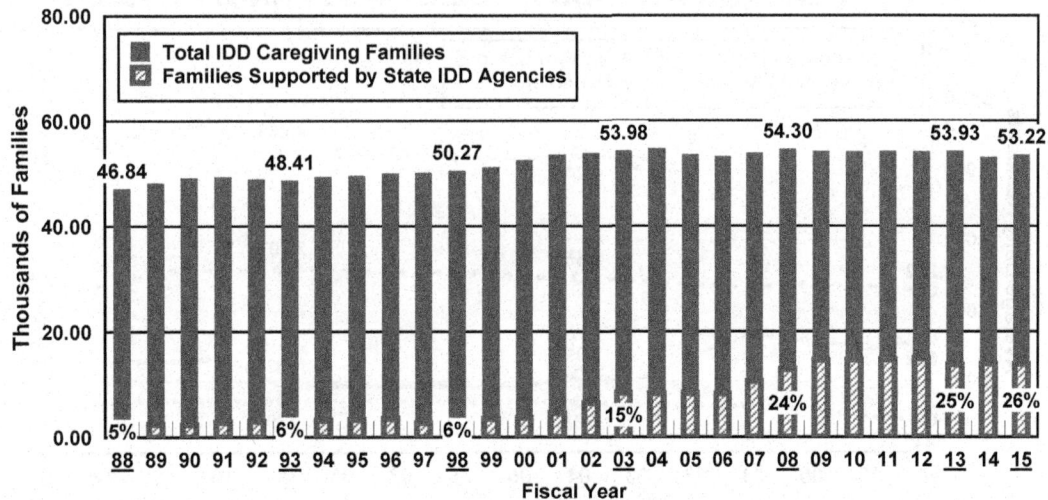

Source: Braddock et al., Coleman Institute and Department of Psychiatry, University of Colorado, 2017.
http://stateofthestates.org

MISSISSIPPI

TOTAL PUBLIC IDD SPENDING FOR SERVICES: FY 1977-2015

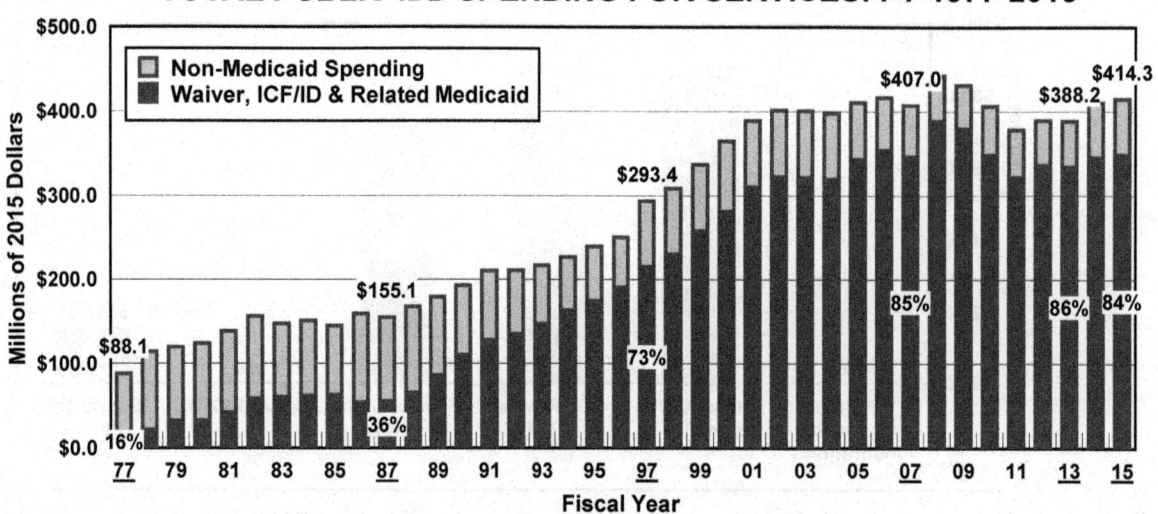

FISCAL EFFORT FOR IDD SERVICES: FY 1977-2015

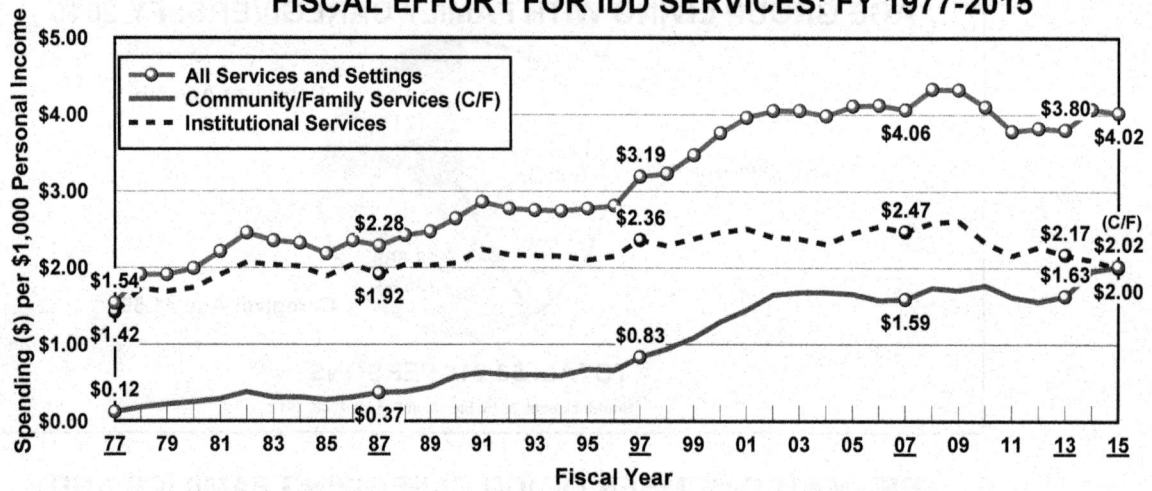

PERSONS WITH IDD BY SIZE OF SETTING: FY 1998-2015

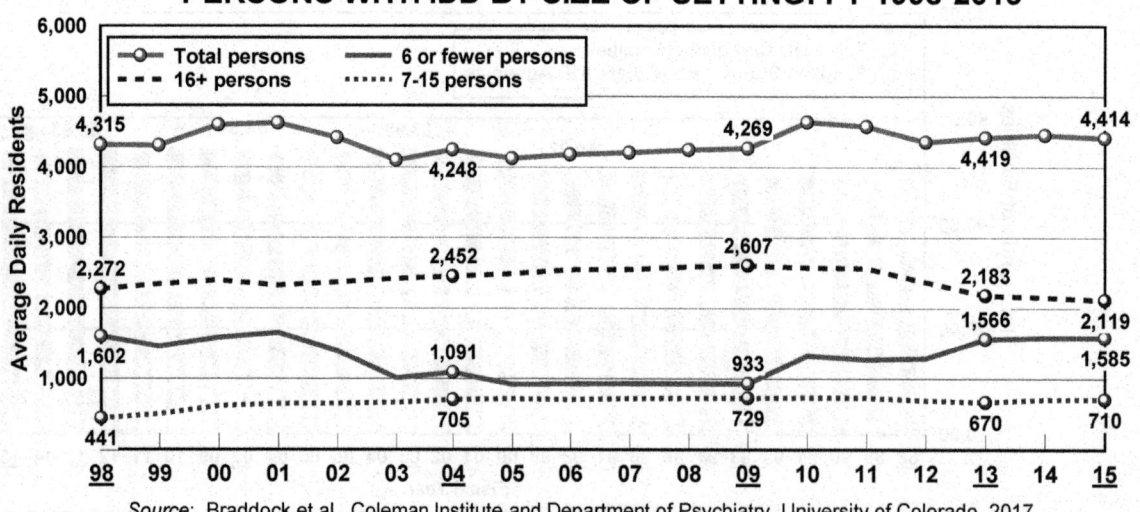

Source: Braddock et al., Coleman Institute and Department of Psychiatry, University of Colorado, 2017.
http://stateofthestates.org

MISSISSIPPI

FEDERAL IDD MEDICAID SPENDING BY REVENUE SOURCE

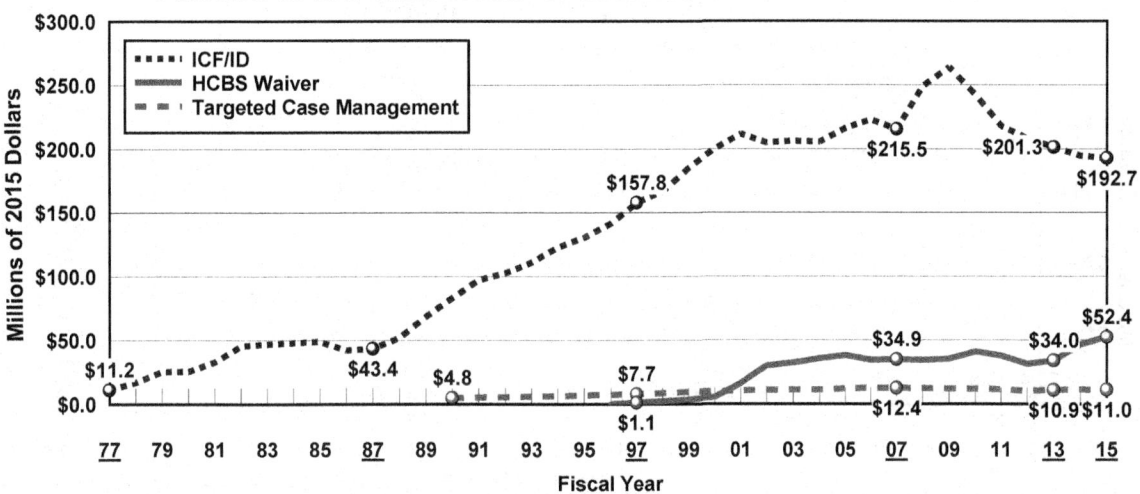

FEDERAL-STATE MEDICAID AS A PERCENTAGE OF TOTAL IDD SPENDING IN FY 2015

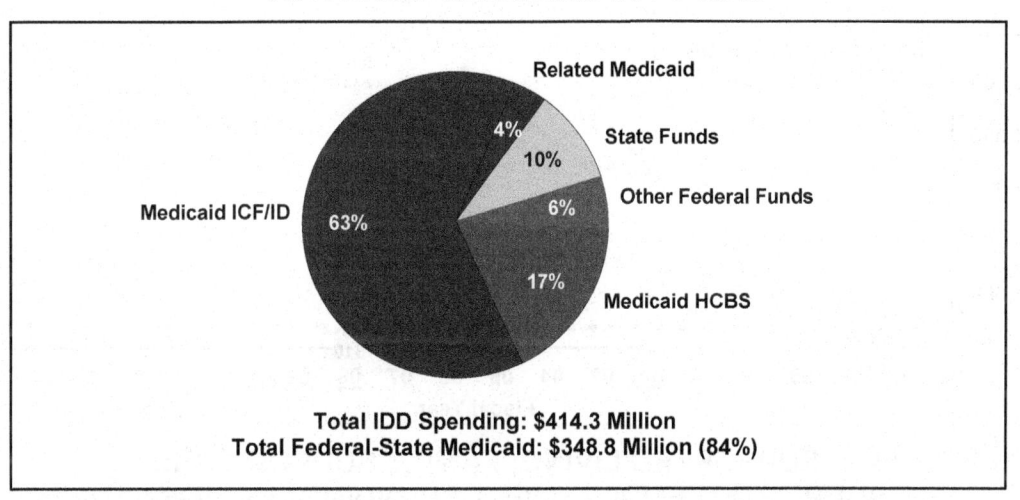

Total IDD Spending: $414.3 Million
Total Federal-State Medicaid: $348.8 Million (84%)

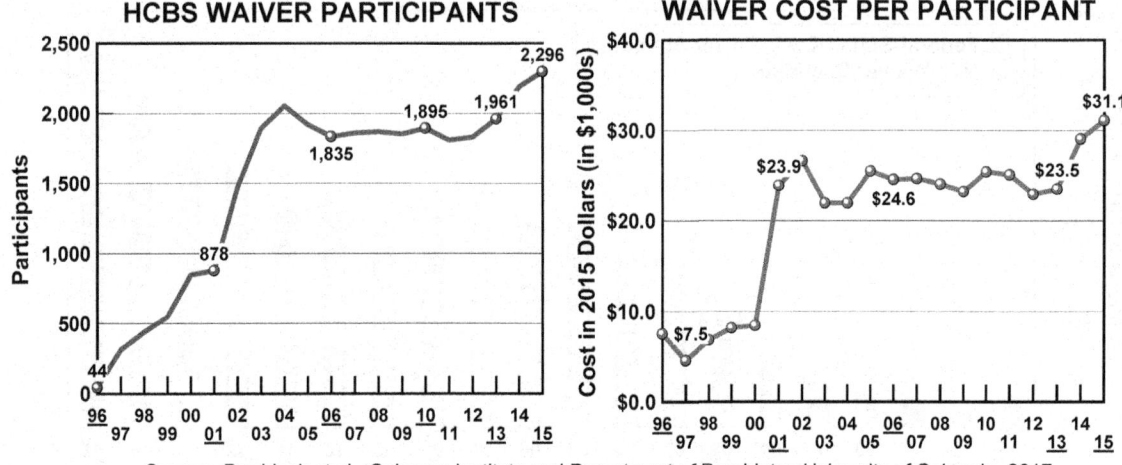

Source: Braddock et al., Coleman Institute and Department of Psychiatry, University of Colorado, 2017.
http://stateofthestates.org

MISSISSSIPPI
INDIVIDUAL AND FAMILY SUPPORT
SPENDING: FY 1996-2015

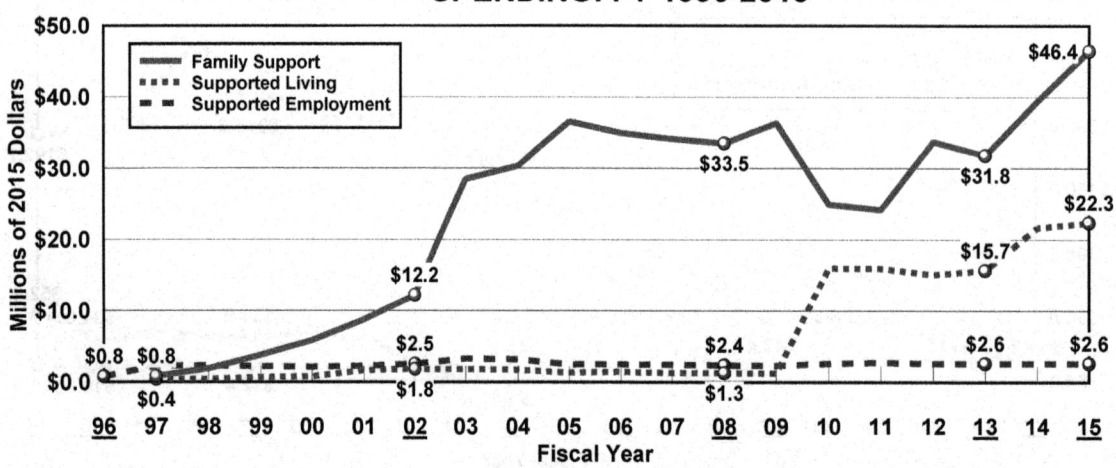

PARTICIPANTS: FY 1996-2015

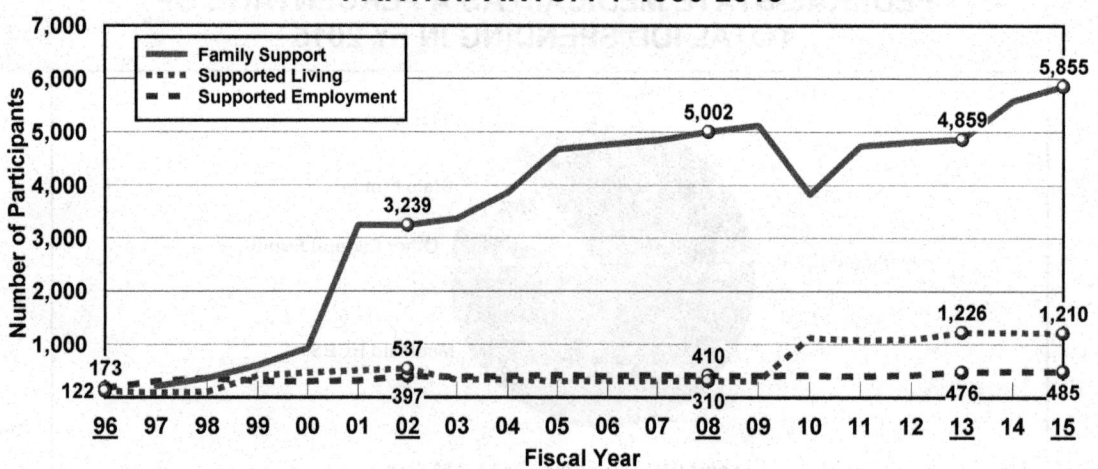

SUPPORTED LIVING, FAMILY SUPPORT AND SUPPORTED EMPLOYMENT SPENDING: FY 1996-2015

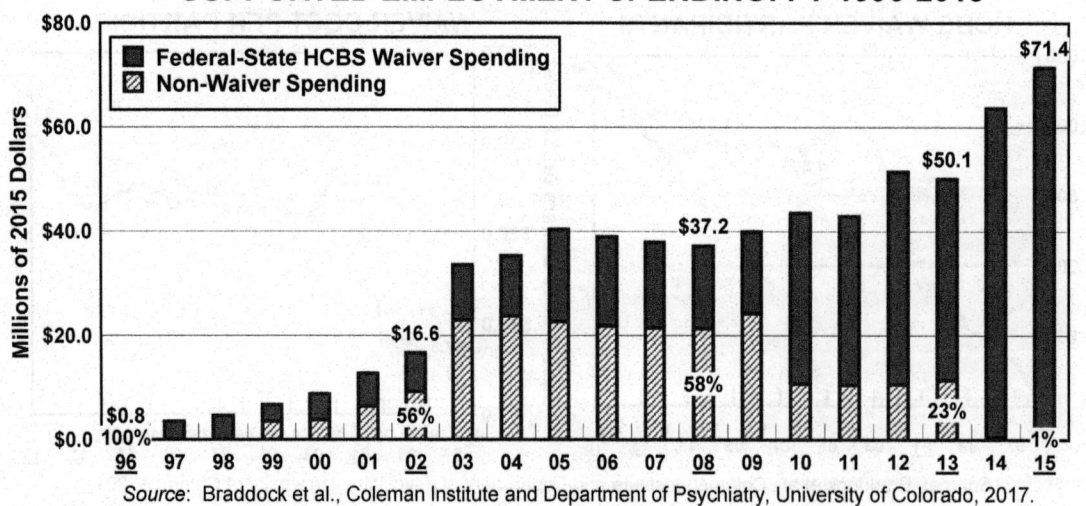

Source: Braddock et al., Coleman Institute and Department of Psychiatry, University of Colorado, 2017.
http://stateofthestates.org

MISSISSIPPI

ANNUAL COST OF CARE BY RESIDENTIAL SETTING: FY 2015

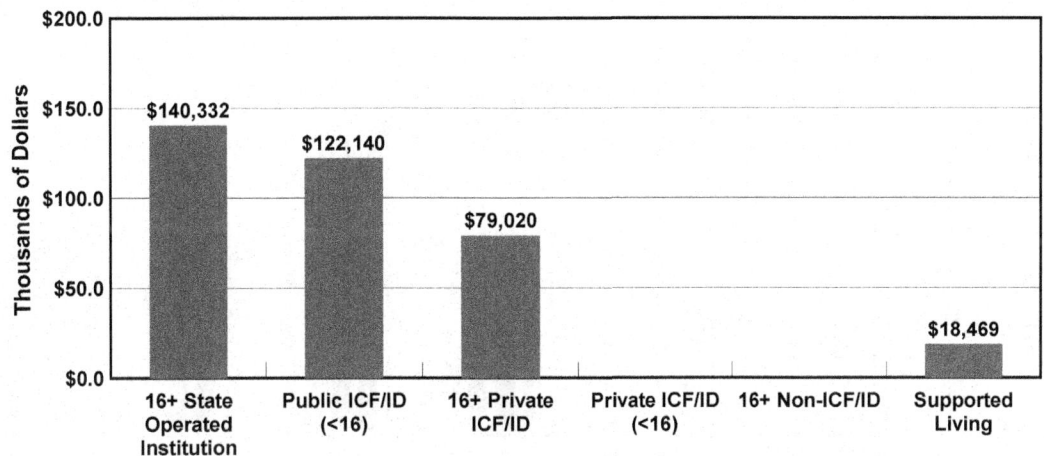

ESTIMATED NUMBER OF INDIVIDUALS WITH IDD BY AGE GROUP LIVING WITH FAMILY CAREGIVERS: FY 2015

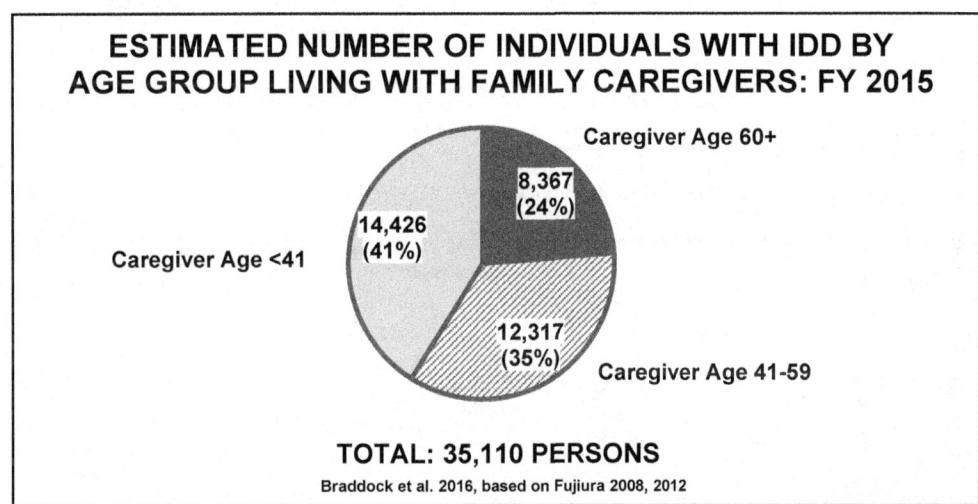

TOTAL: 35,110 PERSONS
Braddock et al. 2016, based on Fujiura 2008, 2012

ESTIMATED NUMBER OF IDD CAREGIVING FAMILIES AND FAMILIES SUPPORTED BY IDD AGENCIES: FY 1988-2015

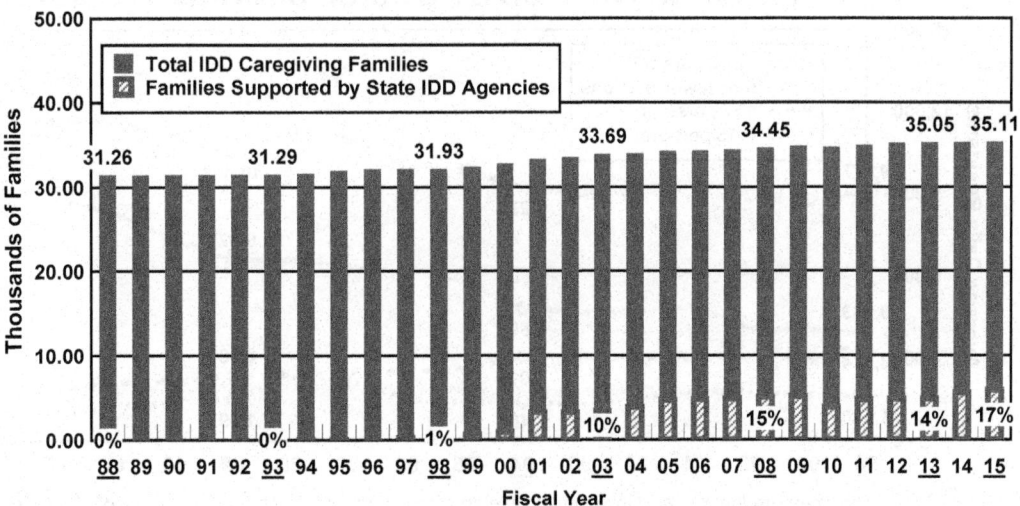

Source: Braddock et al., Coleman Institute and Department of Psychiatry, University of Colorado, 2017.
http://stateofthestates.org

MISSOURI

TOTAL PUBLIC IDD SPENDING FOR SERVICES: FY 1977-2015

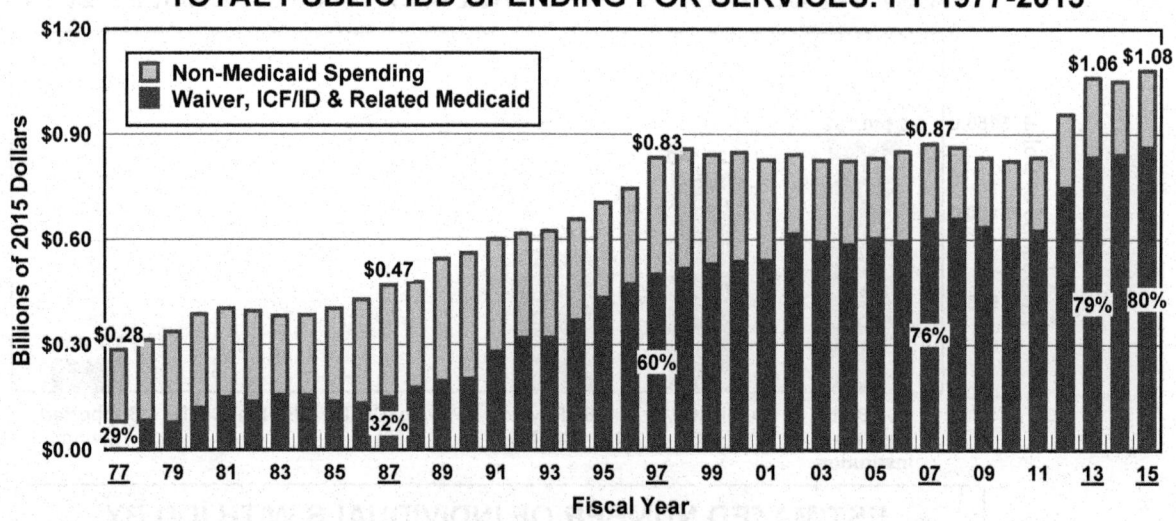

FISCAL EFFORT FOR IDD SERVICES: FY 1977-2015

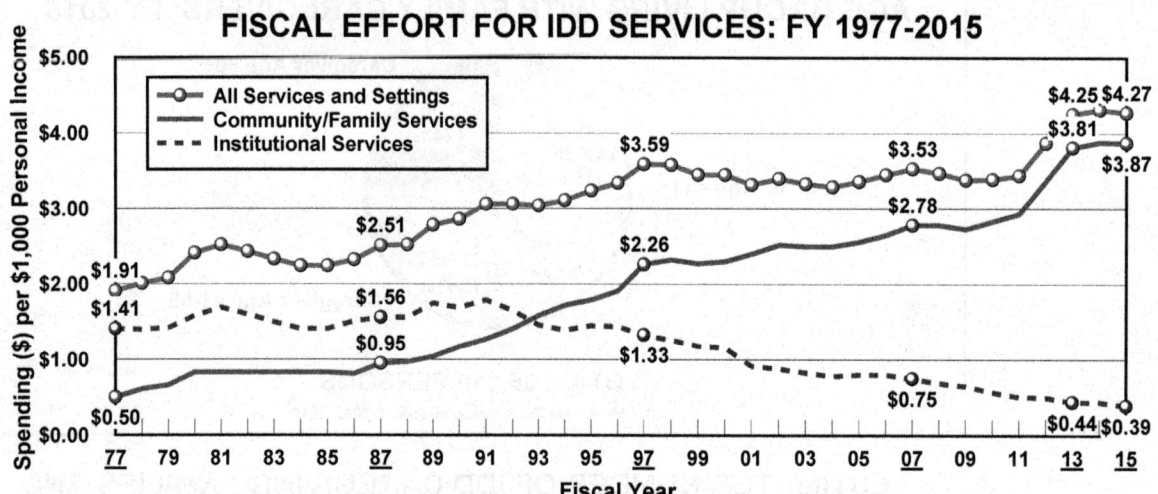

PERSONS WITH IDD BY SIZE OF SETTING: FY 1998-2015

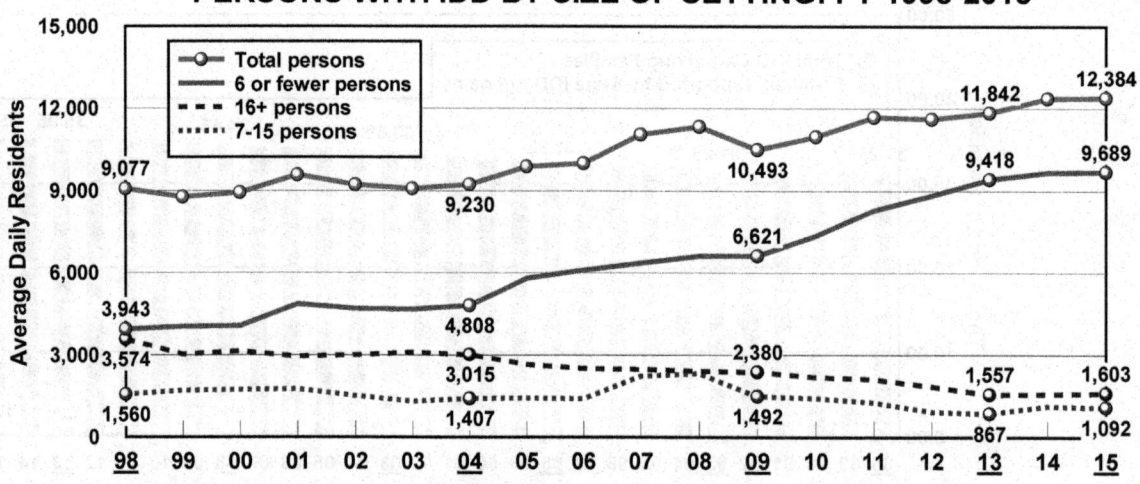

Source: Braddock et al., Coleman Institute and Department of Psychiatry, University of Colorado, 2017.
http://stateofthestates.org

MISSOURI

FEDERAL IDD MEDICAID SPENDING BY REVENUE SOURCE

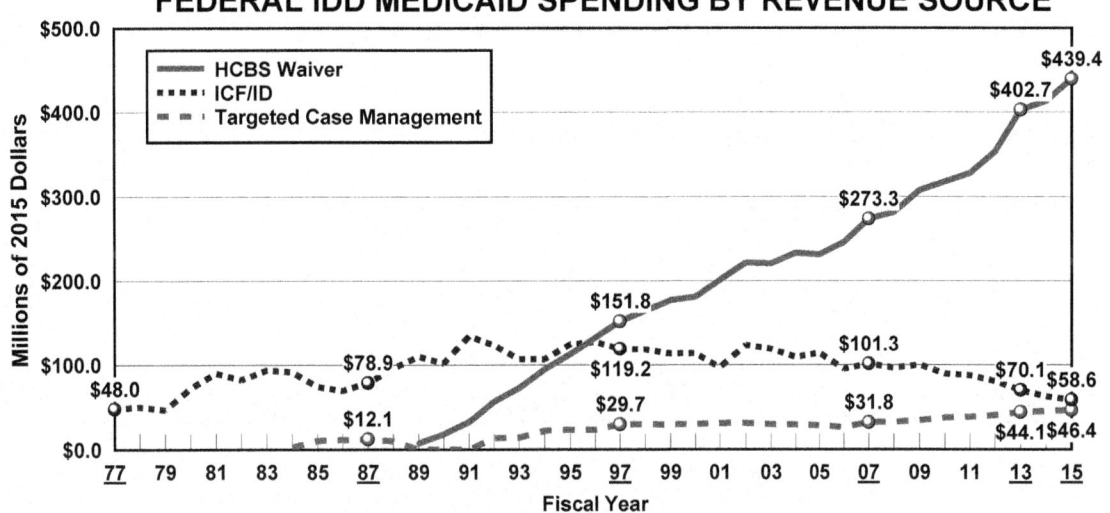

FEDERAL-STATE MEDICAID AS A PERCENTAGE OF TOTAL IDD SPENDING IN FY 2015

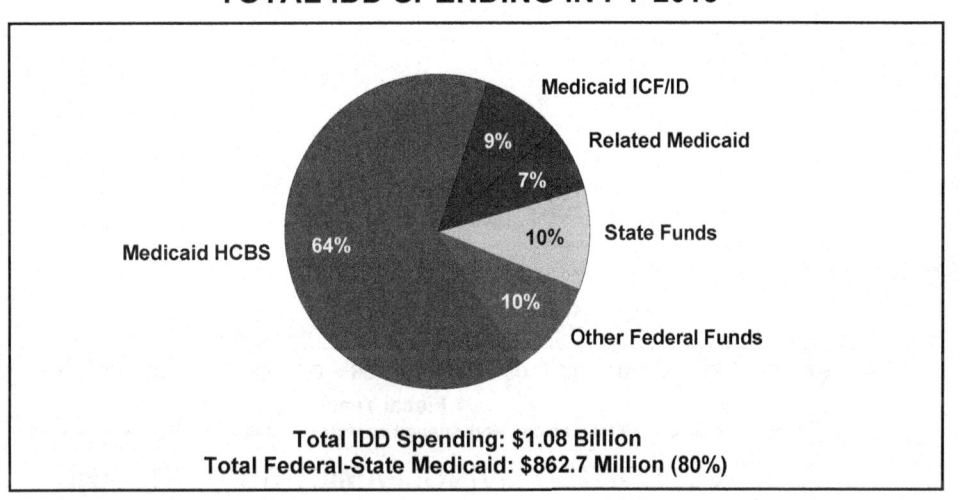

Total IDD Spending: $1.08 Billion
Total Federal-State Medicaid: $862.7 Million (80%)

HCBS WAIVER PARTICIPANTS / WAIVER COST PER PARTICIPANT

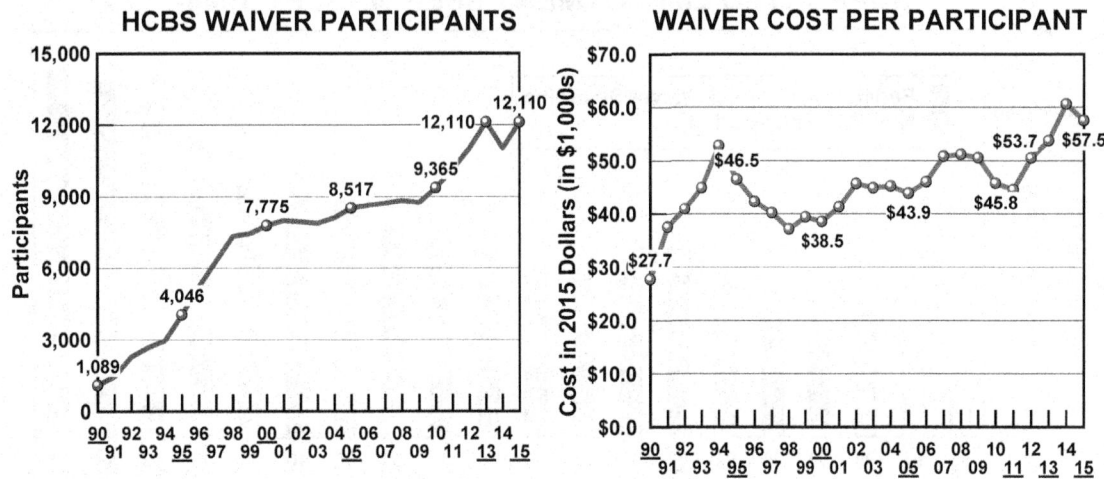

Source: Braddock et al., Coleman Institute and Department of Psychiatry, University of Colorado, 2017.
http://stateofthestates.org

MISSOURI

INDIVIDUAL AND FAMILY SUPPORT
SPENDING: FY 1996-2015

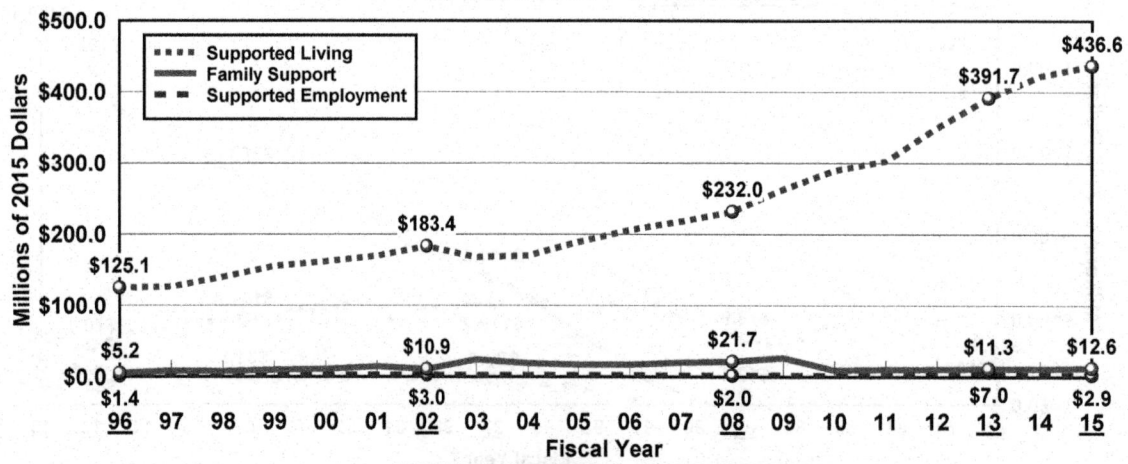

PARTICIPANTS: FY 1996-2015

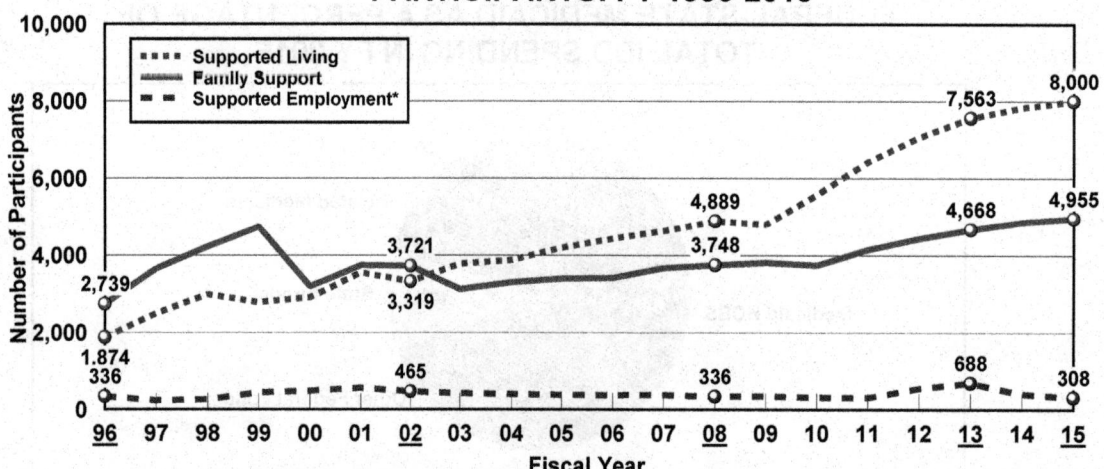

*Does not include 1,019 follow-along work support workers in 2014 and 1,317 workers in 2015.

SUPPORTED LIVING, FAMILY SUPPORT AND SUPPORTED EMPLOYMENT SPENDING: FY 1996-2015

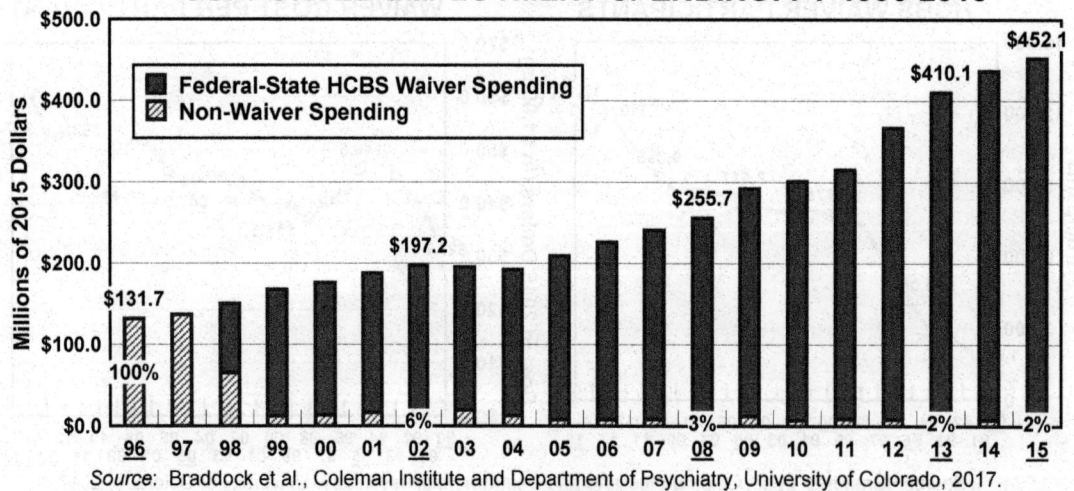

Source: Braddock et al., Coleman Institute and Department of Psychiatry, University of Colorado, 2017.
http://stateofthestates.org

MISSOURI

ANNUAL COST OF CARE BY RESIDENTIAL SETTING: FY 2015

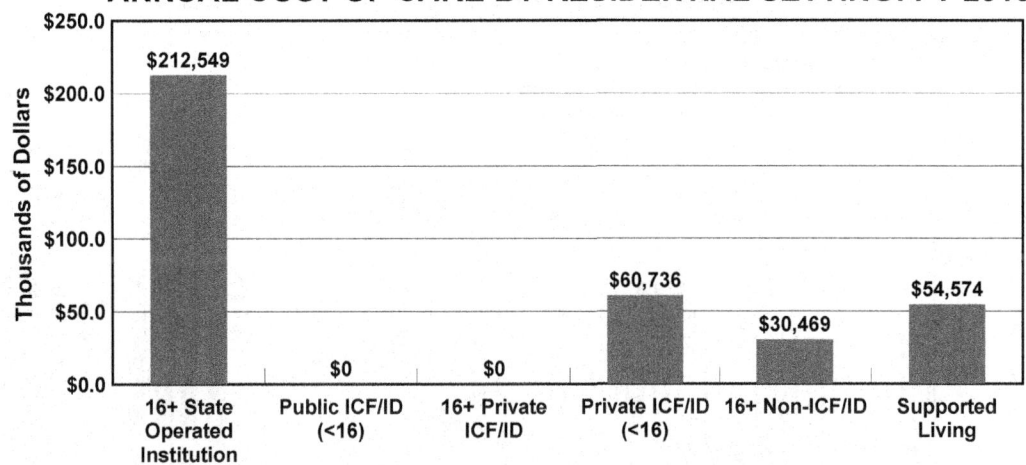

ESTIMATED NUMBER OF INDIVIDUALS WITH IDD BY AGE GROUP LIVING WITH FAMILY CAREGIVERS: FY 2015

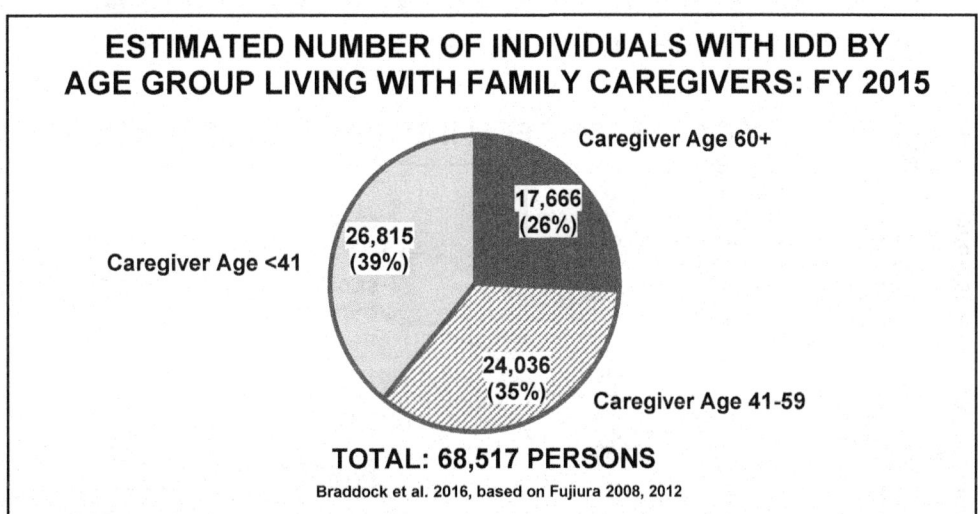

TOTAL: 68,517 PERSONS
Braddock et al. 2016, based on Fujiura 2008, 2012

ESTIMATED NUMBER OF IDD CAREGIVING FAMILIES AND FAMILIES SUPPORTED BY IDD AGENCIES: FY 1988-2015

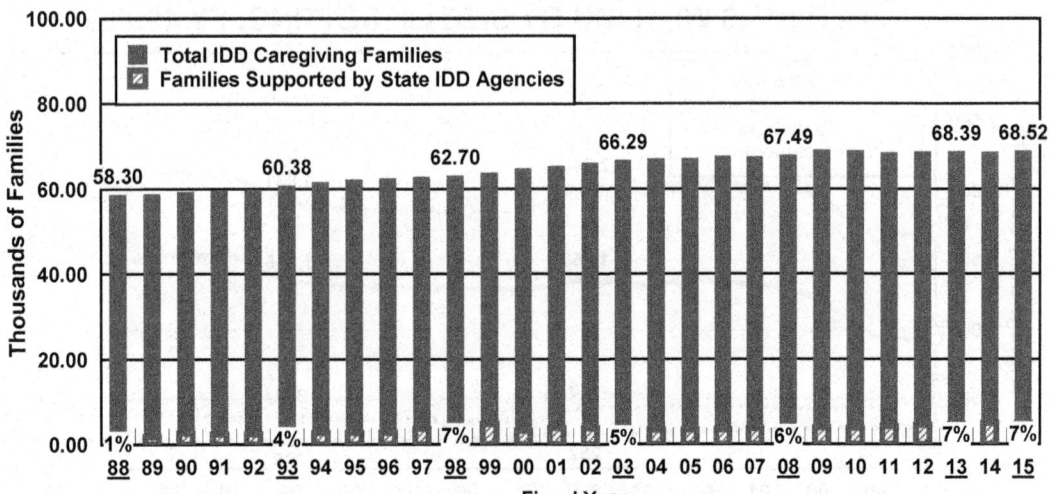

Source: Braddock et al., Coleman Institute and Department of Psychiatry, University of Colorado, 2017
http://stateofthestates.org

MONTANA

TOTAL PUBLIC IDD SPENDING FOR SERVICES: FY 1977-2015

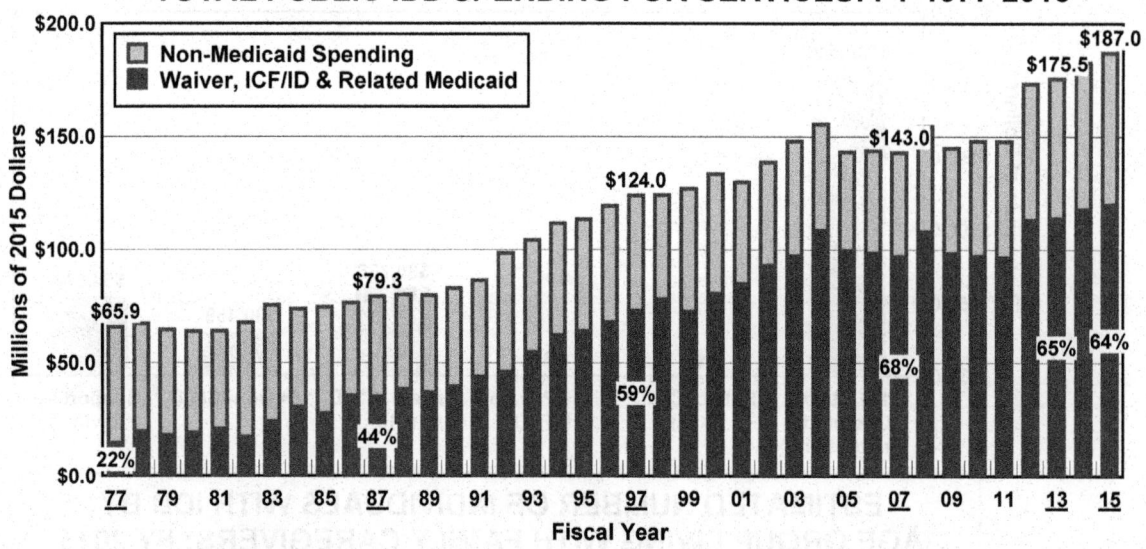

FISCAL EFFORT FOR IDD SERVICES: FY 1977-2015

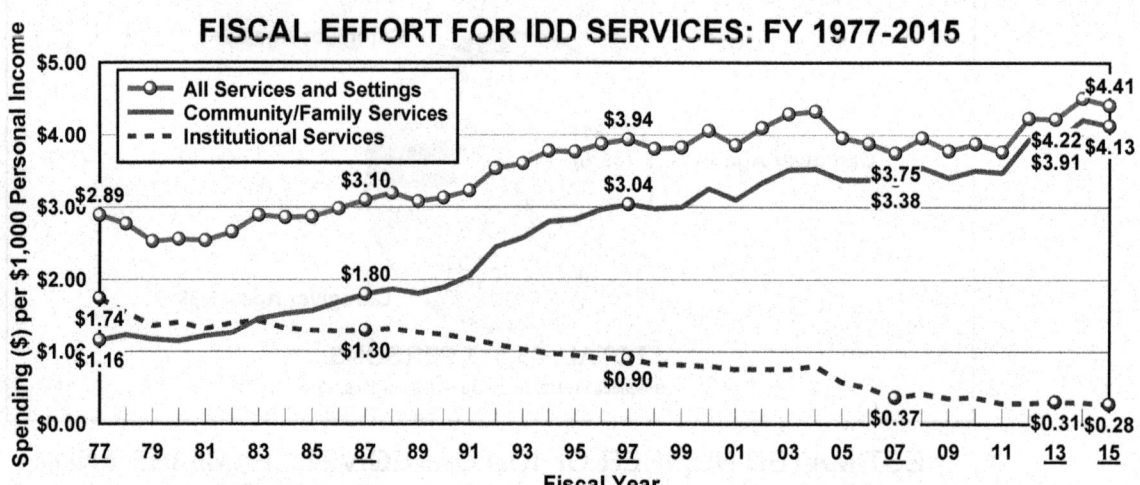

PERSONS WITH IDD BY SIZE OF SETTING: FY 1998-2015

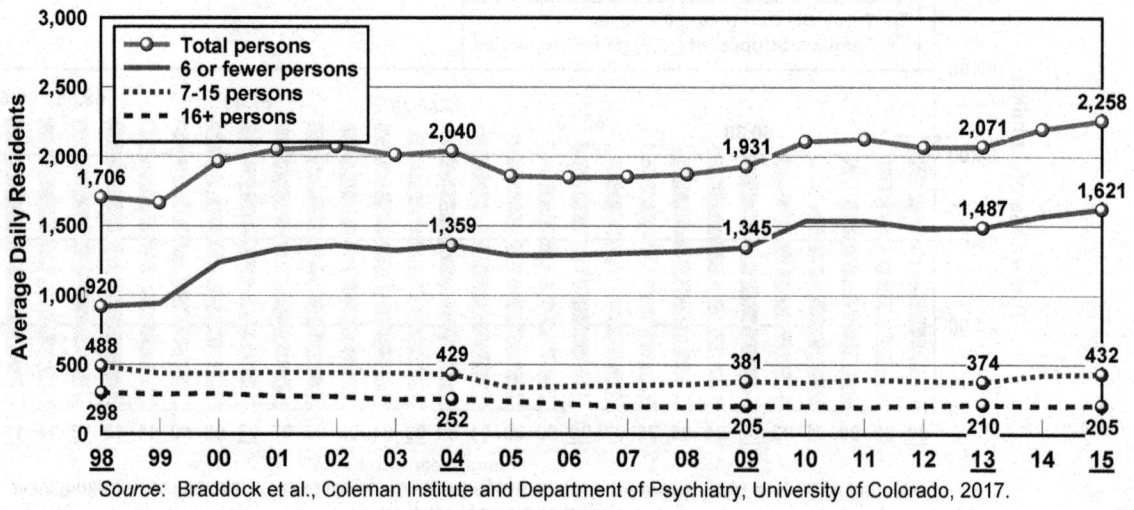

Source: Braddock et al., Coleman Institute and Department of Psychiatry, University of Colorado, 2017.

http://stateofthestates.org

MONTANA

FEDERAL IDD MEDICAID SPENDING BY REVENUE SOURCE

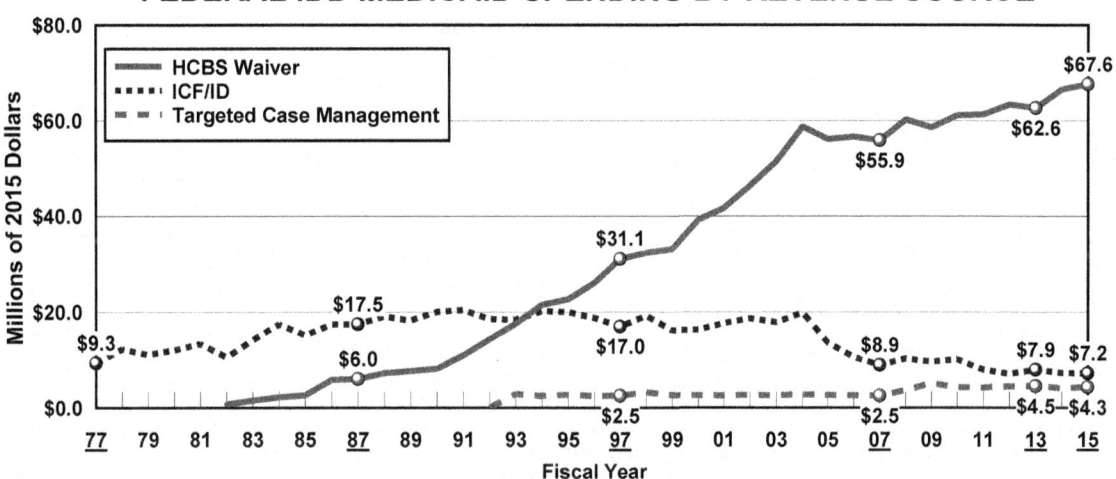

FEDERAL-STATE MEDICAID AS A PERCENTAGE OF TOTAL IDD SPENDING IN FY 2015

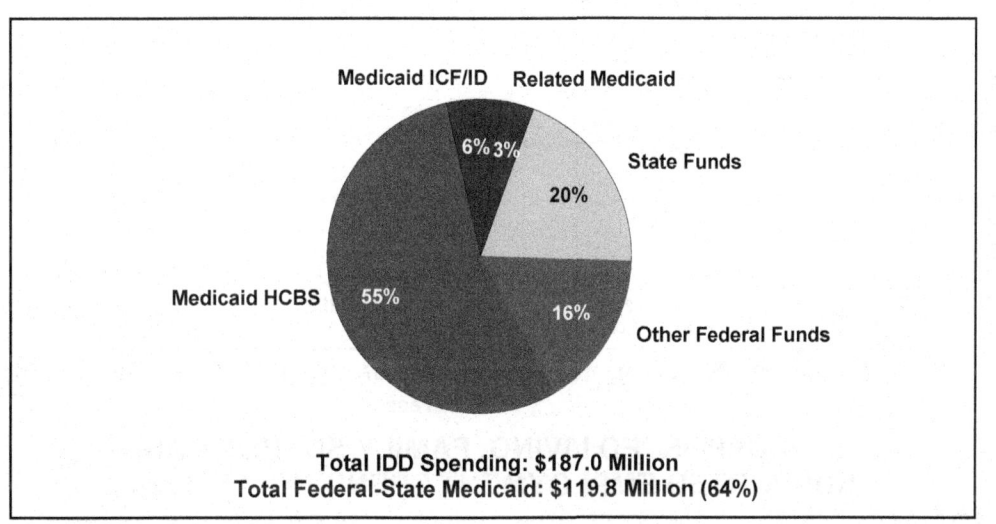

Total IDD Spending: $187.0 Million
Total Federal-State Medicaid: $119.8 Million (64%)

HCBS WAIVER PARTICIPANTS / WAIVER COST PER PARTICIPANT

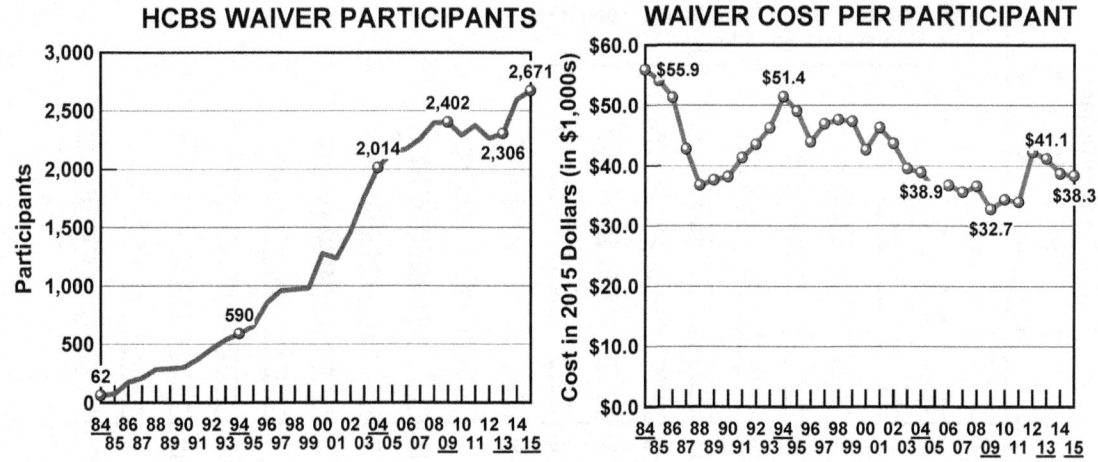

Source: Braddock et al., Coleman Institute and Department of Psychiatry, University of Colorado, 2017.
http://stateofthestates.org

MONTANA

INDIVIDUAL AND FAMILY SUPPORT
SPENDING: FY 1996-2015

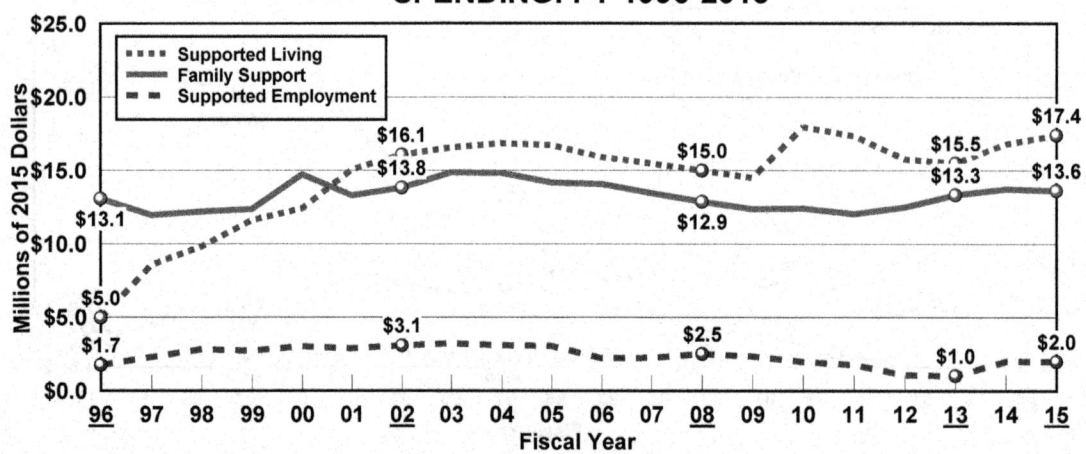

PARTICIPANTS: FY 1996-2015

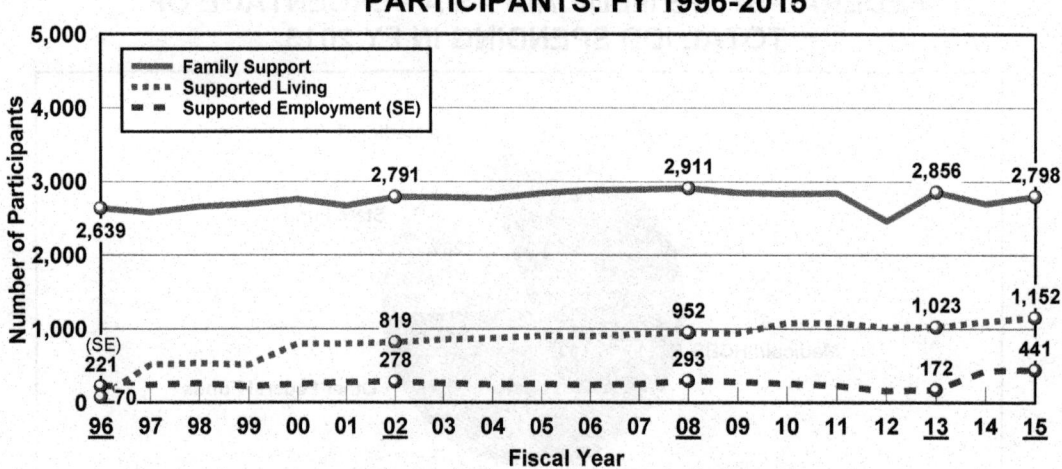

SUPPORTED LIVING, FAMILY SUPPORT AND SUPPORTED EMPLOYMENT SPENDING: FY 1996-2015

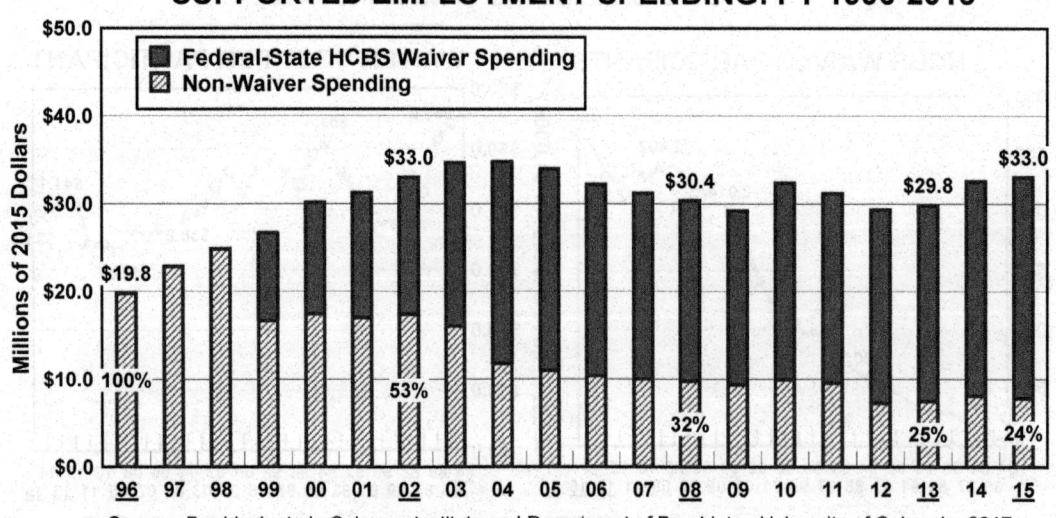

Source: Braddock et al., Coleman Institute and Department of Psychiatry, University of Colorado, 2017.
http://stateofthestates.org

MONTANA

ANNUAL COST OF CARE BY RESIDENTIAL SETTING: FY 2015

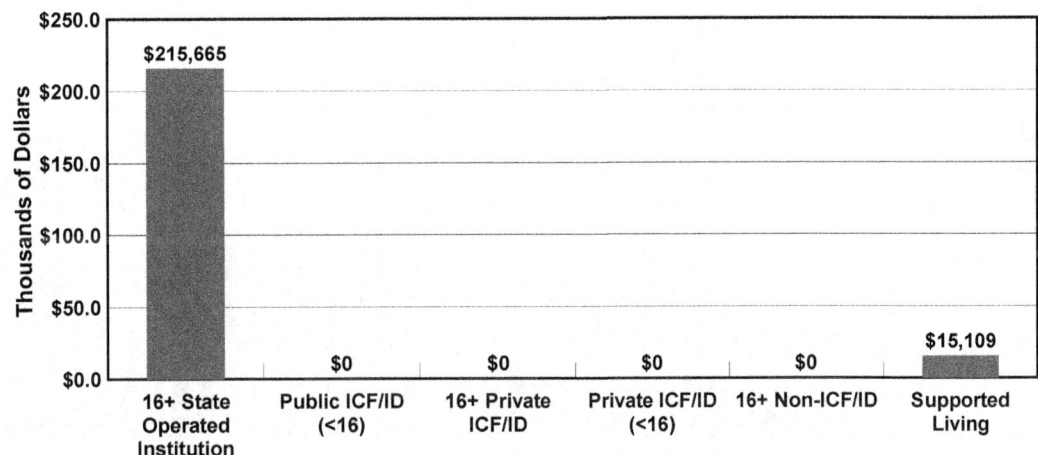

ESTIMATED NUMBER OF INDIVIDUALS WITH IDD BY AGE GROUP LIVING WITH FAMILY CAREGIVERS: FY 2015

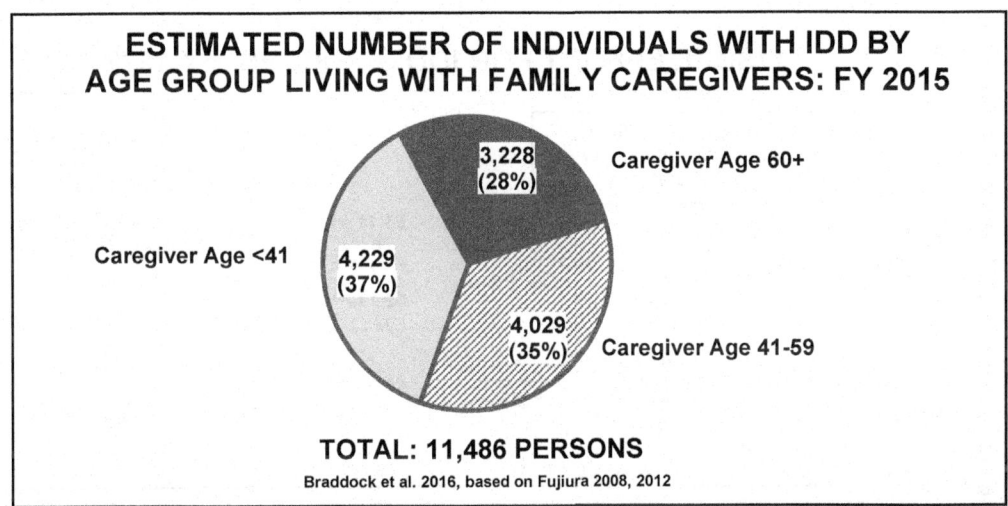

TOTAL: 11,486 PERSONS

Braddock et al. 2016, based on Fujiura 2008, 2012

ESTIMATED NUMBER OF IDD CAREGIVING FAMILIES AND FAMILIES SUPPORTED BY IDD AGENCIES: FY 1988-2015

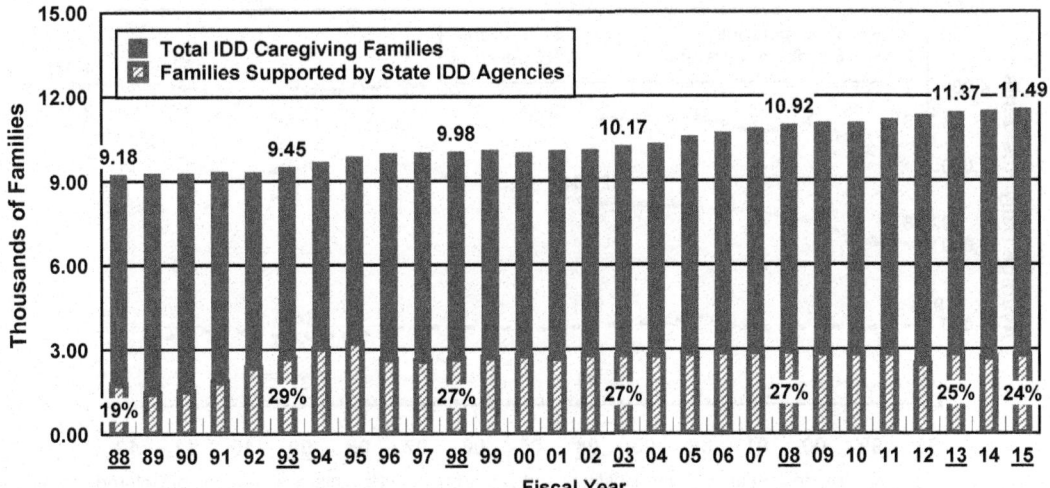

Source: Braddock et al., Coleman Institute and Department of Psychiatry, University of Colorado, 2017.
http://stateofthestates.org

NEBRASKA

TOTAL PUBLIC IDD SPENDING FOR SERVICES: FY 1977-2015

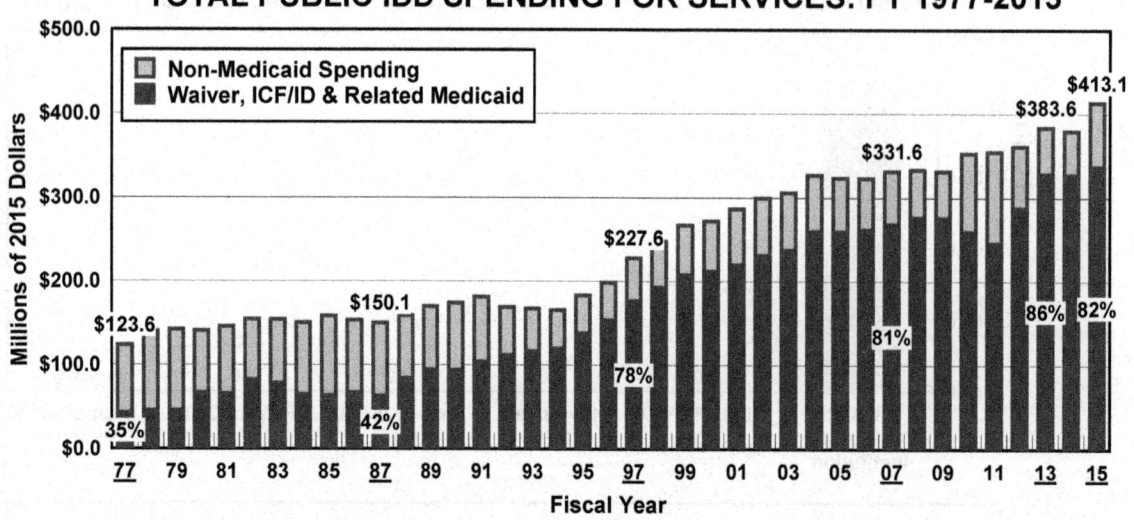

FISCAL EFFORT FOR IDD SERVICES: FY 1977-2015

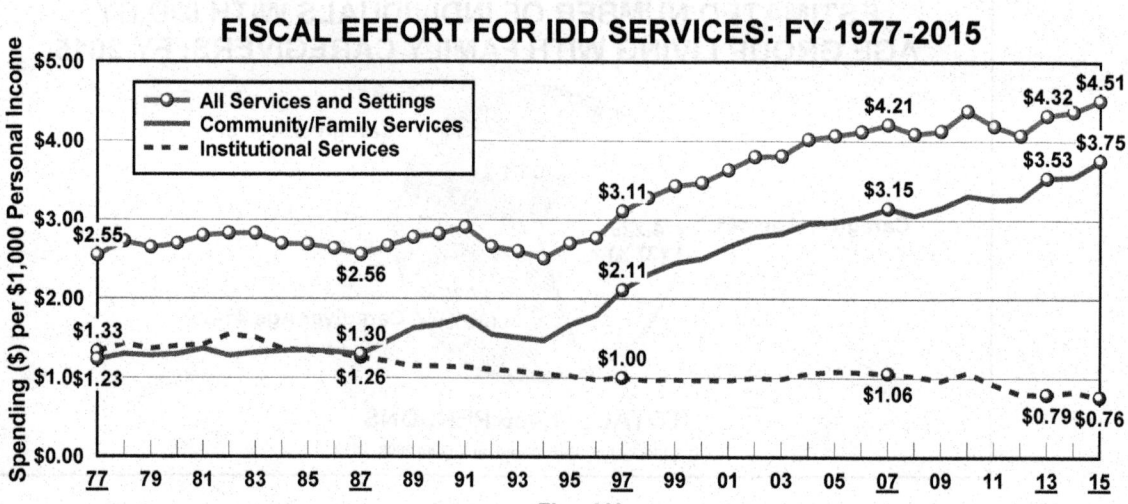

PERSONS WITH IDD BY SIZE OF SETTING: FY 1998-2015

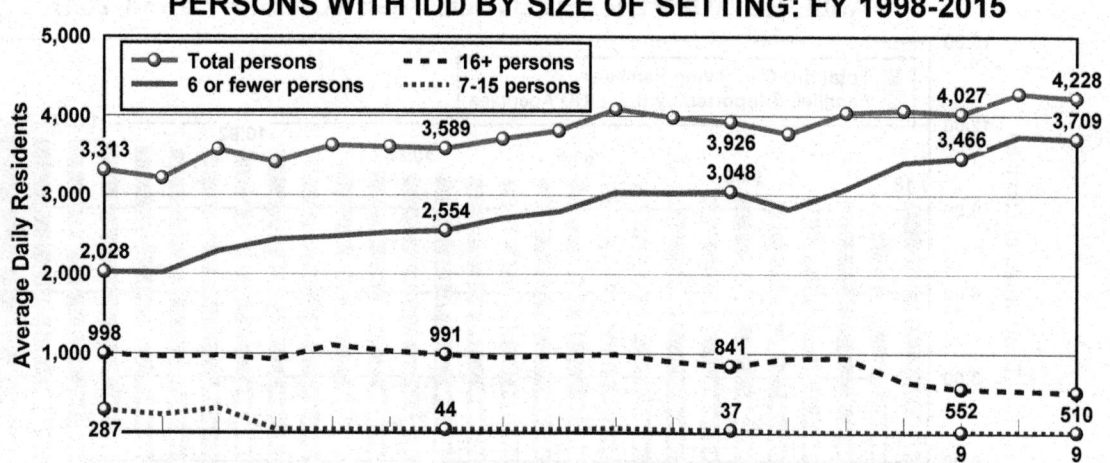

Source: Braddock et al., Coleman Institute and Department of Psychiatry, University of Colorado, 2017.

http://stateofthestates.org

NEBRASKA

FEDERAL IDD MEDICAID SPENDING BY REVENUE SOURCE

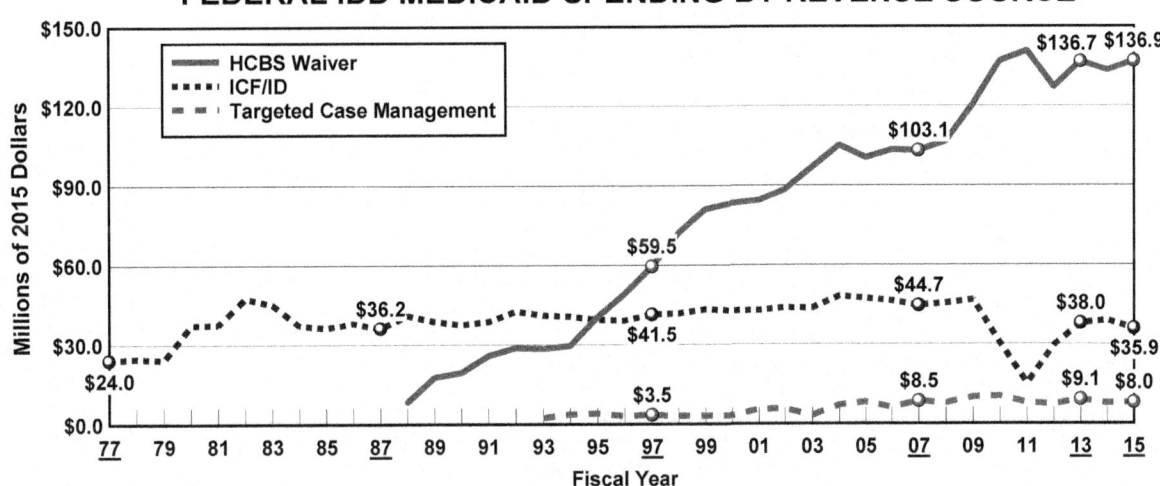

FEDERAL-STATE MEDICAID AS A PERCENTAGE OF TOTAL IDD SPENDING IN FY 2015

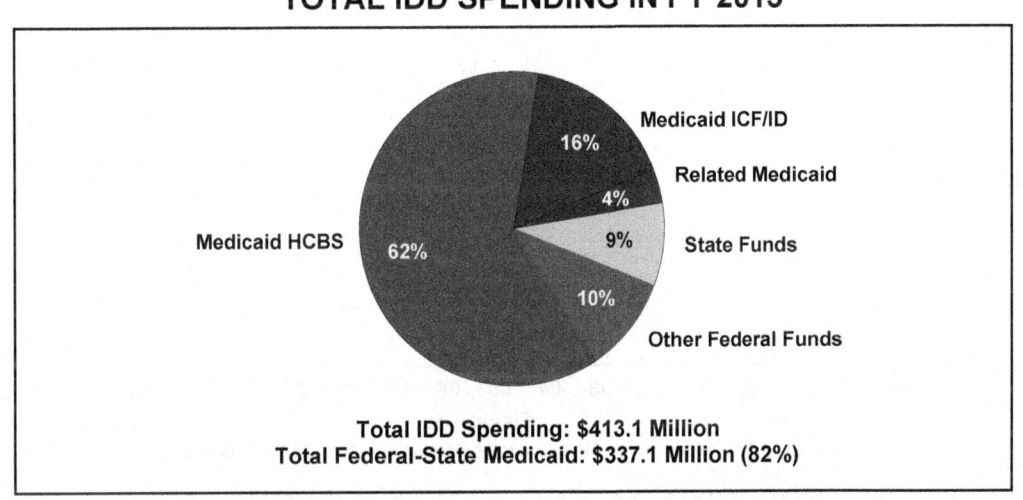

Total IDD Spending: $413.1 Million
Total Federal-State Medicaid: $337.1 Million (82%)

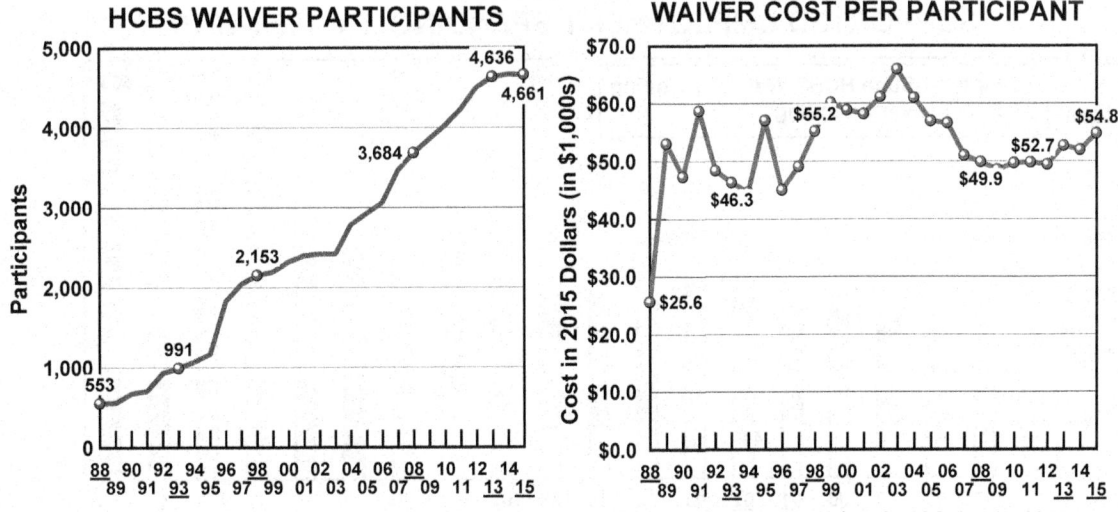

Source: Braddock et al., Coleman Institute and Department of Psychiatry, University of Colorado, 2017.
http://stateofthestates.org

NEBRASKA

INDIVIDUAL AND FAMILY SUPPORT
SPENDING: FY 1996-2015

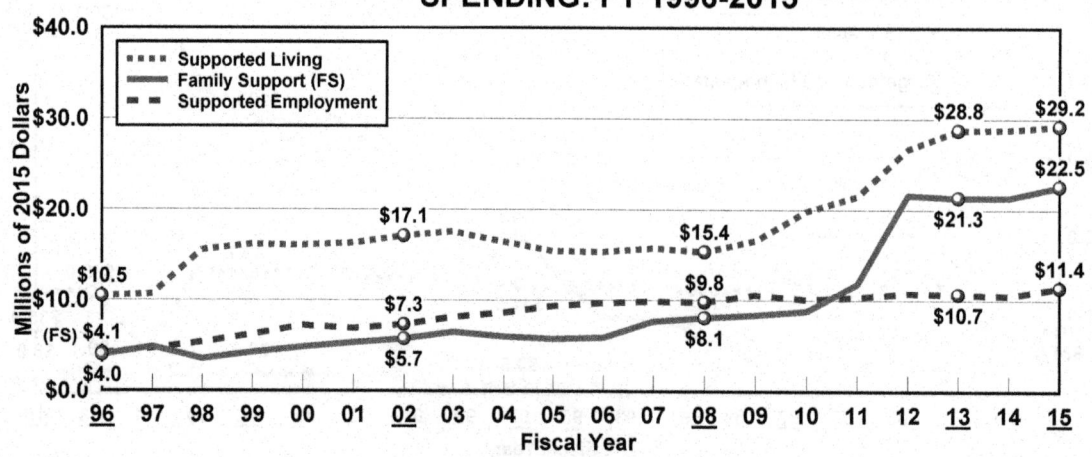

PARTICIPANTS: FY 1996-2015

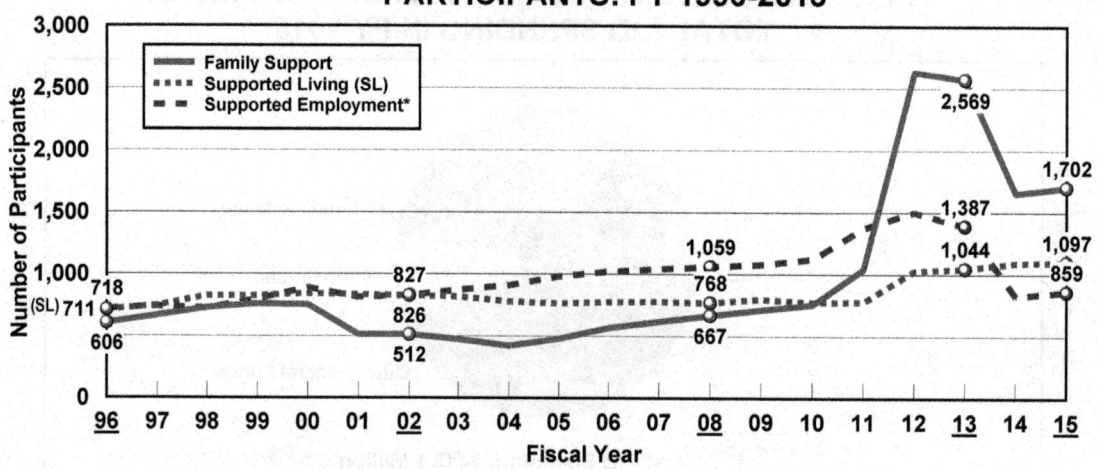

*Does not include 134 follow-along work support workers in 2014 and 135 workers in 2015.

SUPPORTED LIVING, FAMILY SUPPORT AND SUPPORTED EMPLOYMENT SPENDING: FY 1996-2015

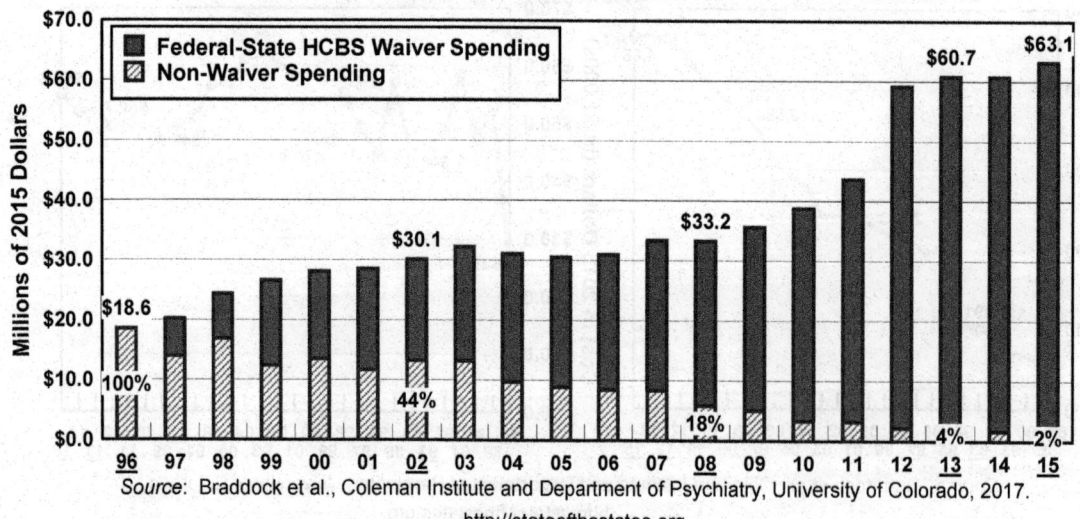

Source: Braddock et al., Coleman Institute and Department of Psychiatry, University of Colorado, 2017.
http://stateofthestates.org

NEBRASKA

ANNUAL COST OF CARE BY RESIDENTIAL SETTING: FY 2015

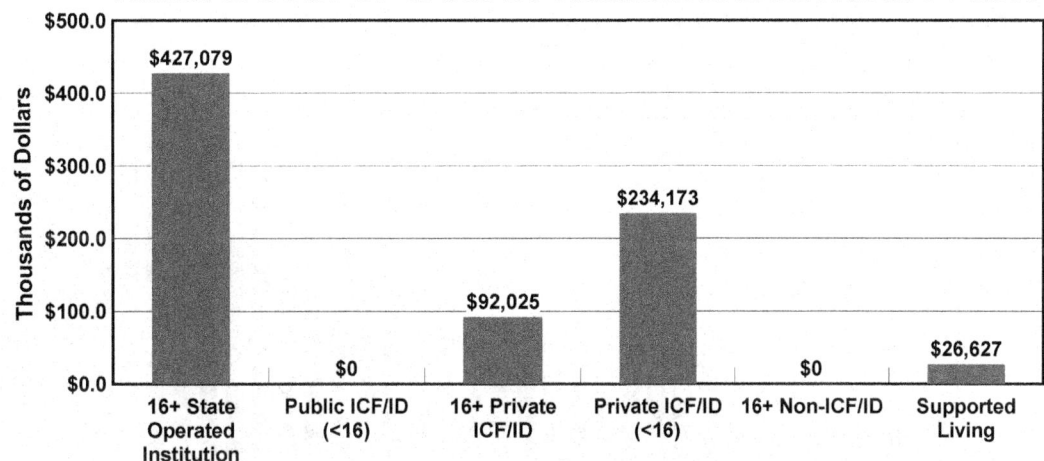

ESTIMATED NUMBER OF INDIVIDUALS WITH IDD BY AGE GROUP LIVING WITH FAMILY CAREGIVERS: FY 2015

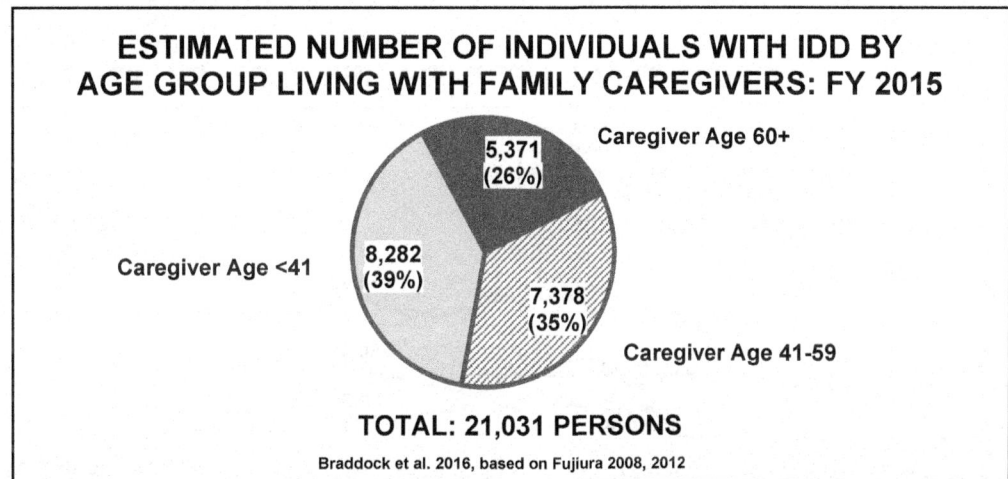

TOTAL: 21,031 PERSONS

Braddock et al. 2016, based on Fujiura 2008, 2012

ESTIMATED NUMBER OF IDD CAREGIVING FAMILIES AND FAMILIES SUPPORTED BY IDD AGENCIES: FY 1988-2015

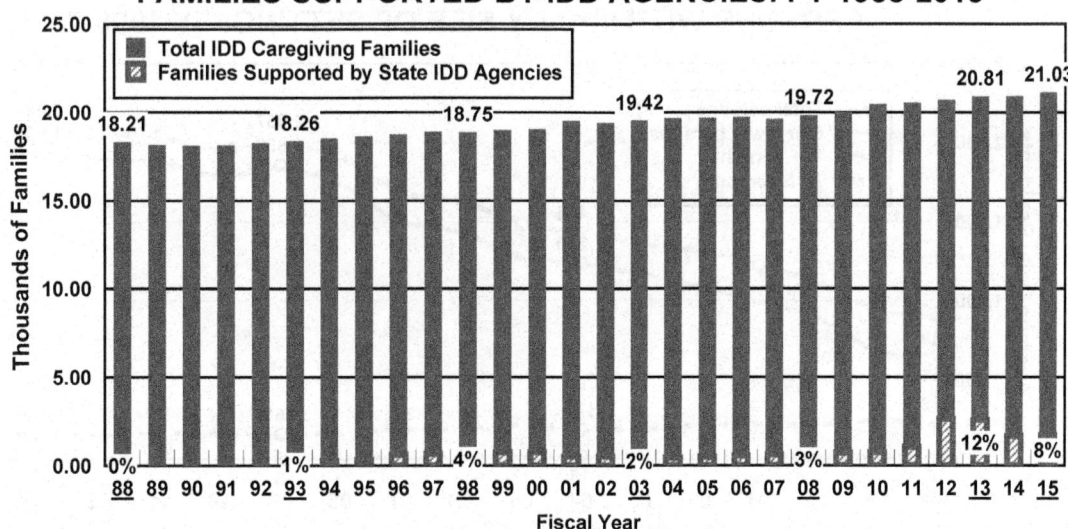

Source: Braddock et al., Coleman Institute and Department of Psychiatry, University of Colorado, 2017.
http://stateofthestates.org

NEVADA

TOTAL PUBLIC I/DD SPENDING FOR SERVICES: FY 1977-2015

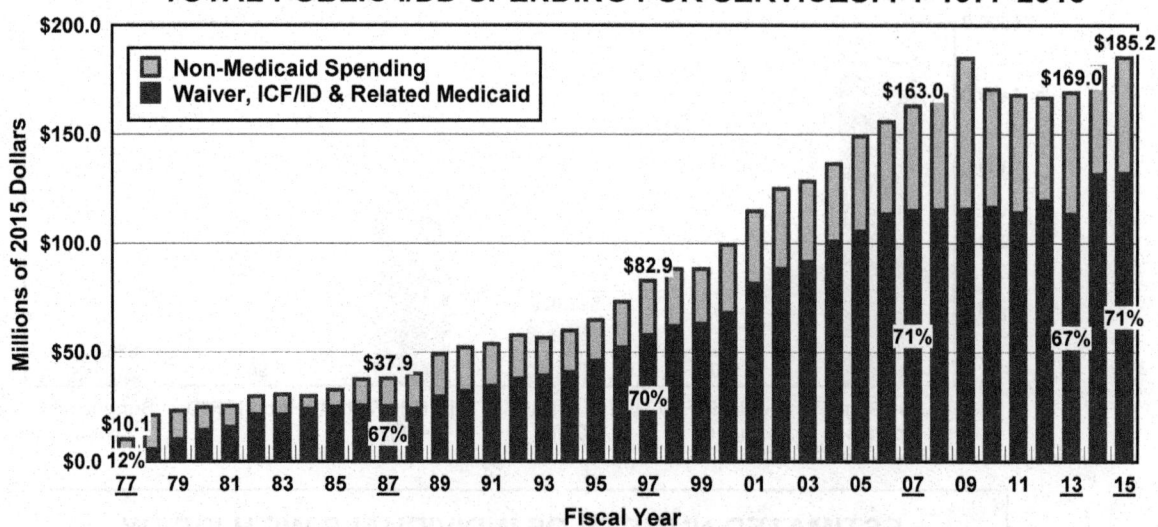

FISCAL EFFORT FOR I/DD SERVICES: FY 1977-2015

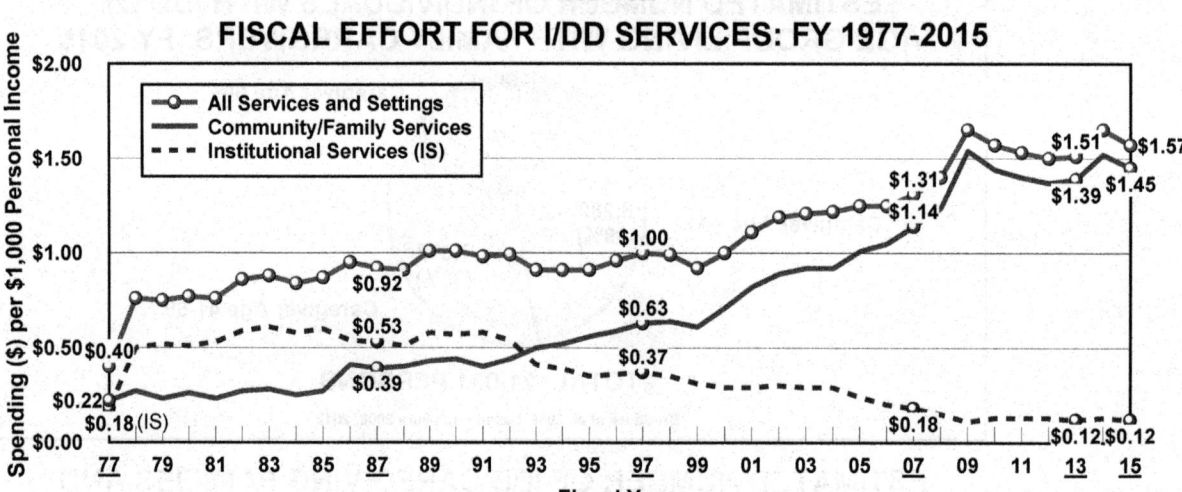

PERSONS WITH I/DD BY SIZE OF SETTING: FY 1998-2015

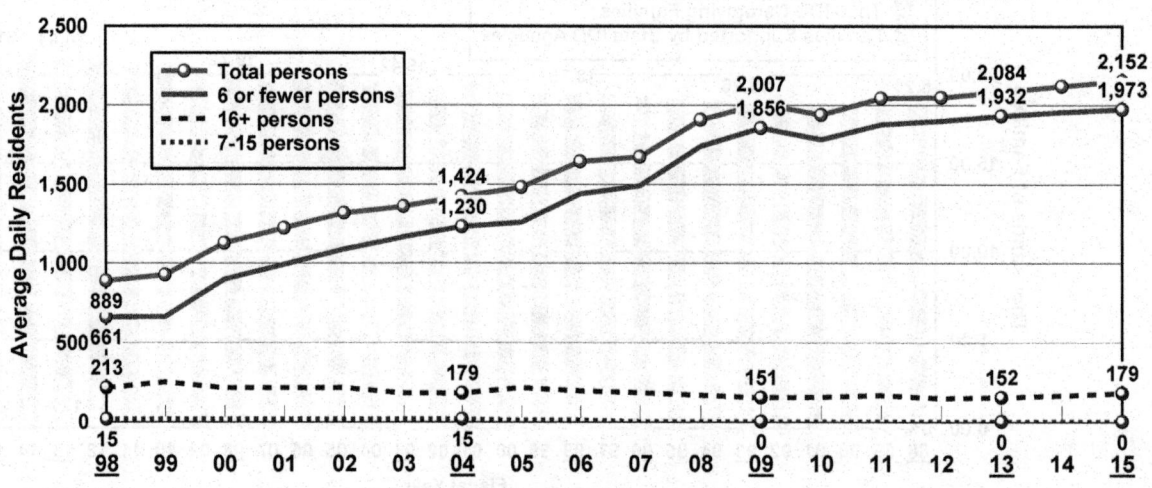

Source: Braddock et al., Coleman Institute and Department of Psychiatry, University of Colorado, 2017.

http://stateofthestates.org

NEVADA

FEDERAL I/DD MEDICAID SPENDING BY REVENUE SOURCE

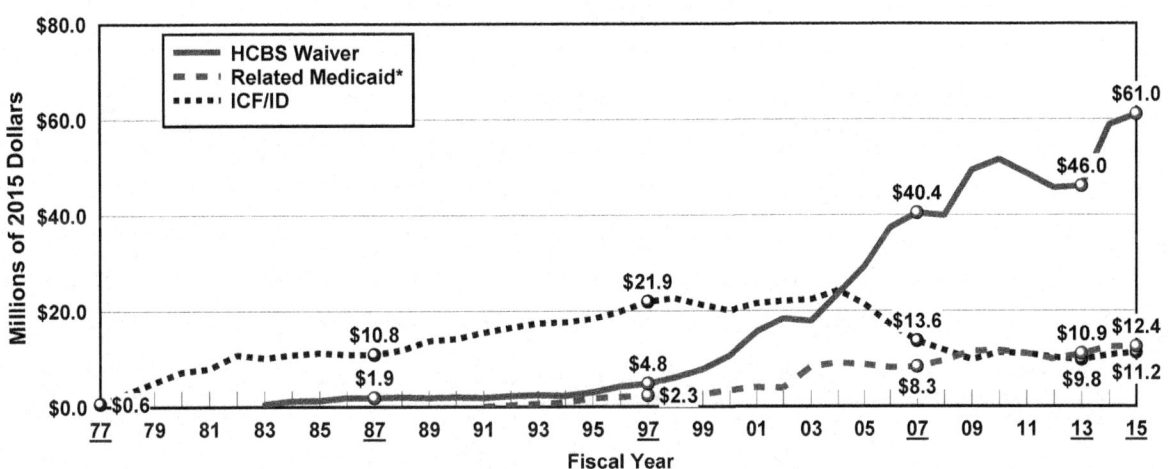

*In 2015, "Related Medicaid" was targeted case management ($4.2 million), personal assistant ($4.1 million) and administration ($4.1 million).

FEDERAL-STATE MEDICAID AS A PERCENTAGE OF TOTAL I/DD SPENDING IN FY 2015

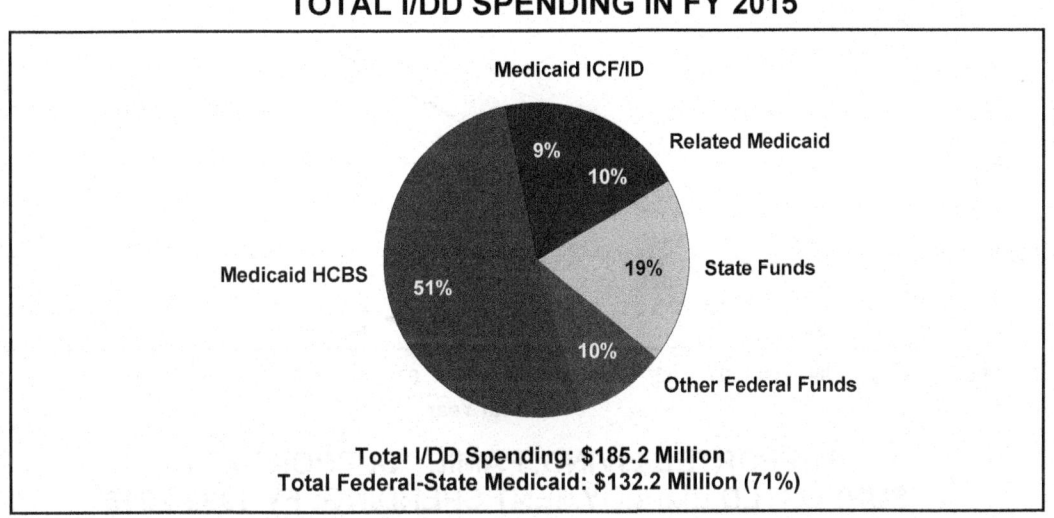

Total I/DD Spending: $185.2 Million
Total Federal-State Medicaid: $132.2 Million (71%)

HCBS WAIVER PARTICIPANTS / WAIVER COST PER PARTICIPANT

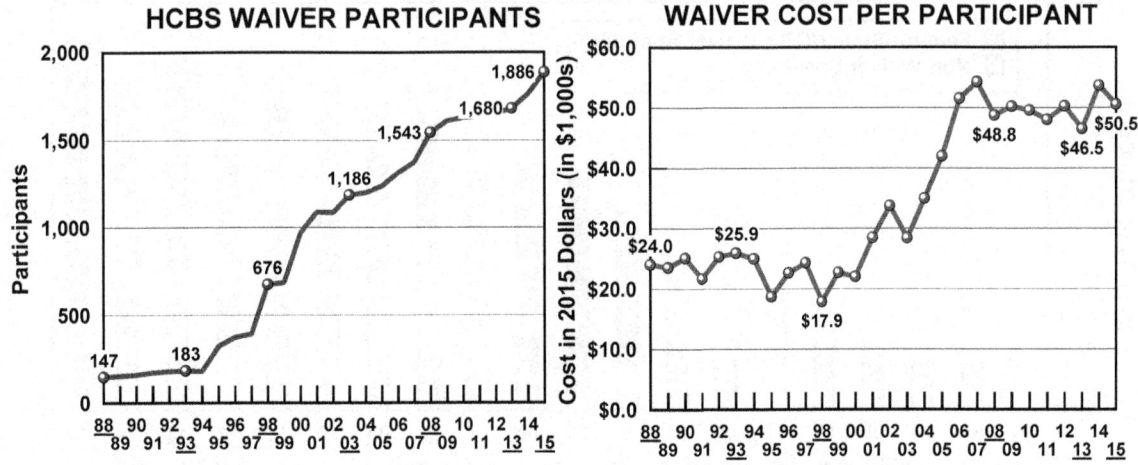

Source: Braddock et al., Coleman Institute and Department of Psychiatry, University of Colorado, 2017.
http://stateofthestates.org

NEVADA
INDIVIDUAL AND FAMILY SUPPORT
SPENDING: FY 1996-2015

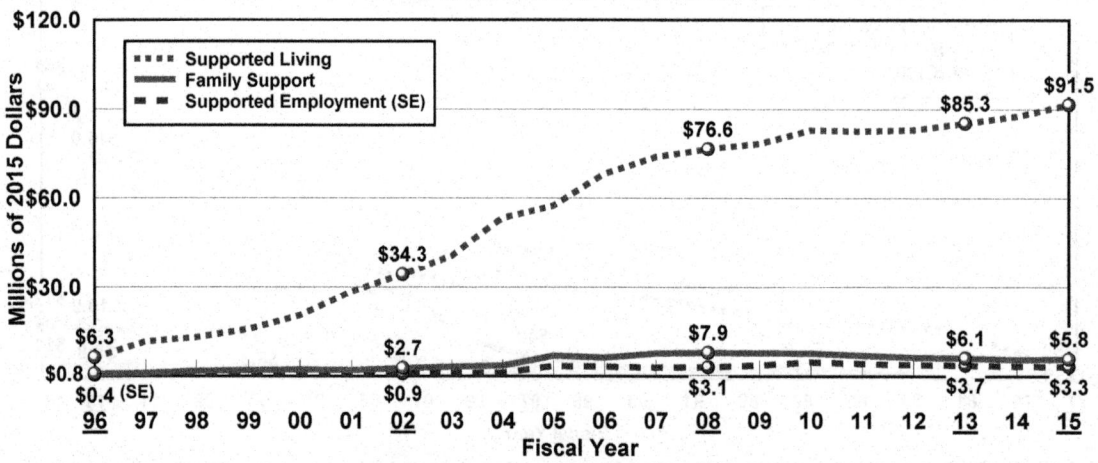

PARTICIPANTS: FY 1996-2015

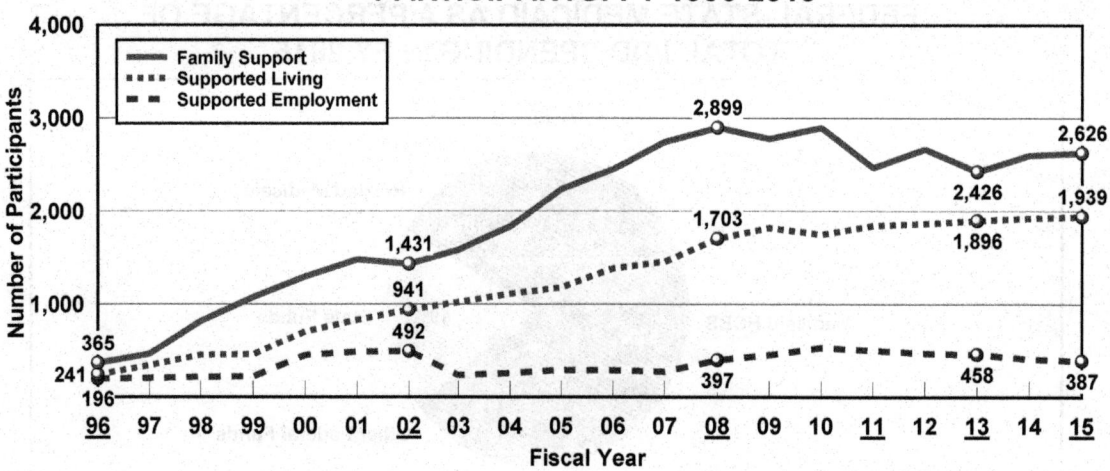

SUPPORTED LIVING, FAMILY SUPPORT AND SUPPORTED EMPLOYMENT SPENDING: FY 1996-2015

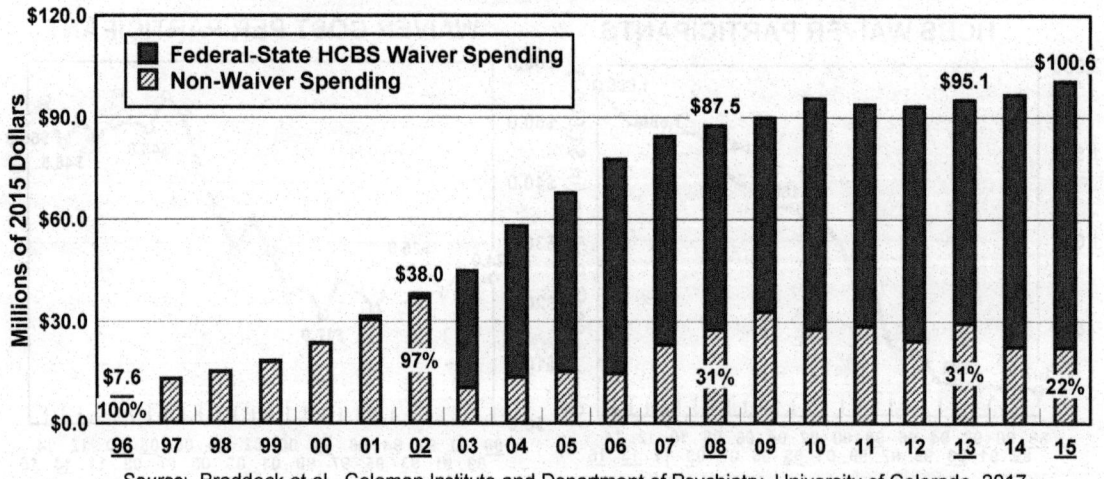

Source: Braddock et al., Coleman Institute and Department of Psychiatry, University of Colorado, 2017.
http://stateofthestates.org

NEVADA

ANNUAL COST OF CARE BY RESIDENTIAL SETTING: FY 2015

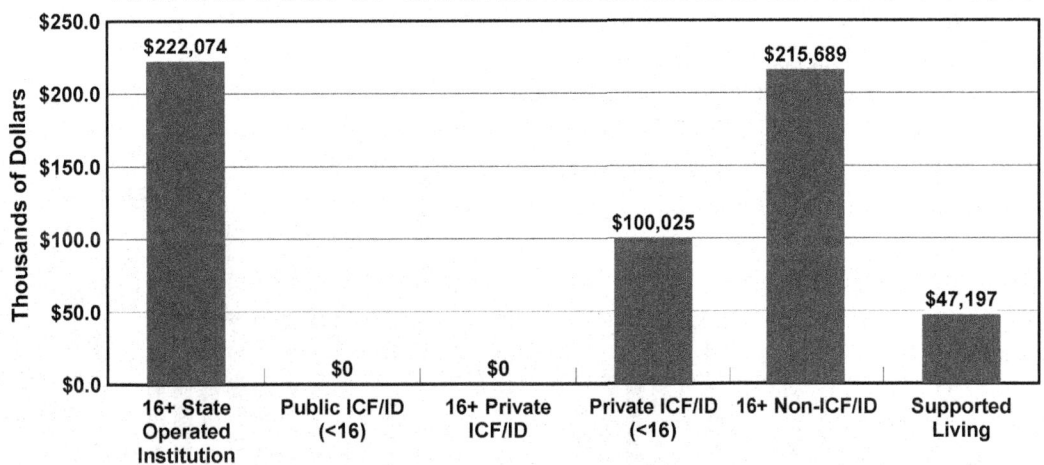

ESTIMATED NUMBER OF INDIVIDUALS WITH I/DD BY AGE GROUP LIVING WITH FAMILY CAREGIVERS: FY 2015

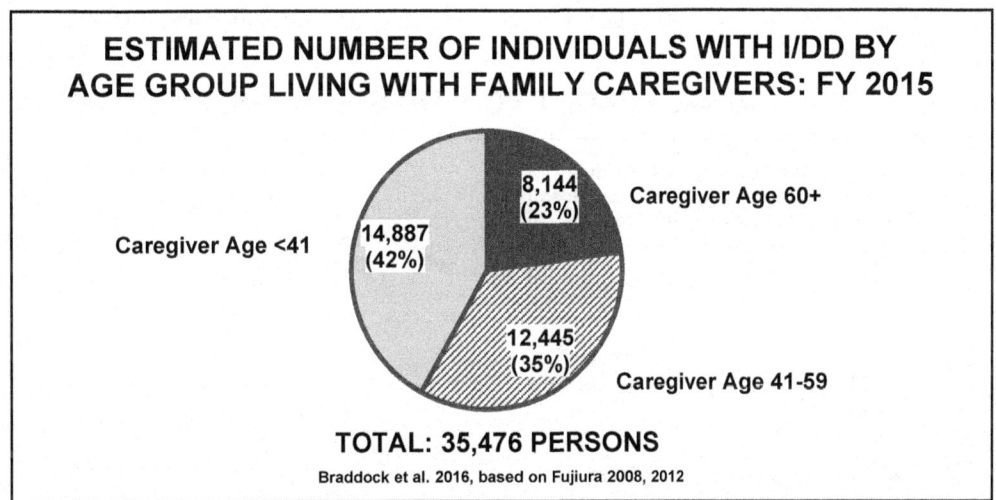

TOTAL: 35,476 PERSONS

Braddock et al. 2016, based on Fujiura 2008, 2012

ESTIMATED NUMBER OF I/DD CAREGIVING FAMILIES AND FAMILIES SUPPORTED BY I/DD AGENCIES: FY 1988-2015

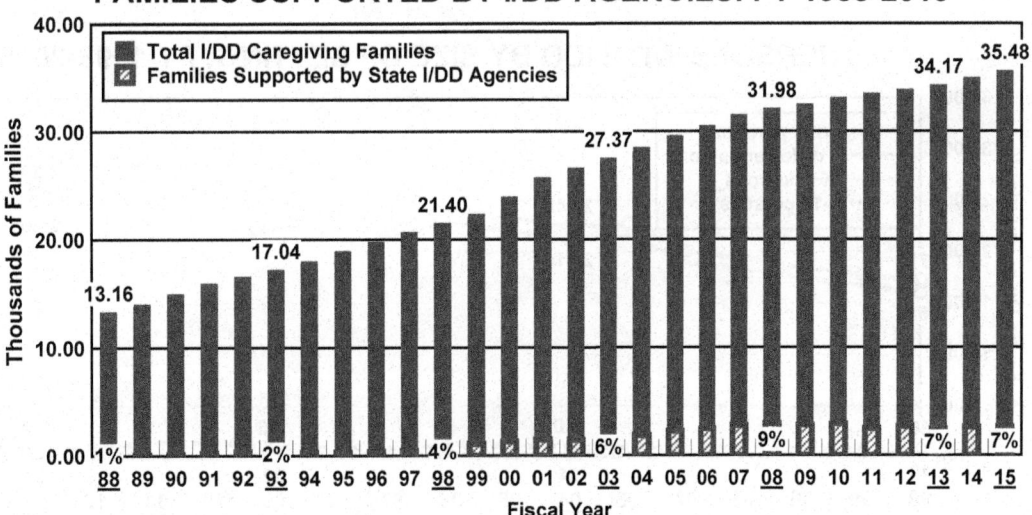

Source: Braddock et al., Coleman Institute and Department of Psychiatry, University of Colorado, 2017.

http://stateofthestates.org

NEW HAMPSHIRE

TOTAL PUBLIC IDD SPENDING FOR SERVICES: FY 1977-2015

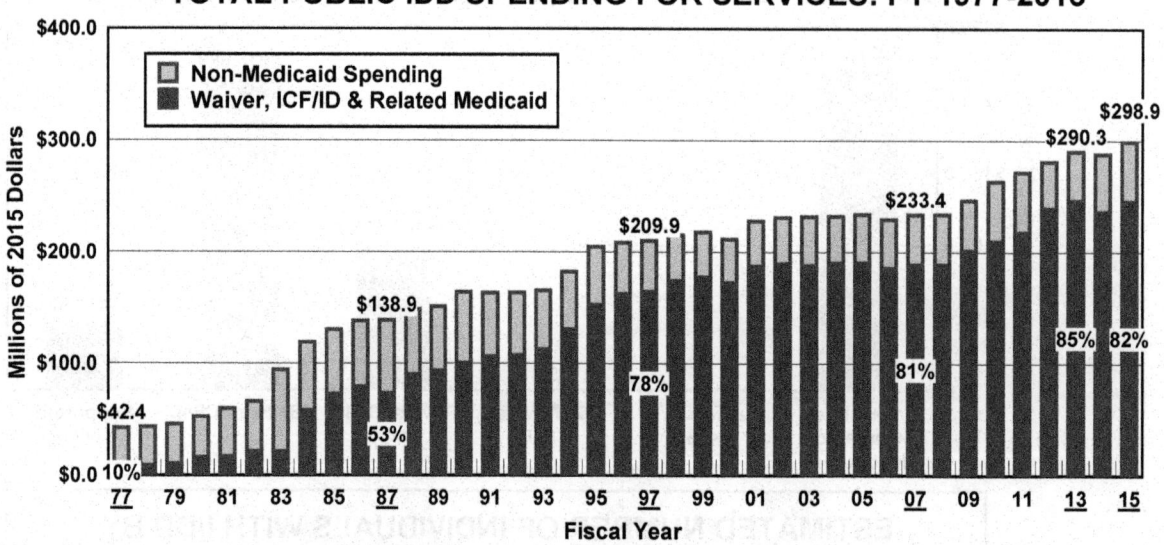

FISCAL EFFORT FOR IDD SERVICES: FY 1977-2015

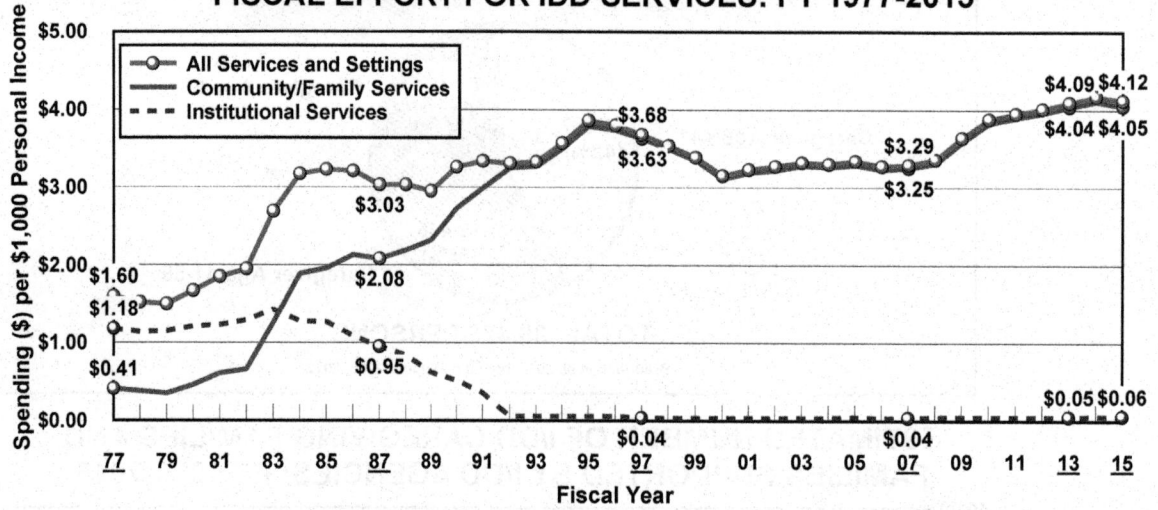

PERSONS WITH IDD BY SIZE OF SETTING: FY 1998-2015

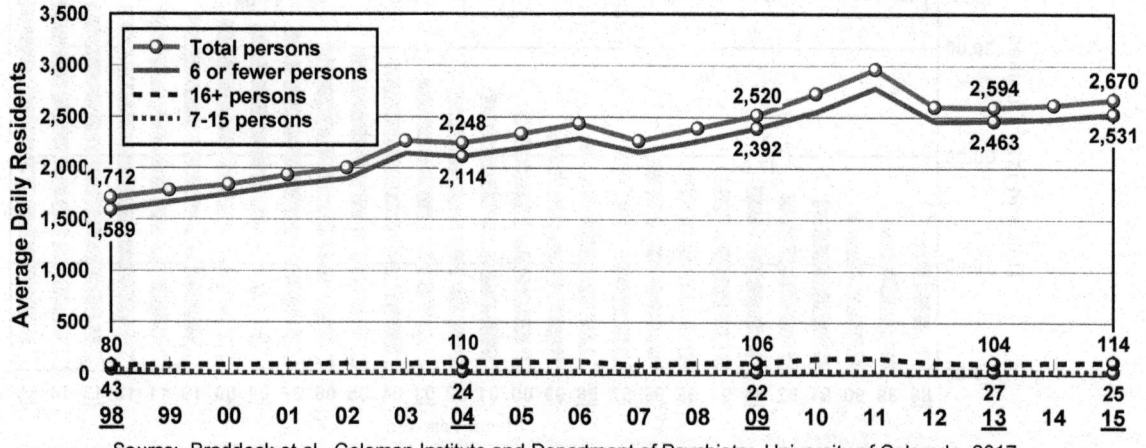

Source: Braddock et al., Coleman Institute and Department of Psychiatry, University of Colorado, 2017.
http://stateofthestates.org

NEW HAMPSHIRE

FEDERAL IDD MEDICAID SPENDING BY REVENUE SOURCE

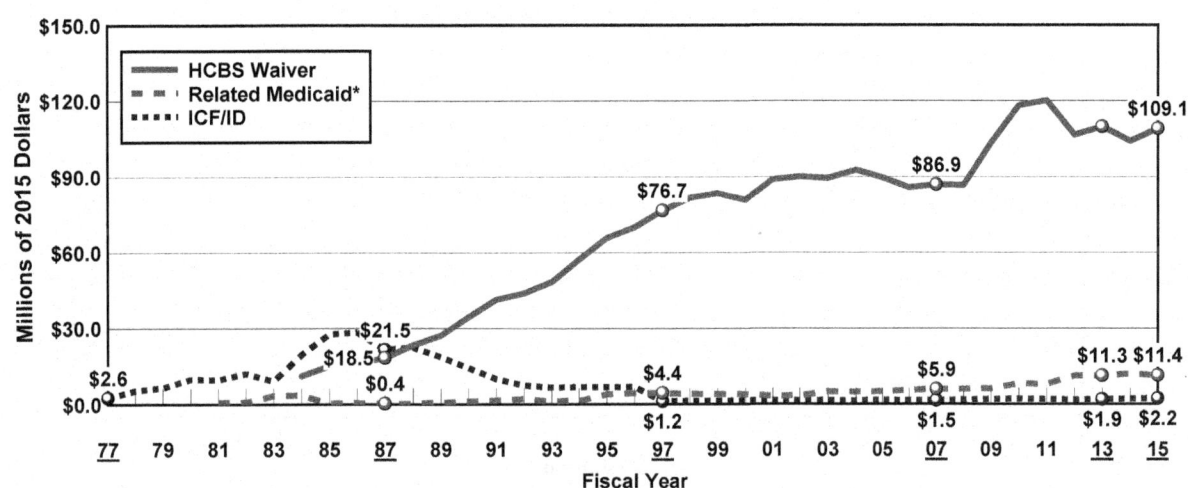

*In 2015, "Related Medicaid" was clinical rehabilitation ($9.2 million) and targeted case management ($2.2 million).

FEDERAL-STATE MEDICAID AS A PERCENTAGE OF TOTAL IDD SPENDING IN FY 2015

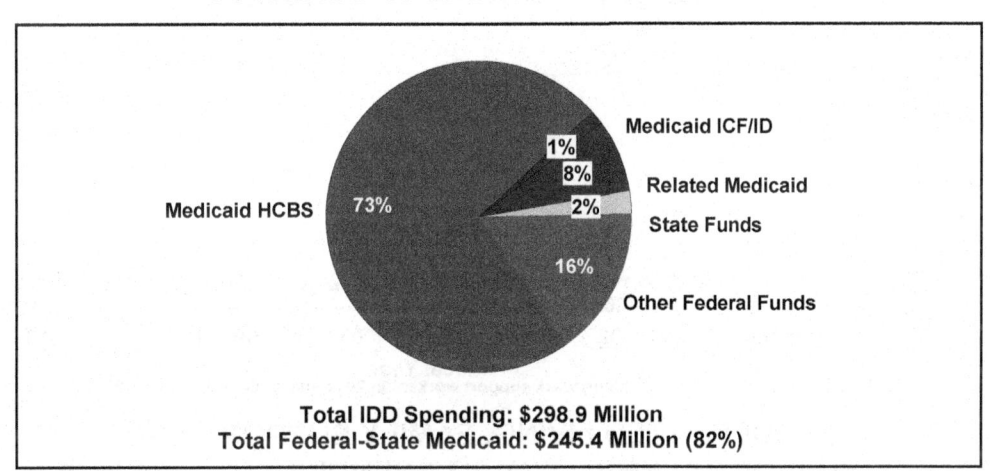

Total IDD Spending: $298.9 Million
Total Federal-State Medicaid: $245.4 Million (82%)

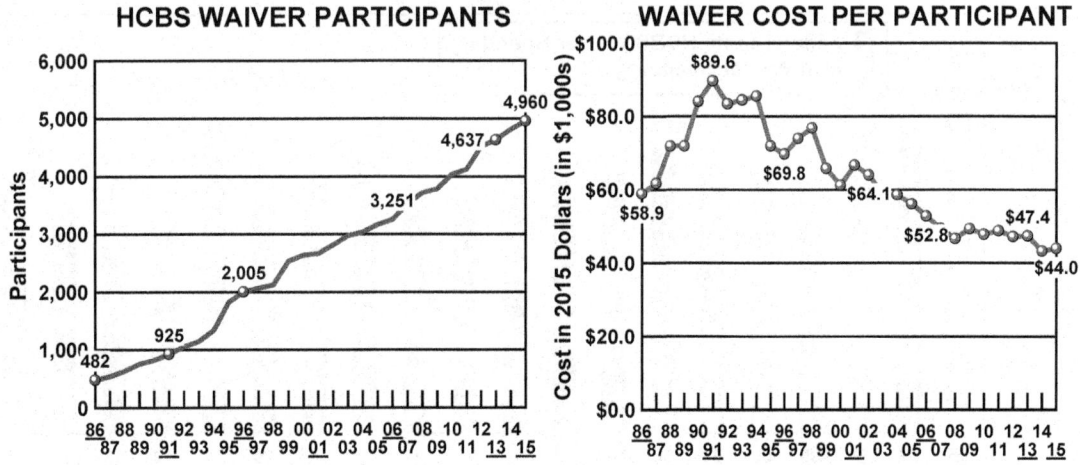

Source: Braddock et al., Coleman Institute and Department of Psychiatry, University of Colorado, 2017.
http://stateofthestates.org

NEW HAMPSHIRE
INDIVIDUAL AND FAMILY SUPPORT
SPENDING: FY 1996-2015

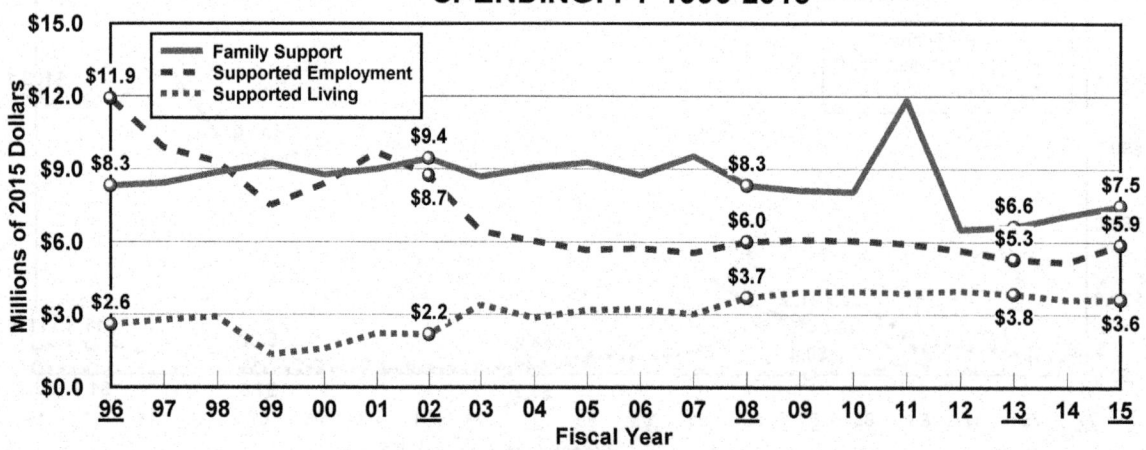

PARTICIPANTS: FY 1996-2015

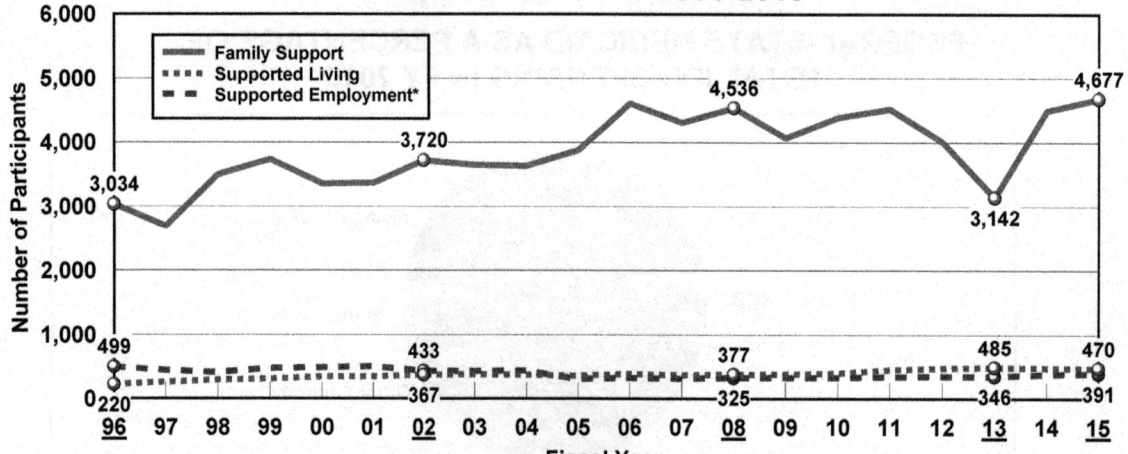

*Does not include 1,418 follow-along work support workers in 2014 and 1,454 workers in 2015.

SUPPORTED LIVING, FAMILY SUPPORT AND SUPPORTED EMPLOYMENT SPENDING: FY 1996-2015

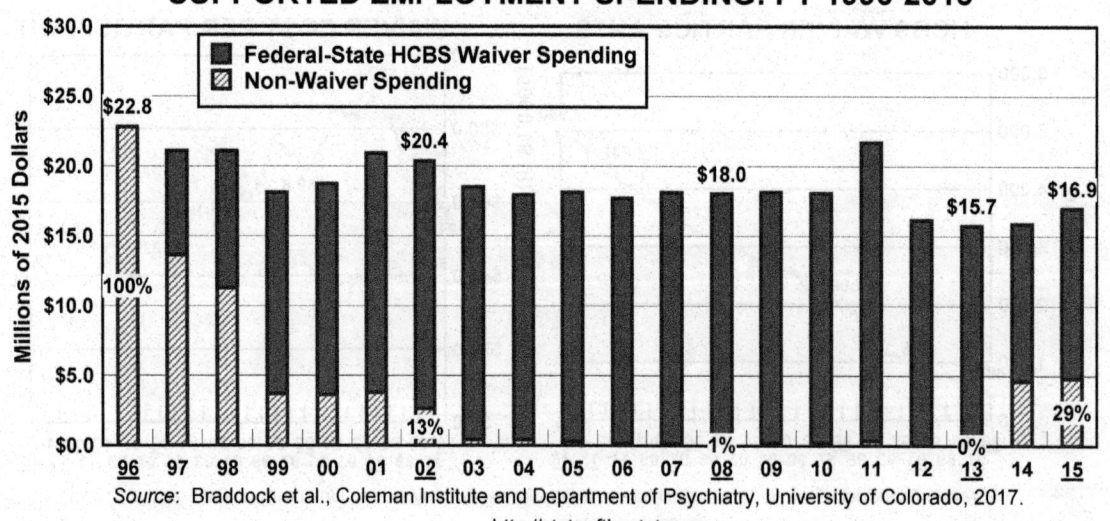

Source: Braddock et al., Coleman Institute and Department of Psychiatry, University of Colorado, 2017.
http://stateofthestates.org

NEW HAMPSHIRE

ANNUAL COST OF CARE BY RESIDENTIAL SETTING: FY 2015

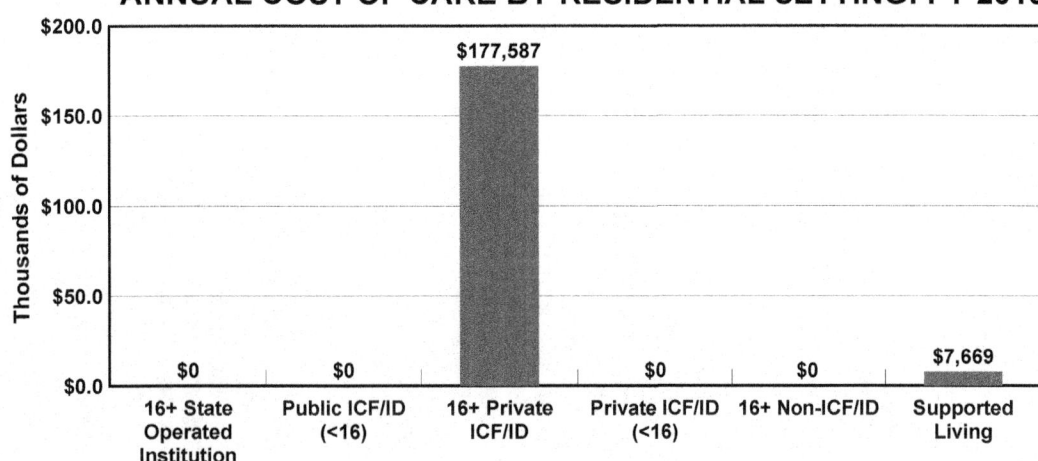

ESTIMATED NUMBER OF INDIVIDUALS WITH IDD BY AGE GROUP LIVING WITH FAMILY CAREGIVERS: FY 2015

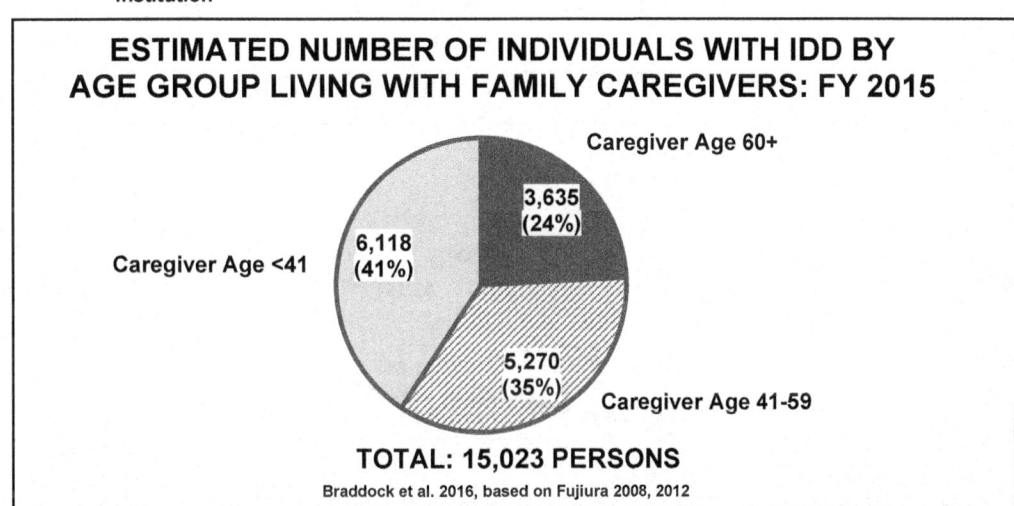

TOTAL: 15,023 PERSONS

Braddock et al. 2016, based on Fujiura 2008, 2012

ESTIMATED NUMBER OF IDD CAREGIVING FAMILIES AND FAMILIES SUPPORTED BY IDD AGENCIES: FY 1988-2015

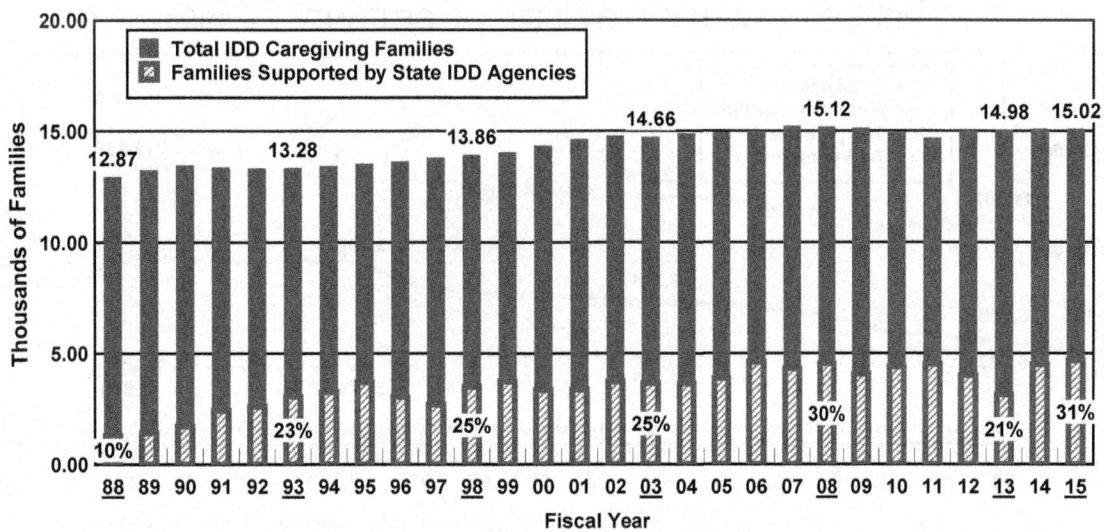

Source: Braddock et al., Coleman Institute and Department of Psychiatry, University of Colorado, 2017.
http://stateofthestates.org

NEW JERSEY

TOTAL PUBLIC IDD SPENDING FOR SERVICES: FY 1977-2015

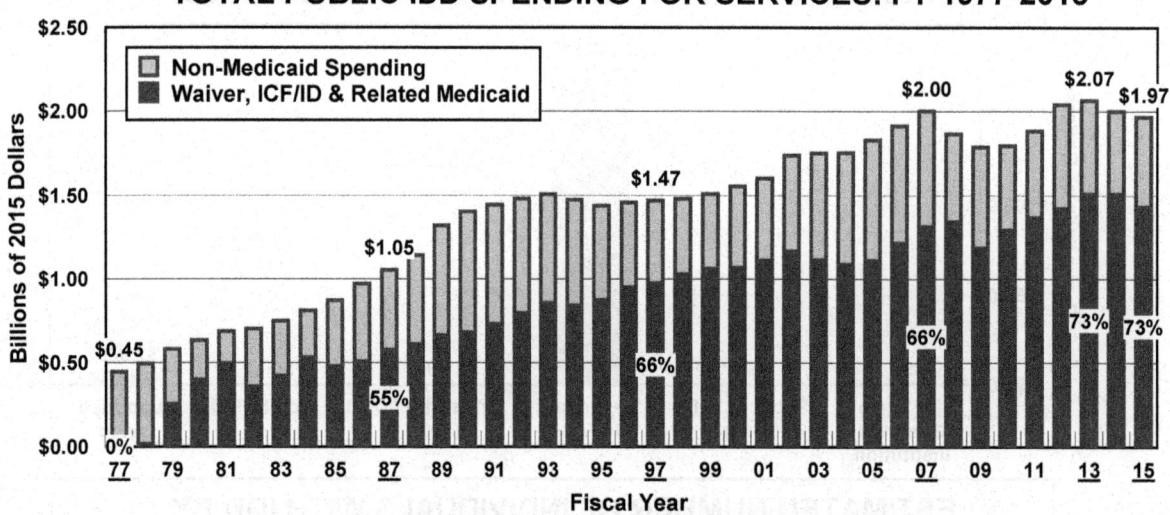

FISCAL EFFORT FOR IDD SERVICES: FY 1977-2015

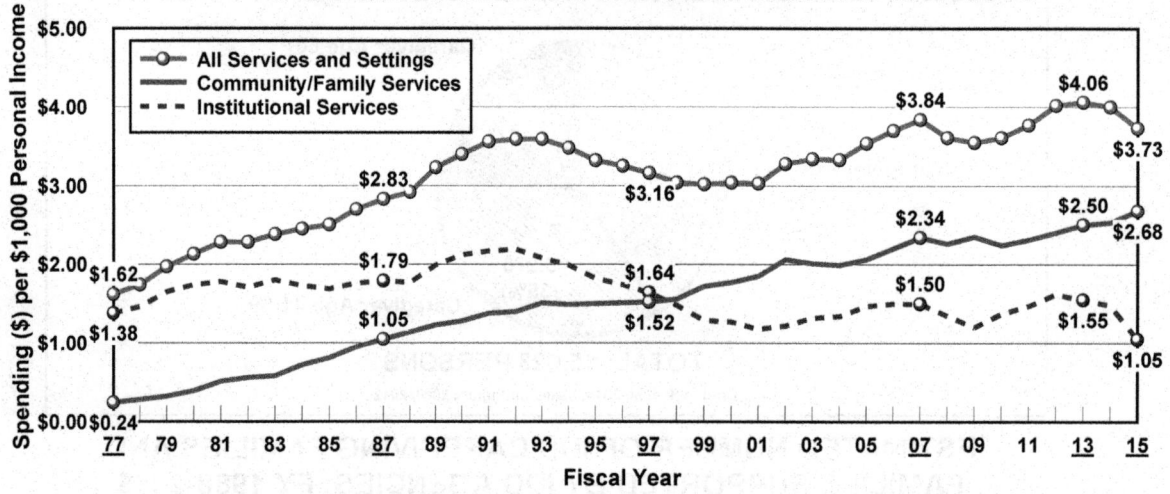

PERSONS WITH IDD BY SIZE OF SETTING: FY 1998-2015

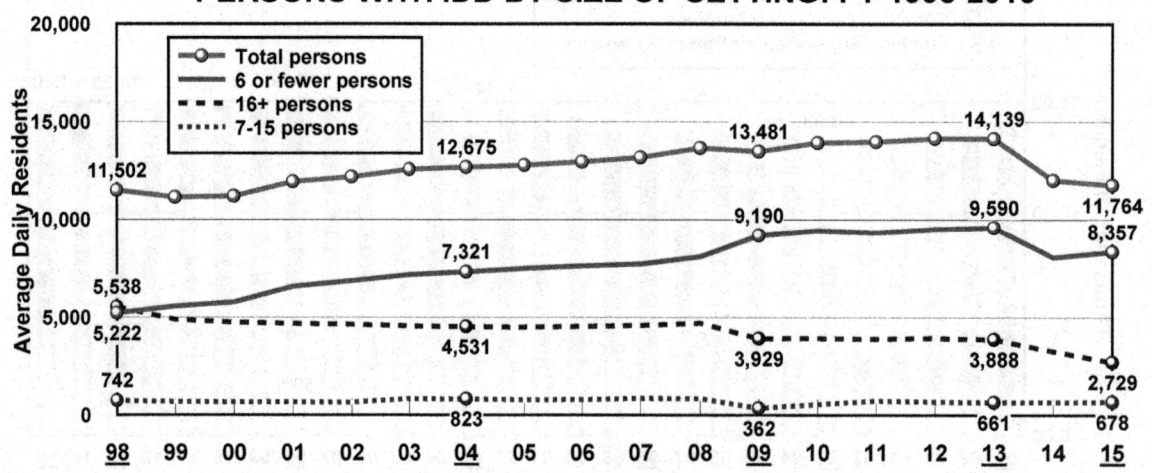

Source: Braddock et al., Coleman Institute and Department of Psychiatry, University of Colorado, 2017.
http://stateofthestates.org

NEW JERSEY

FEDERAL IDD MEDICAID SPENDING BY REVENUE SOURCE

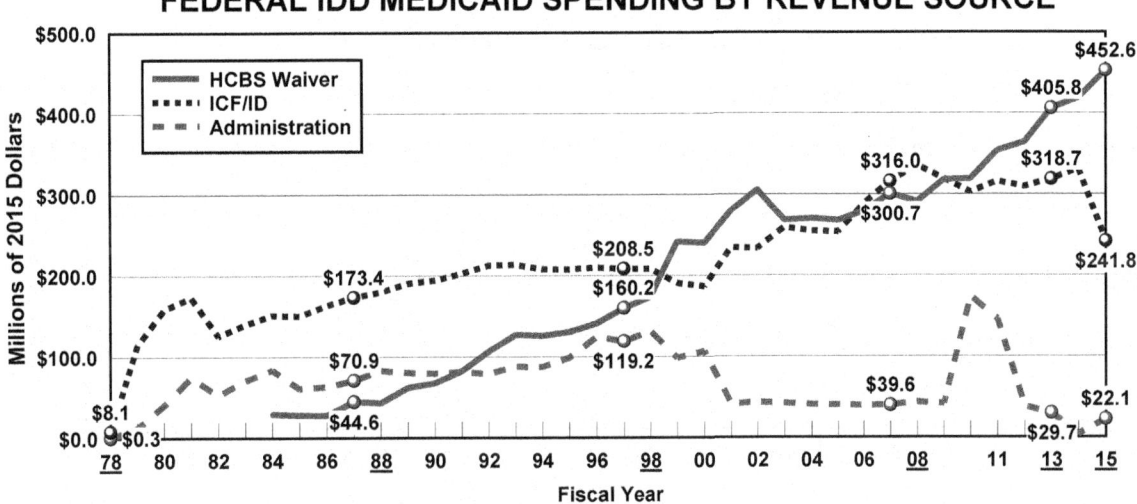

FEDERAL-STATE MEDICAID AS A PERCENTAGE OF TOTAL IDD SPENDING IN FY 2015

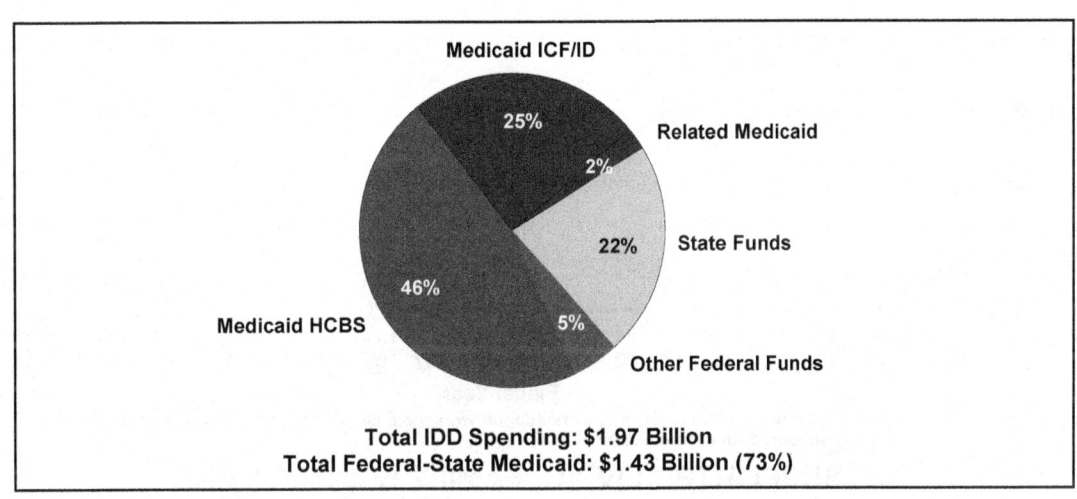

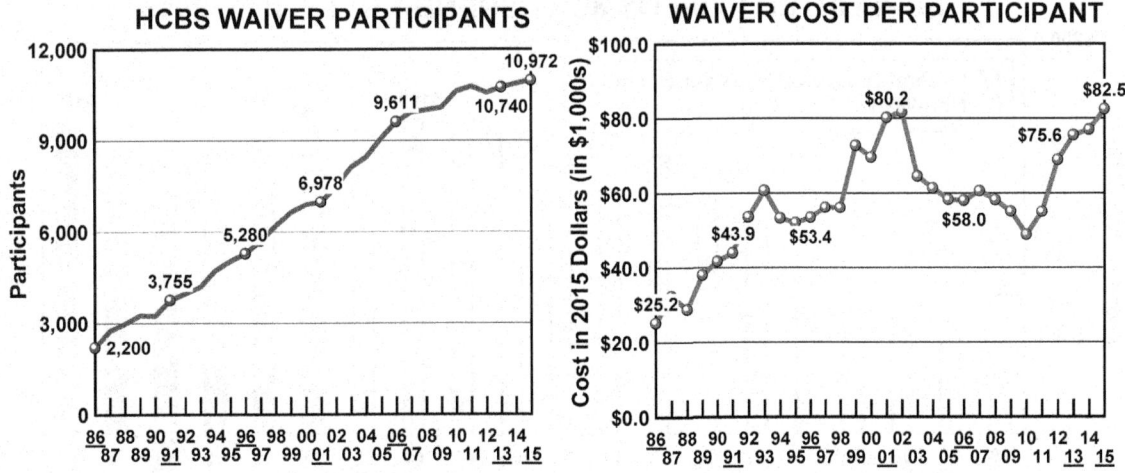

Source: Braddock et al., Coleman Institute and Department of Psychiatry, University of Colorado, 2017.
http://stateofthestates.org

NEW JERSEY
INDIVIDUAL AND FAMILY SUPPORT
SPENDING: FY 1996-2015

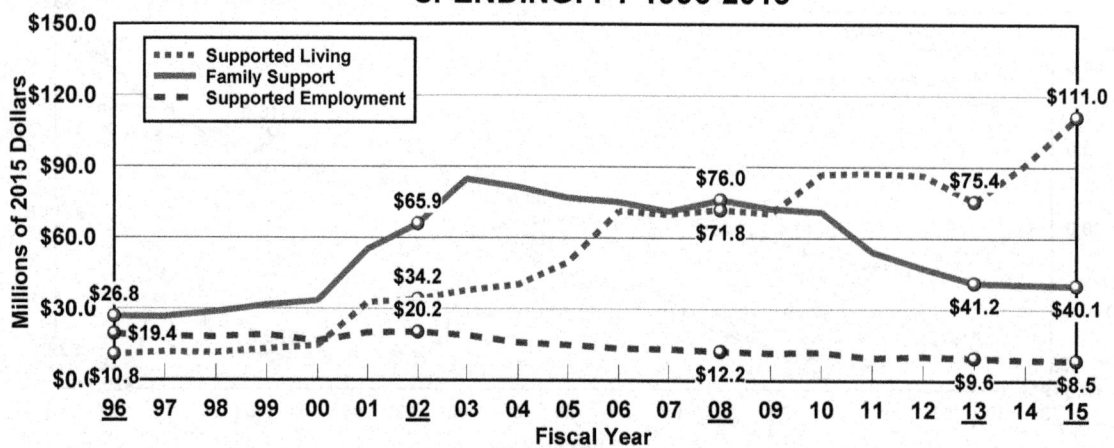

PARTICIPANTS: FY 1996-2015

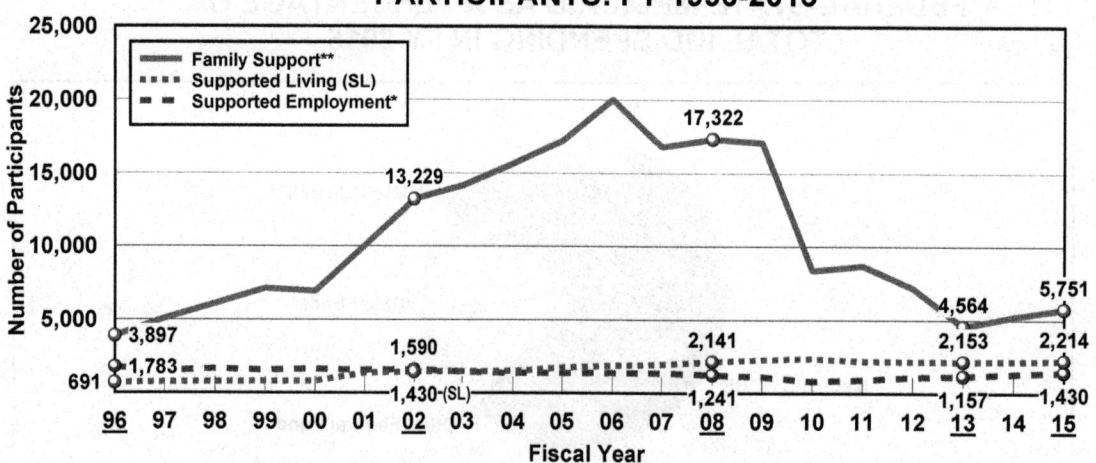

*Does not include 1,127 follow-along work support workers in 2014 and 1,158 workers in 2015.
**Family support cash subsidies terminated in 2009.

SUPPORTED LIVING, FAMILY SUPPORT AND SUPPORTED EMPLOYMENT SPENDING: FY 1996-2015

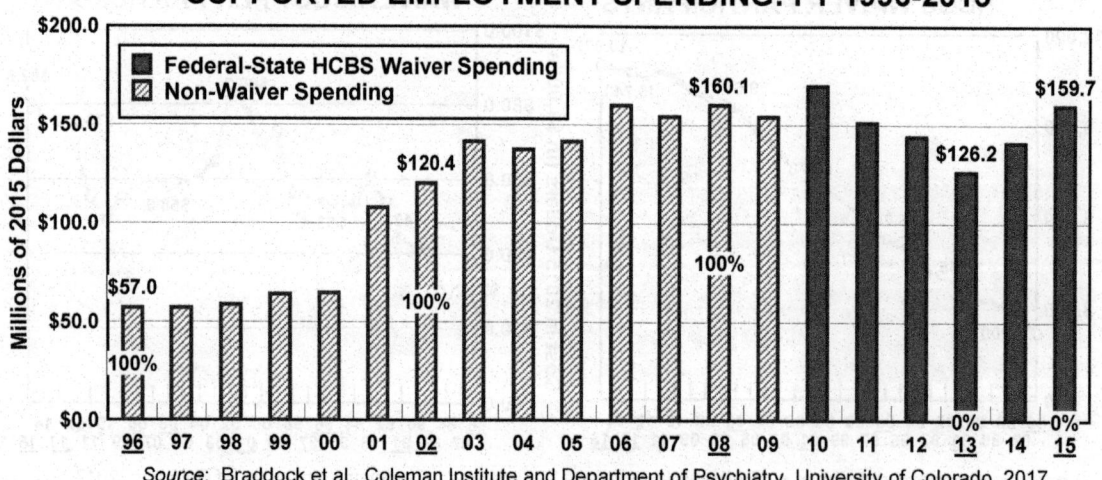

Source: Braddock et al., Coleman Institute and Department of Psychiatry, University of Colorado, 2017.
http://stateofthestates.org

NEW JERSEY

ANNUAL COST OF CARE BY RESIDENTIAL SETTING: FY 2015

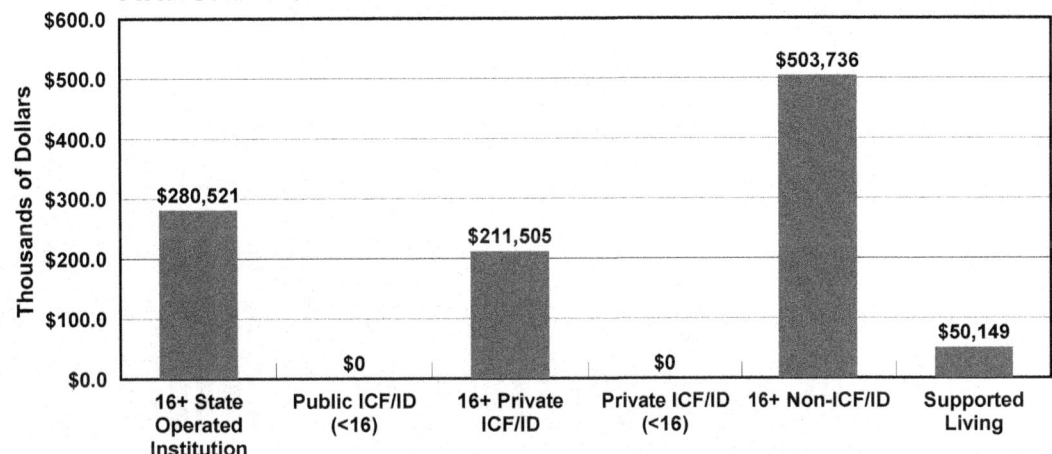

ESTIMATED NUMBER OF INDIVIDUALS WITH IDD BY AGE GROUP LIVING WITH FAMILY CAREGIVERS: FY 2015

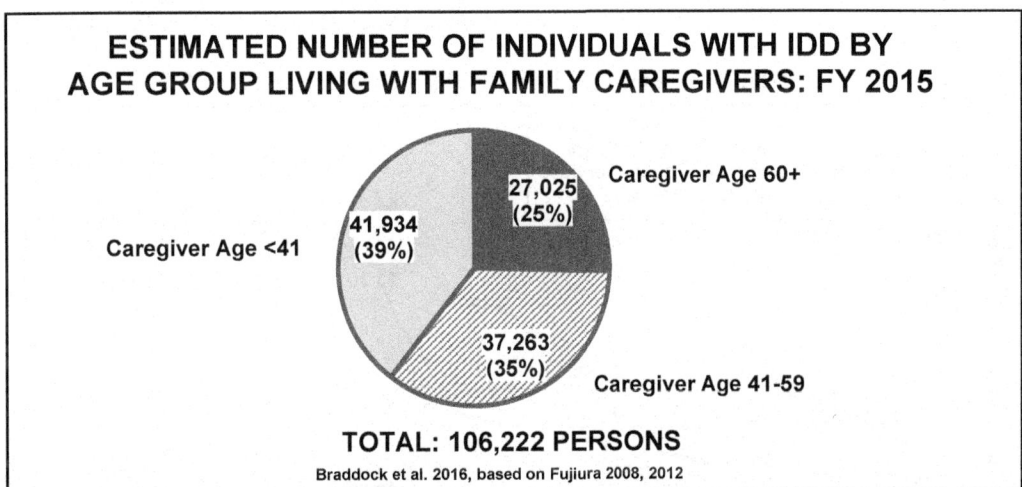

TOTAL: 106,222 PERSONS

Braddock et al. 2016, based on Fujiura 2008, 2012

ESTIMATED NUMBER OF IDD CAREGIVING FAMILIES AND FAMILIES SUPPORTED BY IDD AGENCIES: FY 1988-2015

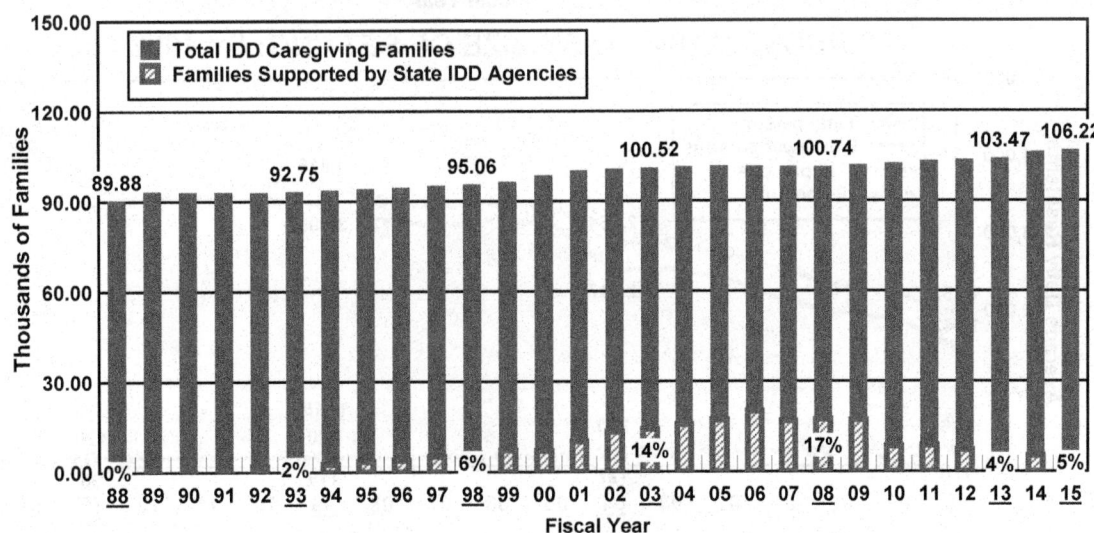

Source: Braddock et al., Coleman Institute and Department of Psychiatry, University of Colorado, 2017.

http://stateofthestates.org

NEW MEXICO

TOTAL PUBLIC IDD SPENDING FOR SERVICES: FY 1977-2015

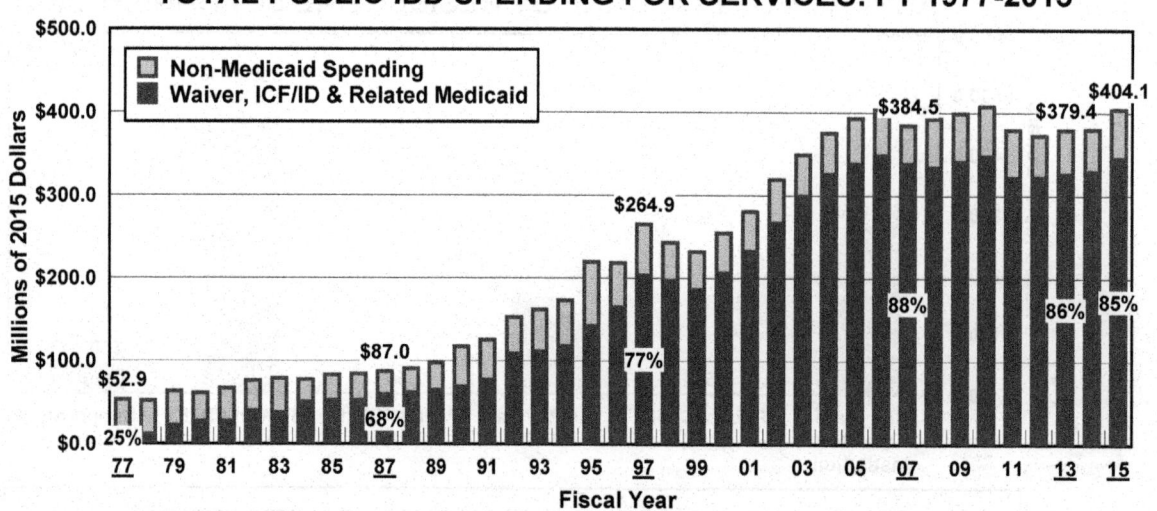

FISCAL EFFORT FOR IDD SERVICES: FY 1977-2015

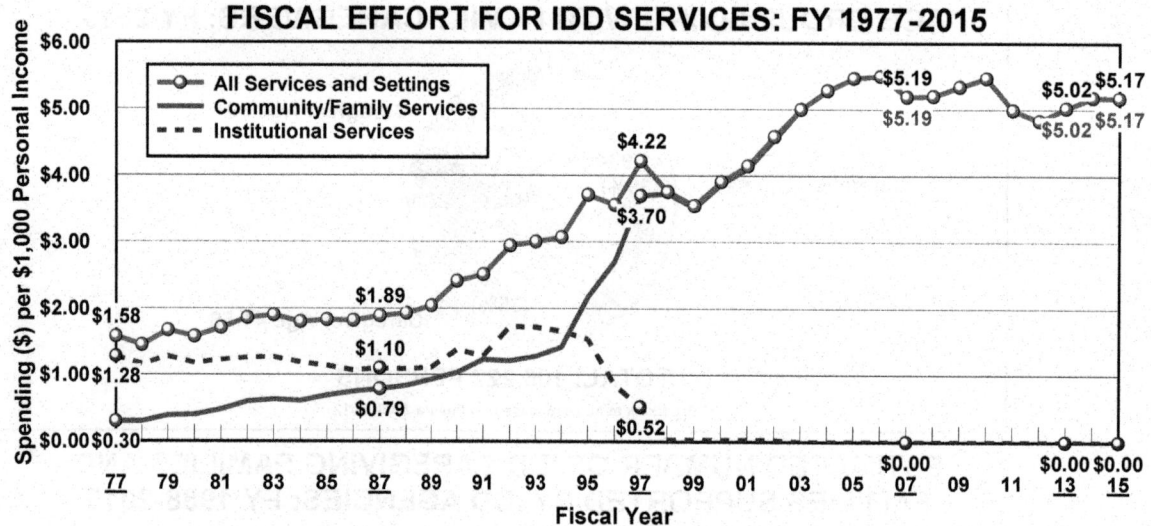

PERSONS WITH IDD BY SIZE OF SETTING: FY 1998-2015

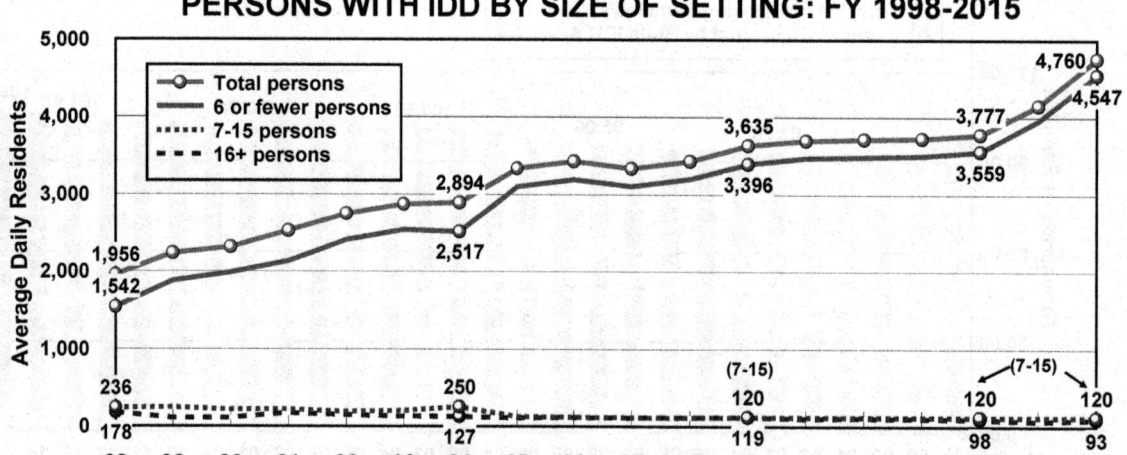

Source: Braddock et al., Coleman Institute and Department of Psychiatry, University of Colorado, 2017.
http://stateofthestates.org

NEW MEXICO

FEDERAL IDD MEDICAID SPENDING BY REVENUE SOURCE

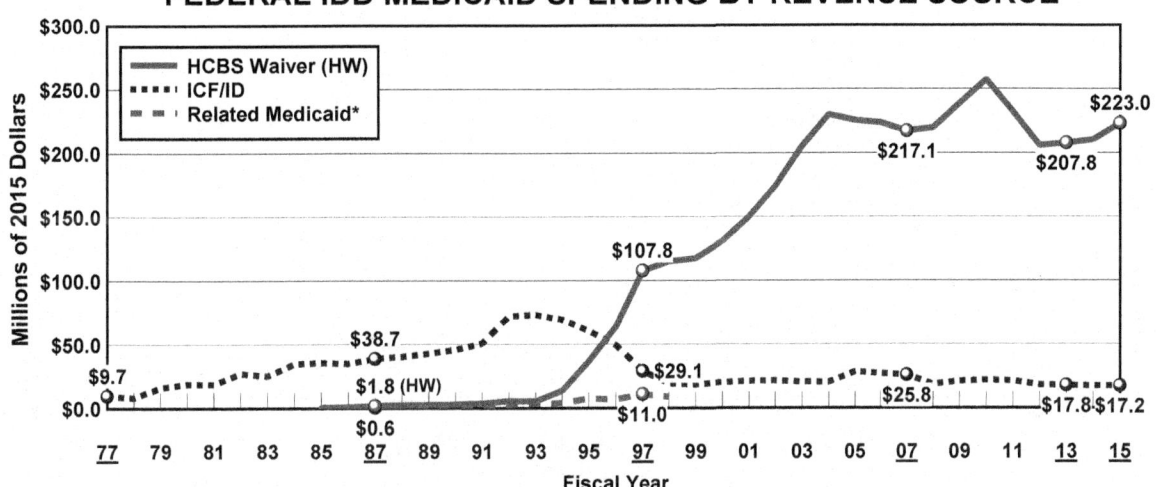

*Between 1986 and 1998, "Related Medicaid" was targeted case management and model 50/200 waiver.

FEDERAL-STATE MEDICAID AS A PERCENTAGE OF TOTAL IDD SPENDING IN FY 2015

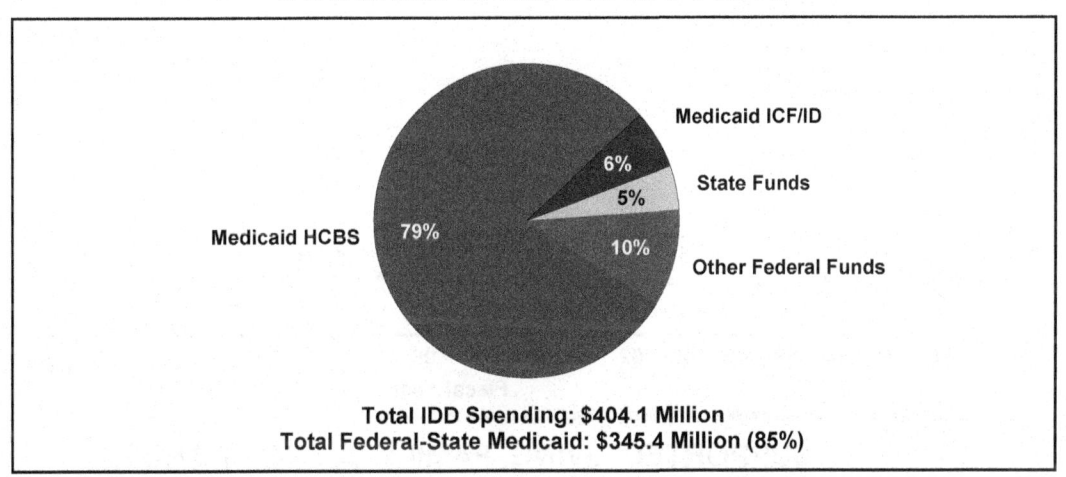

Total IDD Spending: $404.1 Million
Total Federal-State Medicaid: $345.4 Million (85%)

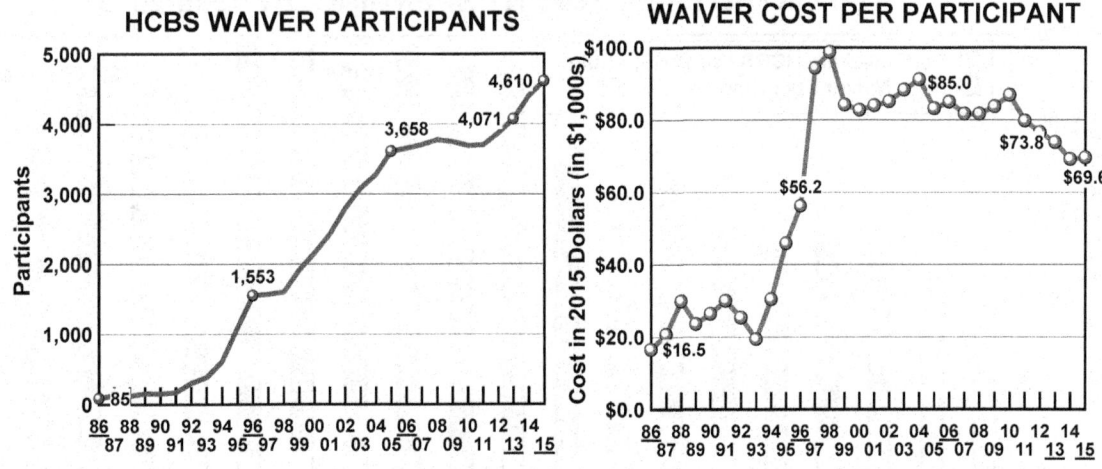

Source: Braddock et al., Coleman Institute and Department of Psychiatry, University of Colorado, 2017.
http://stateofthestates.org

NEW MEXICO INDIVIDUAL AND FAMILY SUPPORT

SPENDING: FY 1996-2015

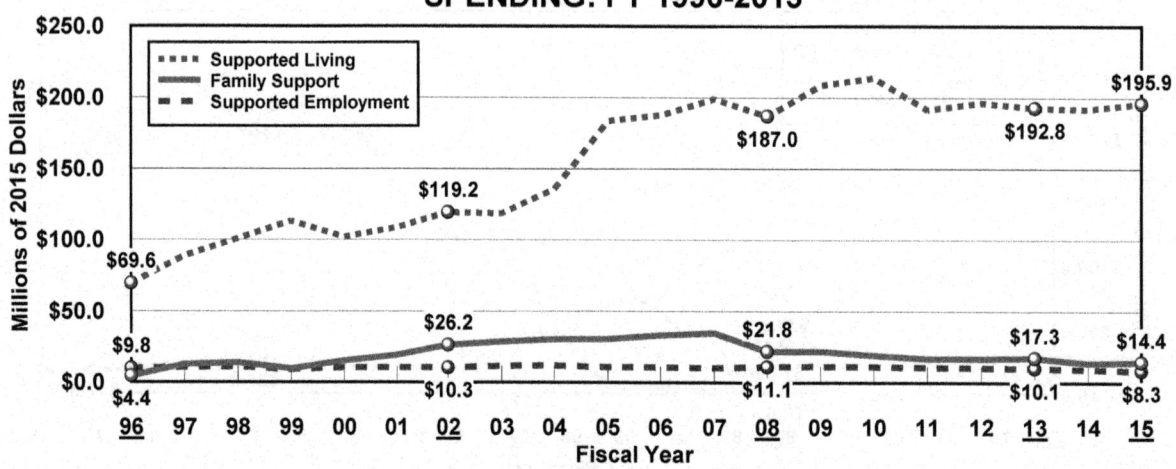

PARTICIPANTS: FY 1996-2015

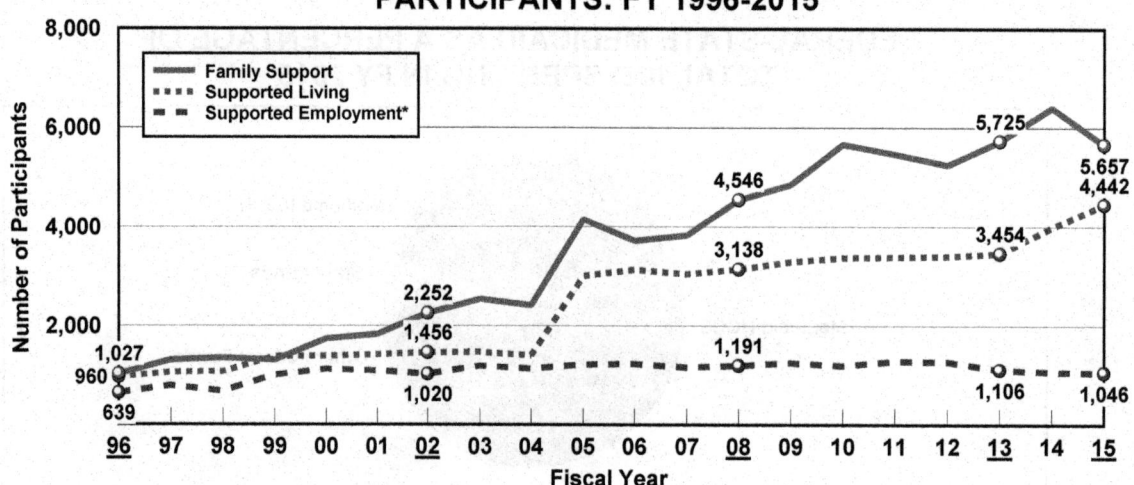

*Does not include follow-along work support workers: 133 in 2014 and 188 in 2015.

SUPPORTED LIVING, FAMILY SUPPORT AND SUPPORTED EMPLOYMENT SPENDING: FY 1996-2015

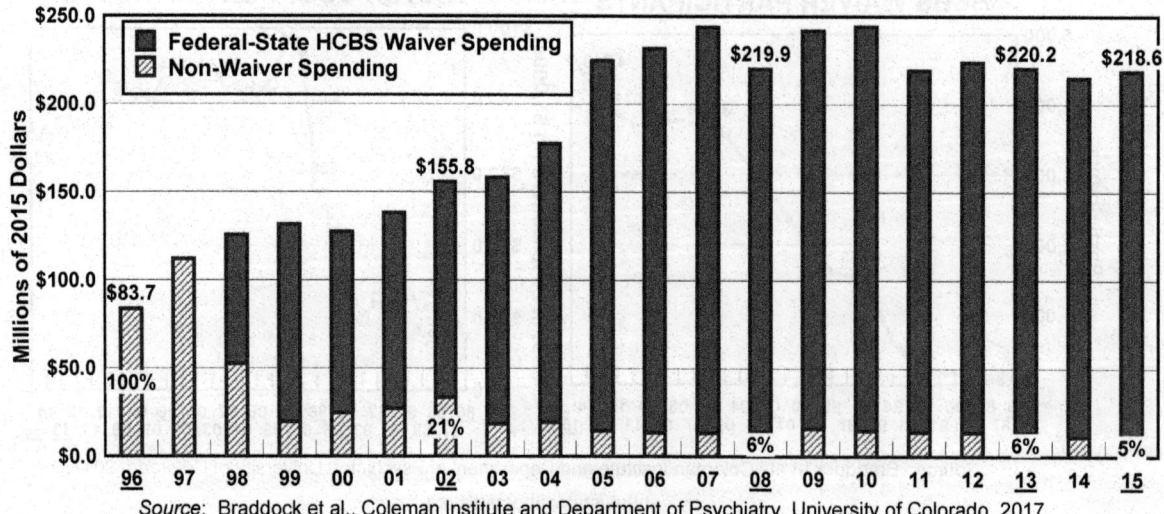

Source: Braddock et al., Coleman Institute and Department of Psychiatry, University of Colorado, 2017.
http://stateofthestates.org

NEW MEXICO

ANNUAL COST OF CARE BY RESIDENTIAL SETTING: FY 2015

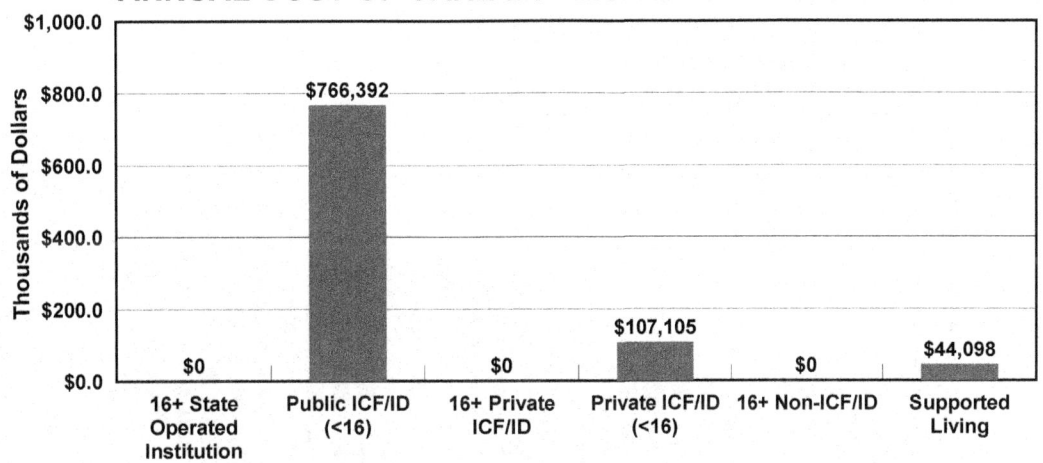

ESTIMATED NUMBER OF INDIVIDUALS WITH IDD BY AGE GROUP LIVING WITH FAMILY CAREGIVERS: FY 2015

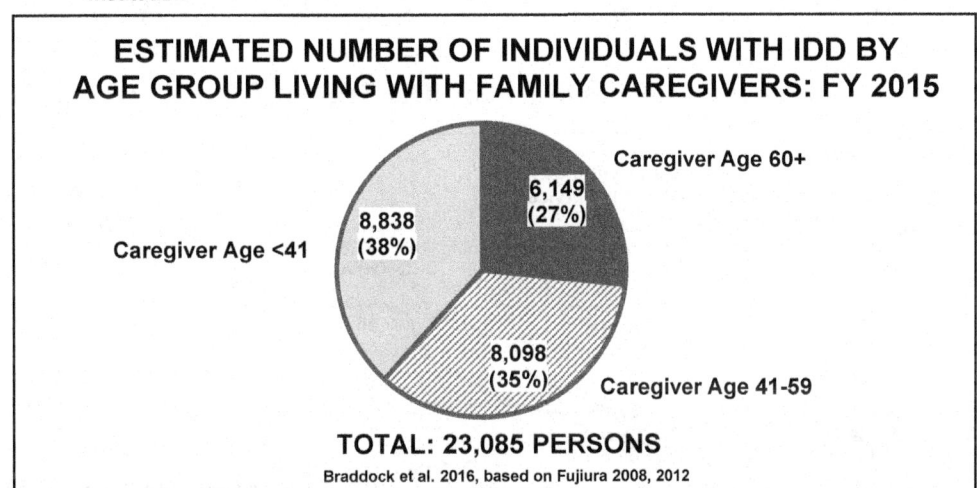

TOTAL: 23,085 PERSONS
Braddock et al. 2016, based on Fujiura 2008, 2012

ESTIMATED NUMBER OF IDD CAREGIVING FAMILIES AND FAMILIES SUPPORTED BY IDD AGENCIES: FY 1988-2015

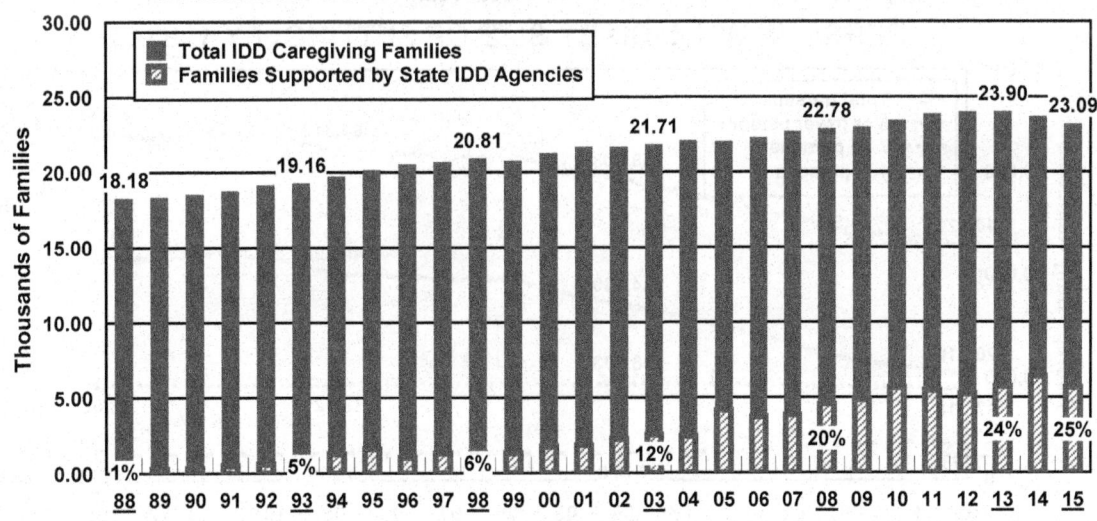

Source: Braddock et al., Coleman Institute and Department of Psychiatry, University of Colorado, 2017.
http://stateofthestates.org

NEW YORK

TOTAL PUBLIC IDD SPENDING FOR SERVICES: FY 1977-2015

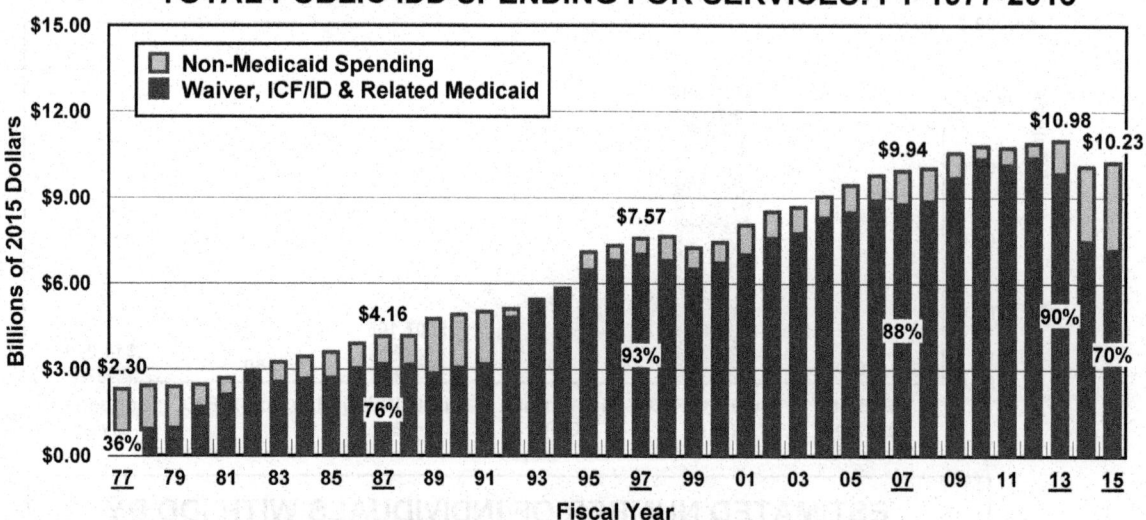

FISCAL EFFORT FOR IDD SERVICES: FY 1977-2015

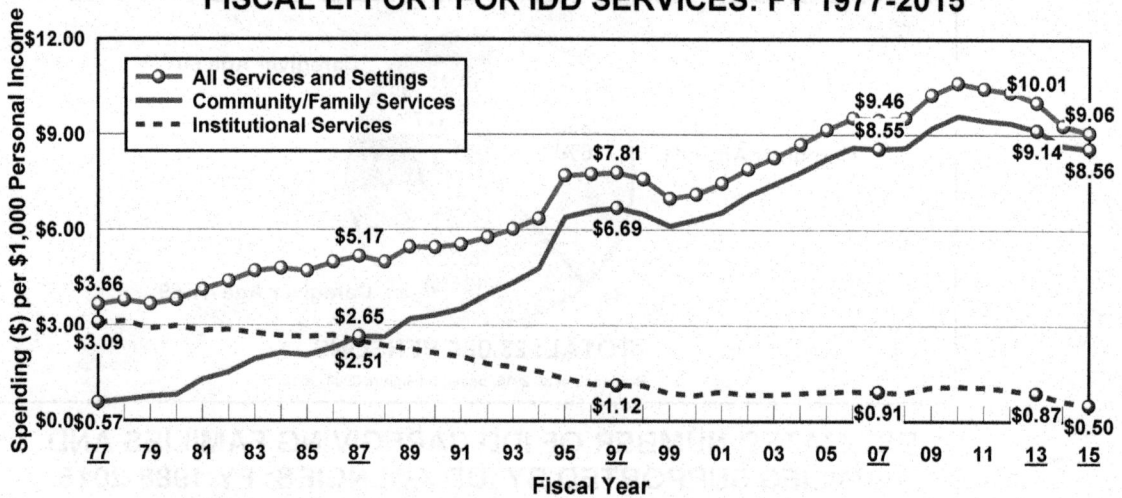

PERSONS WITH IDD BY SIZE OF SETTING: FY 1998-2015

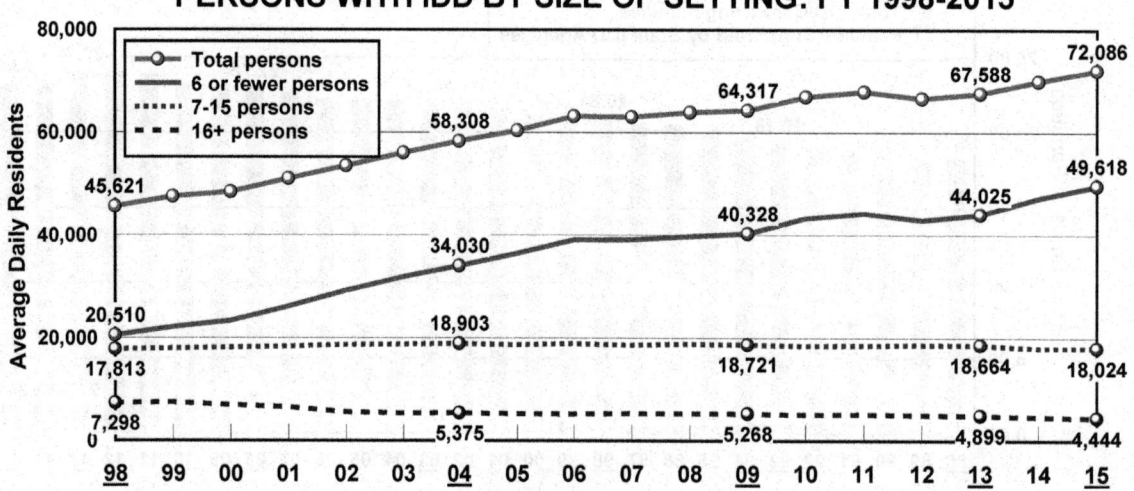

Source: Braddock et al., Coleman Institute and Department of Psychiatry, University of Colorado, 2017.
http://stateofthestates.org

NEW YORK

FEDERAL IDD MEDICAID SPENDING BY REVENUE SOURCE

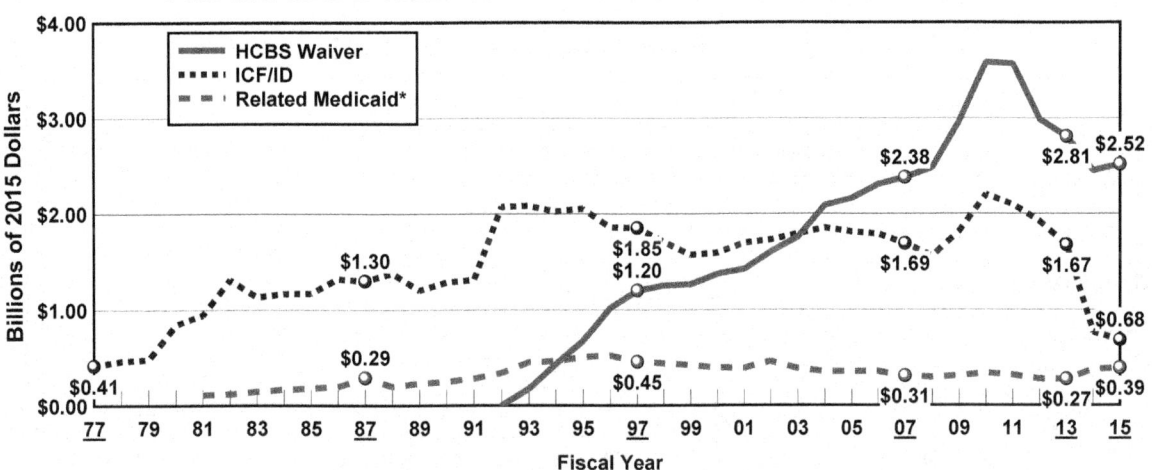

*In 2015, "Related Medicaid" was clinic rehabilitation ($6.3 million), targeted case management ($110.5 million), personal assistance ($204.4 million) and administration ($67.7 million).

FEDERAL-STATE MEDICAID AS A PERCENTAGE OF TOTAL IDD SPENDING IN FY 2015

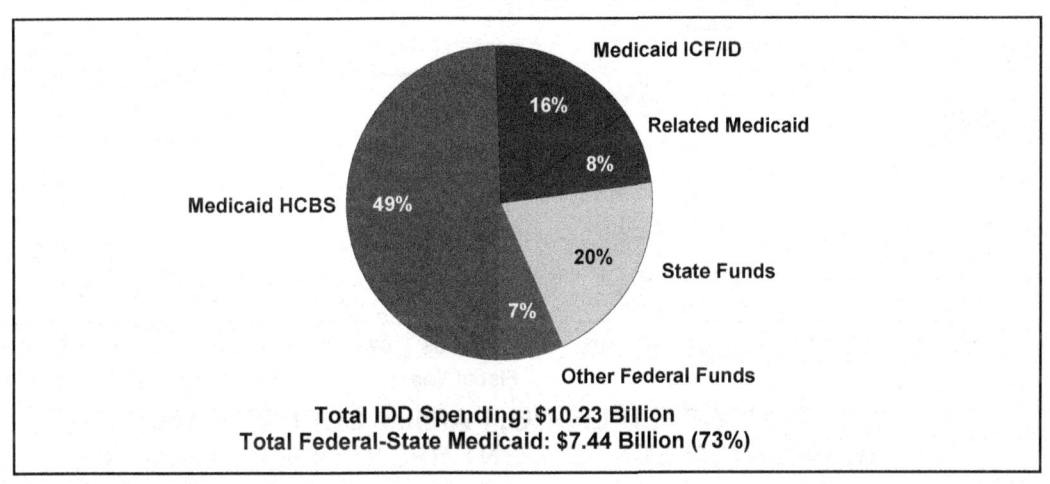

Total IDD Spending: $10.23 Billion
Total Federal-State Medicaid: $7.44 Billion (73%)

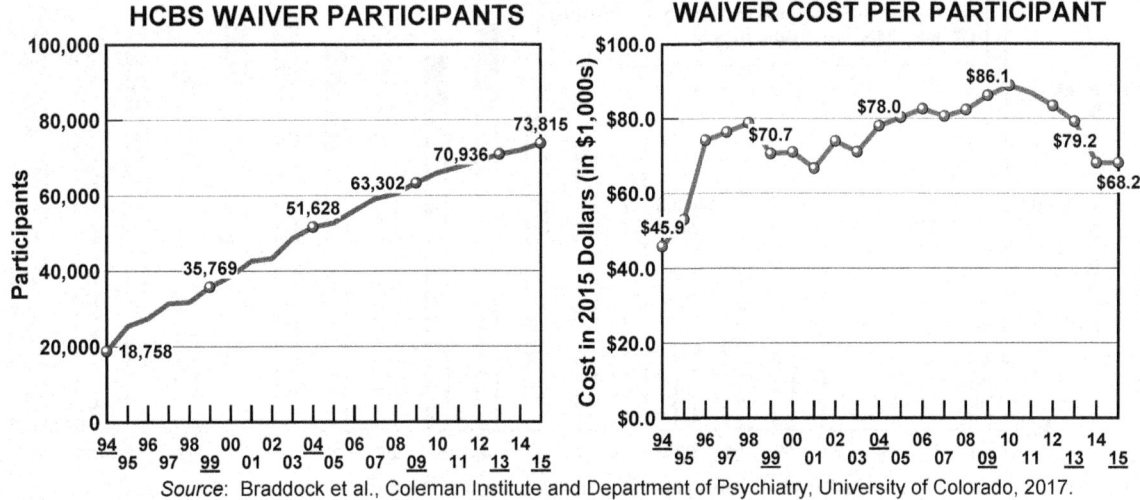

Source: Braddock et al., Coleman Institute and Department of Psychiatry, University of Colorado, 2017.
http://stateofthestates.org

NEW YORK

INDIVIDUAL AND FAMILY SUPPORT

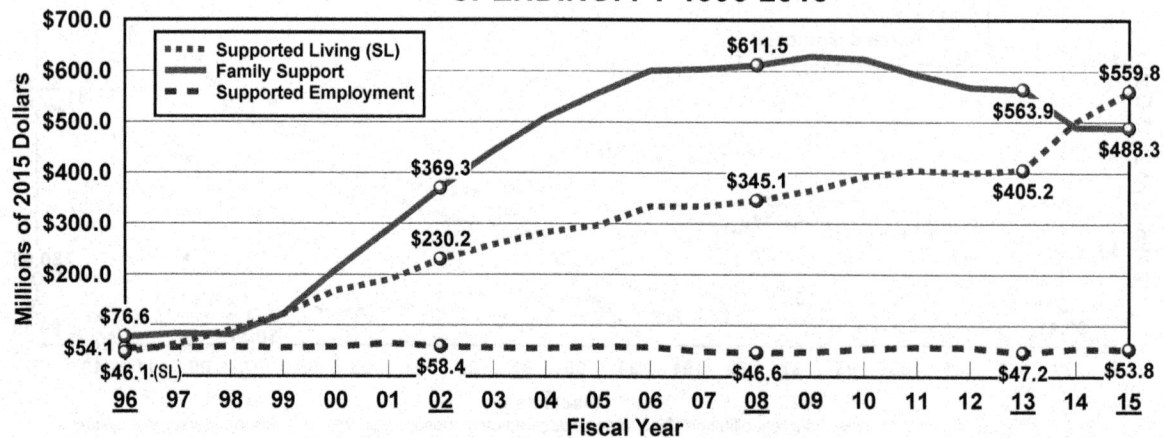

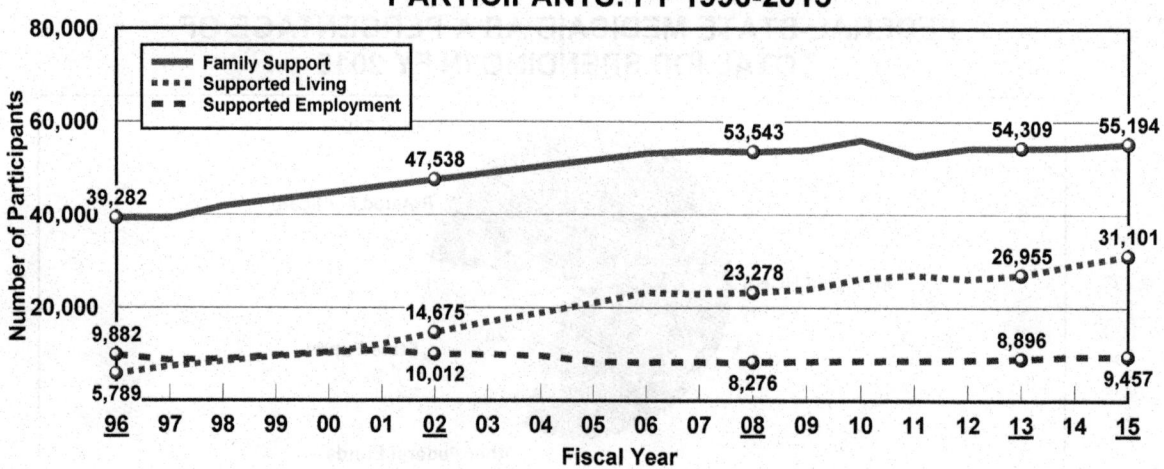

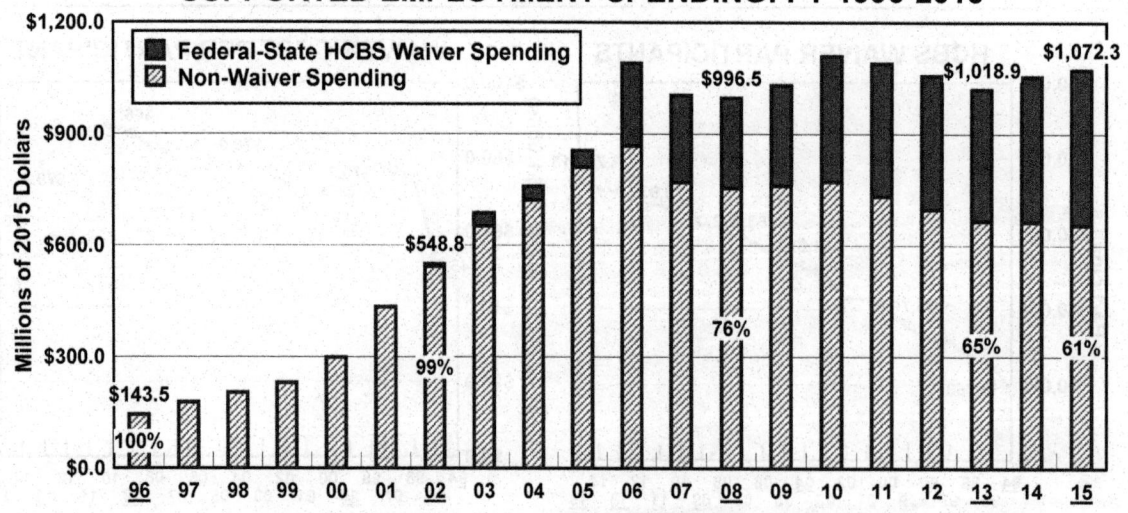

Source: Braddock et al., Coleman Institute and Department of Psychiatry, University of Colorado, 2017.
http://stateofthestates.org

NEW YORK

ANNUAL COST OF CARE BY RESIDENTIAL SETTING: FY 2015

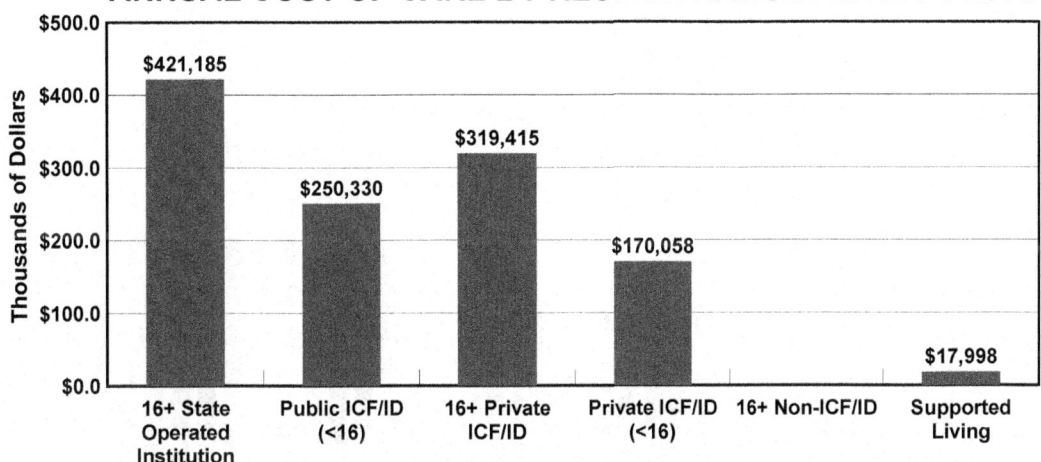

ESTIMATED NUMBER OF INDIVIDUALS WITH IDD BY AGE GROUP LIVING WITH FAMILY CAREGIVERS: FY 2015

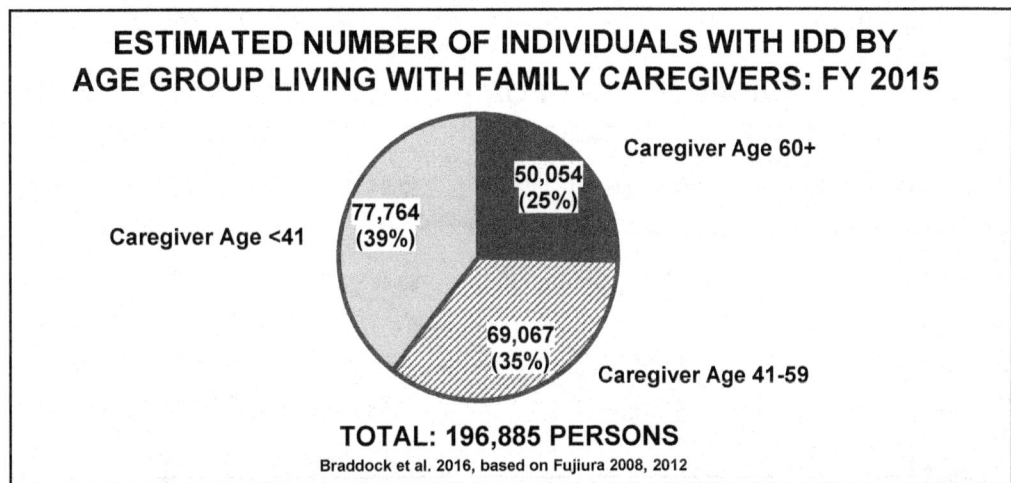

TOTAL: 196,885 PERSONS
Braddock et al. 2016, based on Fujiura 2008, 2012

ESTIMATED NUMBER OF IDD CAREGIVING FAMILIES AND FAMILIES SUPPORTED BY IDD AGENCIES: FY 1988-2015

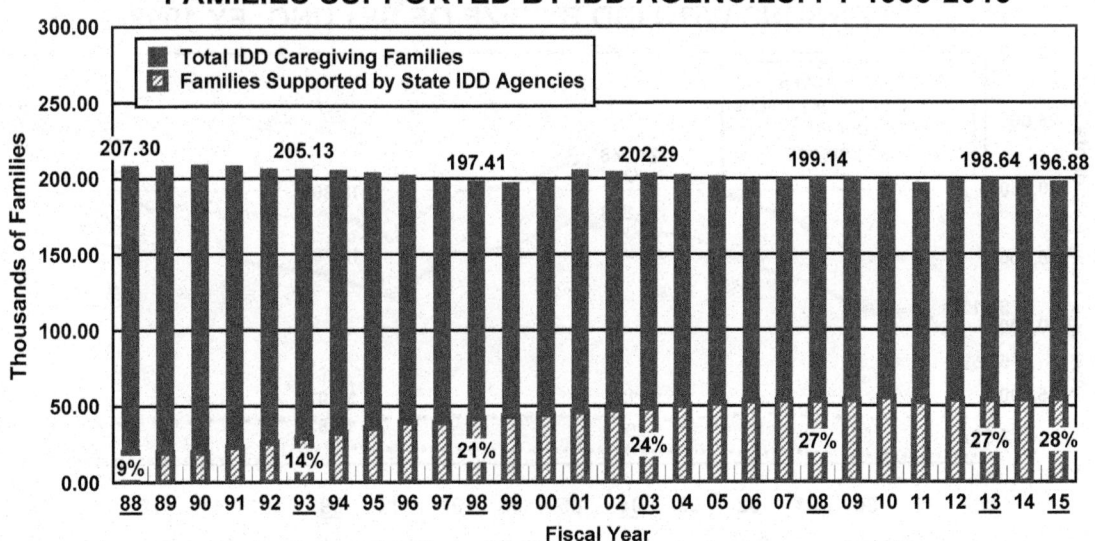

Source: Braddock et al., Coleman Institute and Department of Psychiatry, University of Colorado, 2017.
http://stateofthestates.org

NORTH CAROLINA

TOTAL PUBLIC IDD SPENDING FOR SERVICES: FY 1977-2015

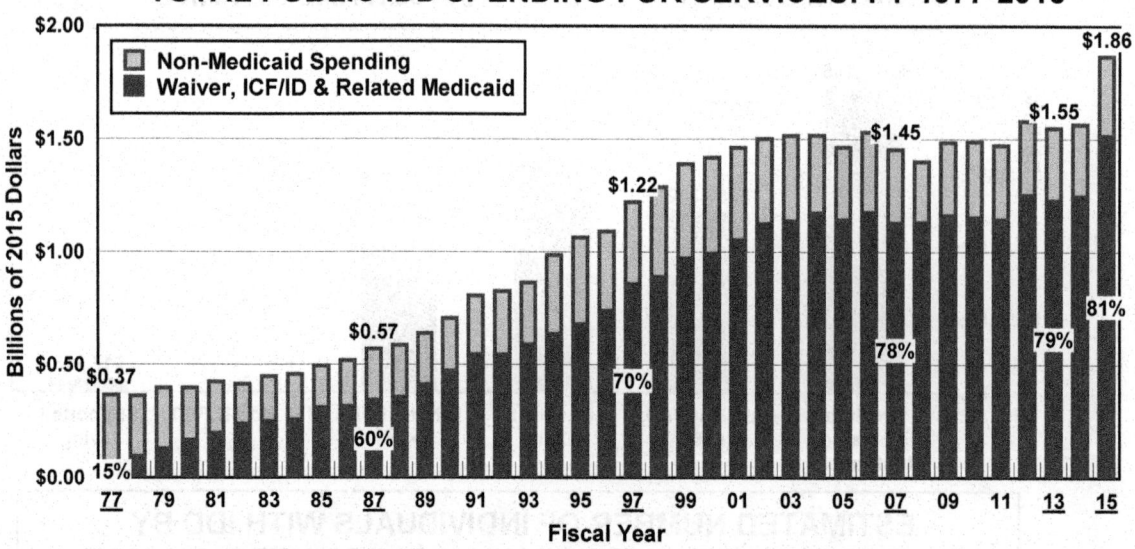

FISCAL EFFORT FOR IDD SERVICES: FY 1977-2015

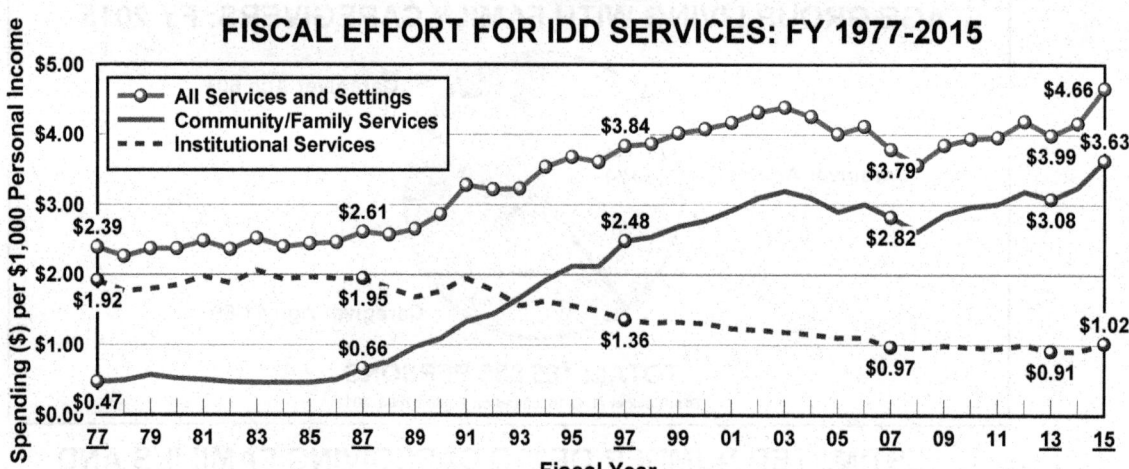

PERSONS WITH IDD BY SIZE OF SETTING: FY 1998-2015

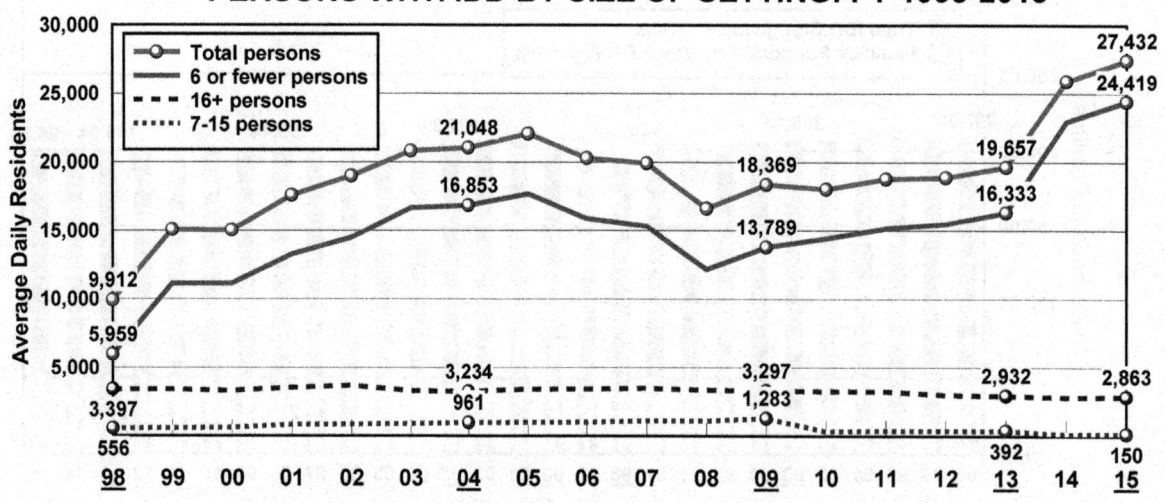

Source: Braddock et al., Coleman Institute and Department of Psychiatry, University of Colorado, 2017.
http://stateofthestates.org

NORTH CAROLINA

FEDERAL IDD MEDICAID SPENDING BY REVENUE SOURCE

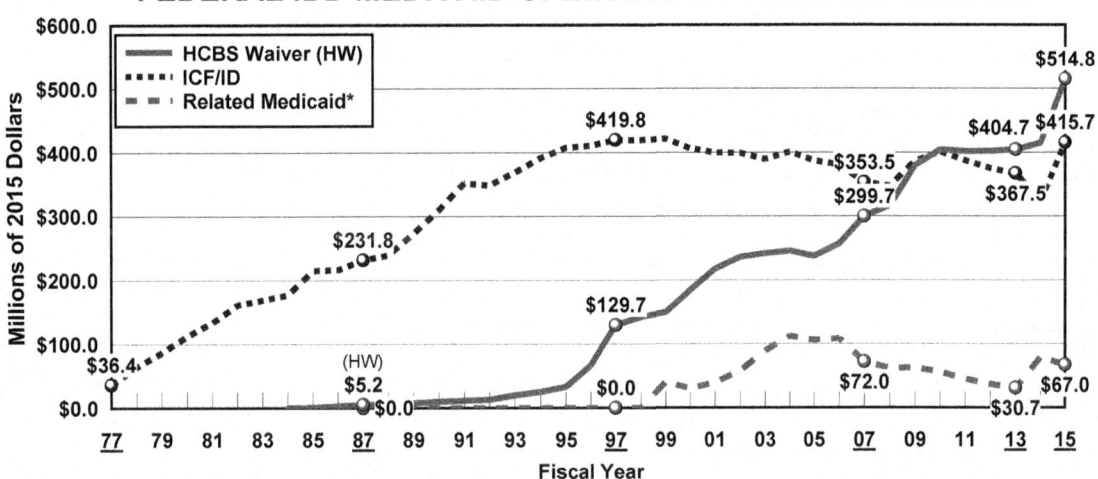

*In 2015, "Related Medicaid" was targeted case management ($66.9 million) and administration ($0.47 million).

FEDERAL-STATE MEDICAID AS A PERCENTAGE OF TOTAL IDD SPENDING IN FY 2015

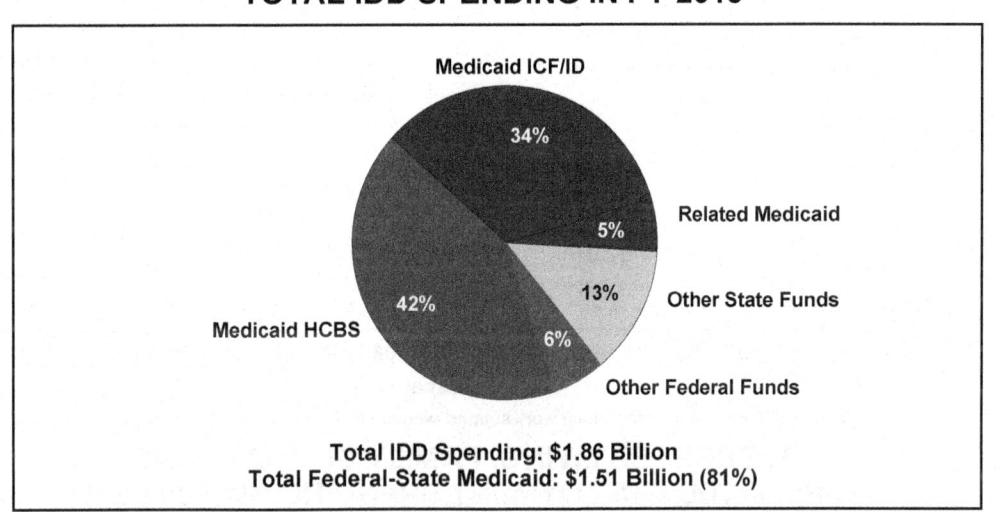

Total IDD Spending: $1.86 Billion
Total Federal-State Medicaid: $1.51 Billion (81%)

HCBS WAIVER PARTICIPANTS · WAIVER COST PER PARTICIPANT

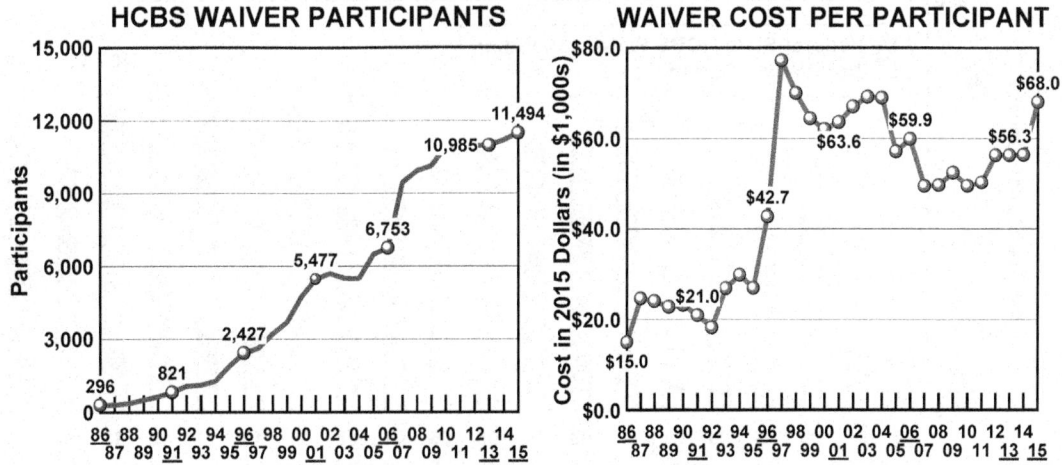

Source: Braddock et al., Coleman Institute and Department of Psychiatry, University of Colorado, 2017.
http://stateofthestates.org

NORTH CAROLINA
INDIVIDUAL AND FAMILY SUPPORT
SPENDING: FY 1996-2015

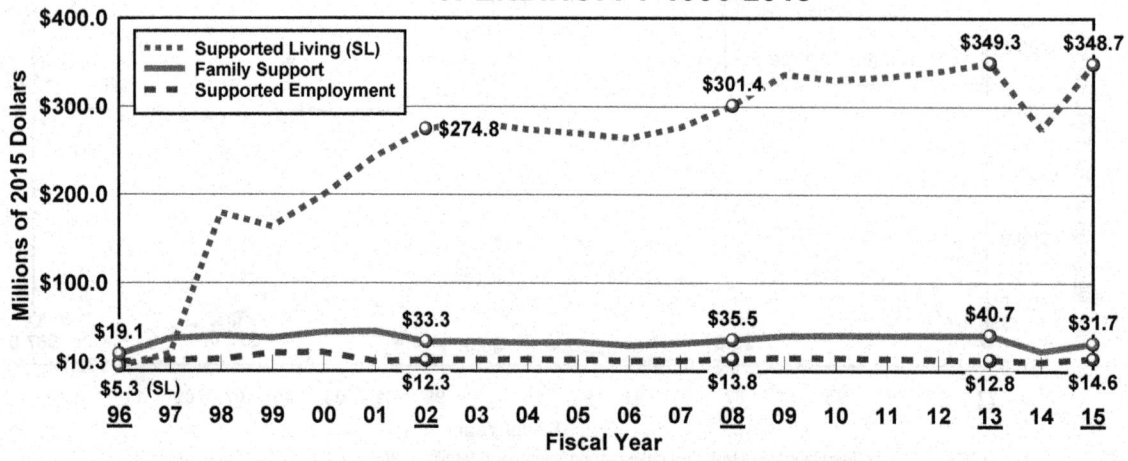

PARTICIPANTS: FY 1996-2015

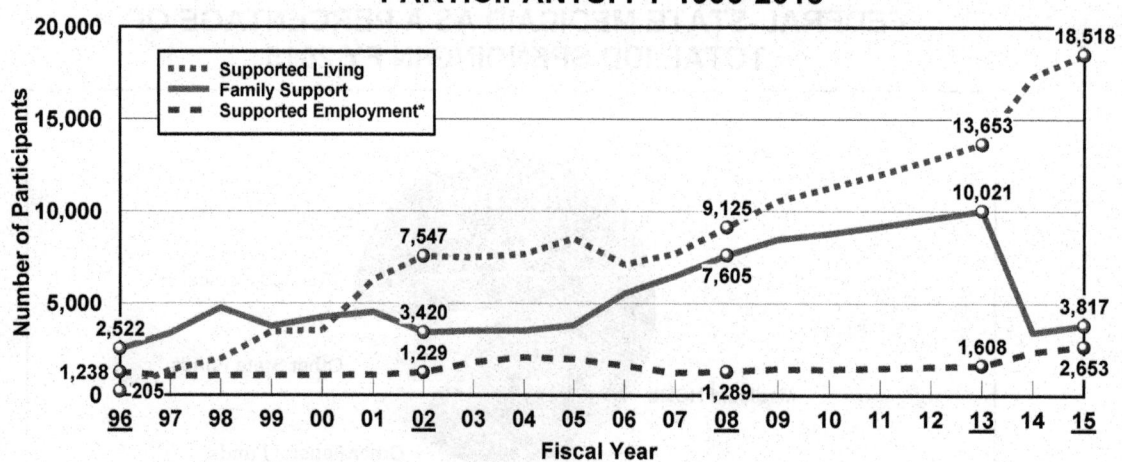

*Does not include 620 follow-along work support workers in 2014 and 1,013 workers in 2015.

SUPPORTED LIVING, FAMILY SUPPORT AND SUPPORTED EMPLOYMENT SPENDING: FY 1996-2015

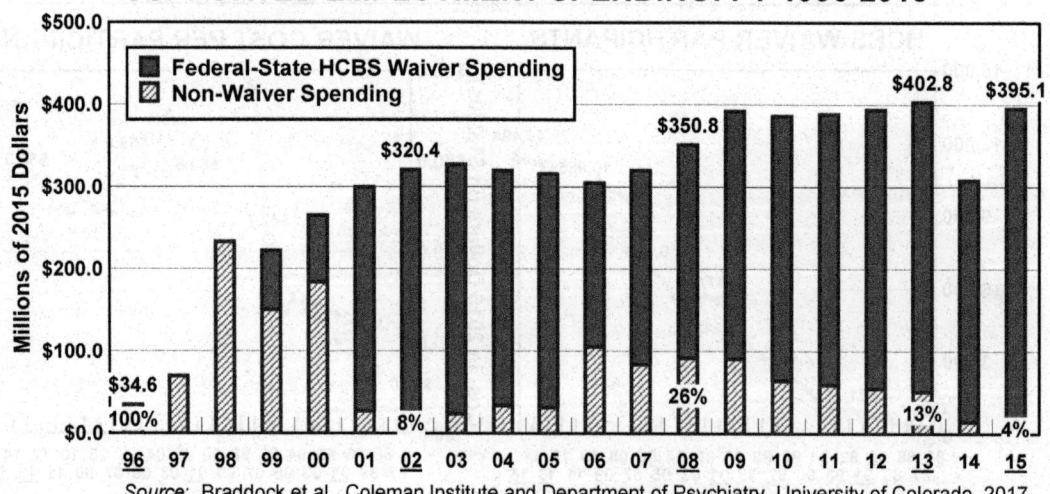

Source: Braddock et al., Coleman Institute and Department of Psychiatry, University of Colorado, 2017.
http://stateofthestates.org

NORTH CAROLINA

ANNUAL COST OF CARE BY RESIDENTIAL SETTING: FY 2015

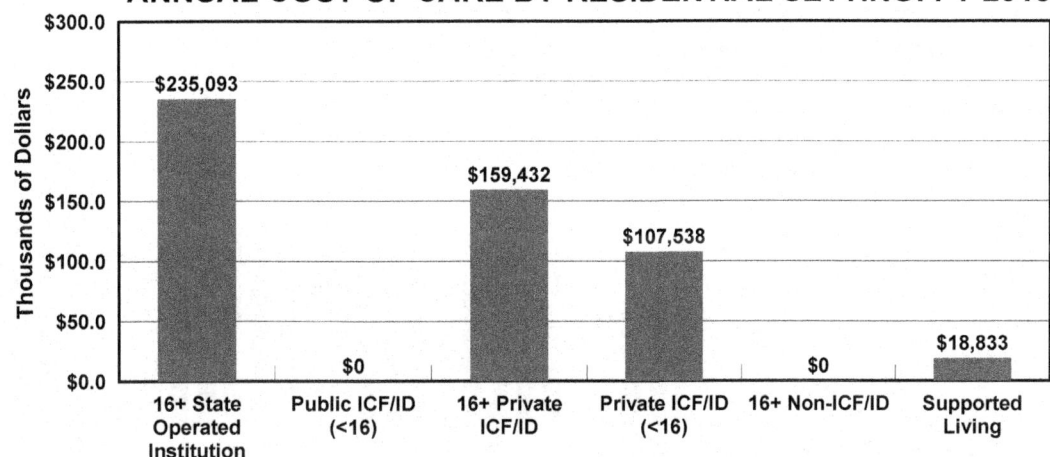

ESTIMATED NUMBER OF INDIVIDUALS WITH IDD BY AGE GROUP LIVING WITH FAMILY CAREGIVERS: FY 2015

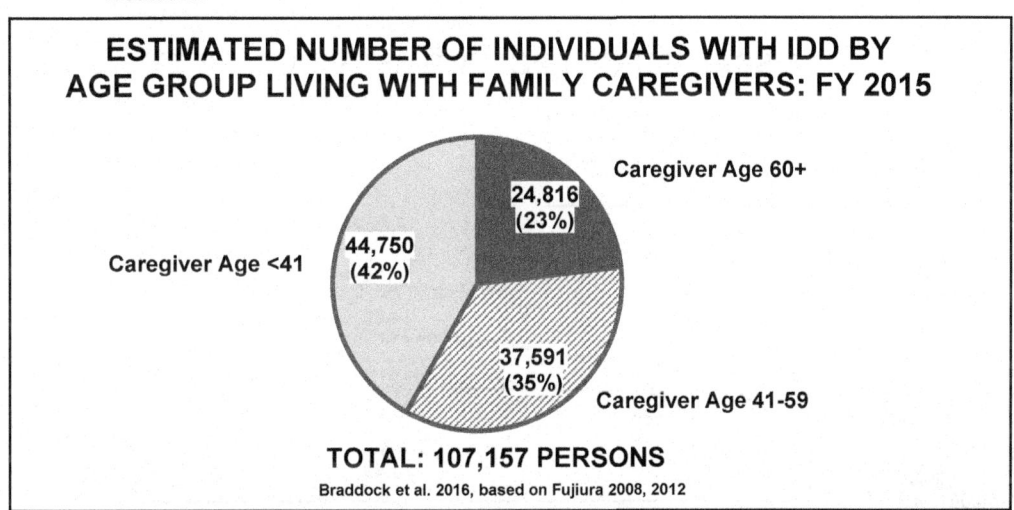

TOTAL: 107,157 PERSONS
Braddock et al. 2016, based on Fujiura 2008, 2012

ESTIMATED NUMBER OF IDD CAREGIVING FAMILIES AND FAMILIES SUPPORTED BY IDD AGENCIES: FY 1988-2015

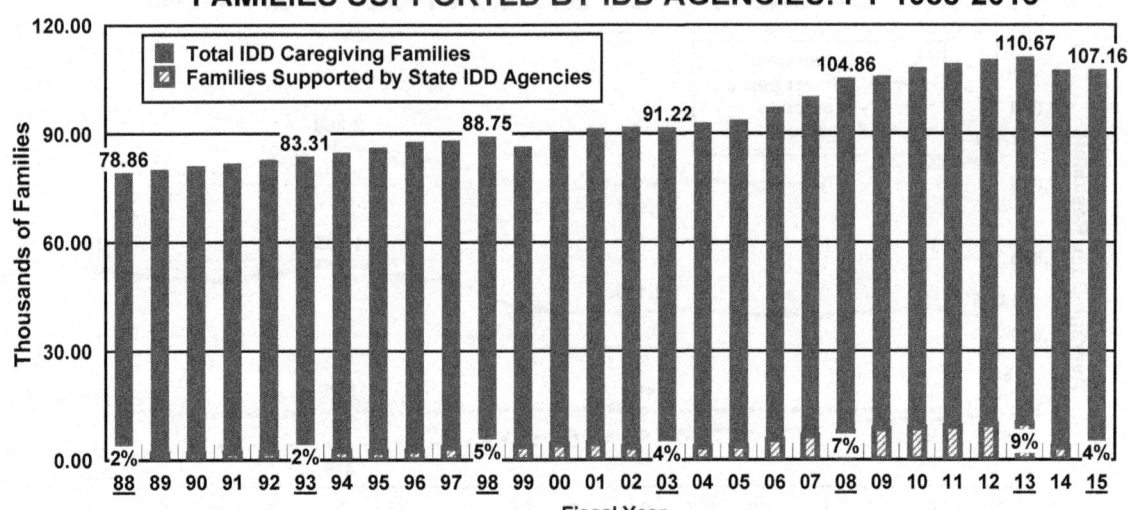

Source: Braddock et al., Coleman Institute and Department of Psychiatry, University of Colorado, 2017.

http://stateofthestates.org

NORTH DAKOTA

TOTAL PUBLIC IDD SPENDING FOR SERVICES: FY 1977-2015

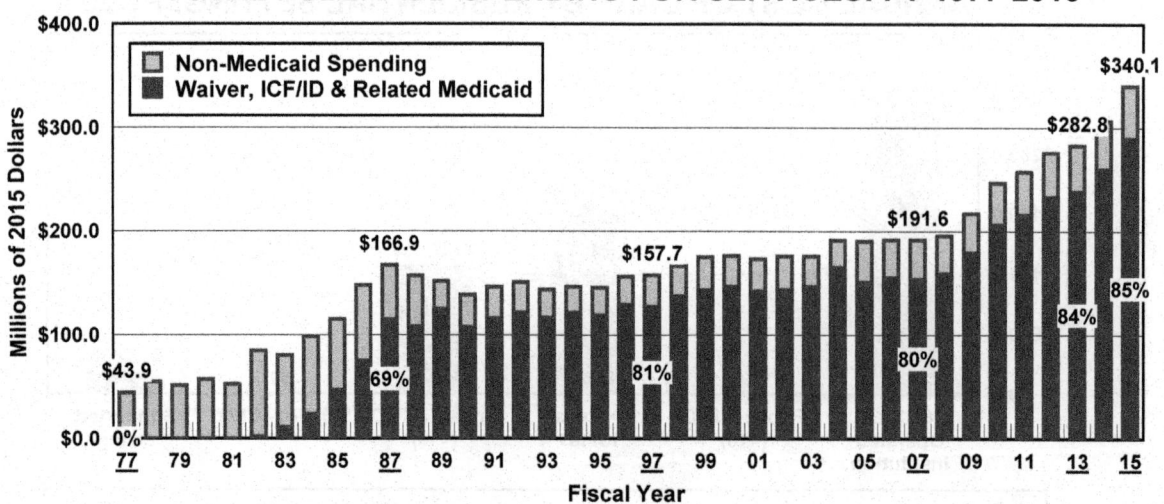

FISCAL EFFORT FOR IDD SERVICES: FY 1977-2015

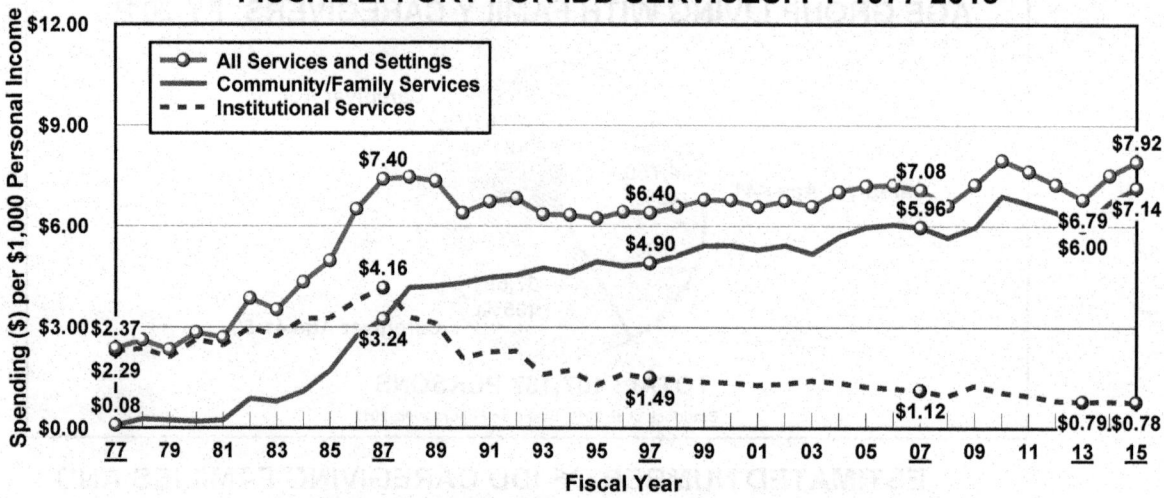

PERSONS WITH IDD BY SIZE OF SETTING: FY 1998-2015

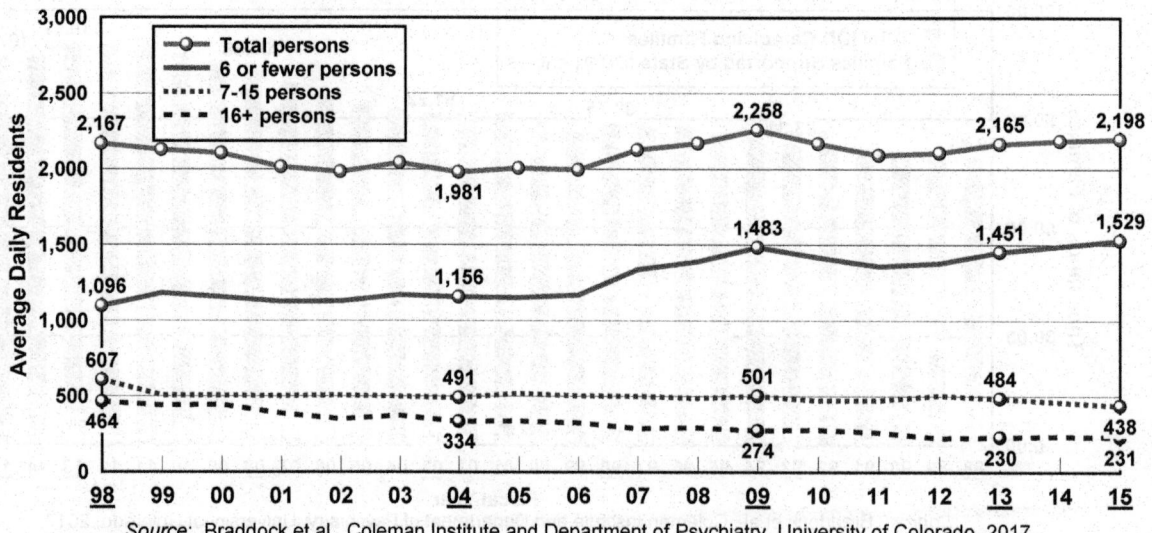

Source: Braddock et al., Coleman Institute and Department of Psychiatry, University of Colorado, 2017.
http://stateofthestates.org

NORTH DAKOTA

FEDERAL IDD MEDICAID SPENDING BY REVENUE SOURCE

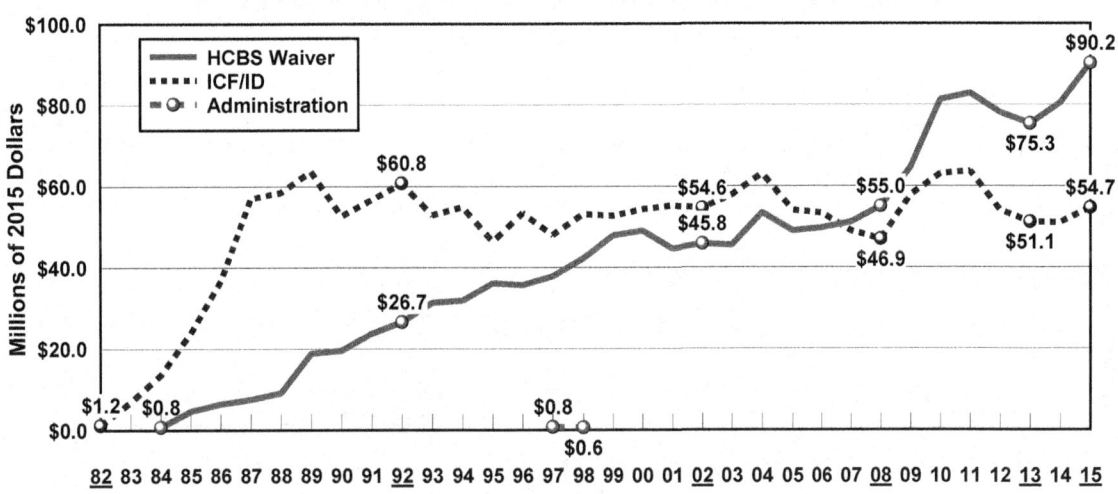

FEDERAL-STATE MEDICAID AS A PERCENTAGE OF TOTAL IDD SPENDING IN FY 2015

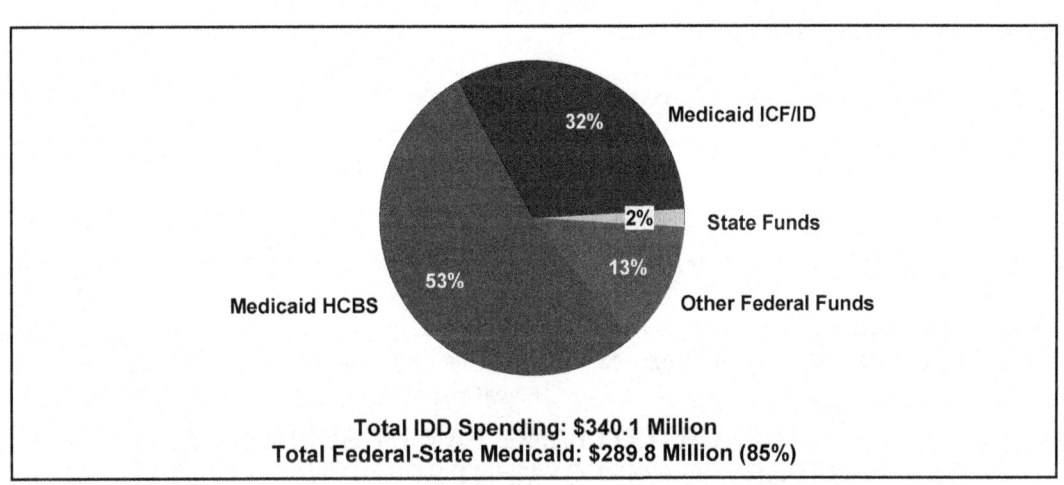

Total IDD Spending: $340.1 Million
Total Federal-State Medicaid: $289.8 Million (85%)

HCBS WAIVER PARTICIPANTS / WAIVER COST PER PARTICIPANT

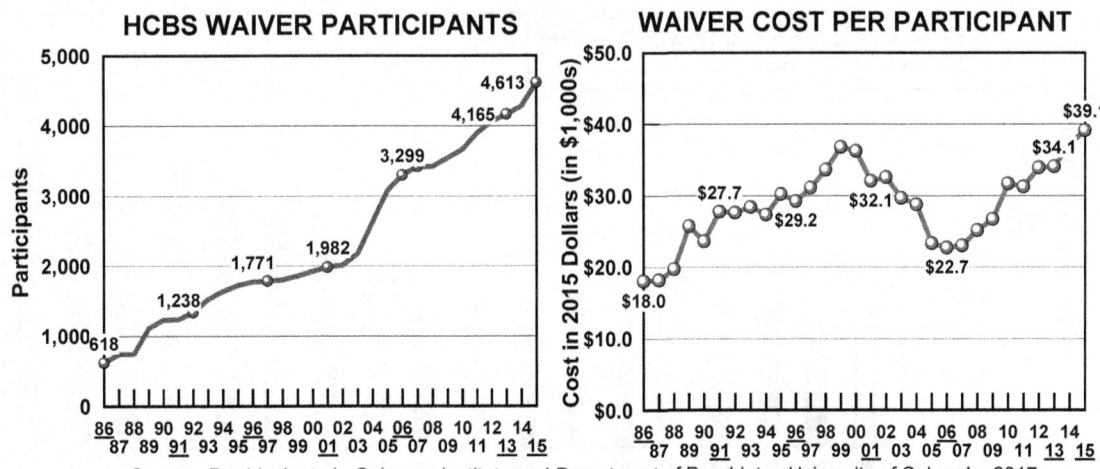

Source: Braddock et al., Coleman Institute and Department of Psychiatry, University of Colorado, 2017.
http://stateofthestates.org

NORTH DAKOTA
INDIVIDUAL AND FAMILY SUPPORT
SPENDING: FY 1996-2015

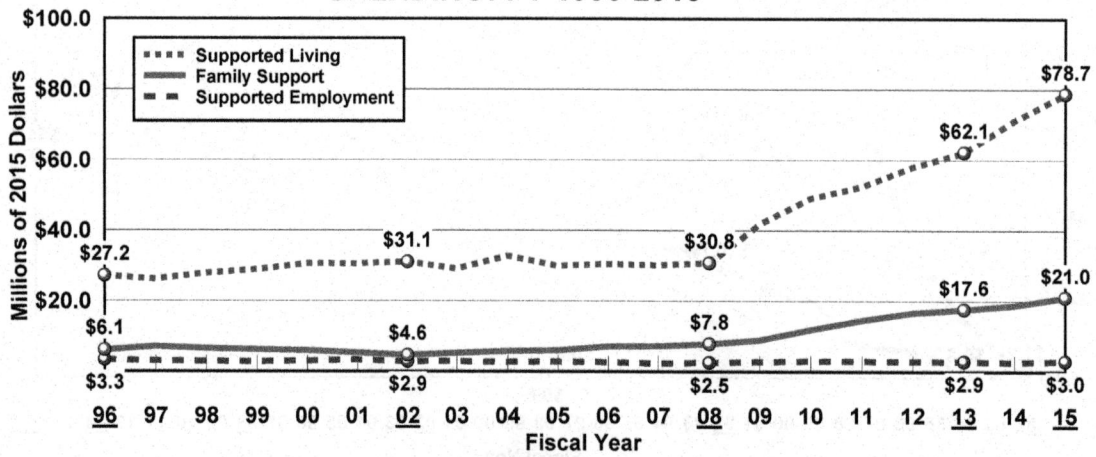

PARTICIPANTS: FY 1996-2015

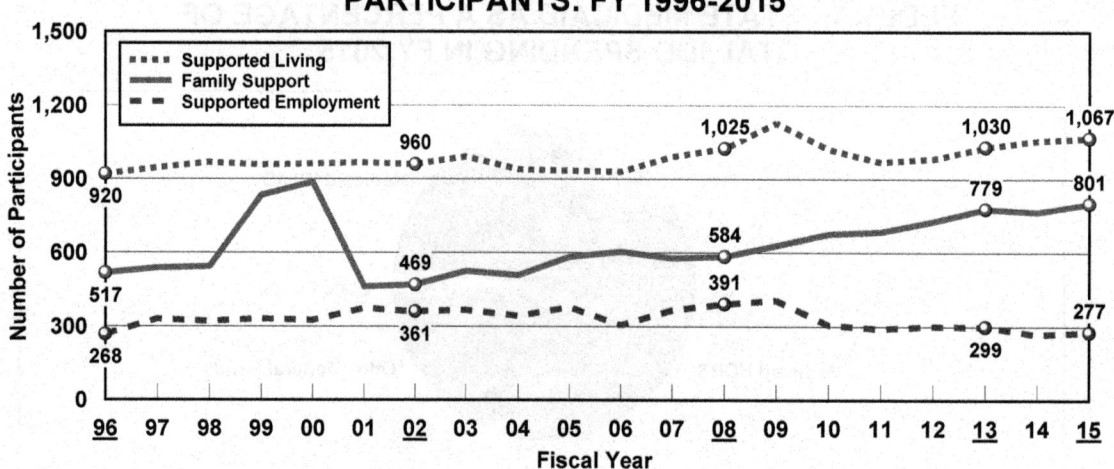

SUPPORTED LIVING, FAMILY SUPPORT AND SUPPORTED EMPLOYMENT SPENDING: FY 1996-2015

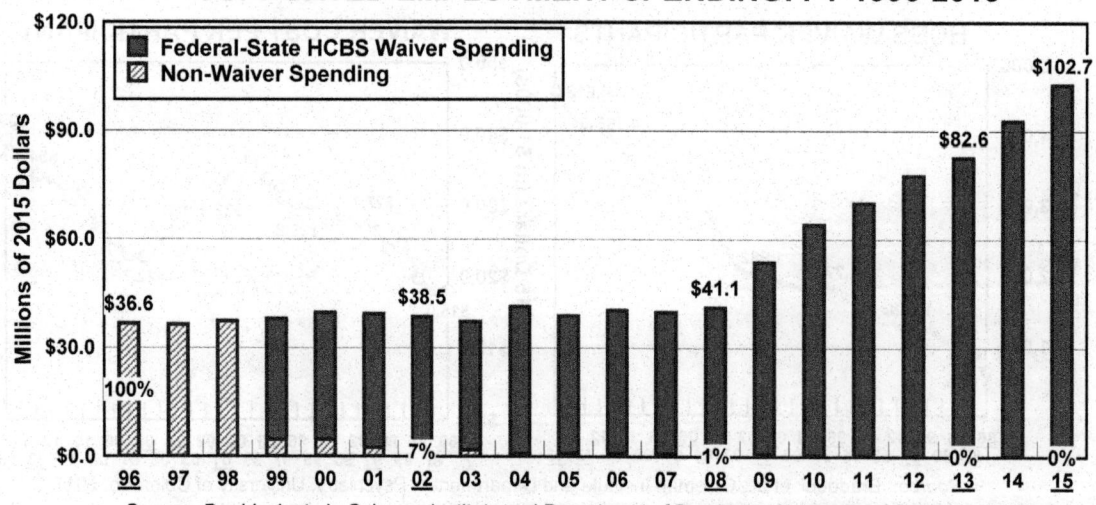

Source: Braddock et al., Coleman Institute and Department of Psychiatry, University of Colorado, 2017.
http://stateofthestates.org

NORTH DAKOTA

ANNUAL COST OF CARE BY RESIDENTIAL SETTING: FY 2015

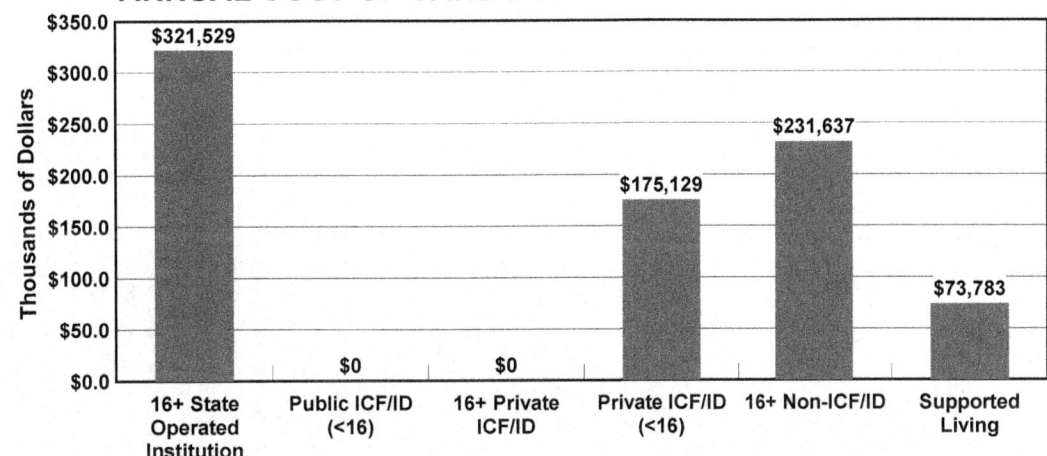

ESTIMATED NUMBER OF INDIVIDUALS WITH IDD BY AGE GROUP LIVING WITH FAMILY CAREGIVERS: FY 2015

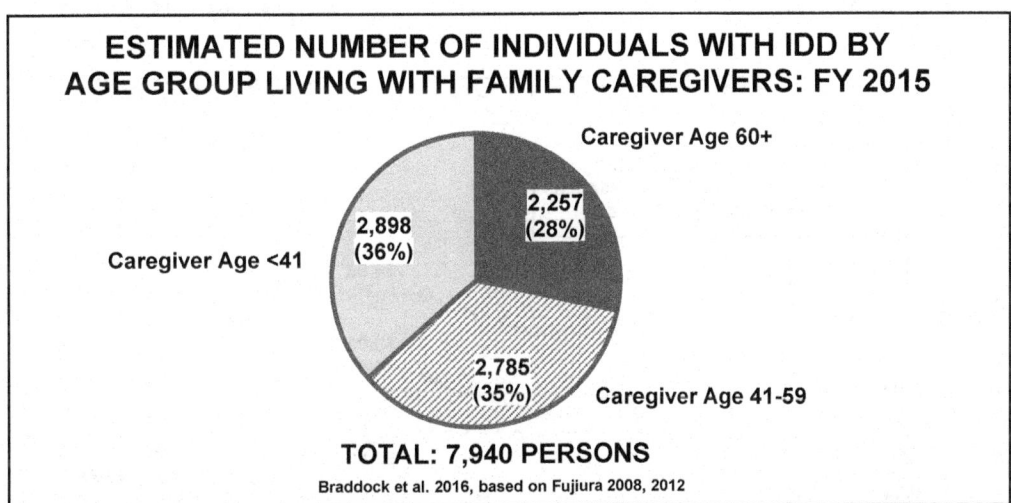

TOTAL: 7,940 PERSONS

Braddock et al. 2016, based on Fujiura 2008, 2012

ESTIMATED NUMBER OF IDD CAREGIVING FAMILIES AND FAMILIES SUPPORTED BY IDD AGENCIES: FY 1988-2015

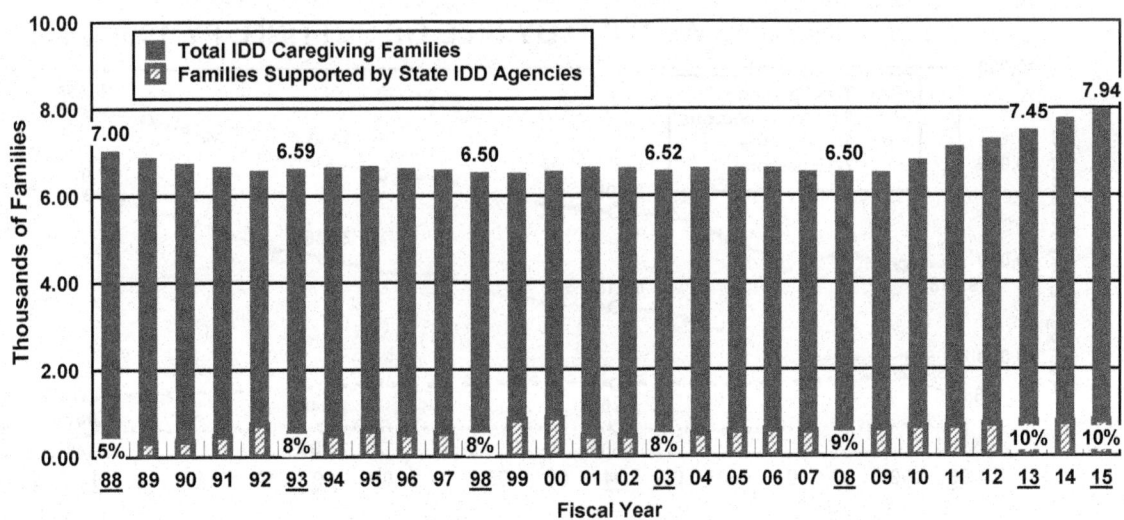

Source: Braddock et al., Coleman Institute and Department of Psychiatry, University of Colorado, 2017.

http://stateofthestates.org

OHIO

TOTAL PUBLIC IDD SPENDING FOR SERVICES: FY 1977-2015

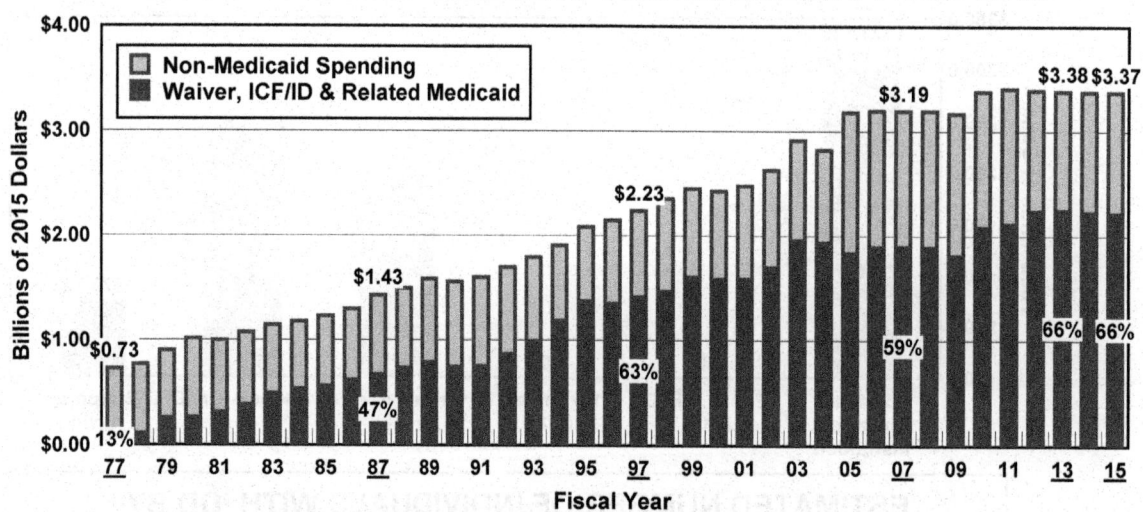

FISCAL EFFORT FOR IDD SERVICES: FY 1977-2015

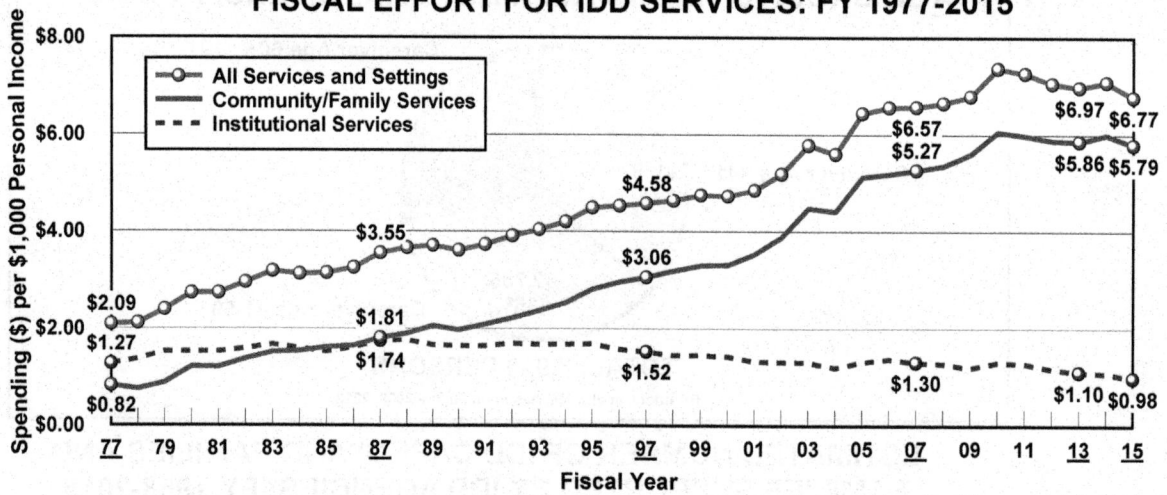

PERSONS WITH IDD BY SIZE OF SETTING: FY 1998-2015

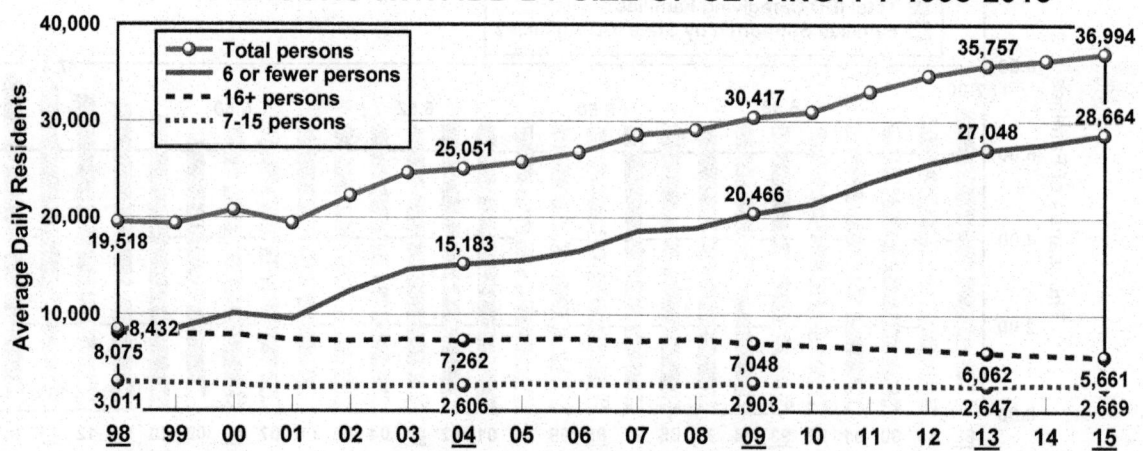

Source: Braddock et al., Coleman Institute and Department of Psychiatry, University of Colorado, 2017.
http://stateofthestates.org

OHIO

FEDERAL IDD MEDICAID SPENDING BY REVENUE SOURCE

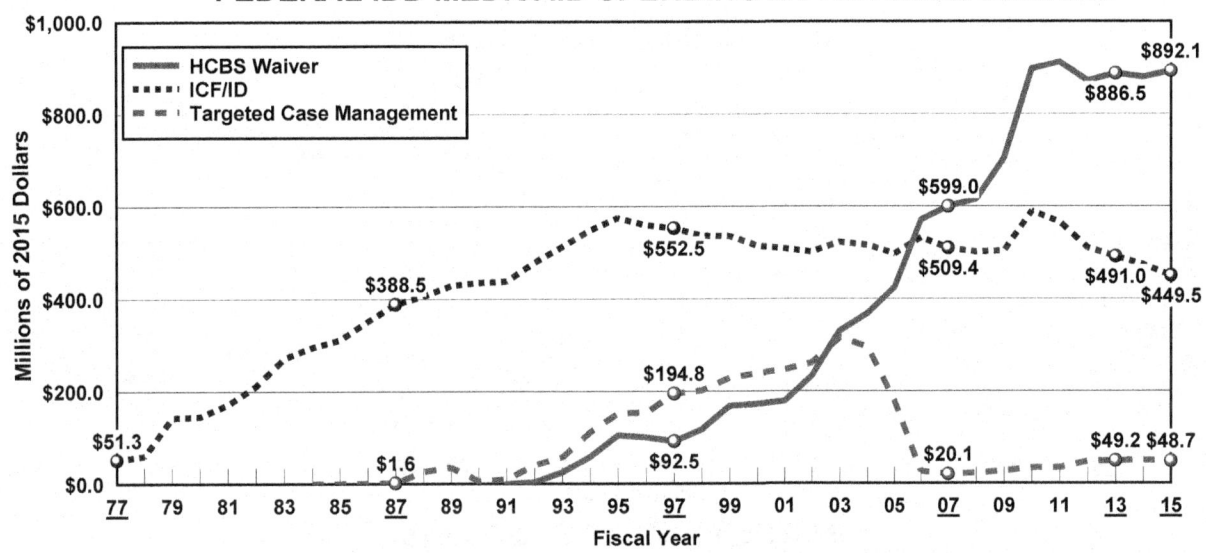

FEDERAL-STATE MEDICAID AS A PERCENTAGE OF TOTAL IDD SPENDING IN FY 2015

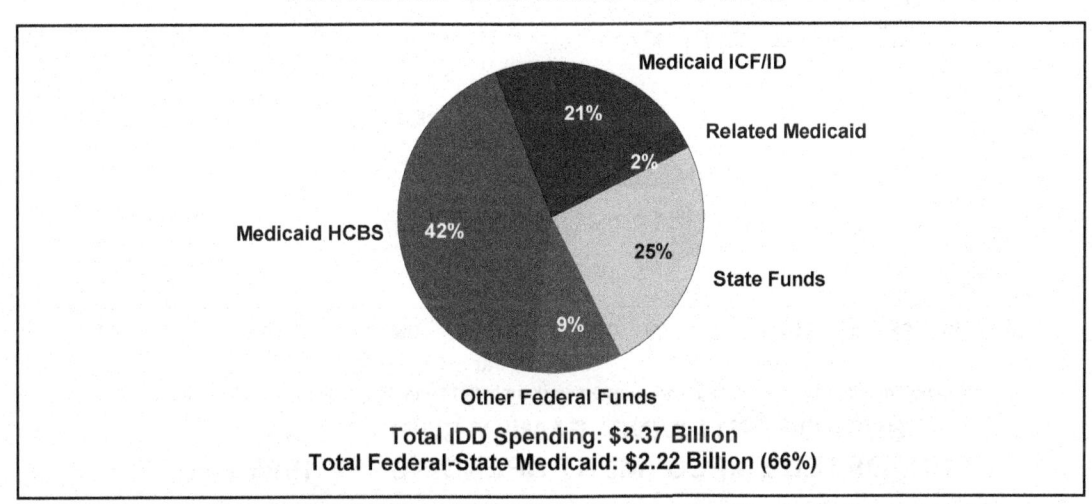

Total IDD Spending: $3.37 Billion
Total Federal-State Medicaid: $2.22 Billion (66%)

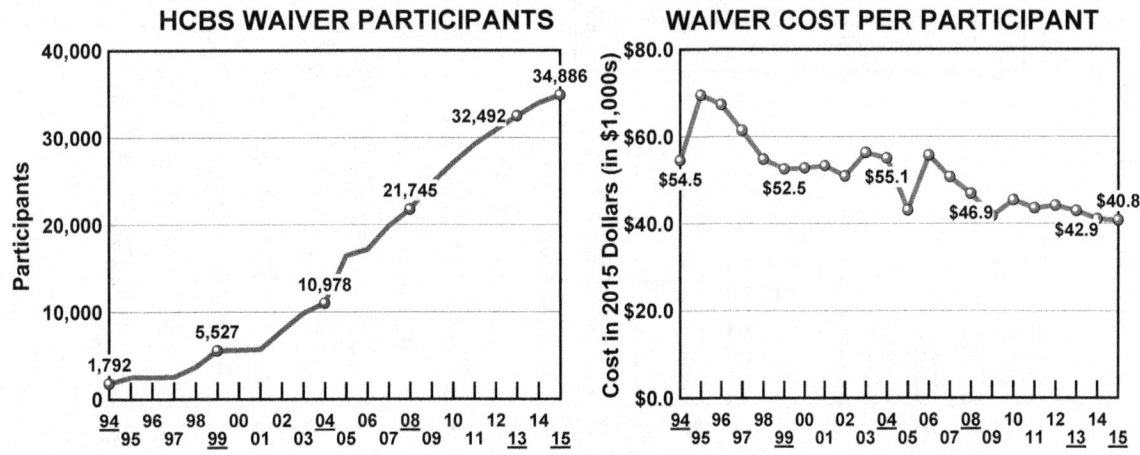

Source: Braddock et al., Coleman Institute and Department of Psychiatry, University of Colorado, 2017.
http://stateofthestates.org

OHIO
INDIVIDUAL AND FAMILY SUPPORT

SPENDING: FY 1996-2015

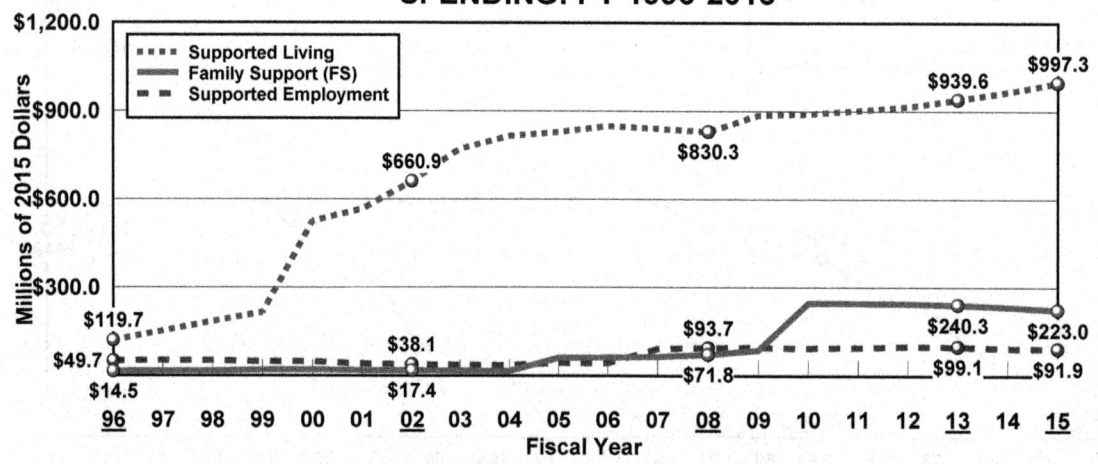

PARTICIPANTS: FY 1996-2015

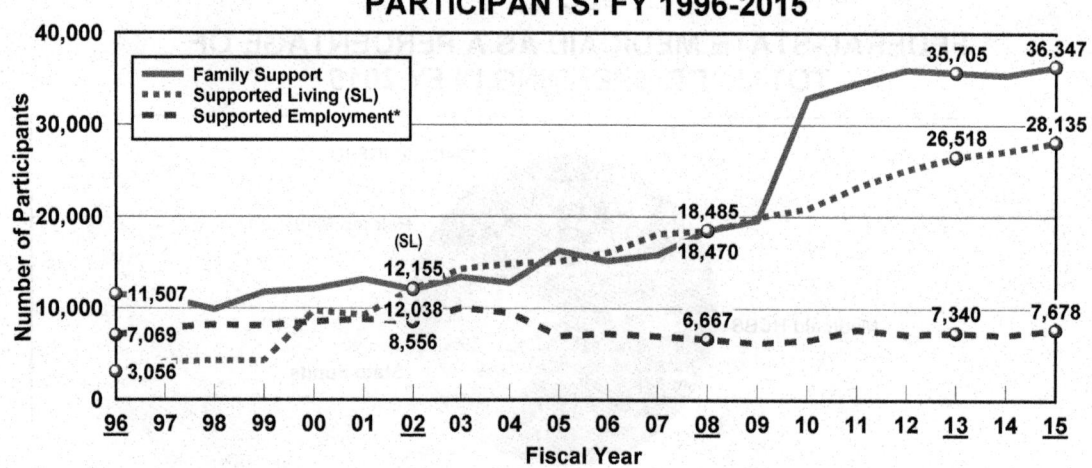

*Does not include 510 follow-along work support workers in 2014 and 830 workers in 2015.

SUPPORTED LIVING, FAMILY SUPPORT AND SUPPORTED EMPLOYMENT SPENDING: FY 1996-2015

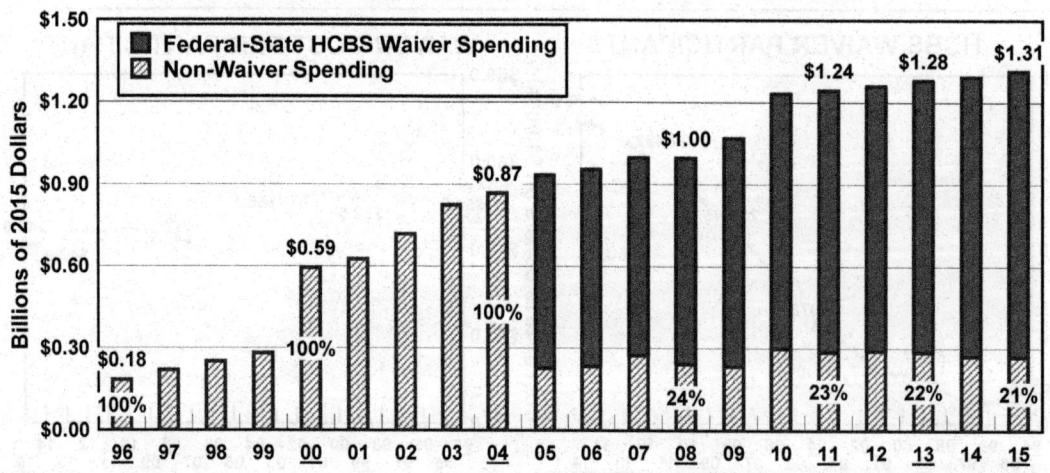

Source: Braddock et al., Coleman Institute and Department of Psychiatry, University of Colorado, 2017.
http://stateofthestates.org

OHIO

ANNUAL COST OF CARE BY RESIDENTIAL SETTING: FY 2015

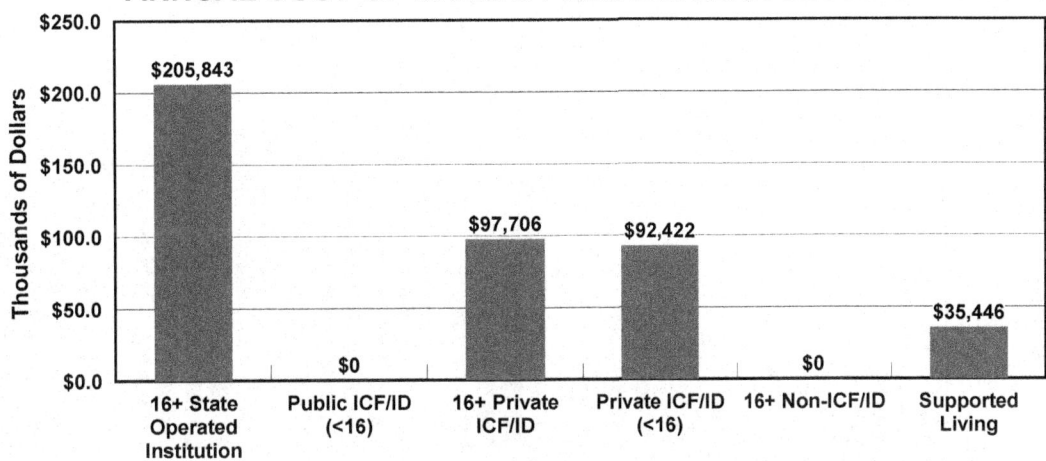

ESTIMATED NUMBER OF INDIVIDUALS WITH IDD BY AGE GROUP LIVING WITH FAMILY CAREGIVERS: FY 2015

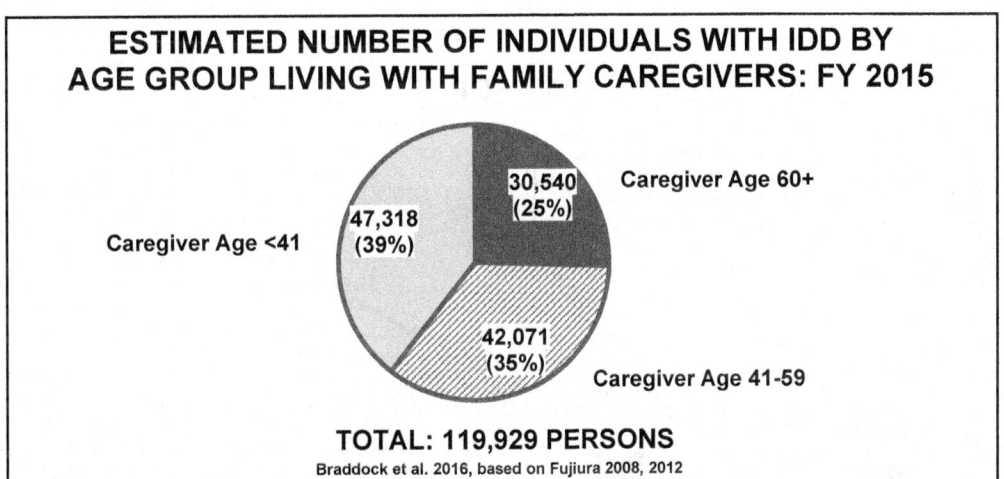

TOTAL: 119,929 PERSONS
Braddock et al. 2016, based on Fujiura 2008, 2012

ESTIMATED NUMBER OF IDD CAREGIVING FAMILIES AND FAMILIES SUPPORTED BY IDD AGENCIES: FY 1988-2015

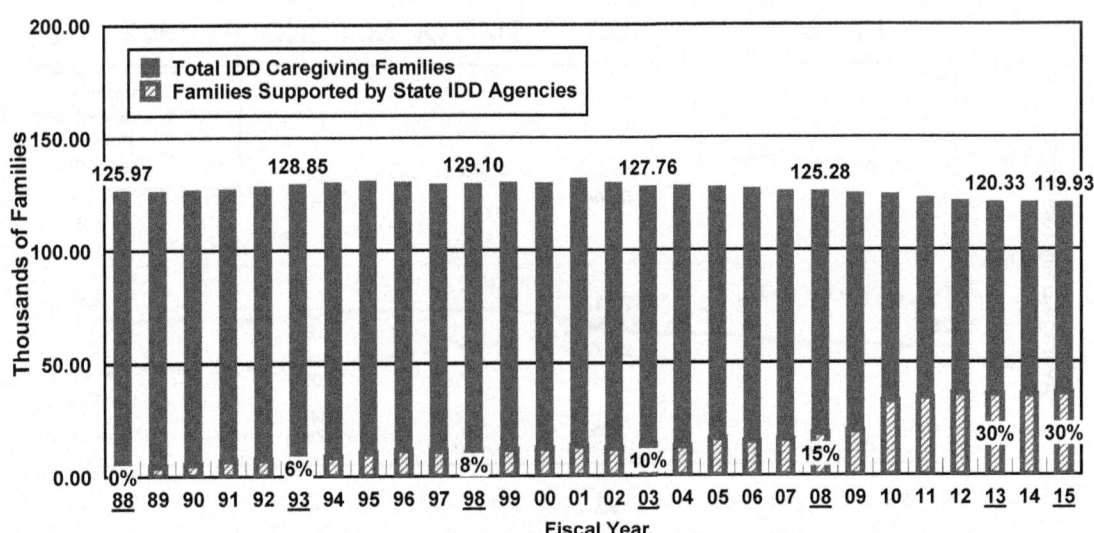

Source: Braddock et al., Coleman Institute and Department of Psychiatry, University of Colorado, 2017.
http://stateofthestates.org

OKLAHOMA

TOTAL PUBLIC IDD SPENDING FOR SERVICES: FY 1977-2015

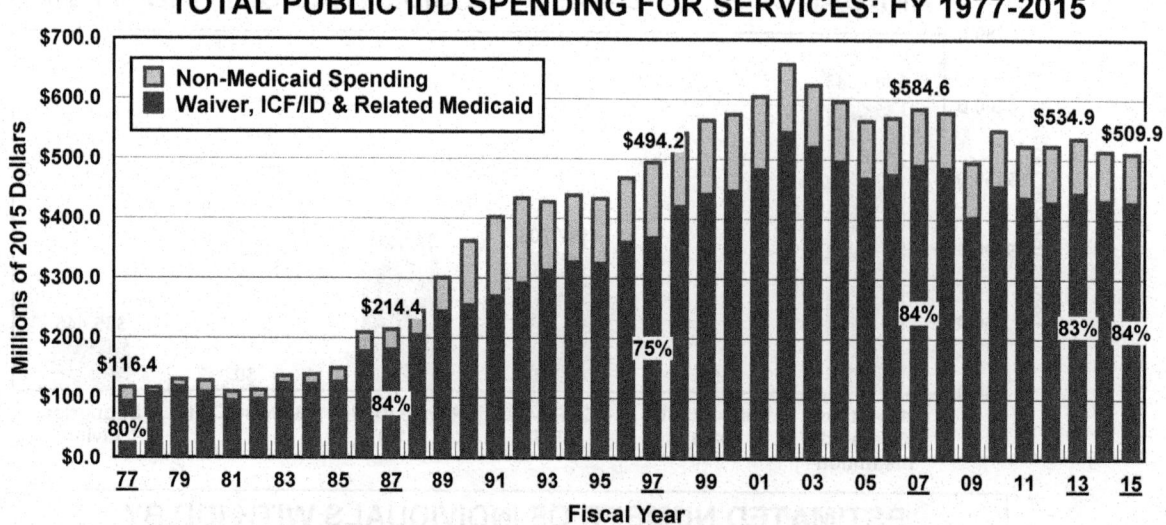

FISCAL EFFORT FOR IDD SERVICES: FY 1977-2015

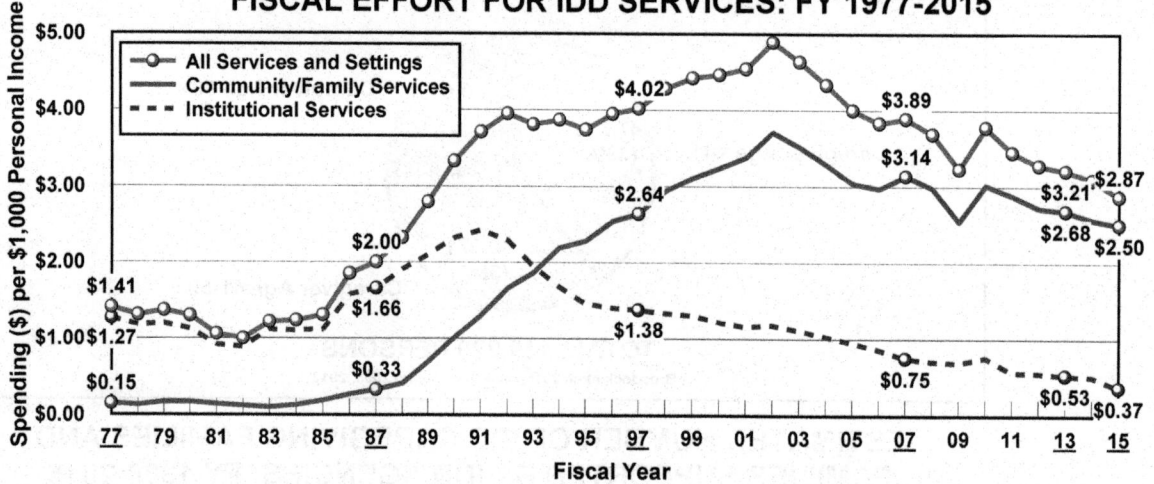

PERSONS WITH IDD BY SIZE OF SETTING: FY 1998-2015

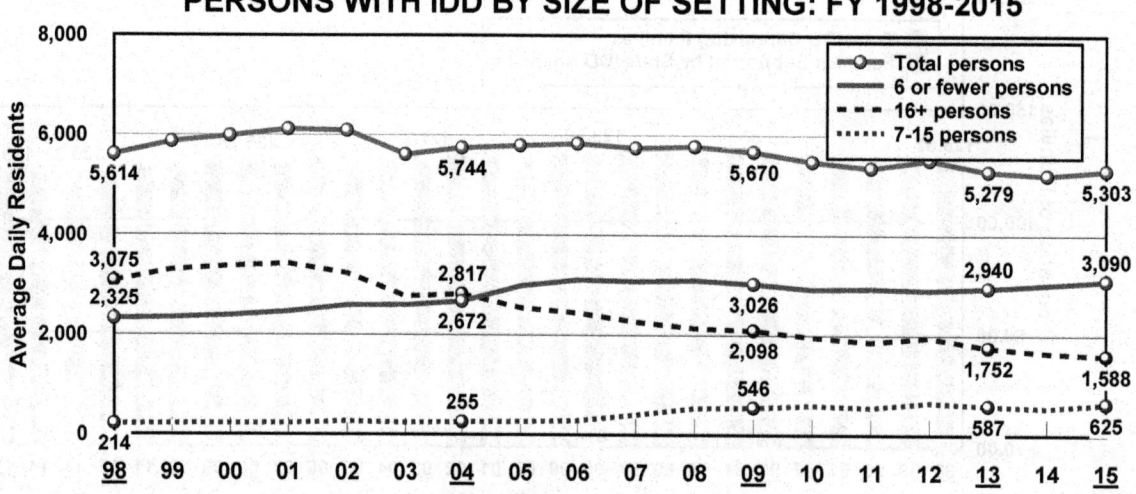

Source: Braddock et al., Coleman Institute and Department of Psychiatry, University of Colorado, 2017.
http://stateofthestates.org

OKLAHOMA
FEDERAL IDD MEDICAID SPENDING BY REVENUE SOURCE

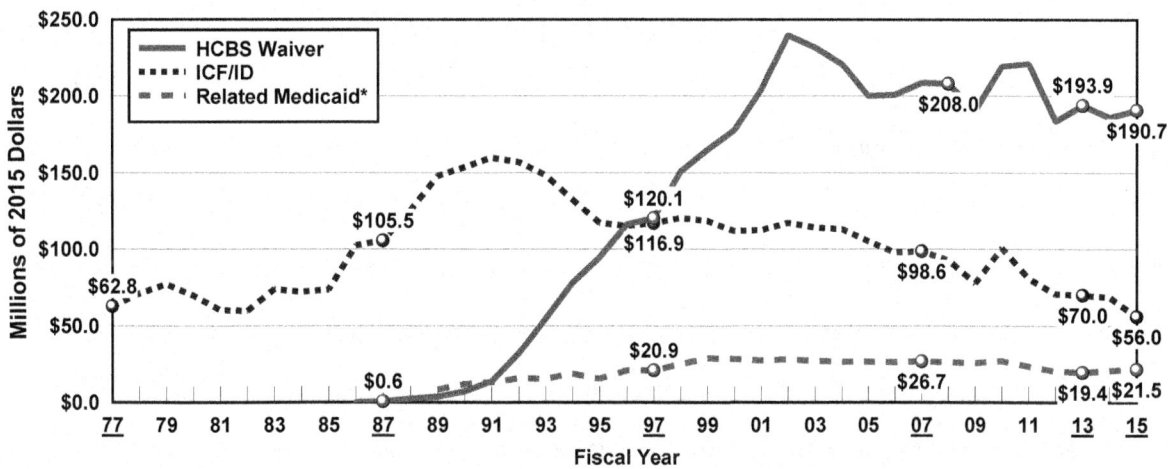

*In 2015, "Related Medicaid" was targeted case management ($12.6 million) and administration ($8.9 million).

FEDERAL-STATE MEDICAID AS A PERCENTAGE OF TOTAL IDD SPENDING IN FY 2015

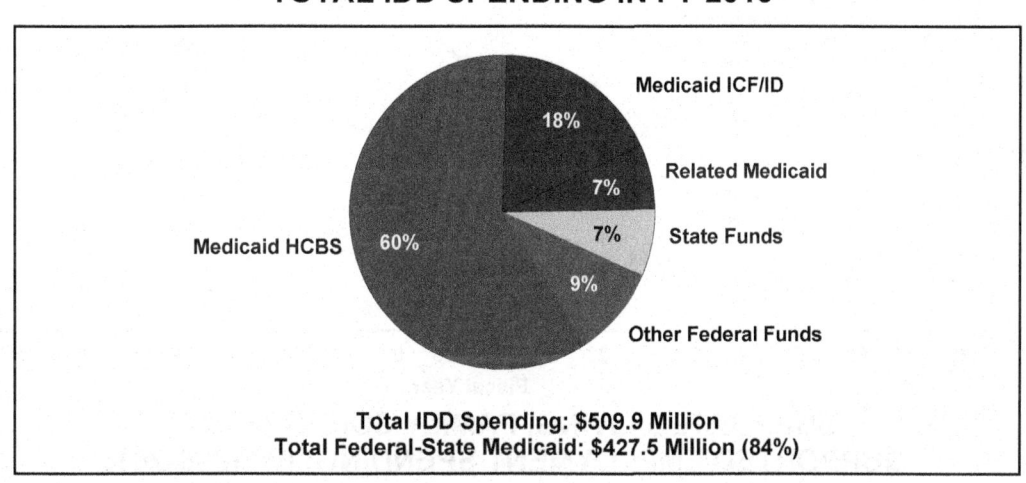

Total IDD Spending: $509.9 Million
Total Federal-State Medicaid: $427.5 Million (84%)

HCBS WAIVER PARTICIPANTS

WAIVER COST PER PARTICIPANT

Source: Braddock et al., Coleman Institute and Department of Psychiatry, University of Colorado, 2017.
http://stateofthestates.org

OKLAHOMA
INDIVIDUAL AND FAMILY SUPPORT

SPENDING: FY 1996-2015

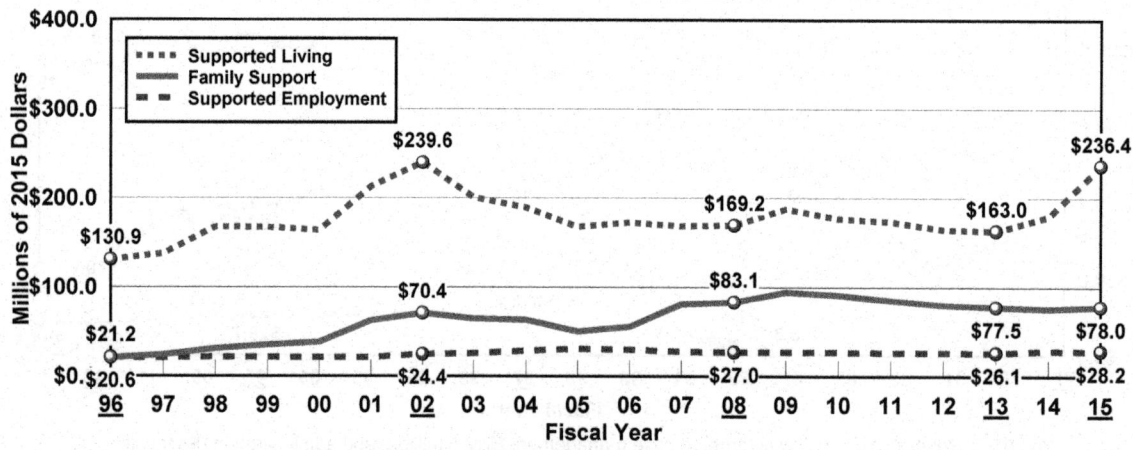

PARTICIPANTS: FY 1996-2015

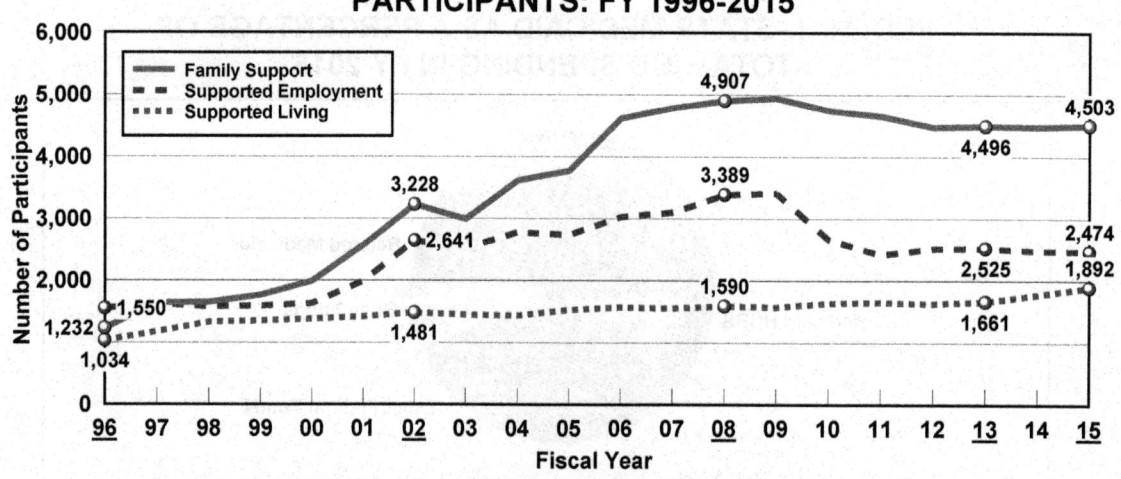

SUPPORTED LIVING, FAMILY SUPPORT AND SUPPORTED EMPLOYMENT SPENDING: FY 1996-2015

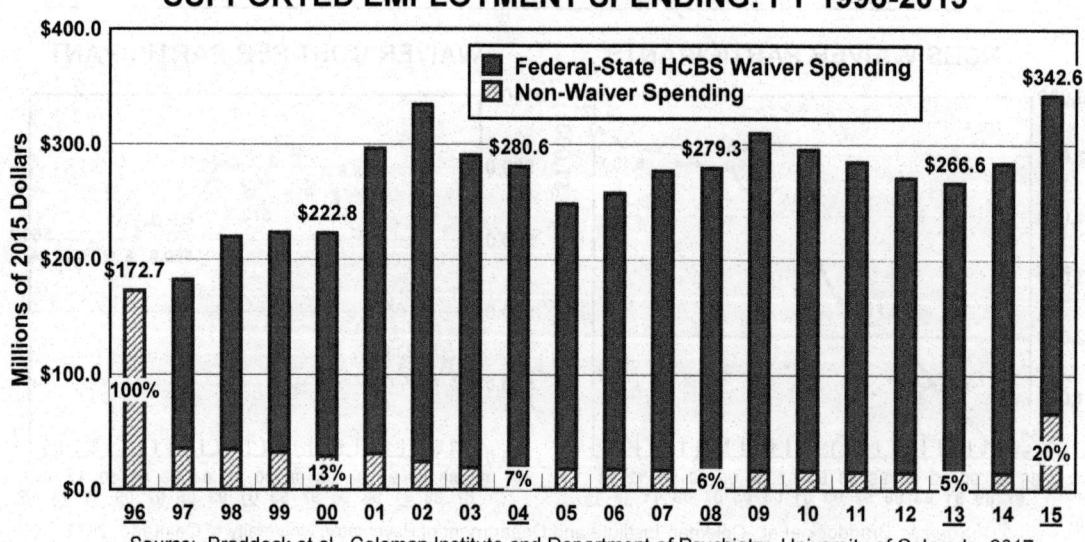

Source: Braddock et al., Coleman Institute and Department of Psychiatry, University of Colorado, 2017.
http://stateofthestates.org

OKLAHOMA

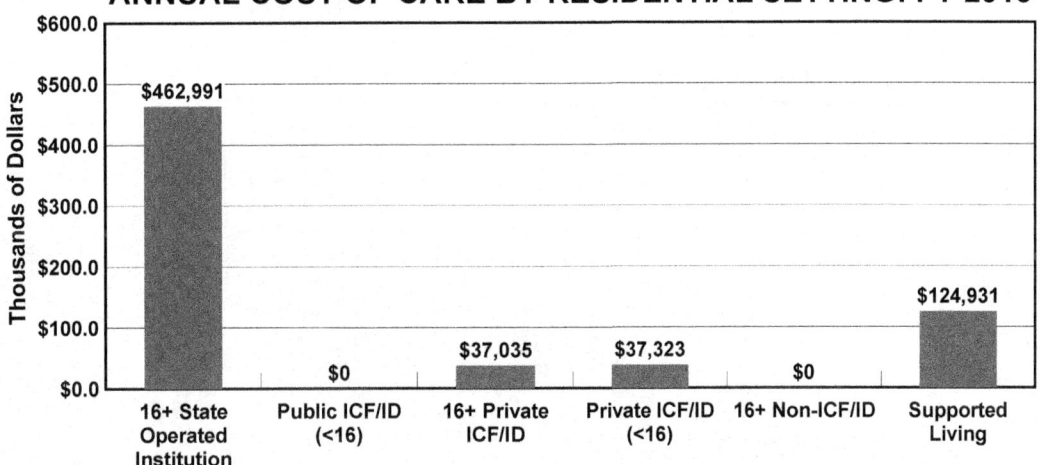

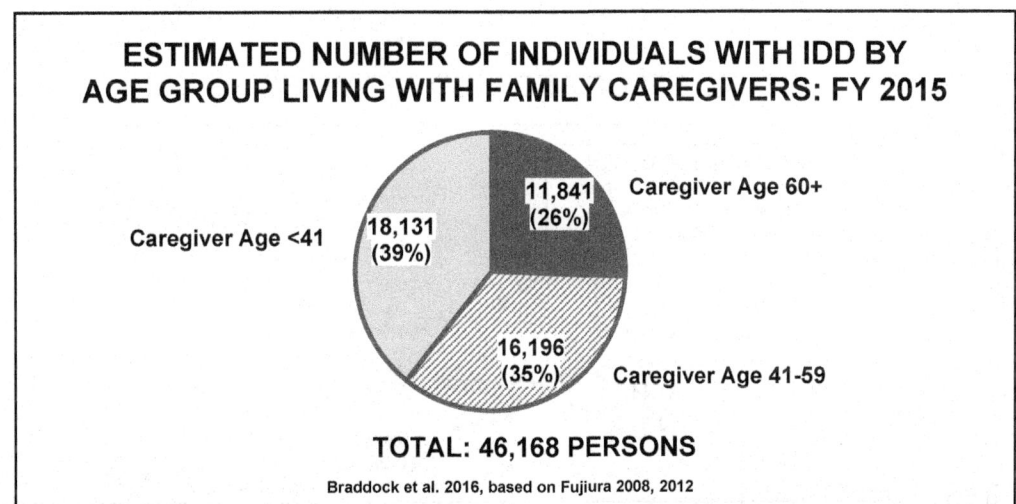

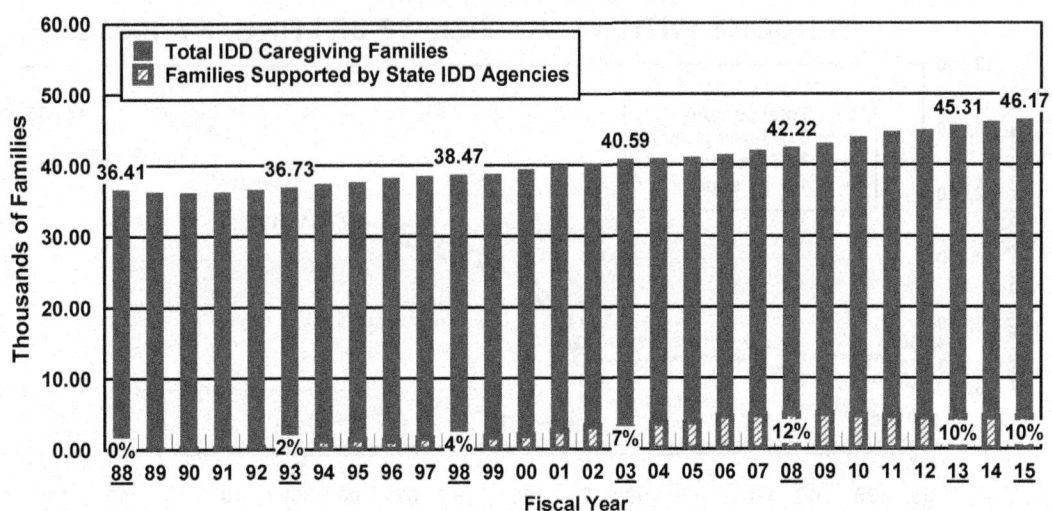

Source: Braddock et al., Coleman Institute and Department of Psychiatry, University of Colorado, 2017.
http://stateofthestates.org

OREGON

TOTAL PUBLIC IDD SPENDING FOR SERVICES: FY 1977-2015

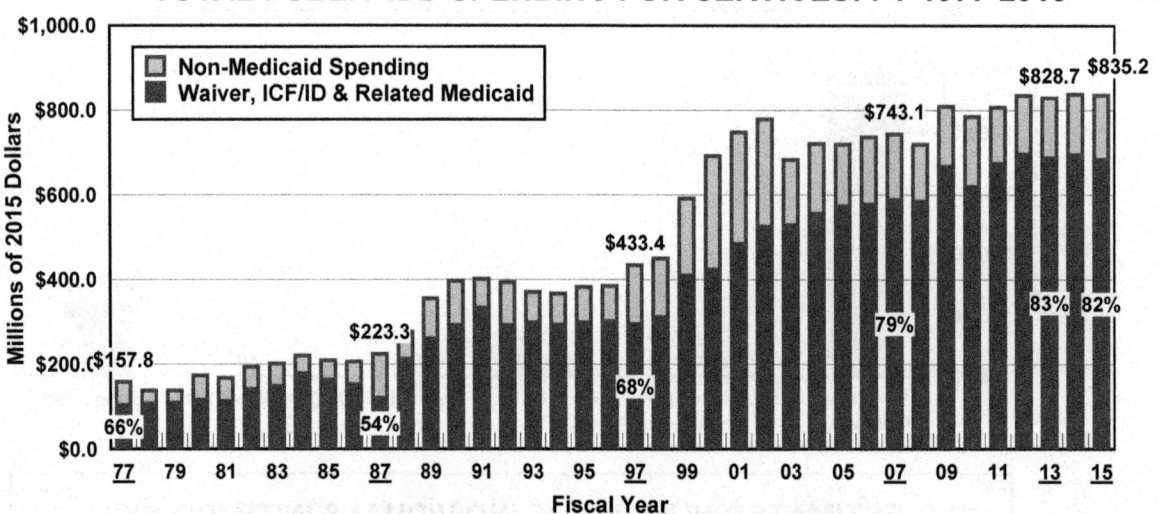

FISCAL EFFORT FOR IDD SERVICES: FY 1977-2015

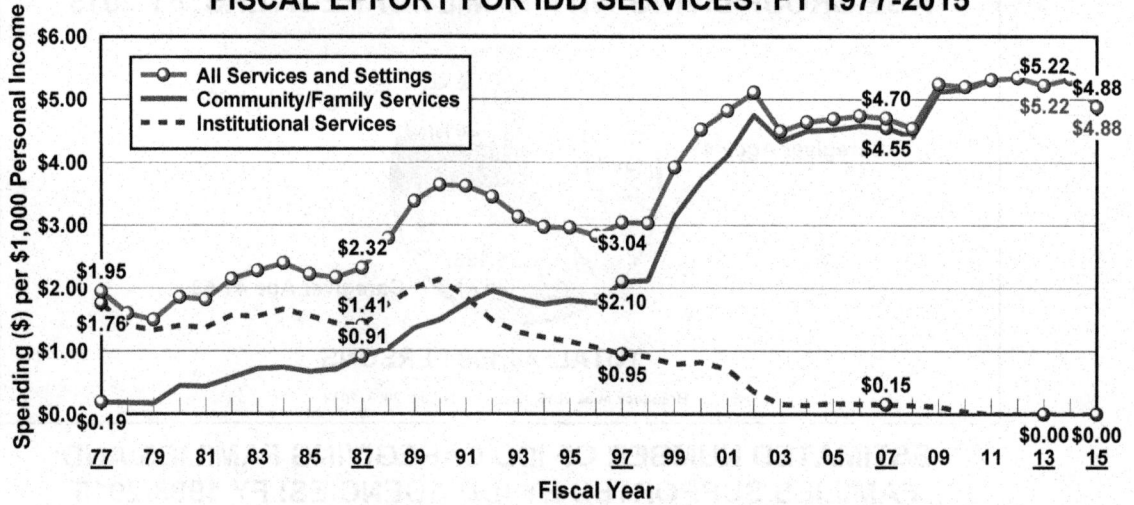

PERSONS WITH IDD BY SIZE OF SETTING: FY 1998-2015

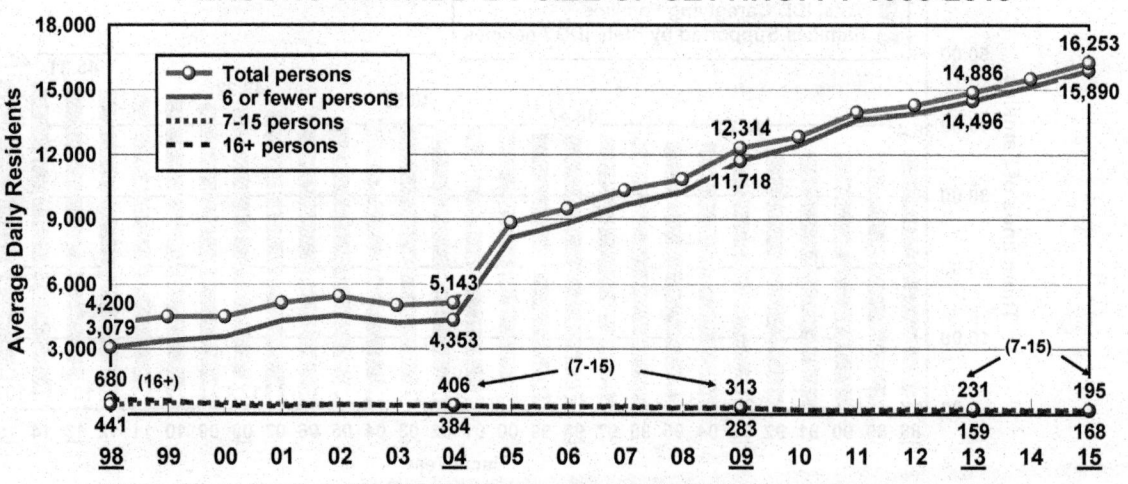

Source: Braddock et al., Coleman Institute and Department of Psychiatry, University of Colorado, 2017.
http://stateofthestates.org

OREGON

FEDERAL IDD MEDICAID SPENDING BY REVENUE SOURCE

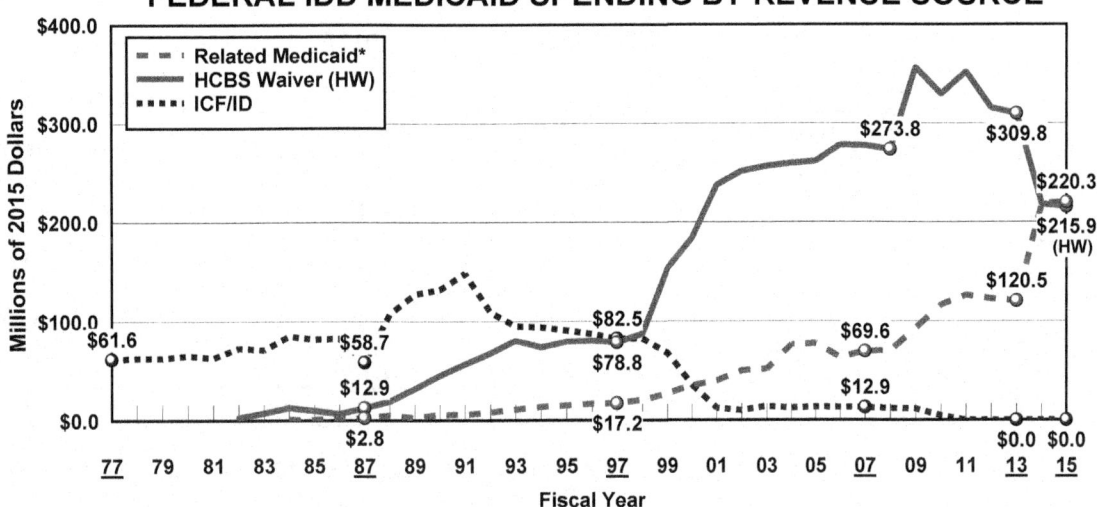

*In 2015, "Related Medicaid" was targeted case management ($29.7 million), personal assistance ($178.3 million) and administration ($12.3 million).

FEDERAL-STATE MEDICAID AS A PERCENTAGE OF TOTAL IDD SPENDING IN FY 2015

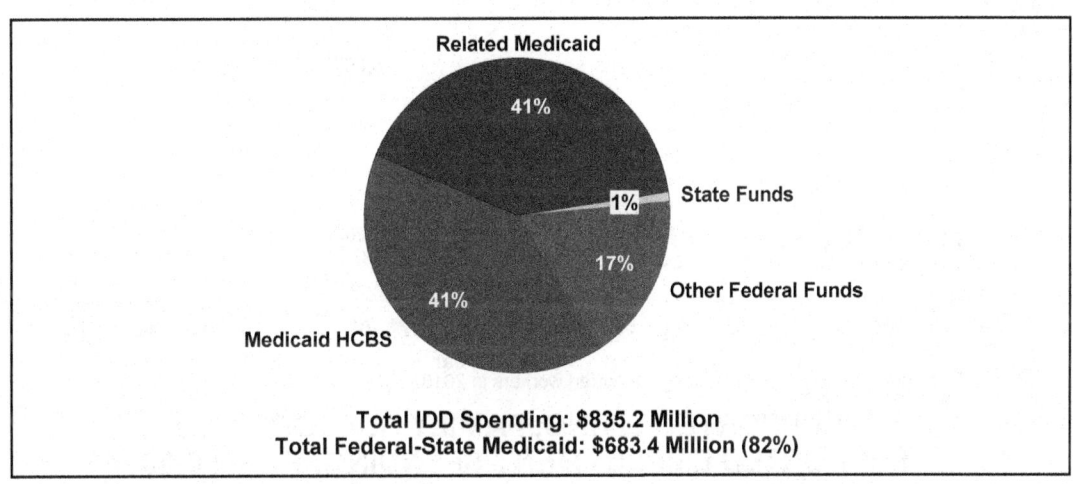

Total IDD Spending: $835.2 Million
Total Federal-State Medicaid: $683.4 Million (82%)

HCBS WAIVER PARTICIPANTS / WAIVER COST PER PARTICIPANT

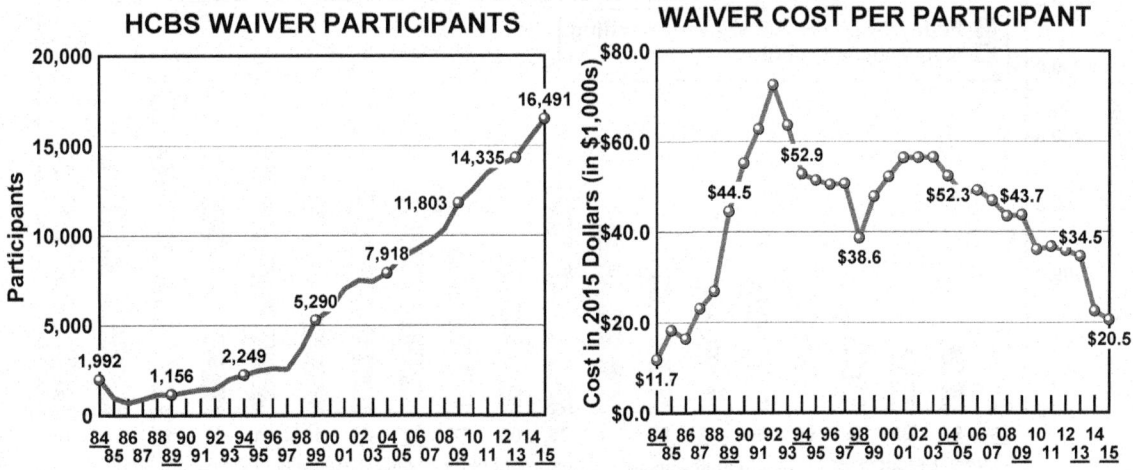

Source: Braddock et al., Coleman Institute and Department of Psychiatry, University of Colorado, 2017.
http://stateofthestates.org

OREGON
INDIVIDUAL AND FAMILY SUPPORT
SPENDING: FY 1996-2015

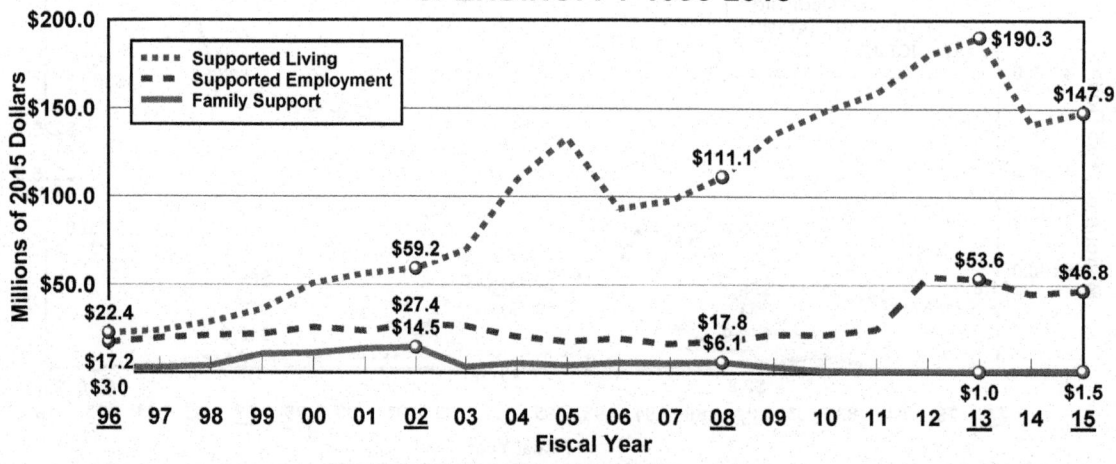

PARTICIPANTS: FY 1996-2015

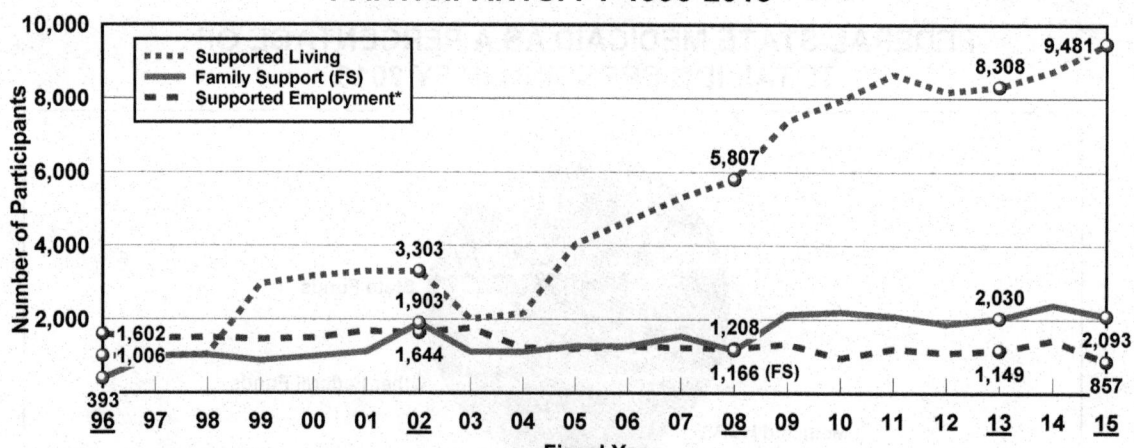

*Does not include 577 Follow-along supported workers in 2015.

SUPPORTED LIVING, FAMILY SUPPORT AND SUPPORTED EMPLOYMENT SPENDING: FY 1996-2015

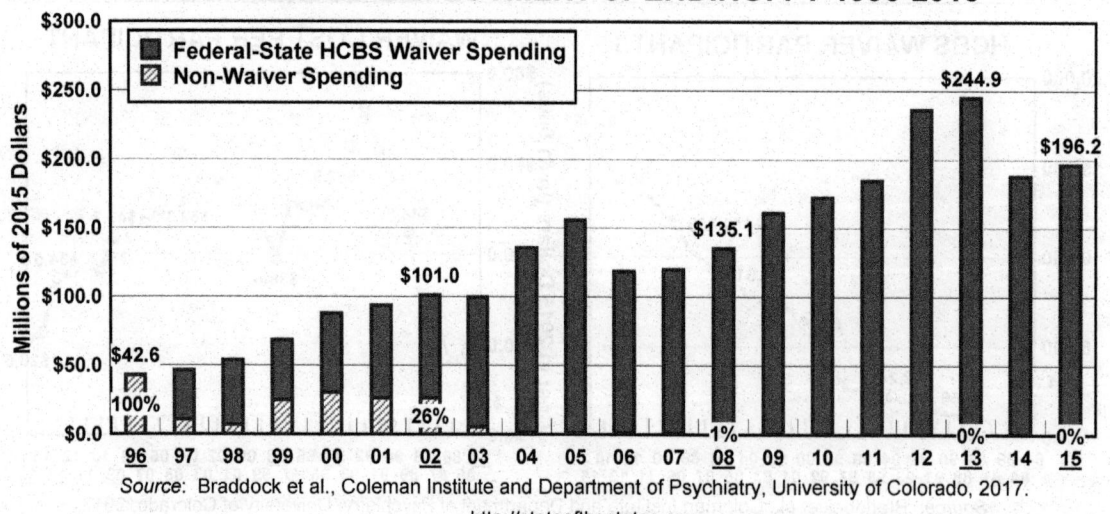

Source: Braddock et al., Coleman Institute and Department of Psychiatry, University of Colorado, 2017.
http://stateofthestates.org

OREGON

ANNUAL COST OF CARE BY RESIDENTIAL SETTING: FY 2015

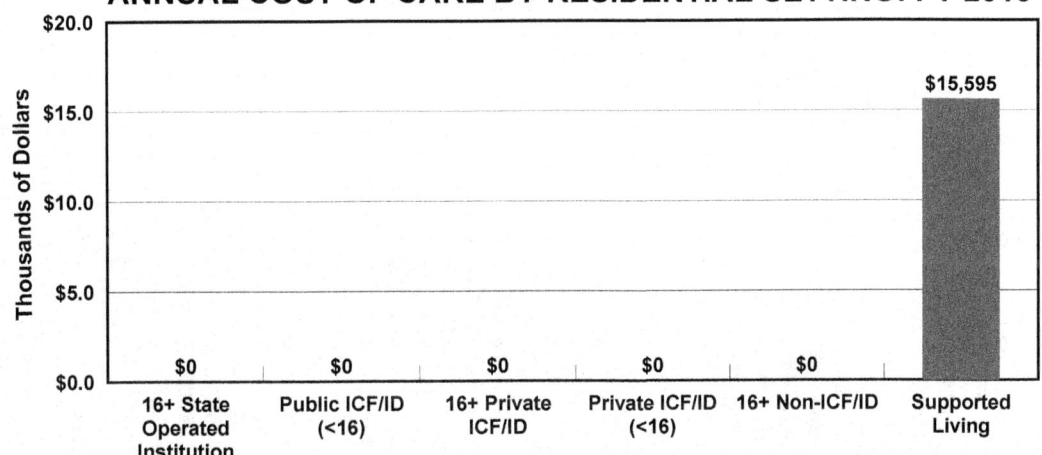

ESTIMATED NUMBER OF INDIVIDUALS WITH IDD BY AGE GROUP LIVING WITH FAMILY CAREGIVERS: FY 2015

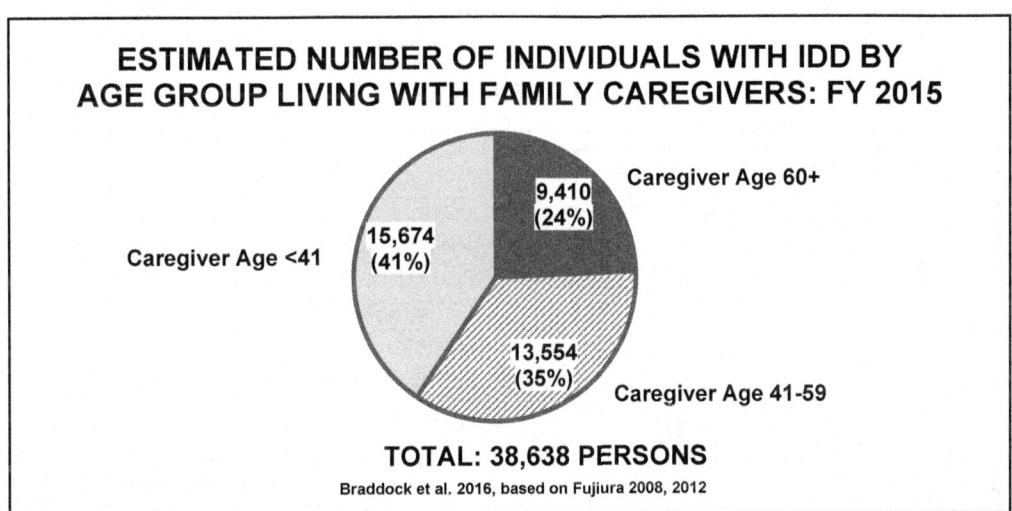

TOTAL: 38,638 PERSONS

Braddock et al. 2016, based on Fujiura 2008, 2012

ESTIMATED NUMBER OF IDD CAREGIVING FAMILIES AND FAMILIES SUPPORTED BY IDD AGENCIES: FY 1988-2015

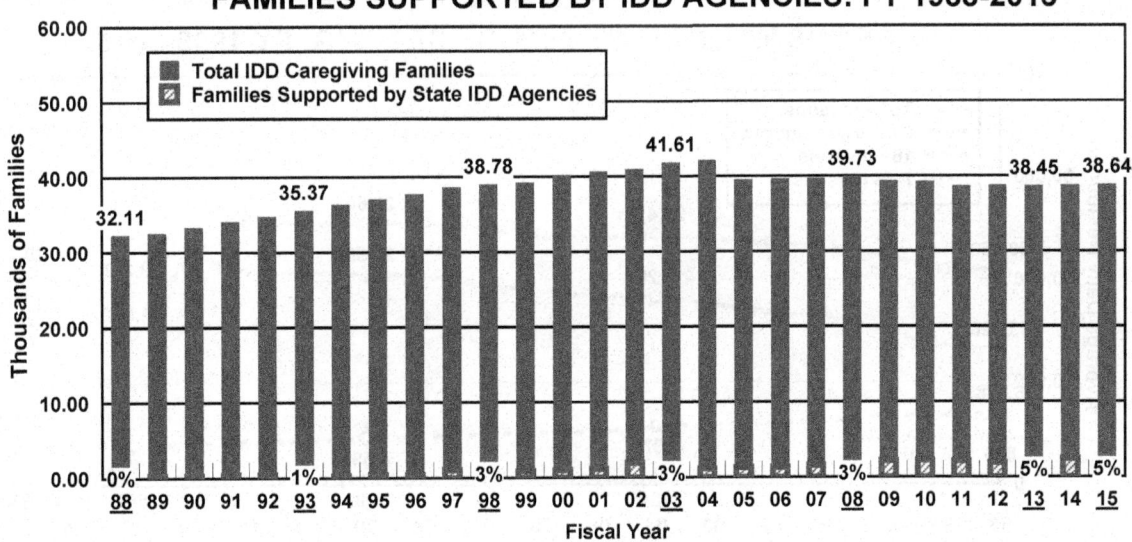

Source: Braddock et al., Coleman Institute and Department of Psychiatry, University of Colorado, 2017.
http://stateofthestates.org

PENNSYLVANIA

TOTAL PUBLIC IDD SPENDING FOR SERVICES: FY 1977-2015

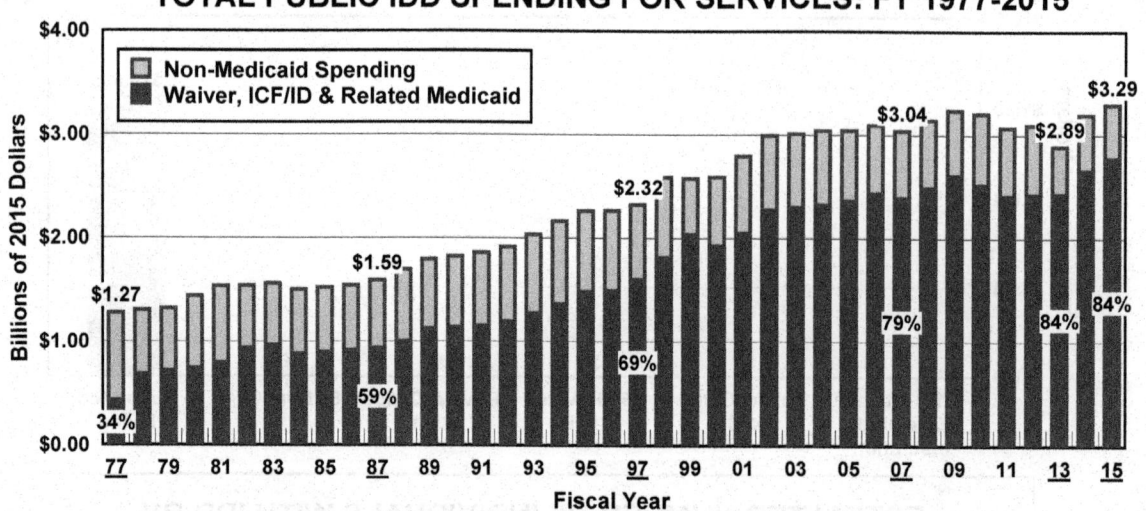

FISCAL EFFORT FOR IDD SERVICES: FY 1977-2015

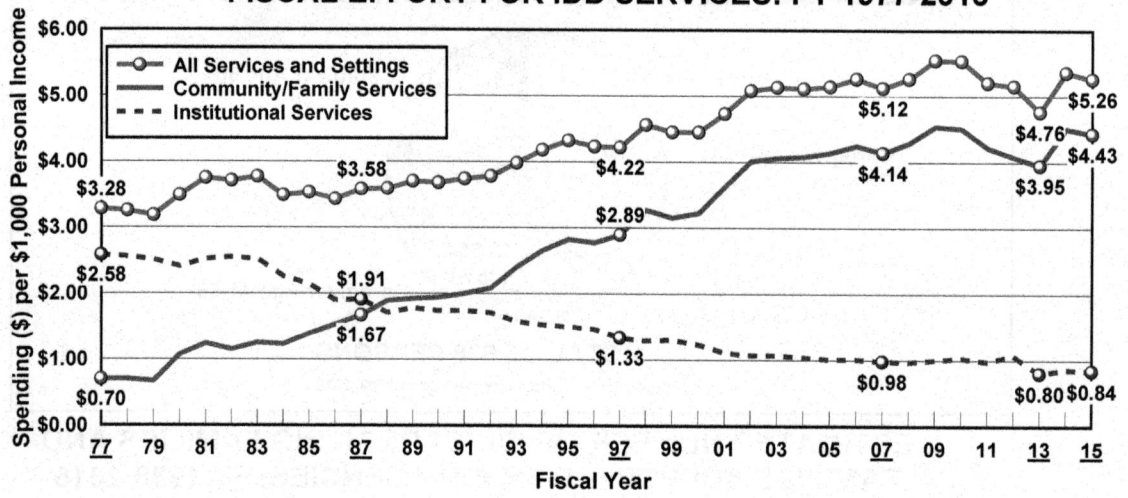

PERSONS WITH IDD BY SIZE OF SETTING: FY 1998-2015

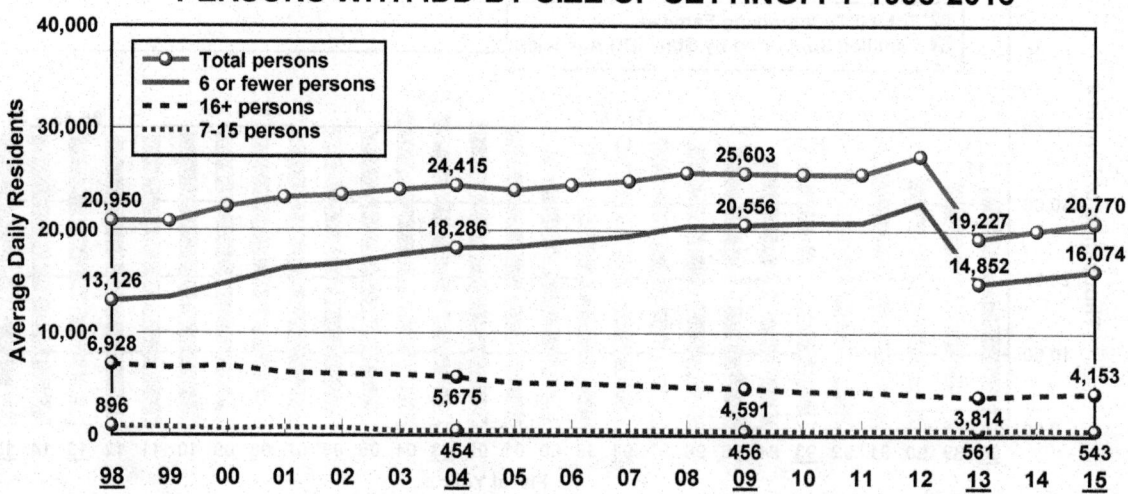

Source: Braddock et al., Coleman Institute and Department of Psychiatry, University of Colorado, 2017.
http://stateofthestates.org

PENNSYLVANIA

FEDERAL IDD MEDICAID SPENDING BY REVENUE SOURCE

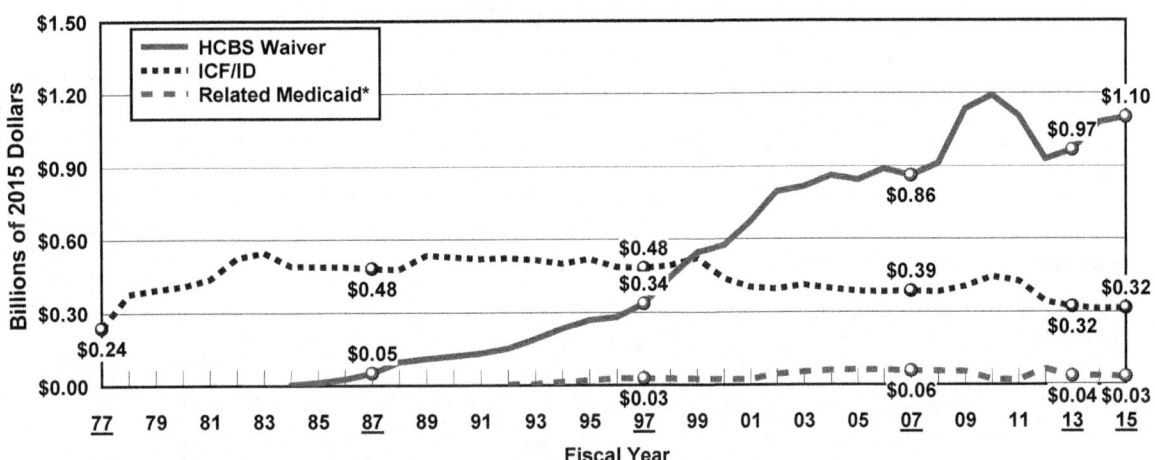

*In 2015, "Related Medicaid" was targeted case management ($9.4 million) and administration ($24.7 million).

FEDERAL-STATE MEDICAID AS A PERCENTAGE OF TOTAL IDD SPENDING IN FY 2015

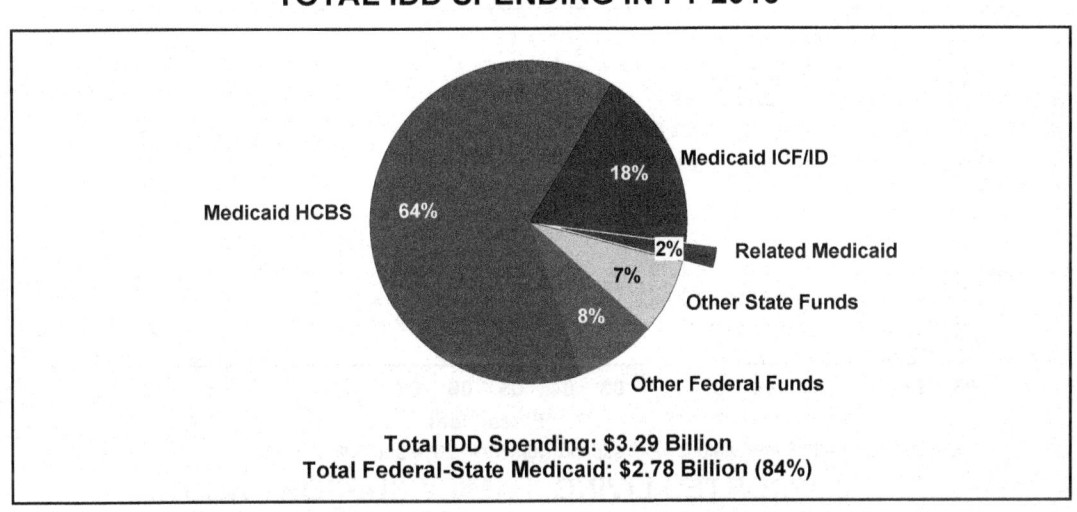

Total IDD Spending: $3.29 Billion
Total Federal-State Medicaid: $2.78 Billion (84%)

HCBS WAIVER PARTICIPANTS / WAIVER COST PER PARTICIPANT

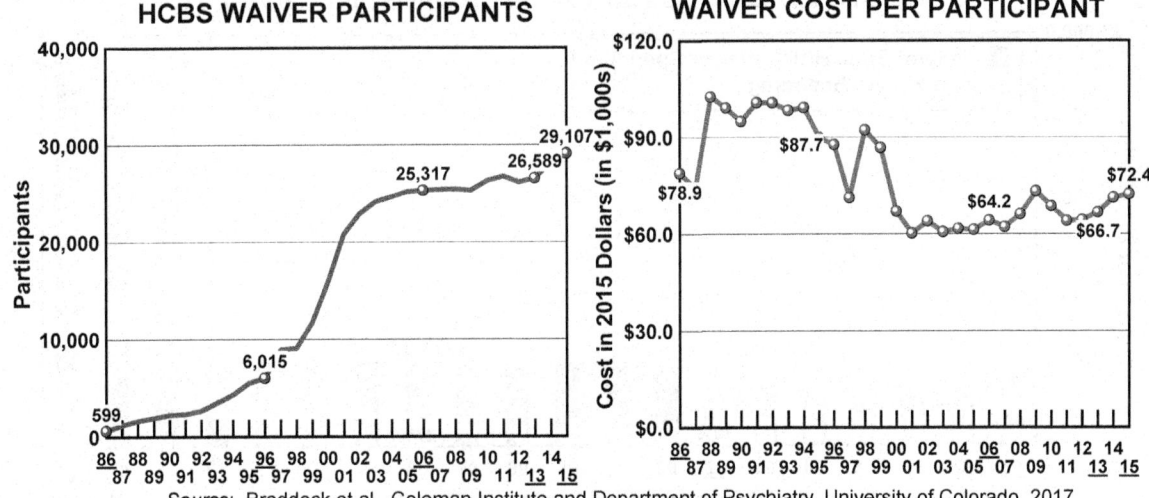

Source: Braddock et al., Coleman Institute and Department of Psychiatry, University of Colorado, 2017.
http://stateofthestates.org

PENNSYLVANIA
INDIVIDUAL AND FAMILY SUPPORT
SPENDING: FY 1996-2015

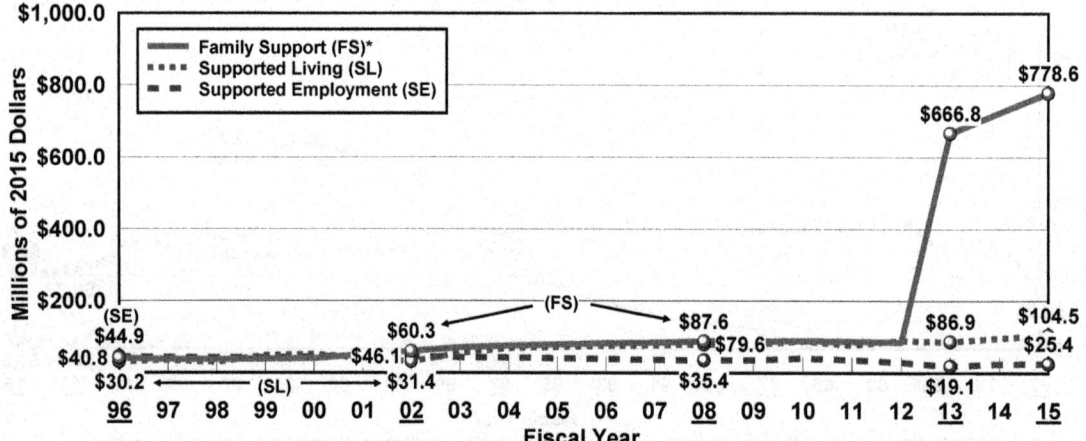

*Large growth in family support spending (2013-2015) reflects waiver funding for adults in the family home.

PARTICIPANTS: FY 1996-2015

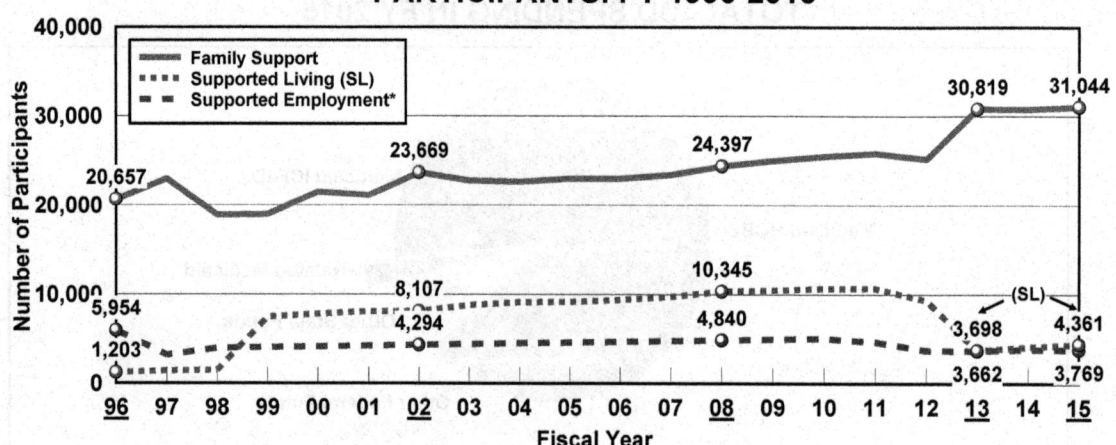

*Does not include 628 follow-along work support workers in 2014 and 538 in 2015.

SUPPORTED LIVING, FAMILY SUPPORT AND SUPPORTED EMPLOYMENT SPENDING: FY 1996-2015

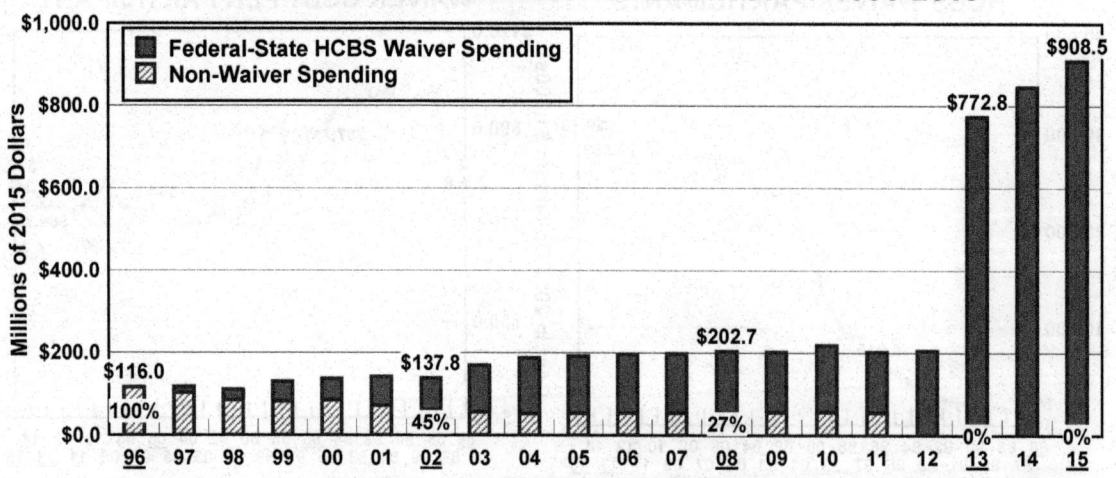

Source: Braddock et al., Coleman Institute and Department of Psychiatry, University of Colorado, 2017.
http://stateofthestates.org

PENNSYLVANIA

ANNUAL COST OF CARE BY RESIDENTIAL SETTING: FY 2015

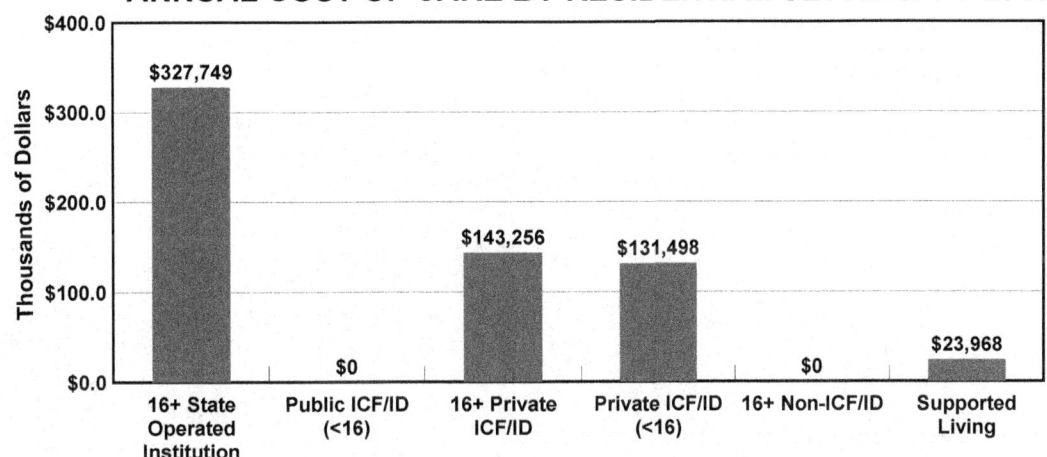

ESTIMATED NUMBER OF INDIVIDUALS WITH IDD BY AGE GROUP LIVING WITH FAMILY CAREGIVERS: FY 2015

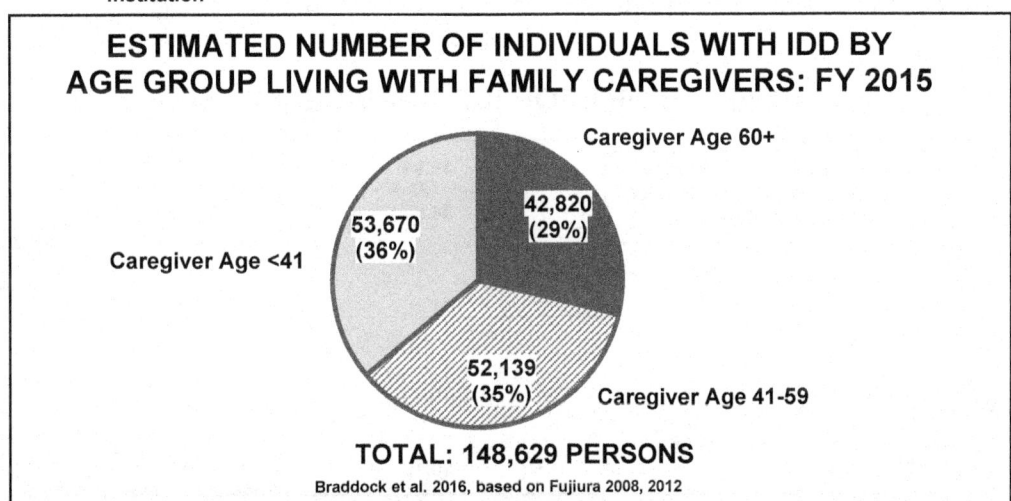

TOTAL: 148,629 PERSONS

Braddock et al. 2016, based on Fujiura 2008, 2012

ESTIMATED NUMBER OF IDD CAREGIVING FAMILIES AND FAMILIES SUPPORTED BY IDD AGENCIES: FY 1988-2015

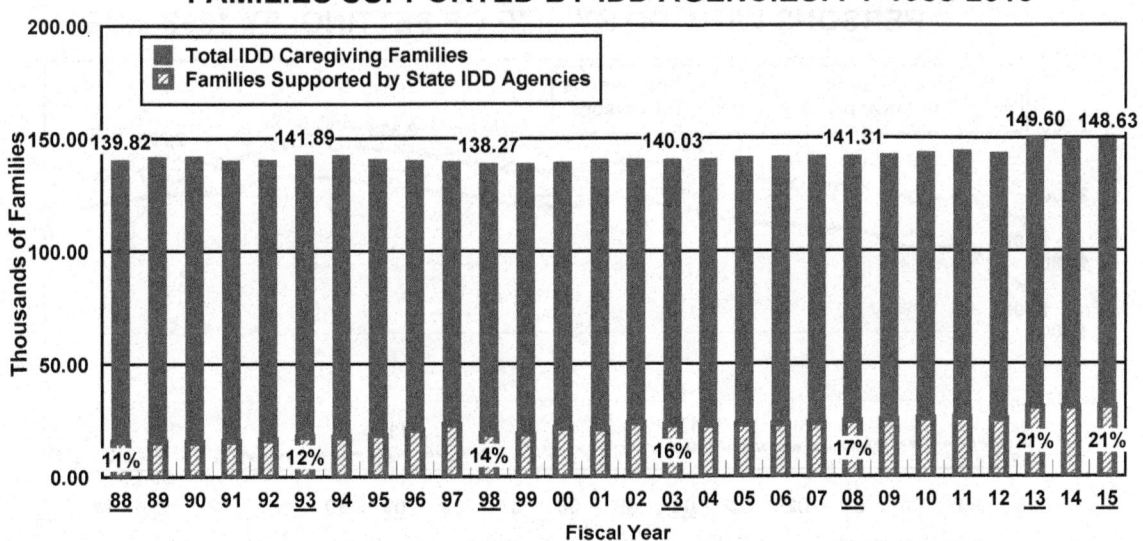

Source: Braddock et al., Coleman Institute and Department of Psychiatry, University of Colorado, 2017.
http://stateofthestates.org

RHODE ISLAND

TOTAL PUBLIC IDD SPENDING FOR SERVICES: FY 1977-2015

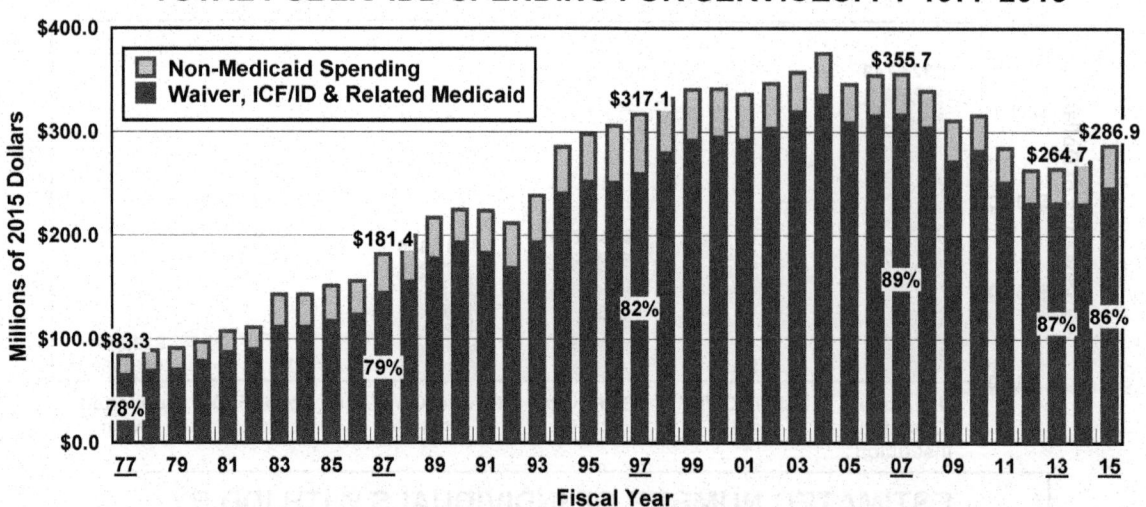

FISCAL EFFORT FOR IDD SERVICES: FY 1977-2015

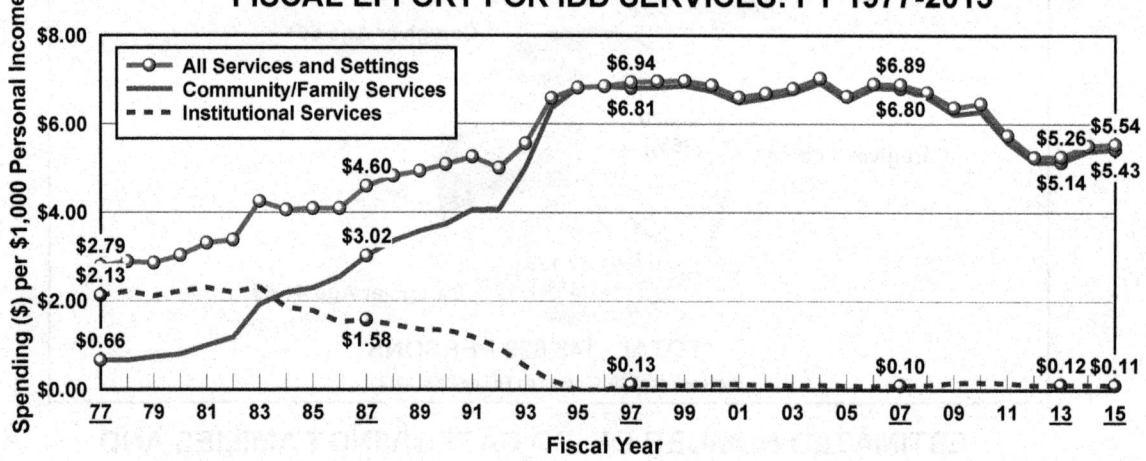

PERSONS WITH IDD BY SIZE OF SETTING: FY 1998-2015

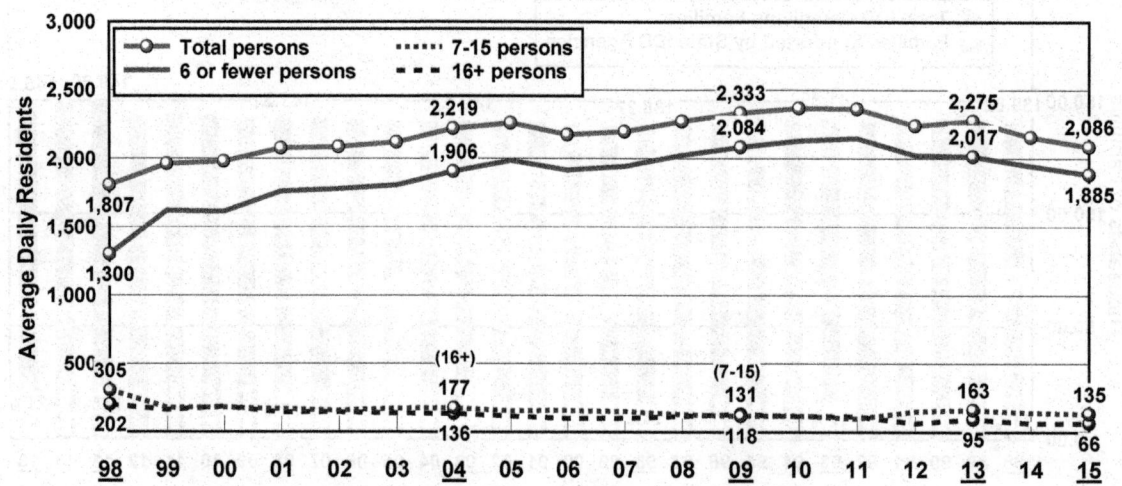

Source: Braddock et al., Coleman Institute and Department of Psychiatry, University of Colorado, 2017.
http://stateofthestates.org

RHODE ISLAND

FEDERAL IDD MEDICAID SPENDING BY REVENUE SOURCE

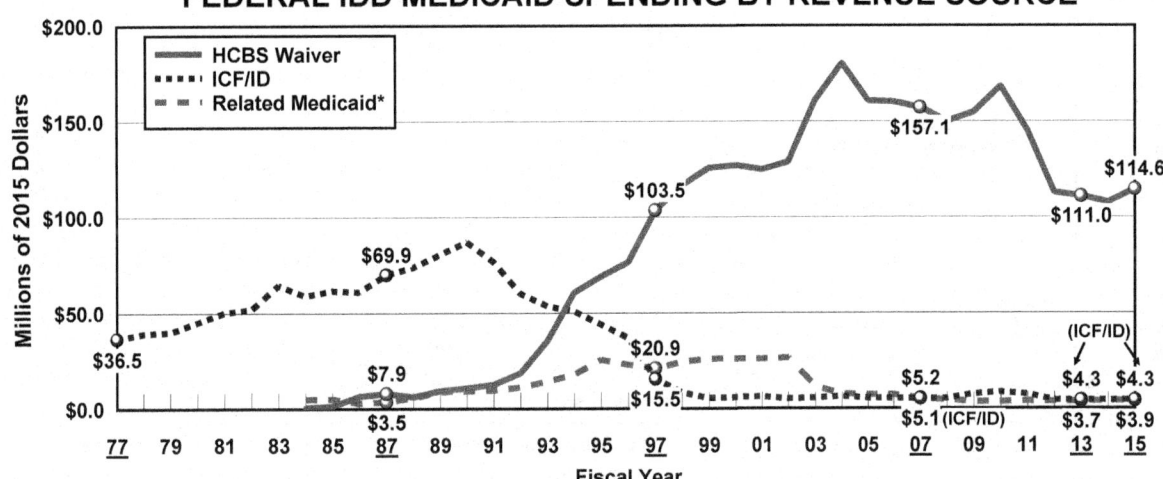

*In 2015, "Related Medicaid" was clinic rehabilitation ($0.4 million) and administration ($3.5 million).

FEDERAL-STATE MEDICAID AS A PERCENTAGE OF TOTAL IDD SPENDING IN FY 2015

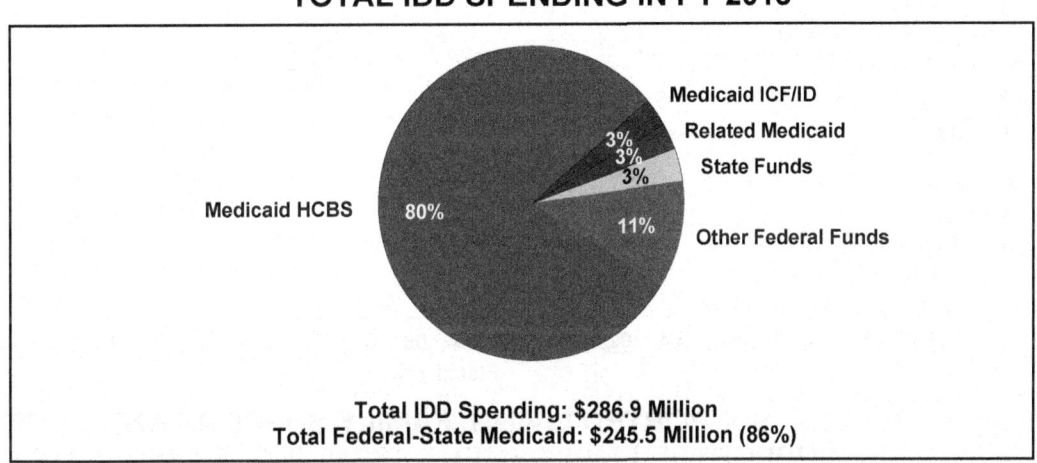

Total IDD Spending: $286.9 Million
Total Federal-State Medicaid: $245.5 Million (86%)

HCBS WAIVER PARTICIPANTS / WAIVER COST PER PARTICIPANT

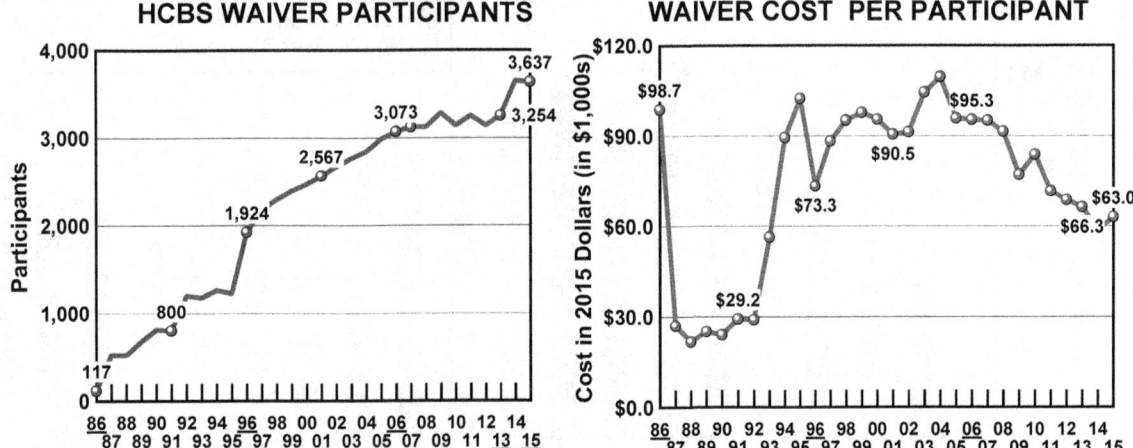

Source: Braddock et al., Coleman Institute and Department of Psychiatry, University of Colorado, 2017.
http://stateofthestates.org

RHODE ISLAND

INDIVIDUAL AND FAMILY SUPPORT
SPENDING: FY 1996-2015

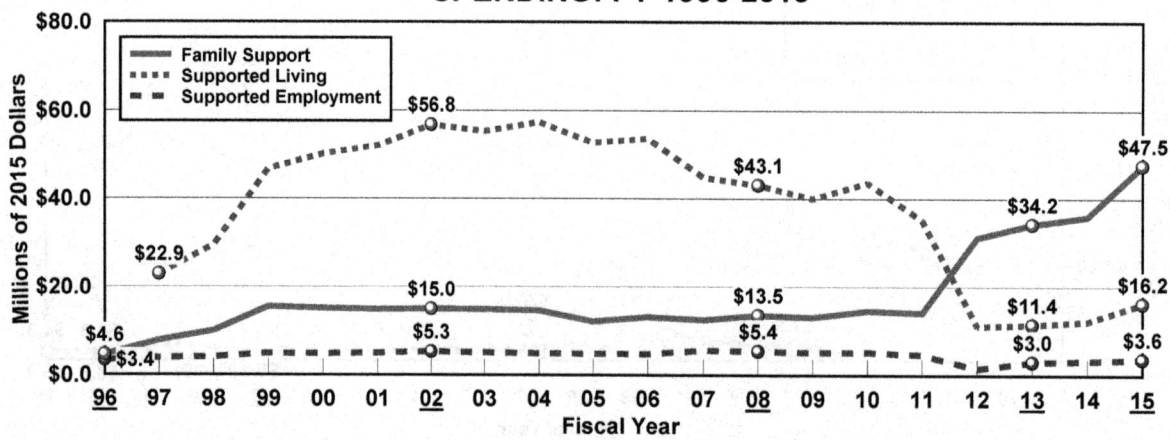

PARTICIPANTS: FY 1996-2015

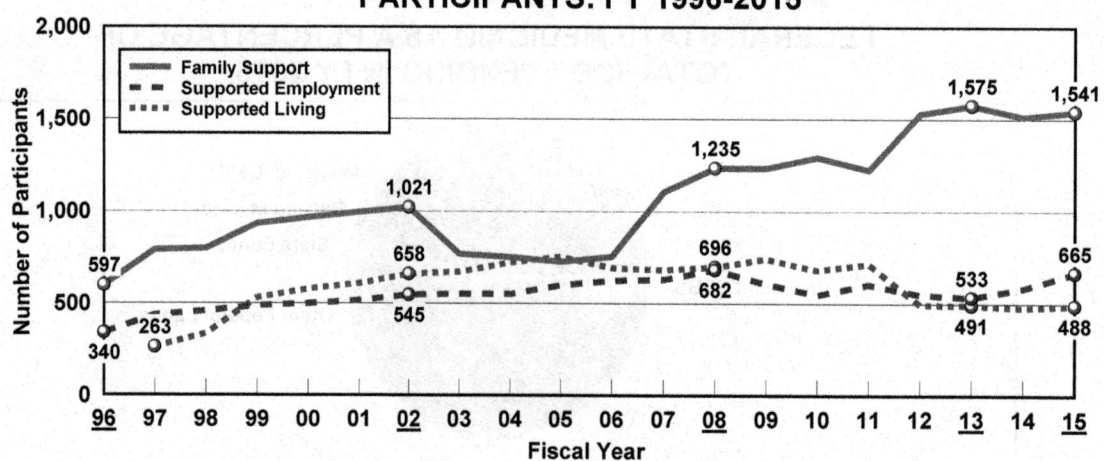

SUPPORTED LIVING, FAMILY SUPPORT AND SUPPORTED EMPLOYMENT SPENDING: FY 1996-2015

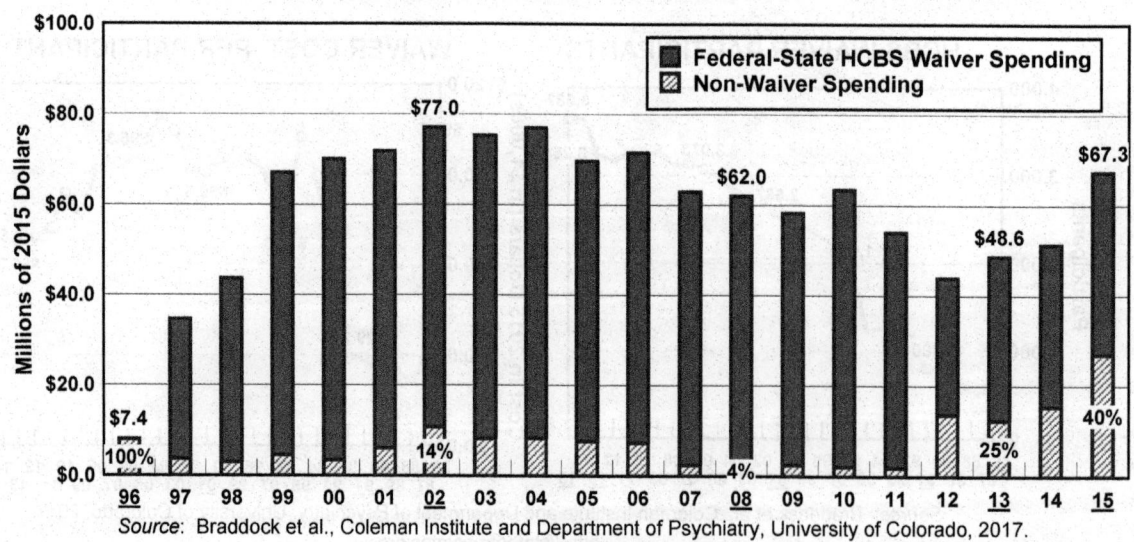

Source: Braddock et al., Coleman Institute and Department of Psychiatry, University of Colorado, 2017.
http://stateofthestates.org

RHODE ISLAND

ANNUAL COST OF CARE BY RESIDENTIAL SETTING: FY 2015

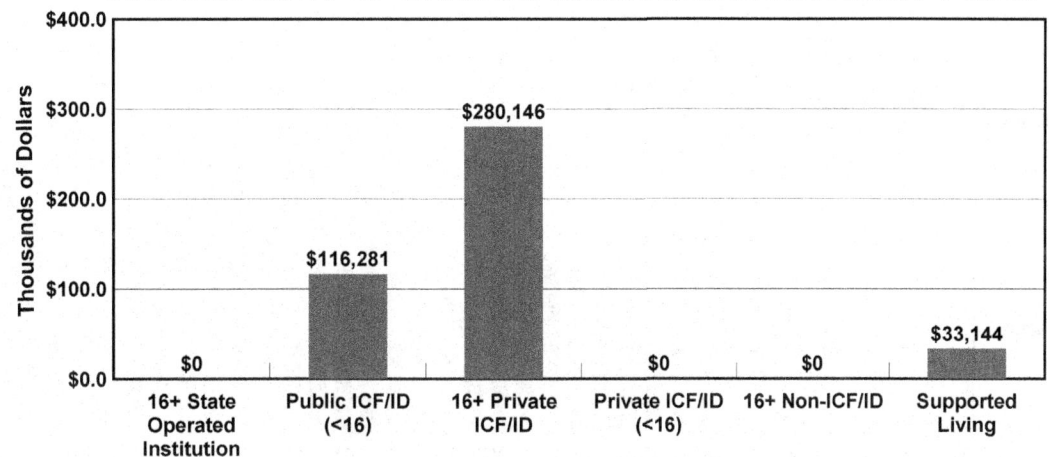

ESTIMATED NUMBER OF INDIVIDUALS WITH IDD BY AGE GROUP LIVING WITH FAMILY CAREGIVERS: FY 2015

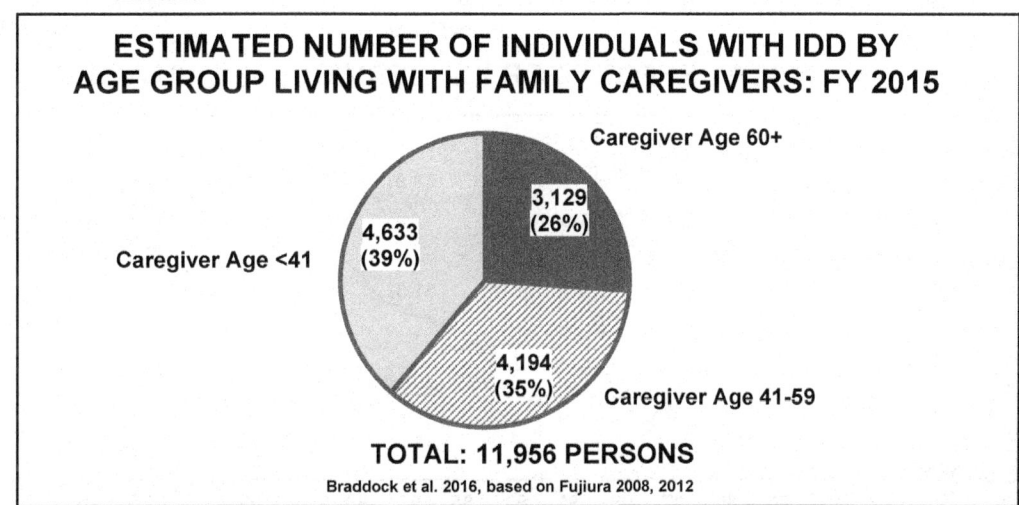

TOTAL: 11,956 PERSONS

Braddock et al. 2016, based on Fujiura 2008, 2012

ESTIMATED NUMBER OF IDD CAREGIVING FAMILIES AND FAMILIES SUPPORTED BY IDD AGENCIES: FY 1988-2015

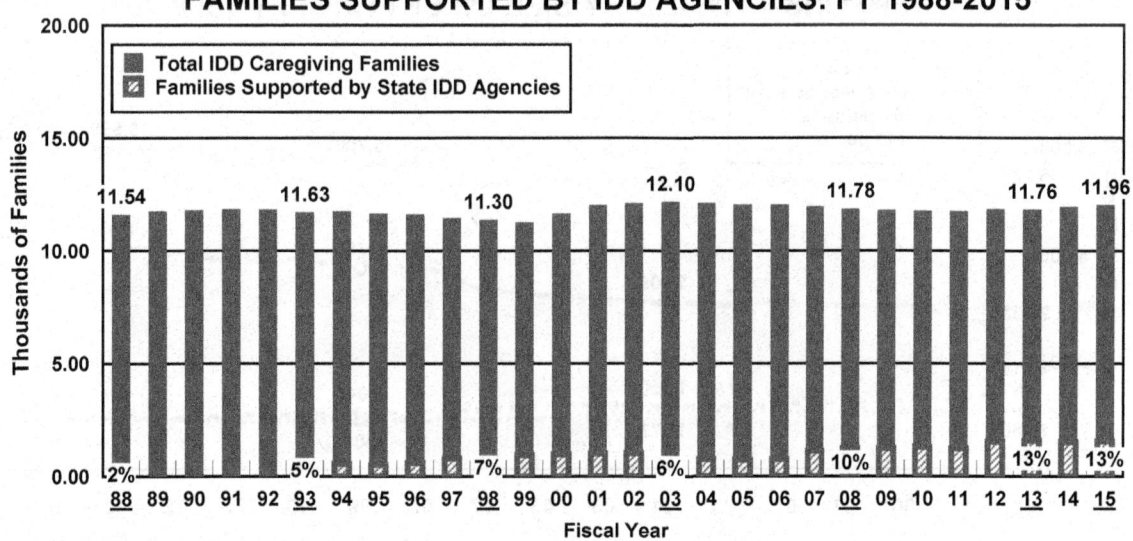

Source: Braddock et al., Coleman Institute and Department of Psychiatry, University of Colorado, 2017.

http://stateofthestates.org

SOUTH CAROLINA

TOTAL PUBLIC IDD SPENDING FOR SERVICES: FY 1977-2015

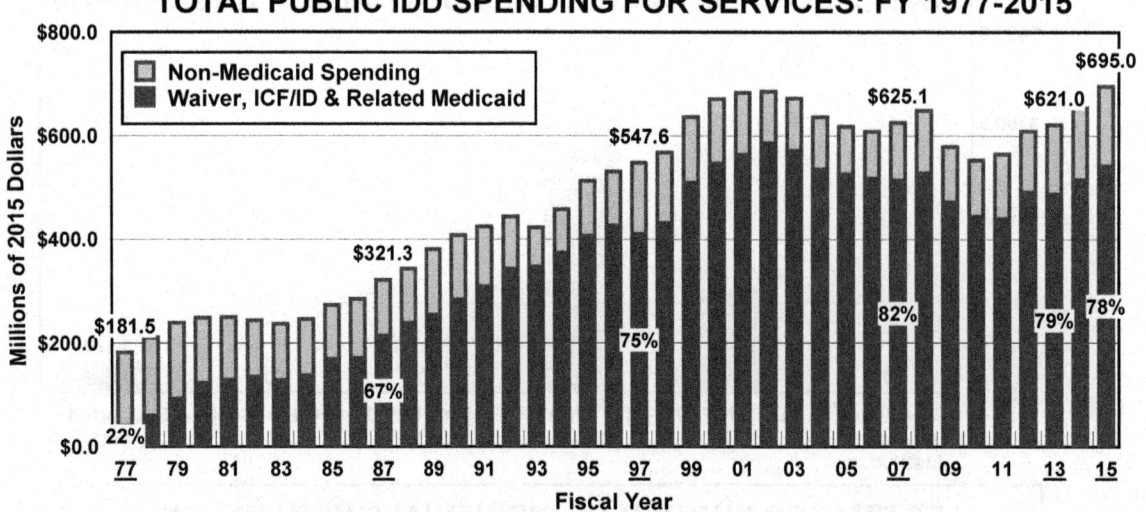

FISCAL EFFORT FOR IDD SERVICES: FY 1977-2015

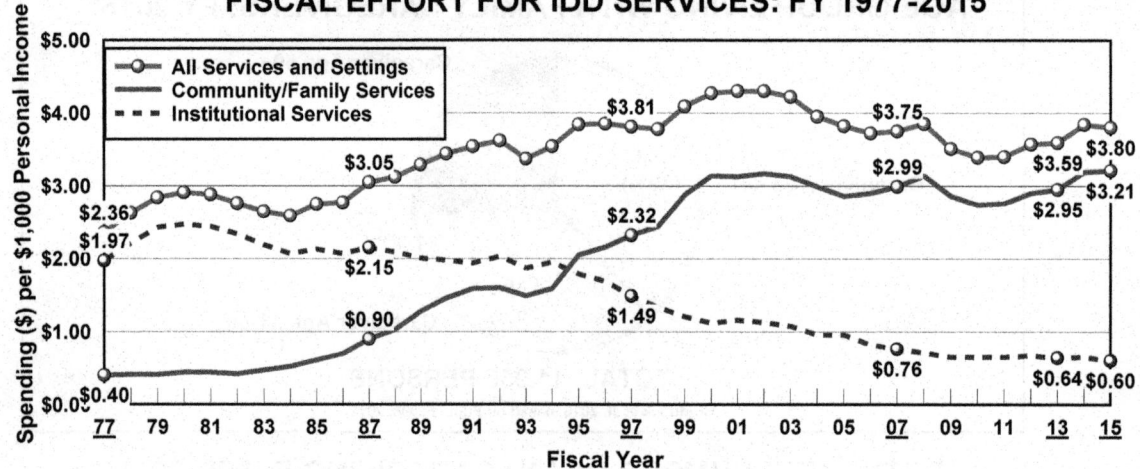

PERSONS WITH IDD BY SIZE OF SETTING: FY 1998-2015

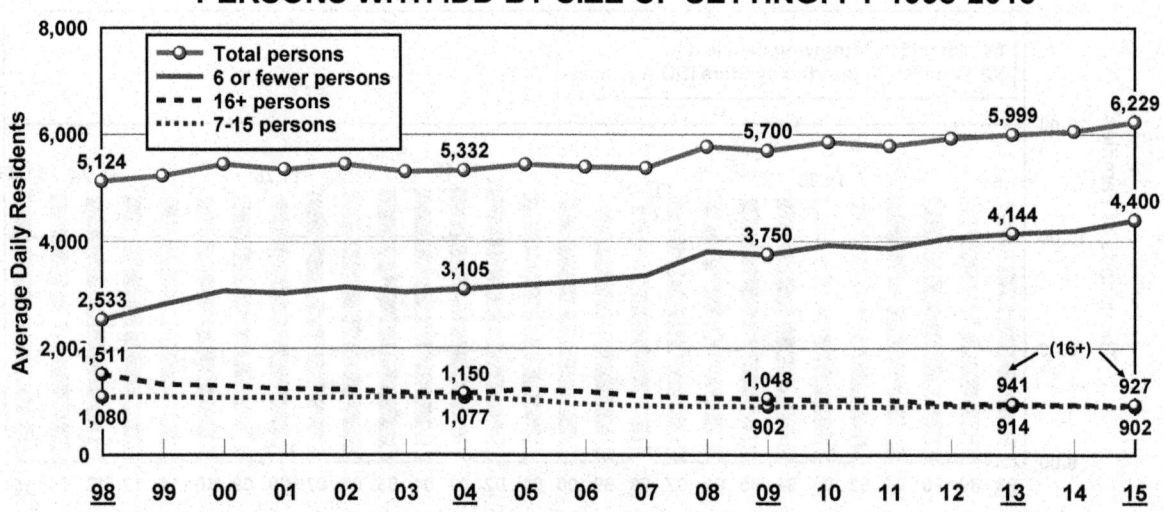

Source: Braddock et al., Coleman Institute and Department of Psychiatry, University of Colorado, 2017.
http://stateofthestates.org

SOUTH CAROLINA

FEDERAL IDD MEDICAID SPENDING BY REVENUE SOURCE

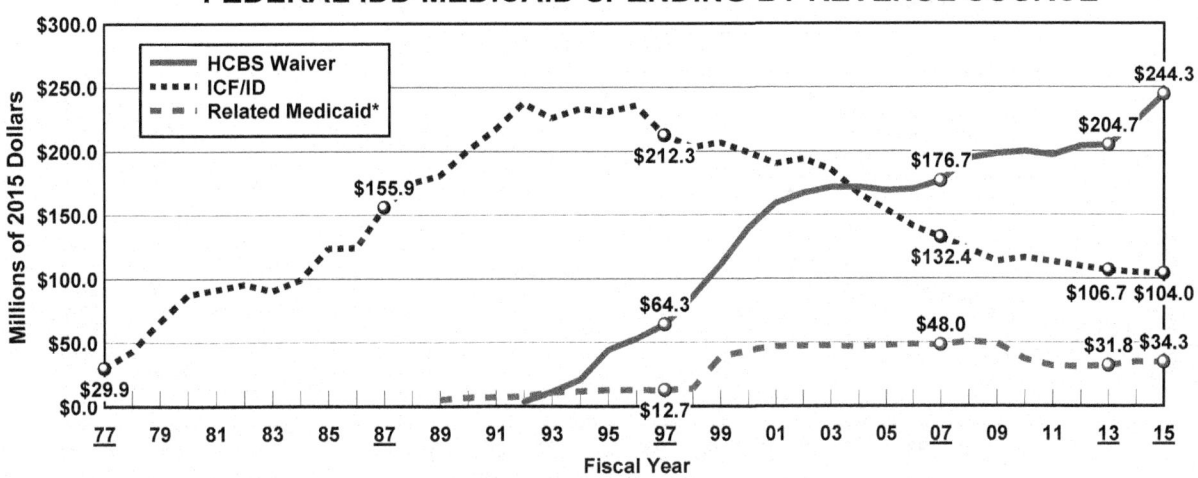

*In 2015, "Related Medicaid" was clinic rehabilitaion ($16.7 million) and targeted case management ($17.5 million).

FEDERAL-STATE MEDICAID AS A PERCENTAGE OF TOTAL IDD SPENDING IN FY 2015

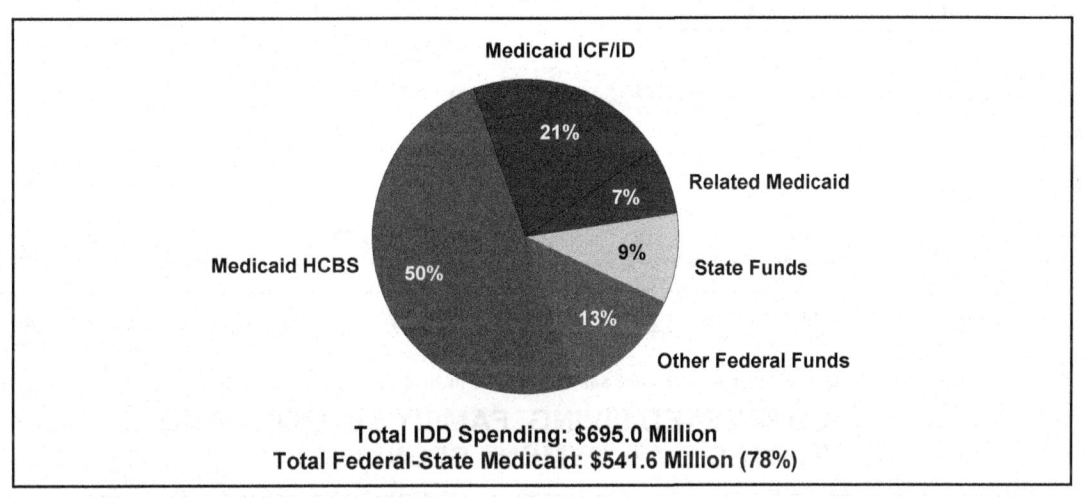

Total IDD Spending: $695.0 Million
Total Federal-State Medicaid: $541.6 Million (78%)

HCBS WAIVER PARTICIPANTS / WAIVER COST PER PARTICIPANT

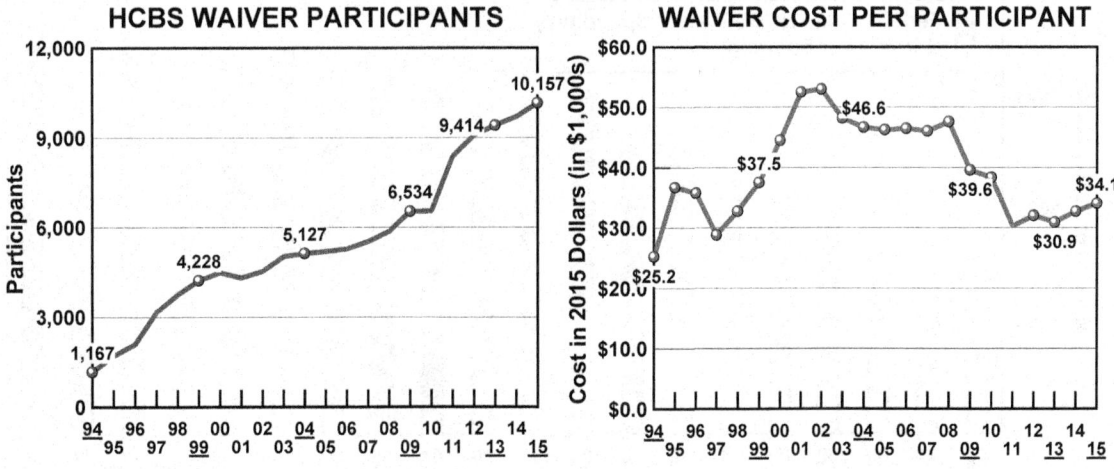

Source: Braddock et al., Coleman Institute and Department of Psychiatry, University of Colorado, 2017.
http://stateofthestates.org

SOUTH CAROLINA
INDIVIDUAL AND FAMILY SUPPORT
SPENDING: FY 1996-2015

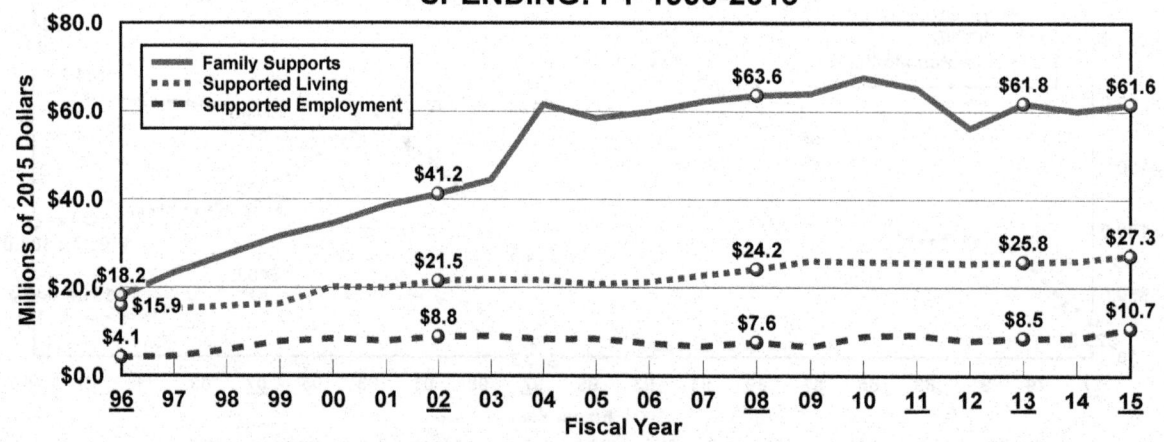

PARTICIPANTS: FY 1996-2015

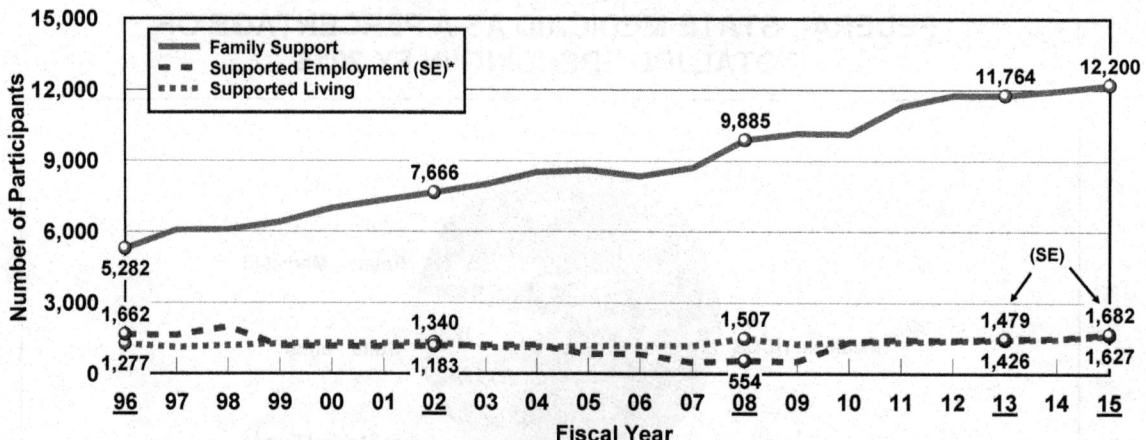

*Does not include 507 follow-along work support workers in 2014 and 629 workers in 2015.

SUPPORTED LIVING, FAMILY SUPPORT AND SUPPORTED EMPLOYMENT SPENDING: FY 1996-2015

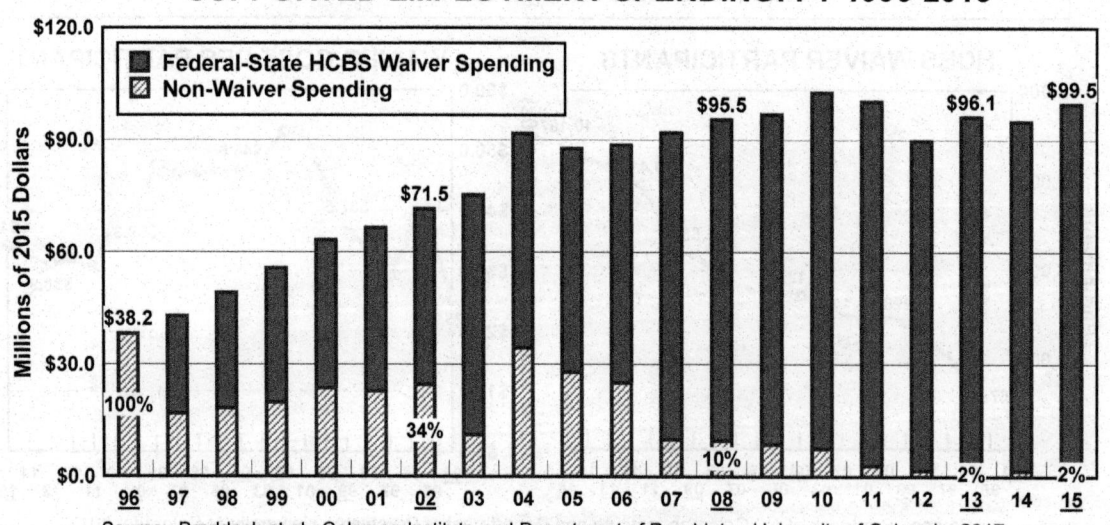

Source: Braddock et al., Coleman Institute and Department of Psychiatry, University of Colorado, 2017.
http://stateofthestates.org

SOUTH CAROLINA

ANNUAL COST OF CARE BY RESIDENTIAL SETTING: FY 2015

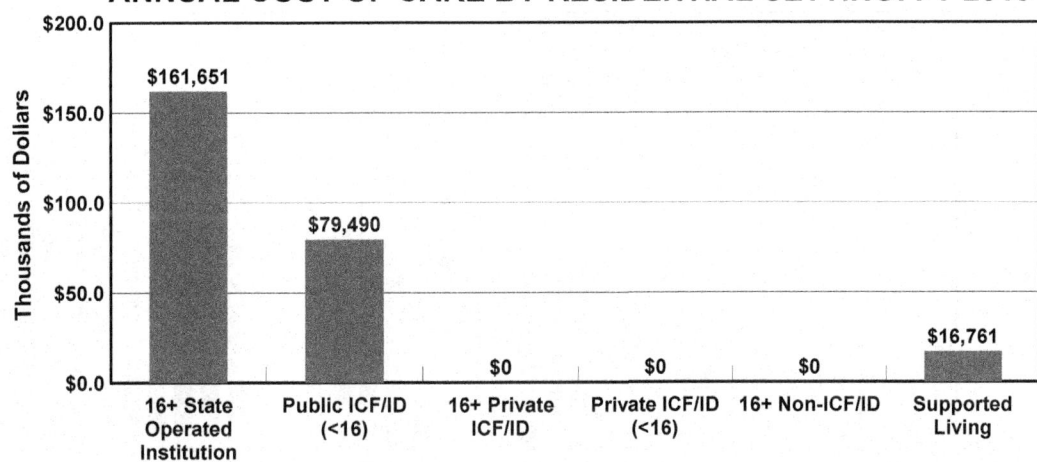

ESTIMATED NUMBER OF INDIVIDUALS WITH IDD BY AGE GROUP LIVING WITH FAMILY CAREGIVERS: FY 2015

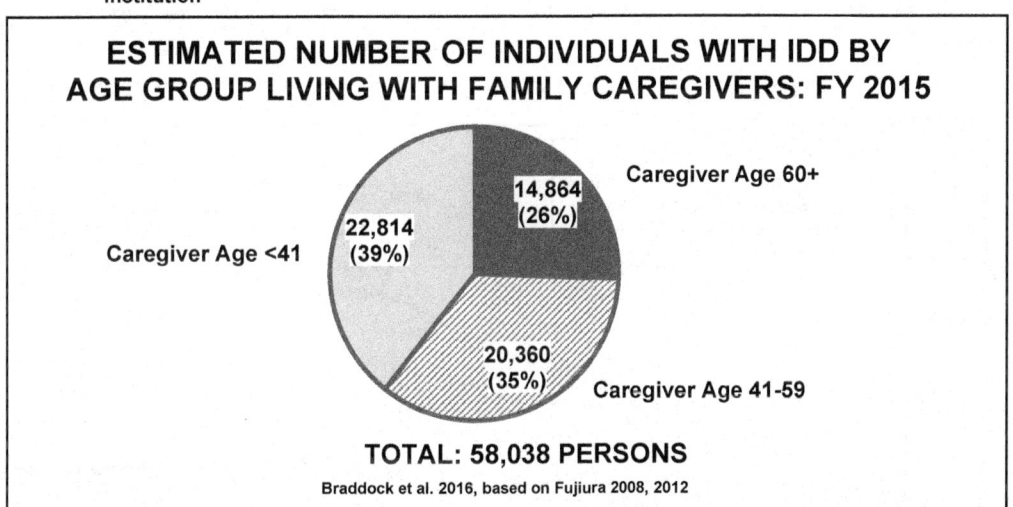

TOTAL: 58,038 PERSONS

Braddock et al. 2016, based on Fujiura 2008, 2012

ESTIMATED NUMBER OF IDD CAREGIVING FAMILIES AND FAMILIES SUPPORTED BY IDD AGENCIES: FY 1988-2015

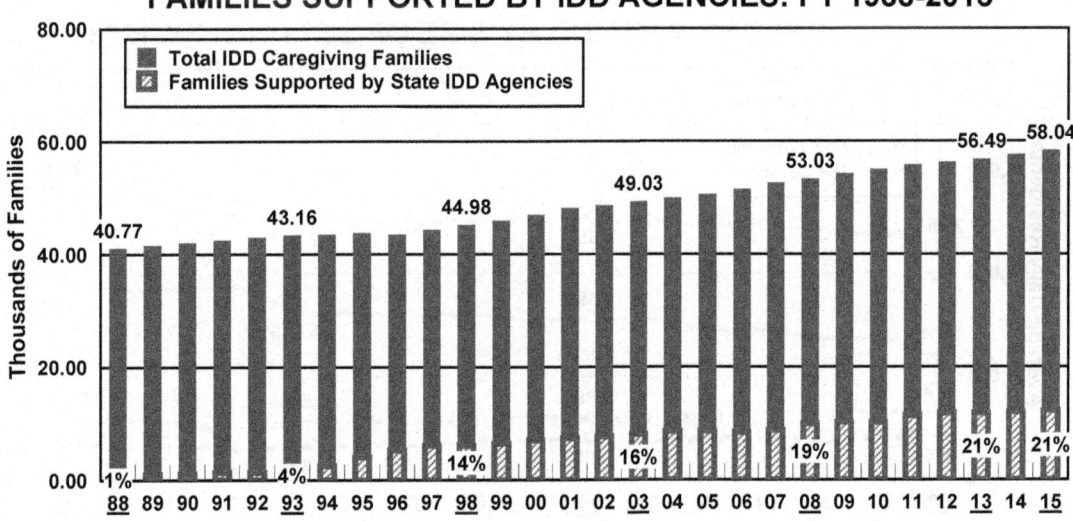

Source: Braddock et al., Coleman Institute and Department of Psychiatry, University of Colorado, 2017.
http://stateofthestates.org

SOUTH DAKOTA

TOTAL PUBLIC IDD SPENDING FOR SERVICES: FY 1977-2015

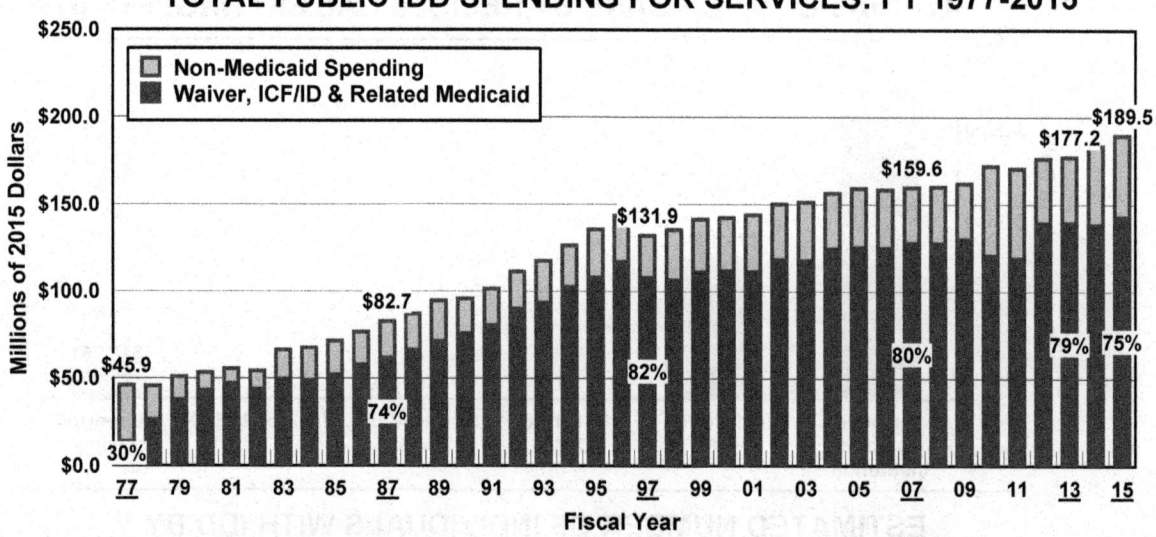

FISCAL EFFORT FOR IDD SERVICES: FY 1977-2015

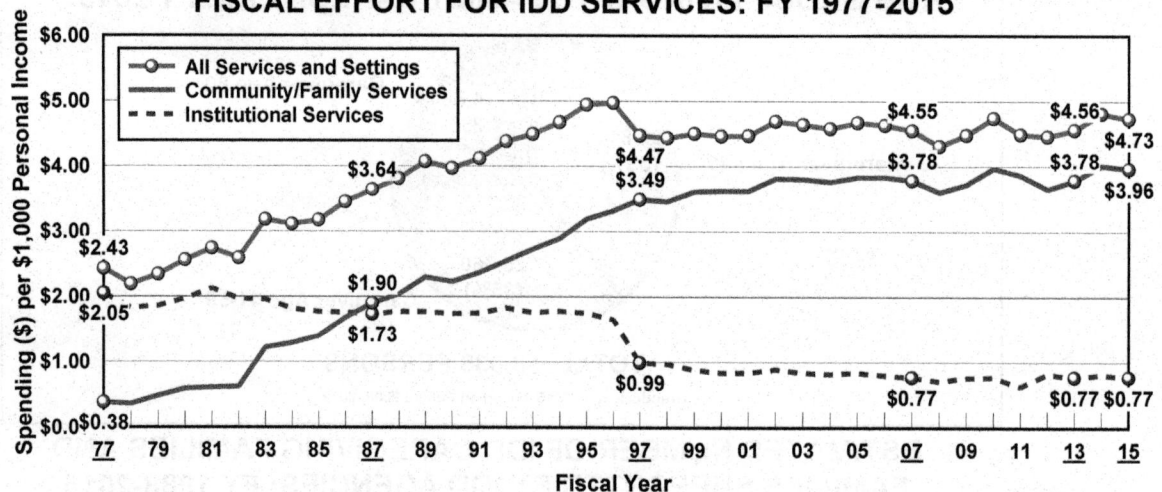

PERSONS WITH IDD BY SIZE OF SETTING: FY 1998-2015

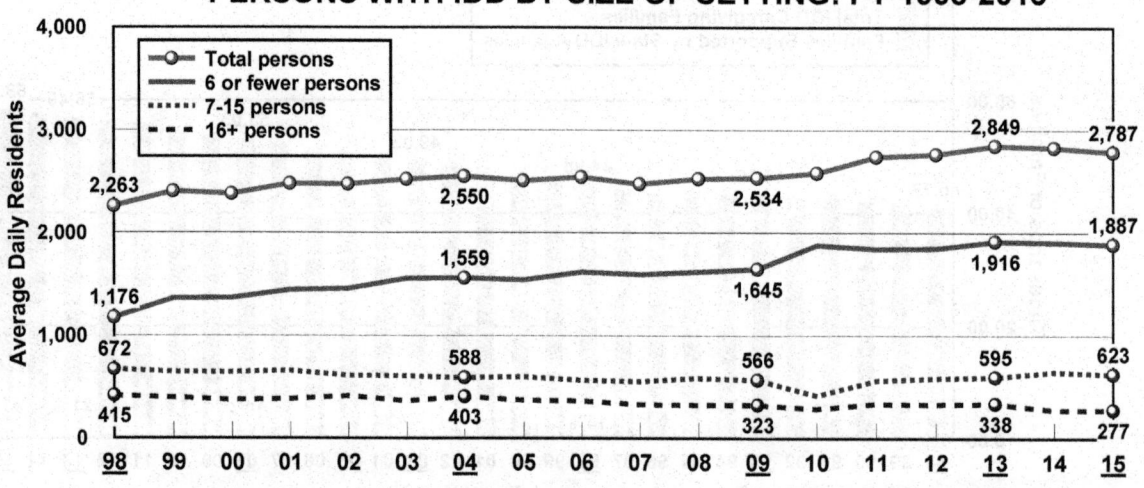

Source: Braddock et al., Coleman Institute and Department of Psychiatry, University of Colorado, 2017.
http://stateofthestates.org

SOUTH DAKOTA

FEDERAL IDD MEDICAID SPENDING BY REVENUE SOURCE

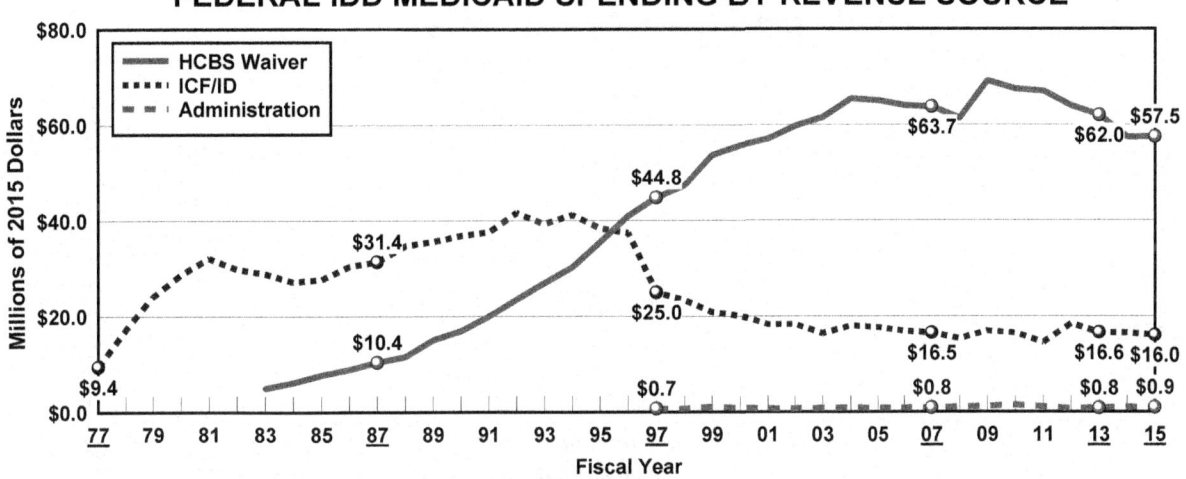

FEDERAL-STATE MEDICAID AS A PERCENTAGE OF TOTAL IDD SPENDING IN FY 2015

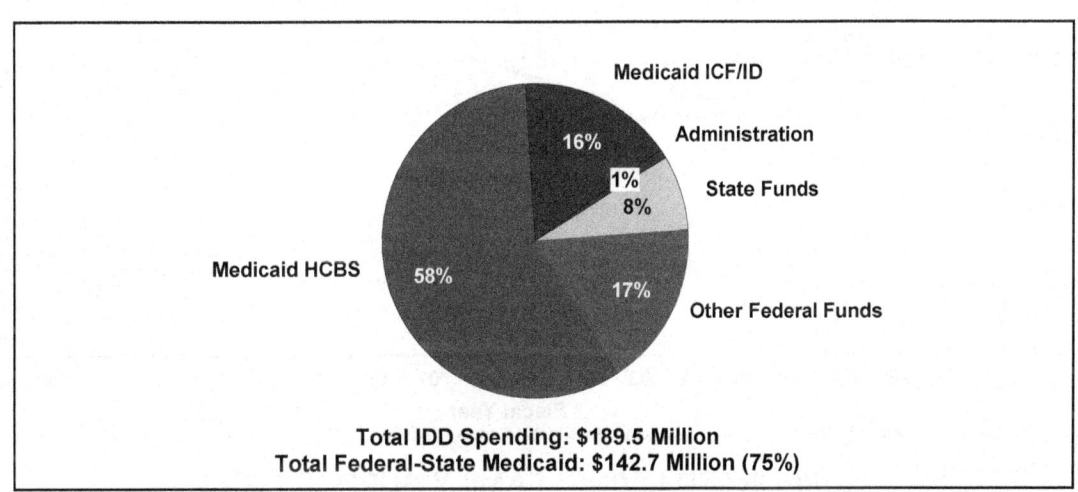

Total IDD Spending: $189.5 Million
Total Federal-State Medicaid: $142.7 Million (75%)

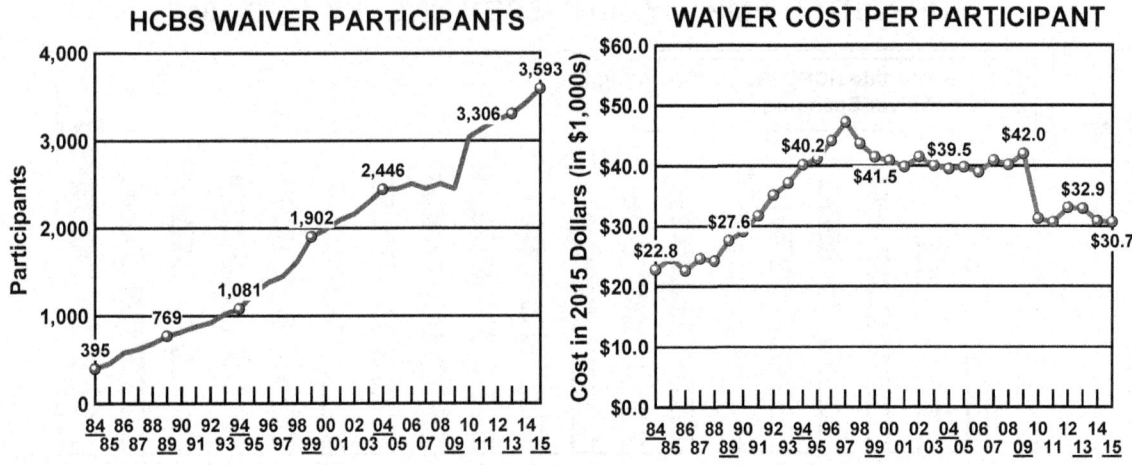

Source: Braddock et al., Coleman Institute and Department of Psychiatry, University of Colorado, 2017.
http://stateofthestates.org

SOUTH DAKOTA
INDIVIDUAL AND FAMILY SUPPORT
SPENDING: FY 1996-2015

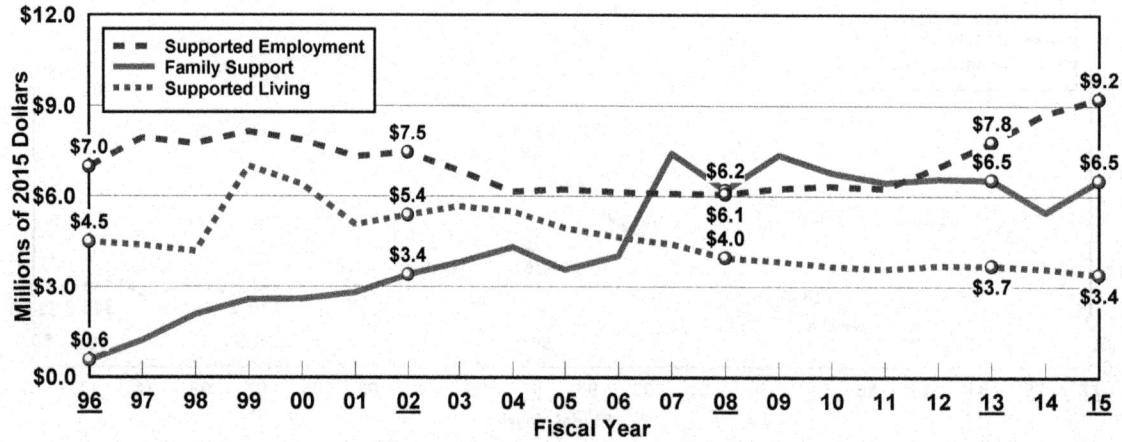

PARTICIPANTS: FY 1996-2015

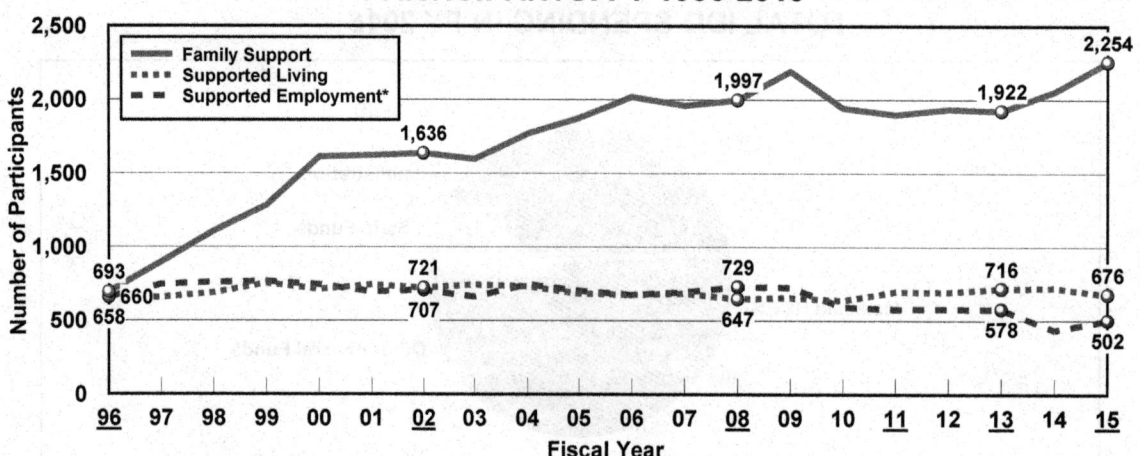

*Does not include 156 follow-along work support workers in 2014 and 147 workers in 2015.

SUPPORTED LIVING, FAMILY SUPPORT AND SUPPORTED EMPLOYMENT SPENDING: FY 1996-2015

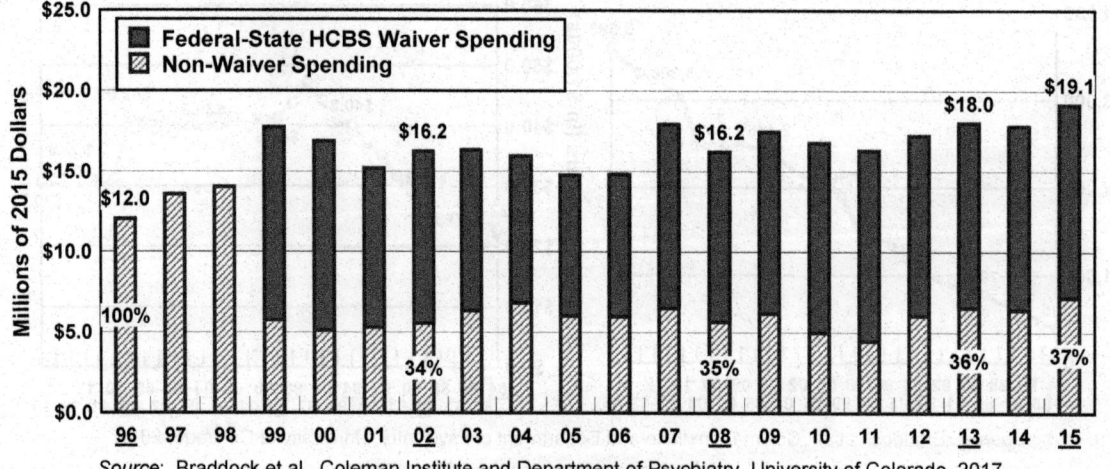

Source: Braddock et al., Coleman Institute and Department of Psychiatry, University of Colorado, 2017.
http://stateofthestates.org

SOUTH DAKOTA

ANNUAL COST OF CARE BY RESIDENTIAL SETTING: FY 2015

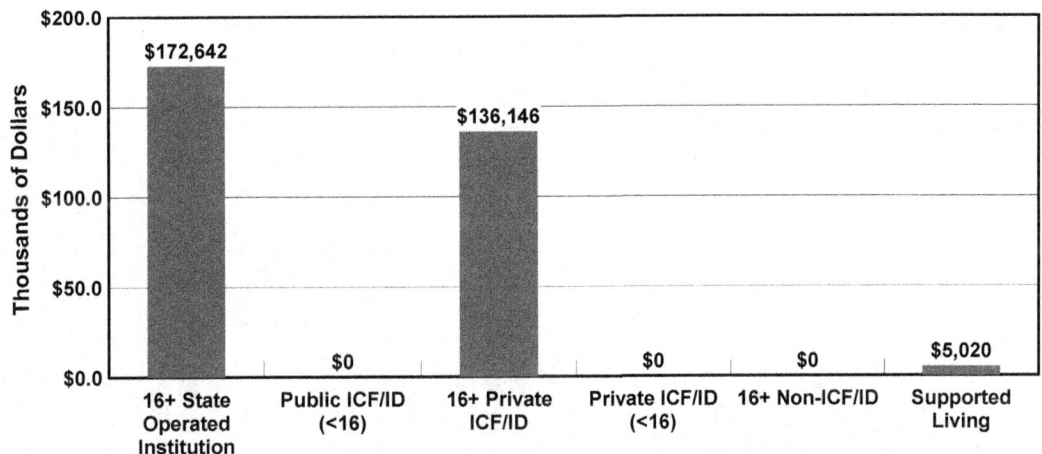

ESTIMATED NUMBER OF INDIVIDUALS WITH IDD BY AGE GROUP LIVING WITH FAMILY CAREGIVERS: FY 2015

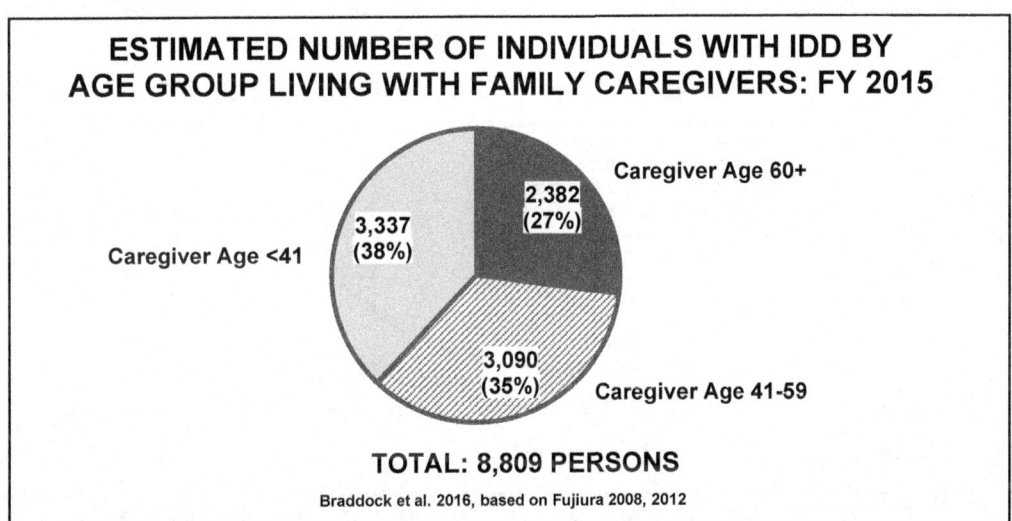

TOTAL: 8,809 PERSONS

Braddock et al. 2016, based on Fujiura 2008, 2012

ESTIMATED NUMBER OF IDD CAREGIVING FAMILIES AND FAMILIES SUPPORTED BY IDD AGENCIES: FY 1988-2015

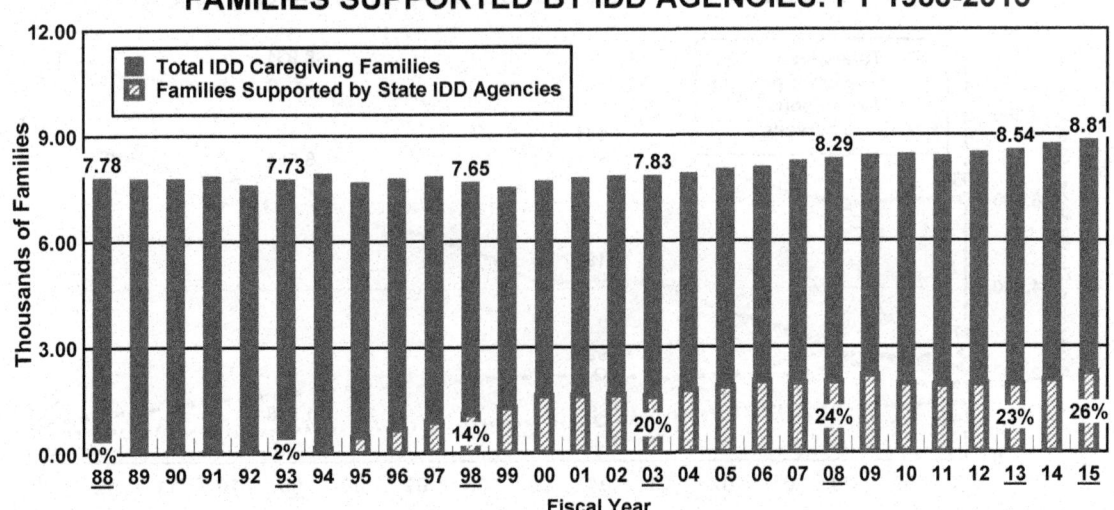

Source: Braddock et al., Coleman Institute and Department of Psychiatry, University of Colorado, 2017.
http://stateofthestates.org

TENNESSEE

TOTAL PUBLIC IDD SPENDING FOR SERVICES: FY 1977-2015

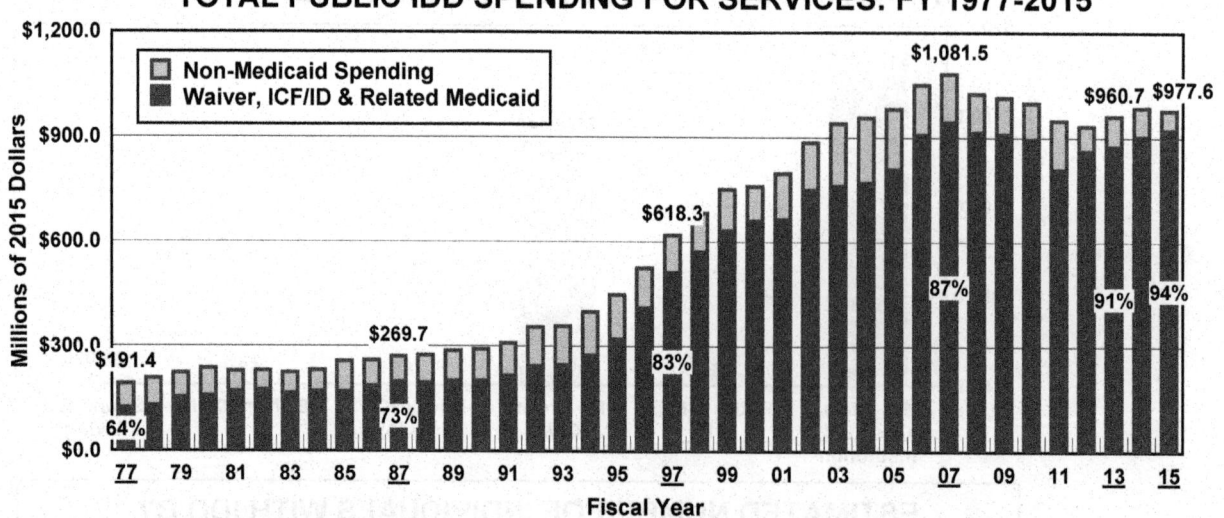

FISCAL EFFORT FOR IDD SERVICES: FY 1977-2015

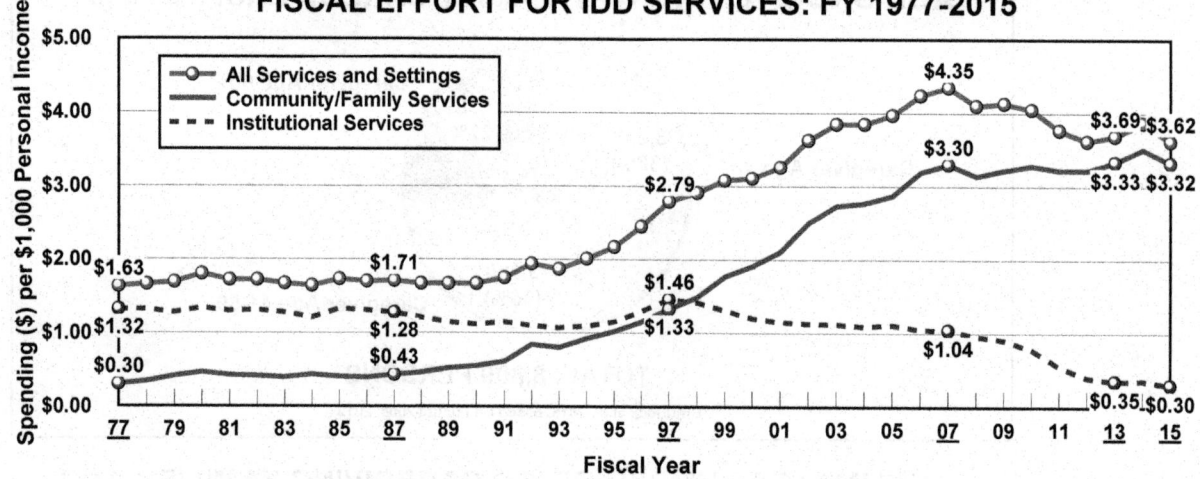

PERSONS WITH IDD BY SIZE OF SETTING: FY 1998-2015

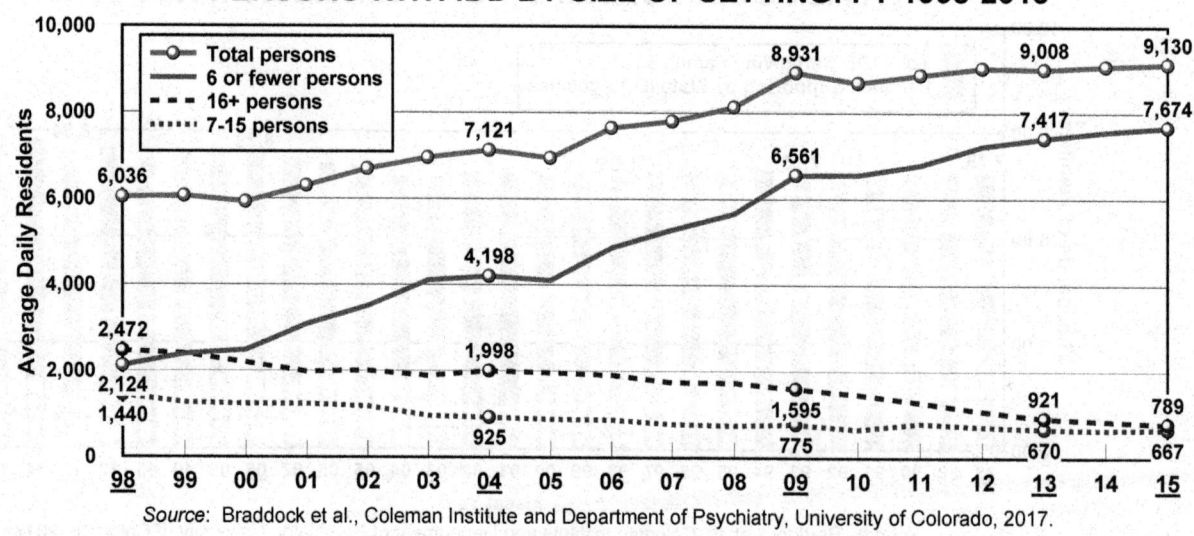

Source: Braddock et al., Coleman Institute and Department of Psychiatry, University of Colorado, 2017.
http://stateofthestates.org

TENNESSEE

FEDERAL IDD MEDICAID SPENDING BY REVENUE SOURCE

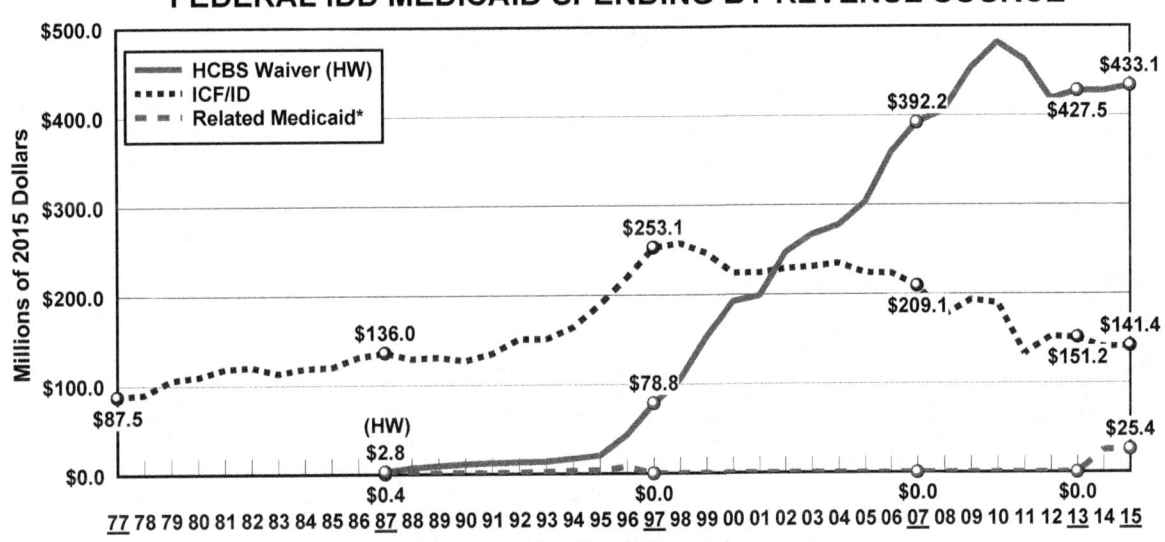

*From 1987 to 1996, "Related Medicaid" was model 50/200 waiver.

FEDERAL-STATE MEDICAID AS A PERCENTAGE OF TOTAL IDD SPENDING IN FY 2015

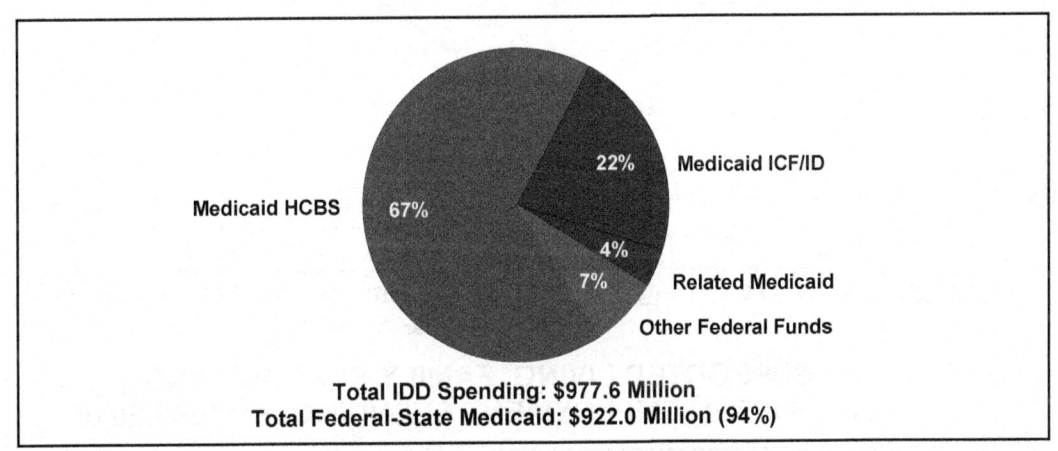

Total IDD Spending: $977.6 Million
Total Federal-State Medicaid: $922.0 Million (94%)

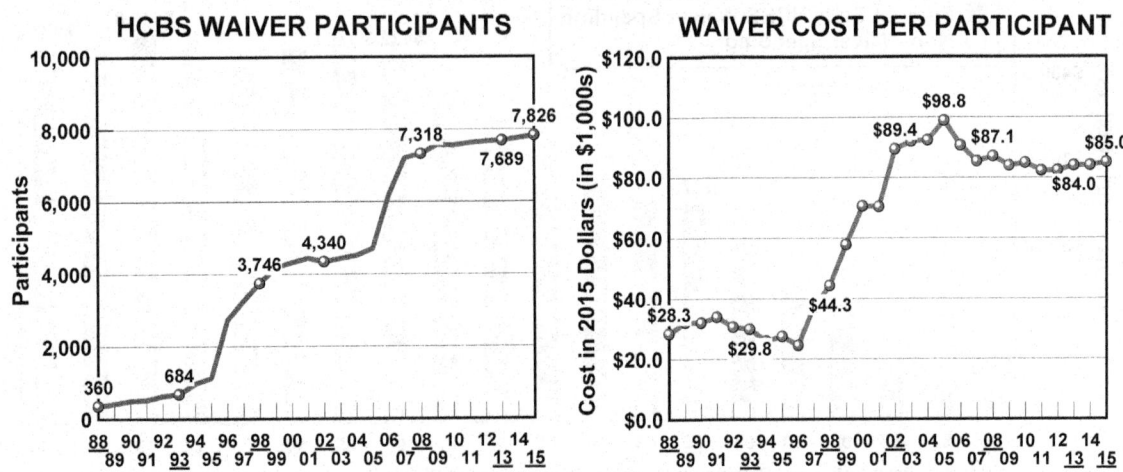

Source: Braddock et al., Coleman Institute and Department of Psychiatry, University of Colorado, 2017.
http://stateofthestates.org

TENNESSEE
INDIVIDUAL AND FAMILY SUPPORT
SPENDING: FY 1996-2015

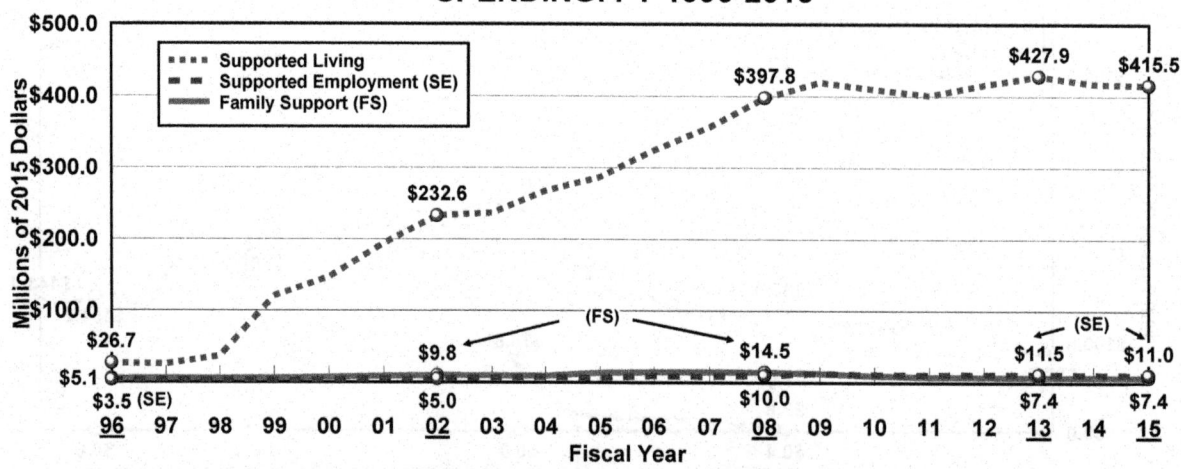

PARTICIPANTS: FY 1996-2015

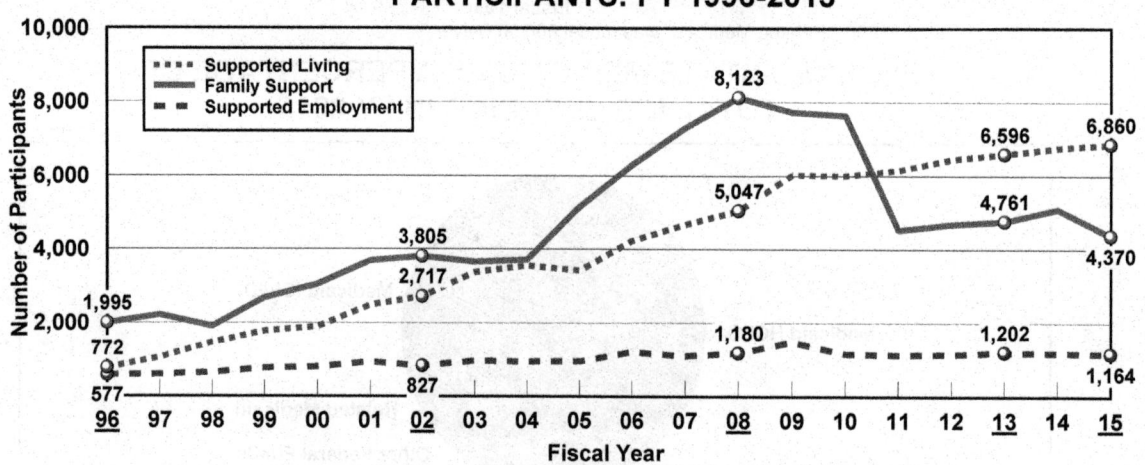

SUPPORTED LIVING, FAMILY SUPPORT AND SUPPORTED EMPLOYMENT SPENDING: FY 1996-2015

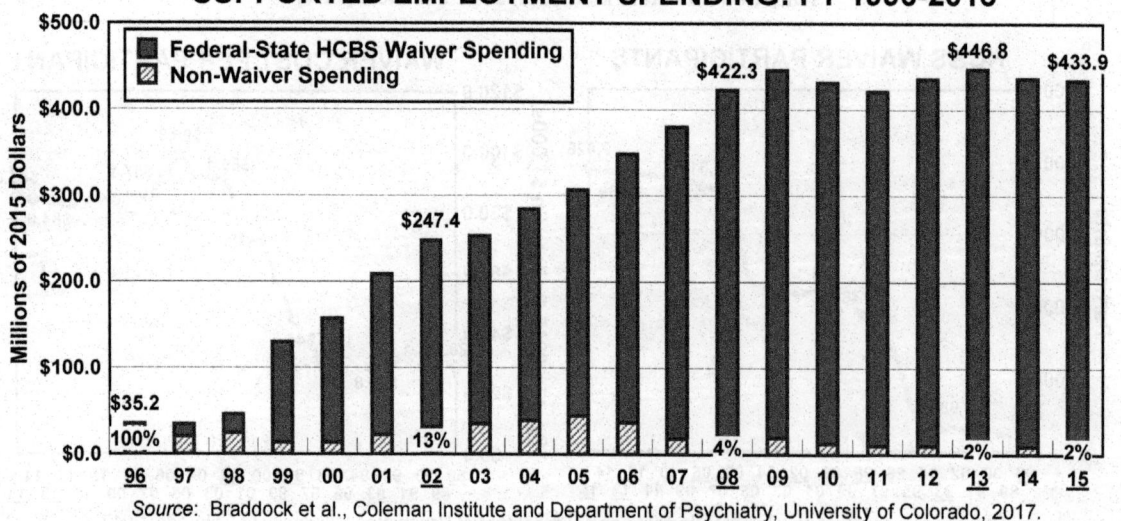

Source: Braddock et al., Coleman Institute and Department of Psychiatry, University of Colorado, 2017.
http://stateofthestates.org

TENNESSEE

ANNUAL COST OF CARE BY RESIDENTIAL SETTING: FY 2015

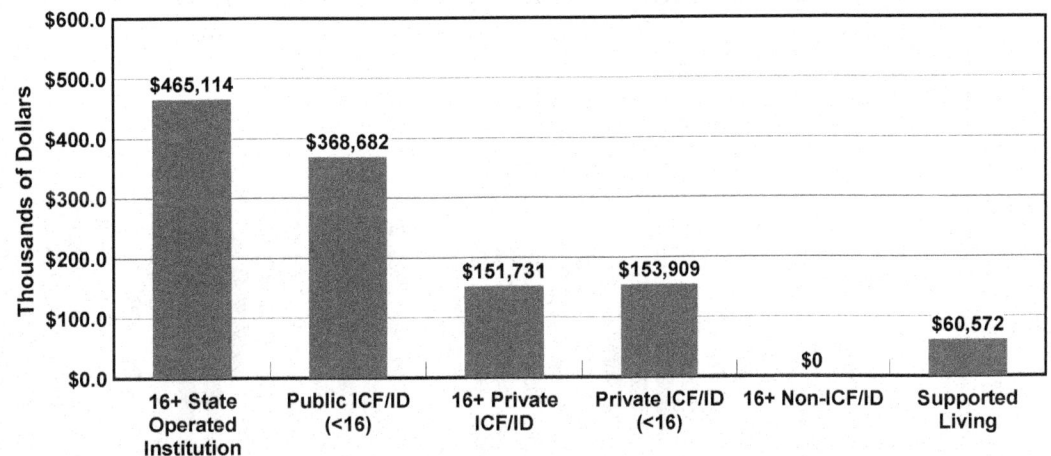

ESTIMATED NUMBER OF INDIVIDUALS WITH IDD BY AGE GROUP LIVING WITH FAMILY CAREGIVERS: FY 2015

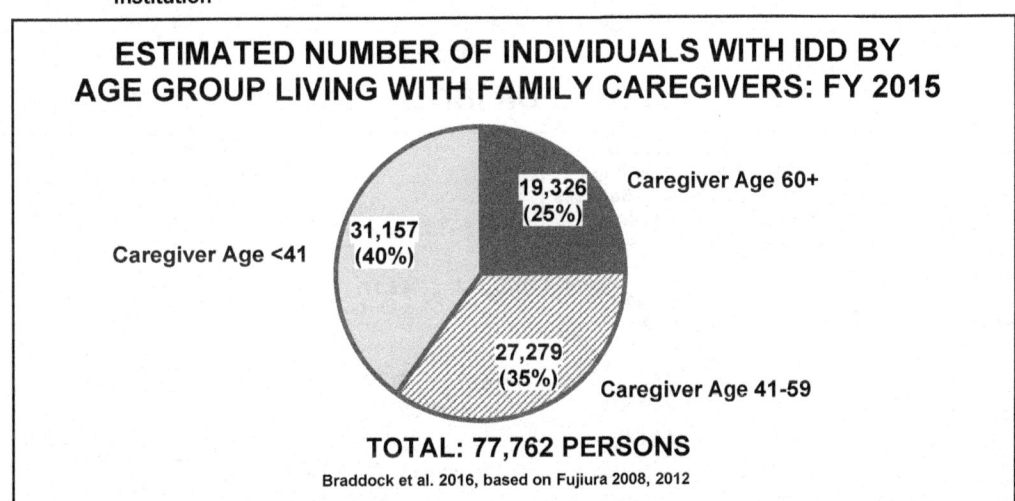

TOTAL: 77,762 PERSONS

Braddock et al. 2016, based on Fujiura 2008, 2012

ESTIMATED NUMBER OF IDD CAREGIVING FAMILIES AND FAMILIES SUPPORTED BY IDD AGENCIES: FY 1988-2015

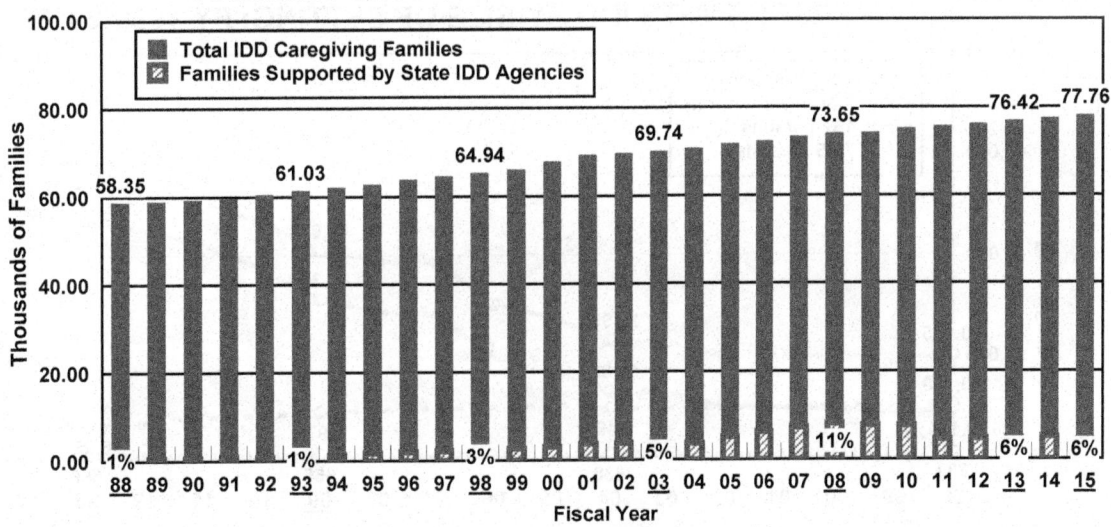

Source: Braddock et al., Coleman Institute and Department of Psychiatry, University of Colorado, 2017.

http://stateofthestates.org

TEXAS

TOTAL PUBLIC IDD SPENDING FOR SERVICES: FY 1977-2015

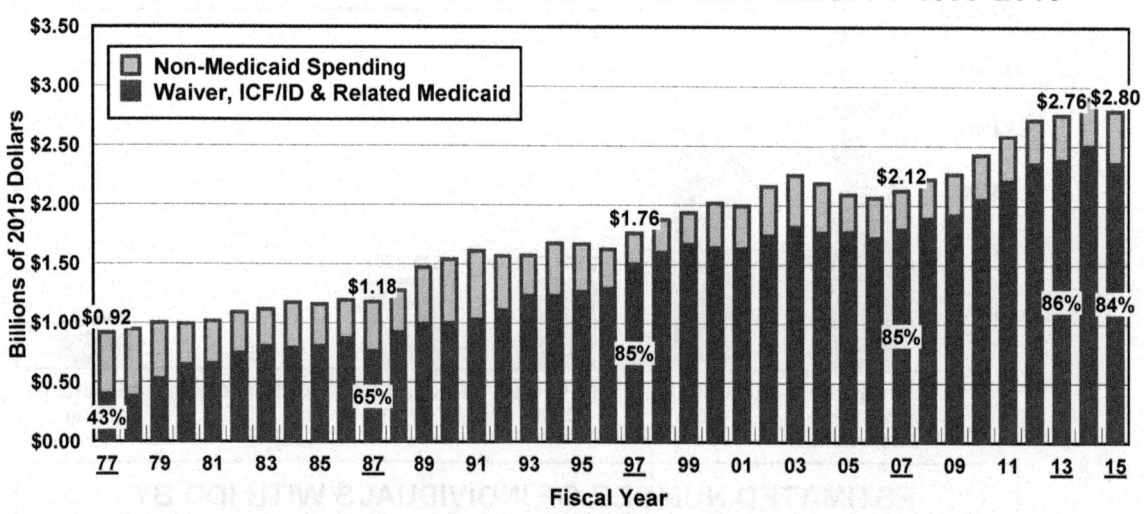

FISCAL EFFORT FOR IDD SERVICES: FY 1977-2015

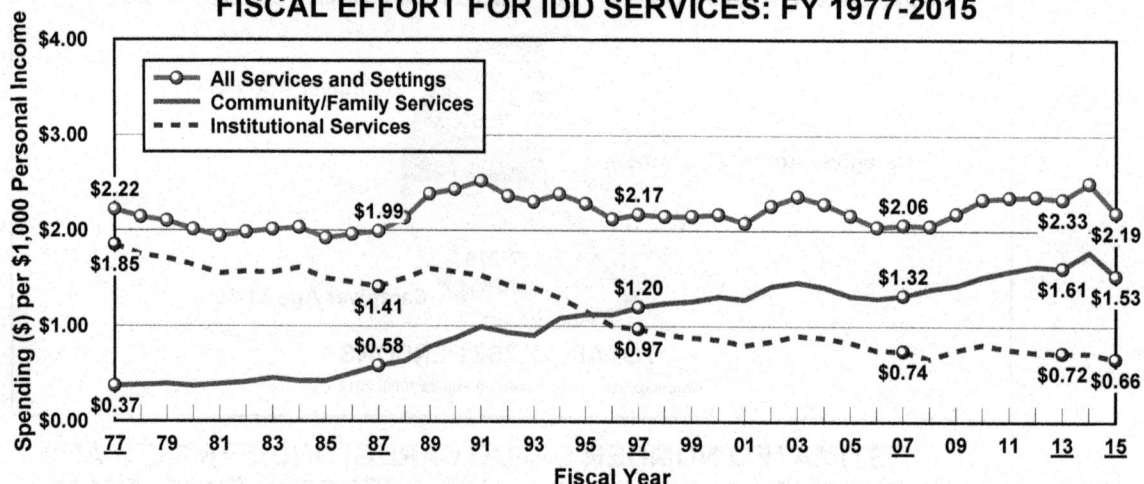

PERSONS WITH IDD BY SIZE OF SETTING: FY 1998-2015

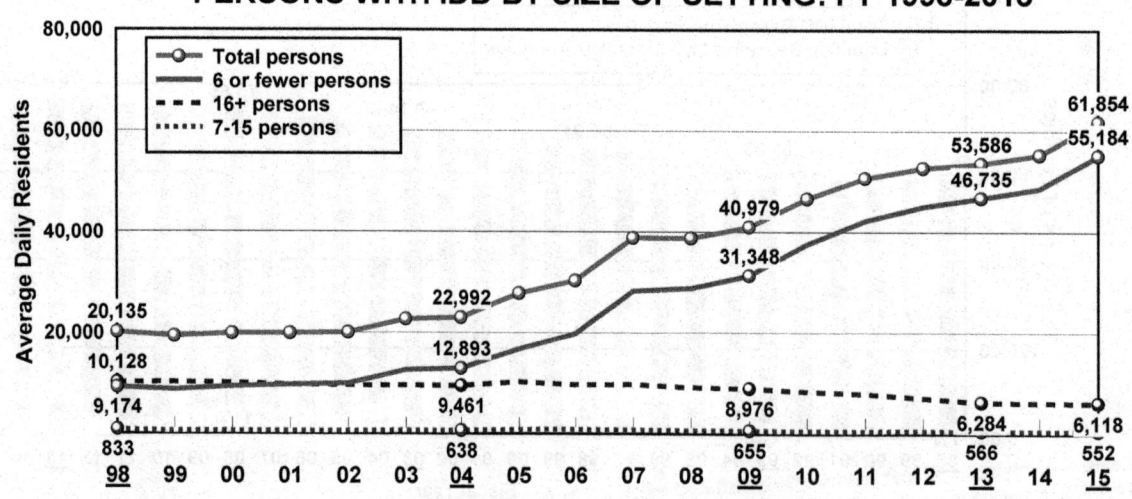

Source: Braddock et al., Coleman Institute and Department of Psychiatry, University of Colorado, 2017.
http://stateofthestates.org

TEXAS

FEDERAL IDD MEDICAID SPENDING BY REVENUE SOURCE

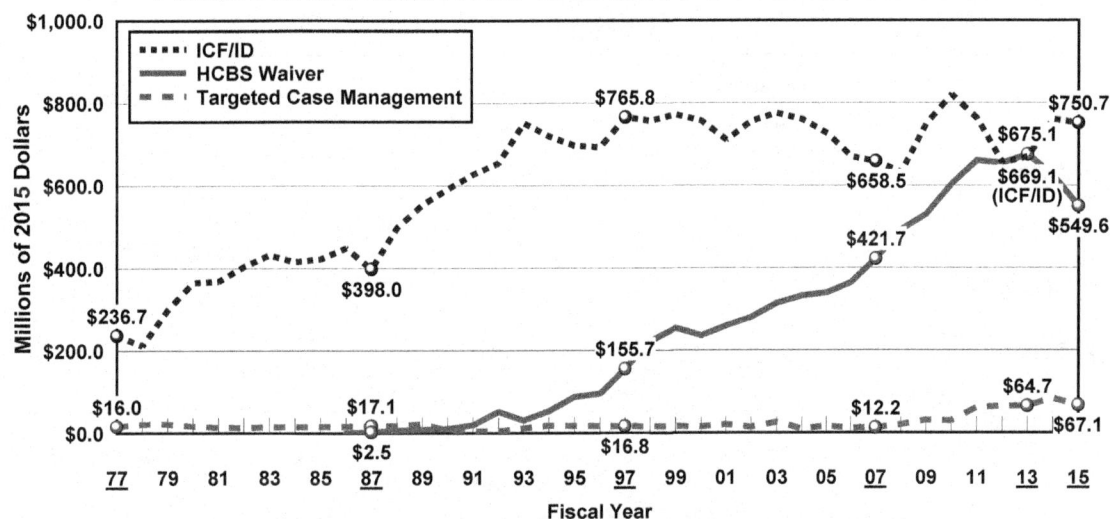

FEDERAL-STATE MEDICAID AS A PERCENTAGE OF TOTAL IDD SPENDING IN FY 2015

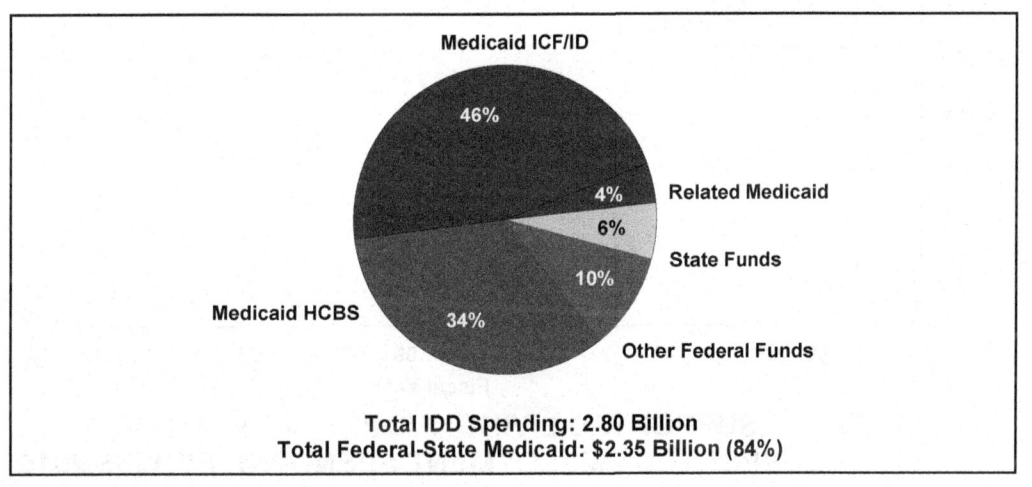

Total IDD Spending: 2.80 Billion
Total Federal-State Medicaid: $2.35 Billion (84%)

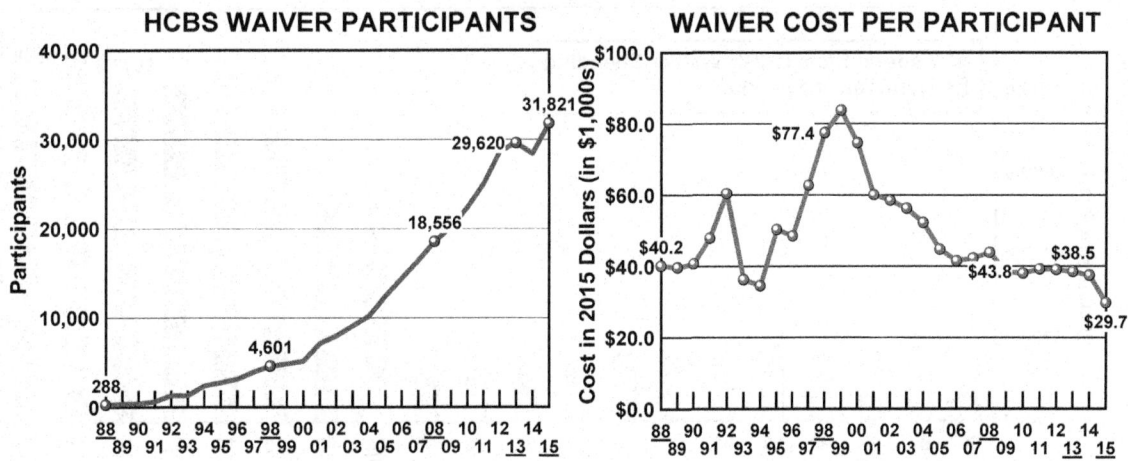

Source: Braddock et al., Coleman Institute and Department of Psychiatry, University of Colorado, 2017.
http://stateofthestates.org

TEXAS

INDIVIDUAL AND FAMILY SUPPORT
SPENDING: FY 1996-2015

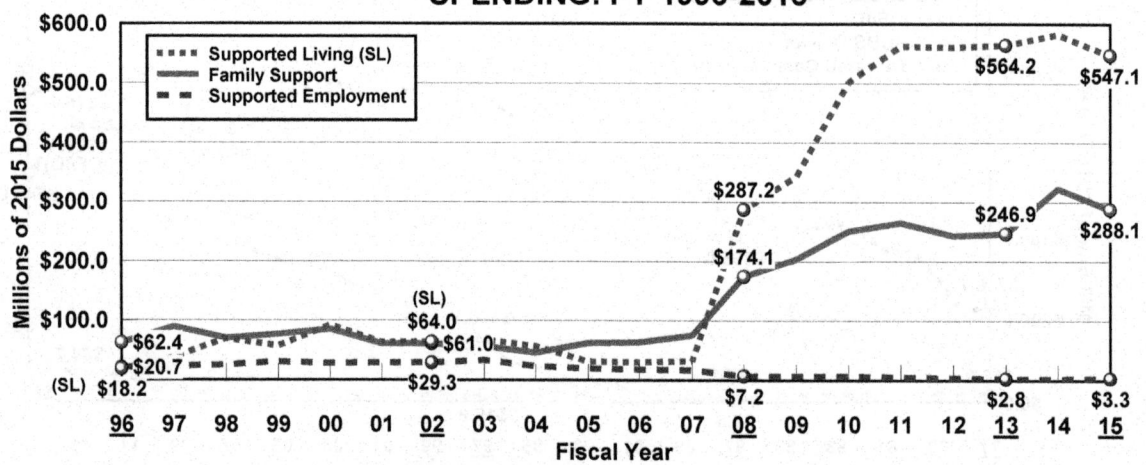

PARTICIPANTS: FY 1996-2015

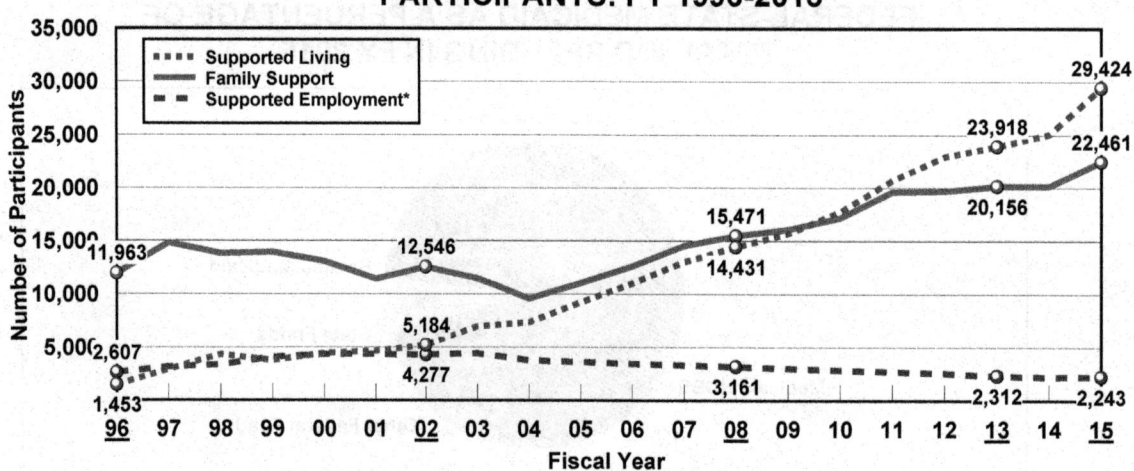

SUPPORTED LIVING, FAMILY SUPPORT AND SUPPORTED EMPLOYMENT SPENDING: FY 1996-2015

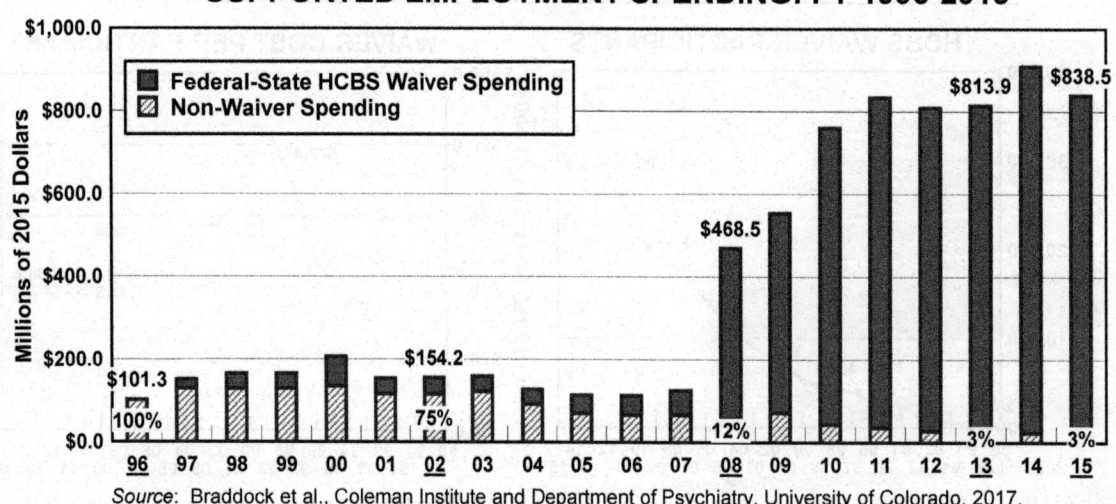

Source: Braddock et al., Coleman Institute and Department of Psychiatry, University of Colorado, 2017.

http://stateofthestates.org

TEXAS

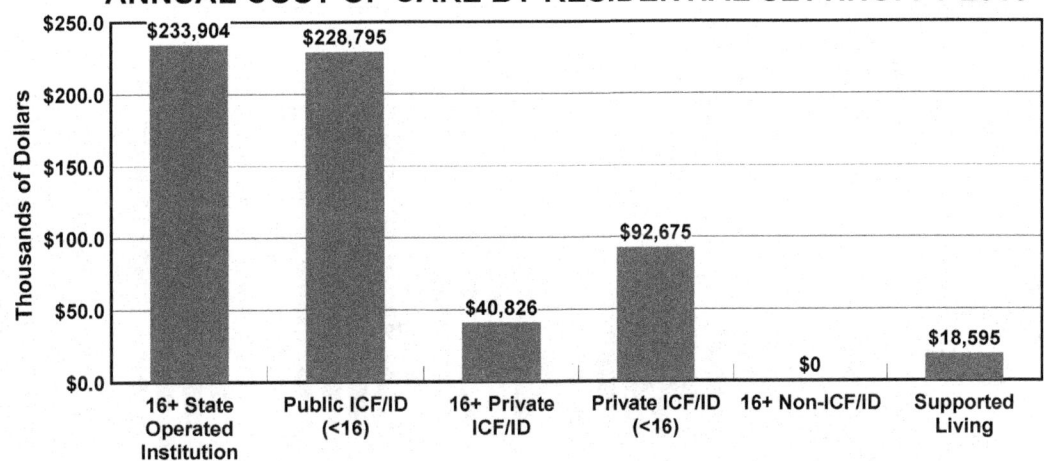
ANNUAL COST OF CARE BY RESIDENTIAL SETTING: FY 2015

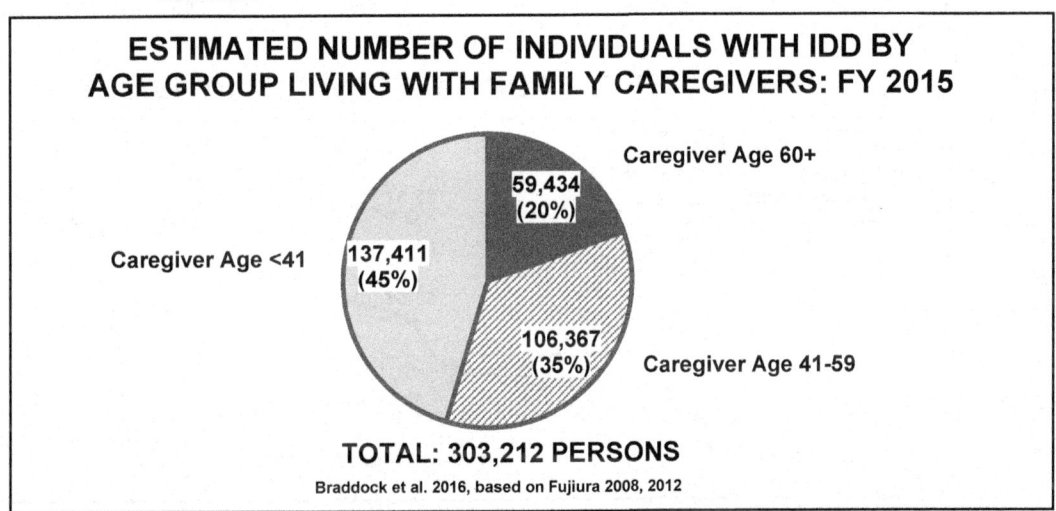
ESTIMATED NUMBER OF INDIVIDUALS WITH IDD BY AGE GROUP LIVING WITH FAMILY CAREGIVERS: FY 2015

TOTAL: 303,212 PERSONS

Braddock et al. 2016, based on Fujiura 2008, 2012

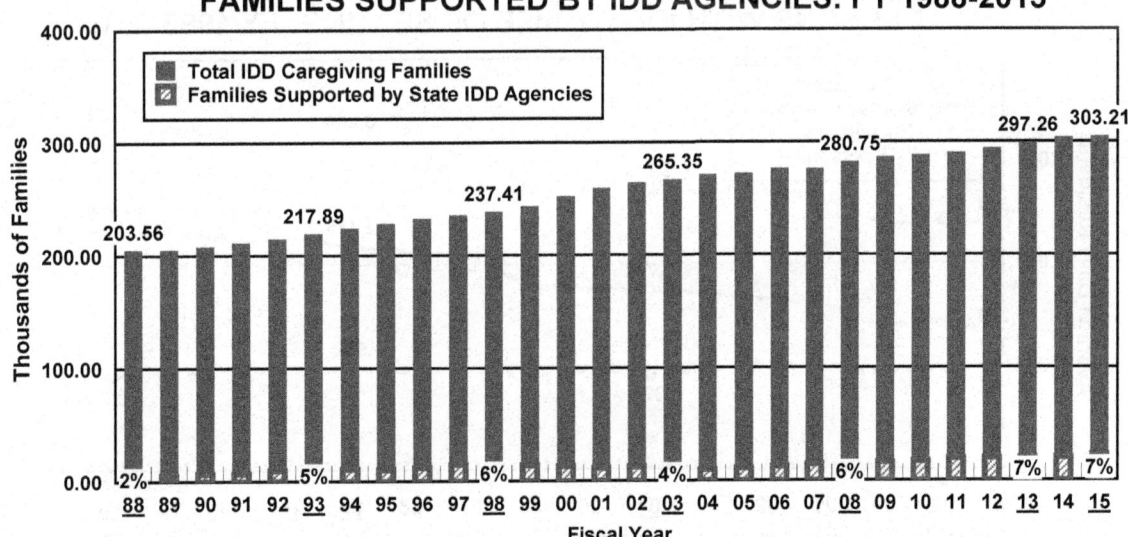
ESTIMATED NUMBER OF IDD CAREGIVING FAMILIES AND FAMILIES SUPPORTED BY IDD AGENCIES: FY 1988-2015

Source: Braddock et al., Coleman Institute and Department of Psychiatry, University of Colorado, 2017.
http://stateofthestates.org

UTAH

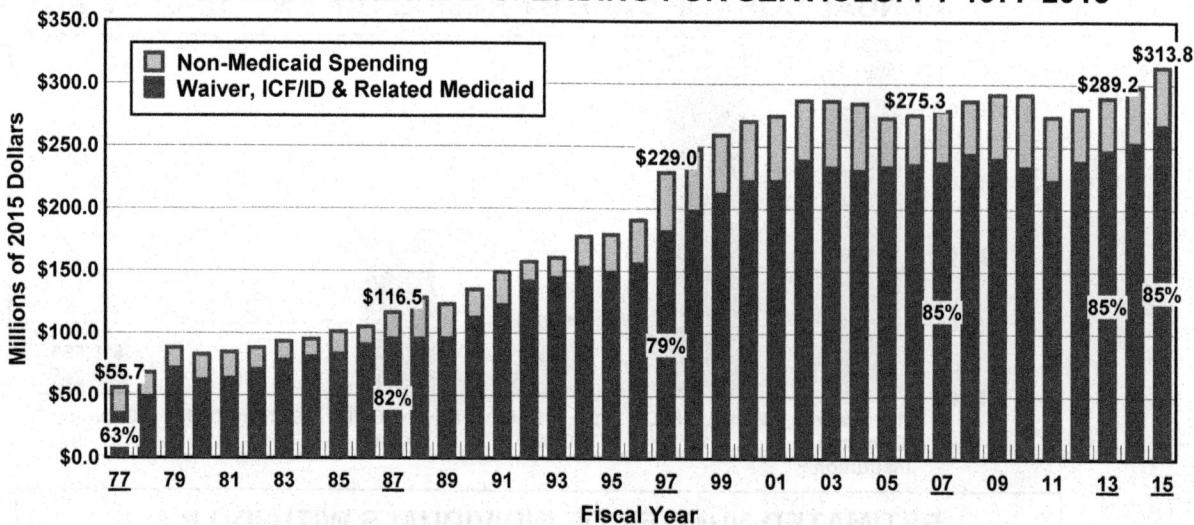

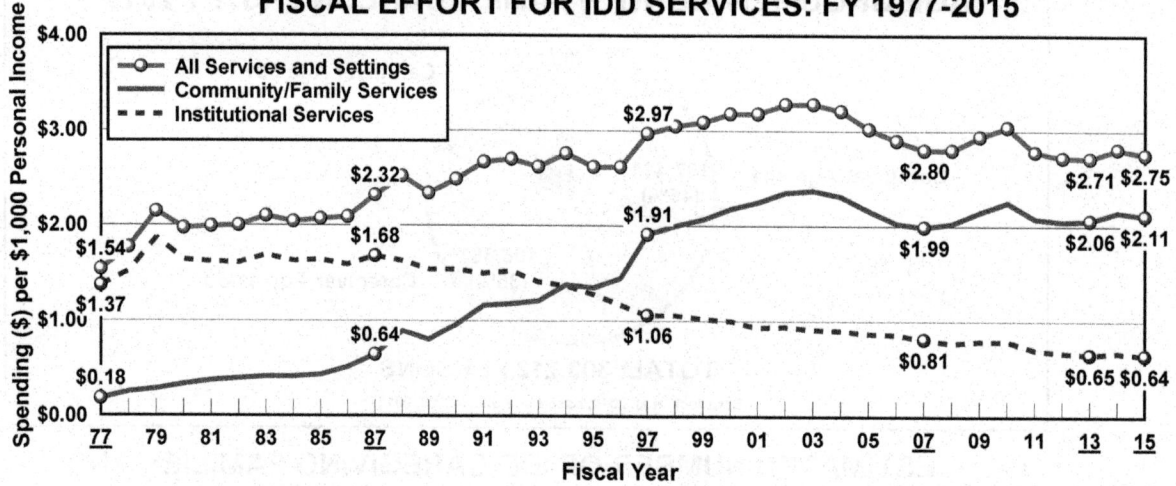

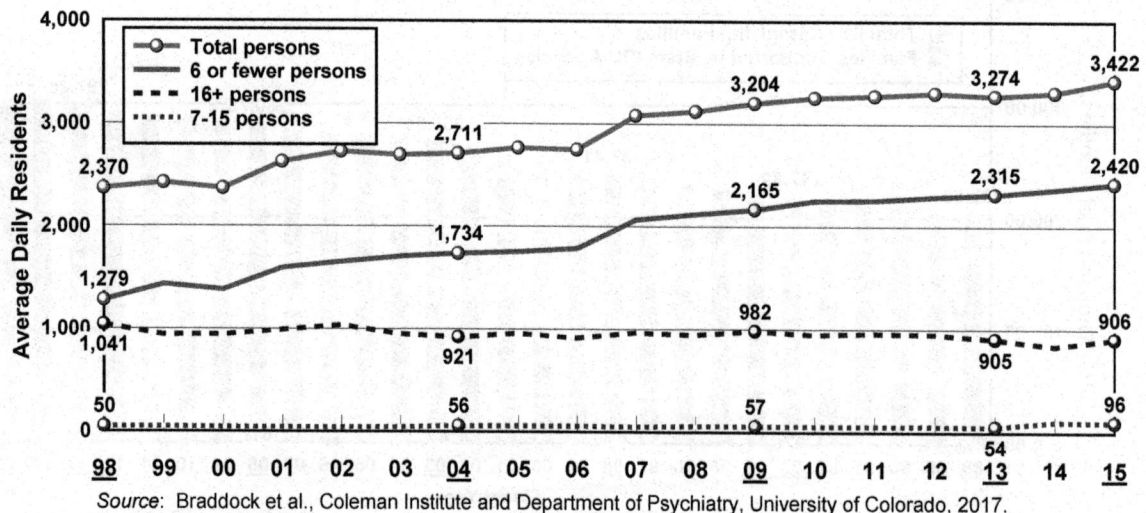

Source: Braddock et al., Coleman Institute and Department of Psychiatry, University of Colorado, 2017.
http://stateofthestates.org

UTAH

FEDERAL IDD MEDICAID SPENDING BY REVENUE SOURCE

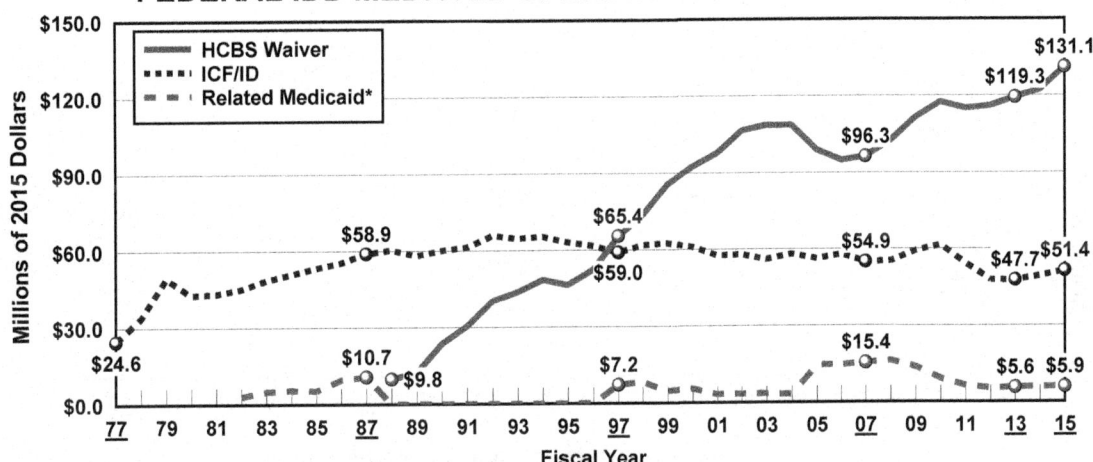

*In 2015, "Related Medicaid" was personal assistance ($1.5 million) and administration ($4.4 million).

FEDERAL-STATE MEDICAID AS A PERCENTAGE OF TOTAL IDD SPENDING IN FY 2015

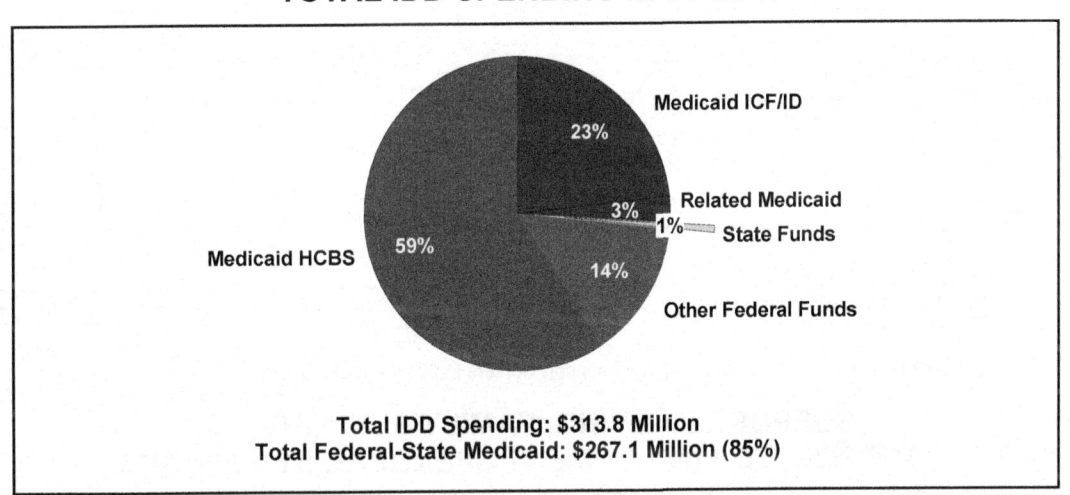

Total IDD Spending: $313.8 Million
Total Federal-State Medicaid: $267.1 Million (85%)

HCBS WAIVER PARTICIPANTS / WAIVER COST PER PARTICIPANT

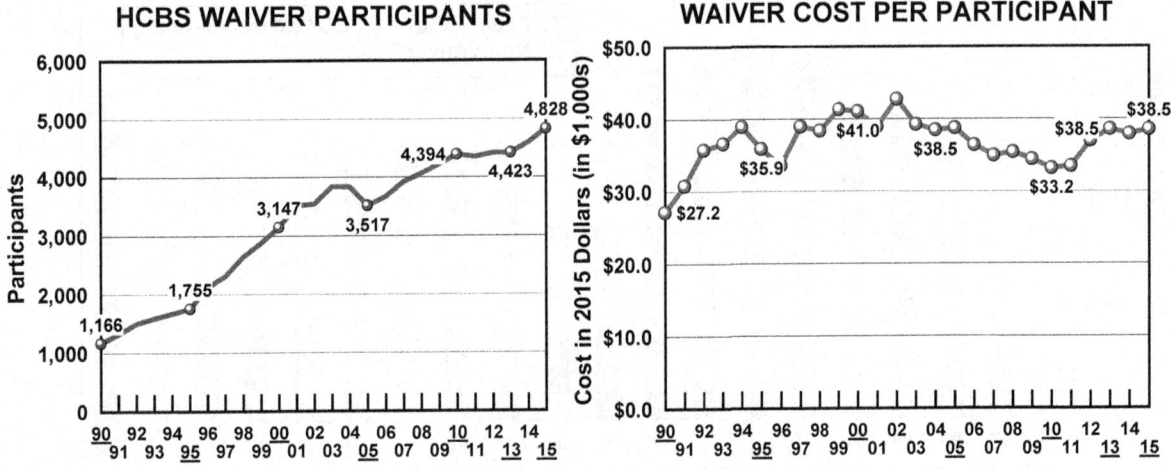

Source: Braddock et al., Coleman Institute and Department of Psychiatry, University of Colorado, 2017.
http://stateofthestates.org

UTAH

INDIVIDUAL AND FAMILY SUPPORT
SPENDING: FY 1996-2015

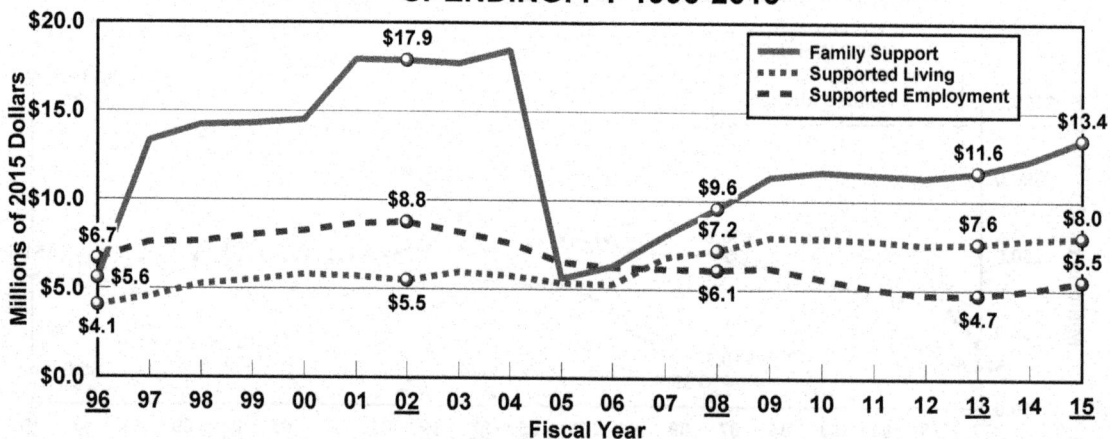

PARTICIPANTS: FY 1996-2015

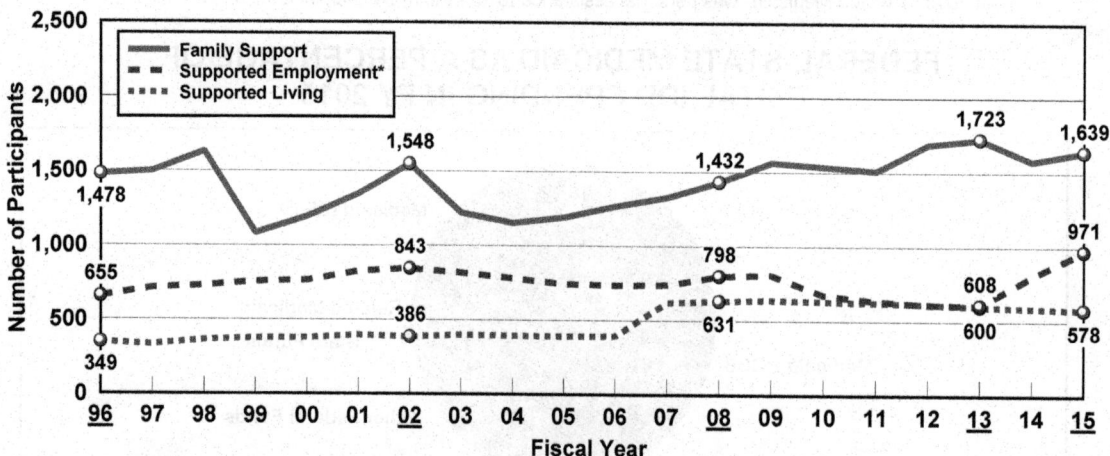

*Does not include 267 follow-along work support workers in 2014 and 282 in 2015.

SUPPORTED LIVING, FAMILY SUPPORT AND SUPPORTED EMPLOYMENT SPENDING: FY 1996-2015

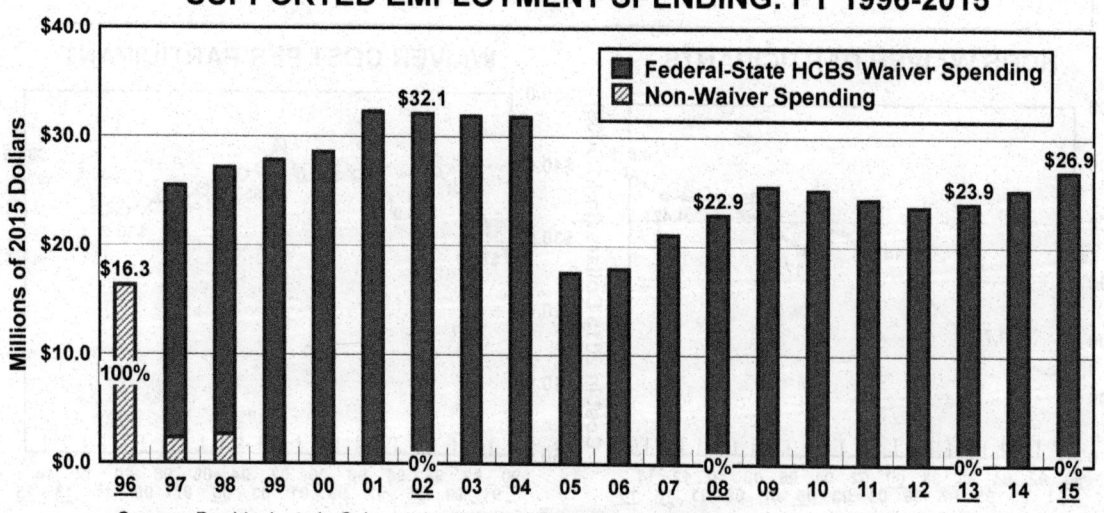

Source: Braddock et al., Coleman Institute and Department of Psychiatry, University of Colorado, 2017.
http://stateofthestates.org

UTAH

ANNUAL COST OF CARE BY RESIDENTIAL SETTING: FY 2015

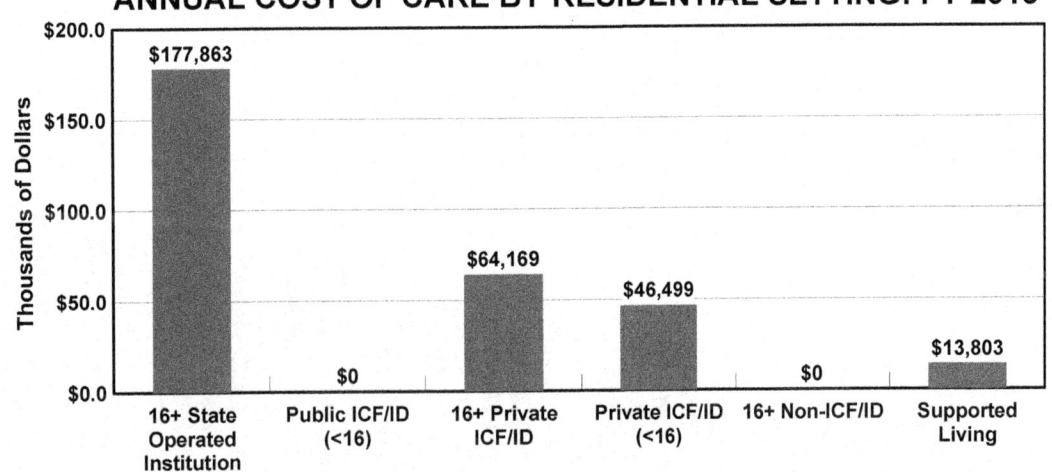

ESTIMATED NUMBER OF INDIVIDUALS WITH IDD BY AGE GROUP LIVING WITH FAMILY CAREGIVERS: FY 2015

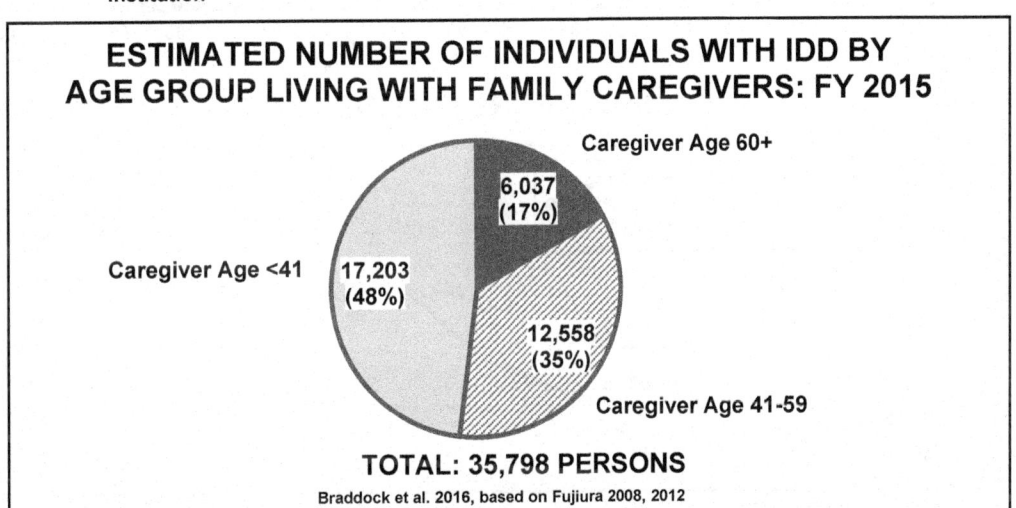

TOTAL: 35,798 PERSONS

Braddock et al. 2016, based on Fujiura 2008, 2012

ESTIMATED NUMBER OF IDD CAREGIVING FAMILIES AND FAMILIES SUPPORTED BY IDD AGENCIES: FY 1988-2015

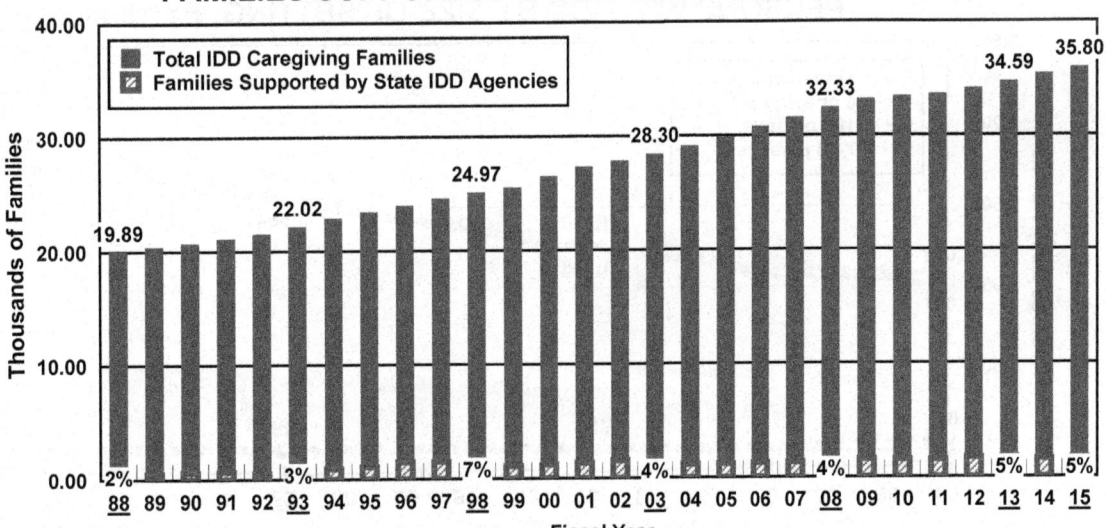

Source: Braddock et al., Coleman Institute and Department of Psychiatry, University of Colorado, 2017
http://stateofthestates.org

VERMONT

TOTAL PUBLIC IDD SPENDING FOR SERVICES: FY 1977-2015

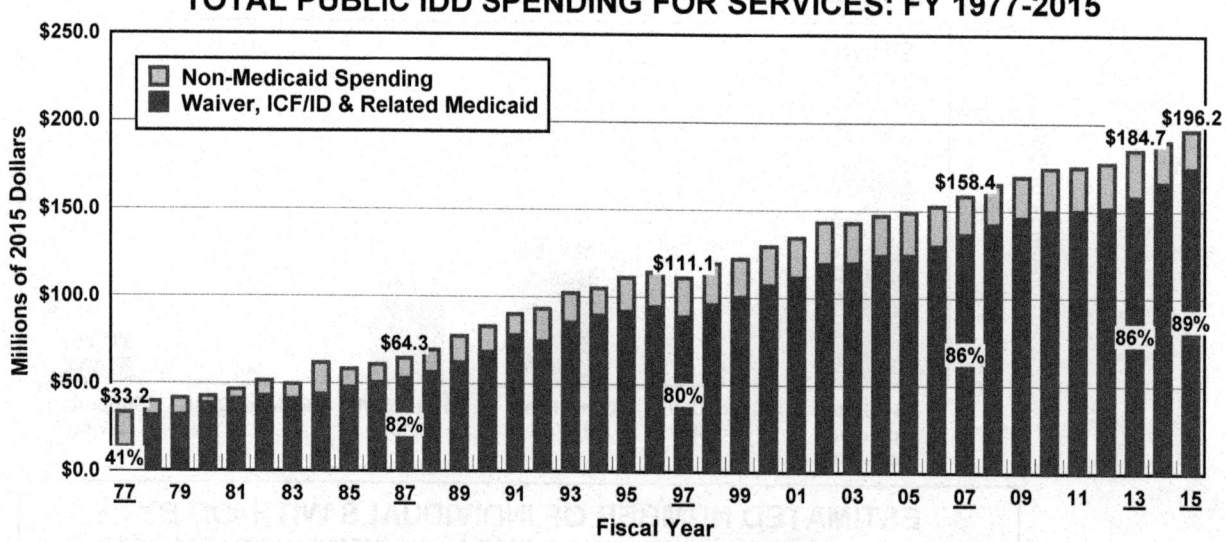

FISCAL EFFORT FOR IDD SERVICES: FY 1977-2015

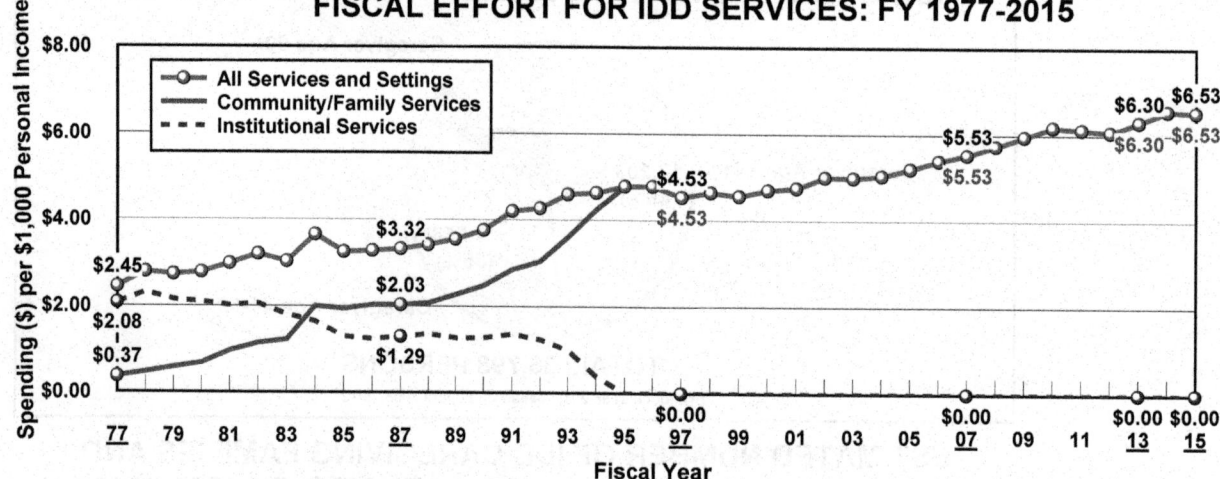

PERSONS WITH IDD BY SIZE OF SETTING: FY 1998-2015

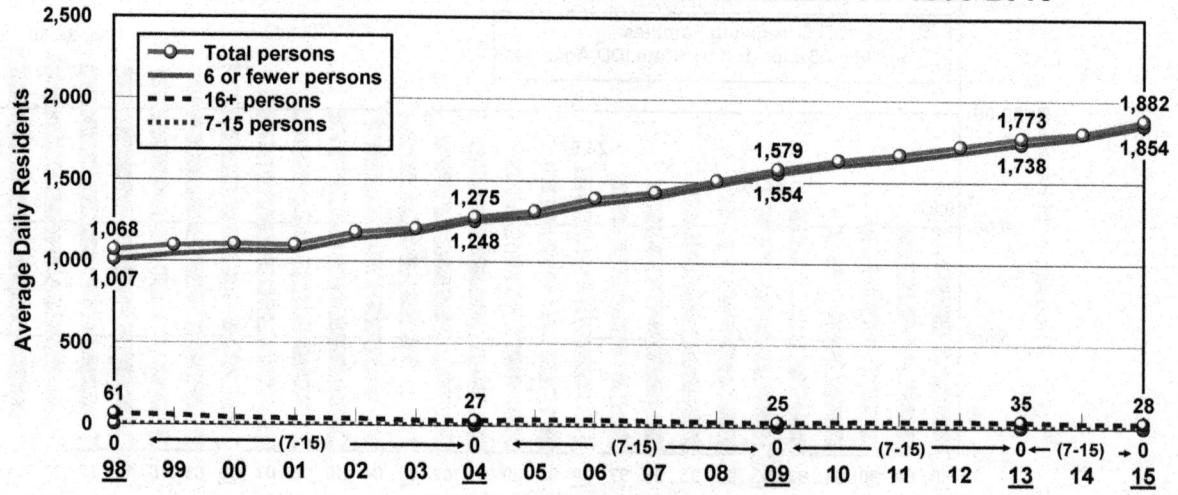

Source: Braddock et al., Coleman Institute and Department of Psychiatry, University of Colorado, 2017.
http://stateofthestates.org

VERMONT

FEDERAL IDD MEDICAID SPENDING BY REVENUE SOURCE

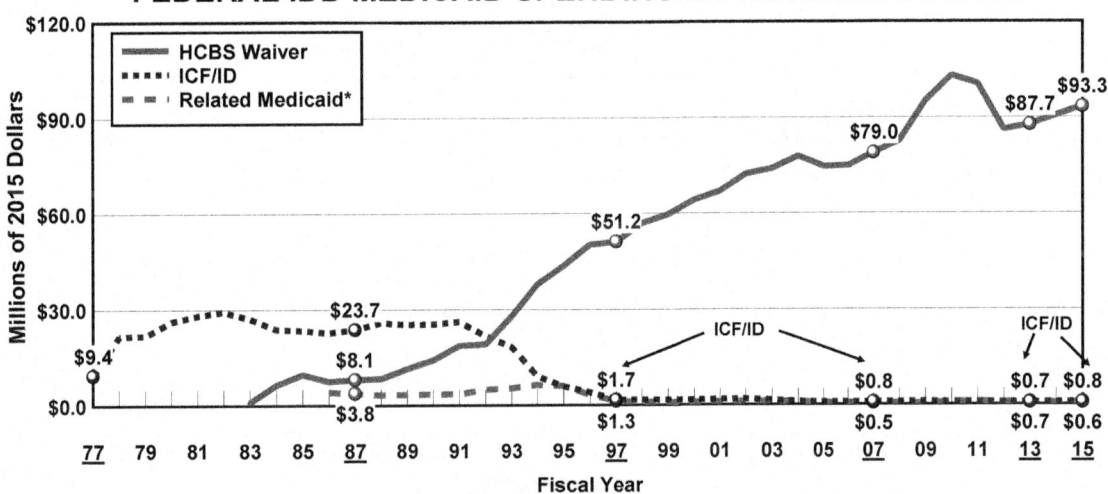

*In 2015, "Related Medicaid" was targeted case management ($0.05 million) and clinic rehabilitation ($0.55 million).

FEDERAL-STATE MEDICAID AS A PERCENTAGE OF TOTAL IDD SPENDING IN FY 2015

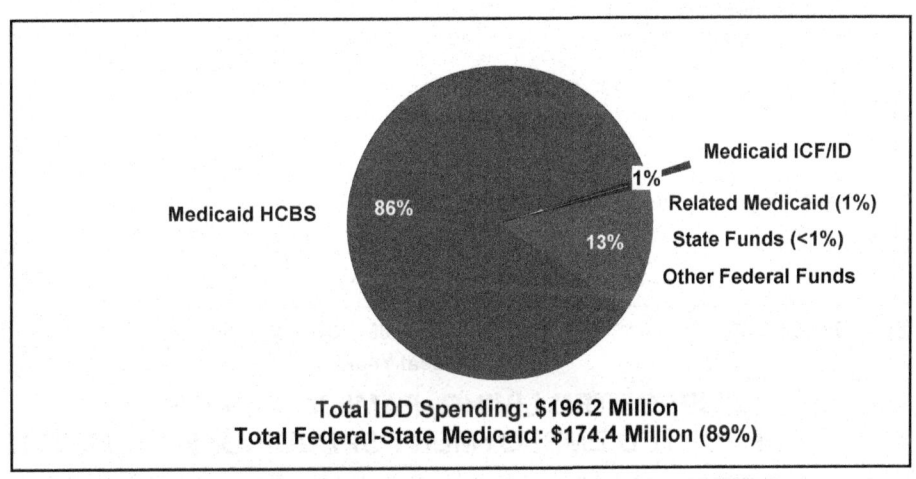

Total IDD Spending: $196.2 Million
Total Federal-State Medicaid: $174.4 Million (89%)

HCBS WAIVER PARTICIPANTS / WAIVER COST PER PARTICIPANT

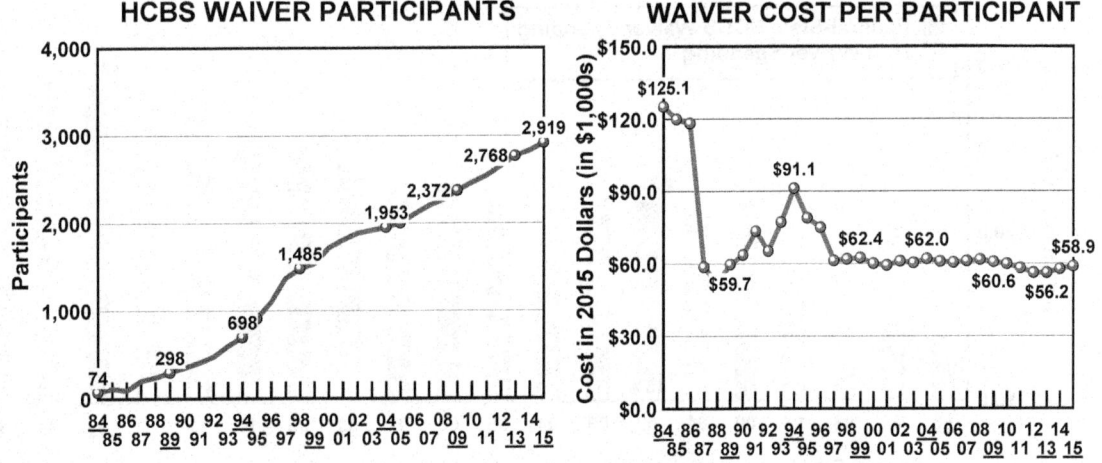

Source: Braddock et al., Coleman Institute and Department of Psychiatry, University of Colorado, 2017.
http://stateofthestates.org

VERMONT

INDIVIDUAL AND FAMILY SUPPORT
SPENDING: FY 1996-2015

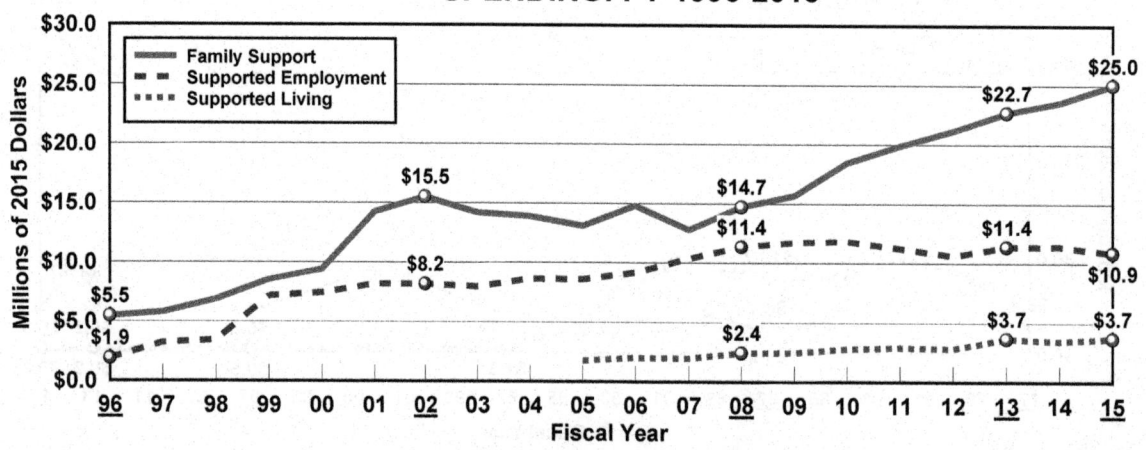

PARTICIPANTS: FY 1996-2015

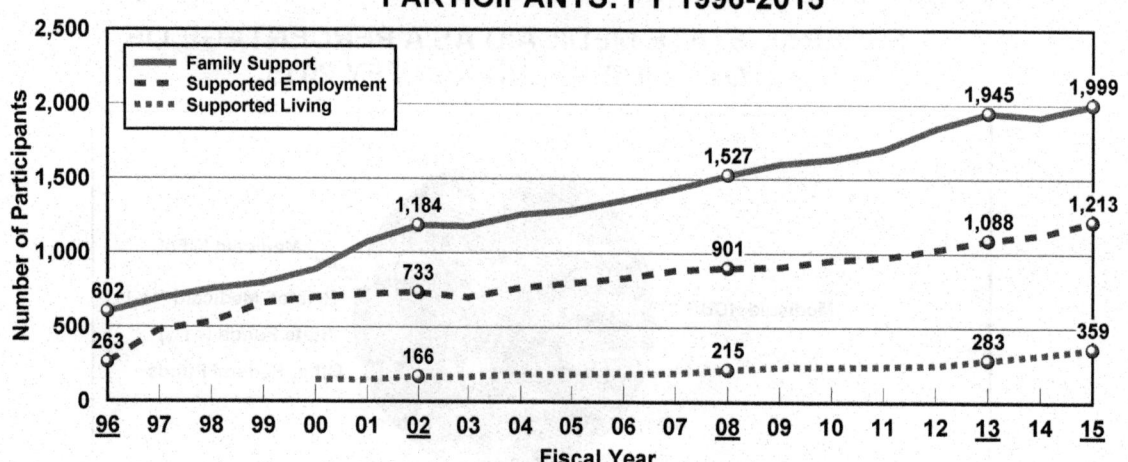

SUPPORTED LIVING, FAMILY SUPPORT AND SUPPORTED EMPLOYMENT SPENDING: FY 1996-2015

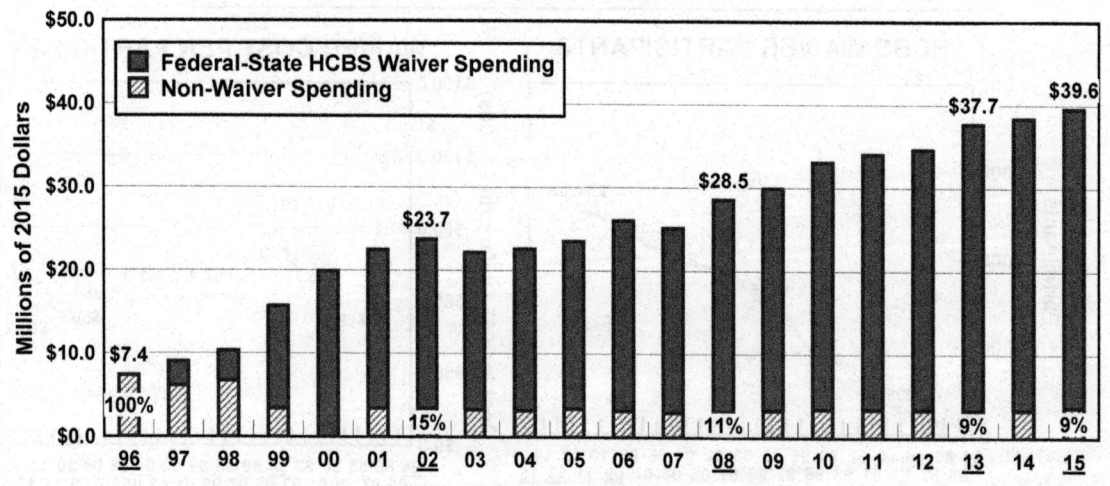

Source: Braddock et al., Coleman Institute and Department of Psychiatry, University of Colorado, 2017.
http://stateofthestates.org

VERMONT

ANNUAL COST OF CARE BY RESIDENTIAL SETTING: FY 2015

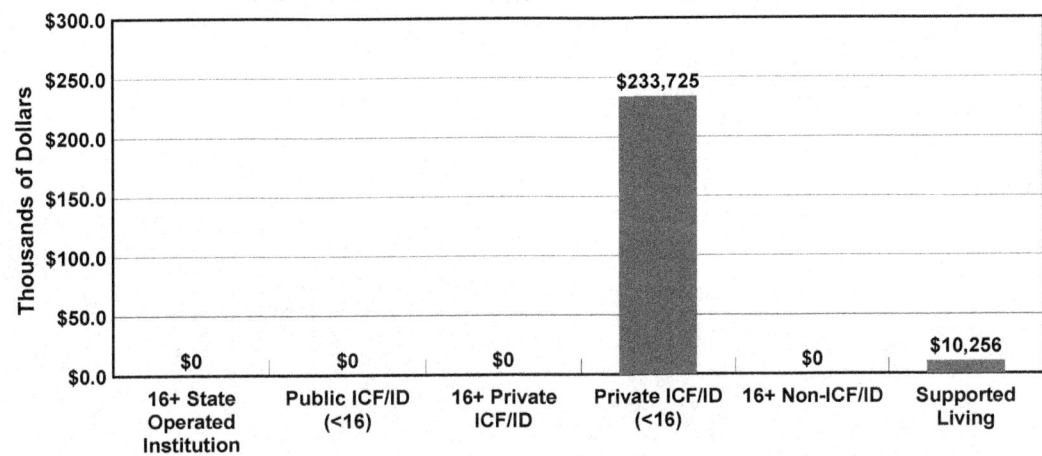

ESTIMATED NUMBER OF INDIVIDUALS WITH IDD BY AGE GROUP LIVING WITH FAMILY CAREGIVERS: FY 2015

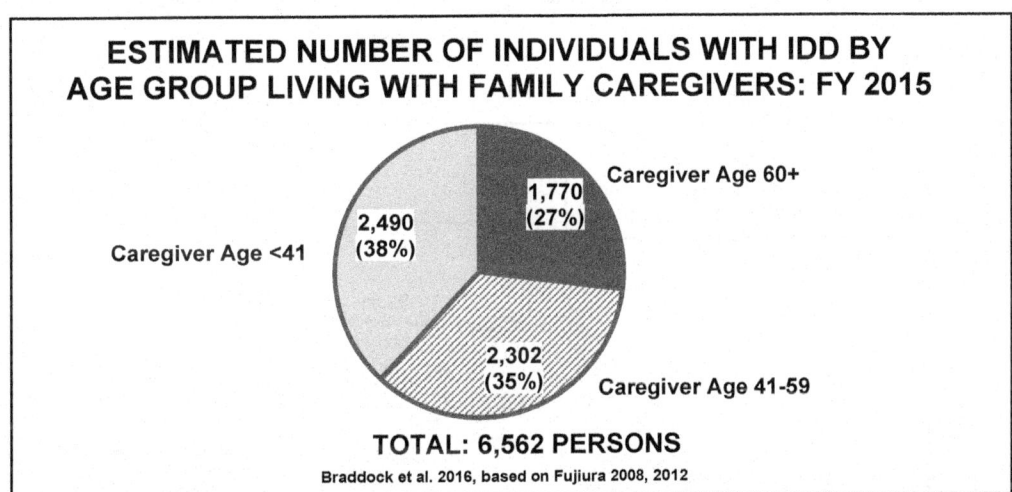

TOTAL: 6,562 PERSONS

Braddock et al. 2016, based on Fujiura 2008, 2012

ESTIMATED NUMBER OF IDD CAREGIVING FAMILIES AND FAMILIES SUPPORTED BY IDD AGENCIES: FY 1988-2015

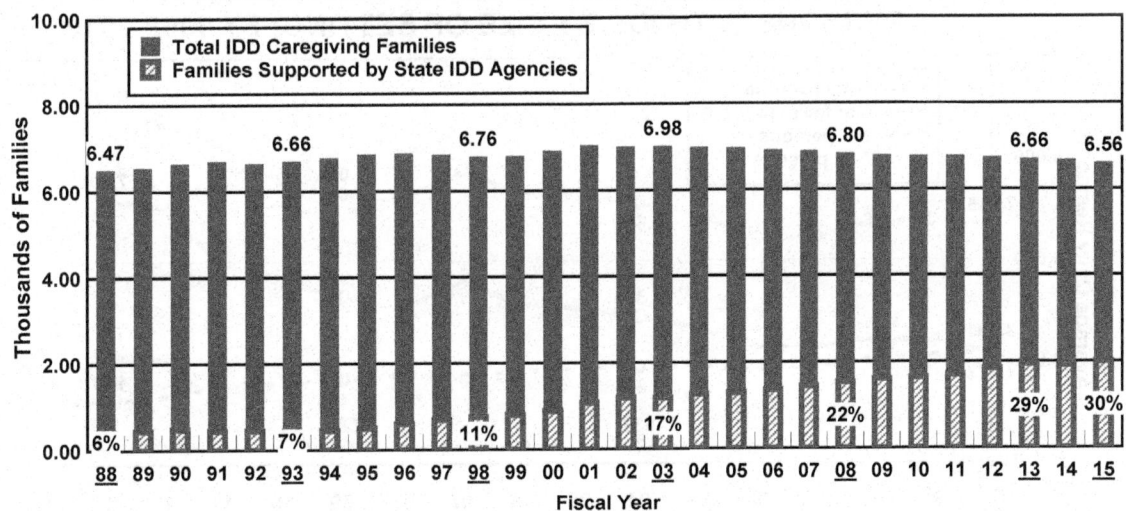

Source: Braddock et al., Coleman Institute and Department of Psychiatry, University of Colorado, 2017.

http://stateofthestates.org

VIRGINIA

TOTAL PUBLIC IDD SPENDING FOR SERVICES: FY 1977-2015

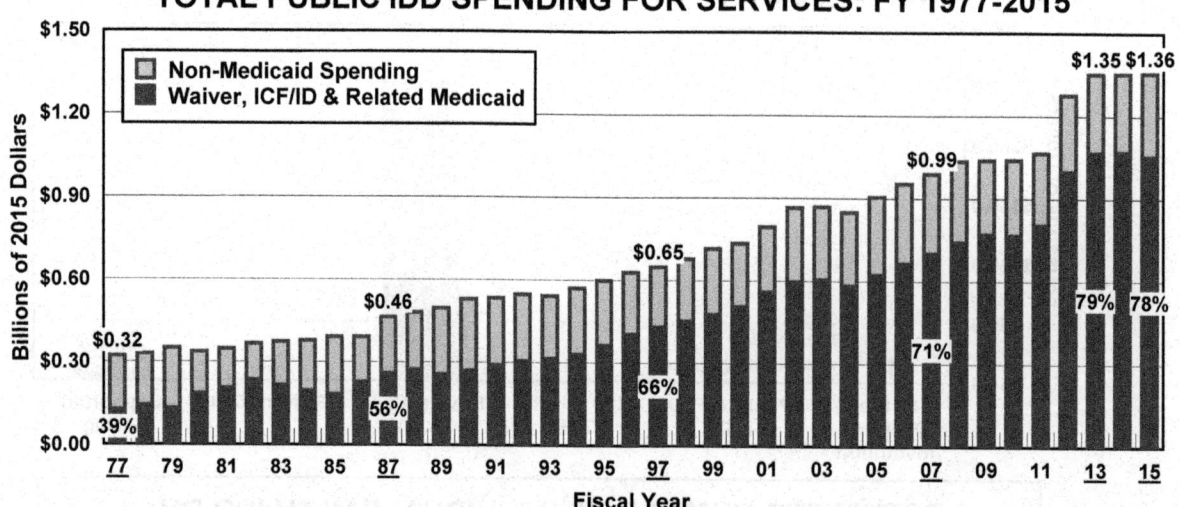

FISCAL EFFORT FOR IDD SERVICES: FY 1977-2015

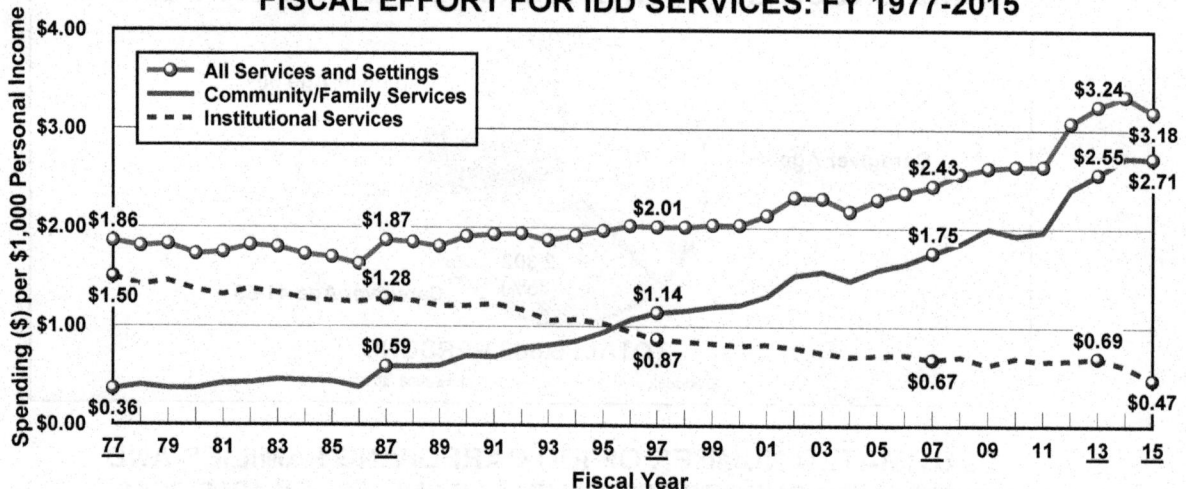

PERSONS WITH IDD BY SIZE OF SETTING: FY 1998-2015

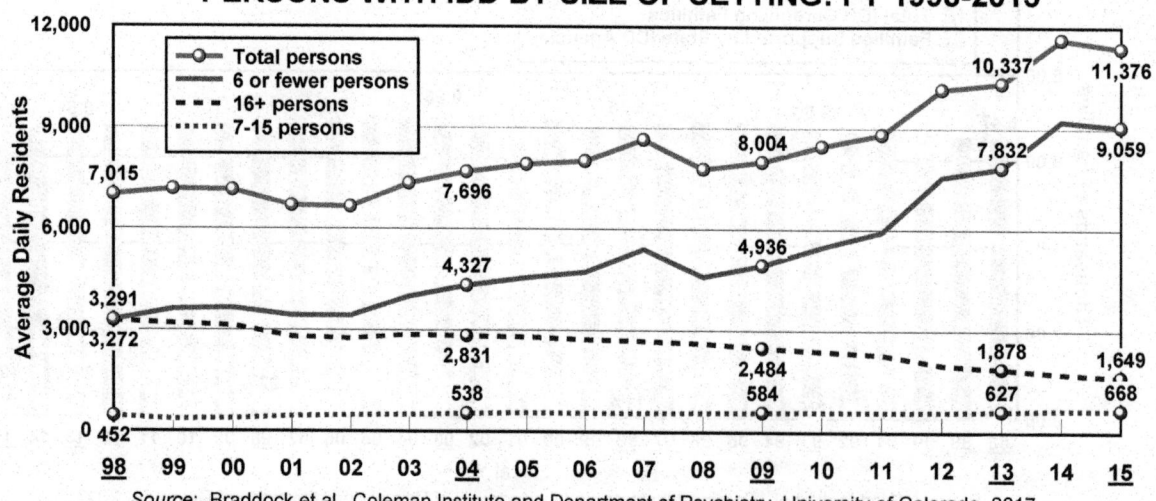

Source: Braddock et al., Coleman Institute and Department of Psychiatry, University of Colorado, 2017.
http://stateofthestates.org

VIRGINIA

FEDERAL IDD MEDICAID SPENDING BY REVENUE SOURCE

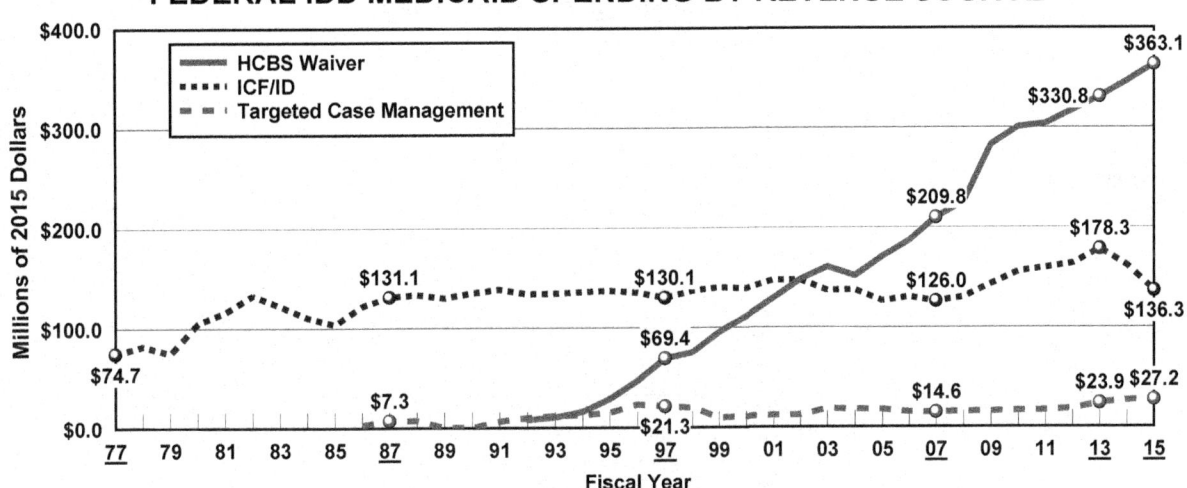

FEDERAL-STATE MEDICAID AS A PERCENTAGE OF TOTAL IDD SPENDING IN FY 2015

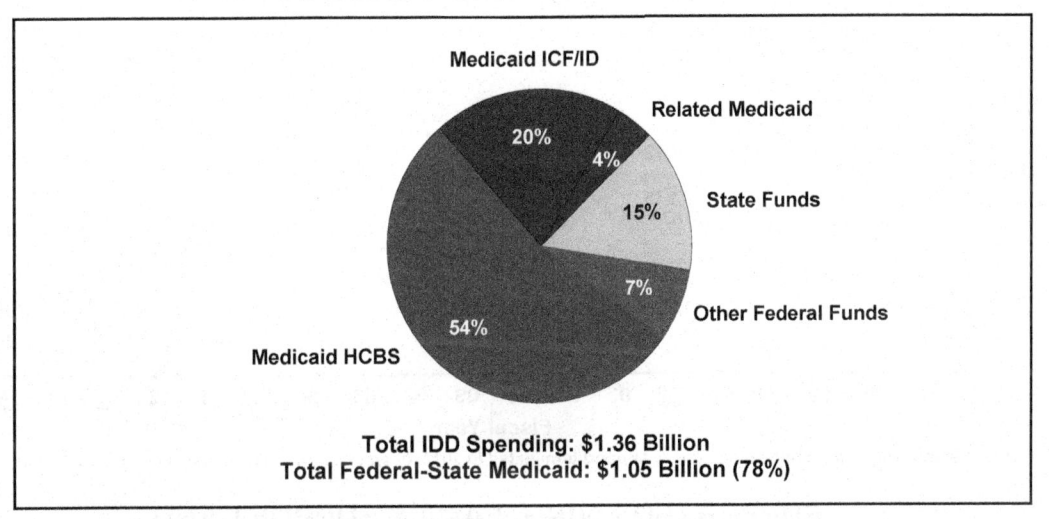

Total IDD Spending: $1.36 Billion
Total Federal-State Medicaid: $1.05 Billion (78%)

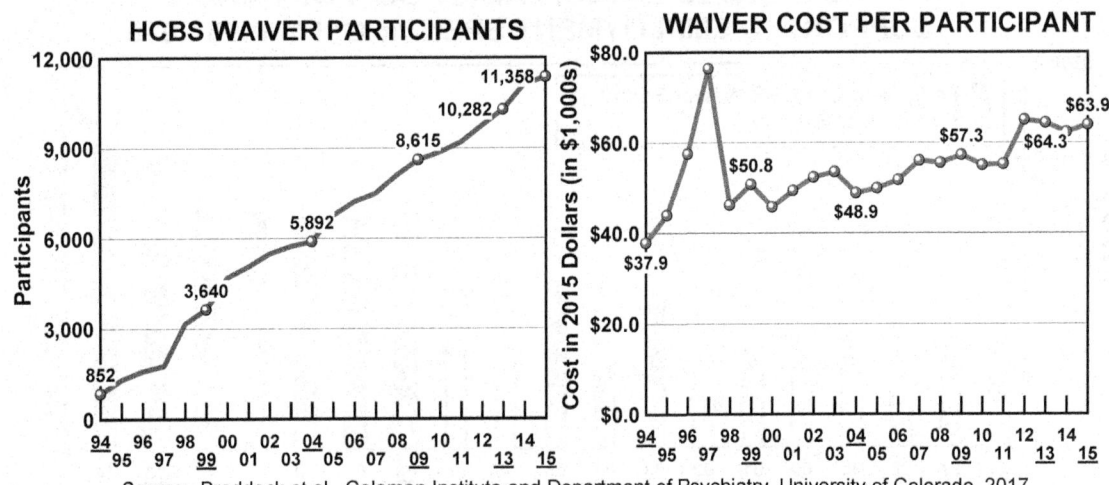

Source: Braddock et al., Coleman Institute and Department of Psychiatry, University of Colorado, 2017.

http://stateofthestates.org

VIRGINIA

INDIVIDUAL AND FAMILY SUPPORT
SPENDING: FY 1996-2015

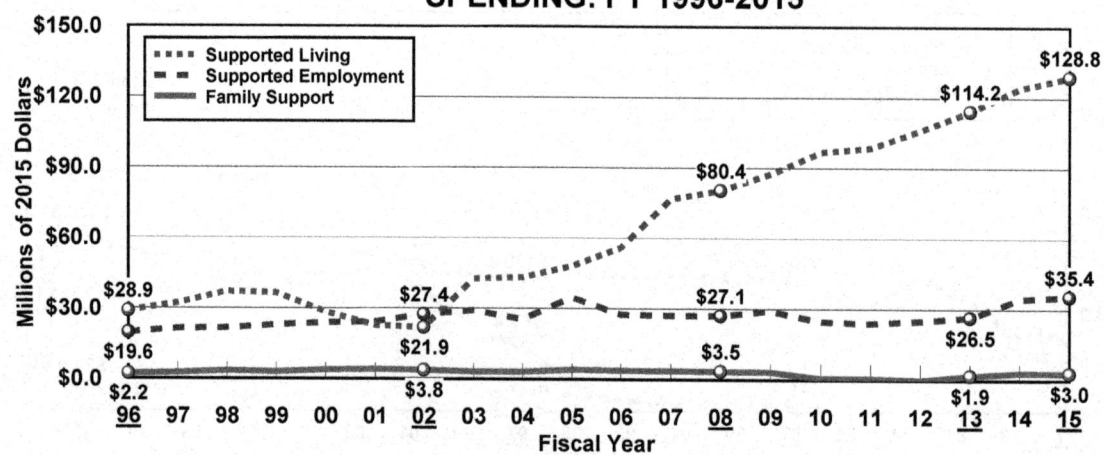

PARTICIPANTS: FY 1996-2015

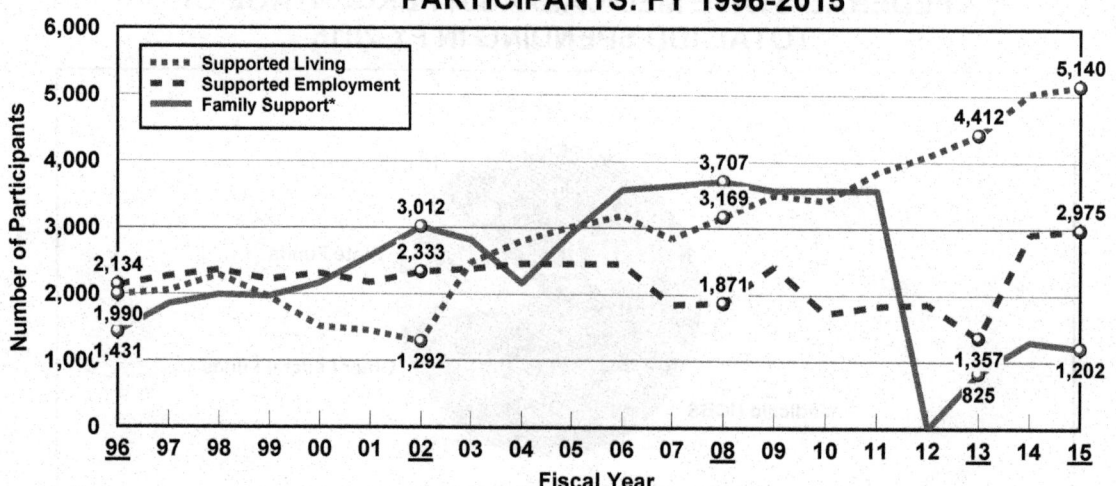

*Due to state general fund reductions, family support terminated in 2012; however, new cash subsidy implemented 2013.

SUPPORTED LIVING, FAMILY SUPPORT AND SUPPORTED EMPLOYMENT SPENDING: FY 1996-2015

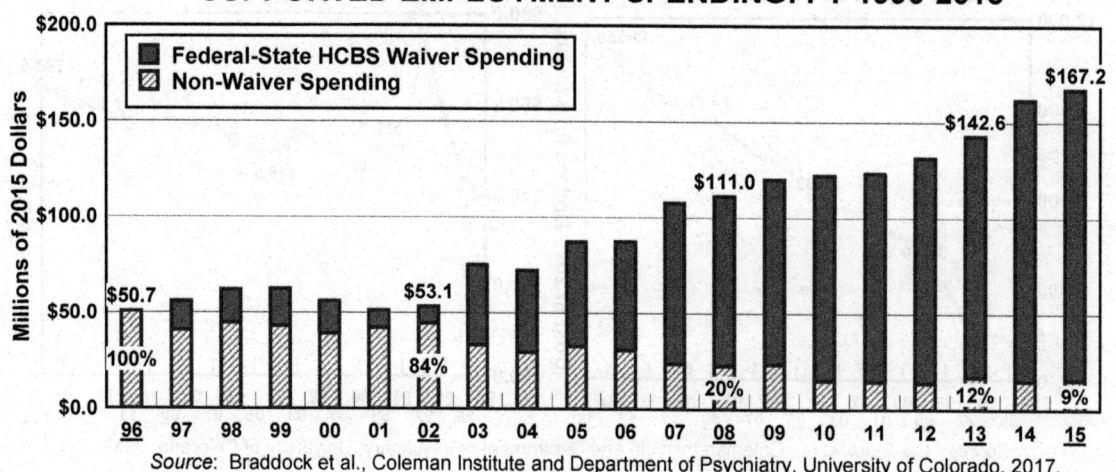

Source: Braddock et al., Coleman Institute and Department of Psychiatry, University of Colorado, 2017.
http://stateofthestates.org

VIRGINIA

ANNUAL COST OF CARE BY RESIDENTIAL SETTING: FY 2015

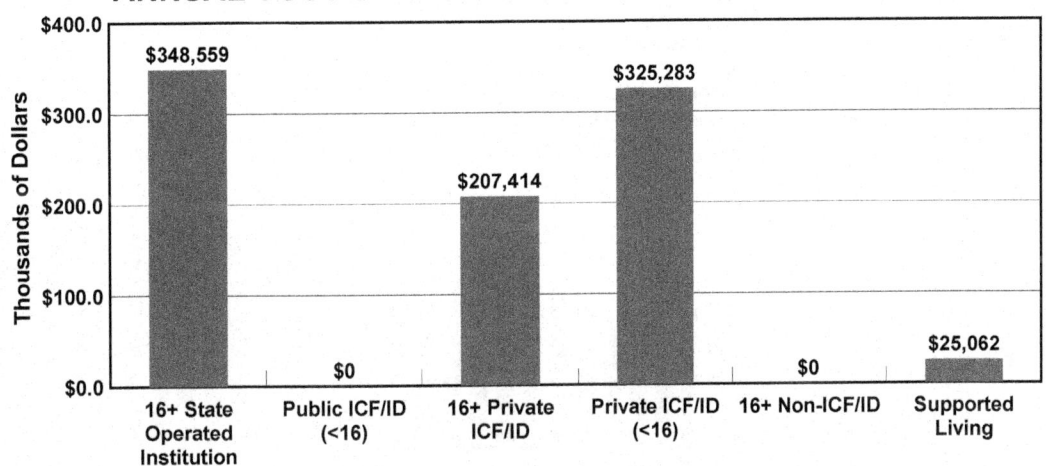

ESTIMATED NUMBER OF INDIVIDUALS WITH IDD BY AGE GROUP LIVING WITH FAMILY CAREGIVERS: FY 2015

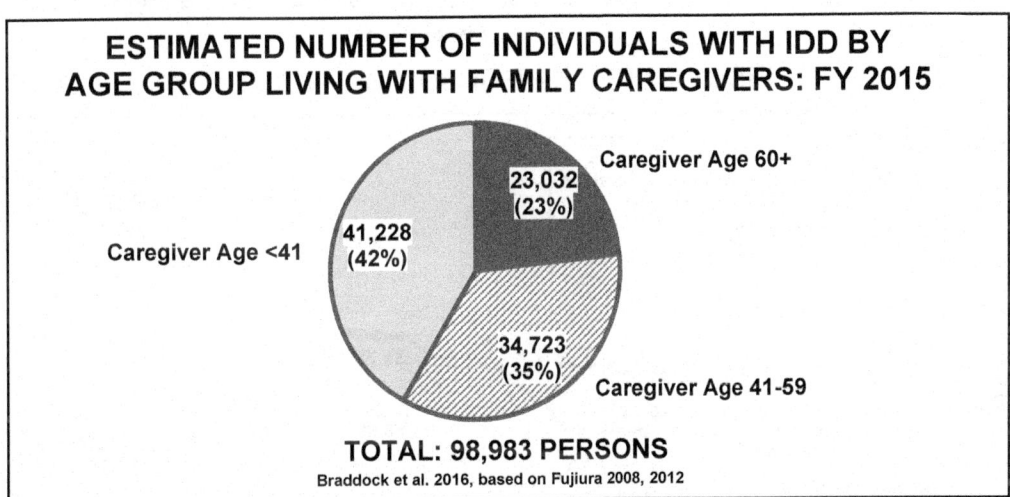

TOTAL: 98,983 PERSONS
Braddock et al. 2016, based on Fujiura 2008, 2012

ESTIMATED NUMBER OF IDD CAREGIVING FAMILIES AND FAMILIES SUPPORTED BY IDD AGENCIES: FY 1988-2015

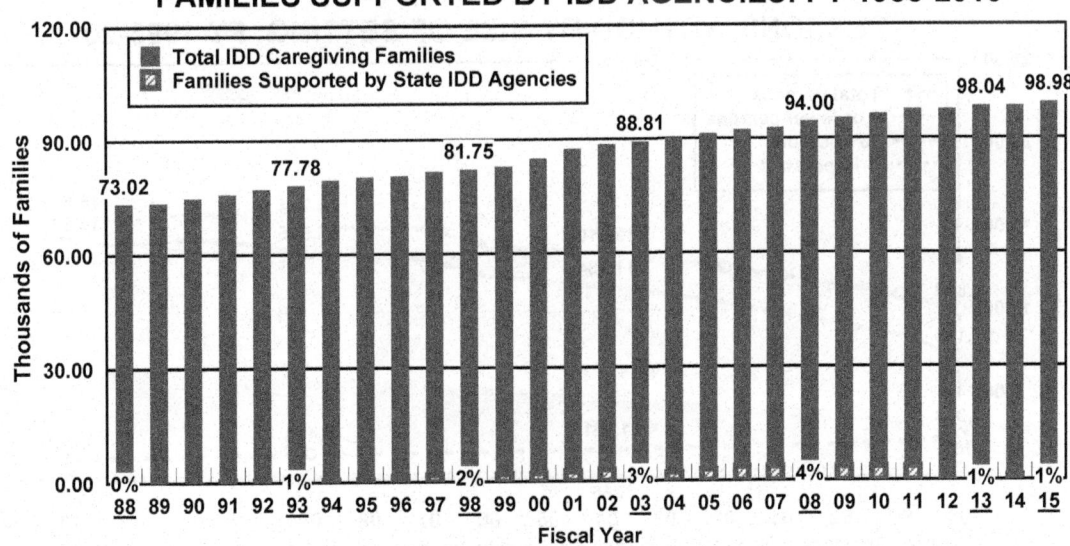

Source: Braddock et al., Coleman Institute and Department of Psychiatry, University of Colorado, 2017.
http://stateofthestates.org

WASHINGTON

TOTAL PUBLIC IDD SPENDING FOR SERVICES: FY 1977-2015

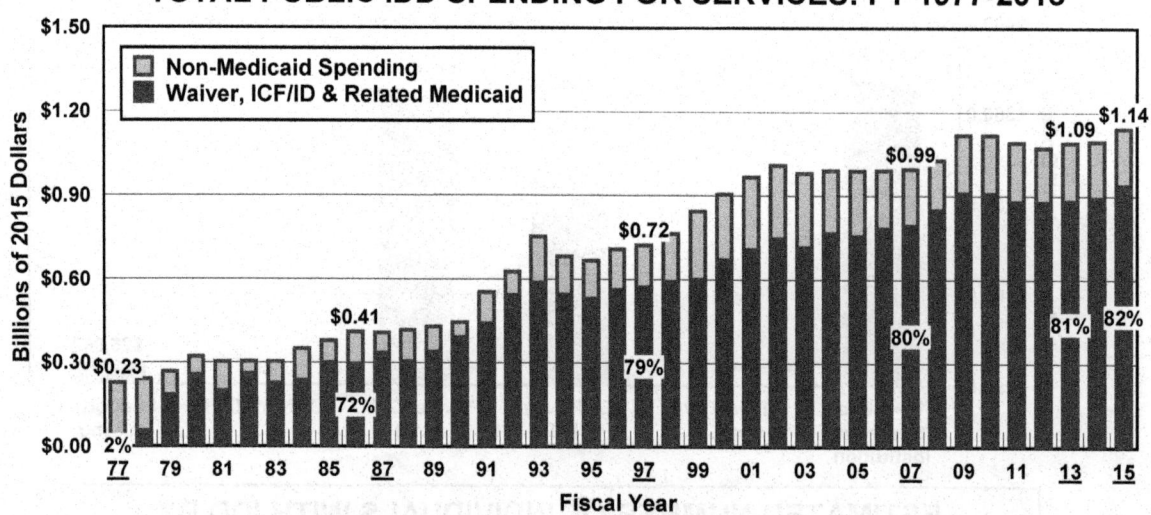

FISCAL EFFORT FOR IDD SERVICES: FY 1977-2015

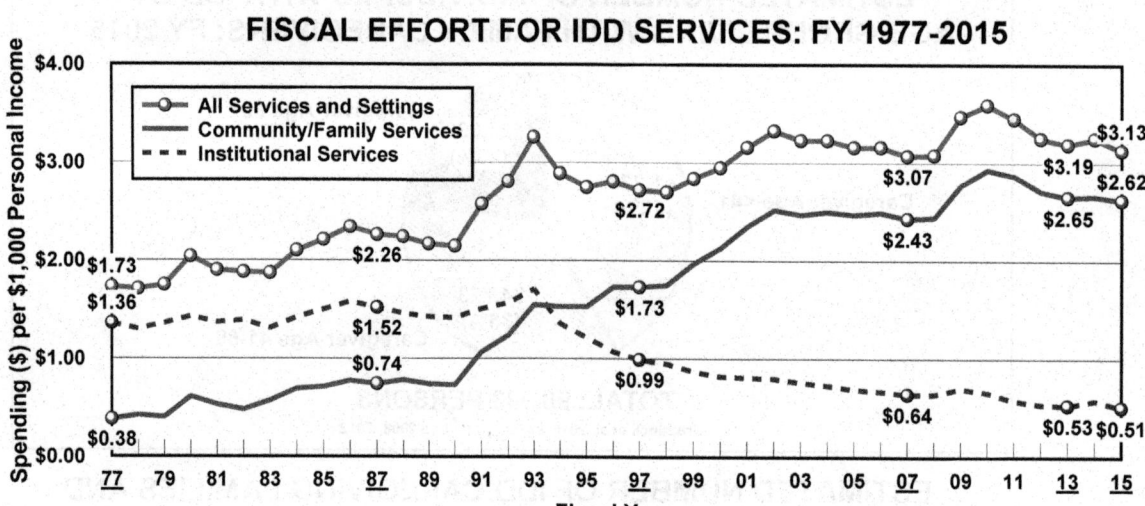

PERSONS WITH IDD BY SIZE OF SETTING: FY 1998-2015

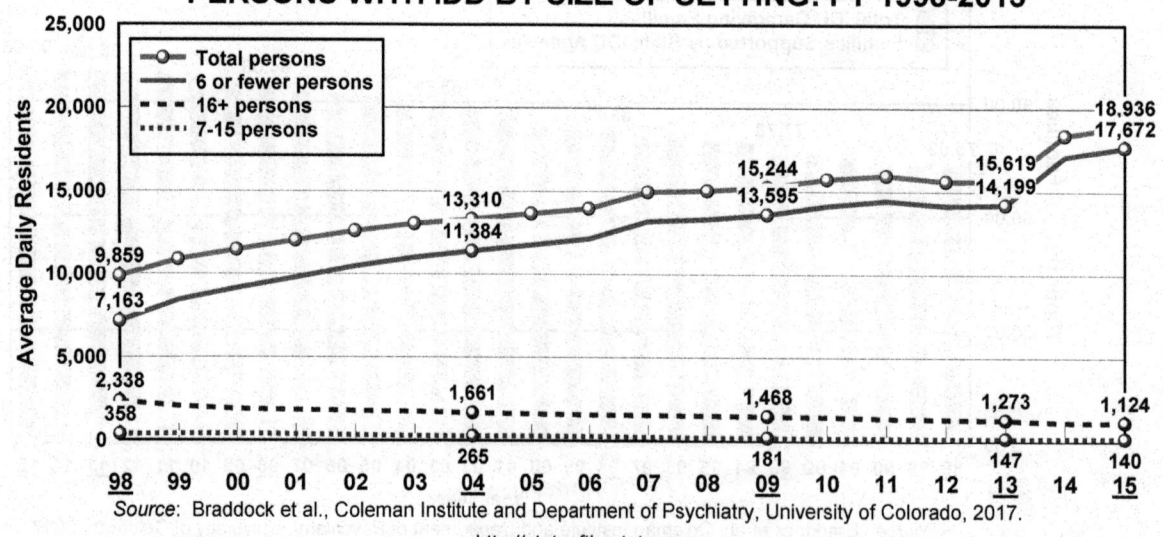

Source: Braddock et al., Coleman Institute and Department of Psychiatry, University of Colorado, 2017.
http://stateofthestates.org

WASHINGTON

FEDERAL IDD MEDICAID SPENDING BY REVENUE SOURCE

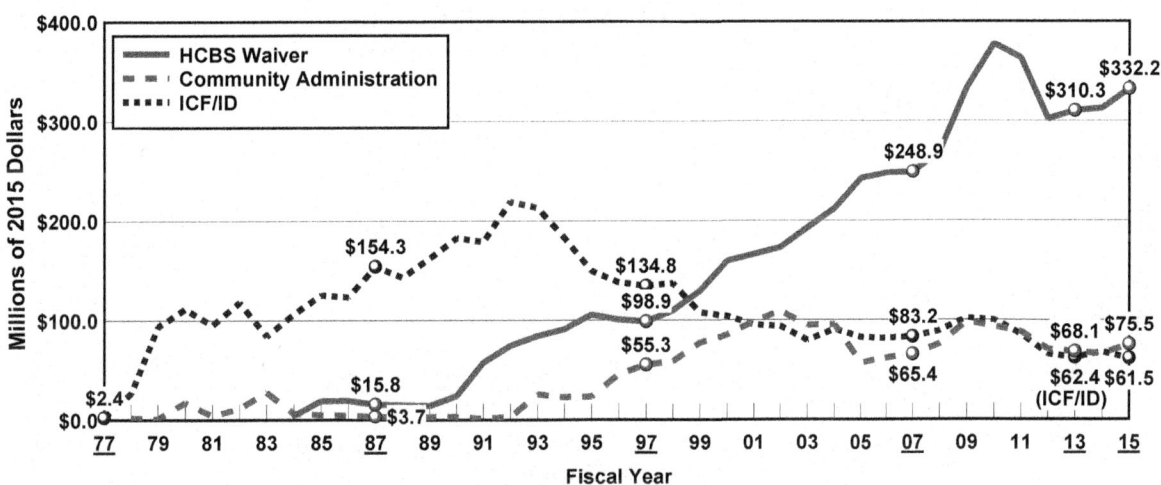

FEDERAL-STATE MEDICAID AS A PERCENTAGE OF TOTAL IDD SPENDING IN FY 2015

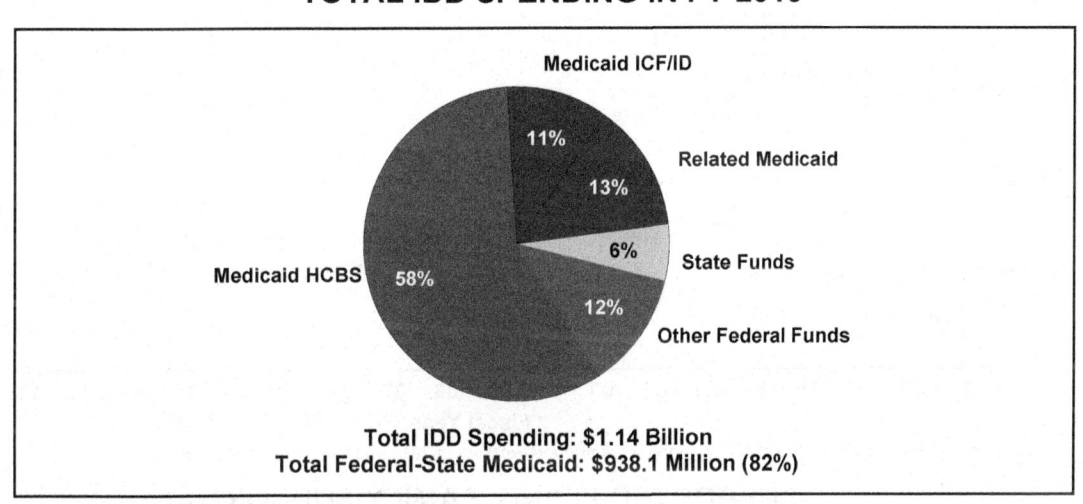

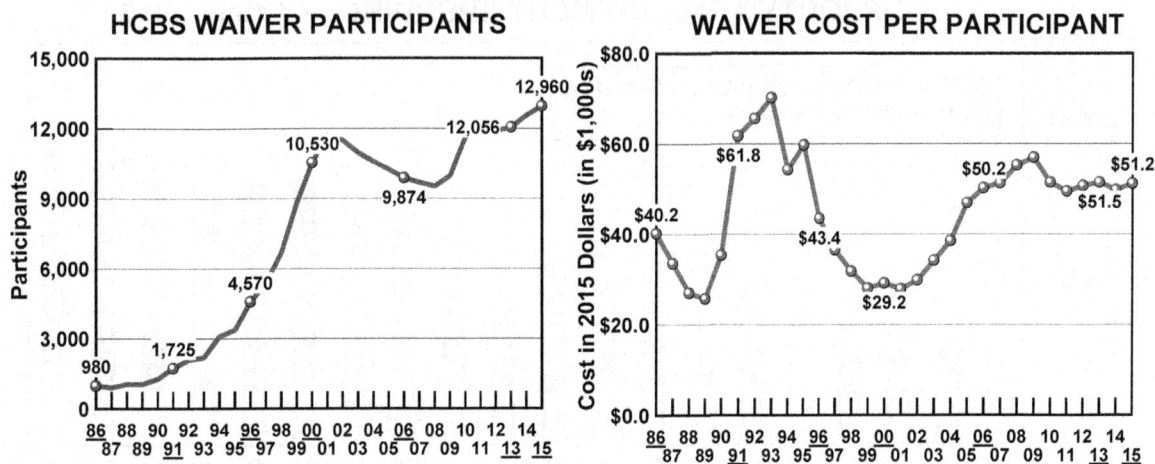

Source: Braddock et al., Coleman Institute and Department of Psychiatry, University of Colorado, 2017.
http://stateofthestates.org

WASHINGTON
INDIVIDUAL AND FAMILY SUPPORT
SPENDING: FY 1996-2015

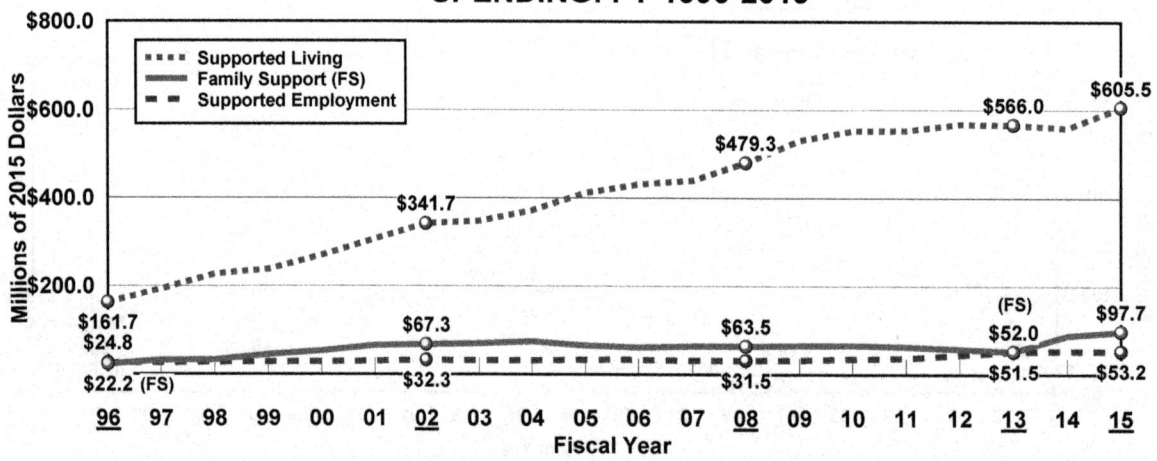

PARTICIPANTS: FY 1996-2015

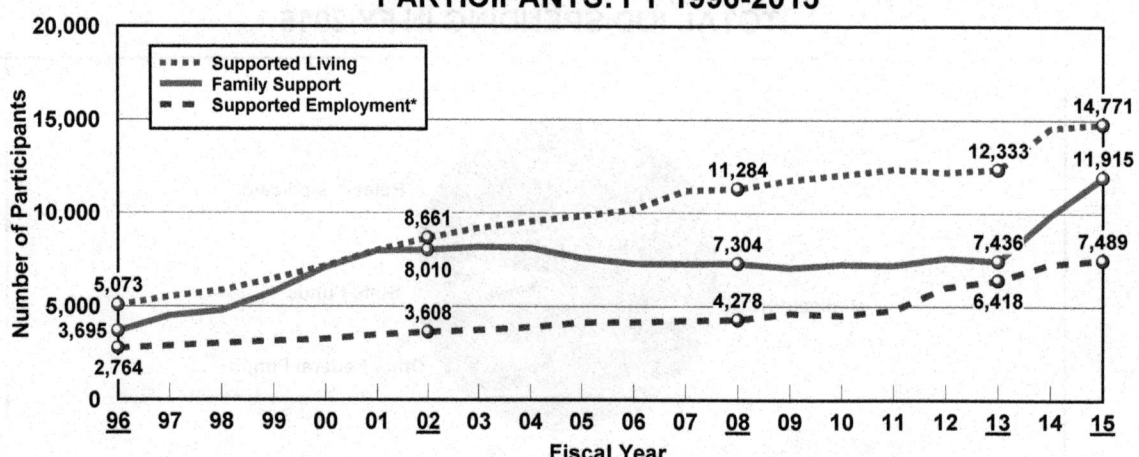

*Does not include 590 follow-along work support workers in 2014 and 863 workers in 2015.

SUPPORTED LIVING, FAMILY SUPPORT AND SUPPORTED EMPLOYMENT SPENDING: FY 1996-2015

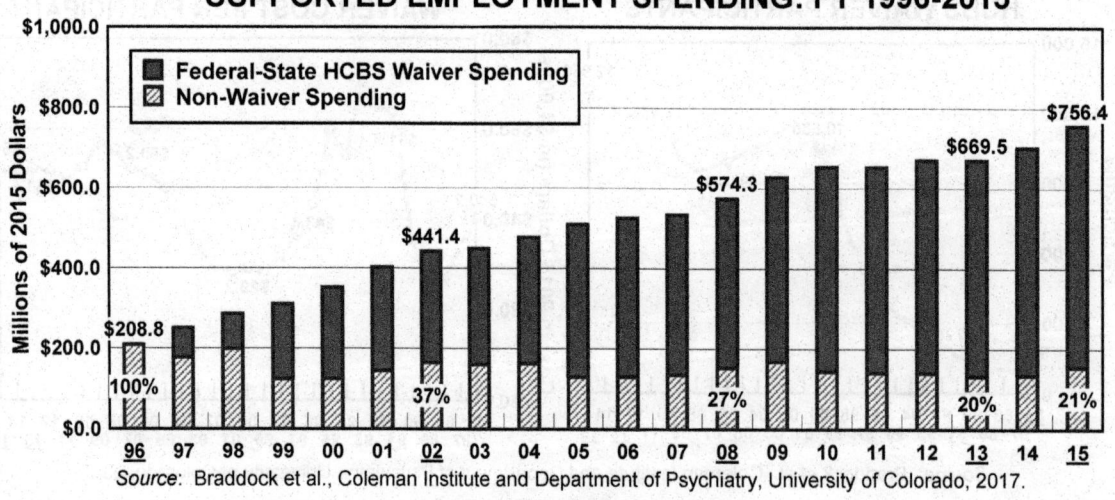

Source: Braddock et al., Coleman Institute and Department of Psychiatry, University of Colorado, 2017.
http://stateofthestates.org

WASHINGTON

ANNUAL COST OF CARE BY RESIDENTIAL SETTING: FY 2015

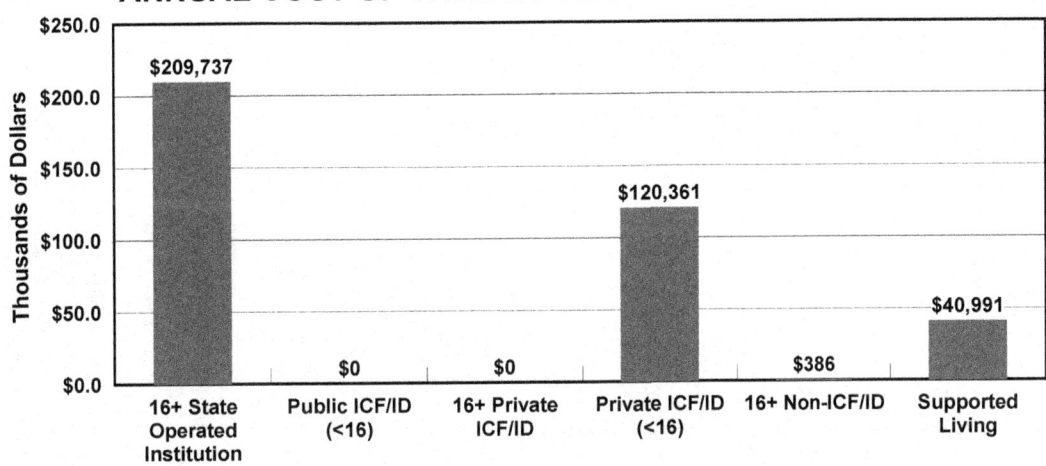

ESTIMATED NUMBER OF INDIVIDUALS WITH IDD BY AGE GROUP LIVING WITH FAMILY CAREGIVERS: FY 2015

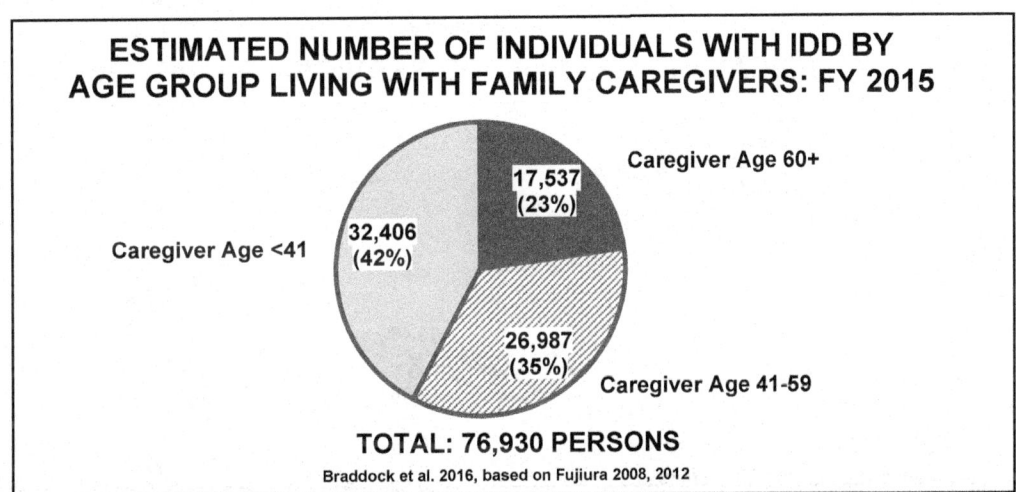

TOTAL: 76,930 PERSONS

Braddock et al. 2016, based on Fujiura 2008, 2012

ESTIMATED NUMBER OF IDD CAREGIVING FAMILIES AND FAMILIES SUPPORTED BY IDD AGENCIES: FY 1988-2015

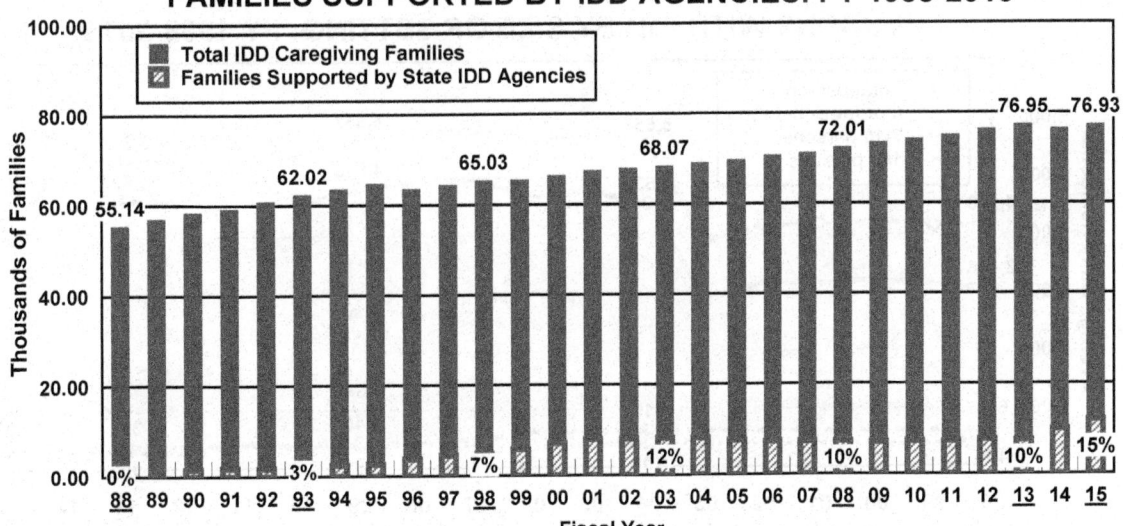

Source: Braddock et al., Coleman Institute and Department of Psychiatry, University of Colorado, 2017.
http://stateofthestates.org

WEST VIRGINIA

TOTAL PUBLIC IDD SPENDING FOR SERVICES: FY 1977-2015

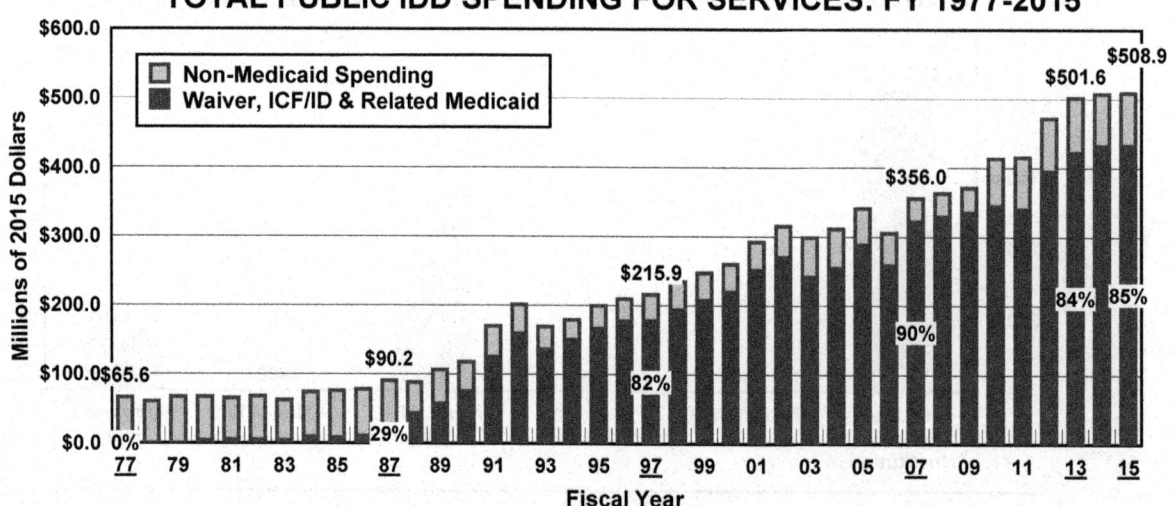

FISCAL EFFORT FOR IDD SERVICES: FY 1977-2015

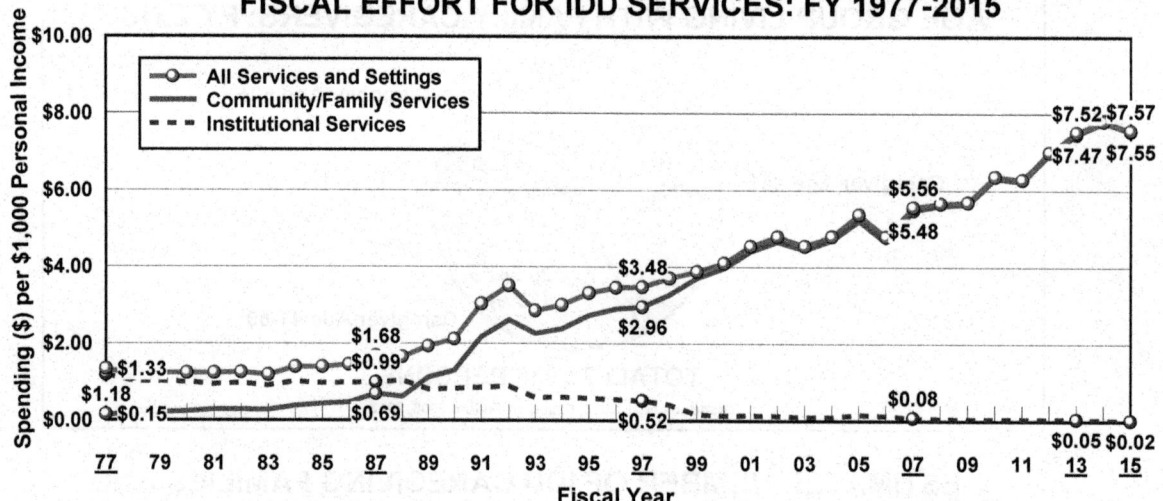

PERSONS WITH IDD BY SIZE OF SETTING: FY 1998-2015

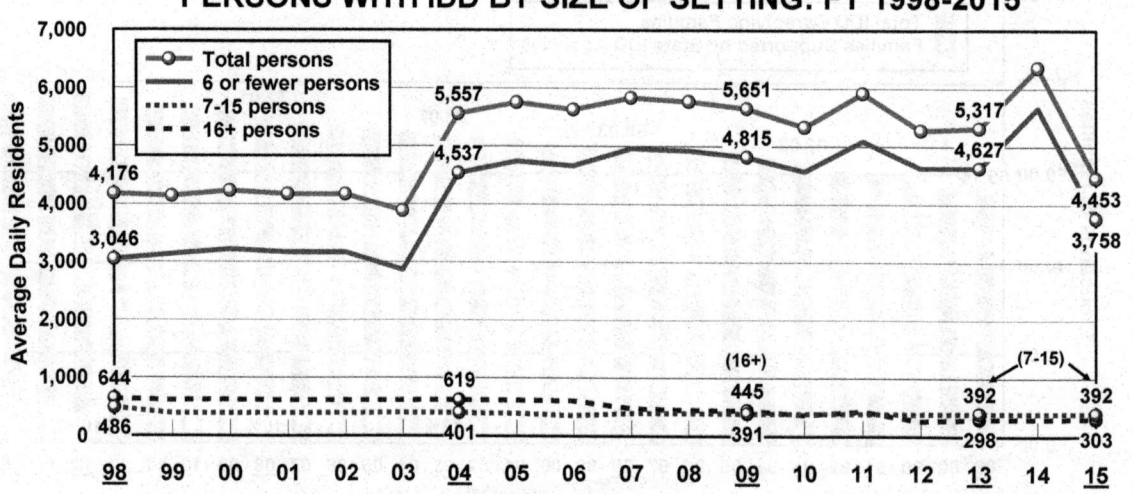

Source: Braddock et al., Coleman Institute and Department of Psychiatry, University of Colorado, 2017.
http://stateofthestates.org

WEST VIRGINIA

FEDERAL IDD MEDICAID SPENDING BY REVENUE SOURCE

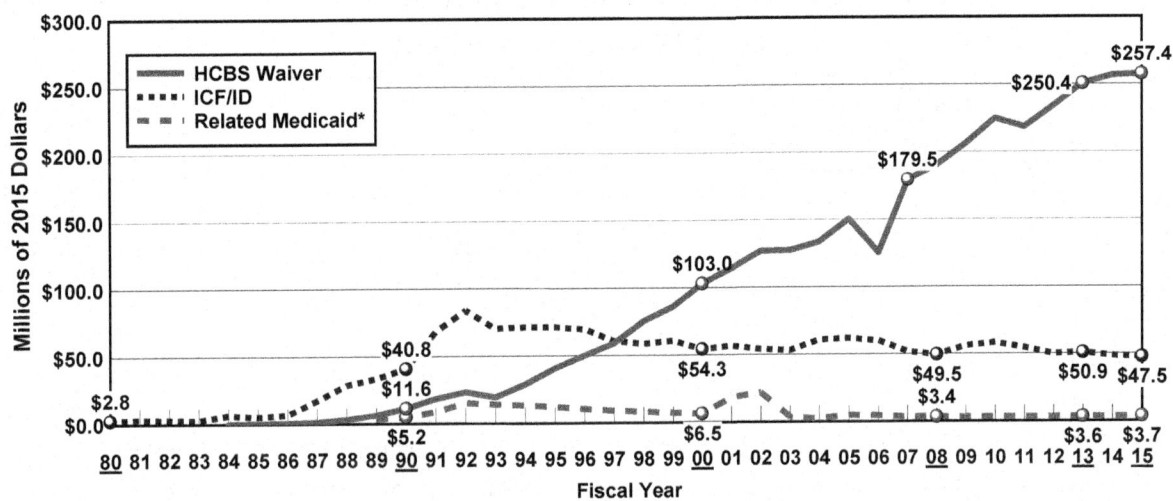

*In 2015, "Related Medicaid" was targeted case management ($0.3 million), clinic rehab ($0.4 million), and personal assistance (3.0 million).

FEDERAL-STATE MEDICAID AS A PERCENTAGE OF TOTAL IDD SPENDING IN FY 2015

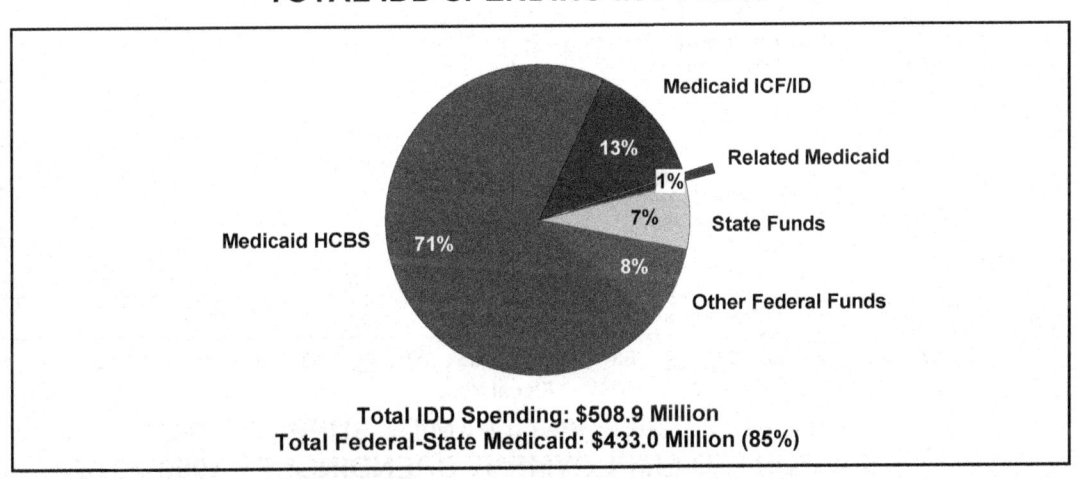

Total IDD Spending: $508.9 Million
Total Federal-State Medicaid: $433.0 Million (85%)

HCBS WAIVER PARTICIPANTS / WAIVER COST PER PARTICIPANT

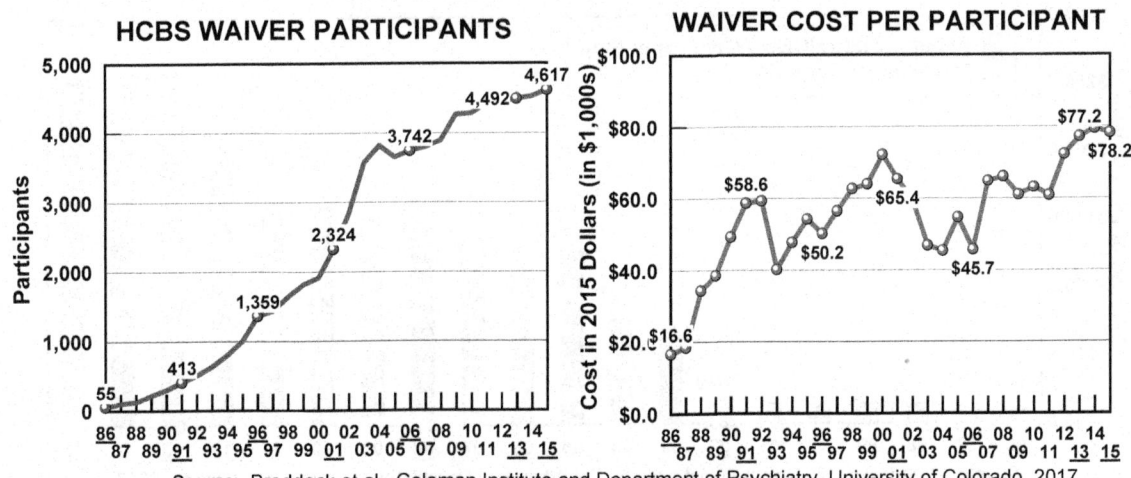

Source: Braddock et al., Coleman Institute and Department of Psychiatry, University of Colorado, 2017.
http://stateofthestates.org

WEST VIRGINIA

INDIVIDUAL AND FAMILY SUPPORT
SPENDING: FY 1996-2015

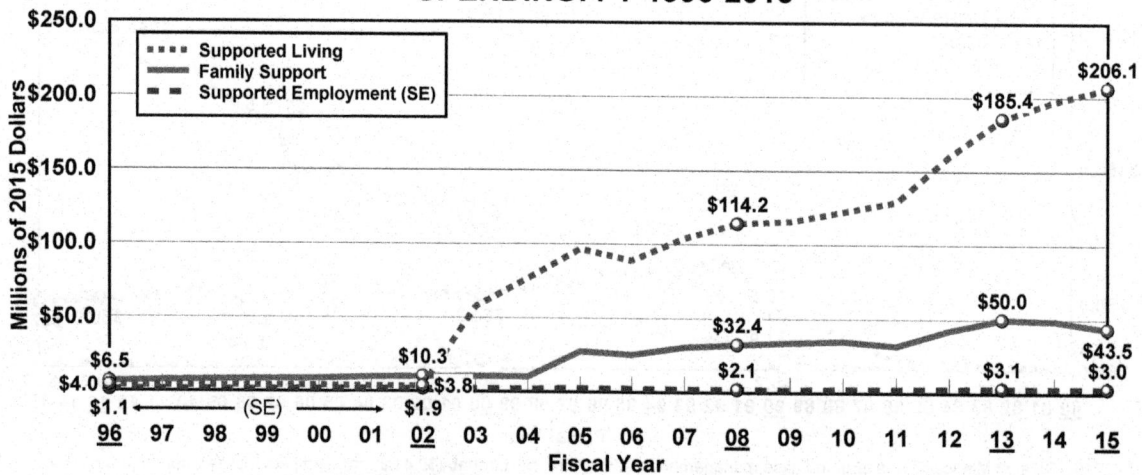

PARTICIPANTS: FY 1996-2015

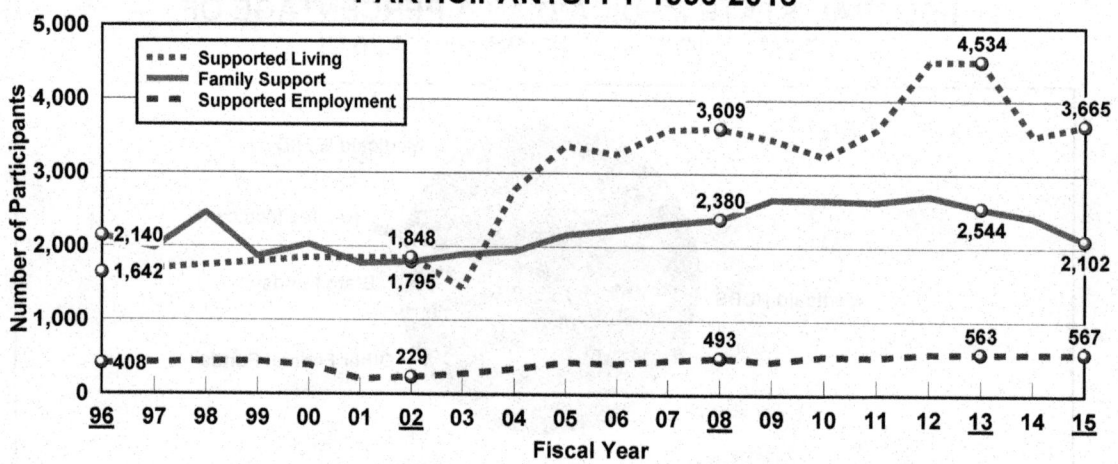

SUPPORTED LIVING, FAMILY SUPPORT AND SUPPORTED EMPLOYMENT SPENDING: FY 1996-2015

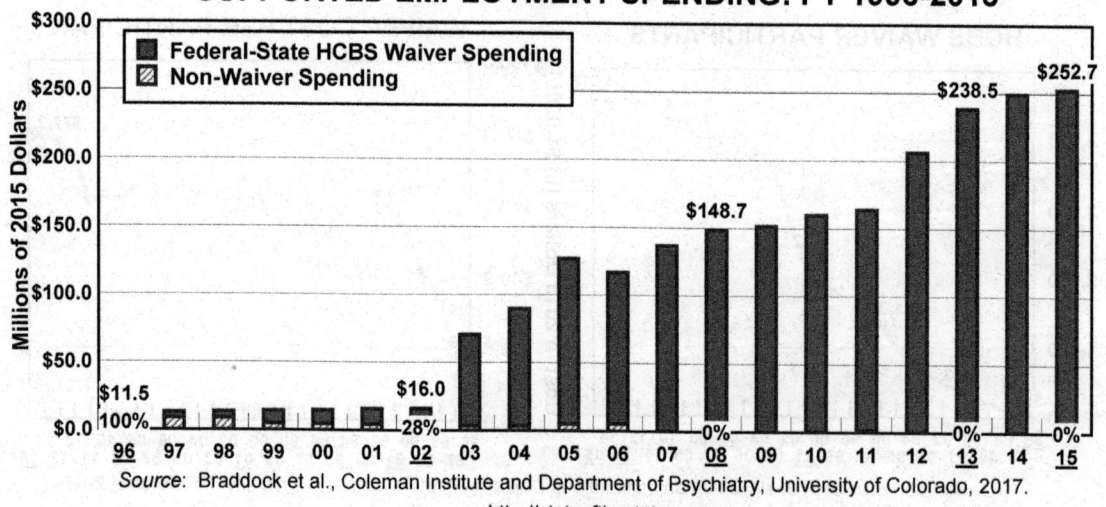

Source: Braddock et al., Coleman Institute and Department of Psychiatry, University of Colorado, 2017.
http://stateofthestates.org

WEST VIRGINIA

ANNUAL COST OF CARE BY RESIDENTIAL SETTING: FY 2015

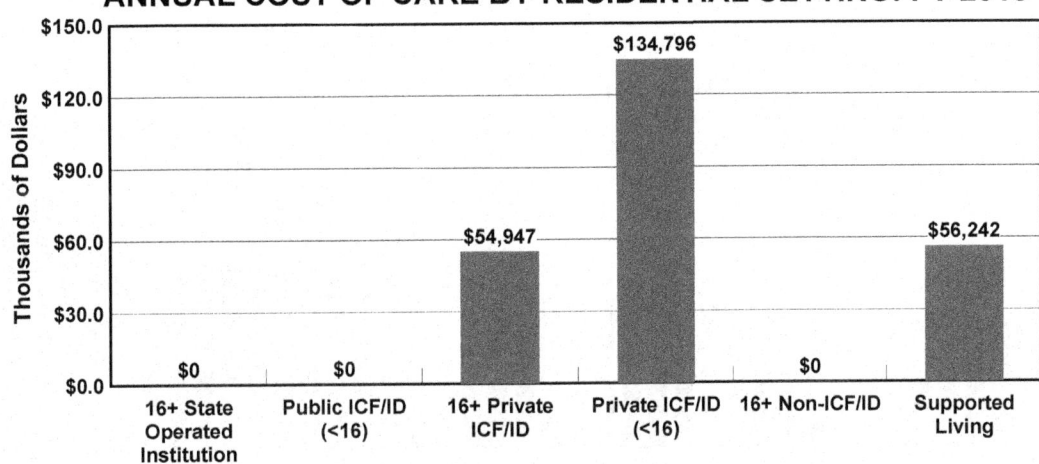

ESTIMATED NUMBER OF INDIVIDUALS WITH IDD BY AGE GROUP LIVING WITH FAMILY CAREGIVERS: FY 2015

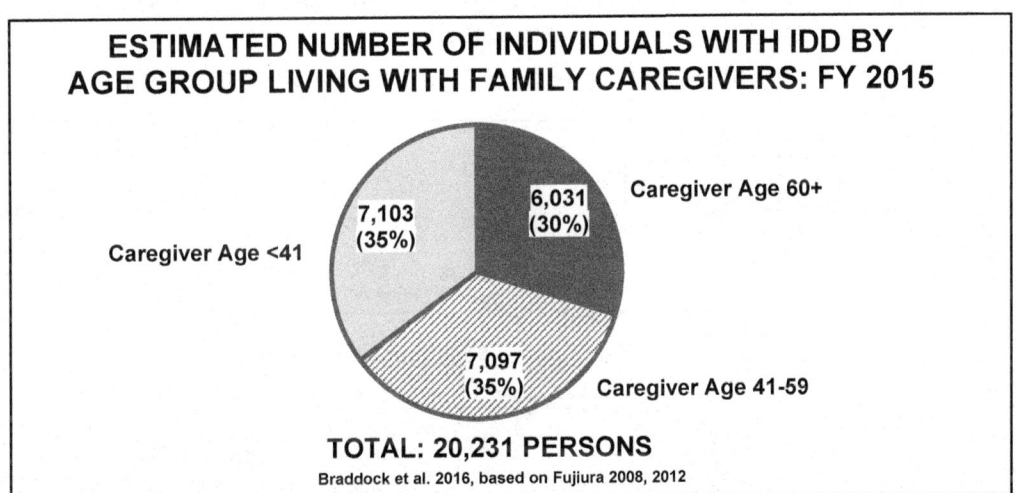

TOTAL: 20,231 PERSONS
Braddock et al. 2016, based on Fujiura 2008, 2012

ESTIMATED NUMBER OF IDD CAREGIVING FAMILIES AND FAMILIES SUPPORTED BY IDD AGENCIES: FY 1988-2015

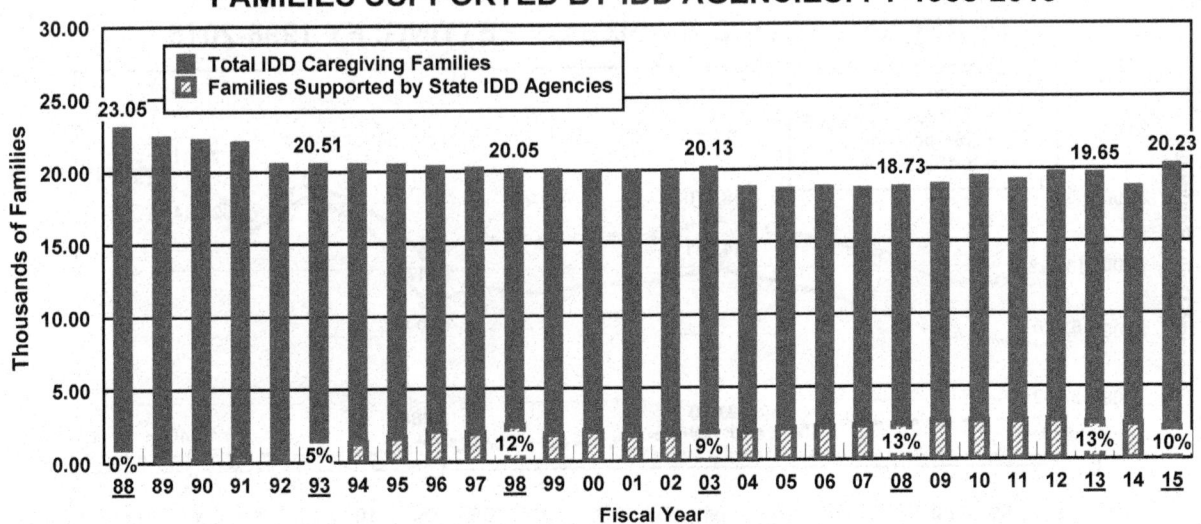

Source: Braddock et al., Coleman Institute and Department of Psychiatry, University of Colorado, 2017.
http://stateofthestates.org

WISCONSIN

TOTAL PUBLIC IDD SPENDING FOR SERVICES: FY 1977-2015

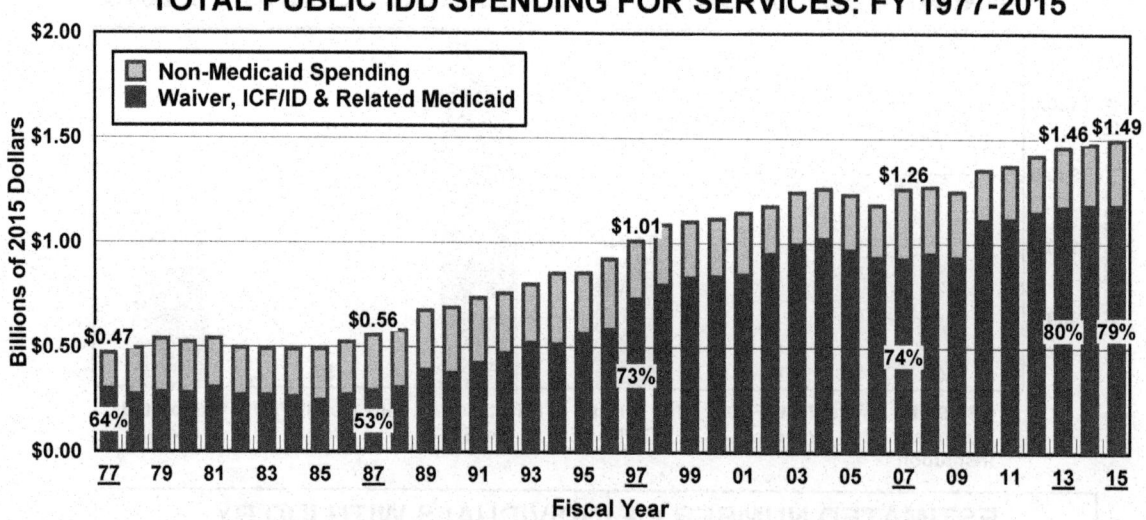

FISCAL EFFORT FOR IDD SERVICES: FY 1977-2015

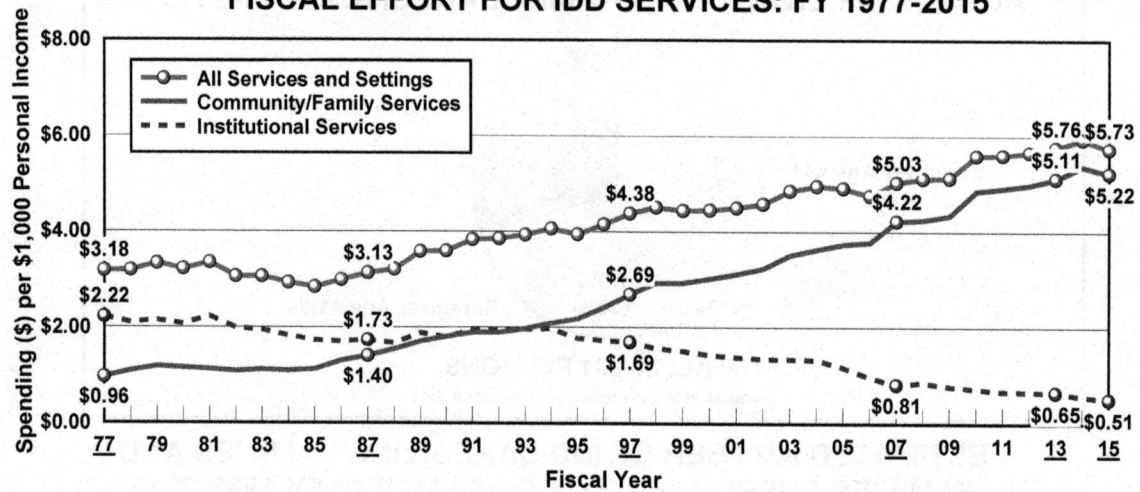

PERSONS WITH IDD BY SIZE OF SETTING: FY 1998-2015

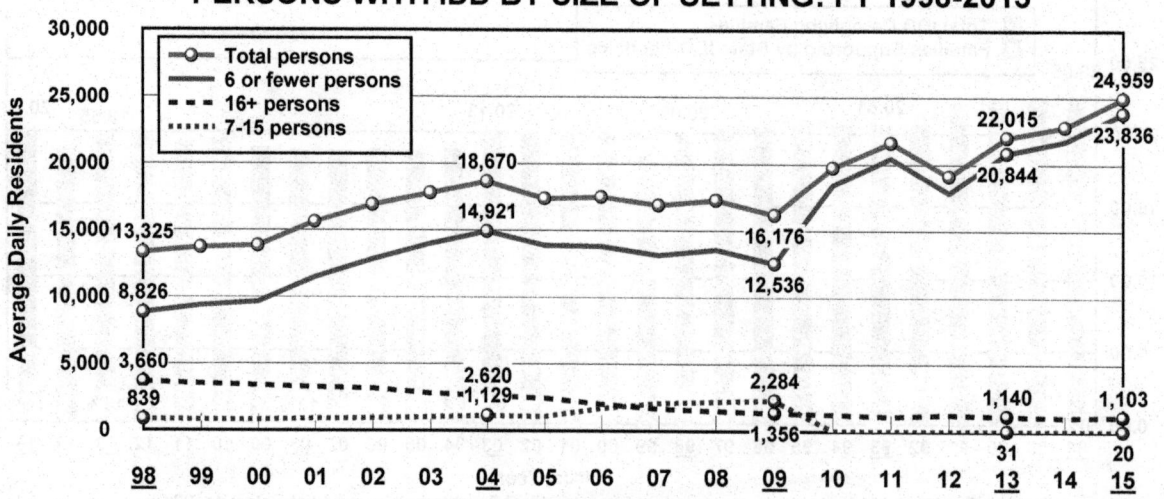

Source: Braddock et al., Coleman Institute and Department of Psychiatry, University of Colorado, 2017.

http://stateofthestates.org

WISCONSIN

FEDERAL IDD MEDICAID SPENDING BY REVENUE SOURCE

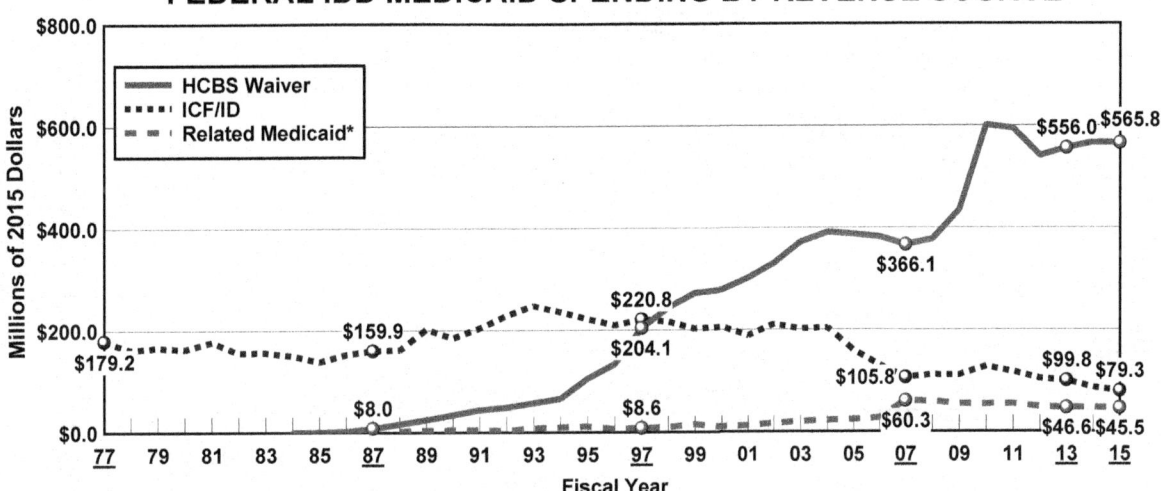

*In 2015, "Related Medicaid" was targeted case management ($0.6 million) and personal assistance ($44.9 million).

FEDERAL-STATE MEDICAID AS A PERCENTAGE OF TOTAL IDD SPENDING IN FY 2015

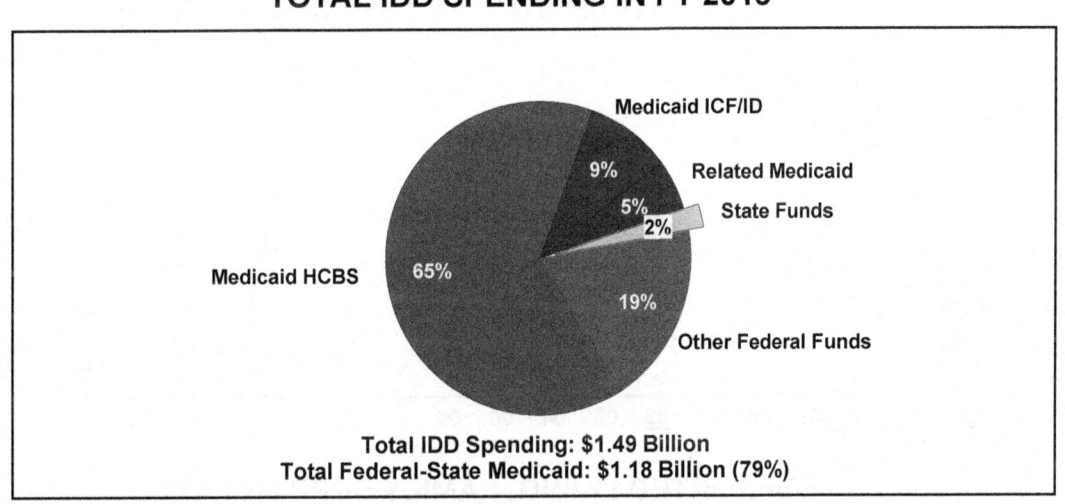

Total IDD Spending: $1.49 Billion
Total Federal-State Medicaid: $1.18 Billion (79%)

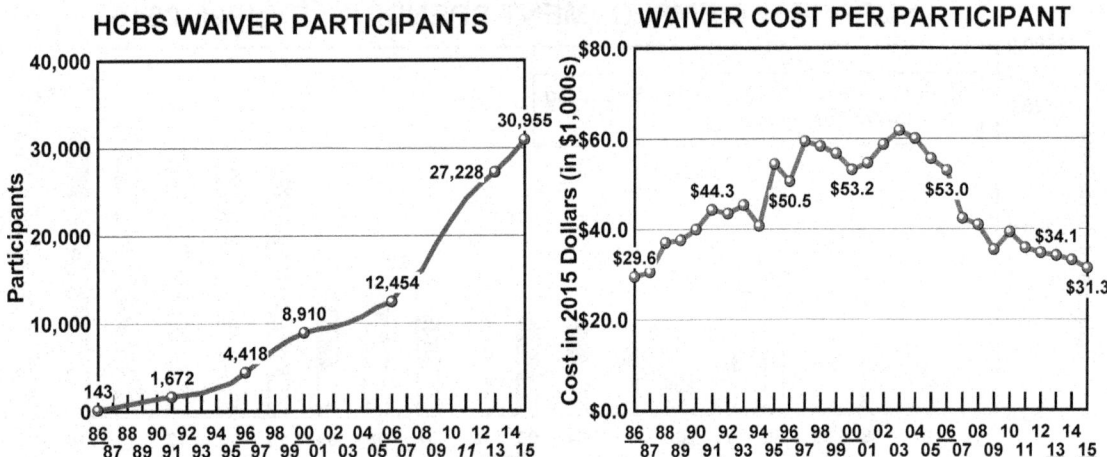

Source: Braddock et al., Coleman Institute and Department of Psychiatry, University of Colorado, 2017.
http://stateofthestates.org

WISCONSIN
INDIVIDUAL AND FAMILY SUPPORT
SPENDING: FY 1996-2015

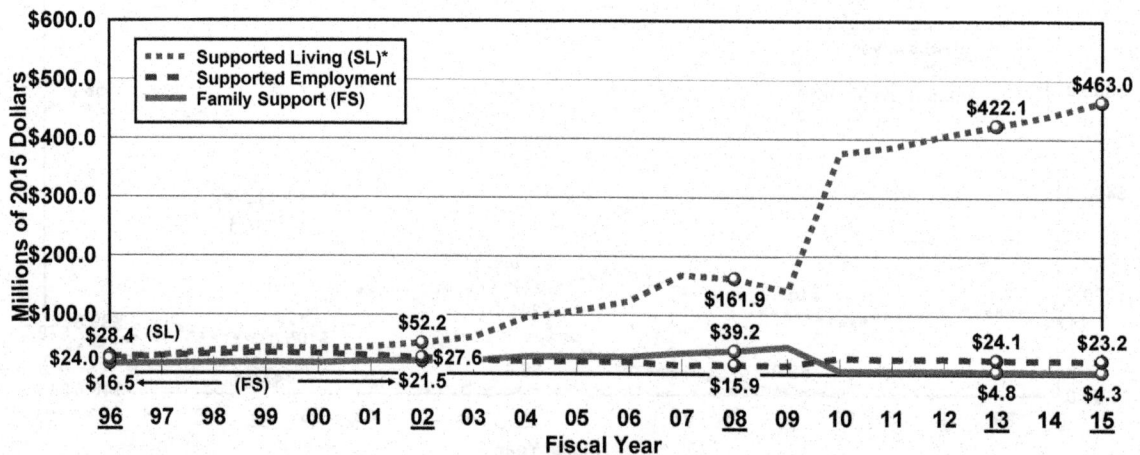

*Wisconsin implemented a redesign of its long-term care system that replaced county-based Waiver programs with managed care programs (Family Care, Family Care partnership, & PACE). As a result of this change, funding for Family Support was re-classified by the State as Supported Living.

PARTICIPANTS: FY 1996-2015

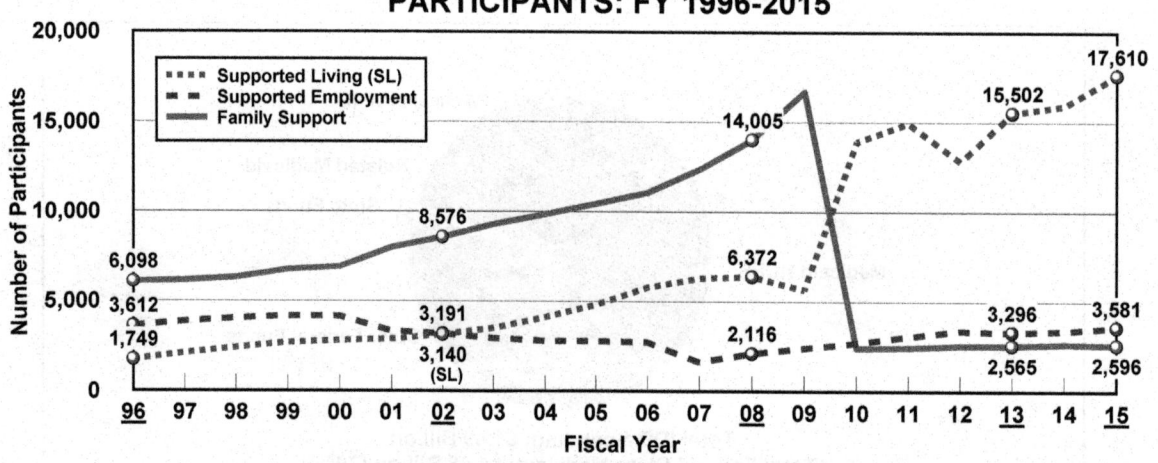

SUPPORTED LIVING, FAMILY SUPPORT AND SUPPORTED EMPLOYMENT SPENDING: FY 1996-2015

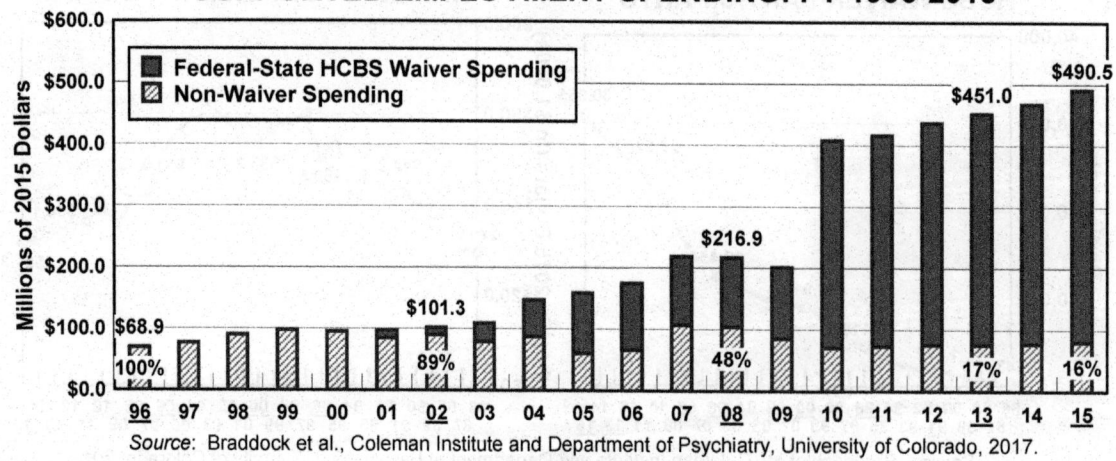

Source: Braddock et al., Coleman Institute and Department of Psychiatry, University of Colorado, 2017.
http://stateofthestates.org

WISCONSIN

ANNUAL COST OF CARE BY RESIDENTIAL SETTING: FY 2015

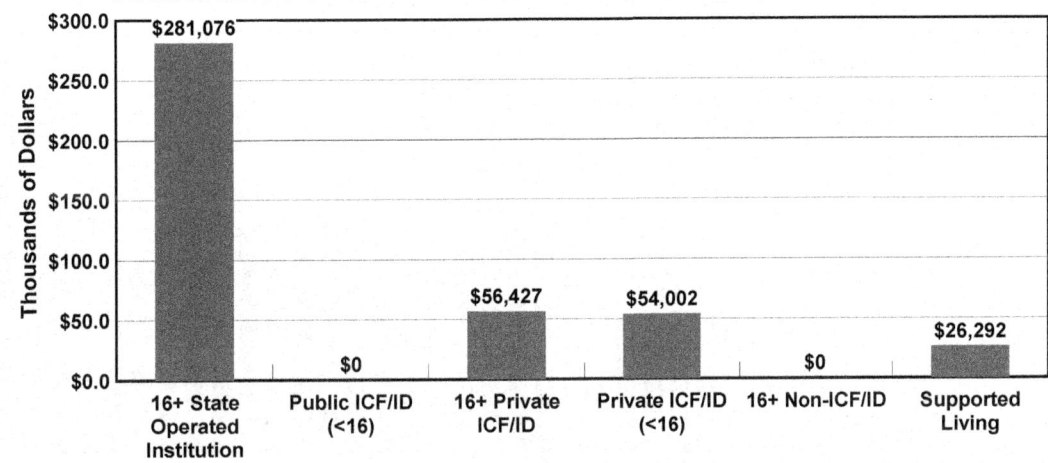

ESTIMATED NUMBER OF INDIVIDUALS WITH IDD BY AGE GROUP LIVING WITH FAMILY CAREGIVERS: FY 2015

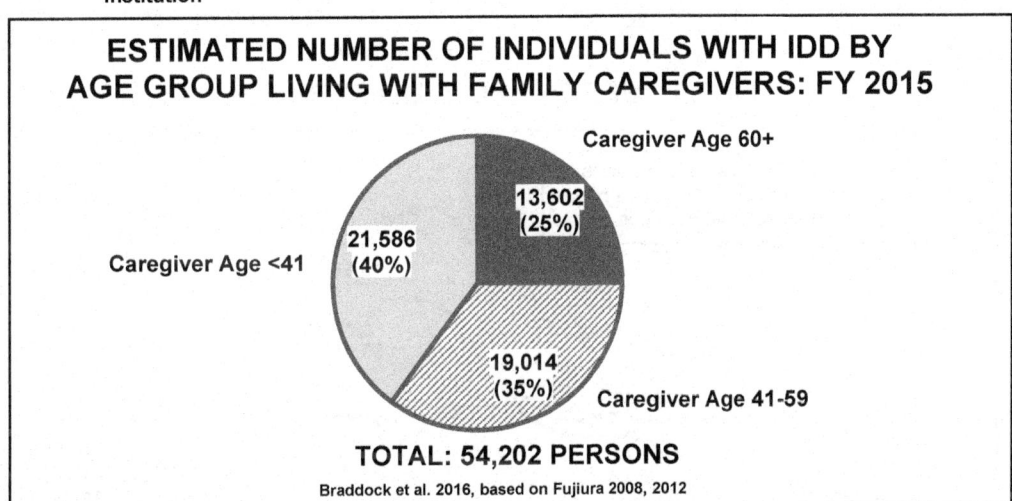

TOTAL: 54,202 PERSONS

Braddock et al. 2016, based on Fujiura 2008, 2012

ESTIMATED NUMBER OF IDD CAREGIVING FAMILIES AND FAMILIES SUPPORTED BY IDD AGENCIES: FY 1988-2015

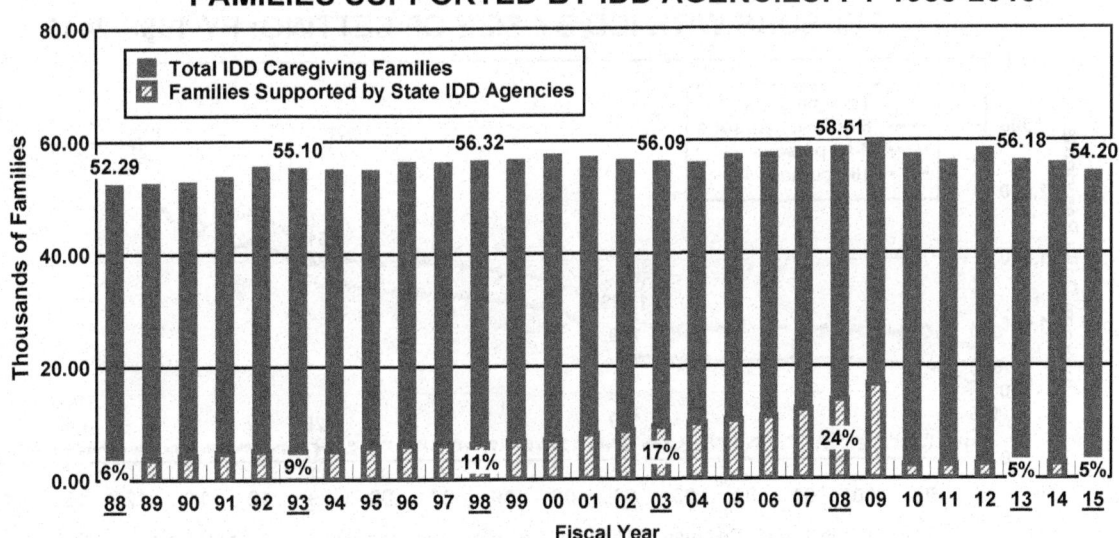

Source: Braddock et al., Coleman Institute and Department of Psychiatry, University of Colorado, 2017.
http://stateofthestates.org

WYOMING

TOTAL PUBLIC IDD SPENDING FOR SERVICES: FY 1977-2015

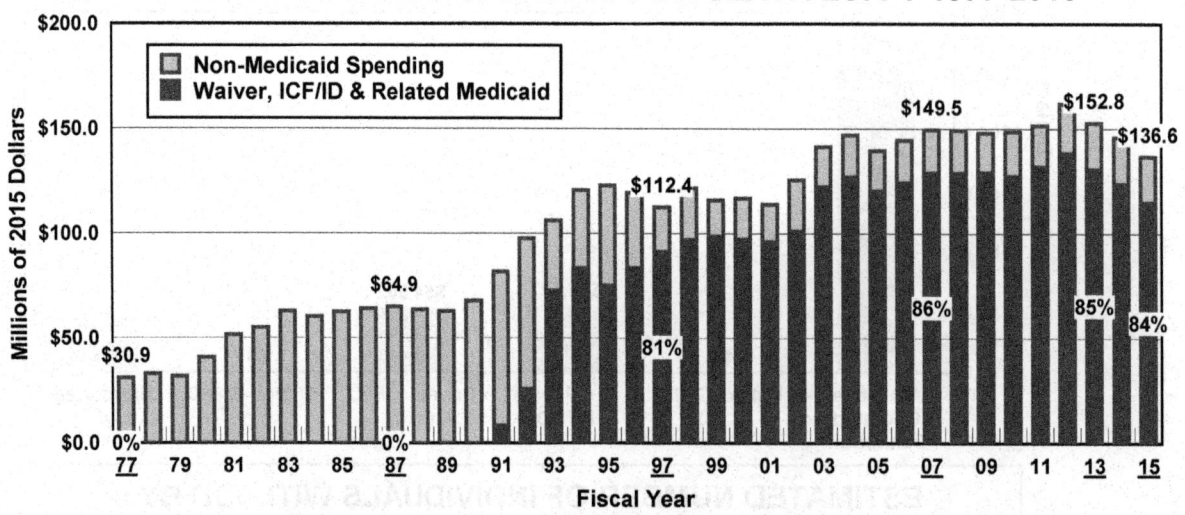

FISCAL EFFORT FOR IDD SERVICES: FY 1977-2015

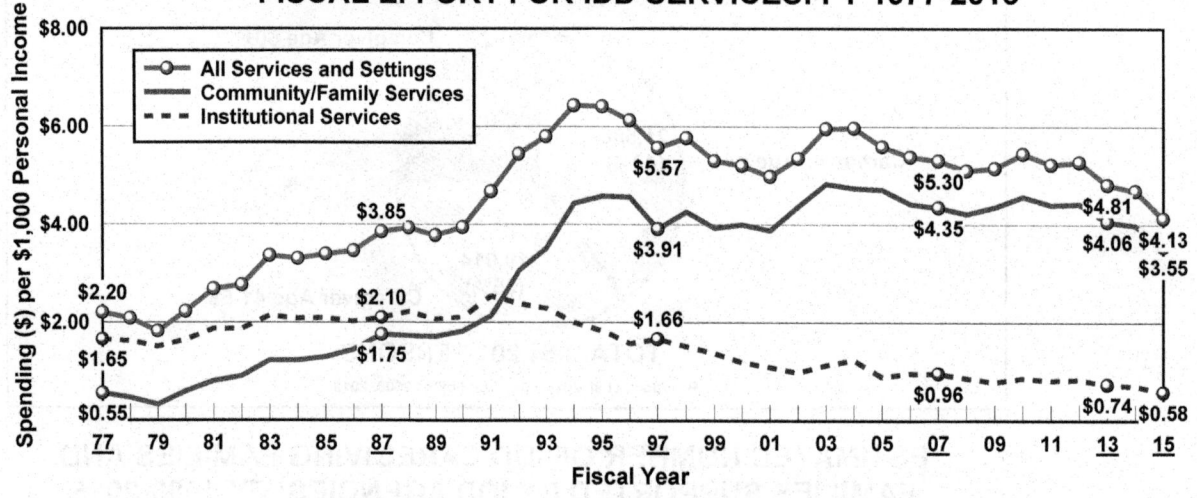

PERSONS WITH IDD BY SIZE OF SETTING: FY 1998-2015

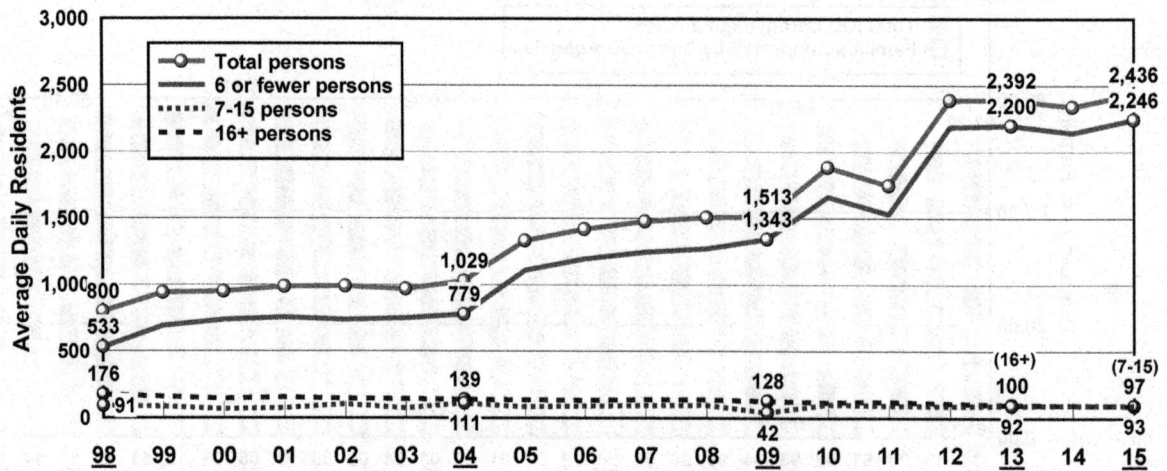

Source: Braddock et al., Coleman Institute and Department of Psychiatry, University of Colorado, 2017.
http://stateofthestates.org

WYOMING

FEDERAL IDD MEDICAID SPENDING BY REVENUE SOURCE

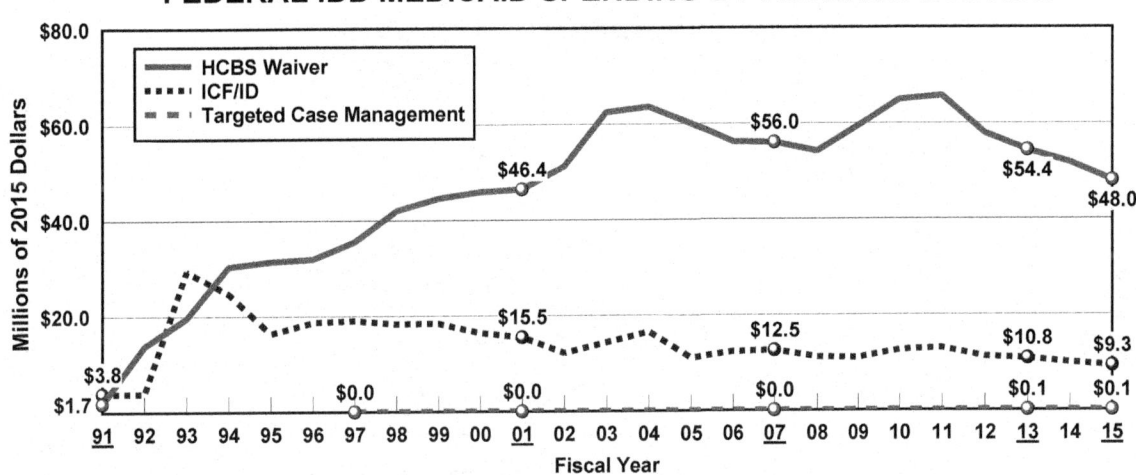

FEDERAL-STATE MEDICAID AS A PERCENTAGE OF TOTAL IDD SPENDING IN FY 2015

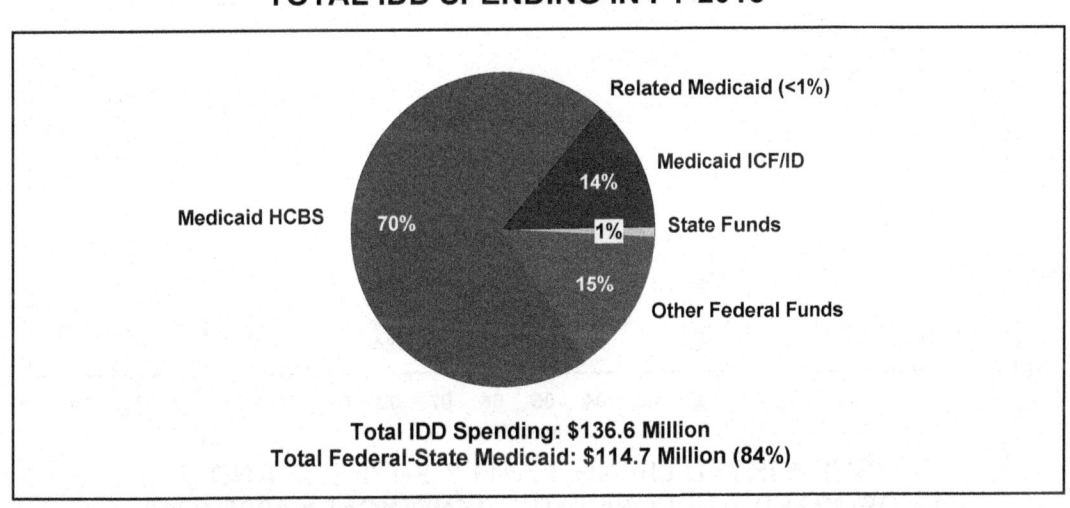

Total IDD Spending: $136.6 Million
Total Federal-State Medicaid: $114.7 Million (84%)

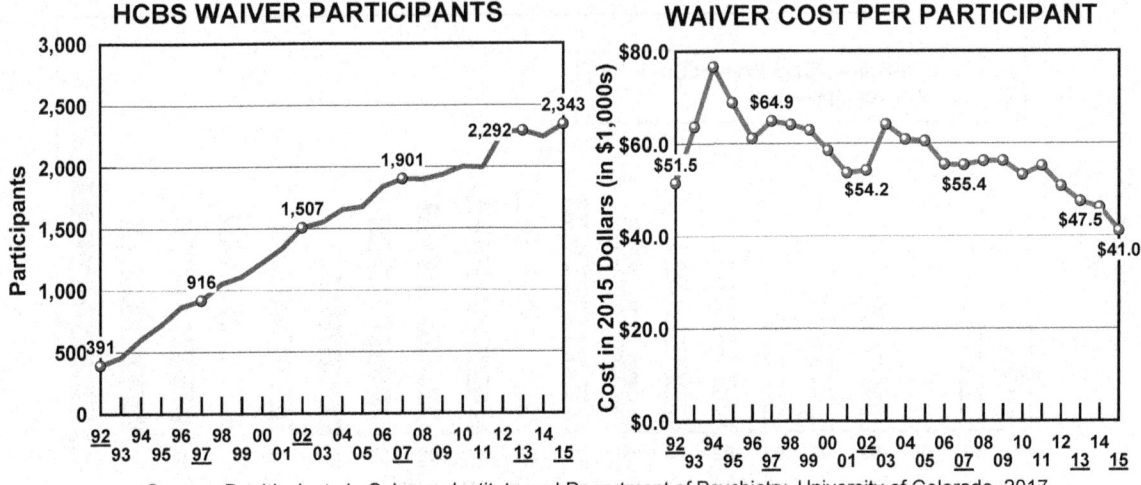

Source: Braddock et al., Coleman Institute and Department of Psychiatry, University of Colorado, 2017.
http://stateofthestates.org

WYOMING
INDIVIDUAL AND FAMILY SUPPORT
SPENDING: FY 1996-2015

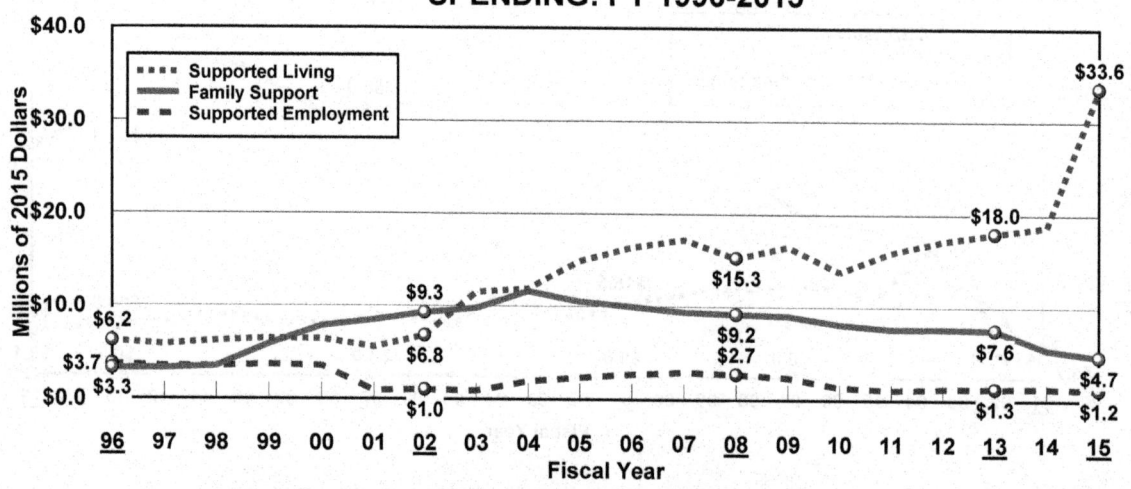

PARTICIPANTS: FY 1996-2015

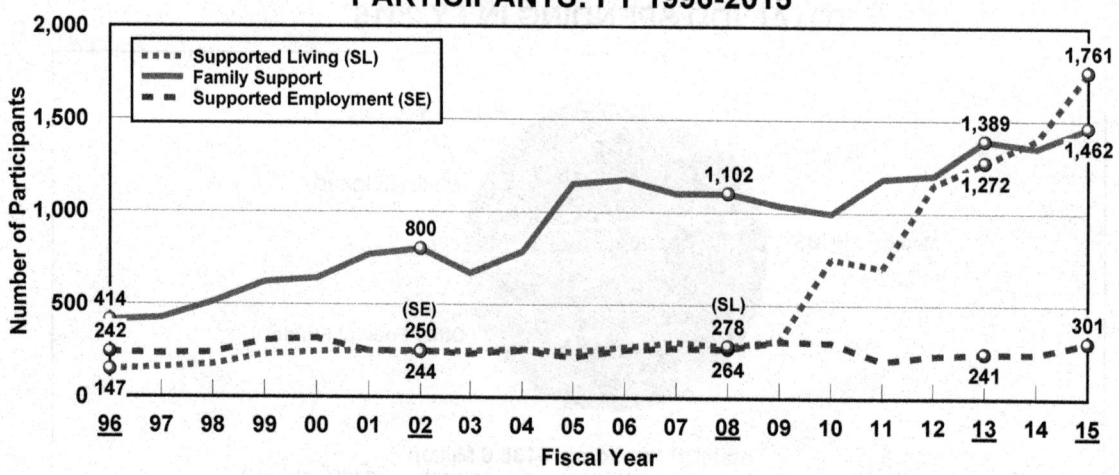

SUPPORTED LIVING, FAMILY SUPPORT AND SUPPORTED EMPLOYMENT SPENDING: FY 1996-2015

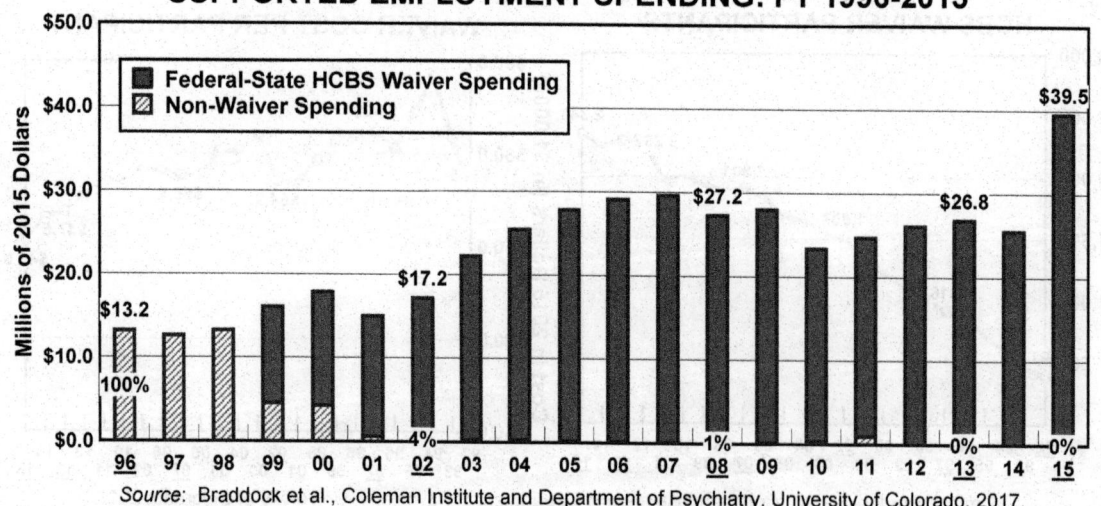

Source: Braddock et al., Coleman Institute and Department of Psychiatry, University of Colorado, 2017.
http://stateofthestates.org

WYOMING

ANNUAL COST OF CARE BY RESIDENTIAL SETTING: FY 2015

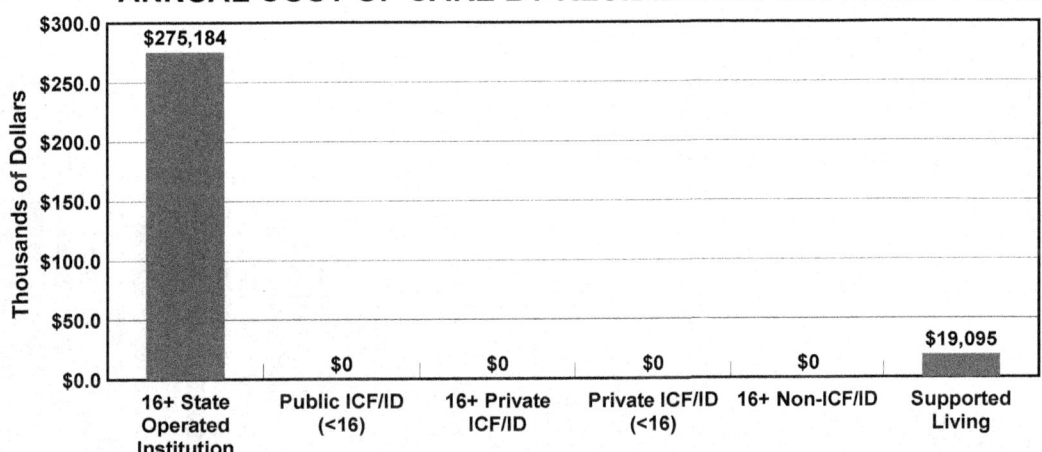

ESTIMATED NUMBER OF INDIVIDUALS WITH IDD BY AGE GROUP LIVING WITH FAMILY CAREGIVERS: FY 2015

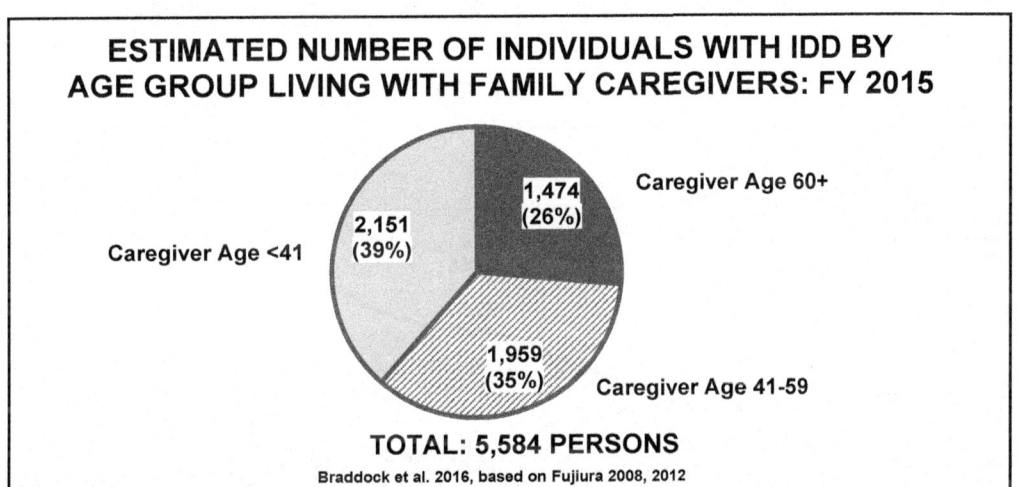

TOTAL: 5,584 PERSONS

Braddock et al. 2016, based on Fujiura 2008, 2012

ESTIMATED NUMBER OF IDD CAREGIVING FAMILIES AND FAMILIES SUPPORTED BY IDD AGENCIES: FY 1988-2015

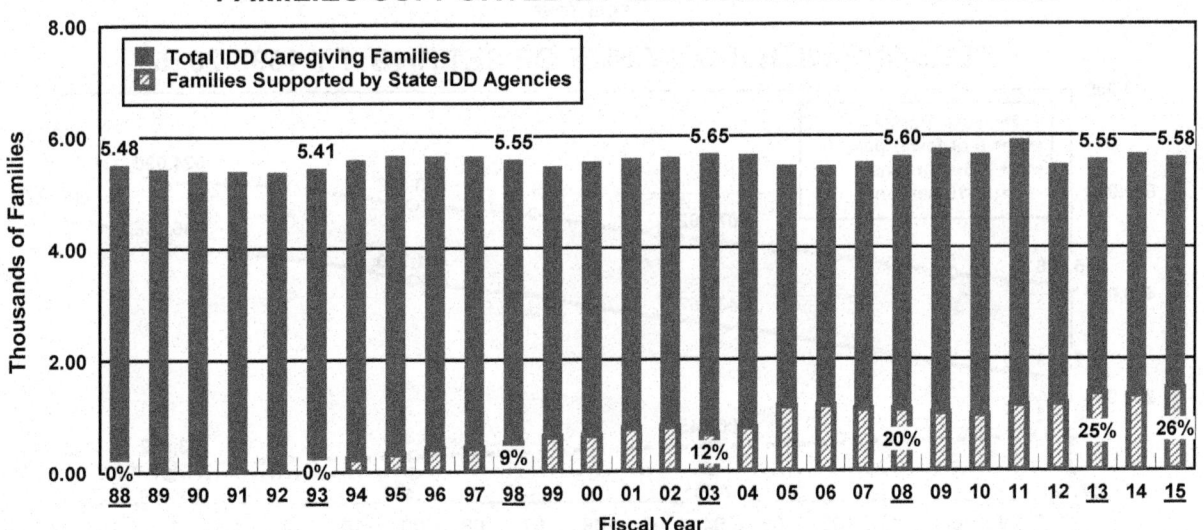

Source: Braddock et al., Coleman Institute and Department of Psychiatry, University of Colorado, 2017.

http://stateofthestates.org

UNITED STATES

TOTAL PUBLIC IDD SPENDING FOR SERVICES: FY 1977-2015

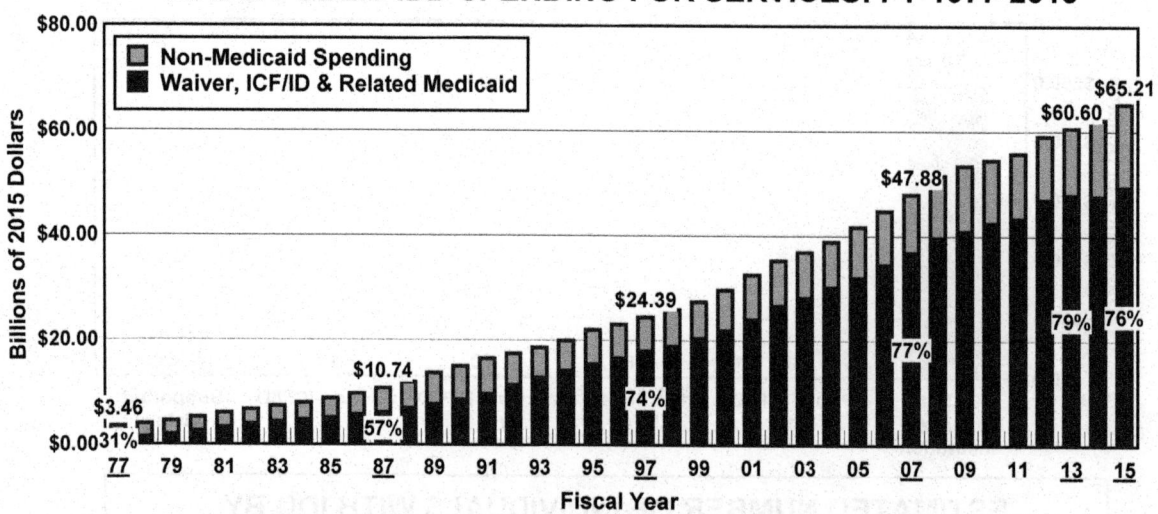

FISCAL EFFORT FOR IDD SERVICES: FY 1977-2015

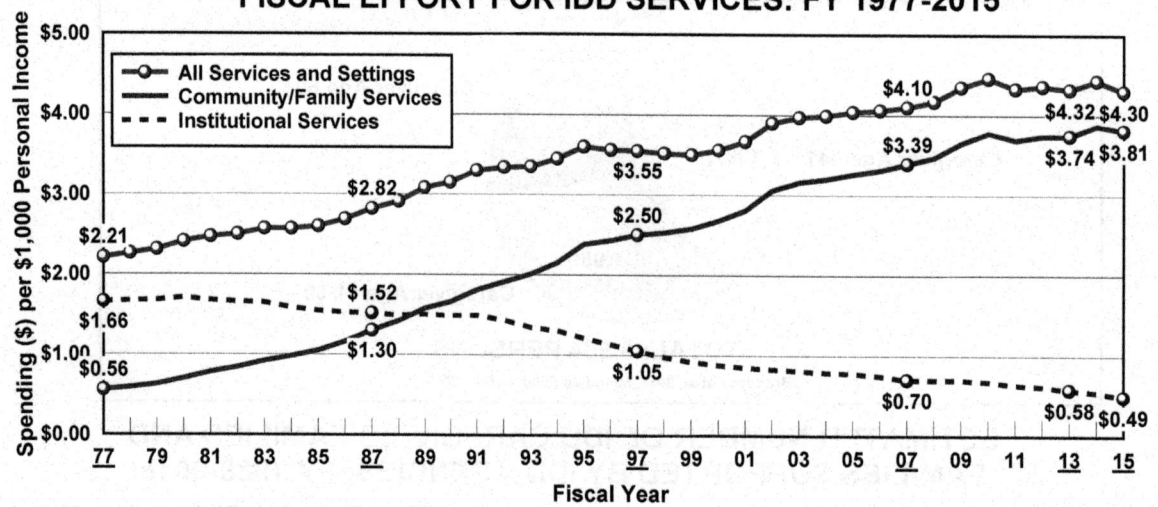

PERSONS WITH IDD BY SIZE OF SETTING: FY 1998-2015

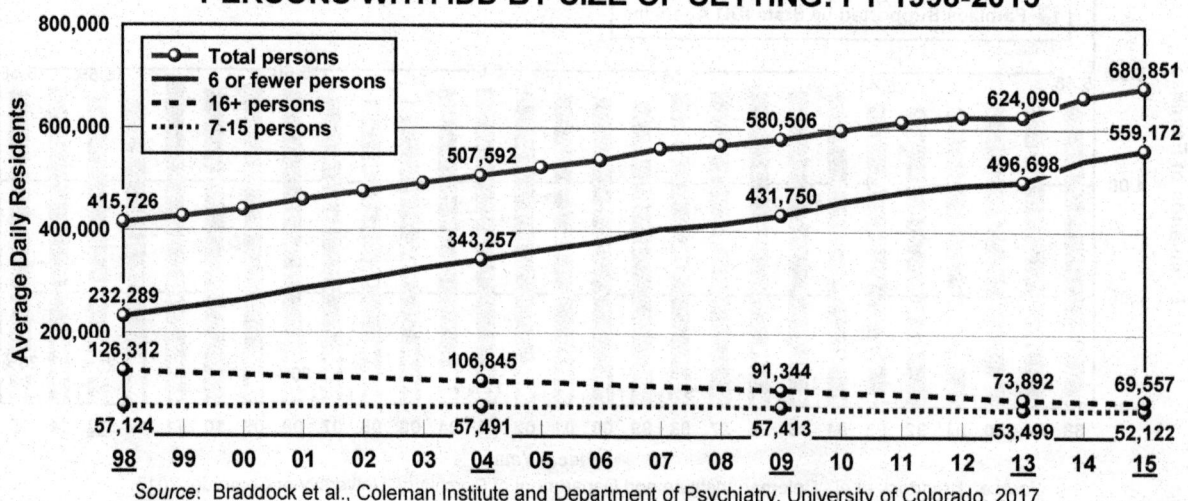

Source: Braddock et al., Coleman Institute and Department of Psychiatry, University of Colorado, 2017.
http://stateofthestates.org

UNITED STATES

FEDERAL IDD MEDICAID SPENDING BY REVENUE SOURCE

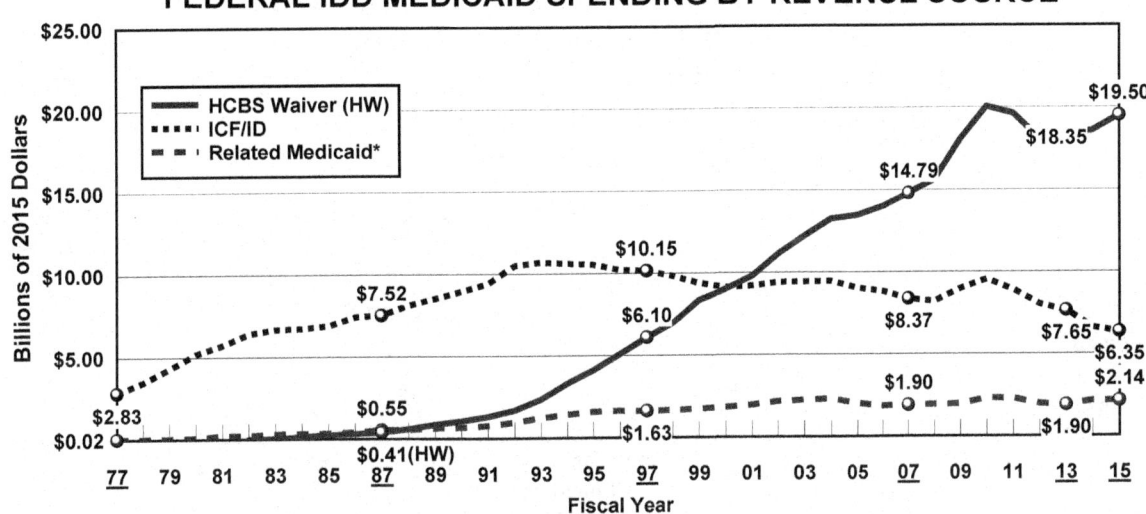

*In 2015, "Related Medicaid" was targeted case management ($0.71 Billion), personal assistance (0.57 Billion), clinic rehabilitation (0.29 Billion) and administration ($0.58 Billion).

FEDERAL-STATE MEDICAID AS A PERCENTAGE OF TOTAL IDD SPENDING IN FY 2015

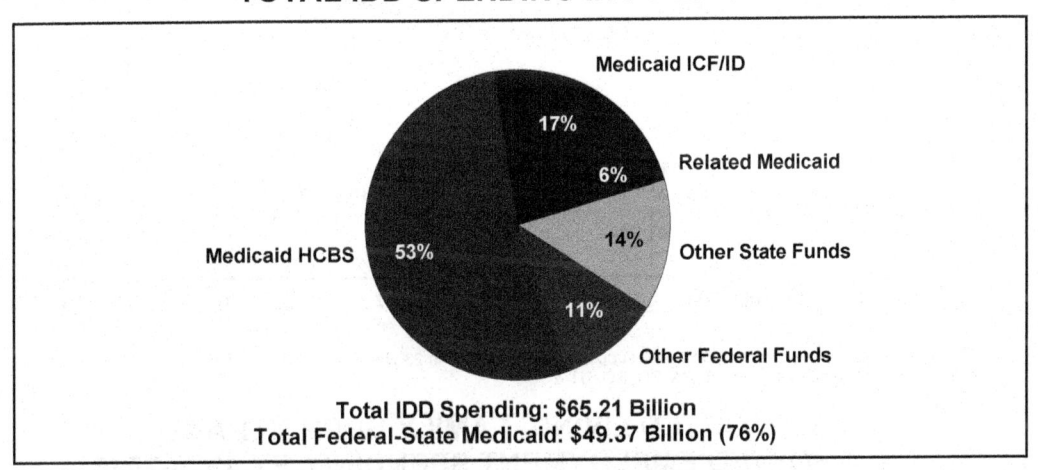

Total IDD Spending: $65.21 Billion
Total Federal-State Medicaid: $49.37 Billion (76%)

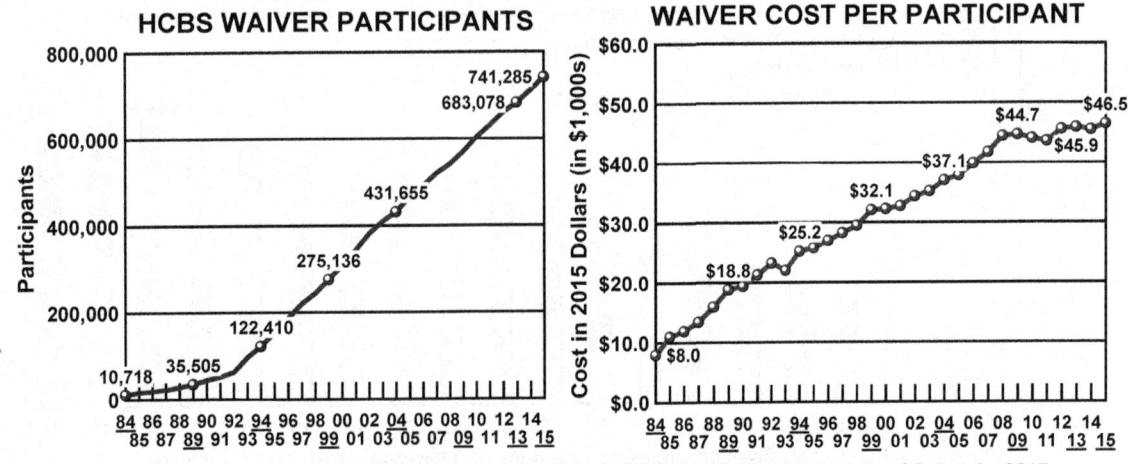

Source: Braddock et al., Coleman Institute and Department of Psychiatry, University of Colorado, 2017.
http://stateofthestates.org

UNITED STATES

INDIVIDUAL AND FAMILY SUPPORT
SPENDING: FY 1996-2015

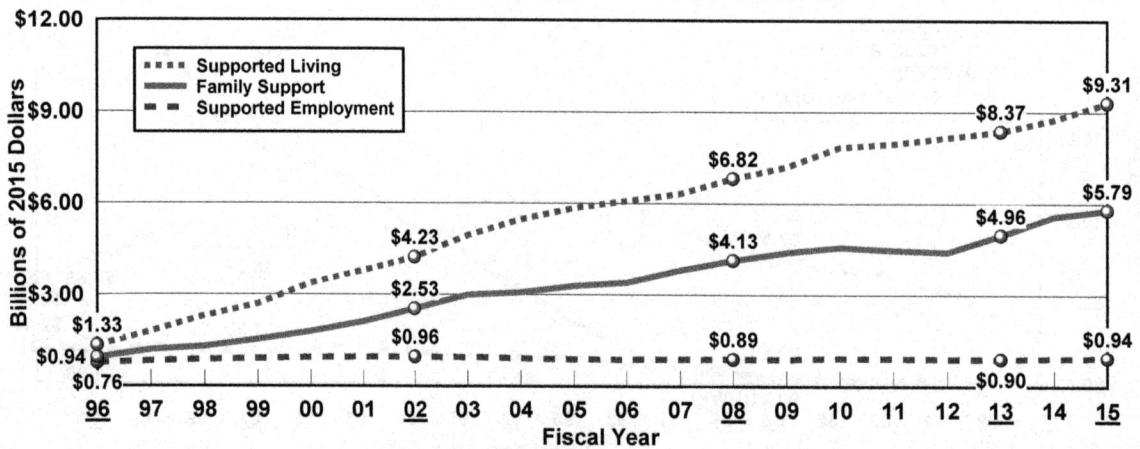

PARTICIPANTS: FY 1996-2015

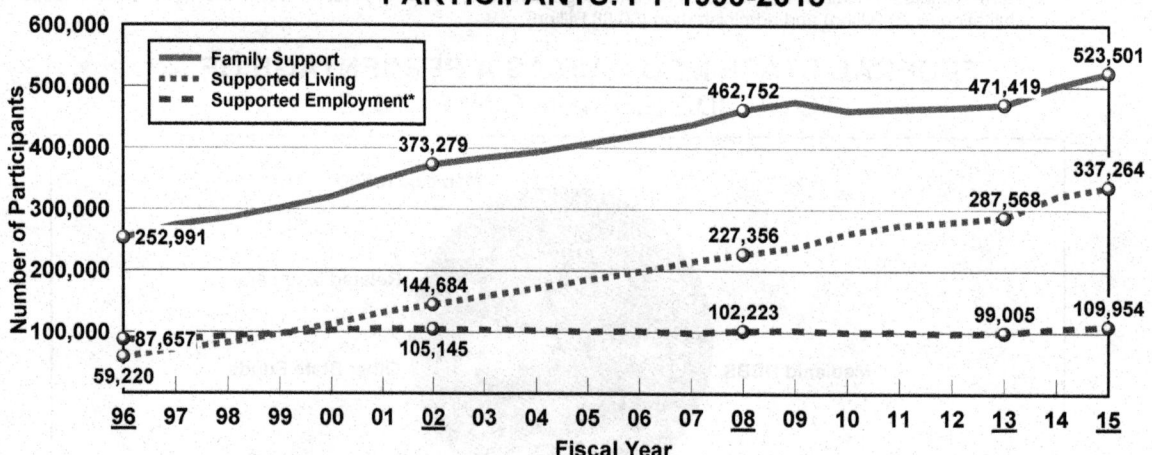

*Does not include 15,640 follow-along work support workers in 2015 in 23 states: AZ, CO, CT, DE, DC, HI, KS, LA, ME, MI, MO, NE, NH, NJ, NM, NC, OH, OR, PA, SC, SD, UT & WA.

SUPPORTED LIVING, FAMILY SUPPORT AND SUPPORTED EMPLOYMENT SPENDING: FY 1996-2015

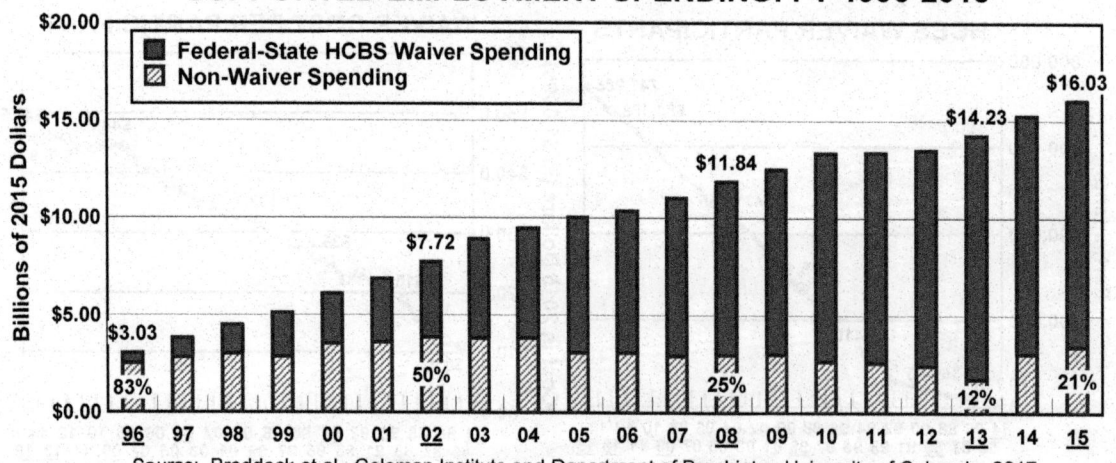

Source: Braddock et al., Coleman Institute and Department of Psychiatry, University of Colorado, 2017.
http://stateofthestates.org

UNITED STATES

ANNUAL COST OF CARE BY RESIDENTIAL SETTING: FY 2015

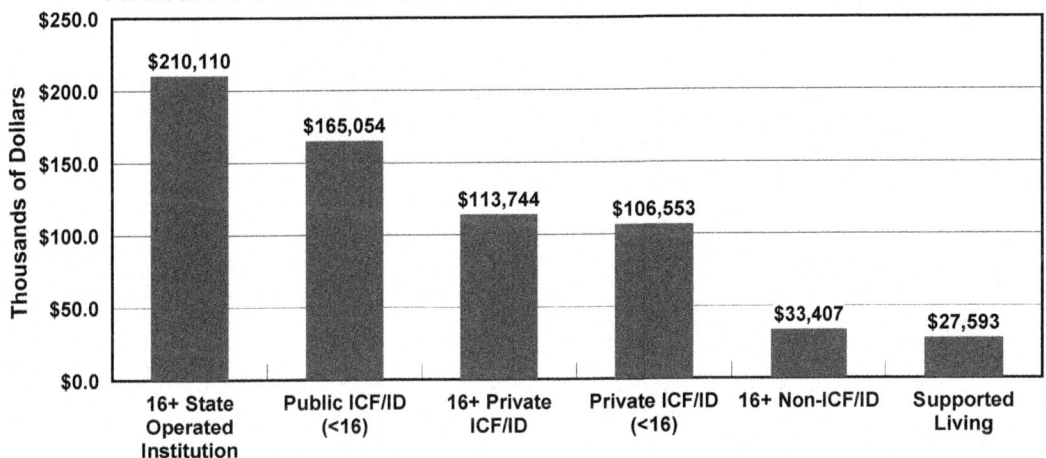

ESTIMATED NUMBER OF INDIVIDUALS WITH IDD BY AGE GROUP LIVING WITH FAMILY CAREGIVERS: FY 2015

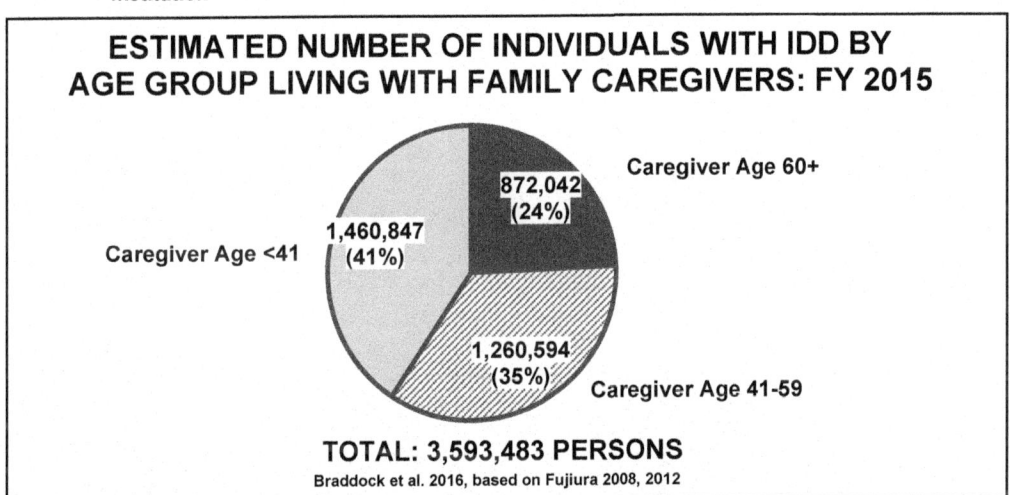

TOTAL: 3,593,483 PERSONS
Braddock et al. 2016, based on Fujiura 2008, 2012

ESTIMATED NUMBER OF IDD CAREGIVING FAMILIES AND FAMILIES SUPPORTED BY IDD AGENCIES: FY 1988-2015

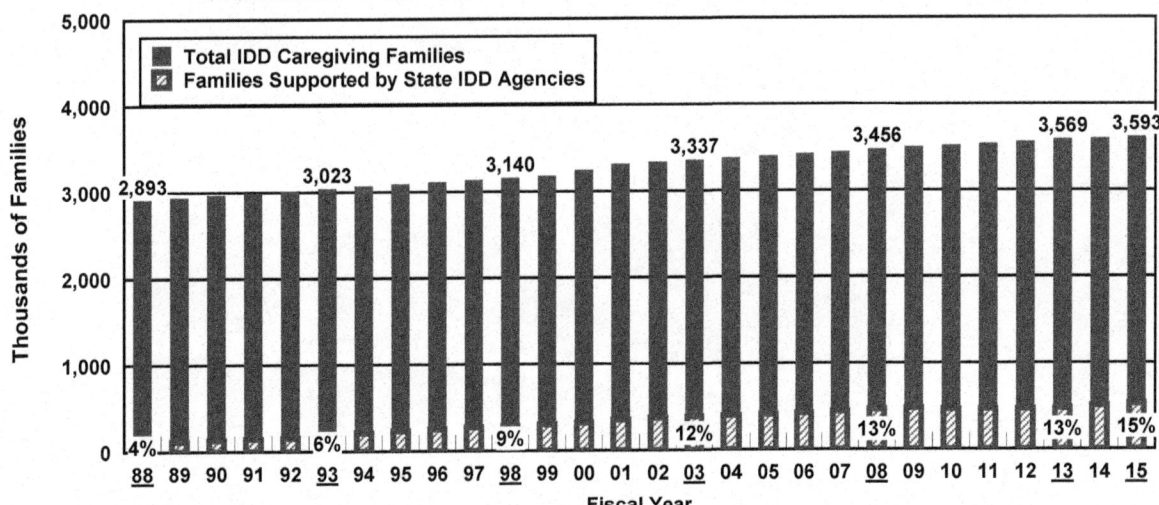

Source: Braddock et al., Coleman Institute and Department of Psychiatry, University of Colorado, 2017.
http://stateofthestates.org

APPENDICES

I. *The Rights of People With Cognitive Disabilities to Technology and Information Access* (The Declaration) 243

II. Representative Organizations Endorsing the *Declaration of the Rights of People with Cognitive Disabilities to Technology and Information Access*. 244

III. AAIDD Article Reprint:
Braddock, D., Hoehl, J., Tanis, S., Ablowitz, E., & Haffer, L. The rights of people with cognitive disabilities to technology and information access. *Inclusion, 1*(2), 95–102. 252

APPENDICES

I. *The Rights of People with Cognitive Disabilities to Technology and Information Access* (The Declaration)

The Rights of People with Cognitive Disabilities to Technology and Information Access

Whereas

- Twenty-eight million United States citizens have cognitive disabilities such as intellectual disability; severe, persistent mental illness; brain injury; stroke; and neurodegenerative disorders such as Alzheimer's disease;

- People with cognitive disabilities are entitled to inclusion in our democratic society under federal laws such as the Americans with Disabilities Act (ADA), the Developmental Disabilities Assistance and Bill of Rights Act (DD Act), the Individuals with Disabilities Education Act (IDEA), Section 504 of the Rehabilitation Act, and under state and local laws;

- The disruptive convergence of computing and communication technologies has substantially altered how people acquire, utilize, and disseminate knowledge and information;

- Access to comprehensible information and usable communication technologies is necessary for all people in our society, particularly for people with cognitive disabilities, to promote self-determination and to engage meaningfully in major aspects of life such as education, health promotion, employment, recreation, and civic participation;

- The vast majority of people with cognitive disabilities have limited or no access to comprehensible information and usable communication technologies;

- People with cognitive disabilities must have access to commercially available devices and software that incorporate principles of universal design such as flexibility and ease of use for all;

- Technology and information access by people with cognitive disabilities must be guided by standards and best-practices, such as personalization and compatibility across devices and platforms, and through the application of innovations including automated and predictive technologies;

- Security and privacy must be assured and managed to protect civil rights and personal dignity of people with cognitive disabilities;

- Enhanced public and private funding is urgently required to allow people with cognitive disabilities to utilize technology and access information as a natural consequence of their rights to inclusion in our society;

- Ensuring access to technology and information for the 28 million people with cognitive disabilities in the United States will create new markets and employment opportunities; decrease dependency on public services; reduce healthcare costs; and improve the independence, productivity, and quality of life of people with cognitive disabilities.

Therefore

We hereby affirm our commitment to equal rights of people with cognitive disabilities to technology and information access and we call for implementation of these rights with deliberate speed.

View endorsers of this document and join us at: colemaninstitute.org/declaration

© 2013 Coleman Institute for Cognitive Disabilities

II. Representative Organizations in the U.S. and Abroad Endorsing the *Declaration of the Rights of People with Cognitive Disabilities to Technology and Information Access*

#	Organization	Location
1	Ability Beyond	Bethel, CT
2	Ability Building Services	Yankton, SD
3	AbleLink Technologies, Inc.	Colorado Springs, CO
4	Access Services	Fort Washington, PA
5	ACT - Alternative Community Training	Columbia, MO
6	Additional Kare for Kids	Allen, TX
7	ADEC	Elkhart, IN
8	Advocacy Center of ILLINOIS	Charleston, IL
9	Advocacy Denver	Denver, CO
10	AHRC	New York, NY
11	All About You, LLC	Ada, OK
12	Alliance	Denver, CO
13	Alpha One	S. Portland, ME
14	Alternative Community Training (ACT)	Columbia, MO
15	American Association on Health and Disability	Rockville, MD
16	Amer. Assoc. on Intellectual and Develop. Disabilities	Washington, D.C.
17	American Ntwrk. of Comm. Options and Resources	Alexandria, VA
18	Amicus	Bangor, ME
19	AngelSense	Fairfield, CT
20	ao Strategies	Rolling Meadows, IL
21	APSE	Rockville, MD
22	ARC of Oswego County	Fulton, NY
23	Arc of Philadelphia	Philadelphia, PA
24	Arc of the Arts	Austin, TX
25	Arc of West Central CO	Delta, CO
26	Arc of Westchester	White Plains, NY
27	Arc of Westchester	Hawthorne, NY
28	ARCA	Albuquerque, NM
29	Architects Of Diversity	Cody, WY
30	Ark Regional Services	Laramie, WY
31	ARRM	South Saint Paul, MN
32	Asset Consulting, LLC	Portland, OR
33	Assistive Technology Partners	Denver, CO
34	Association for Individual Development	Aurora, IL
35	Association of Assistive Technology Act Programs	Washington, DC
36	Association of University Centers on Disabilities	Silver Spring, MD
37	Autism Society of America	Bethesda, MD
38	Autistic Global Initiative	San Diego, CA
39	Autistic Self Advocacy Network	Washington, DC
40	Avenues to Independence	Park Ridge, IL
41	AXIS, Inc.	Minnesota, MN
42	Beach Center on Disability, University of Kansas	Lawrence, KS
43	Beneficial Designs, Inc.	Minden, NV
44	Bethesda Institute	Watertown, WI
45	Bethesda Lutheran Communities	Castle Rock, CO
46	Bethesda Lutheran Communities	Cortland, IL
47	Bethesda Lutheran Communities	Frankenmuth, MI
48	Bethesda Voices Public Policy Advocates	Watertown, WI
49	Black Hills Works	Rapid City, SD
50	Bost, Inc.	Fort Smith, AR
51	Boulder Valley School District	Bloomfield, CO
52	Branches, LLC	Bangor, ME

53	Bridges of Colorado	Aurora, CO
54	Bright Star Learning	Brussels, Belgium
55	Burton Blatt Institute, Syracuse University	Syracuse, NY
56	CapGrow Partners	Chicago, IL
57	CaraSolva, Inc.	Boulder, CO
58	CAU	Elizabeth, NJ
59	CCCPCA Family Resource Center	Carroll, IA
60	cCore Media	Algonquin, IL
61	CCRI	Moorehead, MN
62	Center for Accessible Information	West Bloomfield, MI
63	Center for Disabilities	Sioux Falls, SD
64	Center for Disabilities Services	Joliet, IL
65	Center for Enriched Living	Riverwoods, IL
66	Center on Human Policy	Syracuse, NY
67	Central Aroostook Association	Presque Isle, ME
68	CereScan Corp.	Littleton, CO
69	Champaign Residential Services, Inc.	Lima, OH
70	Champaign Residential Services, Inc.	Troy, OH
71	Champaign Residential Services, Inc.	Urbana, OH
72	Charles Lea Center	Spartanburg, SC
73	Cheyenne Village	Colorado Springs, CO
74	Children's Odyssey	Portland, ME
75	Chimes Delaware	Newark, DE
76	Christensen Group Insurance	Minnetonka, MN
77	Christian Family Ministries The Lambs Fold	Joliet, IL
78	Citizens of Maine, LLC	Hampden, ME
79	Clearbrook	Arlington Hts, IL
80	Coast Rehabilitation Services	Warrenton, OR
81	Coastal Opportunities	Camden, ME
82	Coastal Opportunities	Camden, ME
83	CO-CANDO	Glenwood Springs, CO
84	Cognitopia	Eugene, OR
85	Coleman Colorado Foundation	Boulder, CO
86	Coleman Institute for Cognitive Disabilities, CU	Boulder, CO
87	Collaborative Industries	Lincoln, NE
88	Colorado Bluesky Enterprises	Pueblo, CO
89	Colorado Cross Disability Coalition	Denver, CO
90	Colorado Developmental Disabilities Council	Denver, CO
91	Colorado Respite Coalition	Denver, CO
92	Commonwealth Case Management	Monticello, KY
93	Community Access Unlimited, Inc.	Elizabeth , NJ
94	Community Alternatives Unlimited	Chicago, IL
95	Community Connections, Inc.	Winner, SD
96	Community Drive	Brighton, MI
97	Community Link	Boulder, CO
98	Community Partners	Lewiston, ME
99	Community Partners	Biddeford, ME
100	Community Support Services, Inc.	Salem, OR
101	Community Support Services, Inc.	Biddeford, ME
102	Concurrence Consulting	Denver, CO
103	Consort. for Citizens with Disabilities Techn. Wrkgrp.	Washington, DC
104	Consulting on Quality	Laporte, CO
105	Continuum of Colorado	Englewood, CO
106	CORE Labor Source	Boulder, CO
107	Cornerstone Services, Inc.	Joliet, IL

108	The Council on Quality and Leadership (CQL)	Towson, MD
109	CreateAbility Concepts, Inc.	Fishers, IN
110	CRSI	Paulding, OH
111	CRSI	Troy, OH
112	CRSI	Lima, OH
113	CRSI	Urbana, OH
114	CRSI	Springfield, OH
115	CRSI	Defiance, OH
116	CTF Illinois	Champaign, IL
117	DAC, Inc.	DeWitt, IA
118	Danville Services of Oregon, LLC	Portland, OR
119	DDA	Vancouver, BC, Canada
120	DDRC	Lakewood, CO
121	DDSME	Belleville, IL
122	Delaware Creative Housing, Inc.	Delaware, OH
123	Delta Alpha Pi Honor Society- Beta Zeta Chapter @ Indiana University of PA	Indiana, PA
124	Delta Community Supports, Inc.	Blue Bell, PA
125	Denver VAMC	Denver, CO
126	Developmental Connections	Branson, MO
127	Developmental Disabilities	Richmond, BC, Canada
128	Developmental Disabilities Assoc.	Richmond, BC, Canada
129	Developmental Disabilities Nurses Association	Elmwood Park, IL
130	Developmental Pathways	Aurora, CO
131	Developmental Pathways	Englewood, CO
132	Developmental Services Center	Champaign, IL
133	Developmental Services of Dickson County	Dickson, TN
134	Developmental Services of NW Kansas, Inc.	Hays, KS
135	Devereux	Devon, PA
136	Disability Law Center of Utah	Salt Lake City, UT
137	Disability Law Colorado	Denver, CO
138	Disability Rights Washington	Seattle, WA
139	Disability Section of the American Public health	Multiple Cities, U.S.
140	Disability Services	Boulder, CO
141	Discover Goodwill of Southern and Western	Colorado Springs, CO
142	DJK Enterprises, Inc.	Ada, OK
143	Doglet Captioning	N. Vancouver, BC, Canada
144	Dolle Communications	Newport Beach, CA
145	Downeast Horizons	Ellsworth, ME
146	Dragonfly Heart Massageand Yoga Therapy	Denver, CO
147	Dungarvin	Colorado Springs, CO
148	Dungarvin Minnesota, LLC	Mendota Heights, MN
149	DylanListed LLC	Dallas, TX
150	East Tennessee Technology Access Center, Inc.	Knoxville, East TN
151	Easter Seals Iowa	Des Moines, IA
152	Eastern Colorado Services	Sterling, CO
153	Education Intelligence, Inc.	Nashville, TN
154	EEOC	Denver, CO
155	Elmhurst Inc.	Bath, ME
156	Emmaus Homes, Inc.	St. Charles, MO
157	Ennovysions	Cleveland, OH
158	Equal Employment Opportunity Commission	Denver, CO
159	Exceptional Persons, Inc.	Waterloo, IA
160	Expect ExtraOrdinary, Inc.	Pittsfield, IL
161	Extreme Sports Camp	Aspen, CO
162	F.R.E.E.	Patchogue, NY
163	Families Matter, Inc.	Hallowell, ME

164	Family & Children Services of Silicon Valley	Palo Alto, CA
165	Family Residences & Essential Enterprises	St. James, NY
166	Family Residences & Essential Enterprises	Old Bethpage, NY
167	Family Residences & Essential Enterprises	Hauppauge, NY
168	Family Residences & Essential Enterprises, Inc.	Sayville, NY
169	Family Residences & Essential Enterprises	East Meadow, NY
170	FAYCO Enterprises, Inc.	Vandalia, IL
171	FCRS	Columbus, OH
172	ForgetMeNots Design	Superior, CO
173	Fox Run Golf Club	Johnstown, NY
174	FREE, Day Services East	East Setauket, NY
175	Garvin County Community Living Center, Inc.	Pauls Valley, OK
176	GMS	Westbrook, ME
177	Goldie B. Floberg Center	Rockton, IL
178	Good Shepherd Center for Exceptional Children	Hazelcrest, IL
179	Goodwill Industries of Northern New England	Portland, ME
180	Green Valley Association	Island Falls, ME
181	Group Main Stream	Westbrook, ME
182	GROW in America	West Frankfort, IL
183	GROW in Illinois	Bement, IL
184	Grow in Illinois	Chicago, IL
185	GROW in Illinois	Champaign, IL
186	Grow in Illinois	Reddick, IL
187	Guam System for Assisstive Technology	Mangilao, Guam
188	Hammer Residences, Inc.	Wayzata, MN
189	HANDLE By the Bay	San Francisco, CA
190	Harvard Law School Project on Disability	Cambridge, MA
191	Havar	Athens, OH
192	Hawaii Self-Advocacy Advisory Council	Ewa Beach, HI
193	Heritage Christian	Rochester, NY
194	Heritage Christian Services	Rochester, Buffalo, NY
195	Hills & Dales	Dubuque, IA
196	Homeward Bound	Plymouth, MN
197	Hope Association	Rumford, ME
198	Hope Association	Mexico, ME
199	Horizons Specialized Services	Steamboat Springs, CO
200	Hybrid Pedagogy, Inc.	Madison, WI
201	I Break Websites, LLC	Broomfield, CO
202	IAC	New York, NY
203	IHECP	Denver, CO
204	IHS services,Inc	Worthington, OH
205	Illinois Network of Ctrs. for Independent Living	Springfield, IL
206	Illinois Valley Industries, Inc.	Morris, IL
207	Imagine!	Erie, CO
208	Imagine!	Boulder, CO
209	Imagine!	Longmont, CO
210	Imagine!	Lafayette, CO
211	In the Driver's Seat	Rochester, NY
212	Incl. Design Research Ctr. at Ontario College of Art and Design U.	Toronto, Ontario, Canada
213	Infinitec - An enterprise of UCP Seguin of Greater	Tinley Park, IL
214	Innovative Opportunities, Inc.	Lima, OH
215	Innovative Resources for Independence	Queens Village, NY
216	Innovative Services, Inc.	Green Bay, WI
217	Innov. Solutions for Disadvantage and DIsability	Atlanta, GA
218	Institute for Matching Person and Technology	Webster, NY

219	Inst. on Dis. and Human Dev., U. Ill. at Chicago	Chicago, IL
220	International Friends for the Developmentally	Winfield, IL
221	Iowa Association of Community Providers	Urbandale, IA
222	Iowa Coalition for Integrated Employment	Des Moines, IA
223	Iowa Developmental Disabilities Council	Des Moines, IA
224	Iri, Inc.	Queens, NY
225	Jefferson County	Littleton, CO
226	Jefferson County Adult Protection Services	Golden, CO
227	JFK Partners	Denver, CO
228	Jill Tullman & Associates, LLC	Centennial, CO
229	Kankakee County Training Center	Bradley, IL
230	Kansas University Center on Developmental	Lawrence, KS
231	Karcher Foster Care	North Branch, MN
232	Keon	Peekskill, NY
233	Key Medical Supply	Shoreview, MN
234	Keystone Alliance	Chicago, IL
235	KFI	Portland, ME
236	Kids Together, Inc.	Coopersburg, PA
237	KIFDD	Seoul, Korea
238	Know Me, LLC	Chapel Hill, NC
239	Kreider Services	Dixon, IL
240	Laradon	Denver, CO
241	LEAP	Farmington, MR
242	Lehman Disability Planning	Denver, CO
243	LEND Illinois	Chicago, IL
244	Liberty	Amsterdam, NY
245	Liberty	Niskayuna, NY
246	Liberty Enterprises	Palatine Bridge, NY
247	Liberty Enterprises, Montgomery County ARC.	Amsterdam, NY
248	Life's Plan, Inc.	Lisle, IL
249	LifeStyles Academy	Palos Park, IL
250	Lifeworks, Inc.	Norwood, MA
251	Limitless Possibilities	Oshkosh, WI
252	Little City Foundation	Palatine, IL
253	Living Innovations	Saco, ME
254	Living Resources Corporation	Albany, NY
255	Living Well Disability Services	Eagan, MN
256	LivingLinks	Mankato, MN
257	LSUHSC-Human Development Center	New Orleans, LA
258	LTO Ventures	Henderson, NV
259	Lutheran Services in America Disability Network	Washington, DC
260	Maine Assoc. for Community Service Providers	Hallowell, ME
261	McComb Consulting and Government Relations	Chester, MD
262	Medical Management Enterprises, Inc.	Gonzales, LA
263	MediSked, LLC	Rochester, NY
264	Mercarik, Inc.	Falcon Heights, MN
265	Mercer Residential Services, Inc.	Celina, OH
266	Mercy College	Hawthorne, NY
267	Michigan Assisted Living Association	Livonia, MI
268	Michigan Disability Rights Coalition	Eastg Lansing, MI
269	Missouri Assistive Technology	Blue Springs, MO
270	Missouri Developmental Disabilities Council	Jefferson City, MO
271	Modem	Geel, Belgium
272	Monarch	Albemarle, NC
273	Mondo Mediaworks	Brattleboro, VT
274	Morrison Center	Scarborough, ME

275	Mountain Valley Developmental Services	Glenwood Springs, CO
276	NADD	Kingston, NY
277	Natl. Assn. of Qualified Dev. Dis. Prof.	Joliet, IL
278	Natl. Inst. For People with Disabiliities of NJ	Jersey City, NJ
279	Natl. Inst. For People with Disabiliities	New York, NY
280	Nat'l Jt. Comm. for the Communication Needs of Persons with Severe Disabilities	Sylva, NC
281	New Day Enterprises, Inc.	La Grande, OR
282	New Hope Center, Inc.	Dolton, IL
283	New Hope Village	Carroll, IA
284	NHS	Chisolm, MN
285	NHS Human Services	Pittsburgh, PA
286	Night Owl Support Systems, LLC	Madison, WI
287	Nipd NJ	New City, NY
288	No Boundaries Case Management	Lexington, KY
289	Northeast Occupational Exchange	Bangor, ME
290	Northern Aroostook Alternatives, Inc.	Van Buren, ME
291	NYSACRA	Albany, NY
292	Oasis4HE, L3C	Hyde Park, UT
293	Ocss -NC	Statesville, , NC
294	OHI	Hudson, ME
295	OHI	Brownville, ME
296	OHI	Bangor, ME
297	OHI	Etna, ME
298	OHI	Clifton, ME
299	OHI	Charleston, ME
300	OHI	Winterport, ME
301	OHI	Hermon, ME
302	OHI	Glenburn, ME
303	OHI	Brewer, ME
304	OHI	Bangor, ME
305	Ohio Developmental Disabilities Council	Columbus, OH
306	OHO SIBS	Charleston, WV
307	Oklahoma ABLE Tech	Stillwater, OK
308	Oklahoma Community-Based Providers, Inc.	Oklahoma City, OK
309	OPARC	Montclair, CA
310	Open Avenues	Rogers, AR
311	Open Doors Organization	Chicago, IL
312	Orange Grove Center	Chattanooga, TN
313	OT KIDS CAN	San Jose, CA
314	OTAC	San Jose, CA
315	PAR	Harrisburg, PA
316	PASCO	Lakewood, CO
317	Pathway Enterprises, Inc.	Medford, OR
318	PEAK Parent Center	Colorado Springs, CO
319	PEAT	Arlington, VA
320	Peer Action Disability Support (PADS)	Cedar Rapids, IA
321	People First of Larimer	Fort Collins, CO
322	People First of Marshall Mo.	Marshall, MO
323	People First of Marshall Mo.	Carrollton, MO
324	Personal Onsite Development	Auburn, ME
325	Phi	Bangor, ME
326	Play Learn Earn	Palm Beach, FL
327	Port Resources	South Portland, ME
328	Progress Industries, Inc.	Newton, IA
329	Progressive Careers & Housing	Olympia Fields, IL
330	Progressive Community Services	St. Joseph, MO
331	Project Janus, Inc.	San Angelo, TX
332	Puerto Rico Assistive Technology Program	San Juan, Puerto Rico

#	Organization	Location
333	Putnam County Comprehensive Serv. Inc.	Greencastle, IN
334	Qsac	New York, NY
335	Quality Trust for Individuals with Disabilities	Washington, DC
336	Quantum Solutions	Petersburg, IL
337	Ray Graham Association	Lisle, IL
338	Rcald	New City, NY
339	Residential Resources	Scarborough, ME
340	RESNA	Arlington, VA
341	RHD	Philadelphia, PA
342	RIX Research & Media, U. of East London, UK	London, UK
343	Rockland Cnty. Assn. for Learning Disabilities	Nanuet, NY
344	Rocky Mountain Down Syndrome Association	Denver, CO
345	Rocky Mountain Human Services	Denver, CO
346	Rouses Group Home, Inc.	Stoneville, NC
347	Rush University Medical Center	Chicago, IL
348	Ryan Law Firm, LLC	Denver, CO
349	Salty's pub	Clifton park, RI
350	Sanford School of Medicine Ctr. for Disabilities	Sioux Falls, SD
351	Security Partners, LLC	Lancaster, PA
352	SEEC	Silver Spring, MD
353	Self Advocates Becoming Empowered	Mansas City, MO
354	Self-Advocacy Association of New York State	Schenectady, NY
355	Sengistix	Mendota Heights, MN
356	Sertoma Centre, Inc.	Alsip, IL
357	Shore Community Services, Inc.	Skokie, IL
358	Sibling Leadership Network	Boulder, CO
359	SimplyHome, llc	Asheville, NC
360	Smergut consulting	New York, NY
361	Solace Healthcare	Denver, CO
362	So. Illinois Community Support Services	New Baden, IL
363	Southwest Community Services	Tinley Park, IL
364	Southwest Disabilities Services	Hazel Crest, IL
365	Space2Create	Loveland, CO
366	Special Family Support	Chicago, IL
367	Special Kids Special Families	Colorado Springs, CO
368	SpecialNeedsinmycity.com	Modesto, CA
369	Spectrum Foundation of Colorado	Lafayette, CO
370	Spurwink Services	Portland, ME
371	SRVS	Memphis, TN
372	Stahlman Family	Littleton, CO
373	Suburban Access, Inc.	Homewood, IL
374	Super Host Hotels. Inc	Albany, NY
375	Supportive Living, Inc.	Woburn, MA
376	Susan H Spater MD, PC	Port Washington, NY
377	Tarjan Center at UCLA, 11075 Santa Monica, Blvd.,	Ste 200, Los Angeles, CA
378	Taskar Center for Accessible Technology	Seattle, WA
379	Tech4Impact	Johnston, IA
380	Texas Technology Access Program	Austin, TX
381	The Arc	Washington , DC
382	The Arc Arapahoe & Douglas	Centennial, CO
383	The Arc California	Sacramento, CA
384	The Arc Jackson County	Medford, OR
385	The Arc of Anchorage	Anchorage, AK
386	The Arc of Colorado	Denver, CO
387	The Arc of Greater Cleveland	Cleveland, OH
388	The Arc of Illinois	Frankfort, IL
389	The Arc of Indiana	Indianapolis, IN

#	Organization	Location
390	The Arc of Mississippi	Jackson, MS
391	The Arc of Nebraska	Lincoln, NE
392	The Arc of Philadelphia	Philadelphia, PA
393	The Arc of Philadelphia	Philadelphia, PA
394	The Arc of South Carolina	Columbia, SC
395	The Arc of South Carolina	Cayce, SC
396	The Arc of the Capital Area	Austin, TX
397	The Arc of the Pikes Peak Region	Colorado Springs, CO
398	The Arc of the U.S.	Washington, DC
399	The Arc PPR	Lakewood, CO
400	The Arc: Greater Houston Chapter	Houston, TX
401	The Arc-Jefferson, Clear Creek & Gilpin Counties	Lakewood, CO
402	The Association for Community Living	Springfield, MA
403	The Brain Injury Alliance of Colorado	Denver, CO
404	The Charlotte White Center	Dover Foxcroft, ME
405	The Hope Institute for Children and Families	Springfield, IL
406	Lawrence B. Taishoff Ctr. for Incl. Higher Ed.	Syracuse, NY
407	Legal Ctr. for People with Dis. and Older People	Denver, CO
408	The National Ctr. on Disability & Access to Ed.	Logan, UT
409	The Phoenix Residence, Inc.	West St. Paul, MN
410	The Progress Center	Norway, ME
411	The Rehabilitation Institute	Westbury, NY
412	The Resource Center	Jamestown, NY
413	The Resource Exchange	Colorado Springs, CO
414	THRIVE Center	Aurora, CO
415	Tommie Cares	Mt Kisco, NY
416	TRI	Westbury, NY
417	Trillium Services, Inc.	Minneapolis, MN
418	Trinity Services	Joliet, IL
419	Trinity Services, Inc.	New Lenox, IL
420	UCP Seguin of Greater Chicago	Cicero, IL
421	United Cerebral Palsy Association of San Diego	San Diego, CA
422	University of Colorado	Boulder, CO
423	University of CO-Parking & Transport. Services	Boulder, CO
424	University of Colorado Boulder	Boulder, CO
425	University of Colorado Denver	Denver, CO
426	U. of Guam Ctr. for Excellence in DD Education, Research and Service (CEDDERS)	Mangilao, Guam
427	University of South Florida	St Petersburg, FL
428	Unlimited Possibilities of Colorado	Greeley, CO
429	Uplift, Inc.	Gardiner, ME
430	US dept of VA	Denver, CO
431	Values Into Action	Media, PA
432	Venture Community Services	Sturbridge, MA
433	Verland	Moon Twp., PA
434	VERTESS	Tucson, AZ
435	Vision for EQuality, Inc.	Philadelphia, PA
436	Waban	Sanford, ME
437	Welcome Change Productions	New York, NY
438	Westchester independent living center	White Plains, NY
439	Westchester Institute for Human Development	Valhalla, NY
440	Wild River Consulting Corp.	Bethel, ME
441	Will-Grundy Center for Independent Living	Joliet, IL
442	wli	Bowling Green, OH
443	YAI	New York, NY
444	YAI Network	New York, NY
445	Yes She Can, Inc.	White Plains, NY
446	Young Adult Institute, Inc. (YAI)	New York, NY

III. AAIDD Article Reprint:
Braddock, D., Hoehl, J., Tanis, S., Ablowitz, E., & Haffer, L. The rights of people with cognitive disabilities to technology and information access. *Inclusion, 1*(2), 95–102.

Abstract

Information and communication technologies are ubiquitous and valuable tools for billions of people worldwide today. Yet people with cognitive disabilities, particularly individuals with intellectual and developmental disabilities, have quite limited access to such technologies. This article presents the case for mounting significant efforts to advance the rights of millions of people with cognitive disabilities to technology and information access. A formal statement of these rights is presented, formulated by professionals and consumers representing a variety of disciplines and perspectives. The statement is currently endorsed by numerous national, state and local organizations in the developmental disabilities field in the United States. Your comments and participation are invited and appreciated.

The Rights of People With Cognitive Disabilities to Technology and Information Access

Cognitive disabilities include intellectual and developmental disabilities; autism spectrum disorders; severe, persistent mental illness; brain injury; stroke; Alzheimer's disease; and other dementias. An estimated 28.5 million Americans, more than nine percent of the U.S. population, had a cognitive disability in 2012. People with cognitive disabilities worldwide are believed to exceed 630 million individuals, according to recent World Health Organization estimates (2011).

The prevalence of people with cognitive disabilities living in developing nations substantially exceeds their presence in developed nations. This is primarily because the vast majority of the world's population resides in poor countries with limited access to medical care and educational opportunities. However, there is considerable cause for optimism.

Advances in technology and information science have positively impacted the potential for learning and information access for all people, including people with cognitive disabilities. As Eric Schmidt and Jared Cohen (2013) observed in their book, *The New Digital Age:*

Soon everyone on earth will be connected. With five billion more people set to join the virtual world, the boom in digital connectivity will bring gains in productivity, health, education, quality of life and myriad other avenues in the physical world—and this will be true for everyone, from the most elite users to those at the base of the economic pyramid (p.13).

People with cognitive disabilities comprise a very significant component of "the base of the economic pyramid" in all countries, not just in the developing world. Reducing barriers for people with cognitive disabilities who cannot readily access or utilize information and communication technologies without significant support therefore becomes an extremely important objective in the context of Schmidt and Cohen's prediction.

The pace of the digital age is expected to accelerate rapidly through new innovations in cloud computing, which lends itself exceedingly well to the development of customized, personal platforms to fit varied interests and competencies (Coleman, 2013). Highly individualized cloud computing platforms are expected to become formidable tools analogous to "utilities" fostering inclusion and promoting quality of life of people with cognitive disabilities. Areas of potential positive impact of cloud-based initiatives include not only improved personal communications, but also health promotion, disease prevention, enhanced social interaction, and individualized supported employment opportunities such as remote job coaching.

A particularly provocative question must also be addressed about the future of over one billion people with disabilities worldwide, including those 630 million individuals with cognitive disabilities. How effectively, and how soon, can human-centered computational support technologies be adapted or uniquely developed and properly disseminated to match the unique needs and preferences of individuals with cognitive disabilities? People with cognitive disabilities, in fact, comprise over 60% of the world's total estimated population of people with disabilities. They also often present quite unique challenges for technologists developing personalized human-computer interfaces.

People with sensory disabilities and their advocates have promoted the benefits and adoption of technology and information access for their constituencies much more intensely and effectively than cognitive disability advocates and consumers. The diffusion of captioning online video content and screen readers are two recent examples of effective advocacy by sensory disability constituencies and subsequent responsiveness by industry. People with cognitive disabilities and their parents, friends, and professional support personnel, have not been nearly as effective as sensory disability constituencies in promoting access to personalized technologies and information to meet their unique access needs.

Writing in the inaugural issue of the journal, *Inclusion*, Gomez (2013), immediate past president of the American Association on Intellectual and Developmental Disabilities (AAIDD), drew attention to this point in stating that "focusing on friendship networks for people with (intellectual) disabilities represents a paradigm shift from skills development to social inclusion" (p.1). Thus, the key related question becomes how can greater attention to cognitive disability and technology be generated to promote diffusion of innovation in inclusion to enhance friendship networks, general social participation, employment, education, health and general communications?

One obvious objective is to stimulate greater attention nationally and worldwide to the possibilities now at hand for people with cognitive disabilities through technology while simultaneously championing their rights as citizens to access such technologies in home, school and workplace. On October 21, 2010 at the University of Colorado's Coleman Institute for Cognitive Disabilities Tenth Annual National Conference on Cognitive Disability and Technology, the following question was posed by the lead author of this article and conference chair to one of the most respected civil rights attorneys in the history of our field, Thomas Gilhool. As Gilhool was introduced to a national audience from over 40 states, he was asked: "Forty years after *Pennsylvania Association of Retarded Children [PARC]* v. *Commonwealth of Pennsylvania*, is there an emerging right to technology and information access for people with cognitive disabilities, including intellectual and developmental disabilities?"

Gilhool, formerly chief counsel of the Public Interest Law Center of Philadelphia, Secretary of Education of the Commonwealth of Pennsylvania, and University of Southern California law professor, argued the seminal case in a Philadelphia Federal Court in 1971 that led to establishing the right to a public education for children with disabilities (Pennsylvania Association for Retarded Children V. Commonwealth of Pennsylvania, 1971), and ultimately led to the enactment by the federal government of the Education for All Handicapped Children's Act in 1975 and its successor legislation, The Individuals With Disabilities Education Act (IDEA) in 2004.

In a poignant response to the question about access to technology, Gilhool stated that he believed a right to technology access by people with cognitive disabilities was ascendant in the United States today– potentially enabling a future with far better access to appropriate education, community living and employment opportunities. He encouraged the 500 participants at our conference in Colorado that day to advance this issue with further thought and action.

The Coleman Institute subsequently engaged Gilhool and Syracuse University law professor Peter Blanck, head of the Burton Blatt Institute. We asked them both to explore the implications of existing legal precedents to the rights to education, habilitation and community living as those established rights might inform, and possibly encompass, evolving law and policy pertaining to inclusive technology and web access rights for individuals with cognitive disabilities. This research was commissioned by the Coleman Institute and will be published in book form by Cambridge University Press in 2014. British law instructor Eliza Varney recently authored an important, complimentary international treatise published by Cambridge University Press as well. *Disability and Information Technology: A Comparative Study in Media Regulation* (2013) comparatively and meticulously examined information and communications technology (ICT) regulation across four international domains: Canada, European Union, United Kingdom, and the United States). In addressing the rationale for access to information and technology by people with disabilities, she stated that:

The regulatory approach for the ICT (Information and Technology) sector should perceive persons with disabilities not only as consumers but also as citizens with democratic expectations of effective access to information. Furthermore, the regulatory framework should be based on a clearly defined framework of principles such as equality of citizenship and the protection of human dignity (p.38).

We concur, and Ms. Varney will deliver a keynote address at the Coleman Institute Conference on Cognitive Disability and Technology on October 2, 2013 in Colorado.

To build on the groundwork already done towards documenting the rights of people with cognitive disabilities to technology and information access, in the fall of 2012, the Coleman Institute convened a group of leaders in the United States representing numerous national disability associations and disciplines in cognitive disability, computer science, technology, engineering, special education, disability studies, rehabilitation, psychology, philosophy, philanthropy, and law and public policy. Together we crafted and collectively endorsed *The Rights of People with Cognitive Disabilities to Technology and Information Access*, which appears at the end of this article along with a list of its authors and the initial organizational endorsers of that document*. This document is being officially released internationally through the new AAIDD journal, *Inclusion*, and at the Coleman Institute's October 2, 2013 conference in Colorado where approximately 500 attendees from over 40 states and abroad will have the opportunity to endorse it. Additional supporters may endorse the document online at the Coleman Institute's website (http://www.colemaninstitute.org)

The Rights of People with Cognitive Disabilities to Technology and Information Access is a statement of principles. It builds on the history of community integration rights for people with intellectual and developmental disabilities established in law, policy and practice through decades of advocacy by parents, people with disabilities themselves, and conscientious professionals in the field (Syracuse University, 1979). Centuries of abuse, social isolation, prejudice and incomprehensible discrimination toward people with cognitive disabilities and their families are being addressed in our nation today, albeit at a painstakingly slow pace and unevenly across individual states, cities, communities and neighborhoods. In fact, advocacy by people with cognitive disabilities themselves and their siblings and parents, through organizations like *Self Advocates Becoming Empowered* and the *Sibling Leadership Network*, are playing larger roles in advancing the rights of people with cognitive disabilities today. And *The Arc of the United States*, sixty-one years after its initial formation, retains significant vitality and nationwide influence across virtually all states and in many local communities.

To date, these three advocacy organizations are among those who have officially endorsed our Statement. Other boards of directors of national organizations endorsing *The Rights of People with Cognitive Disabilities to Technology and Information Access* include those from the American Association on Intellectual and Developmental Disabilities (AAIDD), The American Network of Community Options and Resources, The Arc (United States), Beach Center on Disability at the University of Kansas, the Burton Blatt Institute at Syracuse University, the Coleman Colorado Foundation and Coleman Institute for Cognitive Disabilities at the University of Colorado, the Institute on Disability and Human Development at the University of Illinois at Chicago, the Kansas University Center on Developmental Disabilities, Self Advocates Becoming Empowered, and the Westchester Institute for Human Development, New York. AAIDD, it is noted, had the foresight to establish a Technology Special Interest Group (SIG) 15 years ago and continues today to define and lead key aspects of the field by creating and disseminating new knowledge about services and supports.

As signatories of the document presented herein, we are honored and grateful that leading organizations in the intellectual and developmental disabilities field are charter signatories of *The Rights of People with Cognitive Disabilities to Technology and Information Access*. Their collective endorsements signal substantial momentum to advance the right to technology and information access and to act forthwith to implement those rights.

Inclusion and *choice* are indeed cornerstones of the disabilities field today. Their implementation in the United States, incomplete it may be, spans several decades of commitments to deinstitutionalization and community integration, implementation of the right to education nationally, promulgation and implementation of the Syracuse University Community Imperative (1979), and enactment and implementation of the Americans with Disabilities Act of 1990 and the Developmental Disabilities and Bill Of Rights Act of 1975. Inclusion and choice have also driven the self-determination movement by people with developmental disabilities to new heights of independence and productivity (Wehmeyer, Agran, Hughes, Martin, Mithaug, & Palmer, 2007).

Advancing the rights of people with cognitive disabilities to technology and information access is an extremely important next step in the worldwide implementation of inclusion and choice. Modern and developing societies are capable of moving more rapidly toward an inclusive future through the diffusion and application of information and communication technology supports. In this spirit, we present our statement of *The Rights of People with Cognitive Disabilities to Technology and Information Access*.

Figure 1
The Rights of People With Cognitive Disabilities to Technology and Information Access

WHEREAS:

Twenty-eight million United States citizens have cognitive disabilities such as intellectual disability; severe, persistent mental illness; brain injury; stroke; and neurodegenerative disorders such as Alzheimer's disease;

People with cognitive disabilities are entitled to inclusion in our democratic society under federal laws such as the Americans with Disabilities Act (ADA), the Developmental Disabilities Assistance and Bill of Rights Act (DD Act), the Individuals with Disabilities Education Act (IDEA), Section 504 of the Rehabilitation Act, and under state and local laws;

The disruptive convergence of computing and communication technologies has substantially altered how people acquire, utilize, and disseminate knowledge and information;

Access to comprehensible information and usable communication technologies is necessary for all people in our society, particularly for people with cognitive disabilities, to promote self-determination and to engage meaningfully in major aspects of life such as education, health promotion, employment, recreation, and civic participation;

The vast majority of people with cognitive disabilities have limited or no access to comprehensible information and usable communication technologies; People with cognitive disabilities must have access to commercially available devices and software that incorporate principles of universal design such as flexibility and ease of use for all;

Technology and information access by people with cognitive disabilities must be guided by standards and best-practices, such as personalization and compatibility across devices and platforms, and through the application of innovations including automated and predictive technologies; Security and privacy must be assured and managed to protect civil rights and personal dignity of people with cognitive disabilities;

Enhanced public and private funding is urgently required to allow people with cognitive disabilities to utilize technology and access information as a natural consequence of their rights to inclusion in our society;

Ensuring access to technology and information for the 28.5 million people with cognitive disabilities in the United States will create new markets and employment opportunities; decrease dependency on public services; reduce healthcare costs; and improve the independence, productivity, and quality of life of people with cognitive disabilities.

THEREFORE, BE IT RESOLVED THAT:

We the undersigned hereby affirm our commitment to equal rights of people with cognitive disabilities to technology and information access and we call for implementation of these rights with deliberate speed.

INITIAL ENDORSING ORGANIZATIONS

AbleLink Technologies
AbleLink Technologies was founded in 1997 specifically to address the significant need for research-based cognitive support technologies for individuals with cognitive disabilities and those experiencing cognitive decline. The team has been built purposefully with individuals representing relevant fields of expertise including human services, human factors, rehabilitation technology, software engineering, occupational therapy, and clinical and experimental psychology.

American Association on Intellectual and Developmental Disabilities
Since 1876, the American Association on Intellectual and Developmental Disabilities (AAIDD) has been providing worldwide leadership in the field of intellectual and developmental disabilities. AAIDD is the oldest and largest interdisciplinary organization of professionals and citizens concerned about intellectual and developmental disabilities in the world.

American Network of Community Options and Resources
The American Network of Community Options and Resources (ANCOR) is a national, nonprofit trade association representing more than 800 private community providers of services to people with disabilities. Combined, they serve over 400,000 individuals with disabilities and work to shape policy, share solutions, and strengthen community.

The Arc
The Arc is the largest national community-based organization advocating for and serving people with intellectual and developmental disabilities and their families. They encompass all ages and all spectrums from autism, Down syndrome, Fragile X and various other developmental disabilities. With more than 140,000 members and more than 700 state and local chapters nationwide, they are on the front lines to ensure that people with intellectual and developmental disabilities and their families have the support they need to be members of the community. Founded in 1950, The Arc was comprised of a small group of concerned and passionate parents and community members who would be a catalyst for changing the public perception of children with disabilities. For the past 60 years, The Arc has continued to grow and evolve along with the changing needs and issues people with disabilities and their families face.

ASSET Consulting
ASSET Consulting (Applying Systems, Software, and Engineering Technology) helps organizations adopt, market, or develop emerging technologies. For over 20 years, ASSET Consulting has specialized in applications for long-term care and people with cognitive disabilities. Clientele include service providers, technology vendors, academic institutions, trade associations, and government agencies. The mission of ASSET Consulting is to advance the effective use of emerging technology in service of social needs.

Assistive Technology Partners, University of Colorado
Assistive Technology Partners was established in 1989 and is part of the Department of Physical Medicine and Rehabilitation, School of Medicine, University of Colorado. It encompasses programs in four major areas: clinical services, outreach and information services, research and engineering, education and professional development. Assistive Technology Partners provides a unique integration of capabilities and services for persons with disabilities and associated professional affiliations.

Beach Center on Disability, University of Kansas
The Beach Center on Disability is a multi-disciplinary research and training center committed to making a significant and sustainable positive difference in the quality of life of individuals and families affected by disability and the professionals who support them. Its staff of approximately 40 professors, researchers, educators, doctoral students, and support personnel carry out research, technical assistance, and undergraduate, masters, and doctoral training. Its staff focuses on families, family quality of life, and family support; public policy in special education and disability services; school reform, with emphasis on inclusion of students with and without disabilities in general education; conceptualizing self-determination and its application to people with disabilities; conceptualizing and defining intellectual disability; defining

and measuring supports and support needs; technology use by people with cognitive disability; and positive behavioral supports and services.

Burton Blatt Institute, Syracuse University

The Burton Blatt Institute (BBI) at Syracuse University reaches around the globe in its efforts to advance the civic, economic, and social participation of people with disabilities. BBI builds on the legacy of Burton Blatt, former dean of Syracuse University's School of Education and a pioneering disability rights scholar, to better the lives of people with disabilities. BBI has offices in Syracuse, Washington, D.C., and Atlanta. Given the strong ties between one's ability to earn income and fully participate in their communities, BBI's work focuses on two interconnected Innovation Areas: Economic Participation and Community Participation. Through program development, research, and public policy guidance in these Innovation Areas, BBI advances the full inclusion of people with disabilities.

Coleman Colorado Foundation

The Coleman Colorado Foundation (CCF) supports the Coleman Institute for Cognitive Disabilities' activities through a private endowment and sustained annual contributions by the founding donors, William T. and Claudia L. Coleman. The CCF is a 501 (c) (3) public charity classified as a 509 (a) (3) supporting organization to the University of Colorado.

Coleman Institute for Cognitive Disabilities, University of Colorado

The Coleman Institute for Cognitive Disabilities' mission is to catalyze and integrate advances in science, engineering, and technology to promote the quality of life and independent living of people with cognitive disabilities. The Coleman Institute for Cognitive Disabilities was established in 2001 by the Regents of the University of Colorado. A private endowment and sustained annual contributions by their founding donors, William T. and Claudia L. Coleman, support the Institute's activities through the Coleman Colorado Foundation (CCF).

Imagine!

Imagine! was established in 1963 as a private, not-for-profit organization and as the first community-centered board (CCB) in Colorado. In addition to serving as a state CCB, Imagine! provides services designed to incorporate people with developmental, cognitive and physical challenges into the fabric of their communities. Services include educational and therapeutic services, job training and placement, recreation and leisure activities, opportunities for community living, behavioral health services, technology solutions and support for families.

Institute for Matching Person and Technology

The Institute for Matching Person and Technology was formed to better match users of technologies with the most appropriate devices for their use. The Institute works to enhance the situation of technology users through research, assessment, training and consultation. The Matching Person and Technology (MPT) assessment process is one means for providing a more personal approach to matching person and technology.

Institute on Disability and Human Development, University of Illinois at Chicago

The Institute on Disability and Human Development (IDHD), a University Center for Excellence in Developmental Disabilities Education, Research, and Service (UCEDD) is dedicated to promoting the independence, productivity and inclusion of people with disabilities into all aspects of society. The mission is addressed by conducting research and disseminating information about disability to academicians, policymakers, businesses, government agencies, service providers and the general public. The IDHD also provides an extensive array of clinical and community service activities and, through the Department of Disability and Human Development and other academic departments, offers interdisciplinary pre-service training. The values of cultural diversity, consumer choice and self-determination are emphasized across the life span in all training, public service, and research activities of the IDHD.

Kansas University Center on Developmental Disabilities

The Kansas University Center on Developmental Disabilities (KUCDD), established in 1969, is a component of the Life Span Institute at the University of Kansas. The KUCDD maintains facilities on the University's main campus in Lawrence, at the KU Medical Center in Kansas City, and in Parsons. In addition to these primary sites, the KUCDD supports affiliated projects in many Kansas communities and provides training and other types of support to all regions of the state. As a University Center for Excellence in Developmental Disabilities (UCEDD) funded by the Administration on Developmental Disabilities, the core functions of the KUCDD are: pre-service training, research, information dissemination, and community services.

The National Center on Disability and Access to Education
The National Center on Disability and Access to Education (NCDAE) exists to address issues of technology and disability in education policies and practices to enhance the lives of people with disabilities and their families. NCDAE works on policy, research, training and technical assistance, and dissemination of information. NCDAE accomplishes its purpose through an affiliate network of over 500 national and international partners in education, business and industry, and government.

Self Advocates Becoming Empowered
Self Advocates Becoming Empowered (SABE) is the self-advocacy organization for people with developmental disabilities in the United States. It consists of local, state, and national components. Founded in 1990, the organization promotes the full inclusion of people with developmental disabilities in the community throughout the 50 states. Their non-profit advocacy organization is run by a board of self-advocates representing 9 regions of the country.

Sibling Leadership Network
The Sibling Leadership Network's (SLN) mission is to provide siblings of individuals with disabilities the information, support, and tools to advocate with their brothers and sisters and to promote the issues important to them and their entire families. The Network promotes a broad network of siblings nationally who share the experience of disability and people concerned with sibling issues by connecting them to social, emotional, governmental, and provisional supports across the lifespan. This enables them to be effective advocates with their brothers and sisters, and to serve as change agents for themselves and their families.

Westchester Institute for Human Development
Westchester Institute for Human Development is a leader in addressing major social and health issues affecting people with disabilities and vulnerable children. WIHD addresses majo social and health issues by developing and delivering medical, clinical and support services to individuals, their families and caregivers. As one of only 67 University Centers for Excellence in Developmental Disabilities, WIHD creates better futures for these individuals through the creation and dissemination of innovative research, professional leadership education and best practices trainings.

*Acknowledgement of co-authors of the Statement on The Rights of People With Cognitive Disabilities to Technology and Information Access: Twenty-four people participated in the Coleman Institute Preconference Workshop on Cognitive Disability and Technology. The event was held in Broomfield, Colorado on November 16, 2012. Discussion at that event centered on the merit, content and dissemination strategy of a formal statement to advance the development, access and utilization of technology by people with cognitive disabilities in the United States. A formal statement was collectively drafted and revised over the course of the following year. That Statement appears as Figure 1 of this article as *The Rights of People With Cognitive Disabilities to Technology and Information Access.*

Enid Ablowitz, Coleman Institute for Cognitive Disabilities, University of Colorado

Rodney Bell, ASSET Consulting, LLC, Portland OR

Peter Blanck, Burton Blatt Institute, Syracuse University

Cathy Bodine, Department of Rehabilitation Medicine, CU-Denver School of Medicine

David Braddock, Coleman Institute for Cognitive Disabilities, Office of the President and Department of Psychiatry, University of Colorado

Claudia Coleman, Coleman Colorado Foundation

William T. Coleman, Coleman Colorado Foundation

Daniel K. Davies, AbleLink Technologies, Inc., Colorado Springs

Mark Emery, Imagine! Colorado

Cathy Enfield, Self-Advocates Becoming Empowered

Laura Haffer, Coleman Institute for Cognitive Disabilities, Boulder, CO

Richard Hemp, Coleman Institute for Cognitive Disabilities and CU Department of Psychiatry

Jeffery Hoehl, Coleman Institute for Cognitive Disabilities and CU-Boulder Department of Computer Science

Clayton Lewis, Coleman Institute for Cognitive Disabilities and CU-Boulder Department of Computer Science

Margaret A. Nygren, American Association on Intellectual and Developmental Disabilities, Washington, DC

David O'Hara, Westchester Institute for Human Development, Westchester, NY

Renee Pietrangelo, American Network of Community Options and Resources, Alexandria, Virginia

Mary Kay Rizzolo, Institute on Disability & Human Development, University of Illinois-Chicago

Cyndi Rowland, Center for Persons with Disabilities, Utah State University, Provo

Marcia Scherer, University of Rochester and Institute for Matching Person and Technology

Emily Shea Tanis, Coleman Institute for Cognitive Disabilities and Department of Psychiatry, University of Colorado

Michael L. Wehmeyer, Department of Special Education, Kansas University Center on Developmental Disabilities, and Beach Center on Disability, University of Kansas

Greg Wellems, Imagine! Colorado

Ann Cameron Williams, The Arc, Washington, DC

References

Braddock, D. (2013). Testimony on Long Term Care and Developmental Disabilities in the United States. Washington, DC: Hearings Before the United States Congress Bipartisan Long Term Care Commission, Dirksen Federal Building, July 17, 2013.

Coleman, III., W.T. "The Greatest Inflection Point: The Cloud and People with Cognitive Disabilities" Presentation at the National Institute on Standards and Technology, Washington DC, 2013.

Gomez, S. C. (2013). The vision for inclusion. *Inclusion*, 1(1). 1–4.

Schmidt, E. & Cohen, J. (2013). *The New Digital Age: Reshaping the Future of People, Nations and Business*. New York: Knopf.

Syracuse University Center on Human Policy (1979). *The Community Imperative: A refutation in support of institutionalizing anybody because of mental retardation*. Syracuse: Author.

Varney, E. (2013). *Disability and Information Technology*. Cambridge: Cambridge University Press.

Wehmeyer, M., Agran, M., Hughes, C., Martin, J. Mithaug, D.E., & Palmer, S. (2007). *Promoting self-determination in students with developmental disabilities*. New York: Guilford.

World Health Organization (2011). *World Report on Disability*. Geneva: Health Organization Press.

Author:
David Braddock, david.braddock@cu.edu, Coleman Institute for Cognitive Disabilities University of Colorado, Boulder, 3825 Iris Ave., Suite 200, Boulder, CO 80301; **Jeffery Hoehl** Coleman Institute for Cognitive Disabilities, University of Colorado, Boulder; **Shea Tanis,** Coleman Institute for Cognitive Disabilities, University of Colorado, Boulder; **Enid Ablowitz** Coleman Institute for Cognitive Disabilities, University of Colorado, Boulder; **Laura Haffer** Coleman Institute for Cognitive Disabilities, University of Colorado, Boulder